Von Braun

Von Braun

DREAMER OF SPACE, ENGINEER OF WAR

Michael J. Neufeld

ALFRED A. KNOPF NEW YORK 2007
IN ASSOCIATION WITH THE NATIONAL AIR AND SPACE MUSEUM
SMITHSONIAN INSTITUTION

THIS IS A BORZOI BOOK
PUBLISHED BY ALFRED A. KNOPF

www.aaknopf.com

Portions of chapter fourteen were originally published in
somewhat different form as "The End of the Army Space
Program: Interservice Rivalry and the Transfer of the von Braun
Group to NASA, 1958–1959" in *The Journal of Military History*
(July 2005). Portions of chapters ten and eleven were originally
published in somewhat different form as " 'Space Superiority':
Wernher von Braun's Campaign for a Nuclear-Armed Space
Station, 1946–1956" in *Space Policy* (2006).

Owing to limitations of space, permissions to reprint previously
published material can be found following the index.

Library of Congress Cataloging-in-Publication Data

Neufeld, Michael J., [date]
Von Braun : dreamer of space, engineer of war /
by Michael J. Neufeld.—1st ed.
p.   cm.
"This is a Borzoi book."
Includes bibliographical references.
ISBN 978-0-307-26292-9
1. Von Braun, Wernher, 1912–1977.   2. Rocketry—United
States—Biography.   3. Rocketry—Germany—Biography.
4. Astronautics—United States—Biography.   5. Rockets
(Ordnance)—Research—Germany—History—20th century.
I. Title.
TL781.85.V6N48 2007
629.4092—dc22   2007005711
[B]

Manufactured in the United States of America
Published September 26, 2007
Reprinted One Time
Third Printing, November 2007

FOR KAREN

A fiery chariot, borne on buoyant pinions,
sweeps near me now! The time has come for me
to pierce the ether's high, unknown dominions,
to reach new spheres of pure activity!
This godlike rapture, this supreme existence,
can I, but now a worm, deserve and earn?
Yes, resolute to reach some brighter distance,
on earth's fair sun my back I turn!
So let me dare those gates to fling asunder
which every man would fain go slinking by!
'Tis time, through deeds the word of truth to thunder,
that in their courage men with the high gods may vie.

—GOETHE, *Faust: Part One*, lines 702–13,
translated by Bayard Taylor

CONTENTS

Preface and Acknowledgments   ix
A Note on the Name and on Terms   xv

PROLOGUE: *A Romantic Urge*   3
CHAPTER ONE: *The Wheel of Progress (to 1925)*   7
CHAPTER TWO: *Sonny Boy (1925–32)*   21
CHAPTER THREE: *The Black Sedan (1932–34)*   49
CHAPTER FOUR: *How Much Do You Want? (1935–37)*   74
CHAPTER FIVE: *His Indisputable Genius (1937–39)*   89
CHAPTER SIX: *Future Dreams (1939–42)*   115
CHAPTER SEVEN: *A Pretty Hellish Environment (1942–44)*   135
CHAPTER EIGHT: *A Young Man, of Very Germanic Appearance
        (1944–45)*   167
CHAPTER NINE: *Morning in the Desert (1945–46)*   199
CHAPTER TEN: *Mars Project (1946–49)*   223
CHAPTER ELEVEN: *Space Superiority (1950–54)*   246
CHAPTER TWELVE: *We Could Do It! (1954–57)*   279
CHAPTER THIRTEEN: *The Seer of Space (1957–58)*   311
CHAPTER FOURTEEN: *I Aim at the Stars (1958–60)*   333
CHAPTER FIFTEEN: *Before This Decade Is Out (1960–63)*   354
CHAPTER SIXTEEN: *You're an Optimist, but Then, So Am I
        (1963–67)*   391
CHAPTER SEVENTEEN: *A Pretty Emotional Moment (1967–69)*   414
CHAPTER EIGHTEEN: *For Him, a World Was Falling Apart
        (1969–72)*   434
CHAPTER NINETEEN: *The Heavens Declare the Glory of God
        (1972–77)*   458
EPILOGUE: *A Faustian Shadow*   473

Notes   479
Significant Abbreviations Used in the Notes   547
Bibliography and Archival Sources   549
Index   563

PREFACE AND ACKNOWLEDGMENTS

During the centennial of aviation in 2003, the U.S. trade journal *Aviation Week and Space Technology* held a vote among its engineer- and pilot-dominated readership for the "100 Stars of Aerospace"—the hundred most important people in the history of flight. In that poll Wernher von Braun came out number two, after the Wright brothers. This result, which was doubtlessly influenced by the American majority in the poll sample, nonetheless is a testimonial to von Braun's historical importance, at least in the eyes of his former peers: aerospace engineers and managers. The result was doubly interesting because von Braun's name has been slowly vanishing from the consciousness of the general public. Outside the space community and those concerned about Nazi secret weapons and their manufacture by concentration camp labor, hardly anyone under age forty knows his name today. But Wernher von Braun is too seminal a figure in the development of ballistic missiles and space vehicles to be forgotten, especially as his Third Reich career raises the most fundamental questions regarding the moral responsibility of scientists and engineers in the twentieth century—and the twenty-first.

Despite his undoubted importance, the question must be asked: why another biography? There are quite a few books about him already. Nonetheless, for twenty years it has been my conviction that no life of von Braun exists, in English or German, that is simultaneously accurate, readable, and rigorously researched in primary sources. Half a dozen biographies have been published since I began working on German rocketry in mid-1987, some of them substantial, yet nothing has changed in that regard. At least three of those new books are hagiographies (saintly lives), as friends, colleagues, and space enthusiasts attempt to perpetuate the hero worship that grew up around von Braun during the Cold War. Of the recent critical treatments, one in English and two in German, all are short and all are based largely on secondary sources. Moreover, the German biographies, old and new, are (perhaps understandably) weighted toward the Nazi period, yet he spent half his life and two-thirds of his professional career in the United States. On the American side, the basic competence even to research his German life has often been lacking; with one exception, that of von Braun's close friend Ernst Stuhlinger, English-language biographers have been unable to read German. The result is books that are often inaccurate and ill-informed about German history. Even when they discuss his American career, however, errors abound and sophisticated analysis is lacking.

Professional scholars have for the most part avoided the topic, in part because Wernher von Braun is a difficult biographical subject. A command of two languages and national histories is essential, as is at least some familiarity with rocket and space technology. Moreover, he lost almost all his personal possessions in 1945, including his correspondence, and the same fate befell his parents. He salvaged only a small remnant of the things that meant most to him, with the result that his papers begin, for all intents and purposes, at age thirty-three, upon his arrival in the United States. For the second half of his life, the biographer's problem is the inverse: his papers are quantitatively huge (over two hundred linear feet) yet clogged with trivia. Compounding these problems, the majority of his papers are in Huntsville, Alabama, and have been hard to access because the institution that owns them, the U.S. Space and Rocket Center, has lacked resources and has had a protective attitude toward its founder—von Braun.

A second set of problems is the inaccessibility of his widow, his children, and his American relatives, who have been unwilling to be interviewed even by his friendly biographers. As the author of *The Rocket and the Reich: Peenemünde and the Coming of the Ballistic Missile Era* (1995), a critical history of von Braun's German army rocket program, I had no chance to talk to them. Nor, after the publication of that book, would his former German colleagues speak to me any longer, although the National Air and Space Museum does possess twelve oral history interviews that I did with them beforehand.

Rich archival and interview resources are nonetheless available upon which I could base this biography. For the German period, there are the impersonal but informative records of the Peenemünde project, the core of the material I used for *The Rocket and the Reich*, plus old and new research in German and American war crimes trial records. In the 1950s von Braun wrote several short memoirs and gave several interviews about the Weimar and Nazi periods, sources that are problematic but invaluable. I found more information in his postwar correspondence and in memoirs of Peenemünde colleagues. By exploiting his father's reminiscences and the genealogy he wrote and by tracking down obscure archival sources in Germany, I was also able to dig up new information on von Braun's family, upbringing, and schooling. As for the American period, it was a matter of investing five years in U.S. archives to sort the wheat from the chaff in his papers and in the massive government files available in the National Archives and at NASA. I was able to interview several American colleagues of von Braun's as well, plus draw upon the voluminous oral history resources, mostly on the 1960s, collected by the space agency and by my museum. Another fundamental source is the archival collection left by Wernher von Braun's father in Germany, which contains illuminating postwar letters from his son.

The result, I hope, is as full, balanced, and accurate an accounting of von Braun's life as is possible to compile from the surviving sources. Perfect factual accuracy is a chimera: no historian can guarantee it. When one is as dependent on memoir material for key moments in his life as one is with von Braun, that is even more the case. Nor, considering the controversial nature of the evidence and the moral judgments that come into play, can my assessments of his actions and motivations in the Third Reich be the only possible ones. Still, I would hope that the reader at least finds this work to be a credible and stimulating interpretation of a truly amazing life.

The debts I accumulated in the research and writing of this book are legion. Everyone mentioned in *The Rocket and the Reich*'s acknowledgments I must thank again. But for the sake of relative brevity, I will focus on those who made important contributions to the present book.

Once again I must begin with the National Air and Space Museum and the Smithsonian Institution, as the institutional and financial support I have received from them made this book possible. Two Smithsonian Scholarly Studies Grants provided travel money, without which I never would have been able to complete archival work in Germany and the United States. The museum's Collections and Research Department, headed by Ted Maxwell, and the division chairs of Aeronautics (before I transferred in 1999) and Space History (thereafter)—Tom Crouch, Dom Pisano, Allan Needell, and Roger Launius—were unstinting in their support for this research as part of my curatorial job. Affiliation with the museum also afforded me access to archives, historical locations, and people that otherwise might have been inaccessible.

The museum's vibrant intellectual community has not dimmed since I arrived in 1988, but I owe a particular debt to five colleagues. David DeVorkin not only commented on every single draft chapter, but he has stimulated thought in many conversations, notably by giving me the benefit of his own experience as a biographer. Tom Crouch, himself a distinguished biographer, has read sections and shaped my thinking about Wernher von Braun in ways too numerous to count. We collaborated on a joint paper in 1994 and had been talking about how to write this book even before that. After Roger Launius came to the museum in 2002, he commented on all the chapters, and as NASA chief historian before that time, he facilitated access to space agency archives. In recent years James David has provided me with much counsel and help in finding National Archives records and filing FOIA requests. Finally, Frank Winter has shared with me his detailed knowledge of the early rocket pioneers and the often obscure sources about them, ever since I wrote my first letter to NASM in 1987.

During my research in Germany on Wernher von Braun's family and childhood, I had no more enjoyable and helpful companions than Holger Steinle of the Deutsches Technikmuseum and his wife, Irmgard Johannson. Not only did they host me innumerable times at their restored estate house in Wolfradshof, giving me a better feeling for the old life on the land, but the house turned out to be only a few kilometers from the von Quistorp estates of von Braun's mother and wife. Our first coup was finding his grandparents' graves at Crenzow (now Krenzow). Holger also drove me on the two most memorable excursions during the research for this book: visits to von Braun's boarding schools at Ettersburg and Spiekeroog and to the Silesian house of his parents, which is in a difficult-to-find location off the main road of an obscure Polish village.

Among archivists, I have to single out Irene Wilhite of the U.S. Space and Rocket Center, who reboxed the von Braun Papers there and facilitated access to them although she did not agree with my perspective. At the NASA History Division in Washington, D.C., Jane Odom, Colin Fries, and John Hargenrader were unstinting in their aid, as was Charlie Reeves at the National Archives Southeast Region, and Marilyn Graskowiak, Kristine Kaske, Brian Nicklas, Kate Igoe, and all my other colleagues at the NASM Archives Division. I would also like to thank Phil Edwards of the SI Libraries, Bruce Kirby and the reading room staff at the Library of Congress Manuscript Division, Shelly Kelly of the University of Houston–Clear Lake, Tammy Gobert of the RPI Archives, Tom McFarland of the Florida Institute of Technology Library, Mike Wright of NASA/MSFC, David Smith of the Walt Disney Archives, and the staffs of the National Archives at College Park, the Ford and Carter presidential libraries, and the Bundesarchiv Koblenz, plus all the other institutions listed in the Bibliography and Archival Sources section in the back of this book.

For assistance in finding and providing materials regarding the concentration camp prisoners and war crimes, I am especially indebted to the French Dora survivors Yves Béon, George Jouanin, and Pierre Sellier, and to Yves Le Maner, director of La Coupole; Jens-Christian Wagner, director of the Kz-Gedenkstätte Mittelbau-Dora; and Eli Rosenbaum, director of the Office of Special Investigations, U.S. Department of Justice.

Many friends and colleagues provided documents, pointed out sources, or stimulated thought, including Frank Stucke (who gave me his research notes and contacts), Guillaume de Syon (who more than once went out of his way to do research for me), Dwayne Day (who gave me many photocopies), Ron Doel and John Krige (who read chapters), Andrew Dunar, Stephen Waring, Fred Durant, Fred Ordway, Tom Lehrer, Lee Saunders, Torsten Hess, Volker Koos, Johannes Weyer, Manfred Bornemann, Burghard Ciesla, Dieter Hoffmann, Rainer Eisfeld, T. D. Dungan, Lawrence Peterkin, Asif Siddiqi, Andrew Williams, Oliver Halmburger, Paul Dickson, Wayne Biddle, Bob Kraemer, Jacob Neufeld, David Spires, Alvin Gilens, Dirk Zache, Arthur Behn, Bernd Jordan, Hartwig Henke, Bernhard Müller, Joachim Zwanzig, Harald Tresp, Olaf Przybilski, Karlheinz Rohrwild, Daniel Uziel, Terry Cornell, Doyle Piland, Dave Clary, David Onkst, Herb Rochen, Bill Henoch, Robert Smith, Jürgen Matthäus, Evelyn Zagenhagen, and Diane McWhorter. I apologize if I have forgotten anyone. I would also like to sincerely thank Carola, Christina, and Christoph-Friedrich von Braun, children of Sigismund, who were willing to give me interviews, discuss the family history, and allow access to their father's memoirs and to the papers of Magnus von Braun Sr. in their possession.

For permission to quote excerpts, I would like to thank the U.S. Space and Rocket Center for the Wernher von Braun Papers in Huntsville and the Bundesarchiv Koblenz for the Magnus von Braun Papers. Len Bruno of the Library of Congress was kind enough to track down the documents that proved that almost all of the Wernher von Braun Papers there are in the public domain. For photo permissions, I am beholden to the National Air and Space Museum, the Musée de la Résistance et de la Déportation, the Stiftung Deutsche Landeserziehungsheime, the Ullstein Bilderdienst, Christoph von Braun, Bernd Jordan, the U.S. Space and Rocket Center, Doris Dornberger and Sanford Greenburger Associates Inc., Wolfgang Fleischer, the Bundesarchiv Koblenz, Picture Press, and the *Spiegel* Bildarchiv.

Finally, I have to thank most of all my wife, Karen L. Levenback, for her love, support, and unstinting professional advice during the decade that I have worked on this book, and our cats Newt, Kepler, and the late Missy Birch, who provided welcome interruptions during the many long hours at the computer.

A NOTE ON THE NAME AND ON TERMS

English speakers routinely mispronounce Wernher von Braun's name. In German it is something like: "Vairn-er fon Brown" (with a rolled "r"). He accepted the Anglicized pronunciation of his first name (which is an old-fashioned spelling of Werner) and of the *von* that indicated he was from the nobility, but he never accepted "Brawn." *Braun* means and is pronounced "Brown."

Von Braun and his associates called their chief German accomplishment the A-4, for Aggregat 4, the fourth rocket in their series. Vergeltungswaffe 2 (Vengeance Weapon 2), or V-2, was the Propaganda Ministry's name for it. Since the rocket became known by the latter designation after it was deployed as a weapon in the fall of 1944 and it was the standard usage in America, I have, by and large, used A-4 before 1944–45 and V-2 afterward.

One term you will not find in this book is "rocket scientist." There has been a deep-rooted failure in the English-speaking media and popular culture to grapple with the distinction between science and engineering. Although the boundaries are fuzzy, and a leading historian of technology has argued that all we have now is a unitary "technoscience," I still find it useful to think of a spectrum. On one end is basic science, which aims at achieving an understanding of the laws of nature without regard for their practical application, and at the other is engineering, which is about creating technological devices to shape the world to human purposes. Although Wernher von Braun got a doctorate in physics in 1934, he never worked a day in his life thereafter as a scientist. He was an engineer and a manager of engineers, and he used that vocabulary when he was talking to his professional peers. Thus the correct term is "rocket engineer."

Von Braun

A Romantic Urge

That guy upstairs wants to go to the moon.... That's his passion—interplanetary travel. Whether it will be war or peace on earth comes after that for him. —JAMES HAMILL[1]

Late in 1950 *The New Yorker* sent one of its writers, Daniel Lang, to the Deep South—to the small, segregated city of Huntsville, Alabama. Little more than a sleepy Bible Belt cotton town before the U.S. Army began setting up its major rocket center there the previous spring, Huntsville still had fewer than twenty thousand people and no public bars; the only place anyone could buy a drink was in a private club. The object of Lang's interest was thirty-eight-year-old "Professor Wernher von Braun, a scientist who served Hitler as head of the experimental guided-missile station at Peenemünde." Although not yet a household name, or a face recognizable from national TV, von Braun had already acquired a certain notoriety as the technical head of the Third Reich's V-2 missile project and as the leader of more than one hundred Germans who had come to work for the United States under Project Paperclip. After first meeting Major James Hamill, von Braun's superior at Redstone Arsenal, Lang went upstairs to see the rocket engineer.

> As we entered, von Braun rose from the desk and strode buoyantly toward us. He is a startlingly handsome man, over six feet tall, blue-eyed, blond, athletic-looking. His expression struck me as exuberant rather than reflective, and his manner as that of a man accustomed to being regarded as indispensable. He shook my hand energetically. "I will pick you up at your hotel after dinner and drive you to my house, where we will talk," he said.[2]

As arranged, von Braun took Lang home, where they arrived "shortly after eight o'clock. His wife, an extremely pretty young woman, met us at the door and anxiously asked my indulgence for the appearance of the place." They were in the midst of packing to move to a new house. Sitting in a dimly lit living room, with a large, "gloomy" Rembrandt reproduction on the wall, and with bourbon and sodas on the coffee table between them, von Braun and Lang discussed his background, his parents, and his youthful fascination with space. He particularly remembered an article in a late-1920s German astronomy magazine "that described an imaginary trip to the moon. . . . It filled me with a romantic urge. Interplanetary travel! Here was a task worth dedicating one's life to! Not just to stare at the moon and the planets but to soar through the heavens and actually explore the mysterious universe! I knew how Columbus had felt."[3]

While a university student, von Braun had been part of an impoverished amateur rocket group in Berlin. One day in early 1932 a "black sedan" pulled up outside the Raketenflugplatz (Rocketport) and three passengers got out.

> They were in mufti [civilian clothes], but mufti or not, it was the Army. . . . That was the beginning. The Versailles Treaty hadn't placed any restrictions on rockets, and the Army was desperate to get back on its feet. We didn't care much about that, one way or the other, but we needed money, and the Army seemed willing to help us. In 1932, the idea of war seemed to us an absurdity. The Nazis weren't yet in power. We felt no moral scruples about the possible future use of our brainchild. We were interested solely in exploring outer space. It was simply a question with us of how the golden cow could be milked most successfully.[4]

This bald statement of amoral opportunism was virtually identical to something he wrote in a manuscript memoir several months earlier. When that memoir was finally published in 1956, von Braun's editors were careful to edit these words out; with Lang, however, he was not yet so cautious. The reporter's implicit question was one that would haunt von Braun throughout his American career: had he not made a Faustian bargain, a pact with the devil, when he had aligned himself with the German army and ultimately with Hitler? Was he not bothered by the moral implications of working for that regime or of building weapons while wishing to go into space? To Lang, von Braun could offer only that he had never regretted accepting the German army's offer, that technology must march onward or industrial society would collapse, and that only "religion" could reform human morals sufficiently that mankind might survive its own science and technology. His conversion to a more-than-nominal Christianity, he acknowledged, had been quite recent, postdating his arrival in the States in September 1945.[5]

The question still resonates: was Wernher von Braun a twentieth-century Faust? The revelations since the 1960s about his membership in the SS, and his involvement in the exploitation of concentration camp labor, have only increased the force of this question.[6] This biography suggests that few engineers or scientists of that century fit the role so well—he actually got his resources and power from a devilish regime, unlike the Allied scientists who developed the atomic bomb. His life is not, however, that of the classical Faust of the sixteenth-century morality tales and Christopher Marlowe's play, in which the learned doctor simply sells his soul for all eternity in return for earthly powers and pleasures. Rather he resembles Goethe's Faust, who ultimately uses his infernal powers to build great engineering works for what he believes to be the betterment of mankind. He accepts the slavelike workers Mephistopheles provides. When a happy old couple, Philemon and Baucis, stand in the way of Faust's land reclamation project on the North Sea, he asks Mephistopheles to remove them, resulting in their deaths. Faust is upset but scarcely guilty, for he cannot accept personal responsibility. His soul is nonetheless saved by the intervention of angels who outwit Mephistopheles and his crew, but it is redeemed only after he reaches heaven, as an act of divine grace.[7]

In von Braun's case, he accepted the ample resources offered by the Third Reich to build rockets, believing that it would lead to a glorious new future for himself, and humankind, in space. When the cost turned out to be the enslavement and murder of thousands, something he did not want or suggest, he was unhappy, perhaps even appalled; but that did not divert him from his rocket projects or his ambitions. The U.S. Army became his deus ex machina, rescuing him from the potential consequences of his actions. Appropriately enough, in the early 1950s von Braun was fond of quoting a passage from Goethe in which Faust expresses a desire to fly through the heavens—his lifelong obsession.[8]

The importance of von Braun's career in rocket engineering and space exploration is by no means limited, however, to this bargain. Although his followers, and many others who have written about him, have often exaggerated his role in American missile and space programs, he was the most influential spaceflight advocate and rocket engineer of the twentieth century. Others pioneered the idea of the rocket as the key to space, and others held higher jobs in the world's missile and rocket programs: he could never become NASA Administrator because of his Nazi past; nor was his job ever as powerful as that of Sergei Pavlovich Korolev, the chief designer in the Soviet Union. But no one played so great a role both in selling the idea of spaceflight and in making it come true. His historic role rests on four fundamental achievements: (1) as technical director of the V-2 project, he led the design and construction of the world's first large rocket and its first ballistic missile; (2) as chief advocate for space travel in the 1950s, in *Collier's* magazine, and on Walt Disney's TV program, he helped sell the American and Western public on the feasibility of that seemingly utopian proposition; (3) as technical director of the U.S. Army's missile facility in Huntsville, he was instrumental in the launching of the first American satellite in 1958; and (4) as director of NASA's Marshall Space Flight Center, also in Huntsville, he was the consummate manager of the gigantic Saturn booster project that sent two dozen Apollo astronauts to the Moon between 1968 and 1972.

Wernher von Braun was a master popularizer, a talented writer, and a brilliant speaker. But the foundation of his achievements was his performance as a charismatic engineering manager, technological entrepreneur, and system builder.[9] Although he made some specific technical contributions to rocket engineering, none were of fundamental importance; his genius was organizational leadership. He was one of a cohort of technically trained Second World War managers who harnessed scientists and engineers into the service of giant new weapons projects—figures like J. Robert Oppenheimer at Los Alamos. But almost uniquely von Braun made the transition from one side to the other, and he continued his role as an engineering leader in the United States during the Cold War—by far the most prominent ex-Nazi to do so. In his twenty-seven years in the U.S. Army and NASA, he successfully managed nuclear missile and space launch vehicle projects of ever-increasing scale and importance. But after the moon landings, and his move from Huntsville to Washington, he found himself cut off from his role as an impresario of huge technological projects and increasingly uncomfortable in a society no longer strongly committed to expensive human spaceflight programs. He escaped to the corporate world, but his life was soon cut short by cancer.

Von Braun has often been depicted as a saint or a devil, as a hero of spaceflight or as a Nazi war criminal. It is comforting to pigeonhole him as either white or black, because then one does not have to deal with his ambiguity and complexity, or the ambiguity and complexity of the moral and political choices offered to scientists and engineers in the modern era. One thing is, however, clear: the foundation of his remarkable career as engineering manager and space visionary was his romantic ambition to explore space, if possible personally. How this son of the Prussian landholding aristocracy, this title-holding baron, became a spaceflight fanatic, a military engineer, a Nazi opportunist, a devout Christian, a media star, a patriotic German, *and* a patriotic American is a fascinating story and one that is the subject of this book.

CHAPTER ONE

The Wheel of Progress

TO 1925

Demagoguery and democracy are brothers in etymology and spirit . . . for the German ear the word democracy *awakens memories of complete chaos after the First [World] War.*
—MAGNUS FREIHERR VON BRAUN[1]

When Wernher von Braun was about ten years old, his tall, elegant mother, Emmy Freifrau (Baroness) von Braun, asked him what he would like to do with his life. "I want to help turn the wheel of progress" was his answer, a response that sounded odd and surprising to her, coming out of the mouth of a small boy. An unusually abstract statement, it prefigured a lifetime of fascination with science and technology.[2]

Equally surprising, it came from the mouth of a true son of the Junkers—the noble caste that had once dominated the Prussian civil service, officer corps, and landowning elite. Engineering and science were not careers that Junker sons often chose, even in the 1920s. It seemed to reflect some inner compulsion of Wernher's, but it also reflected the tenor of the times—a time of dramatic technological and political change. He had been born in 1912, in a traditional prewar world; his massively built, mustachioed father, Magnus Freiherr von Braun, had been a rapidly ascending civil servant in the empire of Kaiser Wilhelm II, while his intellectually gifted mother was the orphaned daughter of an estate owner. Less than ten years later his father would be forced out of the civil service in the political turmoil of the new Weimar Republic. The family moved to the modern world city of Berlin. Yet as much of a maverick and a Berliner as Wernher von Braun would turn out to be, his Prussian Junker upbringing influenced his values, his abilities, and his choices—more so, in fact, than his father would later be willing to credit.

Of his parents' two families, the von Brauns and the von Quistorps, the former was of much older aristocratic stock. Magnus von Braun, who inherited from his father the hobby of genealogical research, eventually traced the male line back to 1285, although in all probability an ancestor had battled the Mongols at Liegnitz in 1241. The von Brauns arose from the soil of Silesia, a verdant and rolling province on both sides of the Oder River, east of the Czech heartland of Bohemia and Moravia. In 1573 the Holy Roman emperor elevated two of them to the rank of *Reichsfreiherr* (imperial baron) for their military accomplishments.[3]

Magnus von Braun came, however, from an even more distant outpost of Germandom, East Prussia—a province that would disappear from the map in 1945, when Stalin divided it between the Soviet Union and Poland. In 1738 one descendant of the family, Gotthard Freiherr von Braun, entered Prussian service as a lieutenant in the garrison of the province's capital city of Königsberg (now Kaliningrad, Russia). There he married the daughter of a wealthy local burgher. His fifth child, Sigismund, also a Prussian officer, purchased the estate of Neucken, about fifty kilometers southwest of the city, in 1803 and erected a new house—Magnus von Braun's ancestral home. One of the family's close acquaintances in Königsberg had been the philosopher Immanuel Kant; the silver sugar spoon he gave to Sigismund as a wedding present was a holy object in the glass cabinet of the mansion, along with a golden snuffbox from Czar Alexander I of Russia. But in February 1807, not long after the house was finished, Napoleon fought the bloody and inconclusive Battle of Preussisch Eylau against the czar's army around Neucken. Napoleon's troops killed or stole all the farm animals, wrecked the estate buildings, and plundered the house, although valuables like Kant's spoon were successfully carried away or hidden. It took the family years to recuperate economically from the damage—but the starvation and death inflicted on the estate's enserfed peasantry were much worse.[4]

On the seventy-first anniversary of the battle, 7 February 1878, a boy, Magnus Alexander Maximilian, was born at Neucken. His father was Lieutenant Colonel Maximilian Freiherr von Braun, who had inherited the estate in part because no fewer than three of his brothers, as Prussian officers, were killed in the 1866 war against Austria-Hungary. Military values and a fervent loyalty to the Hohenzollern kings of Prussia—who, after 1871, became emperors of the new, Prussian-dominated Germany—were the heart of the values taught on the estate. Magnus was the youngest of five; his brothers Friedrich (Fritz) and Siegfried both became army officers. While Fritz had to terminate his career to take over Neucken shortly before World War I because of the failing health of their father, Siegfried served all through the war, ending as colonel of the Third Guards Regiment. He was forced into other employment only because of the military's drastic down-sizing as a result of the Versailles Treaty.[5]

Acceptable career choices for sons of the Prussian nobility were limited. Every able-bodied male was expected to at least serve a stint in the army before returning to estate agriculture, if there was a prospect of an inheritance—which in the nineteenth century was usually limited by primogeniture to the eldest son. Of course, a young man also had the possibility of marrying into an estate or, less often, accumulating enough wealth to buy one. As Prussia's bureaucracy expanded from the eighteenth century on, however, the higher civil service and diplomatic corps opened up as employment possibilities for younger sons. Unlike the British aristocracy, all children of the Prussian aristocracy, male and female, inherited the father's title, with the result that there were a lot of barons, countesses, and the like who usually lived well as a result of the privileges afforded them but had no landed property.

Daughters in this very patriarchal society inevitably faced even more limited choices. Outside of marriage, about the only prospects they had were to remain with the family as a maiden aunt and sister, or to become a nurse or administrator in a church-based hospital or charity institution. As the Junkers (outside of parts of Silesia) were aggressively Lutheran, the option of taking holy orders was unavailable. Magnus von Braun's oldest sibling, Magdalene (born 1865), remained at Neucken her whole life, whereas Adele eventually became the head of a children's sanatorium on the Baltic coast of East Prussia. Neither ever married.[6]

Old age often puts a nostalgic glow on one's memories of childhood. Magnus von Braun's memoirs, completed in American exile in the late 1940s and early 1950s, are no exception in that regard. He described Neucken as a patriarchal utopia: "the whole estate thought of itself as a large family. . . . Neighborly love . . . was natural and inevitable and at the same time Christian in nature. Patriarchal life on the land bound the people together into a tight community of fate." The housing of Neucken's laborers was, he conceded, "still primitive in my earliest youth," but nonetheless it was better than the conditions he later witnessed in eastern Europe—not to mention those of blacks and Mexicans in Texas and Alabama. (Prussia had abolished serfdom in the early decades of the century, not necessarily to the benefit of the peasants, who often lost their land.) Raised in a stable, hierarchical, rural society in which dissent was rare, Magnus von Braun never saw any need to question a state of affairs in which the Junkers ran local government as their private preserve and most villages were wholly owned appendages of the estates. Indeed, his memoir forthrightly states his reactionary, monarchist, elitist politics—there had always been, and would always be, rulers and ruled; equality was unnatural. In the 1960s he told one of his grandsons, "This democracy thing is just a passing fad."[7]

Educated by a tutor at Neucken until the age of ten, he was then sent to Königsberg to receive the traditional elite education of the humanistic Gymnasium, with a heavy emphasis on languages—in the upper grades, a lot of Latin and Greek. He apparently showed some talent; after graduating on Easter 1896, he made his way to the old, venerable University of Göttingen in north-central Germany to study law, the mandatory path into the civil service. With his baronial title and with a healthy stipend from his father, Magnus was able to join an elite dueling fraternity, the Corps Saxonia, "which was made up almost exclusively of landed nobles." In the old fraternity tradition, he did not study very hard but rather demonstrated his manliness by drinking and dueling. Graduating in spring 1899, he took his civil service entry exams in Königsberg and then did his one-year military service as an officer in the old Prussian royal city of Potsdam, outside Berlin. Again, his connections were the best: he entered the Hohenzollerns' elite infantry regiment, the First Foot Guards. Kaiser Wilhelm II's sons served in this regiment, and Magnus's eldest brother, Fritz, was a captain in the Guards' Rifle Battalion, which was responsible for the army's first experiments with machine guns. Apparently the young Magnus made such a good impression that, when he finished his service in the fall of 1900, the officers of the regiment made him a reserve lieutenant. The rank and uniform, like the elite fraternity membership, were of great value in Imperial German society.[8]

Returning to the civil service track, he then served the long, unpaid apprenticeship that led to the second exam and a permanent and paying position—a system designed to allow only the propertied access to the higher ranks. After serving in various places in eastern and western Prussia, he passed the assessor's exam in 1905, although not with flying colors. But he showed initiative, a talent for dealing with people, and the imagination to grapple with the new industrialized world far outside the realm of the Junkers. The Junkers' anticapitalism is often exaggerated, but their view of the world was often circumscribed by their narrow self-interest as big landowners and as members of a ruling elite. Magnus von Braun spent a year and a half as deputy to the county commissioner (*Landrat*) in the Ruhr city of Essen, which was dominated by the Krupps, the armaments and steel barons. Then he arranged a six-month leave to study trade and city administration in London in 1907, working at a voluntary position in the office of a German bank in the world center of finance and trade. This experience catapulted him into higher circles upon his return home. A chance conversation in Berlin resulted in his diversion from the traditional civil service justice track into the Prussian Trade Ministry, where he served as an adjutant to the minister, Clemens Delbrück. In late 1909 he met Emmy von Quistorp at a reception at the minister's house and was immediately smitten. Only seven or eight months later, on 12 July 1910, they married at her family's estate, Crenzow, in western Pomerania, near the small cities of Anklam and Greifswald—and only twenty kilometers from what would later become the Baltic coast rocket center of their second child, Wernher.[9]

The von Quistorps came from the same Junker landowning class as the von Brauns, but their roots in the nobility and the military were not nearly as deep. As burghers, without the noble *von*, they rose to prominence in the old Hanseatic city of Rostock as theologians, university professors, and merchants. In 1765 Dr. Bernhard Friedrich Quistorp came to Greifswald as a theology professor and Protestant pastor and became "general superintendent" of the last northern German territory ruled by Sweden. (It became Prussian in 1815.) His son, Johann Gottfried, earned a doctorate too, and as an entrée into the landed class, he bought an estate twenty-five kilometers away on the flat, open coastal plain near the estuary of the Peene River. In 1782 he became the first *von* Quistorp when the Hapsburg emperor ennobled him in Vienna. A grandson bought the nearby estate of Crenzow and Zarrenthin in 1819–20, giving up the first, and the next heir, named August (grandfather of Emmy), acquired the estate of Bauer and Wehrland, five kilometers away, in 1867 because favorable grain prices had allowed the family fortunes to flourish. With August von Quistorp's death in 1877, the first son, Wernher (born 1856), inherited Crenzow, and the second, Ulrich, received Bauer and Wehrland, setting up two neighboring branches of the von Quistorps. Both estates would become important in Wernher von Braun's life.[10]

Wernher von Quistorp was more than successful in following the prescribed course of the Prussian nobility: he attended university, served in the cavalry, and married Marie von Below, possessor of a famous Prussian aristocratic name and sister to two well-known diplomats. As a West Pomeranian estate holder, Wernher von Quistorp took a leading role in the agricultural credit cooperatives that served as banks for landowners, and he was appointed to the Prussian House of Lords. Yet he clearly had inherited the Quistorps' intellectual tradition. He pursued his education through to a law doctorate, but his true passion was ornithology, in which he became an important amateur scientist. According to his son-in-law Magnus von Braun, his collection of bird eggs "was one of the largest and most valuable in Germany. His correspondence with many ornithologists secured him superior knowledge in this area."[11]

He passed along his passion for natural history to his oldest child, Emmy Melitta Cécile, who was born on 3 November 1886 in Crenzow. After tutoring, she went to elite finishing schools in Berlin and London for two years. But a family tragedy forced her to return home: the premature death of her mother in Palermo, Sicily, in early 1903, presumably as a result of tuberculosis. The now sixteen-year-old Emmy became secretary for the estate and joined in her father's ornithological research.

> She knew every bird in the forest by its song or individual calls. She knew all the birds and also plants by their Latin names—and never forgot them. She was an expert in the area of mushrooms; thus the sciences of nature and the forest were for her always sources of a pure and great joy. *Astronomy* was an especially beloved subject.[12]

So says her future husband. But her father also died too young, in 1908 at the age of fifty-two, and he was buried in Crenzow's park alongside his wife; the two graves can still be found there today. The second child, Hans, inherited the estate. Emmy also had a younger sister, Irmengard, who married a Count Schlieffen, another famous Prussian name, and a younger brother, Alexander, who took a doctorate of laws and became a banker.[13] When Emmy von Quistorp was put on the Berlin marriage market during the social season of 1909–10, she had a quick and happy result. Through all the successes, troubles, and trials that would ensue, her union with Magnus von Braun would prove to be strong and loving.

Early in the spring of 1911 Magnus von Braun heard that one of his cherished ambitions would be realized: he was to become a county commissioner, "the goal of every government assessor. It promised independence, responsibility, freedom and creative possibilities unlike almost any other administrative post." In the Prussian hierarchy, a county commissioner occupied a key intermediate position as the local representative of the state government but also as the chief executive of the local administration. The pay was not very good, 3,600 Reichsmarks ($860) per year, the same as he had received from his father at the university, plus an inadequate allowance for horse and carriage—one had to have an independent income. The county and town was Wirsitz, in the Bromberg district of Posen province. The population of the county was only half German, and one of his jobs would be to suppress Polish nationalist activity. Immediately after Germany lost the Great War, Wirsitz became the border town of Wyrzysk in a resurrected

Poland. After the Second World War an even more massive loss of German territory put it deep inside the Polish Republic.[14]

Magnus von Braun's assumption of the post of county commissioner had to be delayed a month, until May, due to a happy event—on 15 April 1911 Emmy gave birth to Sigismund Maximilian Wernher Gustav Magnus in Zehlendorf, a wealthy suburb of Berlin. Two months later she and Sigismund joined Magnus in the Wirsitz apartment, which was located in the "county commissioner's office, an ugly brick building from the second half of the 19th century."

The rooms were far from elegant and so dark that Magnus sought permission to cut a new window into the east wall of the bedroom for light. Emmy immediately became pregnant again, and on 23 March 1912 she bore Wernher Magnus Maximilian Freiherr von Braun in the apartment, again fortunately without complications. Although she quickly adapted to the roles of mother and wife of the county commissioner, the transition was not easy for the intellectually gifted young woman. Four decades later she told a younger American friend: "I was very intense about life. Always soaring upward and falling down. It was very hard upon me to restrain and compose myself for the disciplines of household management, looking after my husband and rearing my boys. But little by little I calmned [sic] down and managed."[15]

Wirsitz scarcely figured in the later memory of Wernher von Braun, who was five when the family moved away. Fifty years later his father asserted that "Wernher was a remarkable child. When he was four he could read a newspaper upside down and right side up." A childhood friend, whose father administered a Prussian state domain, remembered riding a pair of donkeys with a three- or four-year-old Wernher. In a memoir written late in life, Sigismund recalled that the two brothers knew all the horses by name, and that living in Wirsitz, and later at Crenzow, gave them a strong connection to nature. His parents' close and happy relationship, he also observed, afforded their sons a great sense of security; they were close to their parents all their lives.[16]

When Wernher was scarcely over two, world war erupted, with disruptive consequences for the family. On 29 June 1914 Magnus von Braun's driver rushed into his office exclaiming, "The heir to the Austrian throne has been murdered. Now there will be war." The county commissioner pooh-poohed the idea, as did most people. But the uneducated man was prescient, and a month later the Austrian ultimatum to Serbia provoked a dangerous crisis. Emmy von Braun had taken the two boys to Krakow, then an Austrian city on the border of the Russian Empire, and on 28 July Magnus wrote urging her to go to Zinnowitz, a Baltic Sea resort (where Wernher would later live). They soon returned to Wirsitz, where Magnus supervised the local army mobilization. Farther to the east, invading Russian troops occupied Neucken for one day in August 1914, forcing the von Braun relatives to flee. But the Russians quickly withdrew after being outmaneuvered and then humiliated at the Battle of Tannenberg by Generals Paul von Hindenburg and Erich Ludendorff. In November threatening Russian troop movements farther west caused Emmy von Braun to make a quick trip to Berlin, carrying all the monetary instruments of the county savings and loan to be deposited in a bank for safekeeping. Magnus stayed behind with "our two small boys[,] . . . an uncomfortable feeling, but their flight would have caused panic" in the local population. Soon, however, the Russians were forced to withdraw, a forerunner of disastrous defeats on the Eastern Front that would lead to the collapse of the czarist empire in 1917.[17]

Early in 1915 Magnus von Braun was once again drawn into high politics by a chance meeting in the capital. His old boss, Delbrück, now state secretary of the Reich Interior Office, requested his services as adjutant, and Magnus von Braun reluctantly acceded to his wartime duty. He commuted back and forth to Wirsitz, as the war made it impossible to find an adequate replacement as county commissioner. Expenses were heavy as Emmy, Sigismund, and Wernher came repeatedly to stay with him in rented, furnished rooms in Berlin, bringing with them some of the household servants.[18]

If the family's existence was peripatetic and uncertain in the two years before mid-1917, it became only more so in the two years following. During that summer the kaiser appointed a new chancellor, Georg Michaelis, who was more to the liking of Hindenburg and Ludendorff, who had ascended to the supreme command of the army in 1916 and now exercised a "silent dictatorship" over the country. Magnus von Braun claims to have been the one to suggest the rather obscure official in food administration. In September 1917, as a reward, Michaelis made him his press secretary, the first ever in the Reich Chancellery. Magnus von Braun received a huge increase in pay, from 4,800 to 14,000 marks per year, but the job was to be very short-lived. Michaelis quickly found himself in over his head and was widely seen as the incompetent lackey of the generals. He was forced to resign in early November. Von Braun had to resign too and was shipped off to the political equivalent of Siberia: as a reserve officer, he was called into the army to serve as an administrator in the occupied territories in Lithuania and Poland, leaving Berlin on frigid New Year's Day 1918. That summer he was finally replaced as county commissioner of Wirsitz, but the family must have moved away before Christmas 1917. Emmy, Sigismund, and Wernher stayed in Crenzow throughout 1918, where she helped administer the estate of her brother Hans, a prisoner of war in Britain. They saw Magnus only on rare visits home.[19]

In the chaotic conditions that followed the czarist collapse and the rise of a tenuous Bolshevik dictatorship in central Russia, the talented forty-year-old quickly ascended into higher positions in the expanding German occupation zone; Magnus even applied on 26 August 1918 to purchase a landed estate in Lithuania. But victory in the east was negated by the loss of the war on the Western Front and the collapse of Austria-Hungary in the fall, leading to a revolutionary uprising of German soldiers and sailors, the abdication of the kaiser on 9 November, and the armistice in the west two days later. At the end of 1918 Magnus von Braun was sent back to a country in turmoil. Early in the new year the now socialist-controlled Prussian Interior Ministry, in which he was still a civil servant, sent him to be the acting police chief of the major Pomeranian port city of Stettin, only eighty kilometers from Crenzow. There he had to negotiate with the local workers' and soldiers' council, and although Magnus von Braun was a monarchist out of sympathy with the new republic, he apparently had skill dealing with people and crises. In the spring he was called to Berlin again as personnel chief in the Interior Ministry. The revolution had led to bloody fighting in the city's streets, and it certainly created administrative turmoil and an extremely heavy workload. "Before one o'clock in the morning I scarcely ever stopped work," he recalled. Emmy and the two boys stayed in Crenzow, which made sense given the dangerous situation but also because she was expecting another child. On 10 May 1919 she gave birth in Greifswald to their third and last son, Magnus Hans Alexander Maximilian, seven years younger than Wernher, and destined to follow him into rocketry.[20]

Stability apparently returned in September 1919, when Magnus Sr. "was kicked upstairs" after left-wing deputies in the Prussian Parliament attacked his conservative personnel policies. He was appointed district chief (*Regierungspräsident*) of Gumbinnen, in his native East Prussia. Now known as Gusev, Russia, Gumbinnen was a small city near the Lithuanian border, in a region much troubled by the Russian civil war and the secession of the Baltic states. In the Prussian system the district chief was the next level up from the county commissioner and reported to the provincial governor; Magnus was one of three in East Prussia. The family moved to Gumbinnen and inhabited the elaborately decorated, thirty-six-room official apartment in the government building. Wernher and Sigismund were put into grade school for the first time, at the age of seven and eight respectively; a surviving photo shows Wernher as a cherubic blond boy in a sailor suit, together with his classmates, one of whom had no shoes. (The elementary grades in Germany were the only level at which students of different social classes might mix.) The two boys had been tutored by an aunt while at Crenzow.[21]

Once again the turbulent politics of the era intervened to send the family packing. On 13 March 1920 extreme right-wing troops with swastikas on their vehicles rolled into Berlin, drove out the democratically elected Reich and Prussian governments, and installed the coup leader, Wolfgang Kapp, as chancellor. Magnus von Braun knew Kapp, and when the East Prussian governor declared allegiance to the new government, von Braun followed suit, one of the few officials in Germany to do so. Later he explained that he felt that the exposed position of the province, which had been cut off by land from the rest of Germany through the creation of the Polish corridor, plus the declarations of the governor and military commander on the side of the coup regime, had forced his hand. But if Magnus had possessed a democratic sensibility, he would have refused to cooperate. The so-called Kapp Putsch turned out to be a fiasco; within four days the plotters were forced to flee when the trade unions called out a massive general strike in Berlin and across Germany. In the aftermath the Prussian interior minister agreed with socialist demands to suspend all those who declared for the "usurper regime." He appointed an acting replacement for von Braun and put him under investigation with all the others, including a cousin who was a county commissioner. Magnus von Braun was not among those ultimately charged with treason, but he was fined 600 Reichsmarks in the fall and put on permanent suspension without loss of pension—a light punishment typical of the Weimar Republic's wishy-washy response to the far right's challenge. His Prussian civil service career was, however, over. With his excellent connections in conservative circles, he was offered a position as the regional director of the Raiffeisen agricultural credit cooperatives (named after their nineteenth-century founder) for the provinces of Brandenburg and Schleswig-Holstein—a job based in Berlin. Emmy and the three little boys followed him back to the capital in the fall of 1920, where they rented the "garden house" behind the "palace of an Upper Silesian magnate" who lived on the elegant Tiergartenstrasse.[22]

For the young Wernher von Braun, it was a move of fateful importance. Rather than spending the middle years of his childhood in a provincial town on the margins of the Reich, he was exposed to the pulsating energy of a world city of four million people. Berlin was a center for the technological innovations of the interwar years in aviation, radio, electrification, public transport, and railways. It was also a city of raw class contradictions, with a lively underground world of seedy nightclubs, prostitution, and crime, and huge districts of shabby working-class apartment blocks where the majority voted Socialist and many of the rest, Communist. The years up to the end of 1923 were especially chaotic. Although the open street fighting that had begun with the 1918 revolution had ended with the Kapp Putsch, the rapidly accelerating collapse of the Reichsmark, leading to the infamous hyperinflation of 1923, fed speculation and crime and an atmosphere of "anything goes." The city was a magnet for sleaze but also for writers, musicians, intellectuals, artists, and strivers of all kinds. In that it bore a resemblance to New York, and the "Old West" of the city might be compared to the tony Upper East Side fronting Central Park. The von Brauns' street bordered the Tiergarten (Animal Park), the old royal hunting grounds outside the Brandenburg Gate. The famous Berlin Zoo was on the far west end of this great park, next to the booming, trendy "New West" district around the Kurfürstendamm and the Kaiser-Wilhelm Memorial Church.[23]

Because of their father's role in banking, Wernher and his brothers, Sigismund and Magnus Jr., lived in a bubble of upper-class privilege, with a butler, servants, and a grand piano; they were sheltered from the rough edges of Berlin. The period was not, however, without financial anxiety for their parents; Sigismund remembers that the hyperinflation forced them to consult with Emmy's brother Alexander, also a banker, about how to protect their liquid assets from rapid erosion. They looked at the paper every day to find the Reichsmark's value and were shocked by their losses. In November 1923 the mark fell to a value of 4.2 trillion to the dollar, or one-trillionth the prewar gold standard. A glass of beer cost 150 billion marks, a pickle 4 billion. People had to carry huge bundles of paper money to shop, there was mass unemployment and wild speculation, and many of the middle and upper classes lost most of their savings, alienating them further from the republic. Magnus von Braun Sr.'s essentially political memoirs mention almost nothing of this period, however, except that he was named one of the founding members of the Rentenbank, an institution created in October 1923 to invent a substitute mark. During the "stabilization era" of 1924–29, when the Weimar Republic enjoyed a brief respite from crisis, he moved up further, joining the board of directors of the central Reichsbank in 1924 and becoming national director of one of the two Raiffeisen cooperative associations two years later. Around 1924 the family moved to an even more elegant house at In den Zelten 11, on the northeast edge of the Tiergarten, and he also had an official apartment at his office on the Landwehr canal.[24]

Soon after arriving in Berlin in the fall of 1920, Magnus and Emmy von Braun put Sigismund and Wernher into the old royal Wilhelms-Gymnasium, but it was closed down within a couple of years and merged into the very eminent and less conservative French Gymnasium (FG). Also known as the Collège Français, it was originally founded in the late seventeenth century for the Huguenot Protestants who had fled Louis XIV's persecution and settled in Prussia. The FG's building, constructed in the early 1870s, was on the Spree River just east of the Reichstag (parliament building) in the city center. After a period of parallel classes that caused a certain amount of friction, the Wilhelms-Gymnasium's students, including the von Braun boys, were brought up to the FG's standards in French and were merged into classes by grade. Half or more of all classes were in French; in later years Latin and finally Greek were introduced, and also English. As was typical of Gymnasia, science was not a strength. Religious instruction was mandatory, and Sigismund later recalled the onerous requirement that Protestant students had to attend the French-language service every other Sunday in the eighteenth-century French cathedral in the city center.[25]

An unusually high proportion of Jewish boys—around a third of the student body—was nonetheless drawn to the school by its high standards and reputation for tolerance. Some parents of Wilhelms-Gymnasium students sent their children elsewhere because of the liberal and Jewish tone of the school, but the von Brauns appreciated its linguistic strengths—Emmy spoke half a dozen languages, and Magnus at least English and French. The latter's memoir inadvertently reveals a traditional form of social anti-Semitism, but Jewish classmates of Sigismund's remember being welcomed into his home warmly and without prejudice. To arrive at their first class at eight, Wernher and Sigismund probably walked from In den Zelten 11 to school, past the Tiergarten and the Victory Column (which was then in front of the Reichstag building), and then either along the riverbank behind Parliament or through the Brandenburg Gate into Unter den Linden, the famous boulevard. School stopped at two in the afternoon, before the main meal of the day. Their parents also put them into a private gymnastics and sport club in the west end.[26]

Wernher von Braun's self-described "nonconformist streak," his engineering inclinations, and his fascination with "progress" apparently manifested themselves quite early. In one memoir he tells a story that may go back to Gumbinnen: "I have always felt an obsession to build things. At the age of seven I started to build a tree house. At the same time an aunt, thinking to steer me properly, gave me a set of books on ornithology"—a von Quistorp aunt, presumably. "Running out of boards, I loaded my books into a wagon" and went down to a bookstore to sell them off to get money for "materials and tools." However, the bookstore owner kept haggling and stalling until "my mother arrived and swept me and my ornithology library into our car. One does not sell his aunt's present, I learned, even though it is useless. It was a very painful lesson." In about 1924 he formed a mock corporation, the "Germanoford Automobil A.G.," with Beach Conger, an American classmate in school, at a time when Henry Ford was a very popular figure in Germany as well as America. They started to put together a car out of old parts in a garage behind the house and created an elaborate corporate structure on paper, with von Braun as "business manager."[27] With such inclinations, Wernher might well have ended up an engineer even if the family had stayed in the east. But living in Berlin immersed him in an environment of cars, elevated and underground railways, airplanes, and occasional sightings of zeppelins; a few years later it would put him at the center of the small German rocketry and spaceflight movement.

Another critical source of his early fascination with technology and science was the profound influence of his scientifically inclined mother, with whom Wernher had a particularly close relationship. Magnus von Braun tells the following story:

> In the twenties, at a small dinner in Berlin, Privy Councilor Nicodem Caro, inventor of "nitrogen fixation from the air," led my wife to the table. Obviously very excited, he came to me at the conclusion of the meal and said: "I sweated blood at dinner today. Never has a woman put questions to me about my area of specialty, but also about atomic research, that showed such a profound command of the material."[28]

Her serious interest in science led the family to nickname her "Madame Curie," although the favorite family pet name for her was "Buttche," a magical fish in a Grimm fairy tale that keeps granting a fisherman wishes until he and his wife get too greedy. Needless to say, aristocratic social expectations and gender roles left her with virtually no chance to become a scientist, and as fundamentally happy as her marriage was, she was wed to a very conservative man who took male superiority for granted and effectively conveyed traditional masculine values to his sons. Later in life, however, he would give himself virtually no credit, hereditary or otherwise, for the technological and scientific talents of Wernher. Expressing perplexity as to how a world-famous rocket engineer could emerge from a line of Prussian soldiers, landowners, and civil servants, he attributed these talents to the genetic inheritance of the von Quistorps and to the profound influence of his wife. And yet his administrative and political skills, his ability to land on his feet through multiple changes of fortune, and his devotion to traditional Prussian values of honest and loyal state service, almost regardless of who was in power, certainly contributed a great deal to Wernher's personality.[29]

Still, Emmy von Braun was his ideal tutor. But he was always questioning, always inquiring into how things work, to the point of being exasperating. She later said:

> He was like a dry sponge, soaking up every bit of knowledge as eagerly as he could. There was no end of the questions he asked; he really could wear you out quickly! I never succeeded in being cross with him. . . . Whenever I tried to, he would put on his most cherubi[c] smile and talk about something else. He had no problem learning good manners, and he usually practiced them. When he did not, it was just a brief spell of naughtiness, or simply his own way of expressing an exuberant joy of life.[30]

His ability to use his manners and charm to win people over, to get past conflicts and inconvenient problems and move on to "something else," would prove to be one of the defining characteristics of his future career. He may have been a "nonconformist" and, in his middle teens, a bit of a troublemaker, but the aristocratic upbringing and loving family environment had left their imprint. That charm and those manners, which became so important to his charismatic leadership style, were learned in a very supportive, highly cultured, and privileged household. But it was also a very conservative household, one in which his father made clear his distaste for social equality and democracy.

CHAPTER TWO

Sonny Boy

1925–32

For generations the von Braun sons had found careers in the army, the government, or in landholding.... I, the middle child, was the maverick. —WERNHER VON BRAUN[1]

Easter was an important time for Wernher and his older brother, Sigismund, not so much because of the religious holiday but because their birthdays fell at that time, and because the school year had its major midyear break at Easter. School terms ran from October to March and April to July, with a few weeks off between the two. Easter was also a traditional time for church confirmation, something boys and girls normally undertook at about age thirteen or fourteen. So when Wernher completed his confirmation studies and Lutheran church ceremony around the time of his thirteenth birthday, 23 March 1925, his parents gave him a present, although not the gold watch customary for an upper-class boy (something unimaginable in the vast proletarian neighborhoods of Berlin). Instead, at the behest of his mother, they presented him with a small telescope. "This was a hit far beyond our expectations," she said a quarter century later; he took up observing with eagerness. Even with the growth of electric lighting, it was still reasonably dark in the middle of the city then, at least in a large park like the Tiergarten.[2]

The year 1925 would prove to be a critical turning point in Wernher von Braun's life, and not only because the telescope launched a newfound fascination with the Moon, the planets, and the stars. In the fall his parents sent him to an elite boarding school in the hope of harnessing his restless nature. Around the end of the year his discovery of a pioneering treatise would direct his astronomical interests toward building things that might actually allow people to travel into space. By 1932 von Braun had matured into an immensely charming, talented, and driven individual with one seemingly utopian ambition: to pioneer human spaceflight, even to land on the Moon himself.

Despite Wernher's new enthusiasm for astronomy, the spring 1925 term found him in serious trouble in school. The traditional Gymnasium education did not particularly suit him; he later remembered the tedium of learning Latin by translating it into French. But his failure, most notably and ironically, was in mathematics; he simply did not apply himself to learn the subject, preferring instead to tinker in the garage with the homemade car he had started with his friend Beach Conger, or to act as the class clown. Sometime in the spring the FG informed his parents that he would have to repeat the *Untertertia* (the equivalent of eighth grade) because he would fail not only mathematics but also physics. A rare surviving letter from his elderly grandmother, written on 14 June, shows that Wernher's parents had already decided to send him to one of the Lietz boarding schools instead. These institutions had been founded by the educational reformer Hermann Lietz in 1898 on the model of the English public (i.e., private) school at Abbotsholme. Wernher's grandmother was glad to hear of this solution and that "the boy is looking forward to it," but she was concerned that the school might not offer the full course to the *Abitur*—the top high school graduation degree needed for university entrance.[3]

Boarding schools were unusual in Germany, and many had a mediocre reputation as "cramming institutions." The Lietz schools, on the other hand, had established an elite reputation through their founder's pioneering approach to education. Rejecting the rote learning, emphasis on classical languages, and class bias against physical work of the Gymnasium, Lietz combined sports and outdoor activities with crafts like carpentry and rigorous courses in modern languages and literatures, mathematics, and science. By training Hermann Lietz was a Protestant theologian; ideologically he was part of the "conservative revolution" that combined nationalistic German values and criticism of class privilege with a distrust of big cities as corrupters of youth and as threats to the genetic and intellectual health of the nation. Like the German right and much of the middle and upper classes in general, he also detested the socialist labor movement and distrusted parliamentary and party politics. Thus his educational philosophy had elements that pointed in the direction of both advanced liberal education and far-right politics. After Lietz died in 1919, his mantle was assumed by Alfred Andreesen, a teacher who would come to play a central role in Wernher von Braun's life.[4]

Wernher would go to one of the newest Lietz schools, opened in 1923 for the middle grades (seven–ten) at Ettersburg castle, just north of the historic town of Weimar, two hundred kilometers southwest of Berlin. Due to the expanding demand for boarding school places, Andreesen was able to lease a small Baroque hunting palace and chapel of the former microprincipality of Weimar, which had been merged into the new republican state of Thuringia in 1920. Weimar was above all famous for its connection to two great writers of the late eighteenth and early nineteenth centuries, Johann Wolfgang von Goethe and Friedrich Schiller. Goethe, a minister for the grand duke, had allegedly used the Ettersburg at times to work on his masterwork, *Faust*. More recently the city had lent its name informally to the German republic. In early 1919 the National Assembly, which created the new constitution, had fled there to escape battles between left-wing revolutionaries and right-wing army units in Berlin. In October 1925 Wernher arrived at school; a photo presumably from this time shows a young-looking thirteen-year-old boy with classmates, unloading luggage from a horse-drawn wagon. It had probably been sent to the train station to pick them up.

Ettersburg school, which was perched on top of a hill next to a pretty little village, had about eighty boys, one-quarter of whom were in Wernher's grade level. Because of the expensive fees, they were drawn heavily from the wealthy, mostly nonnobles. The fathers were typically large-scale farmers and landowners, businessmen, professionals, and senior civil servants; one member of his class was Hermann Planck, the son of the Nobel Prize–winning physicist Max Planck. Northern German Protestants predominated, reflecting the background of the founder and the tone of his schools, but there was also a minority of Catholics. Noticeable for their absence was any significant number of Jews. As early as 1904 Lietz had had a falling-out with Jewish students and a Jewish teacher as a result of his anti-Semitism; they started alternative, more liberal schools on the same model. Although the prejudice of Lietz and his successor Andreesen was not of the racial Nazi type, it certainly reflected the growing anti-Jewish bigotry of the German right.[5]

The daily routine and structure laid down by Lietz at the outset was still very much in force when von Braun came to Ettersburg. Classes ran from early morning until early afternoon, with a couple of short breaks, followed by the main meal of the day at one p.m., a pause, and then a couple of hours in the late afternoon for the "guilds"—clubs based on mutual interests and skills, including carpentry, metalwork, music, theater, and so on. The guilds were also tasked to do farm or maintenance work around the school. In the evening after supper break, there was "chapel," which typically consisted of readings from great literature, music concerts by the school orchestra, or talks by students on subjects of interest. Sunday was a day off, but there was a mandatory nondenominational Christian service, plus religious instruction in normal class hours. One final and important institution was that of the "family": each teacher had a "family" of students from different grade levels who would eat together, increasing the bond between teachers and students as well as providing patriarchal guidance.[6]

Not long after Wernher settled into his first term at Ettersburg, he noticed in an astronomy or nature magazine a brief mention of a little book called *Die Rakete zu den Planetenräumen* (*The Rocket into Interplanetary Space*). It was the second printing of a short treatise originally published in 1923. The author, Hermann Oberth, was a Gymnasium teacher from the German-speaking minority in Transylvania, which had been part of Hungary before 1918 and of Romania afterward. The young Ettersburg astronomy enthusiast excitedly sent away for a copy in the mail. "When the precious volume arrived I carried it to my room. Opening it I was aghast. Its pages were a hash of mathematical formulas. It was gibberish. I rushed to my teachers. 'How can I understand what this man is saying?' I demanded. They told me to study mathematics and physics, my two worst courses."[7]

The book was indeed difficult, and revolutionary. Originally written as a doctoral dissertation for the University of Heidelberg, it had been rejected by the astronomy institute, not without reason, as inappropriate to the discipline. The book opened with four startling propositions: (1) "With the present state of science and technology it is possible to construct machines that can climb higher than the Earth's atmosphere"; (2) "With further development" it would be feasible to reach orbit, or even escape the Earth; (3) These machines could carry humans, possibly without harmful side effects; and (4) "Under certain economic conditions the construction of such machines could pay for itself," and this could happen "within a few decades." Oberth then proceeded to derive the fundamental equations of the rocket and suggested that liquid-propellant combinations such as liquid oxygen and alcohol, when combined with multiple rocket stages, would provide sufficient energy to launch objects into orbit and beyond—thus breaking out of the obvious limitations of the black-powder fireworks rocket. He also described some of the medical effects of spaceflight, such as acceleration and weightlessness, presented some preliminary designs for experimental vehicles, and described a giant space mirror in orbit that could illuminate the Earth or incinerate enemy installations.[8]

Oberth was not the first to show that the rocket could be the means to get into space. An eccentric German inventor, Hermann Ganswindt, had given a scientifically faulty account of a reaction-motor space vehicle in an 1891 lecture. An obscure Russian schoolteacher, Konstantin Tsiolkovsky, had published a number of articles in his country beginning in 1903. And an

American physicist, Robert Goddard, had created an international newspaper flap in early 1920 when the Smithsonian Institution published his paper "A Method of Reaching Extreme Altitudes." Goddard had studiously avoided discussing his far-reaching ideas about liquid-fuel rockets and manned spaceflight, but he did mention the possibility of hitting the Moon with a cluster of powder rockets; the notion provoked both ridicule and fascination with the technology, especially in the English-speaking world. Each of these spaceflight theorists had worked in complete isolation, and Oberth had discovered Goddard's work only as his book was going to press in 1922. Outside the infant Soviet Union, which already had a growing band of spaceflight enthusiasts, no one had ever heard of Tsiolkovsky until after the publication of Oberth's book. Even *The Rocket into Interplanetary Space* might have languished in obscurity but for the efforts of Max Valier, an Austrian air force veteran, astronomy popularizer, and campaigner for a crackpot astronomical theory. In 1924 Valier published a popular book summarizing (sometimes inaccurately) Oberth's mind-stretching insights: at a time when aircraft could scarcely do 300 km/hr (186 mph), the German-Romanian pioneer was talking about velocities in the tens of thousands. To many, the idea of traveling to the Moon and the planets seemed absurd or at least far off in some utopian future. But in Weimar Germany and Soviet Russia there was more acceptance—the upheavals of the preceding decade had made these cultures unusually open to radical ideas.[9]

One of those who was open-minded was a thirteen-year-old boy in Ettersburg; his fascination with the heavens, inclination toward engineering, faith in progress, burning ambition, and optimistic nature combined to produce a romantic obsession with the idea of exploring space. He expressed his newfound enthusiasm by doing rash experiments with fireworks rockets and dangerous chemicals. Once again von Braun's compulsion to work with his hands and his restless intellect got him into trouble. As the few anecdotes we have come from much later, about all we can say is that these experiments likely took place in 1926–27. One of the best stories comes from a former teacher:

> I still remember very well that very first rocket, which blew up in the faces of Edwin May, Jochen Westphal and Ernst August Saalfeld in the farmyard in Ettersburg, while the inventor, Wernher von Braun, was trying to get launch permission from me, and I was trying to tell him that the experiment couldn't go well, because without controlling the mixture ratio of acetylene and air, there was a constant danger of an explosion.

A classmate who knew him from the earliest days in Berlin recalled that Wernher also started a fire in the woods as a result of some experiment at Ettersburg.[10]

From his family, we hear of stunts with fireworks rockets that he pulled at home during vacations. Late in life Sigismund told this story:

> I can still remember what happened one day when we lived in Berlin. We launched a fireworks rocket from one of those little kiddie wagons with the assumption that it would only probably reach the speed of a pedestrian. It didn't turn out exactly that way. Before we knew it, it had flown out of our hands and crashed through our greenhouse window; the cauliflower was literally covered with broken glass. It was the first time my father was to foot the bill for rocket development.

Subsequently Wernher launched his rockets into a vendor's apples and then into a bakery. His father recalled "broken windows" and "destroyed flower gardens," and his mother "an endless production line of vehicles, some small and powered by old clockworks, others larger and driven by rockets."[11]

Sending him off to boarding school, even one with as many manual activities as the Lietz schools, clearly had not immediately made him less of a misfit. On 14 January 1926 his grandmother wrote his mother: "How will you ever be satisfied with Wernehr? [The old lady never could spell his name right.] He looks so . . . modest and nice in the picture." Thirty years later his mother remarked to him in a letter: "That you got a letter from Heinrich Walter [a former teacher] caused us to laugh out loud. When I think how that camel judged you then: 'You were an asocial element and didn't belong in the school, etc.' Dr. A[ndreesen] was a better pedagogue." The Ettersburg school's dissatisfaction with him was not without cause, however. Wernher's enthusiasm for astronomy and rocketry at first actually reinforced his tendency to be "completely lazy" in any subject that did not engage his interest, according to the daughter of another teacher.[12]

Nor did Wernher's discovery of Oberth remove all doubts from his own mind about his future. The later standard version of his biography, which von Braun himself sometimes promoted, leaves the impression that *The Rocket into Interplanetary Space* instantly changed his life. But a ghost-written memoir he published in 1958 gives a more complex picture; this transformation was not complete until he was sixteen.

> Before that I was torn and troubled. One day I wanted to be a musician, for which ambition I showed some aptitude. Mother and I played four-handed duets and our school orchestra, in which my instrument was

the cello, rendered some creditable music as well as several thin melodies I composed. Next day I would swing toward science. My real hero, I recall, was Copernicus, who first said that the center of our universe was the sun, not the earth, as once supposed.

Indeed, Wernher became quite seriously involved in music in the mid-1920s, learned the cello at Ettersburg, and dreamed at times of becoming a composer, a dream that betrays an inner drive to make his mark on the world and become famous. Three handwritten piano pieces survive in his papers, dating from between November 1927 and April 1928, his last term at that school. They may reflect instruction by the modernist composer Paul Hindemith, to whom his obviously well-connected parents sent Wernher for private lessons when he was home. We have no idea when he began the piano—presumably after they moved to Berlin. It seems apparent that his parents greatly encouraged his musical talents in the mid-1920s, as these were much more socially acceptable in the family and high society than his tinkering, his spaceflight enthusiasm, and his rocket experiments.[13]

It was all to no avail. Whereas Sigismund was the model eldest son, excelling at the FG in languages, literature, and history and quite willingly adopting the role of heir to the family traditions (he would later join the diplomatic service), Wernher was the middle child who rebelled, presumably in part to carve out an independent role and compete for attention from his parents. Birth order in this case seems to have mattered, and the two are classical examples of the roles of first and second children. (Magnus Jr. was only a small boy in this period, but for much of his life he would find himself in the shadow of his overachieving brothers.) Wernher's father recalls

the absolute futility of all my attempts to apply a bit of parental guidance to him. His growth rate was exorbitant, and I often thought I could channel his outbursts of activity toward the more civil goals that were the accepted standards of society. Determination, fatherly strictness, diplomacy—nothing worked. Any attempt to admonish him, or convince him of the inappropriateness of a certain action, ran off not only like a drop of water, but like a drop of mercury, without leaving the faintest trace. I soon gave up—a reaction that really ran against my grain—and resigned myself to watching him grow.

Wernher later said that his father was "completely baffled" by his technical interests but "never ridiculed, opposed or discouraged them." He was fortunate in this respect but also in having a mother who came to actively support his focus on astronomy and rocketry.[14]

If Wernher suffered from indecision in this period, it did not stop his high spirits. An old servant of Dr. Gerd von Below, a relative, later gave a vivid picture of him and his brothers during a visit to the Below estate in eastern Pomerania:

> Wernher was nicknamed "Be[e]thoven" there, because he composed at night and in the morning said: "Aunt Annemarie, I will play something for you." There were two other brothers too. They brought a whole observatory with them, and two shotguns with many shells, and shot at everything in the air and on the ground. They took their whole haul to their room. Then it began to stink to high heaven. They didn't want to be parted from their catch. Managed finally to bring it to the cellar. A lot of their haul they nonetheless took back to Berlin.

Hunting was one of the skills and masculine virtues of the aristocracy that Magnus von Braun conveyed to all his sons. While he was county commissioner in Wirsitz before the war, he made sure to participate in the hunts of the large landowners, both for political reasons and for personal enjoyment. He fortified his position by shooting well, and he boasts in his memoirs of bringing home "ninety pheasants or sixty hares in one day." Wernher would also be a good shot and an enthusiastic hunter for the rest of his life.[15]

The small telescope must also have been used for observing at Ettersburg. One of the few childhood things he saved through the chaos at the end of World War II was a carefully marked and measured diagram of Mercury's transit across the face of the Sun on 10 November 1927. A school friend remembers observing a lunar eclipse with him as well.[16]

Wernher poured his new passion for the heavens into a draft for a popular astronomy book that he wrote out longhand—either in his last period at Ettersburg or in his first year at the new Lietz school that opened on Spiekeroog, a North Sea island, in April 1928. Painstakingly written in his usual, very clear hand, the manuscript fills an amazing 179 pages of a bound school notebook, with color and black-and-white illustrations from magazines pasted in. One of them was of the 100-in (2.5-m) telescope on Mount Wilson, the largest in the world at the time; when he reached California in July 1947, he sent his father a postcard of the instrument inscribed: "1000 greetings from the focus of my youthful dreams." Showing a talent for popular writing that would have a chance to bloom only in the United States, Wernher began his 1928 manuscript with two short poetic epigrams, one from Schiller. He then put the reader far off in deep space, beyond the galaxy, and imagined what it would be like to travel at the speed of light through the stars to the solar system. After looking briefly at the history of astronomy, he treated the tools of the astronomer, how the design of the universe was understood over time, and how the seasons and the sky work. Starting from the Sun, he then began a tour of the solar system. Right in the middle of the Mars section, after discussing the mystery of the "canals," the manuscript abruptly ends in midsentence. Perhaps holidays intervened, and his mind turned elsewhere, or maybe he began to see the futility of the exercise. In any case he put an astounding amount of energy and thought into it, based on the model of popular astronomy books of the 1920s. He clearly had an ambition to make his mark.[17]

Another notebook he managed to save definitely comes from Ettersburg, as its content is not as mature. It includes English words, math exercises, and crossword puzzles he was drafting, but the reason he kept the notebook lies in its drawings of spaceships and rockets and a short piece about Oberth's space mirror. The rocket drawings are almost all variants of the same teardrop design. The most elaborate shows a one-man spacecraft with a human figure, a window in the rounded nose of the teardrop, and an elaborate list over top:

Take Along:
Photogr. equipment. Food f. 100 hours. Tinted glass in var. strengths. Divers suits w. heating and cooling equipment. Oxygen f. 100 hours. Replacement windows and lamps, signal apparatus. Tools. Astr. telescope. Radio equip. Mineral probes, test devices.

Other drawings sketch out the design of the pilot's seat and of a military signal rocket. Lacking is any realistic propulsion system or an allotment of adequate room for it. The drawings are the work of a boy with imaginative engineering ideas but a weak command of the technicalities. Similarly, the essay on the space mirror is essentially just a summary of the last part of Oberth's book, but it too shows a certain engineering imagination as he describes Oberth's scheme to spin the framework of the mirror out of wires of sodium metal. He even got up and gave a speech about the feasibility of spaceflight in the evening "chapel" at Ettersburg—something that stuck in the minds of former teachers and classmates decades later.[18]

It was during the next two years, the years when he went to school in Spiekeroog, that Wernher von Braun's mature personality emerged. He developed a single-mindedness about rocketry and spaceflight, a fanaticism that could lead to blindness about the importance of anything else. He also demonstrated a growing brilliance in math and science, powered by ambition, talent, and a determination to work incredibly hard if it served his goals. Finally, he began to show a leadership ability that brought others along to join in his enterprises.

According to von Braun, whatever doubts he had about his future career were wiped out by the spectacular rocket stunts that Max Valier and Fritz von Opel, the heir to the automobile fortune, initiated in April 1928. During the preceding years the German spaceflight movement had steadily grown. The boldness of Oberth and Valier encouraged the publication of new books by converts like Essen city architect Walter Hohmann and Berlin freelance writer Willy Ley. On 5 July 1927 a society, the Verein für Raumschiffahrt (Society for Space Travel), or VfR, was founded in Breslau, Silesia (now Wro-claw, Poland), at the instigation of Johannes Winkler, a church administrator and frustrated engineer. Winkler also created a society journal, *Die Rakete* (The Rocket). None of this made a deep impression on the German public or media, however, until the energetic Valier found a wealthy sponsor to fund the demonstrations that he thought were needed to pave the way for future rocket planes and spaceships. Fritz von Opel was a dashing playboy in search of publicity and fame and was not committed to spaceflight; he proceeded to use Valier and then push him aside. Their experiments began at the Opel headquarters near Frankfurt in mid-April 1928, using large black-powder solid-fuel rockets to propel a hastily constructed car driven by one of Opel's test drivers. The initial results were less than impressive, but once they used enough rockets, the car accelerated spectacularly, spewing smoke.[19]

These tests had nothing to do with proper technology development, and Hermann Oberth and his closest follower, Willy Ley, viewed them with disdain, but they initiated a *Raketenrummel* (rocket rumble or fad) in the popular media. This fad was given a powerful boost on 23 May when Opel himself drove a new, much sleeker-looking car on the AVUS, a long straight road used for racing in western Berlin; the demonstration was preceded by a radio address. In the aftermath Opel and Valier split up and began a crazy summer of rocket-powered stunts with cars and railcars, all of it chronicled in the newsreels, on the radio, and in newspapers. Others jumped in, tying powder rockets to bicycles and gliders, and Valier himself took it to its hilarious nadir in early 1929 when he piloted a rocket ice sled on a Bavarian lake. Meanwhile the famous director of *Metropolis*, Fritz Lang, announced that he would begin filming a realistic spaceflight movie, *Die Frau im Mond* (*The Woman in the Moon*).[20]

For a teenage space enthusiast, the *Raketenrummel* was fabulous. Inspired by seeing at least a single run of one of Opel's rocket cars, von Braun decided to build his latest and largest rocket vehicle while home on vacation in Berlin, probably after his first term at Spiekeroog ended in July

1928. He modified his old wooden children's wagon and attached half a dozen of the largest fireworks rockets he could buy.

> In a sedate German thoroughfare called the Tiergarten Allee, I aimed the vehicle carefully down the pavement. The day was mild, and many strollers were taking the air. It never occurred to me that they were not prepared to share the sidewalk with my noble experiment.
>
> I got behind the wagon, lighted the fuses, and leaped aside as jets of flame thrust out from the rockets and my wagon began to roll. Unattended, it picked up speed. . . . It swerved this way and that, zigzagging through groups. I yelled a warning and men and women fled in all directions.
>
> I was ecstatic. The wagon was wholly out of control and trailing a comet's tail of fire.

Soon after the rockets burned out, the police showed up and hauled him in for questioning, to his great embarrassment, and then turned him over to his father, who gave him a tongue-lashing and one day's "house arrest." It proved to be the last and most spectacular of his experiments, but it marked his now firmly set determination to "dedicate his life" to space travel.[21]

In the meantime he had begun school on Spiekeroog, the special project and love of Alfred Andreesen. Andreesen was a native of the region—flat, rural country along the North Sea in far northwestern Germany, near the Dutch border—and always felt that a school on the sea would provide a special environment for the fulfillment of Lietz's educational vision of ascetic, energetic living and distance from the corrupting influence of the city. One of the East Frisian barrier islands, Spiekeroog was, and is, little more than a giant sand dune in the sea, and over the centuries it has migrated south and east. In the 1920s, other than fishing and some dairy farming for the local inhabitants, the island's economy depended on the three-month summer season, when well-off natives of the neighboring regions came and stayed at a few resort hotels in the village. Just reaching the island was an effort. The rail line ended inland at the tiny town of Esens, then one had to take a bus to the fishing port of Neuharlingersiel, then catch the once-daily ferry to the island. From the ferry dock there was a horse-drawn railway to the village. But to get to the school one had to walk east almost another kilometer and a half over the dunes. Only luggage and heavier items normally came by wagon.[22]

By the time the first fifty-six pupils, including von Braun, arrived for the school's dedication on 28 April 1928, it had at least reached a habitable state, although the classrooms were not finished and the electricity was on only in some areas. It had been far worse when Andreesen and his staff had shown up earlier that month. Sleeping and eating in primitive conditions, they had at least been able to help get the doors and windows in and, two days before the guests arrived, to dig a well that did not produce briny water. Windblown sand had to be shoveled out of the new, two-story brick structure, which was very much exposed to the elements; trees to act as a windbreak grew up only over the next several years. For some years the only privies were outhouses. An urgent task was dike building on the south and east sides, facing the tidal flats separating the island from the mainland. The guilds all had to take turns moving and dumping sand and brush for the dikes, which were needed to protect the school land from the intrusion of saltwater when heavy storms pushed a flood tide into the lagoon. It was a wild, natural setting, dominated by the sea, the wind, the dunes, and the seabirds, and for the boys it was a exciting adventure. Wernher, who had acquired his basic swimming-lifesaving certificate just before leaving Berlin, no doubt a school requirement, became an enthusiastic lifelong sailor on Spiekeroog. His mother later said, "This must have been a happy time and place for him."[23]

Von Braun came to the school to begin the eleventh grade (*Obersekunda*) of a thirteen-grade system. (One normally graduated at age nineteen for university entrance; other school tracks had pupils leaving at fourteen or sixteen.) By then he was an adolescent obsessed with the dream of flying in space himself, a "romantic urge" propelled by science fiction, the *Raketen-rummel* of 1928–29, and the imaginary Moon trip article he later vividly recalled for Daniel Lang. According to former classmates, he was so focused that he did not bathe properly; finally having enough, they dragged him out and gave him an enforced shower—although whether they used water or sand to scrub him varies according to the teller. Heye Deepen, a native of the island who was often at the school, does not remember von Braun as one of those who went to the beach or village dances to pick up girls in the warm months but rather as part of the group that always stayed at the school; it appears that his later career as a ladies' man did not start until he was well into university. (How much puberty contributed to his difficulties between thirteen and sixteen, we will never know.) In the afterglow of the Apollo 11 Moon landing in 1969, a former Spiekeroog student, Dieter Pohl, recalled

those evenings . . . when I hauled you out of your room, where, surrounded by big piles, you had been working on your [Moon flight] problems. I wanted to take a walk with you on the dunes for a change of pace.

In the process you certainly tried to make clear to me the possibilities you had foreseen for such an enterprise, but I was so caught up in my own concerns that all your efforts were wasted. At the end, as often happened, we both looked at the Moon, but with very different thoughts.[24]

The two no doubt looked at the Moon through the school's new telescope, which had been entirely von Braun's doing. Showing the leadership skills that would later be central to his success as an engineering manager, he organized his own guild for astronomy, and through Andreesen he instigated the purchase of a refractor with a 95-mm (3.7-in) objective lens from a Berlin manufacturer, using funds raised from the Lietz schools' benefactors' society. As he explained in a short article, "The Observatory," in the Lietz magazine in early 1929, the plan was to build a "hut" for the telescope and carry out serious scientific observations under the utterly dark and expansive sky of the North Sea coast, which occasionally had "extraordinarily good observing conditions." (That must have been between the endless periods of gray clouds and rain.) But the digging of the foundation for the square building with a removable roof had so far been delayed by the heavy frost of an unusually severe winter.[25]

In fact, weather conditions during his second term were extremely bad. On 17 November 1928 a terrible storm pushed seawater deep into the as-yet-unprotected areas of the school lands. From mid-January to mid-March the ice buildup was so severe that the ferry could not reach the island. Mail and what few provisions got through had to come via sled across the frozen lagoon; once or twice post and packages came via airplane. While essential food was in adequate supply, and the livestock of the island provided milk, the school ran low on coal, to the point where the temperatures in the building went down to the freezing point, and everyone lived in winter coats. As soon as the ferry restarted on 17 March, the school sent everyone home for Easter holidays. Wernher and his classmates finally completed the concrete foundation and wooden structure of the observatory building in the spring and summer of 1929.[26]

During his first year in Spiekeroog, von Braun was put into the "family" of Dr. Andreesen, who ran the school himself until that terrible winter underlined the difficulties of also heading the foundation from a remote island. The two developed a special relationship, as Andreesen had trained as a mathematician and von Braun had become seriously involved in the subject in his last period at Ettersburg—at least as it applied to rocketry and astronomy. Under Andreesen's personal tutelage, he developed into some-

thing of a prodigy in math and science. In the spring of 1929, because he was
so far ahead, he was given permission to spend his class time working on
special problems or on an independent project of calculations relating to
rocketry.[27]

The partial manuscript "On the Theory of the Long-Range Rocket" is
very likely a product of this work. In it von Braun begins to derive the trajectory equations, based on the laws of Newton and Kepler, for a rocket traveling from point to point on the Earth. Presumably the "long-range rocket"
was intended for the transport of mail and passengers, a popular idea in the
spaceflight movement of the time, as he mentions that ranges under 300 km
(180 mi) were probably not "profitable." But he was certainly also aware
that the rocket could be used to transport high explosives or poison gas for
attacking enemy cities, ideas explicitly discussed by his hero, Hermann
Oberth, in the massively expanded third edition of Oberth's book *Wege zur
Raumschiffahrt* (*Ways to Spaceflight*), in mid-1929.[28] As was the case with
Oberth's space mirror, the military uses of rocket and space technology did
not particularly engage von Braun, but neither did he resist such a prospect.
Coming from a conservative nationalist family and receiving a conservative
nationalist education, he would hardly have thought twice about it, espe-
cially if it were to benefit Germany.

Another article he published in the Lietz school magazine gives insight
into his mind, his political ideas, and his special relationship with Andreesen.
In October 1928 a liberal Frankfurt newspaper published a pair of articles
attacking the rural boarding school movement as having lost its revolutionary edge and its connection to the big cities and the needs of the republic. As
one of the articles was from a teacher and the other from a student, the
authors of the Lietz replies were similarly paired: Alfred Andreesen and
Wernher von Braun. Andreesen's article is aggressive, defending Lietz as a
"conservative revolutionary," denouncing modern, urban mass culture as
inferior, and dismissing the republican political process as narrow, selfish
party politics. Von Braun's follow-up is much blander although well written.
Conceding a number of problems in the boarding schools, he defended the
Lietz schools' upper-class tilt by stating that up to 30 percent of the students
were on partial or full scholarships to help ameliorate elite dominance. He
conceded the right of the state to ask for the education of loyal citizens but
said that "more than anything else one should keep them [the pupils] . . .
free from all party influences, so that they freely and independently make
their own decisions later in life." As for alienation from urban life, he argued
that Lietz was correct to put his schools in the countryside because "the big
city, with all its chaotic excess of diversions and excitements, is not the most

suitable site of learning, as it makes it much more difficult for young people to concentrate." Perhaps he was thinking of himself.[29]

Certainly it is instructive that von Braun never identified himself as a Berliner in later life, although the capital was his home or home base for sixteen years (1920–36). But he had been born in a small town and raised in a Junker tradition that took the superiority of rural life for granted.[30] Von Braun's article bears out the statements of later observers that he was fundamentally apolitical in temperament, but at school and at home he was immersed in an environment of right-wing skepticism about parliamentary democracy. Thus it is not surprising that the Weimar Republic's ultimate collapse would be a matter of indifference to him.

In summer 1929 his increasingly prodigious mathematical and scientific performance and close relationship to Andreesen led to a sudden acceleration of his graduation. He had already become legendary in the school; one frequently told anecdote is that he was sitting in the back of the class working on problems while the mathematics teacher, or a substitute, covered three chalkboards with equations. He suddenly called on Wernher von Braun to explain how he had achieved the result he did, which did not agree with the book; the seventeen-year-old glanced up, went to the board, rubbed out a sign, corrected it, and explained where the teacher had gone astray. When the math teacher took ill, von Braun, with the permission of Andreesen, took over teaching the grade thirteen (*Oberprima*) class, even though he was still in grade twelve. "Suddenly it became my responsibility to see that every classmate should get a passing mark. By day I taught. By night I tutored. Between times I studied my own lessons." According to Elisabeth Kutzer, his German, French, and English teacher in his last year in Spiekeroog, he was a success, covering the material at an appropriate pace; he won his schoolmates' respect. Because of this performance he jumped from twelve to thirteen in midyear and was told that he should try to pass the Prussian *Abitur* exams at the end of the fall-winter term in March 1930. His parents were more than pleasantly surprised that their underachieving son had suddenly become a prodigy.[31]

Before he reached that last semester, he visited Ley, one of the leaders of the spaceflight society, the VfR. Von Braun sought advice on how to contact Oberth and make a career in rocketry. By that time von Braun had been a VfR member for about a year; his name appears on the list of contributors in the September 1928 issue of *Die Rakete*.[32] Perhaps he still thought of physics and astronomy as a possibility, but if he wanted to build his own spaceship, he had to become an engineer. Only institutes of technology (*Technische Hochschulen*) had the right to grant higher degrees in engineering, and even aeronautical engineering was not yet a separate undergraduate major, so mechanical engineering would be the most likely concentration. As for the institution, the Berlin-Charlottenburg Institute of Technology (now the Technical University of Berlin) was one of the best engineering schools in Europe, and it was close to his parents' home. Thus it is no surprise that he would begin there.

After he returned to Spiekeroog in the fall of 1929, he continued his single-minded pursuit of space topics, even while playing cello in the school orchestra, sailing, and studying for exams. In a short letter published in the Lietz school magazine issue on "Pupils as Researchers," he describes his calculations on heat transfer, "a problem . . . that plays an important role in spaceflight." In particular he discusses his investigations of the integral equations of the evaporation of a droplet of liquid in a hot gas—that is, inside the combustion chamber of a liquid-fuel rocket, which Oberth believed was the only technology for getting into space. (Solid fuels had not advanced much beyond fireworks.) This short piece has, however, a certain arrogance about it, as von Braun indicates that ordinary mortals would be bored by a lengthier discussion, and he could not explain it to them anyway. It was an arrogance rooted in the supreme self-confidence he now had acquired as the result of his success. Later in life he would be better at suppressing that arrogance; the self-confidence he radiated was, however, one of the keys to his charisma.[33]

In the very last weeks at Spiekeroog, his obsession with flying in space had a final, comic impact on his classmates. For the Mardi Gras (*Fasching*) follies for 1930, the students put together a movie influenced by Fritz Lang's *Frau im Mond*, the realistic Moon-flight film that had opened with a spectacular Berlin premiere on 15 October. (Von Braun probably did not get a chance to see it until the Christmas holidays.) Elisabeth Kutzer, the language teacher, explains:

> And so the pupils edited together a film from written texts (silent film!), photos with the heads of Spiekeroog students glued on, drawings and so forth. It was supposed to show how, in a search for a "female-free" island (then a real issue!) they first loaded the school on a ship and traveled to an island in the south seas, where in adapting to local customs they once again ran into feminine ways [*Weiblichkeit*], so they put the school on a rocket and shot it to the Moon. But since they ran into the "Frau im Mond" there, the search for an "irreproachable planet [*unbescholtenen Planeten*]" had to go on. Wernher naturally helped with the drawings and photos that were inserted.[34]

The film was a joke, but it reveals the masculine values and misogyny that the culture of a boys' school then took for granted.

Before Wernher von Braun could take his graduation exams in March 1930, the Prussian school authority in Hanover had to approve his admission to them a year earlier than normal. It did so because of his "unusual accomplishments"—presumably in learning and teaching mathematics. For the same reason he received permission to graduate without the yearlong research and writing project normally required for the *Abitur*. After a grueling series of written and oral examinations, he passed, of course. Yet his results were far from stellar, and they signify both his single-minded concentration on his areas of interest and the cost of graduating early. In the four-grade system then in effect—"very good" (A), "good" (B), "satisfactory" (C/D), and "unsatisfactory" (F)—he got only two A's, in math and physics, and three B's, in religion, German, and French. All the rest of his grades were C/D's: history and civics, geography, chemistry, biology, English, Latin, physical education, music, drawing, and "practical work." His overall grade was "good" (B). The committee, which included Andreesen and Kutzer, signed his graduation certificate on 3 April 1930. It was time to go home to Berlin.[35]

Shortly after moving back full time to In den Zelten 11, von Braun began a six-month practicum at the Borsig locomotive and heavy machinery factory in the northwestern suburb of Tegel. It was a requirement of higher engineering education in Germany, leading to the diploma engineer (Dipl. Ing.) degree (usually equated to a master's), that students receive hands-on experience in an industrial setting before or soon after starting university studies. And this he did, enjoying the ironies of the situation, despite having to get up early in the morning, which he disliked his whole life. "My father was a pretty well-to-do bank president. The butler would fix my breakfast at 4:30 a.m. Thereafter, metal lunch box in hand, I would take a trolley car to the factory." After a very long ride he would punch in at seven and work until four. He was treated little differently than an ordinary apprentice. He had to join the metalworkers' union, which was the largest in the Western world and aligned with the Socialists—he may have been the only Junker baron in its ranks. Later he always told one story, that of his first assignment.

> An old master artisan with a huge moustache gave me a piece of iron about the size of a child's head and pointed me towards a workbench. Next to the vise was a rough and a fine file, and an angle-iron. "File a

cube," he said. "All corners must be right angles, all sides equally long, and all surfaces mirror-smooth. The size of the cube is irrelevant."

Week after week, Mr. Moustache came by my work-bench, inspected my work and left me with a single, pitiless word: "Continue!" Soon my fingers were bloody, my back ached and each day brought me closer to despair.

Finally after a month or six weeks came his release—the master approved. The cube had shrunk to the size of a walnut. Afterward von Braun "worked in the foundry, the press and forging plant and the locomotive and turbine assembly plants," an experience that helped foster his lifelong commitment to what he called in America "dirty hands engineering." Only in November 1930 would he begin his first semester at the institute of technology in Charlottenburg, a kilometer to the northwest of the Zoo train station.[36]

While the Borsig job would determine von Braun's daily routine for much of the rest of the year, rocketry and spaceflight naturally consumed his spare time. His return to Berlin provided him with a golden opportunity to become much more involved in the VfR, just as its focus shifted to the capital and to the development of liquid-fuel rocket technology. After Fritz Lang began filming *Frau im Mond* at the UFA studios in Germany's Hollywood, Neubabelsberg, outside Berlin, he had invited Hermann Oberth to take a leave of absence from his teaching job in Romania and be the technical adviser. The black-haired, mustachioed, thirty-four-year-old Oberth arrived in late 1928; after providing input on the sets and the special effects, he was encouraged by Lang to begin developing a liquid-fuel rocket that could make a spectacular demonstration for the opening of the movie.

Finding himself utterly at a loss for lack of practical ability, in the fall of 1929 Oberth began to cast about for assistants among the space enthusiasts. His first, a Russian freelance aviation and space writer later shot in Stalin's purges, proved to be lazy and hopeless with machinery. The second, Rudolf Nebel, was a bit better; a fast-talking World War I fighter pilot from Nuremberg, he actually had received the diploma engineer degree, if under rushed and dubious circumstances after the war. The hawk-nosed Nebel was really more of a con man than an engineer, but he found himself picking up the pieces from a hopelessly ambitious project. Oberth had naively expected to build a stratospheric sounding rocket based on drawing-board principles without ever having built the smallest liquid-fuel rocket motor. When, in spite of trumpeted announcements from UFA's publicists, no rocket materialized after the movie's premiere, a distressed Oberth suddenly left for a rest cure in mid-November 1929. Around this time a number of other early-

1930s rocket experimenters came on the scene. Klaus Riedel, a huge, fun-loving machinist trying to take courses to become an engineer, volunteered to assist them. Rolf Engel, a high school student the same age as Wernher von Braun, showed up on occasion. Von Braun himself, after visiting Ley for the first time in late fall, may have met Riedel, but except for the Christmas holiday he was away at Spiekeroog until early April 1930. By then he had written to Oberth and received an encouraging reply; he fervently hoped to meet his idol.[37]

At the end of 1929 the journal *Die Rakete* collapsed because Johannes Winkler had run it at a loss; the VfR leadership shifted from Breslau to Berlin. Meanwhile Oberth had returned to the capital, as Nebel had been seeking a way to finish the rocket so as to appease UFA. It exploded, however, at the launch site on an army base in Stettin, and Oberth went home to Romania before Christmas. Nebel had established contact with the army to find a place to launch it and now appealed to the military for help, as well as to organizations and individuals ranging from Albert Einstein to Adolf Hitler. In March 1930 Lieutenant Colonel Karl E. Becker of the ballistics and munitions section of Army Ordnance, who was becoming interested in the rocket's military potential, secretly kicked in 5,000 marks to enable the completion of the Oberth device. Seeking to revive the movement, which had lost many members after the *Raketenrummel* petered out and the journal ended, Ley, Nebel, and the leaders of the VfR held membership meetings in March and May and organized an evening of public lectures at the Post Office auditorium on 11 April. Officers from the army attended, along with the now-ancient spaceflight prophet Hermann Ganswindt, the famous science fiction writer Hans Dominik, and many members of the press. But Nebel's public and private promises that the Oberth rocket was ready to launch were a fraud. It was symptomatic of his basic dishonesty.[38]

The eighteen-year-old Spiekeroog graduate arrived just in time to get caught up in this flurry of activity. He was probably at the 11 April event, as a picture shows a young man who looks like him standing with Valier, Ley, Winkler, and Nebel under a spectacular display of the Oberth rocket hanging on a parachute. At one of these meetings he met Rolf Engel, with whom he became fast friends. Von Braun then volunteered to help out at an exhibition connected to the aviation days in Berlin at the end of May. He was thrilled to finally encounter *"mon adoré Professor Oberth,"* as he put it in a postcard to a Swiss friend, while helping the theorist install the exhibit in the Wertheim department store. He then found himself trying to convince housewives to support rocket research, notably by asserting that the first human who would walk on the Moon was already alive. He was not far off—Neil Armstrong would be born in August. A couple of weeks earlier von Braun had been shocked, along with the rest of the rocketry movement and the public, to hear of Max Valier's death. During experiments at the Berlin liquid-oxygen-equipment manufacturer Heylandt, which was financing Valier's new liquid-fuel rocket-car motor, the engine had exploded, piercing one of his major arteries with shrapnel. Von Braun saved the VfR's announcement of the death and pasted it in his scrapbook.[39]

In the aftermath of the funeral and the aviation week exhibit, Rudolf Nebel convinced Oberth to return again to Berlin in July. The Reich Interior Ministry had arranged for them to demonstrate their rocket engine at the Chemisch-Technisches Reichsanstalt (CTR), which, together with its sister institute in physics, was the equivalent of the U.S. Bureau of Standards. The rocketeers were convinced that, with an official government testimonial, it would be much easier to raise money from foundations, corporations, and government agencies. Driven by a burning faith in spaceflight's future, they expected everyone else to share their enthusiasm.[40]

After work at Borsig, von Braun took the streetcar to join Oberth, Nebel, Riedel, Engel, and others at the relatively nearby location.

> I shall never forget those nights at the <u>Reichsanstalt</u>. A water pail, mounted on a grocery scale, surrounded the <u>Kegelduese</u>—a cone-shaped rocket motor of steel with its tiny nozzle protruding from the water and pointing upwards. . . . I can still see [Klaus Riedel] skillfully hurling a gasoline-drenched dustcloth over the nozzle exit and throwing his 200 pounds behind an armored cover plate, just a fraction of a second before the motor ignited with a terrifying bang. Finally there was the professor [Oberth] himself,—thoughtful, tight-lipped, every now and then throwing one of his sarcastically witty remarks into the discussion in his dark Transylvanian accent.

These tests led finally to a public demonstration on 23 July 1930, in which Dr. Ritter of the CTR validated that the little rocket engine had put out a thrust of 6 to 7 kg (13 to 15 lb) for 90 seconds. It was a very modest result in comparison to the promised rocket launch for the army, but the VfR group was proud. However, the most famous product of that miserably cold and wet summer Sunday was a picture that has since been reprinted a thousand times. Standing on the right of the group is a tall Wernher von Braun dressed in a fancy suit with knee breeches.[41]

In spite of all he was doing, during the summer of 1930 he found time to complete a science fiction story, "Lunetta," that he may have drafted in Spiekeroog. Published in the Lietz schools' magazine in the fall, it provides some interesting insights into his talents, obsessions, and blind spots. The story opens with a striking image that von Braun, an aviation as well as space enthusiast, drew directly from the adventures of polar explorers of the late 1920s: "Then night fell over the icy wastes." The narrator is the German pilot of a plane crashed in the Arctic. He and his two companions are found and illuminated by Oberth's giant space mirror, then rescued by a rocket plane sent down from the space station Lunetta ("Little Moon") that accompanies the mirror in its orbit. The writing shows great imagination but, not surprisingly for something written by a teenager, the story has no character development and loses what little plot it has after the first paragraphs. Instead it becomes a loving description of the rocket plane, the experience of launching into space and of weightlessness, and a tour of the interior of Lunetta and its observatory. The influences appear to include not only Oberth but also a mysterious and interesting book published in Berlin in 1929 under the pseudonym Hermann Noordung. Nobody knew who Noordung was, as the former Austro-Hungarian officer died about the time the book was published, but he gave an elaborate description of a space station with an observatory.[42]

Von Braun's short story shows his very romantic, personal engagement with space travel and exploration and a yearning to do those things himself; it is no surprise that "Lunetta" is written in the first person. At the same time the story is divorced from economic and political realities. The story is about technology and the wonders of human progress; the inhabitants of the space station are technocrats who benignly watch over the Earth: "We appeared to the people up here unbelievably small and dejected. . . . We couldn't at first believe it, but a look around soon taught us, that up here on Lunetta nothing was considered impossible anymore." The economic practicalities of sending a rescue plane from orbit and constructing elaborate facilities in space do not enter into the story, any more than they would into his fiction and nonfiction popularizations of the late 1940s and 1950s, with their detailed descriptions of huge space stations and multiship expeditions to the Moon and Mars. The romance of space travel and of advanced technology was enough to convince him that these things should be done.[43]

Soon after the CTR experiments, von Braun was on his own, as rocket activity shut down for more than a month. Oberth departed for Romania, not to return for years, and Nebel and Riedel took off to do rocket tests at the family farm in Riedel's hometown in Saxony. They did not come back until September, at which time Nebel had succeeded in getting permission to take over an abandoned munitions dump on the northern fringes of the city, between Tegel and Reinickendorf. The land, which was bleak and open except for low spots with swamps and stands of trees, was owned by the city, but the massive-walled munitions bunkers were the property of the Defense Ministry. Colonel Becker (as he now was) played a hidden hand in helping Nebel and the VfR rocket group rent the territory for a nominal sum—he was not yet totally fed up with Nebel's publicity-seeking. On 27 September 1930 Nebel and Riedel got the key to the first buildings. Soon thereafter they put up a sign for the Raketenflugplatz (Rocketport or Rocket Airdrome) Berlin, as a newspaper had dubbed it. The two, soon joined by a few others, set up primitive bachelor quarters in the old guardhouse. They settled in for the winter, cooking over small stoves and trying to make some progress with the development of the Mirak (for "minimum rocket"), a very small liquid-fuel device.[44]

That fall and winter not only the weather was turning chillier. Ever since the Wall Street crash of a year before, Germany had been sliding deeper and deeper into depression, with devastating consequences for the political and economic climate. In the spring of 1930 the last Weimar government with a stable parliamentary basis collapsed. The president, the tired old field marshal Paul von Hindenburg, appointed a right-wing chancellor and cabinet dependent on his emergency decree powers and approved a Reichstag election for September. The results were disastrous. Hitler's formerly marginal National Socialist German Workers' Party won more than one hundred seats and became the second-largest party nationally. The Communists also gained much ground. As unemployment steadily climbed, ultimately reaching over six million in late 1932, the Raketenflugplatz both suffered and benefited from the crisis. Nebel's entrepreneurial fund-raising was absolutely crucial to the survival of the amateur rocket group and amounted to tens of thousands of marks in 1930–32, most of it in kind from corporations; but ultimately the depression would greatly limit what he could beg and cajole from benefactors. On the other hand, the desperate state of the Berlin unemployed often allowed Nebel to get free labor in return for meals provided by the Siemens company, and a few craftsmen joined the group and set up house in the buildings. Minimal unemployment and job creation funds also helped keep the idealistic enterprise going.[45]

During those early days von Braun helped to clean out the place and set up shop, at least on weekends and after hours from Borsig. Soon thereafter he began his first semester of mechanical engineering and had to concentrate on basic courses in mathematics, sciences, drafting, and so forth; he could come only once or twice a week for visits. He was in a fundamentally different position from the inner group—he was a rich kid living at home and drawing a monthly stipend of 200 marks (about $50) from his father. At least that was the figure recalled by Rolf Engel decades later, when he expressed irritation with retrospective accounts of von Braun as one of the Raketenflugplatz's central figures. Still, in spite of von Braun's privileged situation, Engel and the others could not help liking him. He was so enthusiastic, funny, charming, and smart; at some point they ironically nicknamed him "Sonny Boy," the title of Al Jolson's syrupy hit song from the sound film *The Singing Fool* (1928), released as *Sonny Boy* in Germany. ("When there are gray skies, I don't mind the gray skies . . . You make them blue, Sonny Boy.")[46]

Another impression of von Braun at this age is given by Willy Ley, who worked in a bank and lived with two aunts to make ends meet:

> Physically he happened to be a perfect example of the type labeled "Aryan Nordic" by the Nazis during the years to come. He had bright blue eyes and light blond hair and one of my female relatives compared him to the famous photograph of Lord Douglas of Oscar Wilde fame. His manners were as perfect as a rigid upbringing could make them. I remember that he spoke rather good French. One day he came in while I was struggling with a Sarabande by Handel; after I finished he sat down and played Beethoven's Moonlight Sonata from memory. There was no doubt even then that he was brilliant. Riedel often asked von Braun to make calculations for him and to assist him in proper dimensioning of injection nozzles, etc.

Engel also mentions that they liked to get him to speak to visiting groups, as he had such a talent for persuasion.[47]

From the Raketenflugplatz, Wernher von Braun gained not only hands-on experience with rocket engines and vehicles but also something of Rudolf Nebel's entrepreneurial and risk-taking style, which contributed to his subsequent success as an engineering manager and system builder. He gives this example from the period of the CTR experiments:

> Nebel coined the expression "boldly asserted is half proven." While Oberth was shy and a bit unsociable, Nebel was what Americans call a "Big Time Operator."
>
> I vividly remember a discussion in which Oberth had opposed the purchase of a certain item from the stock of a vendor, insisting that it had to be specially designed for the purpose. "The modern inventor," was Nebel's reply, "doesn't need much brains. All he needs is an up-to-date classified telephone directory to bring him in contact with special-

ized firms." I could never quite agree with this, but I must confess that I learned a lot from Nebel's way of approaching a problem.

During the early period of the Raketenflugplatz, Nebel took von Braun on "one of his 'acquisition trips.' " The ex–fighter pilot told a director of the giant Siemens firm "about his plans—the liquid rocket motor, the stratosphere, lightning voyages across the oceans, the moon. The man was half amused, half impressed." From this trip they got a supply of welding wire; Nebel then drove to a welding shop and bartered for the services of a skilled welder. Through such activities Nebel was able to acquire enough materials and occasional expert help for the Raketenflugplatz to build a large engine test stand out of the old launch rail for the Oberth *Frau im Mond* rocket. By the spring of 1931 the group was almost ready to launch its first rockets.[48]

With his head in the heavens, von Braun naturally followed the aviation accomplishments of the era with great interest. He had taken his first airplane ride as early as 1925, in an open-cockpit Junkers F13. In 1931 he decided to take up piloting himself—perhaps it would even help him fly in space. To pay for lessons, he used his "first self-earned money," perhaps from writing small articles on rockets for various newspapers. At the end of his first semester, from 3 to 23 March, his nineteenth birthday, he spent three weeks in basic glider training at Wolf Hirth's sailplane school in Grunau, in the Riesengebirge mountains of Silesia. He participated in the bungee-assisted takeoffs of other students, working in the snow, then tried his own short hops, leading to the A and B tests and flights of over two minutes.[49]

Von Braun resided, perhaps only before or after the lessons, at his parents' new estate north of the nearby town of Hirschberg (now Jelenia Gora, Poland). In July 1930, after a merger of the two Raiffeisen associations put Magnus von Braun Sr. out of his main job, he and Emmy had bought the "noble estate" (farm and village) of Oberwiesenthal, fulfilling a longtime, sentimental wish to return to the land, as well as a desire to acquire property for the sons to inherit. A further attraction was his fascination with the historic Silesian roots of the Barons von Braun; Oberwiesenthal was near an estate once owed by a branch of the family. Sigismund, who had graduated from the French Gymnasium in 1929 and apprenticed at a Hamburg bank while preparing for the civil service exams, later described Oberwiesenthal as "rather small" by eastern German standards at 120 hectares (300 acres) but with very low costs. The major enterprise was grazing the calves of villagers on the farm's excellent pasturelands during spring, summer, and fall. The modest but attractive two-story, eighteenth-century plastered-brick house was set in a "delightful, hilly landscape" and quickly became for the three boys a beloved "second home." Until mid-1934, however, Magnus, Emmy, and Magnus Jr. (born in 1919 and also attending the FG) would be in the capital most of the time, going to the estate only during school holidays.[50]

Shortly after Easter 1931, with the glider course behind him, Wernher left to attend the Swiss Institute of Technology (Eidgenössische Technische Hochshule, or ETH). Why he decided to switch from Berlin to Zurich after only one semester, and why he ultimately stayed only one semester, is hard to say, as he never saw fit to comment on these decisions later. In 1947 Willy Ley recalled von Braun saying that he would like to take his doctorate in engineering at Zurich; the ETH had a celebrated aerodynamicist, Jakob Ackeret, so perhaps he was attracted to a university that had a strong aeronautical engineering program. Or maybe he was just participating in the time-honored German tradition of university-hopping. At any rate, at the beginning of April 1931 he moved to the Swiss city and soon thereafter met a multilingual Greek-American medical student, Constantine Generales, in line at the cafeteria. Generales heard someone behind him speaking English and "turned around and faced a tall blond chap who informed me that he had just arrived from Berlin." During lunch von Braun inevitably diverted the conversation to rockets, spaceflight, Hermann Oberth, and Robert Goddard, the mysterious and secretive American pioneer.[51]

A couple of weeks later Generales, who was four years older than von Braun and had graduated from Harvard in 1929, bumped into him again, and von Braun started in again on the topic of Moon rockets. As Generales later recalled:

> To me, this whole thing, as I recall, seemed rather ridiculous, and I began making fun of my friend with "a one-track mind" until he reached into his pocket and pulled out a letter. . . . The envelope was postmarked Berlin. I remember staring at the indecipherable equations pertaining to mathematical problems and solutions in rocket design and propulsion. I was dumbfounded and deeply impressed when I recognized the signature to be that of Professor Albert Einstein. The recipient of the letter I held in my hand was my newly found friend, Wernher Freiherr von Braun.

Now willing to take the whole matter seriously, Generales began immediately to think of the medical implications of rocket flight. "I remember clearly my verbal reaction as I handed back the letter to Wernher with the caution, 'Wenn Du zum Mond gehen willst ist es besser zuerst mit Mäusen zu versuchen.' [If you want to get to the moon, it is better to try with mice first.]"[52]

"Borrowing" a dozen white mice from the biology lab, the two set up a crude centrifuge in von Braun's room, "as it was larger than mine," using the front wheel from Generales's bicycle. They attached four little "hammock-like" bags symmetrically around the wheel, and spun the poor creatures so as to simulate the high g-forces of acceleration. The mice were inert, frightened, and dizzy afterward; some of those spun at higher rates died of internal bleeding, as Generales demonstrated in dissections.

> Right at the height of our activities, a dramatic incident occurred. A mouse accidentally slipped out of its cradle and was dashed against the wall leaving bloody stains at the point of impact. The next day (I believe it was the third day of our experiments), we were not too surprised that the landlady who was not accustomed to the odor of small laboratory animals, noticed "the blood on the wall"; became infuriated; seized my notes as evidence of nonsensical cruelty and torture; and threatened to evict us and notify the police unless we immediately ceased these crazy experiments.

To alleviate their consciences, the two let the remaining mice go free in a field. Several weeks later they joined an enthusiastic crowd outside a Zurich hotel greeting Auguste Piccard after his historic balloon flight to nearly 16 km (over 9 mi), an ascension that started a multinational "race to the stratosphere."[53]

On 15 July 1931, after successfully completing a semester of standard engineering and math courses, with electives in financing industrial research, contemporary social problems, and mathematical geography, von Braun wrote a letter to ETH formally withdrawing from the university in order to resume studies in Berlin-Charlottenburg. But he did not immediately return home; instead he and Generales set out on a trip to Greece in Generales's small, beat-up Opel. Crossing over the Alps, they had to use ice and snow to cool the overheated engine; in Italy a wheel fell off and von Braun unsuccessfully went back to Rome to try to find a wheel bearing. Leaving the vehicle behind in an Italian garage, they took the train to Brindisi and a boat to Corfu. Generales remembers von Braun's outgoing and magnetic personality and how he enjoyed Greek hospitality, but there were "no excesses," and in Zurich and on the road "there were no girls; if you went out with one you expected to be planning to get married." Von Braun's days as a bon vivant bachelor had not yet begun. His German friend was also a scientific skeptic of religion, Generales says, bordering on being an atheist—von Braun's days of Christian devotion were even further in the future. After spending part of August in Greece, the two made their way back to Italy, picked up the car, and drove to Berlin. They arrived in time to witness one of the Raketenflugplatz's increasingly frequent launches. "It was a spectacular sight as the pencil-shaped rocket descended, a small parachute attached to its tail. . . . Wernher, Nebel, Riedel and I raced to the landing spot, crowded into my Opel." When Generales left to continue his studies in Paris, where he did a more sophisticated version of the mice centrifuge experiment, he left the little car for the rocket enthusiasts to use until he came back.[54]

While von Braun was in Zurich, the Raketenflugplatz experimenters had finally flown their liquid-oxygen/gasoline rocket, now dubbed the Repulsor, after the space vehicle in Kurd Lasswitz's classic science fiction novel *Auf zwei Planeten (On Two Planets*, 1897)—a Mars tale eagerly read by von Braun when he was younger. But the honors for flying the first liquid-fuel rocket in Europe (they believed it was the first in the world, as Goddard kept secret his launch in March 1926) went to Johannes Winkler. In 1929, as *Die Rakete* was failing, Winkler had gone to work with Junkers Aircraft in Dessau on assisted-takeoff rockets for heavily loaded airplanes. The little triangular, tubular rocket he flew in February and March 1931, however, was funded by a hat and metalwares manufacturer, Hugo Hückel, a true believer in spaceflight who also had given much money to the Raketenflugplatz. The first Repulsors then flew a couple of months later, with highly variable results. Some went up to as high as a couple of thousand meters and parachuted back to the ground; others went crazy and flew off in unpredictable directions, with sometimes hilarious results. In the fall of 1931 one rocket even crashed inconveniently into the police barracks down the road, provoking a visit by the Berlin police chief and restrictions on launches. These Repulsors had a number of configurations, but they did not look like a stereotypical rocket, as the engine was in the nose, pulling the thin tubular tanks behind, with the tail containing the parachute, if there was one. There was no guidance system, other than some arbitrarily shaped fins, but it was hoped that the "nose drive" system might make the vehicle more stable, and anyway the problems of designing a reliable rocket engine with what materials they had were serious enough. Building any kind of gyro stabilization was far too expensive and difficult to contemplate. Klaus Riedel was the leading designer and engineer, but most of the decisions were made by consensus of those who were around; pragmatic experience, rather than systematic technology development, was their guide. By the end of the year the Raketenflugplatz had carried out 270 engine tests and 87 launches and had received 32 tour groups, 9 of them paying.[55]

Wernher von Braun of course participated again as much as he coul
cessful landings were "frequently followed by a gay drinking part

downtown nightclub," he says, although this raises the question of whether he was paying, given the poverty of those who lived on site. We hear of him using his great powers of persuasion in lectures to visitors, who were charged fees beginning in September. According to Rolf Engel: "Only rarely did he mention the long-range missile, usually only when a visitor asked him a specific question about it. Then he would say naturally, that it was clear that a rocket could be built that could go ten or fifteen thousand kilometers. But he always placed emphasis on spaceflight." With the start of the new semester in November 1931, von Braun again could show up only once or twice a week, but sometimes he would stay overnight on weekends, sleeping in one of the buildings. He nonetheless continued his theoretical work for the Raketenflugplatz, producing an eleven-page, single-spaced primer for the calculation of performance, trajectories, tank size, and size of parachutes, dated 28 February 1932. In addition, his writing talent and desire to proselytize the unconverted led him to draft an article, "The Secret of the Liquid-Fuel Rocket," that was published in one of the leading popular science journals in early June. It too avoided the discussion of military applications, while advocating the long-distance transport of mail and passengers and pushing the question of human spaceflight into the background—a tactic he undoubtedly learned from Rudolf Nebel.[56]

Meanwhile, on his twentieth birthday, von Braun returned to Hirth's glider school in Grunau, Silesia, and completed the course for his C license, soaring for more than eleven minutes on 10 April. One of his fellow students was a tiny, vivacious Silesian almost exactly the same age, Hanna Reitsch, the only woman there. Whether there was any romantic attraction is unclear, but the two certainly became good friends and remained so throughout her remarkable Third Reich career as a test pilot, friend of Nazi leaders, and true believer in Hitler.[57]

It was just after he got back from Grunau that matters took a fundamental turn: the army reappeared on the scene. In the seven years since he had discovered his love for astronomy and space, his mature personality had formed. From a dreamy, talented, privileged little boy with a desire to work with his hands and no strong commitment to school, there developed a determined, pragmatic, energetic, and mathematically skilled young man with one obsession and burning ambition: to build rockets and, if possible, to fly to the Moon. But the charming amateurism of the Raketenflugplatz was reaching its limits, both financially and technically. However little the military applications of rocketry interested him, his upbringing and schooling created no moral or political obstacles to working on such applications. Indeed, when the opportunity opened, he would be the first to seize it.

CHAPTER THREE

The Black Sedan

1932–34

[My colleagues in Germany] all thought that civilized Germans would not stand for anything really rough happening. The reason I took the opposite position was based on observations of rather small and insignificant things. I noticed that the Germans always took a utilitarian point of view. They asked, "Well, suppose I would oppose this, what good would I do? I wouldn't do very much good, I would just lose my influence. Then, why should I oppose it?" You see, the moral point of view was completely absent, or very weak, and every consideration was simply, what would be the predictable consequence of my action. And on that basis did I reach the conclusion in 1931 that Hitler would get into power, not because the forces of the Nazi revolution were so strong, but rather because I thought that there would be no resistance whatsoever. —LEO SZILARD[1]

Wernher von Braun never forgot the "black sedan" that pulled up at the Raketenflugplatz one day in the spring of 1932. Three men in civilian clothes, "who held themselves with suspicious straightness," got out to watch a test of the new, larger "three-liter" Repulsor rocket. He must have known immediately that they were from the military. According to Rudolf Nebel, Colonel Karl Becker and two subordinates from Army Ordnance's ballistics and munitions section, Captains Walter Dornberger and Ernst Ritter (Knight) von Horstig, had dropped in before and after the turn of the year to check out the rocketeers' activities.[2] The new visit, in about mid-April, would be the second critical turning point in von Braun's life. Before the end of 1932 he would begin working on a secret doctoral dissertation for the army. Shortly thereafter Adolf Hitler came to power. Less than three years after the visit, at age twenty-two, von Braun would launch his own rockets for the military, paving the way to gaining even more resources for his beloved technology.

The army's renewed interest in the Raketenflugplatz actually signaled a change of policy. In May 1931 Becker had written a memo to Ordnance's aviation section describing his disillusionment with Nebel. Even after the secret 5,000-mark subsidy in the spring of 1930 had not led to the launch of Oberth's rocket, Ordnance had supported Nebel's request to use the old munitions bunkers in Tegel. But Becker soon came to the conclusion that the freewheeling leader of the rocket group had no interest in the "necessary practicality, quietude and secrecy." Nebel preferred to make himself known "through sensationalistic articles in newspapers and magazines." An unnamed source even described him as "dishonest" in his technical claims, with the result that Ordnance had cut off all contact with him months before the memo.[3]

A congenial officer from western Germany with a doctorate in engineering, the stout, mustachioed Karl Becker was a veteran of the heavy artillery on the Western Front and the leading advocate for the technical training of officers in the Reichswehr (Reich Defense Force). He had read the work of Oberth and Goddard in the 1920s, but his real interest in rocketry began in 1929, at the height of the Weimar *Raketenrummel*. After a year of investigation Becker made his first major presentation to Ordnance on 17 December 1930. Black-powder solid-fuel rockets such as those used in the Valier-Opel rocket cars, Becker thought, might be the basis for a low-cost weapon that could saturate the battlefield with chemical weapons; the much more efficient liquid-fuel rocket might eventually lead to a long-range superweapon—what we would now call a ballistic missile.[4]

The Weimar rocket fad did not alone initiate Becker's interest. The Reichswehr—severely limited by the Versailles Treaty to a lightly armed 100,000-man army, a minuscule 15,000-man navy, and no air force at all—had begun systematically to lay the groundwork for rearmament in 1928. This secret planning built on earlier covert violations of the treaty, especially through a secret alliance with the Soviet Red Army. Tanks, aircraft, and poison gas—weapons denied to Germany—were tested at bases in Russia. The degree to which violation of the treaty was taken for granted in secret rearmament projects, and the intimate relationship between illegal chemical weapons and the early army rocket program, casts much doubt on the oft-repeated cliché that Ordnance's interest in the rocket stemmed from the fact that it was not banned by the treaty. The rocket's legality was a secondary issue; of primary importance was finding new weapons, legal or not, that through cost-effectiveness and surprise might help to compensate for Germany's military weakness.[5]

With the strong backing of Ordnance's leadership, the ballistics and munitions section began to develop battlefield solid-fuel rockets for chemical warfare under the direction of Becker's deputy, Captain von Horstig. Joining him on 1 April 1931 and taking special responsibility for rocketry was another, younger veteran of the heavy artillery, Walter Dornberger. Born in 1895 to a pharmacist in the Hessian city of Giessen, the smiling, balding Dornberger had just finished his diploma engineer degree from the Berlin Institute of Technology under the engineering officer program initiated by Becker. While improving solid-fuel rockets remained Dornberger and von Horstig's focus, the long-range potential of liquid fuels was still of interest. In the fall of 1931 Becker inquired of the Berlin firm of Paul Heylandt, a manufacturer of liquid-oxygen equipment, about purchasing Heylandt's liquid-fuel rocket engine. Heylandt had supported Max Valier's research in the months before the Austrian's accidental death in May 1930; in 1931 he had allowed one of his engineers to build a rocket car, assisted by two men who would become von Braun's deputies, Walter Riedel and Arthur Rudolph. With the Depression deepening and the rocket fad trailing off, the car failed to attract much money at demonstrations, and the engine itself had poor combustion efficiency—so poor, in fact, that Becker decided to authorize Heylandt only to experiment with compressed air to improve nozzle design. During the winter of 1931–32 the three Ordnance officers then expended much energy looking into the claims of a liquid-fuel rocket "inventor" who turned out to be a total fraud.[6]

Under the circumstances, the accomplishments of Rudolf Nebel's group did not appear so bad after all. In response to Nebel's 3 March 1932 offer to demonstrate the launch and successful parachute recovery of his rocket to Ordnance in return for expenses, Becker finally responded on 23 April, presumably after a new visit. The conditions were strict: the launch must take place in complete secrecy at the army's Kummersdorf testing range, 40 km (25 mi) southwest of the Berlin city limit, and the rocket must deploy its parachute and fire a red flare at the top of its trajectory in order to be declared a success. Only under these circumstances would the Raketenflugplatz be awarded the 1,367 marks (about $325) for expenses specified by Nebel; otherwise the rocketeers would get nothing.[7] The obsession with secrecy was characteristic of Becker's approach: the effectiveness of any new weapons would depend on surprise and the acquisition of a significant development lead over any prospective enemies.

In order to accommodate this demand, Nebel formed, as von Braun told

Ley in 1946, "a little conspiracy. [Klaus] Riedel would show off the Repulsor and I (v.B.) would give a short lecture." Nebel kept the whole thing secret from the VfR's board of directors, but he also needed one Raketenflugplatz mechanic to assemble the rocket, who later let the secret slip by complaining about the extra work he had to do. Early in June Nebel received instructions to appear with the rocket at the east entrance to the village of Kummersdorf at four o'clock on the morning of 22 June 1932. The reason for this cloak-and-dagger approach, presumably, was to obscure the sight and destination of the four-meter-long, pencil-thin rocket inside its even longer launch rack, which would be mounted on top of the Raketenflugplatz's Buick. On the appointed night Nebel, Riedel, and von Braun, who must have been skipping classes, left the Raketenflugplatz and drove through the darkened city to the army's proving grounds. One of them followed in a second car, probably Constantine Generales's Opel, carrying the liquid-oxygen container and tools. Dornberger met them at the appointed crossroads, and as dawn began to break, von Braun later explained, he "led us to a remote site on the artillery firing range. The site turned out to be covered with photo-theodolites, ballistic cameras and all sorts of equipment we then never knew existed." To their envy, they also saw the well-equipped solid-rocket test stand built the previous year.[8]

After erecting the long, narrow launch rack next to the car, von Braun, Riedel, and Nebel worked to fill the rocket with liquid oxygen and alcohol, followed by gaseous nitrogen to pressurize the tanks. Becker, von Horstig, and a number of other observers from Ordnance watched the preparations. Around six-thirty a.m., all was ready. The long, strange-looking "nose-drive" rocket rose from its rack, flame spewing from its water-cooled head, which was connected to the narrow tubular body by four fuel and oxidizer lines. At the rear was an egg-shaped parachute and flare container with four little fins. Von Braun comments: "Our joy was short-lived. Soon, the vertical flightpath tilted into a rather shallow trajectory . . . the missile swept horizontally over the trees and crash-landed some 2 or 3 miles away from the launching site, with the parachute still in its casing." The official report shows that the impact was actually only 1.3 km (less than a mile) away; the rocket went through a low cloud deck and reached at most 600 m (about 2,000 ft) in altitude. "We hoped that the show would impress our hosts despite its shortcomings," von Braun continues, "but they were outright disappointed and made no bones about it." The flame had burned through a weld, creating a sideward thrust that threw the rocket off its vertical trajectory, so that it was not even close to meeting the 3.5-km altitude Nebel had promised that morning, not to mention the eight kilometers he had promised earlier. Ordnance concluded once again that Nebel was unreliable and dishonest; payment was out of the question.[9]

In the aftermath of 22 June, Nebel more than once visited Army Ordnance's offices at Jebenstrasse 1, behind the Zoo train station in Berlin, asking for payment or for a development contract. He experienced only frustration. Dornberger later said, "The failure of this demonstration brought home to us . . . how many scientific and technical questions needed answering before we could hope to construct a [liquid-fuel] rocket that could fly efficiently. We had still paid far too little attention to the problem of stability and control." In-house development by the army seemed the way to go, as no amateur group or company appeared competent. But the Raketenflugplatz visits and the failed demonstration had one positive outcome: Wernher von Braun caught their eye. Dornberger, for one, "had been struck during my casual visits to Reinickendorf by the energy and shrewdness with which this fair, tall, young student with the broad massive chin went to work, and by his astonishing theoretical knowledge." Another connection came through von Braun's father, who met von Horstig at a dinner at Reichswehr headquarters and quietly discussed Wernher's future with him, probably several weeks after Magnus Sr. joined the Reich government as agriculture minister during that same month, June 1932.[10]

Thus, one way or another, von Braun came to see Dornberger, von Horstig, and Becker in their offices. In contrast to Nebel's picture of Becker as a hidebound artillerist, the twenty-year-old student found him, according to von Braun's 1950 memoir, "broad-minded, highly intelligent and warm-hearted . . . , a first-rate scientist in an officer's uniform." But Becker demanded a "systematic and scientific" approach.

"How do you measure your propellant consumption, your combustion pressure, your thrust?" I admitted that we hadn't measured these things at all, but hurriedly added that we would be pleased to do so if he would only be good enough to buy us the necessary instruments. "You can't blame us for our approach," I said. "We have to put up a certain amount of showmanship in order to keep our place going."

"It is just this publicity . . . ," Becker replied, "that renders it impossible for us to do business with you. You see, if we are going to make something of military value out of the liquid-fuel rocket, it will all have to be done under extreme secrecy. . . . I am impressed by the enthusiasm of your organisation and I want to give you an opportunity to continue with more adequate means. But not at Reinickendorf. My condition is that you work behind the fence of an Army post.[11]

In another version of this story, von Braun remembered saying that he did not want to leave his friends, so Becker (and Dornberger) said, "Take them along."[12] It is hard to imagine that Becker could have tolerated Nebel, but perhaps the Ordnance officer saw that he otherwise might not get von Braun if the group decided to stick together. The strapping blond student took the offer back to the Raketenflugplatz, where he, Nebel, and Riedel had long debates. Nebel was exasperated—his group invented the technology, how dare those paper pushers attempt to take over? They would just "choke us with their red tape once we go behind their fence." Klaus Riedel, on the other hand, "had been the strongest promoter of the idea of developing space travel within the framework of a self-supporting industrial firm, although he had been always a bit vague about how this wonderful goal could be achieved." As for von Braun,

> I had no illusions whatsoever as to the tremendous amount of money necessary to convert the liquid-fuel rocket from the exciting toy— which in my eyes the Mirak was—to a serious machine that could blaze the trail for the space ship of the future. . . . To me, the Army's money was the only hope for big progress toward space travel. . . .
>
> [I]n these discussions the moral aspect of building rockets for military purposes was never touched. The very thought of a possible war was too absurd in those days. There has been a lot of talk that the Raketenflugplatz finally "sold out to the Nazis." In 1932, however, when the die was cast, the Nazis were not yet in power, and to all of us, Hitler was just another mountebank on the political stage. Our feelings toward the Army resembled those of the early aviation pioneers, who, in most countries, tried to milk the military purse for their own ends and who felt little [sic] moral scruples as to the possible future abuse of their brainchild. The issue in these discussions was merely how the golden cow could be milked most successfully.[13]

While morality may indeed have played no role, von Braun's account of politics at the Raketenflugplatz is inaccurate. Rolf Engel describes arguments between Nazi, Socialist, and Communist supporters, although the rocket fanatics continued to work together harmoniously in the cause of spaceflight. He specifically names Riedel as a believer in a utopian future under Communism, but he does not tell us that he himself gave Soviet intelligence a report on German rocket activities and later offered to work in the USSR, facts that only recently have surfaced in Russian archives. Nebel, meanwhile, was aligned with the hard-right German Nationalist Party and the equally conservative veterans group Stahlhelm (Steel Helmet), and he was the one person at the Raketenflugplatz who trumpeted the military uses of rocketry for the nation. During the summer of 1932 Germany was locked in a life-and-death political crisis—one that led to Magnus von Braun Sr.'s sudden and surprising elevation to Reich minister at the beginning of June. Before joining the cabinet, he had been a member of the Nationalists. Could Wernher von Braun really have been as apolitical and naive as he presents himself?[14]

The answer is a qualified yes. According to Engel, von Braun took no interest in political debates, which he thought only impeded the work, but he "swam . . . in the wake of his father, and thus was inclined towards conservatism and German nationalism." Willy Ley wrote in a 1947 memoir:

> Did we discuss politics? Hardly, our minds were always far out in space. But I remember a few chance remarks which might be condensed into saying that in von Braun's opinion (as of that time) the German Republic was no good and the Nazis ridiculous. That, of course, was simply the political platform of the *Deutsche Adels Gesellschaft* (Society of German Nobility) to which von Braun's father and possibly also Wernher von Braun belonged.[15]

While the last assertion is almost certainly incorrect, Ley, like Engel, captures von Braun's essential nature: obsessed with space and indifferent to party politics but comfortable with his father's values. Wernher von Braun's self-admitted streak of amoral opportunism was certainly one side of his character—one that emerged when it served his personal ambition to be the Columbus of space—but his conservative-nationalist instincts, and the long family tradition of Prussian military and civil service, pushed him in the same direction. If going with the German army was the most important decision of his life, it was not a decision that proved difficult to make. Just as would later be the case in Cold War America, his inherited values and politics coincided with his ambition and his obsessions, making it easy for him to accept military money for the development of rocketry.

The upshot of his discussions with Nebel and Riedel, as one might expect, was that only von Braun would take up Colonel Becker's offer. "The idea was that I might be able to help the Raketenflugplatz from within,—or, if Reinickendorf should fail, I could at least pull my friends onto the platform I would endeavour to establish at an Army post." It is unclear how Becker would have brought more of them into Ordnance, but the brilliant young student had a model to follow: write a secret dissertation in physics at the prestigious Friedrich-Wilhelm (now Humboldt) University in the center of Berlin. During 1930–31, as a part of starting rocket research for the army,

Becker had arranged for Walter Nernst, the Nobel Prize–winning physical chemist who headed the university's Institute of Physics, to assign research topics of interest to his doctoral students. Becker also had a close associate in the institute, Dr. Erich Schumann, who held dual positions as a lecturer in physics and as a researcher in Ordnance's ballistics and munitions section, and in early 1932 Becker was made an honorary professor at the university, an appointment that reflected the growing power of the army and far right in Germany. As von Braun was about to complete the first half of his engineering education at the Institute of Technology in Berlin-Charlottenburg, he would transfer to the University of Berlin after he wrote his *Vorexamen*—his preliminary exams—in the fall. When the new semester began in November, he would enroll in the Institute of Physics and begin working at Kummersdorf on subsidized dissertation research under contract.[16]

In the meantime he and his family had moved from their beautiful house on the margins of the Tiergarten into the even more luxurious house of the Reich minister of food and agriculture, located in the park behind the ministry, just southeast of the Brandenburg Gate. The formation on 1 June of the ultraconservative Papen cabinet, with Magnus von Braun as a member, came in the wake of President Hindenburg's difficult reelection victory over Hitler in the spring. With the nation sinking ever deeper into a catastrophic depression and the totalitarian parties of the left and right growing rapidly, the cabinet of Chancellor Heinrich Brüning had become very unpopular. The last straw for the increasingly senile eighty-five-year-old field marshal and his reactionary advisers was Brüning's ban on the Nazi paramilitary associations SA (Stormtroopers) and SS (Protection Squad) in May, without a similar ban on the paramilitaries of the Socialists and Communists. General Kurt von Schleicher, the head of the Reichswehr's Political Office, succeeded in convincing the president to create a new far-right, nonparty "cabinet of experts," with the aim of bringing the Nazis into the government as a base of mass support that the traditional right lacked. Schleicher became defense minister. For chancellor he found a very conservative Catholic, Franz von Papen, who happened to be a neighbor and friend of Magnus von Braun's. History has not treated Papen kindly. He was a political lightweight and reactionary who, more than anyone except Hindenburg and Schleicher, would be responsible, out of catastrophic miscalculation, for allowing Hitler to become dictator.[17]

Soon after his appointment Papen called up Magnus Freiherr von Braun and asked if he did not wish to join a *"Kabinett von* Gentlemen"—consciously using the English word. Wernher von Braun's father became one of the barons in what was quickly dubbed the "cabinet of barons," a government dominated by Prussian Junkers that seemed a bizarre throwback to the Kaiserreich. In order to curry favor with the Nazis, the Papen cabinet repealed the ban on the SA and SS—leading to a new round of political murders—and called new Reichstag elections for 31 July. Hitler's party became the largest, winning nearly 38 percent of the vote and 230 seats. Eleven days earlier the Papen government had seized control of the state government of Prussia, which covered two-thirds of the nation, further undermining the foundations of the Weimar Republic. Magnus von Braun, a full participant in this constitutionally dubious, undemocratic action, took over the Prussian Agriculture Ministry. On 9 August he wrote a letter to the Nazi agricultural leader, Walther Darré, praising him for sharing many of the same fundamental values. It was part of a campaign to bring the Nazis into the government. Yet Hitler refused to participate in any cabinet merely as a prop for the old right, negotiations collapsed four days later, and the Papen government became ever more isolated and unpopular.[18]

The deeper meaning of all of this certainly passed twenty-year-old Wernher von Braun by. He was proud of his father, enjoyed the privileges that came from their elite social position, and liked showing off the residence. Constantine Generales later remembered the two of them driving his tiny, beat-up Opel through the grand ministry gate. During the visit of a classmate from the Lietz schools, von Braun said, "with a grand gesture to the park: 'The people pay for everything!' " On another occasion he invited Rolf Engel to dinner, but Engel, who barely scraped by at the Raketenflugplatz, found the von Brauns intimidating: "there was a rule that every day the whole family spoke another language, French, Italian, English, Spanish, I think even Portuguese. . . . I knew just a little French, and I always felt a bit lost in the family." After dinner they went to Wernher's room, where the two lay on the floor and von Braun explained the principles of thermodynamics as it applied to rocketry.[19]

Rudolf Nebel hoped to exploit von Braun's new status by putting him on the VfR board of directors. Indeed, he may have included the engineering student in the 22 June Kummersdorf expedition only because von Braun's father had become minister. At the general society meeting held on 24 September, according to Willy Ley, some members objected to the election of a student to the board, although they did not doubt his ability. Ley rose and said, "Gentlemen, if von Braun's age is the only obstacle you can think of, rest assured that that will be bettered every day all by itself." Von Braun was elected.[20]

His position in the VfR leadership quickly became inconvenient, however, as the army began to enclose him in its world of secrecy. Ley noticed that at the time of his election he "simultaneously . . . became less accessible." On 30 September Magnus von Braun Sr. sent Generales a note thanking him for a photo, mentioning that "Wernher is sitting for exams." Five weeks later, on 3 November, he received his diploma certifying that he had passed the "preliminary examination" in "mechanical engineering"; once again his performance in the various subjects ranged from good to merely adequate. He then enrolled at the university with a primary concentration in physics. Two weeks earlier, on 20 October, he had sent in a contract offer to the ballistics and munitions section of Army Ordnance, undoubtedly after careful instruction from Dornberger or the new section head, Major von Horstig. Becker had meanwhile moved up to chief of the Ordnance Testing Division and would be promoted to general on 1 February 1933. The contract, issued on 27 November with an initial length of four months, promised von Braun fourteen marks per workday for the expense of commuting, meals, and accommodation; he could apply weekly to stay at the Kummersdorf officers' club. His task would be the "conception, management of buildup, and, under the direction of Wa Prw 1/I, conduct of experiments on, a liquid-fuel reaction-motor test stand at Main Battery West in Kummersdorf."[21]

On the first day of December he formally reported for work. Although he was not the only or even the most advanced doctoral candidate working on Ordnance rocket projects—Kurt Wahmke, a student of Erich Schumann's, was already completing a dissertation in liquid-fuel rocketry—for all intents and purposes the army's long-range ballistic missile program began that day. Almost exactly two months later Hitler came to power.[22]

For von Braun, starting work at the army's artillery range felt very much like beginning at zero, without the help of his friends. As the liquid-fuel test stand was not yet built,

> one half of a concrete pit with a sliding roof was at my disposal, the other half being occupied by tests with powder rockets. Also, one mechanic was assigned to me. I was instructed to give my work orders to an artillery workshop which turned out to be loaded to capacity with other tasks, mostly of a higher priority than mine. The mechanics as to how my purchase orders were processed through the cumbersome administrative machinery remained for a long time an opaque mystery to me. It was a tough start.[23]

The "one mechanic" was Heinrich "Heini" Grünow, an experienced metalworker from the Raketenflugplatz, hired by Ordnance to help him.

After the war Willy Ley asserted: "One night in 1932, von Braun came to see his old friends of the VfR and complained bitterly about what he called the stupidity of his superiors." In spite of all his theoretical arguments "they insisted on powder as a fuel because of the non-storability of liquid-fuel rockets." Yet the army had also achieved "remarkable results. He spoke of 30,000 yards, but he did not state whether this meant horizontal range or vertical ascent. In the end he added, presumably because he suddenly realized he had talked too much, that experimentation had discontinued." Von Braun later said that when he began at Kummersdorf, Becker and his officers told him nothing about their military reasons for supporting rocketry. As a fervent believer in liquid fuels, he clearly failed to comprehend the logic of the solid-rocket program. In any case, it was the last time he visited the Raketenflugplatz.[24]

Von Braun's initial depression was uncharacteristic; soon he returned to his natural state: enthusiasm. As his first objective he took the development of a liquid-oxygen/alcohol motor of 150-kg (330-lb) thrust, based on scaling up the work at the old amateur site. About a year earlier Klaus Riedel had switched from gasoline to ethyl alcohol in order to reduce burn-throughs in rocket nozzles. Because alcohol is miscible with water, the combustion temperature could be lowered by cutting alcohol concentration, as Hermann Oberth had noted in his books. Von Braun chose an alcohol concentration of 75 percent, and technological momentum, as well as loyalty to his hero Oberth, motivated him to stick with this propellant choice until well into World War II. He made no attempt to study other propellant combinations, most notably storable, hypergolic (self-igniting) ones using highly toxic nitric acid as an oxidizer, which other rocket experimenters in Germany, Russia, and America soon examined. Liquid oxygen was difficult to handle too, with its extreme cold temperatures, evaporative losses, and penchant for causing explosions when it came into contact with organic materials, but it seemed like the obvious oxidizer, and von Braun was familiar with it. It is characteristic of his lifelong engineering style that, notwithstanding his romantic vision of future space technology, he preferred to plow ahead on a pragmatic, even conservative path in rocket development.

Sometime toward the end of winter (Heini Grünow would later remember it as 4 March 1933) he had his first test with the new engine, which was water-cooled and therefore designated 1W. "To everyone's amazement," the test was completely successful, burning for 60 seconds at about 120-to-140-kg thrust. "But I did not have to wait long for the set-backs. Ignition explosions, frozen valves, fire in the cable ducts . . . troubled me and taught me the hard way." The liquid-fuel test stand must have been finished for these tests. It had three concrete sides, plus a sliding roof and metal doors so that it could be closed to create a weatherproof workspace and opened for engine tests. Along with the test stand, von Braun put extensive efforts into developing test instrumentation to chart thrust-time curves, temperatures, pressures, and the like—all the things Becker had asked for in the summer of 1932.[25]

While spending most of his workweeks at Kummersdorf, von Braun commuted back and forth from Berlin in his first car, an ancient, beat-up Hanomag that he got for a hundred marks in late 1932. Sometimes it was parked beside President Hindenburg's grand Mercedes when he was home with his parents, and passersby looked amused when he drove it out of the gate of the Agriculture Ministry with the minister in the passenger seat. The doors were held shut with wire, the starter did not work, and the fenders rattled, but in a society where still only a very small fraction of the population owned automobiles, even this jalopy was a symbol of class. To get to the university, however, he needed only to walk. The Physics Institute building was blocks away from the ministry, very close to the French Gymnasium, his old school, on the Spree River near the Reichstag. But soon after 30 January 1933 the family was forced to move again to another luxury apartment in the Old West of the city: Magnus von Braun Sr. lost his job when a new coalition government was formed with Adolf Hitler as chancellor.[26]

The previous November, with six million unemployed and near-civil-war conditions in the streets, the bankruptcy of Franz von Papen's leadership had led General Schleicher, the conspiratorial defense minister, to convince President Hindenburg to make him chancellor instead. Papen got his revenge by making a new attempt in January to bring the Nazis into a cabinet, this time promising Hitler that he could have the top job. Old-line conservatives, including the leader of the Nationalists, who would take the Agriculture and Industry Ministries, and Papen, who would be vice chancellor, would "frame in" the chancellor and his two Nazi colleagues, preventing a dictatorship. It was a disastrous miscalculation, but one that even Magnus von Braun accepted at the time. While his son would sometimes later depict him as a principled anti-Nazi who quit rather than join, in fact he says in his memoirs: "When I ask myself whether I would have remained with my old friends and colleagues in the Hitler cabinet, my answer is . . . yes. I . . . couldn't see *any other way out*."[27] In fact, the catastrophes of World War II and the Holocaust were avoidable, and if they had been avoided, Wernher von Braun's life would have been completely different. Perhaps his commitment to the reactionary army of a weak republic was no Faustian bargain, but the Nazi seizure of power certainly made it one, if at first only slowly and imperceptibly. Rearmament money would begin to trickle, then pour into the Reichswehr's coffers, and rocketry would be only one of the beneficiaries.

It is unknown whether the enthusiastic rocketeer witnessed any of the dramatic events of early 1933 in central Berlin: the Nazis' torchlight parade directly past the Agriculture Ministry on the night of 30 January, the Reichstag fire of 27–28 February, the mass arrests of Communists and Socialists that followed, the Reichstag's passage of an act giving Hitler dictatorial powers on 23 March (von Braun's twenty-first birthday), the often-thuggish anti-Jewish boycott of 1 April, or the now-infamous book bonfire staged by Nazi students at his university on 10 May. He never mentioned any of these events in his various memoirs and interviews, but he may have seen one or two, and he certainly heard of them. A quarter century later he told the Hollywood producer of a heroic movie being made about his life:

> As a young fellow I was very little interested in the "world around me," and downright naïve in my views of political matters. For example, I did not consider Hitler's rise to power in 1933 as a thing of particular significance except, maybe, that my father lost his job in the process. The fundamental nature of the changes that had taken place in Germany dawned only gradually on me.[28]

As von Braun's statement implies, he observed the Nazis' rapid demolition of civil rights and democratic institutions with indifference—an indifference that could only have been reinforced by his conservative-nationalist upbringing and education. He was, moreover, surrounded by army officers and professors who profited from and supported the Nazi regime. Becker, whose far-right politics reflected those of much of the officer corps, soon established a personal relationship with Hitler, and Erich Schumann, von Braun's doctoral adviser, had close ties to the National Socialist Party in 1932 and joined it in the spring of 1933, when it was politically convenient. The Prussian Education Ministry quickly accepted the retirement request of the old and politically moderate director of the Institute of Physics, Walter Nernst, and removed a large number of younger lecturers and assistants from their jobs under the infamous civil service law of 7 April 1933—one could be fired for having the wrong politics or the wrong racial background. It sufficed for removal to have even one Jewish grandparent. The most distinguished physicist left, Arthur Wehnelt, became acting director. Not many months later Schumann was made professor and director of the Second Institute of Physics, which would concentrate on secret military research in support of his other job: head of an Army Ordnance research section under

Becker since the fall of 1932. None of the changes at the university particularly affected von Braun, except for Schumann's ascent in status, but, again, he must have been aware of them, including the expulsions of Jews from the faculty.[29]

What evidence we have from this period supports von Braun's contention that he "was too wrapped up in rockets" to pay much attention to the political changes happening around him. As his dissertation from spring 1934 shows, due to his talent, energy, enthusiasm, and very hard work, he would make astonishingly rapid progress in not much more than a year after his "tough start." The 1W series of water-cooled engines was followed by a 1B (for *Brennstoff*, "fuel") series in the spring and summer of 1933, which incorporated "regenerative cooling"—the alcohol fuel circulated through a cooling jacket around the aluminum combustion chamber and nozzle to prevent burn-throughs, just as had been done at the Raketenflugplatz shortly before he left. But manufacturing problems resulted in the "implosion" of the combustion chambers and numerous other spectacular failures. "Solidly in Nebel's footsteps," von Braun says, "I grabbed the telephone directory and got in touch with welding experts, instrumentation firms, valve factories and pyrotechnical laboratories." Working with three captains in the ballistics and munitions section—Walter Dornberger, Leo Zanssen, and Erich Schneider—he built particularly close contacts with firms expert in working aluminum and began to travel on business inside Germany, acquiring a great deal of expertise in fabrication.[30]

From the 1B series von Braun moved up to the 2B series of engines with a thrust of 300 kg (660 lb), which would go into his first rocket, the A-1, or Aggregat (Aggregate) 1; the designation was intentionally opaque. After successfully testing this engine numerous times in the fall, early in 1934 he was ready for his first static test of the whole vehicle. "It took us exactly one half year to build this 'A-1 rocket'—and exactly one half second to blow it up. An explosive propellant mixture accumulated in the motor, and delayed ignition led to a detonation which ripped the whole thing to pieces." Very much reflecting the influence of the artillerists he worked for, the person-sized A-1 was to be stabilized in flight by spinning the nose of the vehicle as a large, brute-force gyroscope; unlike the solid-fuel projectiles that Dornberger was developing in parallel to von Braun's work, a liquid-fuel rocket could not be spun as a whole because of the effect on the propellants in the tanks and lines. Underneath the gyro nose was a liquid-oxygen tank made up of a Bakelite-type plastic, mounted on the engine, which itself was immersed inside the alcohol tank to shorten the length of the vehicle. Unfortunately, further static tests on new rockets in the winter months of

1934 showed that the vibrations of the gyro spinning at 9000 rpm cracked the oxygen tank, resulting in leaks into the fuel tank and further explosions. Eventually all four A-1s blew up, wiping out von Braun's plan for launches in early 1934. The basic design would have to be discarded.[31]

Even as von Braun worked very hard at Kummersdorf and at the university, he took time in the summer of 1933 to get his private pilot's license, building on his earlier soaring tickets. He took lessons evenings and weekends at Staaken airfield, west of Berlin, beginning on 20 June and soloed for the first time on 5 July. But completing qualifications for an A2 license, including a cross-country flight, took until the end of August. As for his personal life, we know little. Constantine Generales moved to Berlin to study medicine in the fall of 1932 and stayed until April 1939, but after mid-1933 von Braun had to distance himself from his Raketenflugplatz friends for secrecy reasons. He did see Klaus Riedel a few times before then, however. Riedel's later wife and widow, "Babs," commented: "As a student Wernher also often visited us, and frequently brought girlfriends along, often two at once." For the "startlingly handsome," six-foot-tall, blue-eyed blond, it would be the start of a long career in Germany as a ladies' man.[32]

As the fall semester began at the University of Berlin, he started another activity, horseback riding—with the SS. The only explanation he ever gave is in a secret U.S. War Department deposition done in El Paso, Texas, in 1947, when his formal immigration status was being considered:

> In fall 1933, I joined the SS-horseback riding school of the "Reiter-sturm I" at Berlin-Halensee [in western Berlin, near the Grünewald forest]. I was there twice a week and took riding lessons. The entire outfit never did participate in any activity whatever outside the riding school during my connection with it. In summer 1934, I got my discharge from the "Reitersturm."

An enrollment document shows that he officially became an *SS-Anwärter* (SS applicant) on 1 November 1933. At that time the SS was still a small if fast-rising autonomous unit of the SA, the brown-shirted Storm Troopers who provided the primary muscle for the Nazi Party. The SS cavalry units were an even more specialized subdivision of Heinrich Himmler's black-shirted organization, and the Berlin regiment in particular attracted an unusually high proportion of nobles, a class that had traditionally played a disproportionate role in equestrian sports and the regular cavalry. Combined with the fact that the SS had pretensions to becoming the elite of the new order, it is clear why Wernher von Braun, the Prussian baron, would be attractive to recruiters for Reitersturm I. But why did *he* want to join?[33]

In the absence of evidence, we can do little more than speculate. As a resident of and visitor to country estates, he had had some riding experience. Perhaps the recreational aspect, combined with the social prestige of the SS equestrian units, was enough to attract him. A more likely reason for signing up, not at all incompatible with the others, was the pressure being applied on non-Nazi university students in the fall of 1933 to join SA-affiliated organizations for paramilitary training; for two weeks precisely around the time von Braun joined, the SA allowed any student to sign up for a probationary period. Yet he dropped out immediately after graduating in the summer of 1934, lending credence to the hypothesis of pressure and weak political commitment. Nonetheless, von Braun would have to have worn the black uniform with swastika armband at the riding club, and he would have been subject to ideological indoctrination, as well as training in riding, jumping, basic military skills, and the care of horses.[34]

Further insight into his adaptation to the Nazi regime can be glimpsed through a comment he made decades later about Hitler. He had his first distant encounter with the "Führer" on 21 September 1933, when the chancellor toured Kummersdorf. A photo from that day shows the young rocketeer on the margins of a very large group of army officers and Nazi leaders, including Becker, Hitler, and Air Minister Hermann Göring. Another group photo from early 1934 shows von Braun standing several rows above the dictator on the steps of the Kummersdorf officers' club. Decades later, however, he seems to have forgotten about the 1933 encounter:

> I met Hitler four times. When I saw him from a distance for the first time in 1934, he appeared to me as a fairly shabby fellow. Later when I met him in a smaller circle [in 1939 and 1941], I began to see the format of the man: his astounding intellectual capabilities, the actually hypnotic influence of his personality on his surroundings. It moved one somehow. . . . My impression of him was, here is a new Napoleon, a new colossus, who has brought the world out of its equilibrium. . . . In my last meeting with him [on 7–8 July 1943], Hitler suddenly appeared to me as an irreligious man, a man who did not have the feeling of being responsible to a higher power, someone for whom there was no God. . . . He was completely unscrupulous.

One can perhaps read aristocratic disdain in his dismissal of Hitler as "a fairly shabby fellow." By his own admission, however, he too would be seduced by the Führer cult—at least for a while.[35]

The consolidation of the Nazi dictatorship had another impact on von

Braun's life: he would have to stand by silently as his superiors in Ordnance set out to harass the amateur rocket groups out of existence. From the outset Karl Becker's emphasis on the secret development of surprise weapons meant that he and his subordinates looked on the publicity created by the VfR, the Raketenflugplatz, and other rocket groups with exasperation. They wished to establish an army monopoly over the technology, but there was little they could do about it until the Hitler government had effectively destroyed constitutional rights.

While the campaign against the amateurs did not begin in earnest until the fall of 1933, it had a precursor. In April the political police arrested Rolf Engel for treason in Dessau, where he had gone to set up his own rocket group. Somehow Reichswehr counterintelligence (the Abwehr) got wind of his low-level collaboration with the Soviets, but the evidence that he had done anything illegal was so flimsy that a judge threw the charges out six weeks later—but not before Engel got a case of jaundice in the unhealthy, overcrowded jail conditions during the Nazi seizure of power. Convinced that Dornberger and Becker were behind it, he began to pursue a vendetta against them by going over to the Nazis, eventually becoming a student leader and an SS officer. This vendetta naturally undermined his friendship with von Braun.[36]

Much more troublesome for Ordnance, however, was Rudolf Nebel, who created a new flurry of publicity in June 1933 with his attempted launch near Magdeburg of a scaled-down version of his "pilot rocket." In late fall 1932, just before von Braun left the Raketenflugplatz, Nebel had come back from Magdeburg with a contract from the city fathers promising tens of thousands of marks in loans and support if the city was the site of the launch of the first manned rocket. Typically, Nebel had promised that one of his men, Kurt Heinisch, a friend of von Braun's, would be launched and then parachute out of the rocket; he knew full well that they had little chance of developing a big enough engine to pull it off. (If they had ever tried, they probably would have killed Heinisch.) While the June launch was a fiasco, another version of the smaller rocket was successfully fired outside Berlin in July and August. It was the last hurrah for the Raketenflugplatz.[37]

In the fall the VfR leadership had a falling-out with Nebel, whom they accused of embezzling funds; meanwhile a huge water bill came in to the rocket site that the army refused to pay. Most seriously, the Gestapo raided the Raketenflugplatz, fingerprinted everyone, and hauled Nebel in to warn him that communicating with foreign countries about rocketry would be treason. Nebel responded, as always, by wrapping himself in the red, white, and black flag. He called upon his acquaintance with the leader of the Stahlhelm veterans association, Franz Seldte, now labor minister in the Hitler cabinet, and Seldte in turn pointed him to Ernst Röhm's SA, to which the Stahlhelm had been subordinated by the Nazis. The embittered Rolf Engel also became mixed up in Nebel's attempt to use the Storm Troopers against the army, at a time when the SA was becoming a rival of the Reichswehr. As the VfR's charges against Nebel were not upheld by the prosecutor, the ex–fighter pilot was able to stave off being kicked out of the Raketenflugplatz for many months. Ordnance was forced to keep squelching his initiatives instead, as Nebel wrote to Hitler and other Nazi bigwigs, and succeeded in getting the SA leadership and the post office minister to intercede on his behalf.[38]

Wernher von Braun's superiors did not involve him in their battle with Nebel, but he certainly knew what was going on. In mid-July 1934 he had to give an uncomfortable interview to a Gestapo detective about his relations with the leader of the Raketenflugplatz, who had been briefly arrested during the bloody "Night of the Long Knives," 30 June 1934. Hitler had authorized SS squads to shoot the SA leadership so as to pacify the army and eliminate a perceived threat to his rule; Ordnance added Nebel's name to the arrest list after he stupidly printed an open leaflet discussing the military uses of rocketry. In response to Nebel's claims that von Braun was his liaison man to Ordnance, the young engineer-physicist told the Gestapo that he had not violated secrecy and had neither met nor corresponded with Nebel since February 1933. He had nonetheless kept his place on the VfR's board for some months because his supervisor, Captain Erich Schneider, did not want to make "the remaining members of the board . . . unnecessarily attentive."[39]

However, when the battle between Nebel and the VfR leadership began, he agreed with Schneider that it was time to quit. Klaus Riedel, his close friend,

> called me several times during 1933 in order to ask for advice about bettering the relations between Nebel and Wa A [Ordnance]. In order to avoid telephone discussions of such matters, I met Riedel several times (in all about 5 times, the last ¾ of a year ago [c. October 1933]) and I made him aware that:
>
> 1.) Nebel was personally rejected by Wa A,
> 2.) If Nebel continues his campaign again Wa A he could bring serious consequences upon himself,
> 3.) Nebel should, in his own interest, and in the interest of the subject, avoid publication of technical details and of military applications.

Von Braun thus not only hinted that Nebel faced possible arrest but also laid out Ordnance's policy of press censorship regarding rocketry, which was formalized in a decree from the Propaganda Ministry in April 1934. A couple of months after his one-day arrest, Nebel was finally kicked out of the Raketenflugplatz. Von Braun did not see him again for years.[40]

Meanwhile, because of the fundamental technical problems afflicting the A-1 design, he and his military superiors had decided in the spring of 1934 to redesign the rocket completely—so completely that it would receive a new designation, A-2. The massive rotating gyro would be moved to the middle of the rocket, between the liquid-oxygen tank and the alcohol tank, with its embedded engine. The apparatus for producing nitrogen gas to force the propellants into the engine was moved from inside the liquid-oxygen tank to the nose of the vehicle. To prevent "hard starts" and explosions when too much fuel reached the combustion chamber before ignition, von Braun also had to rework the complicated system for controlling propellant flow. One of the valves he adopted came from the Heylandt company, which had had a small rocket research project going under Ordnance contract since the fall of 1931.[41]

In January 1934 von Braun acquired from Heylandt an engineer who would be one of his right-hand men for many years, Walter Riedel. Riedel (no relation to Klaus) was ten years older than von Braun and had the dry wit for which Berliners were well known. Dornberger's memoir describes him as "a short sedate man with a permanently dignified and serious expression" who provided "the right counterpoise to the rather temperamental—and at that time self-taught—technician, von Braun." In the preceding two years Riedel had pretty much carried the Heylandt rocket effort himself, after gaining experience working with Max Valier (who died in his arms as a result of the May 1930 accident) and with Arthur Rudolph, his assistant on the rocket car project of 1931. In late 1932 Ordnance had contracted the Heylandt company to build a small rocket engine for bench experiments, which Riedel duly completed. But at the end of 1933 the Ordnance officers decided to cut off Heylandt and hire Riedel, so as to focus their resources on von Braun, who was proceeding with such speed and energy. According to von Braun:

> My "marriage" with him proved to be very fertile because of our complementary dispositions. While I found satisfaction in carving out problems and formulating specific tasks, Walter Riedel was an old hand at design work. . . . To me and his colleagues he became a good friend; to his men he was a respected if fatherly boss and they awarded him the honoring sobriquet "Papa."[42]

In Germany there were and are two kinds of engineers: diploma engineers (with a deeper, more theoretical training) and two-year engineers trained at trade schools (with a more hands-on, practical experience with industry). Riedel was one of the latter and provided the brilliant wunderkind, still a novice at design and development, with a lot of paternal advice. Working with Riedel also fostered von Braun's leadership skills, so that he could maintain his authority even when working with colleagues who were much older. It would be the beginning of his primary career as an engineering manager.

As spring finally came to northern Germany, von Braun completed his University of Berlin physics dissertation, "Design, Theoretical and Experimental Contributions to the Problem of the Liquid-Fuel Rocket," in mid-April. A major section on the theory of combustion in a rocket engine can fairly be described as physics, but most of the typescript was actually an engineering treatise on his rocket motors, the A-1 vehicle, and the test instrumentation. Ordnance considered the work so sensitive that the dissertation was given a cover name, "Regarding Combustion Experiments," a boring and opaque pseudotitle that would appear in his graduation paperwork and on his doctoral diploma. Schumann and Wehnelt, his two examiners in physics, were so impressed with the work that they gave it the Latin distinction *"eximium"*—extraordinary, the highest possible grade.[43]

In the German system, however, to complete one's doctorate one also had to undergo an oral examination in four different fields. The examination itself took place on 7 June: first Wehnelt in experimental physics, then Bodenstein in chemistry, then Baeumler in philosophy, and finally Schumann in theoretical physics. Among other topics, Wehnelt asked von Braun about the laws of gases and thermodynamics, Bodenstein about the production of salts, Baeumler about the philosophy of physics in Descartes, Newton, and Leibniz, and Schumann about "quantum statistics, Schrödinger's wave mechanics," acoustics, and "theoretical ballistics." The results were reminiscent of his *Abitur* and his preliminary engineering exams. Schumann, his primary adviser, gave him a "very good" (A), whereas Wehnelt and Baeumler gave him a "good" (B) and Bodenstein a "satisfactory" (C). Due to his accelerated schedule and total focus on his subjects of greatest interest, he once again had done brilliantly in some things and only passably in others. In contrast to the dissertation, his oral received the distinction of "cum laude"—praiseworthy, a middling grade. Yet none of this mattered. At age twenty-two Wernher Freiherr von Braun—as he signed himself in university paperwork—had received a doctorate from one of the most prestigious universities in Germany, and he had written a superb dissertation that laid the foundation for his future career. The original typescript was returned to Ordnance, as it was deemed too secret to be left in university custody.[44]

Graduation did not change von Braun's status at Kummersdorf, where he had begun receiving a monthly salary as a contractor in April 1933; his superiors had clearly decided by the end of 1933 to make him a permanent employee when the budget allowed. He returned to his work almost immediately, but at the end of June 1934 he took a few days off. "On the last day of my vacation, the front pages exploded with news of a scandal in Germany": the purge of the SA. It gave him a "glimmer" of the true nature of the regime, he says, although he remained fundamentally loyal to it. "Later I learned that it [the purge] involved scores of murders that Chancellor Hitler ordered without benefit of any court whatsoever." The SS had sent out hit men to coldbloodedly assassinate old enemies, including General von Schleicher, who was gunned down with his wife in their Berlin home. Vice Chancellor von Papen, now completely powerless, was put under house arrest. Only two months later President Hindenburg died of old age. Hitler took the opportunity to abolish the office, assume the powers, and make himself commander in chief of the armed forces and Führer of the nation.[45]

For Wernher von Braun's parents, the assassination and arrest of acquaintances was frightening. They gave up their Berlin apartment and moved full time to their modest estate in the rolling hills of Silesia, pulling Magnus Jr. out of the French Gymnasium and sending him to Spiekeroog in the fall. (Wernher had rented his own apartment in Berlin's "New West" a little earlier.) Since his exit from the cabinet, Magnus Sr. had been in semiretirement, with only membership on the boards of two national banks to hold him in the capital. He and Emmy continued to move in very high circles, however, visiting Hindenburg and going to elegant dinner parties where foreign ambassadors and Nazi greats would appear, including Hitler, Propaganda Minister Josef Goebbels, and Reichsführer-SS Heinrich Himmler. The elder von Braun also remained on close terms with conservative ministers held over from the Papen and Schleicher cabinets, most notably Justice Minister Franz Gürtner. Whatever Gürtner's reservations about the lawlessness of the regime, he rationalized staying in the job as necessary to prevent someone worse from assuming it. In fact it only made him responsible for many crimes. After 1934 Gürtner continued to visit Oberwiesenthal, where the elder von Braun now focused on farming. "The conversations that we held in my Wiesenthal library in front of a burning fire until deep in the night," Magnus later wrote, "with a glass of good Rhine or Palatine wine in our hands, were for us, including my three sons, a lasting memory."[46]

What did the younger von Brauns learn from sitting by the fire with Hitler's justice minister? We will never know, but the father's anecdote, and Wernher's comments about "scores of murders," implies that they got an inside look at the regime. Wernher once stated that Sigismund "was bitterly Anti-Nazi from the outset." While this may be exaggerated, on 24 July 1935, the day the eldest son took the personal oath to Hitler required of all civil servants, he wrote a rather exceptional comment in his datebook: "anxiety for my humanity." He had recently returned to Germany following a two-year absence, studying for two semesters at the University of Cincinnati in Ohio and then traveling around the world. His American stay and his trip shaped his political attitudes in ways that moved him beyond his father's authoritarian nationalism. He decided to become a diplomat in the hope of promoting international understanding, applied to join the Foreign Office, and was accepted in 1936. Wernher, by contrast, had no deep qualms about the Führer. In June 1935 he told his elder brother that "Hitler [is] a good military leader," which certainly reflected the context he worked in. Although he traveled outside Germany two or three times between 1933 and 1939, the thought of emigration never crossed his mind, as it had for Willy Ley, who used a carefully disguised journalistic trip in early 1935 to escape to the United States permanently. Sigis's stories of that land's technological prowess did, however, later influence Wernher's decision to go there; he told his younger brother, "America is the place for you to build your moon rockets." Magnus Jr., being only fifteen in 1934, would be the one son to actually live at Oberwiesenthal, although he was mostly at Spiekeroog until 1937. He seems to have been captivated by Wernher's interests and personality, like so many others, and he modeled himself on his brother, starting to study chemical engineering in Munich in 1937. He was also young enough to receive a heavier dose of National Socialist indoctrination, serving as a junior Hitler Youth leader at Spiekeroog.[47]

For Wernher von Braun, visits to Oberwiesenthal were but interruptions, however, in the relentless pace of rocket development work at Kummersdorf; he pushed onward to the completion of the A-2. A series of engine tests to prevent ignition explosions in the 300-kg-thrust motor, such as had wrecked the A-1, had begun on 29 May and would continue to 17 October. There was a stark reminder of the dangers of the work, however, in a deadly accident that killed three colleagues. Dr. Kurt Wahmke, who had blazed the trail that von Braun followed, completed his secret dissertation on rocket engine nozzles under Erich Schumann in early 1933. We know little of what he was up to thereafter, except that he was researching liquid-fuel propellants for Schumann. On 16 July 1934 (the very same day von Braun sat down in Berlin to write the memorandum about his interview with the Gestapo) Wahmke decided to try a dangerous experiment: if hydrogen peroxide in high concentration could be mixed with alcohol, it would be an ideal monopropellant, greatly simplifying the complex piping of a liquid-fuel rocket. The propellant would need only to be injected and ignited. He was assisted by one technician and two graduate students. When the engine was ignited, burning was unstable, followed by a small explosion, which propagated backward into the propellant tank. The latter went off like a bomb, the test stand was destroyed, and Wahmke and the two students were killed. Von Braun had first met Wahmke at Kummersdorf in June 1932 during the Raketenflugplatz's failed demonstration launch. But there is little evidence that the accident deeply affected von Braun; he never emphasized the story later. With his usual energy and single-mindedness, he pushed onward, likely writing off the incident as the product of an ill-advised experiment that had little to do with his line of development.[48]

By the end of September 1934 assembly and static testing of the A-2 vehicle were almost complete. According to Captain Walter Dornberger, the officer with whom von Braun had worked most closely on the test stand: "My last day at Kummersdorf was given to a detailed discussion of the rocket A-2—'4.5 calibers long,' as it was called in accordance with artillery tradition." On 1 October Dornberger left to assume command of the first solid-fuel rocket unit in the army. The 11-cm-diameter rockets of his battery were added to a battery of conventional 10-cm "smoke mortars" (*Nebelwerfer*) that could lay down smoke, chemical, and high-explosive barrages. *Nebel* means "smoke" or "fog," but it was also Ordnance's cover name for poison gas. *Nebelwerfer* eventually became the term applied to all solid-fuel artillery rockets of the German army, as they became the primary weapons of the chemical warfare units.[49]

In December two A-2 rockets dubbed *Max* and *Moritz*—after the hell-raising twins in the German cartoon that gave birth to the American strip *The Katzenjammer Kids*—were finally ready for launching. Because room was lacking at Kummersdorf and secrecy was not sufficiently assured, Ordnance decided to fire them on the East Frisian island of Borkum. For von Braun, it would be rather like going home, as the island was in the same North Sea chain as Spiekeroog, only farther west. Demonstrating how much the solid-fuel and liquid-fuel projects were paired in the ballistics and munitions section, the Borkum expedition would also carry out a series of launchings of the unguided 11-cm rockets to explore their effectiveness as an antiaircraft barrage. On 10 December von Braun, Walter Riedel, Heini Grünow, and three others set off for Borkum, presumably in trucks, as they carried the disassembled 12-m (40-ft) launch mast and other equipment. The two rockets were to be shipped directly to the island by the gyroscope firm of Kreiselgeräte in Berlin, with which von Braun's group had begun to work on guidance issues.[50]

On the twelfth he wrote to one of the captains in Berlin, either Leo Zanssen or Erich Schneider, from the Beach Hotel Frisia on the island: "Our expedition has arrived in good shape and has already found helping hands." Certain details still needed to be straightened out, however, as the "Navy Artillery Depot Borkum" had never received Becker's order regarding the expedition, and it was unclear exactly where the theodolites and movie cameras were to be placed on the island. It would take at least a day to string telephone wires to connect the launch site with the measuring sites, he continued, so it was important that an expert from Ordnance arrive by Saturday to help set up the instruments for a launch on the planned date of Tuesday, 18 December. But all looked feasible. He ended the letter with "Weather is so far promising. There is a strong east wind and thus dry and clear weather. The experienced and well-traveled old salts here predict that we will get a clear frost."[51]

Indeed, all worked as planned, and many observers arrived on the island, including Schneider and Zanssen. (Dornberger was not allowed to attend, however, as he had to show off his new battery to the inspector of artillery.) On the eighteenth all was ready at the launch site on the northeast tip of the island, as far from the town as possible. The local population was warned to stay indoors during the launches for secrecy reasons. But the weather was bad. The next morning, 19 December, the wind was still very intense, with gusts up to 15 m/sec (50 mph)—it must have been absolutely frigid for the men on the dunes. "Because of the short time left before Christmas and in view of the fact that a second apparatus was available, around noon it was decided to go ahead with the launching," von Braun's expedition report states. *Max* was filled with alcohol, liquid oxygen, and compressed nitrogen; then they waited until enough liquid oxygen had boiled off to raise the pressure in the tank. When the firing command was given, the results were thrilling. " 'Max' reached a height of about 400 m [1,300 ft] over the clouds, that is about 1700 m [1 mi] in altitude, its burnout point," and then a big gust knocked the rocket into bigger and bigger oscillations until it finally tipped over. It impacted in the sand about 800 m south of the launch site. The whole flight could be followed "with the naked eye," much to everyone's excitement. With a success in hand, the Ordnance crew decided to fire *Moritz* the next morning, whatever the weather. For good photography the launch would be at dawn. Twelve minutes after the sun came up on the twentieth, *Moritz* took off with almost identical and spectacular results. It was later recovered when an airplane observer spotted the rocket sunk deep into the muck of the tidal zone.[52]

Von Braun shared credit with his coworkers, but he felt it was a very personal victory.

> It was for me an uplifting and proud feeling. . . . We had proof that we were on the right road. "Max" and "Moritz" . . . were the first rockets at that time that flew over two kilometers high. What was much more important for me, however, was this: the two were entirely my own work. I designed them myself, I drew every screw on the drafting table, [I] conceived the pressure regulator myself—in short, I had put them together from A to Z.[53]

Four years earlier he had been merely Oberth's "helper" and a hanger-on at the Raketenflugplatz. Now, thanks to the army and the Third Reich, he had done it—he had flown what he thought was the world's most capable liquid-fuel rocket. (He was right about that, even though he knew nothing of Robert Goddard's experiments in the New Mexico desert, not to mention those of the Red Army group around Sergei Korolev in Moscow.) Immediately after the expedition packed up, he took off for a celebratory Christmas vacation in London by catching a ride on a German trawler. He spent a very enjoyable five days, seeing the British Museum and Houses of Parliament and lunching at the Savoy Hotel. Three decades earlier his parents had each spent many months in that city; a decade in the future their son's rockets would be exploding on it.[54]

CHAPTER FOUR

How Much Do You Want?

1935–37

Hardly had the echo of the motors died away in the pine woods than the General [Army Commander in Chief Werner Freiherr von Fritsch] assured us of his full support, provided we used the funds to turn our rocket drive into a serviceable weapon of war. Bluntly and dispassionately he put the all important question: "How much do you want?" —WALTER DORNBERGER[1]

The flawless success of *Max* and *Moritz* gave Wernher von Braun's little liquid-fuel rocket project a big shot in the arm, and it came with excellent timing. In 1935 German rearmament would accelerate further, as Hitler gained confidence that the Western powers would respond with empty rhetoric when he tore up the Versailles Treaty. In March he announced the reintroduction of conscription and unveiled the covert Luftwaffe (air force), which had been forming inside Hermann Göring's Air Ministry. This new, independent air arm would, within a year, provide the impetus for a massive expansion of von Braun's project, one that would lead to the opening of a revolutionary new rocket center on the Baltic coast.

Soon after the New Year, Schneider invited a large number of people both inside and outside Ordnance, including representatives of the air force and navy, to a 15 January presentation of films and data from the Borkum expedition. He, Zanssen, and von Braun would speak. The powerful impression made by the success of the A-2 launches (nothing ever came of using unguided solid rockets in air defense) would have very positive effects on the program's budget and support, but first von Braun had to fend off a potential major diversion of effort resulting from a suggestion made at the meeting. On the eighteenth he wrote a memorandum explaining why Ordnance should not develop an interim weapon of 50-km (30-mi) range based on a scaled-up A-2. While a weapon based on a massive gyro could be developed relatively quickly and would provide a lot of useful experience, he noted, it would derail the existing line of development and create a missile of poor accuracy. It might even be difficult to design such a weapon. Moreover, if it were deployed, it could undermine the "surprise effect" of later, better missiles. It would be better instead to concentrate "all efforts on the main goal of an actively guided long-range projectile device"—for example, a rocket with a "1500 kg [3,300 lb] payload over a 400 km [250 mi] distance" that might also be fired at shorter ranges with even bigger payloads.[2]

Although von Braun later said that Becker and his officers told him nothing about their motivations when he joined in 1932, this memo shows that two years later the project's clear objective was the long-range ballistic missile, stemming from Becker's original program. As for the actual military use to which such a missile might be put, the memo says nothing. Perhaps not surprisingly, the relevant documentation from this period has since disappeared, as Becker and his officers undoubtedly had chemical weapons, as well as high explosives, in mind for the "payload." Oberth himself, it must be remembered, had discussed poison gas rocket attacks on enemy cities in his 1929 book.[3]

With the A-2-style weapon quickly laid to rest, von Braun and his military superiors were able to proceed with their plans for a much larger test vehicle, the A-3, with an inertial guidance system and a 1500-kg (3,300-lb) thrust engine. The new rocket required a greatly expanded test stand complex at Kummersdorf. On 4 February 1935 Major von Horstig sent General Becker a budget for nearly half a million marks for two new test stands (III and IV), with the mobile test rigs and small locomotives needed to move them, plus dedicated office, laboratory, and storage space. The budget included furniture for a new office for von Braun, who was finally made a permanent employee in October 1935. Meanwhile the expanded facilities had acquired a name: Versuchsstelle (Test Center) West, after their position on the Kummersdorf range. As the liquid-fuel rocket project expanded, so did von Braun's management responsibilities; the number of engineers, technicians, and workers under him grew to perhaps a couple of dozen by year's end.[4]

One key subordinate had joined during the Borkum expedition: Walter Riedel's old Heylandt colleague Arthur Rudolph. Born on a farm in the central German state of Thuringia, the balding Rudolph was a trade school engineer six years older than von Braun. He was also a committed Nazi, joining the party and the SA reserve in mid-1931, long before it was opportunistic to do so. Laid off because of the Depression in 1932, he and his old boss at Heylandt, Alfons Pietsch, tried to get support from the Berlin SA commander to build a liquid-fuel rocket engine. In May 1933 Ordnance gave Pietsch a contract to do just that (parallel to the von Braun, Heylandt, and Wahmke projects), but Pietsch later spent the money and disappeared, leaving Rudolph to finish it on his own. After securing another 300 marks from Dornberger, "a lean, starved-looking" Rudolph came to demonstrate his engine at Kummersdorf on 3 August 1934. Although thrust was a little low, it was a success; using a generous interpretation of the rules, von Braun signed the certification. In keeping with the policy of stamping out amateur work and establishing an army monopoly, a policy that could be enforced after the SA purge, Dornberger insisted that Rudolph join them if he wanted to continue to work on rockets. He was soon asked to quit the Storm Troopers (but not the party) as part of the security clearance process. Rudolph became von Braun's right-hand man for manufacturing and fabrication questions, paralleling Walter Riedel's role in design and testing.[5]

Rudolph was a spaceflight enthusiast even before meeting Valier, which forged a real bond with von Braun. As two bachelors staying in rooms at the Kummersdorf officers' club, they would spend many an evening in the lounge during 1935.

> We would sit until midnight or mostly into the morning hours and von Braun would spin his thoughts, his fantastic thoughts of going to the moon, going to Mars, going into . . . space. And I would work with logarithm table and slide rule. He developed his formulas. And we were so fascinated by it that we suddenly noticed, good grief, it is 4 o'clock in the morning! We have to go to bed. Now, of course, we were dead tired in the morning, and von Braun was not one who woke up easily in the morning. He had a hell of a time getting up.

The fact that von Braun had also been close friends with Klaus Riedel, who he once described as "a true Liberal, and a citizen of the world," is an indication of how little political ideology really mattered to the young aristocrat. But politics did intrude when the army made von Braun put his friendship with the Raketenflugplatz Riedel on hold. With work dominating von Braun's life, and secrecy making it impossible to discuss what he was doing with anyone who was not cleared, a friendship with a space enthusiast inside the project was certainly welcome.[6]

When he did drag himself out of bed, his days were usually dominated, as before, by the development of rocket engines, tanks, and plumbing in steel and various aluminum alloys, and by engine testing and test stand construction. The A-3's 1500-kg-thrust engine, which Walter Riedel took the lead in designing, was successfully fired in a steel version by October. But the new rocket also required venturing into new fields, most notably guidance and control. In the summer or fall of 1934 von Braun and his superiors had established contact with a firm secretly owned by the navy, Kreiselgeräte (Gyro Devices). In his 1950 memoir von Braun recalled its technical director, Johannes Maria Boykow, as "one of the strangest and most charming characters I have ever met." A former actor and Austrian naval officer and pilot, Boykow became deeply involved in torpedo development in World War I, leading him into gyroscopic devices for ships and aircraft.

> He was a true genius, but . . . he did not bother much about the mundane engineering phases of his inventions. His company's design office often found it necessary to deviate considerably from his original ideas, and therefore the end products often but vaguely resembled his original proposals. Unfortunately, I found this out only after severe setbacks. When I first met Boykow, I was left spell-bound by his analytic sharpness and imagination and, being a novice in the gyro field myself, I took everything he said for granted.

Boykow began designing a stabilized platform for the A-3 in October 1934, with the aim of creating a control system to maintain the rocket on a vertical trajectory, but he died only about a year later, leaving the firm to complete it. Both the development of this system and its ultimate failure would force von Braun to make himself into a guidance expert.[7]

Early in 1935 he met another striking personality who was to have a profound influence on his future career, and on the Ordnance rocket project: Major Wolfram Freiherr von Richthofen, the new head of development in the Air Ministry. A nephew of the Red Baron and an ace himself with eight Allied aircraft shot down in 1917–18, von Richthofen would later become a field marshal and a top Luftwaffe operational commander. He was also an enthusiastic National Socialist. Probably as a result of a subordinate attending the 15 January presentation, he dropped in at Kummersdorf to check out what the army was doing, and on 6 February he informed the ballistics and munitions section that an official of the Junkers aircraft firm in Dessau had been injured in a rocket engine explosion.[8]

Worried by the potential threat to Ordnance's policy of monopoly and secrecy, Captain Schneider dispatched Leo Zanssen and von Braun for a visit to Junkers a week later. They met company officials and an old acquaintance of von Braun, Johannes Winkler, the VfR founder who had worked on and off with Junkers on rocket-assisted-takeoff devices for heavily loaded aircraft since 1929. After impressing on them Ordnance's secrecy obsession, the two inspected Winkler's work, which they found to be small scale and behind what they were doing at Kummersdorf. Nonetheless, as Winkler was working with different propellants, Zanssen and von Braun did not see unnecessary duplication. A few weeks later they went to Munich to join an Air Ministry group inspecting the experiments of Paul Schmidt, an engineer working on an air-breathing pulse-jet engine, using intermittent combustion, that would eventually lead to the V-1 "buzz bomb."[9]

Von Richthofen continued to foster the rapidly developing alliance between the army and the air force. Reminded by Zanssen in May of the disinterest in the rocket in Ordnance's old aviation section, one of the precursors of the Air Ministry's Development Division, he told Zanssen that he was "of another opinion." The ever-increasing speed and altitude of bombers necessitated the creation of rapid-reaction interceptors that could quickly zoom up to altitude; he had in mind a cooperative program with Junkers leading to a rocket fighter. Ordnance signaled its support for this idea in a 22 May memo that Zanssen drafted.[10]

On 27 June representatives of Junkers, Ordnance, and the Air Ministry met at Kummersdorf to discuss the project. In preparation for the meeting, von Braun wrote a very revealing position paper, one that codified the views of his superiors. As there was no difference in principle between a rocket engine for a missile and one for an aircraft, he stated, it made sense if both were developed in the same place. "Wa.Prw.1 [the ballistics and munitions section] believes that this goal can be achieved through the future creation of an 'experimental rocket establishment.' " The employees of this establishment should be employed by Ordnance or the center, to which the air force should provide development funding, an arrangement that would make the Luftwaffe a rather junior partner. Ordnance's desire for control, however, went even further. "Because the previous development of liquid-fuel rocket propulsion has been financed by the state," von Braun continued, the ballistics and munitions section laid special emphasis on denying industrial firms any drawings or materials regarding the army's rocket development. "Otherwise there is the danger that profit-making opportunities in industry would arise from development the state has carried out at a considerable expense." It was a very statist conception of technological development, one with Prussian army roots more than National Socialist ones. Corporations would be mere contractors to a central government institution, where design and final assembly would be concentrated. In the United States this tradition of in-house military development was called "the arsenal system" and had a long and successful history. In German form the arsenal system would be the context in which von Braun developed his great talent for the management of complex engineering programs.

In the 27 June meeting, Ordnance, Junkers, and the Air Ministry agreed to proceed with the rocket fighter, although a small test aircraft should be built first and perhaps towed into the air for preliminary engine tests. Von Richthofen pointed out, however, that the Air Ministry did not intend to be a junior partner; nor would it make sense to obstruct direct communication between Junkers and Ordnance. Perhaps because of the army's attitude, the Junkers company lost interest in the project and was supplanted in the fall by Heinkel Aircraft, based near the Baltic seaport of Rostock. Its energetic owner, the short, bald, bespectacled Ernst Heinkel, loved setting speed records. On 16 October the young Dr. von Braun traveled with Walter Riedel to meet the firm's owner and his leading designers; two Air Ministry engineers joined them. Ten days later Ernst Heinkel witnessed an engine firing at Kummersdorf.[11]

For von Braun, a pilot as well as a rocket enthusiast, the rocket aircraft program was an exciting prospect. In the fall of 1934, and again in the spring and summer of 1935, he had taken refresher flying courses and at the end of August did a little flying during a visit to the Luftwaffe's main test station of Rechlin. Now he even dreamed of being the test pilot for the first rocket-equipped aircraft, a Junkers Junior biplane with an A-2-type 300-kg-thrust motor. Funded by Dr. Adolf Bäumker's Research Division of the Air Ministry despite Junkers's exit, this project continued as part of a program of investigation into rocket-assisted takeoff for heavily loaded bombers. The Junior was delivered to Kummersdorf in the fall of 1935, and firings began in early 1936. As for the Heinkel project, the objectives quickly converged on developing an engine of about 1000 kg (2,200 lb) thrust and building it into an He 112 piston-engine fighter as a test bed. In order to carry out the necessary engine development, von Braun's group received funds from the Air Ministry for several more designers and metalworkers, as well as for the modification of the test stands.[12]

In late November or early December 1935 matters took an even more exciting turn: the air force decided to back von Braun's idea for an interservice "experimental rocket establishment." Arthur Rudolph remembers his boss asking him to accompany him to the Air Ministry. "We were received by a . . . high official. Bäumker I think was his name. And von Braun in his usual manner made an excellent presentation to him. And before he even finished, Bäumker said, 'Von Braun, I give you five million of Luftwaffe money so you can start the ball rolling.' " The younger man took this offer back to his superiors at the Ordnance Testing Division:

General Becker . . . was wrathfully indignant at the impertinence of the Junior Service.

"Just like that upstart Luftwaffe," he growled, "no sooner do we come up with a promising development than they try to pinch it. But they'll find they're the junior partners in the rocket business!"

"Do you mean," asked [Lieutenant] Colonel von Horstig in astonishment, "that you propose to spend more than five millions on rocketry?"

"Exactly that," retorted Becker, "I intend to appropriate six millions on top of von Richthofen's five!"

In this manner our modest effort[,] whose yearly budget had never exceeded 80,000 marks, emerged into what the Americans call the "big time."

Rudolph was probably right that it was Bäumker, not von Richthofen, as the former had a virtual blank check from Göring at this time to expand Luftwaffe research facilities. To Rudolph, this action was "entirely new, fantastic, unbureaucratic, fast moving, decisive, overwhelming," especially in comparison to the ponderous army bureaucracy. He and von Braun became air force enthusiasts.[13]

Von Braun immediately set off in search of "a suitable site from which it was possible to fire rockets over several hundred miles; safety reasons required this site be situated on the coast." Only the Baltic fit that criterion; Germany then possessed an unbroken coastline almost to Danzig (now Gdansk). His best site on the big island of Rügen, however, turned out to have been purchased for a gigantic beach resort for the German Labor Front, the mandatory Nazi organization for workers and employers. "Christmas 1935 I went home to my father's farm in Silesia," says von Braun, and told his parents about the "new prospects" and the need for a launch site. (The army had never asked him to keep his activities secret from his family, and Dornberger had even given Magnus von Braun, the ex-minister and former reserve officer, a Kummersdorf tour in 1933, to "frequent headshakings" as to how his son had ever acquired "this strange technological bent.") "Why don't you take a look at Peenemünde," his mother suggested. "Your grandfather used to go duck hunting up there." Immediately after the New Year Wernher journeyed north, "and it was love at first sight." The northern tip of the island of Usedom with its dense forests, pristine marshes, and beautiful sand beaches, was a natural haven for wildlife only twelve kilometers from the von Quistorp estates at Crenzow and Bauer. The two services quickly began to plan for a joint facility with an airfield on the western side of the northern peninsula of Usedom and an army rocket development center along the eastern coastline.[14]

Spending millions on rocketry required, however, gaining new political backing and developing a new long-range objective for the army program. In March 1936 General Becker succeeded in pulling Walter Dornberger, now a major, back from his *Nebelwerfer* command so that he could put him in charge of Ordnance rocket development, which was elevated to its own section. A year earlier Becker, as the dean of the new Faculty of Military Technology at the Berlin-Charlottenburg Institute of Technology, had arranged for the younger man to receive an honorary doctorate for his rocketry accomplishments. Now he told him, "If you want more money you have to prove that your [liquid-fuel] rocket is of military value." That same month, March 1936, Hitler successfully remilitarized the Rhineland, over the objections of his generals, and the army commander in chief, General Werner Freiherr von Fritsch, visited Kummersdorf to see a demonstration of the A-2 and A-3 engines. Impressed, he asked, "How much do you want?"[15]

On the air force side, von Richthofen secured the support of the Luftwaffe chief of logistics, General Alfred Kesselring, in a meeting on 1 April; Kesselring had doubtlessly talked to his commander in chief, Hermann Göring. After the two services reached their final agreement in a conference a short time later, the Air Ministry acted with astonishing speed, sending "a senior official" in "a high-powered car" the same day to initiate the purchase of the site from the town of Wolgast.[16]

A few days after Fritsch's visit, Dornberger sat down with von Braun and Walter Riedel to lay out preliminary specifications for the A-4, the world's first ballistic missile. (Later it would be better known as the V-2.) "We conducted a few project calculations," von Braun states, "and found that the largest rocket with a configuration similar to the A-3, that could be shipped without disassembly through railroad tunnels, would be capable of covering a range of 275 kilometers [170 mi], with a payload of one metric ton [2,200 lb]." The engine would need to have up to 25 metric tons of thrust (55,000 lb)—seventeen times that of the A-3! These range and payload specifications met the desires of Dornberger, the heavy artillery veteran.

Artillery's highest achievement to date had been the huge Paris Gun, developed during the First World War. This could fire a 210-millimeter shell with about 23 pounds of high explosive about 80 miles. My idea of a first big rocket was something that could send a ton of explosive over 160 miles—that is, double the range of the Paris Gun.

Becker had worked on that project, and it shaped his perceptions of the potential of the liquid-fuel rocket from the outset. The Paris Gun had been a surprise weapon intended to demoralize the French during the spring 1918 German offensives; although the gun had been far from effective, Becker (and Dornberger) hoped for the desired effect from a new superweapon. Perhaps a radical new technology, combined with a chemical warhead, would spread fear and panic among an enemy population. Through very high accuracy, Dornberger also expected to be able to attack specific larger targets.[17]

Dornberger's appointment as chief of Ordnance rocket development was the beginning of a long, intense, and mutually beneficial relationship with von Braun.

> I had worked under Dornberger since joining the Ordnance Department. But in the early years the contact was rather elastic, since he was also in charge of powder rockets which absorbed most of his time. . . . But now that Peenemuende was getting started, General Becker hurriedly called him back from field duty. . . . From now on, until war's end, he piloted the liquid rocket program courageously and skillfully around all the reefs and barriers that lay in its way.

In another memoir he calls Dornberger his "fatherly friend"—at the time of Fritsch's visit, he was just turning twenty-four. Dornberger's paternal advice, encouragement, and restraint were very important to the brilliant engineer's development as a leader, and von Braun, for his part, functioned best when he reported to a decisive commander. His traditional, rather authoritarian Prussian upbringing, combined with his polished yet unpretentious manner, made his personality an ideal fit with those of his superiors in the officer corps. In two surviving performance evaluations, one by von Horstig in February 1936 and the other by Dornberger in September 1937, he is praised enthusiastically for his tact, humor, manual skill, manufacturing knowledge, engineering creativity, and ability to extract the utmost in efficiency from his subordinates.[18]

An especially vivid picture of von Braun at this age comes from Erich Warsitz, the Luftwaffe's designated test pilot for the rocket-equipped He 112. By the time of Warsitz's visit to Kummersdorf, probably in late 1936 or early 1937, the flights of the Junkers Junior had been canceled because the added rocket motor shifted the aircraft's center of gravity too far back; Ordnance would not let von Braun risk his life as a test pilot in any case. Warsitz arrived at the army facility to witness a test of a rocket-equipped He 112 fuselage and was first directed to "a wooden barracks—a very completely run-down thing—where six or six people sat around a conference table, the only thing in a room that was so filled with cigarette smoke that at first I couldn't recognize anybody." (Von Braun had become a smoker too by this time.) After giving a highly technical lecture on rocketry to the mystified test pilot, von Braun led him to the He 112 fuselage and got into the cockpit, directing Warsitz to stand beside it. After working "innumerable levers, switches and buttons" and enduring a false start, von Braun began a countdown:

> "Three, two one, . . ." Boom! An ear-splitting noise. The full power of the motor's thrust shook the machine in its supports so much that I had to hold onto the rim of the cockpit. I was incredibly impressed and swept away, turned around and saw coming from the fuselage tail a blue-white jet of fire. . . .
>
> During the night that followed, I would find out that von Braun had previously ignited the motor from an observation stand behind a concrete wall thirty or forty meters away. But he and [Walter] Künzel, the leading engineer from Heinkel, who was also present, had agreed that, if they had first showed it [the airplane] to me from behind a concrete wall, I never would have gotten into it.[19]

As evening was coming, von Braun invited Warsitz and Künzel to go to Berlin with him. "We went to his car. I would never have dreamed it could be his vehicle: in the back only half a bumper, the fenders unbelievably banged up, unwashed in three years. . . . I was shaken to think that one could drive in such a car at all." A pile of papers on the passenger seat was needed to hold a large spring from popping up, and there was no door handle or lock. Eventually von Braun wired Warsitz's door to the steering column and took off at a high rate of speed.

> Suddenly, at a dangerous intersection near Kummersdorf, a vehicle approached us from the right. Von Braun drove on with undiminished speed. At that moment there was a noticeable cracking sound. . . . Speechless with fear, I looked at von Braun, who, without taking his foot off the gas, said with complete calm, emphasizing every word: "Gentlemen, that was only a little tap."[20]

They proceeded to the elegant Kurfürstendamm shopping and entertainment street in western Berlin. First von Braun took them to a restaurant, where they ate a hearty stew and talked shop, then to a bar where the waiter knew him and delivered a giant plate of stuffed cabbage, which he wolfed down with a "huge appetite." Then to the "well-known 'Gypsy Cellar,' " where they received a bottle of champagne from a free-spending Dutch prince. Their drinking went on until nearly six o'clock in the morning. They got back in his wreck, and somewhere near the Kaiser-Wilhelm Memorial Church, von Braun stopped, turned to Warsitz, and said:

> "Will you go along with us, and test the rocket in the air?" I: "Yes." He: "Then, Warsitz, you will be a famous man. And later we will fly to the moon together—and you will steer!" We then agreed to use the famil-iar "Du" form with each other, and von Braun told me that I had now been accepted into the conspiracy. But first we must make a bet: namely, whether he would dare to drive three times in the wrong direction around the Memorial Church, and finish it without the police noticing.

Once, twice, almost three times around the circle he drove, before a couple of cops whistled them to a halt. "With his speaking ability and charm, Wernher von Braun soothed the policemen, and kept them so long, that it struck six o'clock and the officials declared that any charges would be dropped because their shift was over." The three then took the cops out for a nightcap in a local bar. Warsitz was completely won over. "I said to myself, one would go through fire for a man with such verve, skill and humor in dealing with peo-ple, and so many formulas in his head—he will reach his goal."[21]

Wernher von Braun had every reason to be a happy-go-lucky young man in 1936–37: research money, respect, and responsibility were flowing his way, and his dreamed-of "experimental rocket establishment" was rising on the shores of the Baltic. When his military service requirement came up in 1936, he even got to fly, spending May, June, and July away from Kummers-dorf at a Luftwaffe flying school in Frankfurt am Oder, east of Berlin. There he flew a wide variety of trainers and was designated an air force reserve pilot; he was exempted from regular service because of the value of his work. He had given up his Berlin apartment, and when he returned to his job, he roomed with a family in the lakeside town of Mellensee so as to be near Kummersdorf. His first official day back, 1 August, was also the day Adolf Hitler opened the Olympic Games in Berlin to enormous public enthusiasm. It was one more propaganda success.[22]

On the tenth von Braun issued an order tightening up the organization of engine testing in view of the "fast work pace of the last few weeks." He now had to be a manager on three fronts at once: developing the A-3, pushing forward the rocket aircraft projects, and planning for Peenemünde's opening in the spring of 1937. Although the A-3's design was finished in the spring of 1936 and secretly patented by Ordnance, there were many challenges to making it work, notably its aerodynamics, its guidance platform, and the jet vanes that would divert the engine exhaust in order to adjust the rocket's attitude. For the He 112 project, another engine initially targeted at 1000 kg (2,205 lb) of thrust, later reduced to 725, had to be developed, along with a complicated tanking and valve system that could be safely operated by a pilot. Finally, together with Dornberger he had to recruit people, both for the short-run needs of Kummersdorf and for the future, much-expanded operation up north. In late 1936 they managed to attract two very important researchers to the A-4 and Peenemünde projects.[23]

Dornberger lured Dr. Walter Thiel away from Erich Schumann's Ordnance research section, where he had replaced Wahmke in the scientific investigation of rocketry, to take charge of the huge challenge of developing the 25-ton-thrust engine. Thiel, a chemical engineer, would prove to be a great asset, revolutionizing the form of rocket motors—von Braun and Riedel's very long, cylindrical combustion chambers were leading to a technological dead end of unwieldy size, inadequate efficiency, and unsolved cooling problems, an indication that detail design was not von Braun's strength. "A pale-complexioned man of average height, with dark eyes behind spectacles with black horn rims," Thiel could be arrogant and highstrung at times, but he was a fount of new ideas.[24]

Meanwhile von Braun campaigned for Dr. Rudolf Hermann, a slender, thirty-one-year-old assistant professor at the Aachen Institute of Technology. Hermann was engaged in cutting-edge research on supersonic aerodynamics, and von Braun had met him in Aachen on 8 January 1936, when he was looking for someone to do wind tunnel research into the A-3's shape, especially its fins. "During my frequent visits to Aachen," von Braun says, "we would sit together in[to] the small hours [of the night] discussing what could be done to put supersonic aerodynamics on an adequate basis for our ambitious rocket projects." The two also shared an enthusiasm for classical music and concerts in Berlin. When Hermann, using tiny models in his small supersonic tunnel, was finally able to produce an A-3 design in fall 1936 that made the vehicle stable at velocities over the speed of sound, Dornberger gave in to von Braun's repeated arguments that Peenemünde would need its own advanced aerodynamics institute with larger wind tunnels. The estimated cost for the institute was 300,000 marks, an already worrying sum, but Dornberger thought he "had enough experience with building to know that there wasn't the least chance of . . . remaining at that figure, especially with von Braun about. It was more likely to cost a million marks." Becker agreed to fund it only if Dornberger could find another Ordnance section that would support the project. After being rebuffed by his old organization, ballistics and munitions (von Horstig had transferred to other duties), Dornberger eventually secured the support of antiaircraft artillery development. Hermann would join them in spring 1937 to begin constructing his dream institute in Peenemünde.[25]

Recruiting for an expanding program also brought opportunities to hire some of the old rocket enthusiasts, but it brought dilemmas as well. The question of what to do with Hermann Oberth had resurfaced in late 1934, after the pioneering theorist and impractical high school teacher, now a true believer in Hitler, had sent in a naive missile proposal from Romania. Zanssen and Schneider, after talking to von Braun, decided in early 1935 that Oberth would never be acceptable, as he lacked engineering training, was cranky and difficult, and was not a German citizen, and hence excluded from knowledge of the supersecret program. Presumably under their instructions, Wernher von Braun drafted a letter advising another branch of Ordnance to string Oberth along rather than refuse him outright, in order to keep him from working for any other power. Oberth refused to go away, however, repeatedly sending dubious emissaries to Germany, including a Nazi member of the Romanian parliament who represented the German minority, and an Italian citizen with a Russian name whom the Ordnance officers treated as a possible spy. Von Braun, still influenced by hero worship and fond memories of working with him in 1930, refused to see what a troublesome person he could be. In a May 1937 memo the young engineer wrote: "Regarding his character, I can only say good things about Oberth. I also know him as a thoroughly nationally minded German." It is a comment as revealing of his own values as of those of Oberth's.[26]

In the fall of 1935, as a part of the first, small expansion of the Kummersdorf crew to accommodate the new Luftwaffe projects, von Braun tried to hire one of Oberth's regular correspondents, Otto Wiemer, a draftsman-designer working for the giant Krupp firm. But when Wiemer came to Berlin to meet von Braun, the two got into a personal conflict over Wiemer's unrealistic demands for pay and promotion. (The civil service did not pay very well.) Von Braun hired a Berlin trade school engineer, Bernhard Tessmann, instead. Afterward Wiemer became a troublemaker who kept complaining about von Braun and campaigning for Oberth.[27]

What is interesting about this minor case is what it reveals about Wernher von Braun's integration into the National Socialist system. Before the two fell out, Wiemer had sent in his "Aryan certificate"—this just after the enactment of the Nuremberg Laws, although the exclusion of Jews began with the civil service law of 1933. When hiring, von Braun naturally had to take Nazi racial decrees into account. In 1936 Wiemer's complaints to a private firm about von Braun's alleged bungling of rocket development led to the first investigation of the Krupp designer's violations of secrecy. Von Braun recommended that, in view of the "probably very serious consequences" that would follow from a formal charge, only a severe warning letter be sent, and this was done. Wiemer's name was added to the list of people, like Oberth, whose mail was opened. After a second indiscretion, however, von Braun drafted a letter in April 1938 to the Abwehr to be signed by the chief of Ordnance Testing and Development. Because Wiemer was "a young idealist" who made his "frivolous remarks" with "a complete disregard for the importance of military secrecy," but not "out of a lack of national-mindedness,"

> Ordnance Testing Division believes it useful if he would be given an appropriate warning through a multi-week imprisonment. The formal filing of charges for negligent treason would probably lead in due course to a complete annihilation of his future, so Ordnance Testing Division therefore asks that this possibility be avoided.

In short, von Braun and his superiors did not want to send him to a concentration camp but thought that some secret police intimidation was in order. As Wiemer had complained to Walter Künzel of Heinkel, who already knew the secret, no case could be made, but Wiemer did receive an unpleasant warning in the form of a visit from the Gestapo. It is clear from von Braun's memorandum that, notwithstanding his limited efforts to protect Wiemer, by 1938 he was well adapted to the military culture of secrecy, to the extreme nationalism of Hitler's Reich, and to the internal workings of its police state.[28]

Despite the trouble with some of the rocket enthusiasts, von Braun was excited to be able to hire four of his former Raketenflugplatz friends for Peenemünde: Klaus Riedel, Hans Hueter, Helmuth Zoike, and Kurt Heinisch (the erstwhile "rocket pilot"), all of whom he had had to avoid for several years. Ordnance had arranged for the giant Berlin electrical firm Siemens to put them "on ice" by giving them jobs in the aircraft autopilot and gyro controls section. But bringing in Riedel raised the problem of what to do with Rudolf Nebel. In mid-1936 the two had been awarded a rocket engine patent they had applied for in 1931. Nebel had taken a routine designer job in another part of Siemens in 1935, after being repeatedly thwarted by Ordnance when he tried to interest firms in rocketry or join the new Luftwaffe. During 1936 Nebel created even more trouble for the army, appealing to the Propaganda Ministry and winning the backing of Dr. Fritz Todt, the chief of autobahn construction and head of the Nazi Party's technology organizations. To buy Nebel's acquiescence, von Braun and Dornberger decided that

Army Ordnance should purchase the rights to the almost worthless patent, specifying that Riedel would join the organization to transfer the knowledge. On 2 July 1937, at General Becker's office in Berlin, Rudolf Nebel and Klaus Riedel signed the contract, which gave them the healthy sum of 75,000 marks (roughly $18,000), which they split two-thirds/one-third after giving 5,000 marks to a couple of others from the Raketenflugplatz. Some months later Riedel finally was able to marry his girlfriend and move north, where he would begin as the head of test stands at the brand-new rocket center.[29]

By the time Wernher von Braun began moving his liquid-fuel rocket group to Peenemünde in April–May 1937, it had grown from 2 people— Heini Grünow and himself—to almost 80 in less than five years. Now, with the addition of Riedel and many others, it would once again grow dramatically. He would have 350 people working for him as chief of Werk Ost (East Works), the army half of the interservice facility. It was an astonishing accomplishment for such a young man, even in a regime dominated by young men. But it was only the beginning. During the next few years the seductions of power, resources, technical achievement, and recognition would only increase—and so would the problems and the dangers.

CHAPTER FIVE

His Indisputable Genius

1937–39

Von Braun's imagination knew no bounds. . . . He reveled in any project that promised to be on a gigantic scale, and, usually, in the distant future. I had to brake him back to hard facts and the everyday. I had to force him to go more deeply into things, to concentrate more, especially in questions of detail.

I knew that as soon as he really applied himself intensively . . . his indisputable genius would find the right answer. He had an almost incredible gift for retaining, out of a profusion of scientific data, literature, discussions, visits to factories, the one important point that concerned our work; for seizing upon it, developing it in his mind, and putting it into action at the right spot.
—WALTER DORNBERGER[1]

Between 1937 and 1939 Wernher von Braun came into his true calling: the management of huge engineering projects, the building of large technological systems. Thanks to the German army's massive investments of money, manpower, and political capital in rocketry, his initial Peenemünde staff of 123 white-collar and 226 blue-collar workers would at least triple, only to triple again early in World War II. After 1938 corporate and university researchers were also integrated in increasing numbers, further propelling fundamental breakthroughs in liquid-fuel propulsion, supersonic aerodynamics, and guidance and control. But the efforts of the growing corps of scientists, engineers, and technicians, within and without the rocket center, would have been wasted but for von Braun's superb technical leadership. Talented, creative engineers and scientists are essential for any program that is attempting to make fundamental technological breakthroughs, but those relatively rare skills are common in comparison to the few who have both superior technical talent and the ability to manage, lead, and inspire large, complex organizations. The remarkable skills that the precocious young engineer had displayed in leading a few dozen people at Kummersdorf he almost effortlessly extended to thousands. The price he paid for his position was his further seduction by, and enmeshment in, the system—late in 1937 he would find himself pressured to join the National Socialist Party.

When Wernher von Braun left the familiar environs of the Berlin region in May 1937, he moved to Zinnowitz, a Baltic coast town on the island of Usedom, where Peenemünde was located. About 200 kilometers north of the capital, Zinnowitz was one of a string of villages that had blossomed in the late nineteenth century as summer beach resorts, mostly for the Berlin bourgeoisie. Farther east were the upscale *Kaiserbäder* (imperial beach resorts) like Bansin, Ahlbeck, and Heringsdorf, made famous by Kaiser Wilhelm II around the turn of the century; farther west of Zinnowitz there were only a couple of smaller, less imposing resorts, ending at Karlshagen.

Beyond Karlshagen, the northwestern tip of the island was almost completely undeveloped before von Braun's mother suggested it in late 1935. Much of the land was forested or swampy and undesirable for farming, and the only population center was the tiny fishing village of Peenemünde— "the mouth of the Peene," a river that flowed into the lagoon behind the western end of Usedom and then emptied into the sea at its northwestern tip. The picturesque little village was absorbed and eventually destroyed by the military development of the joint Luftwaffe-army rocket center that would bear its name. Nearby was Peenemünde-West, the air force airfield and test center, and on the Baltic side, ranging down the coast, was Peenemünde-East, the army facility. Von Braun first lived in Zinnowitz because the center was still a construction site well into 1938 and in places even into 1939.[2]

Especially during those golden prewar summers, the heyday of the Third Reich, von Braun's off-hours could be very pleasant, as he explained to a movie producer in 1959:

> The seashore of Usedom-Island was like the New Jersey coast in the summer: there was a whole string of seaside resorts with nice beach hotels, restaurants, open air dance floors with music bands along the "beach promenade" etc. The bachelors employed at Peenemuende had ample opportunity to make the acquaintance of vacationing girls. There were horses and boats to rent. And there were many lovely inns at the (quieter) "lagoon" side of Usedom Island where one could sip a drink and dance under the sky.

One of those "vacationing girls" was a striking, tanned Norwegian teenager who lied about her age; she fell madly in love with him. He showed less commitment, although twenty years later he remembered her "oh so well." He did not lack for female company.[3]

After September the vacationers withdrew, and the weather was often gray and cold. "In the winter, most of these places were closed down[,] and with wooden shutters in front of most of the windows the whole area looked like 'Cape Cod in February.'" Yet even in the off-season it was sometimes possible to sail on the sheltered lagoon. Sailing had been one of von Braun's passions since at least Spiekeroog; as a teenager he had often used his father's boat on Berlin's lakes. After he moved into "rather fancy bachelor quarters" next to his office in November 1939, he transferred his own boat from the lagoon to a dock in Peenemünde harbor.[4]

The fact that the von Quistorp estates were close by was yet another reason to fall in love with the place. If he wished, he could sail to the mainland dock of "Uncle Allack"—Alexander von Quistorp, his mother's youngest brother, a Berlin bank president who retained the grand, two-story estate house at Bauer, near the lagoon. Wernher was particularly close to Alexander's family, which he knew well from the capital. They resided at Bauer for Easter, other school holidays, and a month in the summer; Werner Jagenow, the son of the gardener, still remembers von Braun's visits there. At least once he landed a Fieseler Storch, a high-wing light plane noted for its short-field capability, in the fields nearby and got stuck in the mud. Von Braun, an avid hunter of ducks and deer on the estates of the region, took the boy out target shooting—he was never one to be a snob with the servants. A kilometer up the road was Bauer-Wehrland, the farm of Hans-Ulrich von Quistorp, a cousin who had purchased the Bauer lands from Alexander, and ten kilometers inland across the flat, open countryside was Emmy von Braun's birthplace of Crenzow, where he had lived with her and Sigis from 1917 to 1919 and where Magnus Jr. had spent his first few months of life. That estate, with its large country house, was still in the possession of Uncle Hans von Quistorp.[5]

Von Braun must have enjoyed living in Zinnowitz—instead of moving to base housing as soon as possible, he stayed two and a half years in his apartment on the hill across the street from the church. Its one minor disadvantage was distance to work. He could either drive the ten kilometers on old two-lane roads or take the "works train" that left from the town's station and traveled along a newly built spur that stopped at the villages of Trassenheide and Karlshagen before going into the closed military area. If he drove, he would first encounter security at the gate just beyond Karlshagen. To the right was the new settlement of very pleasant, steeply roofed, solidly built row houses and apartments being constructed for the staff of both centers as a "model National Socialist community." Its entrance, quickly nicknamed "the Brandenburg gate," was a grandiose piece of Nazi neoclassical architecture, complete with carved stone swastika. The senior engineers and officers, although never von Braun, moved there as the settlement opened up. Passing the last houses, he would drive along a peaceful two-kilometer stretch of road through the mostly coniferous forest, occasionally in sight of the beach dunes; this area would become the site for a new rocket production plant after 1939.[6]

Entering the army development complex, von Braun would pull up next to the main building, Haus 4 (Building 4), a gabled, two-story structure where he had his office. Close by were the newly constructed workshops where whole rockets could be built in-house, as well a liquid-oxygen plant, Rudolf Hermann's Aerodynamics Institute, laboratory buildings, a commandant's office, and some of the usual features of a military base: a canteen, an officers' club, a firehouse, and so on. Reflecting the extravagance of the ongoing rearmament, everything was being built to the highest standards and for the long term. To the north, for two kilometers along the beach, a string of test stands was still under construction. Farthest from the center in the early years was Test Stand I, a towering, massive structure for testing 25-ton engines and whole A-4 rockets. Like the Aerodynamics Institute, it would not be ready for operation until 1939. As Dornberger and von Braun were building for the future, they sized Test Stand I to restrain at least quadruple that thrust—100 metric tons (220,000 lb), the projected impulse of the never-to-be-built successor to the A-4. In the meantime Walter Thiel and his propulsion group remained at Kummersdorf until 1939–40, working on precursors for the 25-ton engine as well as the motors for cooperative aircraft projects with the Luftwaffe.

Security was absolutely central to life at Peenemünde. As had been General Becker's vision from the outset, rocket development was carried out in complete secrecy in order to achieve surprise and maintain a lead over other countries. In modern Pentagon parlance, the rocket project was a "black program," and although a small amount of information did leak to foreign powers through spies in Berlin, for the most part secrecy was very tight in the early years. Locals who did not work on base had little or no idea of what was going on before 1942, when hard-to-conceal A-4 launches began. One of von Braun's secretaries (and girlfriends), Hannelore Bannasch, later said that Peenemünde "was actually a world for itself, a big family. The classification system and the secrecy was very binding. It was a very closed group of good friends."[7]

At the center of that world stood Wernher von Braun. While Peenemünde-

East was not built specifically for him—it was the army's commitment to the ballistic missile as a revolutionary new weapon that was fundamental—the place scarcely could have existed without him. His talent, drive, and managerial ability had brought liquid-fuel rocketry to a much higher level in only a few years, making Becker and his subordinates believe in the technology. He was likely the first to suggest a new center in cooperation with the Luftwaffe, and he was the one who found its location. Inside the army center, he was never the head—there was a commandant and a military administration to report to—but as technical director he was always the heart and soul of the place, the essential figure in the construction of a technological system for the research and development of the world's first ballistic missile. Peter Wegener, a young aerodynamicist sent there in 1943, describes his role:

> I can attest to von Braun's leadership at Peenemünde. It was von Braun who assembled the core team for missile design and construction. He had a vision of the special talents needed for such a new enterprise. He himself was a good general physicist, and he had exceptional engineering talent, a rare combination. . . .
>
> At a meeting of people from several technical areas it quickly became apparent that von Braun knew more than anyone else about the many ingredients of missile design. Every specialist sitting at the table was better versed in his own field, but von Braun had a remarkable grasp of all fields. He could separate important from peripheral items, distinguish what had to come first, make clear decisions, and inspire people to work. He was close to being obsessed with rocket development.[8]

One might only add that "close to" is an understatement. Within him still burned the ambition to fly into space, even to land on the Moon, and rocketry was his way to get there.

If a very high level of technical competence was the foundation of his leadership, his charismatic personality was also central. He had a quick wit and could be very funny; he was very polished, well dressed, tactful, and polite as a result of his elite upbringing; but he also enjoyed profane jokes and getting his hands dirty in a laboratory or on a test stand. He was, in short, "one of the boys," never standing aloof from the blue-collar workers who built the missiles in the large in-house facilities or from the ordinary technicians who tested them in the field. He was an extraordinarily talented listener; throughout his life people testified to his ability to focus his attention completely on the person he was talking to, making them feel like the most important person in the world to him at that moment. He could be "quite mean" and tough, computer expert Helmut Hoelzer has said, if anyone was unprepared, tried to shirk responsibility, or give him a "snow job," but unlike Dornberger or Zanssen he rarely exploded at people. In a famous incident at Peenemünde, rather than humiliating or punishing an engineer who admitted a mistake that caused a rocket to go disastrously astray, von Braun gave him a bottle of champagne, the better to prevent future costly errors and cover-ups. He inspired people by making them feel like pioneers in new territory. According to Georg von Tiesenhausen: "He was capable of creating enthusiasm for things, by his own enthusiasm. People had unlimited confidence in him, that we could accomplish the things we set out to do."[9]

He was Peenemünde-East's star and, for the female population, also its sex symbol. Even before Ernst Kütbach got a job in the measurement section in 1939 at the instigation of his father, his sisters waxed "very enthusiastic about . . . [von Braun's] physique and . . . his charisma." After the start of the war, the relative dearth of females at the center was somewhat alleviated through hiring and the civilian draft, as many young women came as secretaries and as technicians and "computers" in the laboratories—always in subordinate roles. Von Braun, by then living on base, apparently had a string of relationships with his secretaries and others; rumor had it that "the Doctor," as he was widely known, was never alone on his sailboat.[10]

He had a couple of noteworthy flaws as a manager. He was sometimes carried away by enthusiasm, leading him to be flighty and inconsistent. His close associate since 1935, Arthur Rudolph, later said: "[V]on Braun was overflowing with ideas. He had so many ideas, he hardly finished one, he came out with another one and on top of that another one and another one. So Dornberger would say: 'You have too many ideas. I don't need that many. I want this one and that one and that one, so stick to it, fellow.' And he was hard to control, Wernher von Braun." Rudolph, the chief of the fabrication and assembly shops for the first two years, himself became annoyed because von Braun would go directly to his subordinates with new ideas, telling them to make this or that or the other component without ever bothering to tell him. Von Braun also had trouble at first keeping up with paperwork. In July 1938 Dornberger organized a weekend get-together at Peenemünde for his Army Ordnance rocketry section (acronym Wa Prüf 11), including those in his Berlin office and in Kummersdorf. The commemorative booklet issued for the weekend had a gently satirical poem, "Peenemünder A B C," that included the couplets: "*Der Braun führt das Entwicklungsheer, Paperkrieg fällt ihm oftmals schwer* [Braun leads the development army, red tape often drives him crazy]," and "*Das ganze Werk im Stillen lacht, Wenn Wernher die Termine macht* [The whole Works silently laughs, when Wernher his deadlines makes]." His first secretary, Mrs. Lewandowski, "an elderly lady with the manners of a demanding school teacher . . . taught him a lot about orderly office and filing procedures," which was crucial given that virtually everything that crossed his desk was secret or top secret and subject to "very careful logging, mailing and safekeeping regulations." In 1940 von Braun also acquired a very able deputy for administration and the shops, Eberhard Rees, an unassuming but tough-minded mechanical engineer from southwest Germany with experience in heavy industry; Rees would serve under him for thirty years.[11]

The first year at Peenemünde, 1937–38, was marred however by a major conflict with the commandant, General Schneider, first name unknown (not Erich Schneider from the early days of the program). At least thirty years older than von Braun, Schneider was very much set in army bureaucratic ways. He rapidly came into conflict with von Braun, Dornberger, and Rudolph by wishing to meddle in the technical correspondence between Berlin and Peenemünde, and by attacking Rudolph's innovative management methods for purchasing and stockpiling materials. Schneider was ill suited to a project on the cutting edge of technology. Requirements were often poorly known, and speed, rather than economy, was of the essence. By October 1937 von Braun and Dornberger were already knocking heads with Schneider, and the Air Ministry had given notice that it was pulling Peenemünde-West out of the joint center in the spring because of the commandant's interference. The fights went on. On 21 March 1938 von Braun wrote a letter to his parents, the only one known to survive from before 1945:

> I was in Berlin today and had a meeting alone with General Becker. He was very clear and warm, and told me first that I was one of his most valuable and pleasant colleagues and that he especially appreciated my temperament. Regarding the extraordinary sensitivity of S., it would have been better if, on the day in question, I had not allowed myself to become involved in an angry discussion, but rather immediately reported the contested points to Berlin.

Clearly there had been quite a row; von Braun even felt his job was at stake. For Becker, who was about to become chief of Army Ordnance, it was the last straw. Schneider would be sent away and an officer reporting directly to Dornberger would be put in his place. Shortly thereafter Major Leo Zanssen was recalled from his assignment to a solid-fuel rocket battery and appointed commandant. This arrangement had been made possible by the Luftwaffe's pullout, as a general was no longer needed in the post. As a veteran of the early program and Dornberger's close friend, Zanssen was an excellent choice and got on well with von Braun.[12]

The Schneider incident notwithstanding, the young engineer always felt comfortable in a military environment rooted in Prussian tradition, and in the early years of the regime the army also provided a zone of relative autonomy inside the Nazi system. But in justifying his own political behavior after the war, he often exaggerated and romanticized that fact. In 1959 he told his movie producer: "The German Army . . . took great pains to keep the Nazi party and all its tentacles out of its own operations. . . . I worked from 1932 until the middle of the war in an environment that was rather hermetically sealed against any Nazi party infiltration."[13] Yet he could not deny that the local party had enough power over the army in Peenemünde to push him into joining, an event that took place only months after the center opened.

Von Braun officially applied for membership on 12 November 1937 and was given sequential party number 5,738,692. Ten years later he stated in his affidavit for the U.S. Army:

> In 1939, I was officially demanded to join the National Socialist Party. At this time I was already Technical Director of the Army Rocket Center at Peenemuende (Baltic Sea). The technical work carried out there had, in the meantime, attracted more and more attention in higher levels. Thus, my refusal to join the party would have meant that I would have had to abandon the work of my life. Therefor[e], I decided to join. My membership in the party did not involve any political activity.

Why did he give the wrong date? He either lied or subconsciously pushed his entry back in his own mind as part of a self-justification process. What little evidence we have, however, supports his claim that he was pressured to join. In 1937 there was a party campaign to recruit nonmembers in positions of authority and social influence. Membership had been closed in the spring of 1933 after millions of converts and opportunists had flocked to the party during the seizure of power, and it reopened only in 1937 as a part of the process of consolidating the regime and extending its ideological influence. At least one other leading Peenemünde engineer signed up at the time, design bureau chief Walter "Papa" Riedel. Von Braun, like other Peenemünders, was assigned to the local group in Karlshagen; there is no evidence that he did more than send in his monthly dues. But he is seen in some photographs with the party's swastika pin in his lapel—it was politically useful to demonstrate his membership.[14]

As for his attitude toward the National Socialist regime in the late 1930s and early 1940s, there can be little doubt that he was a loyal, perhaps even mildly enthusiastic subject of Hitler's dictatorship. With the Führer going from success to success—eliminating unemployment, tearing up the Versailles Treaty, rearming, reoccupying the Rhineland, and then in 1938 absorbing Austria and the Czech Sudetenland without war—there is no doubt that the regime, but above all Hitler, had become immensely popular. Von Braun, a German nationalist immersed in a military environment, doubtlessly found much he could like about these accomplishments, and little reason to be disturbed, especially in view of how much money had been poured into his beloved rocketry as a result of rearmament. He admitted in a 1952 memoir article that he "fared relatively rather well under totalitarianism," at least until his Gestapo arrest late in the war. Indeed, when he met Hitler again in 1939 and 1941, it should be recalled, he was "moved" by the dictator's "astounding intellectual capabilities, the actually hypnotic influence of his personality on his surroundings."[15]

It is not that von Braun was completely insulated from anti-Nazi views. His father, who was skeptical of the Nazis but was unable to envision a viable alternative, "warned me that it was all going to end in tragedy for Germany and many other people too. But I was too wrapped up in rockets to heed his warning." (If his father indeed made this statement, it must have been after the violent SA purge of 1934, perhaps much after.) Wernher heard dissent from Sigismund too, notably in the summer of 1937, when he visited the Paris World's Fair with Dornberger, a trip that would have been possible only if the two had been cleared as politically trustworthy. A pleasant evening with younger diplomats at the German embassy, where his older brother had been assigned in May, was disrupted when Sigis and his colleagues "declared in open indignation that Hitler's unlimited and unscrupulous foreign policy was on the point of causing a new world conflagration." Dornberger and von Braun were "unbelieving and dismayed." This 1953 story by Wernher von Braun clearly implies that he and Dornberger, like a substantial majority of Germans, then had every faith in the Führer's genius and his declarations of peaceful intentions.[16]

How did von Braun feel about the persecution of the Jews, a very explicit part of Hitler's program? There is absolutely no evidence of anti-Semitic statements or attitudes on von Braun's part, but at the same time there is no evidence that he much cared either. He was fortunate that, Cold War politics being what they were, he was rarely even asked the question until late in life. In 1971 he told a critical letter writer in New York City:

In the early years of Hitler's regime . . . this persecution took many forms but the most obvious was the vilification of the Jewish people in the Nazi press. Most thinking Germans saw this for what it was, creating a necessary scapegoat for the desperate unemployment rate to rally the masses behind the Hitler government. . . . Until the outbreak of the war, Jews were welcomed as officers and enlisted men in the German Army, and social contacts were widely maintained with Jewish friends.

These statements are naive and wrong and show how little von Braun knew or remembered about the Nazi persecution of the Jews twenty-six years after World War II. Like many Germans, both before and after the war, von Braun grossly underestimated the fundamental character of Hitler's anti-Semitic hatred, preferring instead to explain it away as mere scapegoating. The letter continues:

I confess to no deep psychological thinking on this matter during these times. I thought that when the political objective of the anti-Jewish campaign had been reached a new scapegoat would be found. Stalin's series of persecutions . . . seemed to set a most likely pattern. During these years I was, of course, a young engineer with very little interest in politics. . . . I felt very fortunate when I gained support for my work in the form of some money and facilities from the German Army. . . .

I knew that many prominent Jewish, Catholic and Protestant leaders had been jailed for their opposition to the government. I also suspected from the fact that I had lost sight of my own Jewish friends, that many Jews had either fled the country or were being held in concentration camps. But being jailed and being butchered are two different things.[17]

Although the substance of this letter is plausible as an explanation of his attitudes, it also reveals his selective memory, rooted in subconscious processes of self-justification and denial. In his civil service career von Braun had to deal with the requirements for "Aryan" certification, which excluded "full Jews" from civilian and military positions in the army; even Christian half-Jews had increasing difficulties by 1938. Moreover, he certainly was aware of the infamous pogrom of 9–10 November 1938, which has gone down in history as *Reichskristallnacht*—the "Night of Broken Glass"—even though he was in Peenemünde at the time, away from the cities where it happened. He was often in Berlin, the destruction of shops and burning of synagogues was well publicized by Josef Goebbels's Propaganda Ministry, and the excuse for the pogrom was a Polish Jewish boy's assassination of Sigismund's successor at the Paris embassy a couple of months after his brother's recall. (Sigis had been sent to the tropical backwater of Addis Ababa in Italian-occupied Ethiopia as punishment for political unreliability.)[18] As for Wernher's own "Jewish friends," there is no evidence that he had any after he left the French Gymnasium in 1925, so old school chums may indeed be the ones he was thinking about. All in all, his own testimony demonstrates his lack of interest in the persecution of Jews and political opponents. Like much of the population, and even many nominal party members, he had little commitment to Nazi racial theory, but he was willing to ignore or make excuses for what was unpleasant or frightening about the system, because he personally benefited from it and admired its "successes." The historian Ian Kershaw has said: "The road to Auschwitz was built by hate, but was paved with indifference."[19]

As for Peenemünde, however much the armed forces provided a zone of relative autonomy from party interference, signs of Nazi influence or enthusiasm were scarcely absent. Photographs show the settlement's Hitler Youth group marching with drums, uniforms, and banners. Some of von Braun's key assistants and close friends were early, or at least enthusiastic, National Socialists, notably Arthur Rudolph, but also Rudolf Hermann, leader of the local party cell from 1941 to 1943. (On the other hand, according to von Braun, Klaus Riedel "took considerable personal risks and spent substantial amounts of money in helping some Jewish friends to leave the country.") In one of von Braun's more candid moments, he told the producer working on the movie about his life: "I never had any noteworthy trouble with the Nazis among my co-workers. Quite a few of them, of course, were card-bearing party members, but on the politically 'decontaminated' Army base hotheads and bullies did not have a chance, and so they stayed in line." And yet Wilhelm Raithel, a structural engineer drafted into Peenemünde-East in 1940, became structures chief in 1942 because his predecessor was denounced by three colleagues for making a critical remark about the war. The man spent a year in jail and was lucky to stay out of a concentration camp. Raithel had earlier made such a remark himself and was pulled aside by a Peenemünde colleague who flashed the Golden Party Badge, presented for meritorious service, and told him to be careful, because he would not get away with saying things that party members could say. Under the leadership of von Braun and Dornberger, Peenemünde-East may well have been a magical place to many engineers, where they worked on groundbreaking technology in a pampered environment, but it was also a community well integrated into Hitler's Reich.[20]

During the last two years before the war, von Braun may still have had significant free time, but his life was always dominated by work—work he immensely enjoyed. His primary job was to lead the development of the

A-series of rockets and their integral systems, a task that would turn out to be even more difficult and complicated than expected. But the cooperative aircraft rocket projects with the air force remained an important, and often welcome, diversion.

Just before von Braun moved to Usedom in May 1937, the Luftwaffe began a supersecret series of test flights at Neuhardenberg, an obscure air-field east of Berlin. (Peenemünde-West was still a year away from opening.) He and his new friend Erich Warsitz eagerly awaited Warsitz's flights in the Heinkel He 112 single-engine fighter with the 1000-kg-thrust "Braun motor" in its tail, as the Air Ministry dubbed it. But this was not the only objective of the series. In 1936 the ministry had begun to work more closely with the hydrogen-peroxide innovator Hellmuth Walter, whose rocket engines were based on the catalytic decomposition of highly concentrated H_2O_2 into superheated steam and oxygen. In more advanced versions the resulting free oxygen could be burned with a fuel. Although concentrated hydrogen peroxide was potentially explosive and less energetic than Ord-nance's alcohol/liquid-oxygen combination, supercold liquid oxygen would often freeze valves and would always boil off, making long-term storage and military field use problematic. At Neuhardenberg "Walter motors" were to be tested in a small plane and in the first experiments with dual, jettisonable rocket-assisted takeoff pods mounted on a bomber. Later would come flights with a second He 112 outfitted with a larger Walter motor.[21]

After many delays, late on the afternoon of 3 June 1937 Erich Warsitz took off from Neuhardenberg in the He 112 V4 (fourth prototype). As he passed over the field, von Braun and his compatriots saw a small glimmer, then a puff of black smoke, and then the rocket exhaust shot out impres-sively, extending a distance of half the length of the fuselage. After ten or twelve seconds it shut down. Suddenly the plane entered a steep dive—the tail was on fire. Warsitz dove for the ground, landing the airplane on its belly. He quickly exited the cockpit, the fire was put out, and the aircraft was salvaged. It may have flown again later in the year, but the two services soon decided to completely redesign the propulsion system. The airplane would become the test bed for the motor to be installed in a new pure rocket air-craft called the He 176.[22]

As unpromising a beginning as the first flight was, it marked the apogee of the army-Luftwaffe rocket alliance. Early in 1937 its architect, Wolfram von Richthofen, had left to fly for the Luftwaffe in the Spanish Civil War after being subordinated in the Air Ministry to one of Göring's friends, World War I ace Ernst Udet. Later that year flight tests with the Walter-equipped He 112 went more smoothly than those with the "Braun" engine, confirming the ministry's inclination toward hydrogen-peroxide technology. The separation of Peenemünde-East and -West in April 1938 also simplified matters bureaucratically, but further increased the distance between the two services and two centers. In the summer of 1938, when Peenemünde-West chief Uvo Pauls wrote in a memo that "this time, exceptionally," the rebuilt He 112 V4 would be fired in the test stand on the army side because the facilities at West were not yet ready, von Braun wrote an exasperated marginal comment: "This is what we demanded as a conditio sine qua non also for the future. Without the 'ironing out' of the center, using the same people and the same facilities, I refuse to accept responsibility for flight testing." It was an empty threat.[23]

Even more indicative of the Air Ministry's desire to go its own way was the underhanded manner it went about building up an institute around Dr. Eugen Sänger, an Austrian rocket pioneer and visionary of hypersonic space planes. Against the recommendation of von Braun, who saw the slightly older man's work as duplicative of what he was doing, the ministry brought the Austrian to Germany in 1936 and gave him an institute near its new aeronautical research center outside Braunschweig. The ministry even secretly built for Sänger a liquid-oxygen plant and a test stand for a 100-metric-ton-thrust engine, something von Braun and Dornberger did not learn about until 1941–42, by which time the facility had been abandoned for lack of further investment. Long before that happened, von Braun again reacted jealously to Sänger in early 1937, when the air force wanted permission to publish some of the Austrian's work. Von Braun felt it overlapped his own. These flashes of ego are illuminating: apparently he saw Sänger as a threat to his role as *the* pioneer of large-scale rocket technology. In the background probably lurked von Braun's desire to be first into space. At Peenemünde he and Warsitz "often dreamed together of the first manned spaceflight."[24]

Von Braun did not feel the same about Hellmuth Walter. Hydrogen peroxide was inherently limited by its low energy, which made it unsuitable for large rockets. Moreover the two engineers had known each other almost from the time Walter had sent his first rocket-ramjet proposal to Karl Becker in the fall of 1934. Early in the development of the exotic turbopumps that would be needed to feed propellants to the big A-4 motor, von Braun and his subordinates had decided to use a Walter hydrogen-peroxide motor as a "steam generator" to produce the hot gas stream needed to power the turbopumps, as this was simpler than the alternatives. This decision had been reached in the spring of 1936 and made Walter a key supplier and needed ally.[25]

The cooperative program with the Luftwaffe and the Neuhardenberg test series were not all that kept von Braun moving in the summer and fall of 1937: the A-3 was finally coming to fruition. To save travel time, in July the army gave him his first aircraft, a Junkers Junior open-cockpit biplane—the same type used in the rocket aircraft ground tests at Kummersdorf in 1936. His flight log shows numerous trips to airfields in and around Berlin. He did have to fly out of Greifswald, the nearest small city to Peenemünde, an hour away by car, but he could still go back and forth to meetings at Dornberger's office, the Air Ministry, or Kreiselgeräte, the A-3 guidance and control contractor, on the same day. When he landed south of the city his target was Kummersdorf, where Thiel's propulsion group and the test stands were located. That summer the first A-3 vehicles were ready for testing on a special rig there. Actuators simulated disturbing forces on the rockets, so as to test the guidance platforms. Commands sent by the platform would turn the flat jet vanes sticking into the rocket exhaust, which was deflected so as to correct the rocket's course. Everything appeared to work well.[26]

On 1 September Dornberger ordered "Operation Lighthouse" to begin. Its purpose: to launch the A-3s from the Greifswalder Oie, a small Baltic island with a lighthouse lying several kilometers northeast of Peenemünde, "potentially in the first half of November." Von Braun assigned the new head of his measurement unit, Gerhard Reisig, to prepare the complicated launch expedition, which would be much bigger than the one to Borkum three years previously. From the time the Peenemünde site was chosen, Dornberger saw the Oie as ideal for launching in secrecy, as it was even more isolated than the center. But that very isolation, and the primitive character of the Oie, made the transportation and logistical arrangements difficult. Ordnance rented an ancient ferry to carry people and equipment; it could dock only at the tiny fishing port on the south end of the island, where the Halliger family, which farmed some of the land, had a small inn. There was also a barracks for the workers who came to maintain the lighthouse on the north end, overlooking the towering cliffs that faced out to sea on all sides. Leading up from the little harbor to the interior, there was only a dirt road plus small-gauge railway tracks left by the lighthouse authority—they turned out to be a lifesaver when the trucks bogged down in the mud resulting from the constant rain that fall.[27]

As had been true throughout A-3 development, there were more delays due to the complexity of the technology. The rocket was very large and ambitious by the standards of the day: 6.75 m (22 ft) long, and 0.93 m (3 ft) across the antenna ring that surrounded the long, narrow fins. The propulsion system was the 1500-kg (3,300-lb) thrust engine developed at Kummersdorf by von Braun and "Papa" Riedel, still with the very long combustion chamber immersed inside the alcohol tank. The guidance and control system was the one designed by the late Kreiselgeräte director Johannes Boykow, a stabilized platform plus three rate gyros to keep the rocket on a vertical course; it even had early accelerometers to correct for wind forces that might push the A-3s to the side. In the nose of each rocket was one of two scientific payloads: either a suite of temperature and pressure instruments to measure the upper atmosphere during the parachute descent or instruments to measure frictional heating on the vehicle. A small camera would record the measurements by filming an oscilloscope. In an elaborate description of the vehicles dated 29 November 1937—just days before the first launch—von Braun laid out his calculation and fond hope that they would reach a burn-out speed of 500 m/sec (over 1,100 mph, about Mach 1.5) and coast up to an altitude of 20 km (12.5 mi), far exceeding the accomplishments of the A-2s.[28]

Beginning in November, he and Dornberger spent a lot of time on the little island supervising the preparations, which were beset by all kinds of difficulties. It rained, it snowed, and storms kept the ferry from reaching the island. The big tent erected for rocket preparation near the launch site nearly collapsed one night from the weight of snow. "[A]n extraordinary plague of mice and rats" came out to gnaw on the tar papers of the barracks and on the telephone cables laid out between the firing bunkers, the launch site, and the observing and measurement sites. Von Braun and Dornberger "beguiled this nerve-wracking period of waiting with shooting expeditions" that bagged large numbers of the pheasants and rabbits that had free rein on the Oie.[29]

On 1 December Dornberger finally issued his "order of the day": "The launch attempt of Aggregat III/1 'Deutschland' will occur—in so far as weather allows—on 2 December ca. 9:30 AM." Again it was not to be. The actual launch took place two days later, after a series of weather delays and technical problems. At 10:03 a.m. on 4 December, A-3 number 1 "took off like an elevator." In a test of the planned launch method of the later ballistic missile, there was no guide rail; the rocket sat on its tail ring over a blast deflector. For three seconds it rose straight and true, but then the parachute deployed and was dragged behind the accelerating vehicle, burning in the exhaust and throwing the A-3 off course. At 6.5 seconds the engine cut off automatically. After coasting upward for a few seconds, the rocket tumbled back to Earth, crashing 300 m (1,000 ft) from the launch site on the edge of the island. Upon impact, the unburned propellants ignited in "a fairly heavy explosion." There was little left except scrap metal.[30]

Everybody was shocked and also sobered by the safety implications. According to Dornberger, "eye-witness accounts from the staff were wildly contradictory. . . . We decided to venture on a second launching." Number 2 took off on 6 December at 1:37 p.m. and did exactly the same thing: it crashed and exploded in the sea 5 m (16.5 ft) off the steep cliffs. The demolished fragments again gave no clue, but the obvious explanation was a fault in the parachute mechanism. A flare was substituted for the parachute. The weather turned bad, but on 8 December the launch crew managed to get the third A-3 off at 12:15 p.m. Instead of staying on a vertical course, it began to turn into the stiff, cold wind. After four seconds the flare shot out, and at 300 m (1,000 ft) altitude the engine cut off again. Lacking the drag of a burning parachute, the rocket crashed 2 km (1.25 mi) offshore, exploding under water. With little information as to the cause, Dornberger and von Braun decided to launch the fourth and last A-3. There were more weather delays. At last, on the eleventh at 9:57 a.m. number 4 rose and virtually repeated the performance of the third.[31]

Although shocked by the complete and unexpected failure of his dreamed-for launches into the stratosphere, von Braun channeled his energies into a burst of meetings, experimentation, and analysis. His usual Christmas trip home to Oberwiesenthal must have been brief. The last two launches made it clear that the Kreiselgeräte control system simply was too weak to over-power the wind forces acting on the rockets. The jet vanes in the exhaust could not exert enough force to turn the A-3s back to a vertical course because the vehicles were too aerodynamically stable and the vane servo mechanisms too weak. But what caused the parachute circuit to fire after only a few seconds? The initial investigations focused on an electrostatic buildup on the vehicles, somehow caused by the ionized hot gas stream of the rocket exhaust. At Kummersdorf, Thiel's team ran firing tests on an electrically insulated rocket. Von Braun's later A-3 report notes: "These experiments led astoundingly to a totally negative result. In not a single case could the slightest evidence of an electrostatic charging process be observed."[32]

It was only in the first two weeks of January 1938 that he finally came to the conclusion, over the resistance of the Kreiselgeräte engineers, that the stabilized platform was itself at fault. On the A-3 the parachute command was hooked to the platform on the assumption that when the rocket reached its culmination point, it would turn over, upsetting the platform, thereby ejecting the parachute as the A-3 began to fall back to Earth. But the platform was stable only if the vehicle rolled less than 6 degrees per second; otherwise the forces acting on the platform gyros would force them to move to the point where one or the other would slam into the stops at the end of their ranges, causing the platform to lurch and flip over. Gerhard Reisig, the head of the measurement group at the time, remembers how von Braun demonstrated this: "He just told me, since we had one spare platform, . . . Put it up, and put it on something I can turn." So Reisig took the only thing he had, a wooden box, and rigged it up electrically, and called von Braun to come back to the laboratory. "He came over and he just . . . turned it quickly, jumped, the thing tipped over. That was the explanation. But that's typical von Braun. He had some imagination."[33]

For several weeks neither the Peenemünde nor the Kreiselgeräte engineers had believed that the A-3s could roll that fast. Due to lack of experience, the rockets had not been painted in clear patterns that would show movement, as was later the case with the A-4s. Only a careful analysis of the photographs of the flare on the last two shots later documented how far they had turned in a few seconds. Small asymmetries in the fins and body were enough to start them rolling faster than the control system could compensate for—so fast that the platform gyros almost immediately hit their stops. Ultimately the A-3 failures were due to the lack of experience, on the part of both the company and von Braun's group, in the exotic new field of rocket guidance. Kreiselgeräte's background in heavy naval systems was not strictly applicable, and von Braun had started as a novice in 1934–35 and "took everything [Boykow] had said for granted." Leaving propulsion and aerodynamics in the very competent hands of Thiel and Hermann, respectively, von Braun would now begin to educate himself much more thoroughly in the principles of guidance and control.[34]

He and Dornberger made some quick decisions. By 15 January 1938 they decided to redesign the A-3 thoroughly and give it a new, untainted designation, the A-5, as A-4 was already assigned. The A-5 would keep the A-3's propulsion, pressurization, and tank system, which had worked well, but the body and fin design would be discarded and replaced with something that would allow a better control response. Rudolf Hermann's deputy for research, Dr. Hermann Kurzweg, found a broader and shorter shape in early 1938—the shape later familiar from the A-4 missile. The scientific instrumentation would also be discarded—the A-5 would have one purpose only: to test different guidance and control systems. This would have to be done repeatedly, as the A-3s demonstrated that they had become complacent about the need for constant launch testing after the A-2 successes.[35]

Initially, at least, there would be two guidance contractors for the A-5, Kreiselgeräte and the giant electrical firm of Siemens. Just before the Oie expedition, on 9 November, von Braun, Dornberger, Klaus Riedel, and others had visited the Siemens aircraft instruments group in Berlin. This unit was headed by Karl Otto Altvater, a family friend of Riedel, who had given him and three others from the Raketenflugplatz jobs after it was closed. Von Braun lectured on the state of the rocket project and the Kreiselgeräte system, making clear that they were already looking beyond the A-3 guidance system, in which they had confidence, at the radical new requirements for a ballistic missile with a range of 200 to 400 km (125 to 250 mi) and good accuracy that could reach 2000 m/sec (4,400 mph) in only 60 seconds burn time. Thus they were interested in stimulating competitive developments, possibly including radio guide beams. After the very disappointing Oie results, the two sides met again on 24 January in Peenemünde. With hindsight, the Siemens engineers were now able to make a thorough critique of Kreiselgeräte's design, and von Braun and Dornberger encouraged them to design a new system based on different principles. Meanwhile the original contractor had agreed to proceed with a thorough redesign and simplification of its stabilized platform, putting emphasis on control of the roll axis. But both contractors would have to incorporate a means to pitch the rocket over from the vertical to the 45-degree angle needed for an eventual ballistic missile trajectory, an objective that was originally to have been accomplished in further flight tests with a modified A-3 system.[36]

The decision to remain with a contractor-centered approach in the guidance and control field reflected the lack of expertise at Peenemünde in this highly specialized branch of technology, but it really was the exception in Walter Dornberger's vision of the rocket program. Already during the design of the new army rocket center, Dornberger, backed by Becker, had decided to create large shops for building engines and rocket structures, thus greatly reducing outside contracting. (The A-3 engines and tanks had been built by a small Stuttgart company.) The emphasis on supersecrecy and the conviction that it could be done just as well or cheaper in-house, with "everything under one roof," led Dornberger and Becker to a very state-centered approach.

How much this was the case was confirmed by an incident during the Oie expedition. Sometime during the middle of the firings, trapped at the inn by thick fog, Rudolph, von Braun, Dornberger, and Hermann were sitting around discussing how the A-4 could be produced. According to Rudolph, Dornberger said,

> out of the blue sky, "I want to build a . . . production plant for the V-2 [its later name] and the coming big rocket [its successor, with 100 tons of thrust], and you will do that." I say, "Dornberger, for heaven's sake, I'm a development man, not a production man, and you leave this up to industry, don't bother us fellows in development with your new ideas."

And von Braun was of course saying the same thing, even harsher than I did. . . . There was an argument, there was a strong argument. I was so opposed to it.

Neither von Braun nor Rudolph felt that they had any expertise in large-scale production—and they were right; in later years this deficiency would be a major problem for the A-4 program. But this argument would not deflect Dornberger; the Peenemünde production plant began building in 1939. In the meantime the A-3's failure postponed all A-4 plans for at least a year. Before the Oie, Wernher von Braun hoped to launch the world's first ballistic missile by 1940. Afterward the picture was much murkier.[37]

Dornberger and von Braun would soon find themselves replicating the "everything under one roof" philosophy in the guidance field as well, as corporate contracting alone turned out to be inadequate. In January 1938 Altvater's group had warned the Peenemünders that it was unrealistic to expect Siemens to develop and construct three new guidance systems for the A-5 by October; the best they could promise was maybe March 1939. They were actually delivered a year beyond that. Over the course of 1938 Kreiselgeräte also fell further and further behind. An October letter from the company promised the first new stabilized platform system by 1 July 1939, to which an annoyed von Braun wrote in the margin: "First promised: February, then: 1 April, now: July!" In addition to development difficulties, both contractors were heavily burdened with work from their primary services—the Luftwaffe for Siemens, and the navy for Kreiselgeräte—in the context of a mad scramble for rearmament as Hitler brought the country close to war.[38]

Late in 1938 von Braun began to look into further alternatives. He took an interest in a new aircraft autopilot system developed by an engineer at the main Luftwaffe test center at Rechlin, who was to be transferred to the well-established gyro firm of Askania to produce it. When von Braun inquired with that company, it advocated a variant of its simpler torpedo control system using compressed air to transmit commands to the control surfaces. Ultimately that proved to be a waste of time, but in the process of investigating first two, then three, and finally four competing systems, Wernher von Braun had to become his own chief guidance expert and hire new, in-house expertise.[39]

The evolution of the Siemens system also drew von Braun into developing his own guidance and control division. Soon after the January 1938 meeting one of Altvater's key men, Dr. Karl Fieber, proposed a highly original and simplified scheme for missile guidance using only two position gyros bolted to the rocket in place of a stabilized platform that would keep the gyros fixed in space. Although inherently less accurate than a platform, this so-called Vertikant guidance promised to be much lighter, simpler, and cheaper to produce. But given the heavy demands on the Siemens aircraft instruments works, it could take a long time to develop the specialized gyros needed. Siemens also had hydraulic servomotors from aircraft autopilot applications that were a promising alternative to Kreiselgeräte's mechanical systems of rods and gears for transmitting the commands from the control system to the jet vanes. But they too required development for much more demanding rocket applications, drawing on Siemens's resources needed for the regular Luftwaffe autopilot systems. Yet von Braun needed a workable system from Siemens for the A-5 soon. How he solved this problem is illustrative of his willingness to take chances to get things done.

According to Fieber, on the day top Siemens management was to make the decision as to how many Vertikant systems to promise to Peenemünde, probably in the spring of 1938, von Braun came to his laboratory to ask if he might request twenty or twenty-five. Fieber thought that he would be lucky get two or three. In desperation, he told von Braun of a vague, "almost absurd thought" he had had the night before, to use three normal course gyros from aircraft production for the A-5, even though they were neither exact enough nor designed to withstand rocket accelerations. "To my great surprise, he declared then in the conference . . . that the whole problem had been solved through my substitute solution . . . with the course gyros." The company directors approved, but Fieber was floored. He would never have presented such an untested, half-baked idea as a proven fact. "As I objected angrily to Dr. v. Braun afterwards, he slapped me encouragingly on the shoulder and said, smiling: 'But, Dr. Fieber, boldly asserted is half proven!' "—Rudolf Nebel's old saying. "I sweated blood for a couple of weeks, but he had won and was also right in the end, it even worked!"[40]

Elsewhere in his memoir Fieber says this about the young rocketeer's ability:

Von Braun grasped things with lightning speed, had no fear of underdevelopment, problems, expenditure, or risk, and conquered his partner, depending on that person's nature, with hardness or with matchless charm. And when our people accused him of failure to understand the problems and of childish errors—at least in our field, I had to answer: yes, terrible errors, but to my knowledge never one and the same error a second time. These days of extremely fruitful collaboration were among the happiest of my entire career.

Ultimately, however, there would be a cooling in relations with Siemens in 1940–41 as the company insisted that it did not have the capacity to develop the Vertikant system speedily. As Fieber's secret patent was owned by the Reich, von Braun took his concept and the idea of hydraulic servomotors to two gyro firms rich in tradition. But this strategy could work only because meanwhile he had built up his own laboratory at Peenemünde to test and integrate the components.[41]

His decision to build such a laboratory was apparently made in the spring of 1939, as the complexity of all the competing solutions to the guidance problem manifested themselves and as the demands of guided A-5 launches approached. In 1937 von Braun had hired a talented mathematician, Dr. Paul Schröder, to head his small unit responsible for guidance theory, but in one of the few exceptions to the story of von Braun's success with subordinates, he and Schröder did not get along. The mathematician found the engineer arrogant and excessively bold; von Braun found him intolerably pessimistic. In 1939, with Dornberger and Zanssen's permission, von Braun shunted him aside and hired Dr. Hermann Steuding of the Darmstadt Institute of Technology in western Germany to take over the development of the complex calculations of guidance theory. Steuding in turn recommended a Darmstadt colleague, Ernst Steinhoff, as the head of the guidance and control laboratory, to which Dornberger had allocated a million marks. Although Steinhoff was still only working on his dissertation on aircraft instruments, he was of a type reminiscent of Warsitz and of von Braun himself: a dashing pilot bursting with energy. Closely associated with the Air Ministry's glider institute, Steinhoff had been given the ministry's important honorific title of "flight captain" for setting a world's record for distance in a sailplane. An "idealistic" National Socialist, when he came to Peenemünde he was bowled over by the facilities and by the challenge of groundbreaking engineering research on guided missiles. Dornberger happened to be there that day and "was suddenly accosted by a young man apparently in his late twenties, who seized my hands with every appearance of genuine enthusiasm and exclaimed, 'Sir, you must take me! I'm all yours! I want to stay!' " Like Warsitz, Steinhoff became a close friend of von Braun's.[42]

Meanwhile, the frustrating delays to the Kreiselgeräte and Siemens systems led Dornberger and von Braun to launch two unguided A-5s in fall 1938 to test the aerodynamic stability and basic functioning of the rocket. "Operation Lighthouse II" began with the successful launching of the first A-5 on 3 October, just after the Franco-British sellout of Czechoslovakia at Munich ended an extremely tense period; war had appeared imminent. The A-5 success was a great consolation after the A-3 failures, but the lack of a guidance system left the feeling that a lot was left unproven. Afterward the complexity of this launch expedition, which again drew upon borrowed equipment, led von Braun to recommend purchase of the Oie and the ferry and the construction of new buildings that would convert the island into a permanent launch site. These measures would come on top of work already done in the summer of 1938 to build better harbor facilities and concrete launch structures. Dornberger's marginal comment was "Finally!"[43]

The army's rocket chief backed these recommendations, knowing he had strong support from the very top of his service. In early 1938 Hitler had forced out the war minister and the army commander in chief and had taken over supreme command of the armed forces himself. He installed the pliable General Walther von Brauchitsch, an artillerist who happened to be Dornberger's old regimental commander during the Weimar Republic, as head of the army. Shortly thereafter, in March 1938, Karl Becker ascended to the position of chief of Army Ordnance. With these kinds of connections, Dornberger was able to secure complete backing for an accelerated rocket program from the army leadership, allowing a significant expansion of Peenemünde and other related facilities. In late November, Becker got von Brauchitsch to sign an order making that expansion a top priority of the army, even though they had yet to demonstrate a guided A-5 launch. This order allowed Dornberger to begin planning the rocket production plant and von Braun to build up a guidance and control laboratory.[44]

Yet the rocket factory was a project requiring such major allocations of construction manpower and materials that it could not be carried out speedily with the army's backing alone, especially as the quasi-war economy was crashing into its limits. Under Hitler's leadership, rearmament was a poorly coordinated free-for-all among the services, and quite by design, he was the ultimate arbiter. Thus, in hopes of enlisting the Führer's personal enthusiasm, Becker and von Brauchitsch hit upon the idea of inviting him to a rocket demonstration at Kummersdorf, where most of the testing still was taking place. (Hitler never visited the more distant Peenemünde, perhaps for secrecy reasons.) The result was Wernher von Braun's first really close encounter with the dictator, within a day or two of 23 March 1939, the rocket engineer's twenty-seventh birthday.[45]

The Führer arrived at Kummersdorf on a miserable wet, cold, overcast morning; everything was drenched from recent downpours. With him were von Brauchitsch, Becker, and other dignitaries. Dornberger greeted them, gave some introductory remarks about rocketry, and introduced Hitler to his technical experts, von Braun and Thiel. Von Braun noticed that the dictator looked quite energetic and unexpectedly tanned, probably from his mountaintop perch in the Bavarian Alps. Just a week earlier Hitler had entered Prague in a motorcade, after browbeating the Czechoslovak president into allowing a German seizure of the country, in blatant violation of the Munich agreement. On the nineteenth he had had a triumphal homecoming in Berlin staged by Goebbels, complete with spectacular lighting and adoring masses. The dictator was completely preoccupied with foreign policy at this time, a fact that explains much about his behavior at Kummersdorf.[46]

Not long before the visit, Dornberger had ordered von Braun to say nothing about spaceflight. The latter had been known to wax enthusiastic to army dignitaries about the rocket's possibilities beyond the development of the ballistic missile. According to Rudolph, two or three years earlier, after he and Walter Riedel had briefed Becker about the A-3 and A-4, von Braun had given a talk on "going to the moon." Knowing him well, Becker was quite willing to debate him on the details. But Dornberger was afraid that such an outburst with Hitler might well undermine the whole program. Von Braun's role would be limited to briefing the dictator on the technical details of the demonstrations he would see.[47]

First stop on the tour was one of the oldest test stands, where a 300-kg (660-lb) thrust A-2 motor was mounted horizontally. Hitler watched the "pale blue jet of gas, . . . with the supersonic shock waves clearly delineated in colors of varying brightness" (Dornberger) and heard the deafening roar even through thick cotton earplugs. He was impassive. Next was the 1500-kg (3,300-lb) thrust A-3/A-5 engine, suspended vertically, and fired to even greater effect. Again little reaction appeared on his face. They all proceeded to an assembly rig with a cutaway A-3, with the components, tanks, and lines painted in various colors to show the workings. Knowing that Hitler was very interested in the details of weapons technology, von Braun tried to explain as clearly as possible the complicated mechanisms. Silently the Führer walked away, shaking his head.[48]

There was one last display, a suspended A-5 with some of the skin removed. Here Hitler at last showed some life. He asked von Braun about the engine's power and about parachute recovery of the instruments. But he seemed to make another dismissive gesture, as if the A-5 did not impress him at all. As they walked away from the test stand, Hitler suddenly turned to the rocket engineer and said: " 'Even now I still don't know how a liquid-propellant rocket can fly. Why do you need *two* tanks and *two* different propellants.' " Von Braun was astonished. "I believe that I looked at him completely dismayed. I had to accept that my explanation went in one ear and out the other." He was forced to begin all over again and explain the

liquid-fuel rocket in simple terms, hoping he was not sounding too condescending. Hitler did ask about payload; von Braun had to explain that the
A-5 was a test rocket only but that it would soon lead to weapons. It proved
to be an apt transition to the subsequent lecture on the A-4, given by Dornberger to an even more restricted group. Hitler seemed interested but asked
no questions.[49]

At the closing lunch in the mess hall, the Führer sat at the apex of a
U-shaped table and had his usual bland fare of vegetables and mineral water.
He chatted with Becker and seemed a little more interested in the rocket, asking von Braun and Dornberger how long it would take to develop the A-4
(then projected at four years) and if aluminum, in increasingly short supply,
could be replaced with steel. He then issued his one, backhanded compliment
of the whole day, "*Es war doch gewaltig!* (Well, it was grand!)" Mentioning
his acquaintance with Max Valier in Munich in the late 1920s, Hitler dismissed the early space advocate and experimenter as a dreamer. Von Braun,
although entranced by the Führer cult, barely suppressed the urge to say
something. "How much I would have liked to talk about spaceflight"—just
as he would with later American presidents.[50]

Afterward Dornberger found the "whole visit . . . strange, if not down-
right unbelievable." Other visitors were stunned and thrilled by the rocket-
engine firings, yet Hitler seemed barely interested. His mind was engaged
elsewhere, probably mulling over his next foreign conquests; the ballistic
missile was not going to help with those. Notwithstanding his encyclopedic
knowledge of weaponry, it also seemed as if he could not quite comprehend
a technology so far beyond his experience as a World War I veteran. In any
case, the net result of the visit turned out to be zero: the army rocket program was neither hurt nor helped. Ordnance continued to generously fund
the ongoing expansion of Peenemünde out of its own budget, but it would
receive no extra resources or higher priorities from the dictator.[51]

For von Braun, too, the encounter became a strange interlude, a subject
for a good anecdote, rather than a decisive turning point in his career. He
returned to the A-5 and the A-4 but also to the aircraft program, which was
entering a new and exciting phase. The He 112 V4 was almost ready to fly
again with its new, turbopump-driven motor but, more important, Warsitz
at Peenemünde-West had begun taxi tests of the world's first true rocket
plane, the He 176. That aircraft had a Walter hydrogen-peroxide motor, as it
was proving difficult to adapt Ordnance's alcohol/liquid-oxygen technology
to the craft. Because Ernst Heinkel and his designers were more interested
in making an aircraft that could surpass the magical milestone of 1000 km/h
(621 mph) than in building a practical interceptor, the airplane was tiny, only

6 m (20 ft) long and 5 m (16.4 ft) in wingspan. The size made it difficult to design efficient tanks for liquid oxygen, and there were weight limitations on the combustion chamber so that the center of gravity would not be too far back. The complexity of designing a new turbopump system for both the He 112 V4 and for the He 176—the first ever incorporated into a working rocket engine—only added to the delays. By early 1939 the Air Ministry bumped the "Braun motor" from the second prototype to the third and fourth, the He 176 V3 and V4, still under construction.[52]

Throughout 1938 and into 1939 von Braun remained in close contact with Ernst Heinkel and his leading engineers, often flying to the company's headquarters at the relatively nearby Baltic port of Rostock. After the war Heinkel spoke fondly of the enjoyable evenings they had spent at his seaside villa at Warnemünde, outside the city. Von Braun was fascinated by the rocket-aircraft projects, and despite the growing separation between the army and the Luftwaffe, he also had personal and business reasons to remain close to the air force. In early May 1938 he spent another ten days at a training school in Stolp, in eastern Pomerania, improving his skills as a Luftwaffe reserve pilot. He flew a number of trainers and passed his K1 aerobatics license. Afterward he got to fly a wider variety of aircraft out of newly opened Peenemünde-West, most notably a couple of sleek Bf 108 single-engine aircraft that would allow him to make business trips year-round. (He did not fly the open-cockpit Junior from October 1937 to April 1938.) For programmatic reasons it was important to cultivate his Air Ministry connections as well, because of the need to draw on the aviation instruments industry for A-5 and A-4 gyros and equipment; hiring Ernst Steinhoff in July 1939 only helped in that regard. But if the correspondence of the rocket-aircraft engine projects is any indication, over time he delegated more and more of the responsibility to others, preoccupied as he was with guidance development, as well as responsibility for all the other rocket systems of the A series.[53]

On 15 June 1939 Erich Warsitz was finally allowed to fly the Walter-equipped He 176. Solid-fuel rockets had been attached to gliders during the Weimar *Raketenrummel*, and liquid-fuel ones had been installed in piston-engine airplanes like the He 112, but this flight was the first for a true rocket aircraft. It proved to be hair-raising, as Warsitz hit a molehill on the grass airfield, diverting his takeoff roll, then barely cleared the trees. He had to make a fast circuit around the area as he had only two minutes' worth of propellant. As the wings were so small, the He 176's gliding characteristics were dubious, so Warsitz put it down after only 50 seconds. Von Braun almost certainly witnessed the flight, as he was in Peenemünde. Warsitz repeated the feat on the twentieth and twenty-first and then for the last time in front of Hitler at Rechlin on 3 July. The airplane nonetheless was a failed design, and Air Ministry technical chief Ernst Udet was firmly against it. When the war began two months later, he took the opportunity to cancel the project entirely. Meanwhile Warsitz had shifted his attention to the He 178, the world's first turbojet aircraft. On 27 August, just as Germany prepared to attack Poland, he made his historic flight at the Heinkel works at Marienehe, outside Rostock. Warsitz is often forgotten, but the two milestones in ten weeks should put him near the top of any list of famous test pilots.[54]

Recognizing the He 176's limitations, von Braun nevertheless was inspired enough by its flight to send a rocket fighter proposal to the Air Ministry. Dated 6 July 1939, it depicted a larger aircraft that would take off vertically, powered by a main rocket engine of 10 metric tons (22,000 lb) of thrust. It was designed to intercept any bomber, as it could reach an altitude of 8000 m (25,000 ft) in 53 seconds. To sustain speed at altitude for cruising and attack, the airplane would also carry a sustainer motor, the He 176's 725-kg (1,600-lb) thrust one, and would glide back to base. Although a pilot himself, von Braun was so carried away by enthusiasm for the technology that he failed to see vertical takeoff as a frightening proposition: if the engine failed, the pilot was dead. The ministry silently filed it away and moved on to other projects, most notably one that combined the tailless glider designs of Alexander Lippisch with a Walter engine, eventually leading to the Messerschmitt Me 163 Komet rocket fighter. The summer of 1939 turned out to be a critical turning point. Although the He 112 V4 test aircraft would still fly in the first year of the war, the joint army-Luftwaffe rocket aircraft program that had launched Peenemünde was dying a slow death. It would take only Hitler's war to kill it.[55]

CHAPTER SIX

Future Dreams

1939–42

*Before us in a clearing among the pines towered an unreal-
looking missile four stories high. Colonel Dornberger, Wernher
von Braun, and the staff were as full of suspense over this first
launching as we were. I knew what hopes the young inventor was
placing on this experiment. For him and his team this was not the
development of a weapon, but a step into the future of technology.*

—ALBERT SPEER[1]

On Saturday, 19 August 1939, after three days of traveling, Wernher von
Braun landed his Bf 108 at Hirschberg airfield, near his parents' Oberwiesenthal farm, and stayed for two nights. It was a pleasant weekend visit
at the end of a long, golden summer of illusions for the German people. Few
believed war was imminent despite rising government propaganda about
Poland. Almost everyone expected the Führer to pull off another painless
diplomatic victory. Just before midnight on the twenty-first, the day von
Braun returned to Peenemünde and Zinnowitz, the radio gave the stunning
news that Germany had agreed to a nonaggression pact with the arch-
enemy, the "Jewish-Bolshevik" Soviet Union. Everyone assumed that this
was Hitler's coup: now the West would not interfere in the seizure of the
free port of Danzig and parts of Poland lost in 1918. Few knew of Hitler's
true aims: to launch a genocidal war to destroy the Polish state, enslave its
people, and murder many of its leaders and many of its Jews.[2]

Within four days, war measures began: the regime canceled the September party rally, closed the airports, and implemented food rationing. Diplomatic interventions forced Hitler to postpone the attack from 26 August to
1 September, but he would not be denied. The assault began officially at
4:45 a.m. But his central gamble failed. Britain and France would not back
down; the occupation of Czechoslovakia in March had been the last straw. A
war long dreaded by the populace, a conflict with the West that revived

memories of the bloody attrition of the trenches, began two days later. The general German mood was far from enthusiastic; indeed it was mostly depressed and resigned.[3]

For von Braun, the coming of World War II would magnify all the challenges, opportunities, and dangers of the late 1930s. Even more resources and people would pour into the army rocket project, further testing his management virtuosity at so young an age. Inevitably, technological challenges and setbacks would grow as the A-4 came to fruition, magnifying the political pressures upon the project and upon him. In the process he would be asked once again to make a gesture of loyalty to Nazism, a new acknowledgment of his implicit bargain with the Third Reich.

In Peenemünde the call-ups of engineers and technicians to the armed forces had an immediate negative effect. On 30 August von Braun issued an order prioritizing his group's major projects. At the top was Lighthouse III, the launch of guided A-5s with three different control systems; at the bottom of the list were another system and the He 176 tests. In second priority was the A-4 25-ton-thrust engine, versions of which were first fired on Test Stand I in spring 1939, and the He 112 V4, which in any case would require only three men to assist Peenemünde-West in its return to flight.[4]

On 5 September, two days after Britain and France declared war, Dornberger went to the army's new underground headquarters at Zossen, near Kummersdorf, and had the commander in chief, von Brauchitsch, sign an order making the entire Peenemünde project, including the new factory and all its related construction, a top priority for the service. The first objective was to protect the project from massive losses of manpower due to mobilization, but its second was to accelerate the A-4 ballistic missile so that it might be relevant to the war. In return, von Brauchitsch asked for its development to be completed in a breathtaking two years—that is, by September 1941. Becker was doubtlessly behind the order and the schedule. After the quick victory over Poland he asked for a further acceleration, to May 1941. These deadlines, as it turned out, were illusory given the complex and radically new technology needed for the missile, but they had the effect of greatly increasing the pressure on everyone in the project. Hours became even longer; the workload increased. It was one likely reason why von Braun gave up his Zinnowitz apartment in November 1939 and moved into the "rather fancy bachelor quarters" in Building 5, next to his office.[5]

It was immediately clear to Becker and Dornberger that the existing research and development resources were inadequate for such an accelerated schedule, even though Peenemünde-East had more than tripled in size to about twelve hundred employees by the start of the war. The barriers of extreme secrecy had to be lowered a little so as to mobilize the resources of university institutes, which were also threatened by draft call-ups and political demands to show relevance to the war. Becker, a central figure in the rather chaotic science administration of the Third Reich, encouraged his subordinates to make direct contacts with the universities, often to beat the other services to the punch. Meetings were organized at Kummersdorf and Peenemünde by the end of September. Wags up north dubbed the meeting there the *"Tag der Weisheit* [Wisdom Day]," for all the illustrious professors who came to agree on projects, particularly in guidance and control and propulsion. Most were from the engineering-dominated Institutes of Technology (technical universities), particularly Dresden, Darmstadt, and Berlin.[6]

For von Braun, the integration of university researchers became another notable management success. He set the right academic tone, and due to his charisma, brilliance, and sound education in engineering and physics, he was once again able to win over older colleagues skeptical about his age. His later commentary shows how much he enjoyed this dimension of the wartime program:

> Our cooperation with the universities became a most pleasant experience for all concerned. We operated on an entirely democratic basis, with plenty of discussions, symposia and mutual visits. Our contracts were worded in broad terms, because we were anxious to familiarize the institutions accurately with all the practical angles of their particular tasks. This method offered them a wide latitude for their approach and greatly stimulated creative contributions by all involved.[7]

The war also provided another mechanism for mobilizing research resources for the accelerated program: the ability to draft technically qualified people through both military and civilian channels. How the latter could work is illustrated by the recruitment of Helmut Hoelzer, an electrical engineer in Berlin. Shortly after the war began, probably in October, he heard a noise under his window one night. He saw two friends he knew from the Luftwaffe's glider institute near Darmstadt: Ernst Steinhoff, Hermann Steuding, and a third one he did not know, a "young guy, whistled all the time." They invited him out for a beer at a nearby pub. The three friends, all Darmstadt graduates, talked over old times. The third man "was very much more interested in the music and the girls who run around . . . instead of what I had to tell."

And he listened to the music and whistled and was quite happy. After a while, he turned around. "Say, I want to ask you something. You work on wave propagation and things at Telefunken?" I said, "Yes." "What do you do if you have a flying body and you want to keep this flying body on a straight line?" I said, "Well, it just depends on the body. . . . If you take a piano and throw it down the Empire State Building, or if you have an airplane, you have to use different methods. So what kind of flying body is this?" He said, "Well, I can't tell you." I said, "Well, I can't answer it."

In spite of a few such mysterious exchanges, Hoelzer found the man's mind "impressive," although his manner was a bit "arrogant." A couple of weeks later he got a civilian draft notice sending him to Peenemünde, a place he had never heard of. One of the first persons who showed him around was the third man: Wernher von Braun. He wanted Hoelzer to modify Luftwaffe guide-beam technology for the A-5, to keep the rocket from being blown off course by wind. But Hoelzer's work would turn out to be something much more important: an analog computer that would be essential to the success of A-4 guidance and control.[8]

Just about this time Lighthouse III was beginning on the transformed Oie, which now had a permanent set of launch structures, living quarters, communications systems, and tracking outposts. The expedition model of rocket launches was at an end; now much of the crew could go over a day or two in advance. Originally targeted for the summer, the long-awaited A-5 tests with the Kreiselgeräte platform had to be postponed until the parachute recovery system was deemed reliable; indeed the first launch on 24 October was of an unguided A-5 with the sole purpose of testing it. Everything worked fine, although the rocket was not recovered. Once again bad weather and technical problems intervened, so that it was a week before the first guided A-5 was ready to launch. On the thirtieth von Braun flew over to the Oie for the first time in a new Fieseler Storch, allowing him to get to the little island in ten minutes. But more problems led to another delay, so he had to fly over again the following day.[9]

At 10:30 a.m. on 31 October 1939 the A-5, looking to later eyes just like a scaled-down V-2, finally lifted off. For von Braun, "it was an unforgettable sight, as the slim missile rose slowly from its platform, climbing vertically with ever-increasing speed and without the slightest oscillation, until it vanished in the overcast." Through the clouds he could hear "the thundering roar of its jet." After 22 seconds he pushed a button to send the radio command to cut off the engine, "then all was silence." Thirty seconds later he sent further commands to open the braking and main parachutes. "We held our breaths. Five minutes later, joyous cries . . . [all] over the island. There was the missile again, straight overhead, descending on its parachute! It finally drifted into the water, less than 200 feet off shore." Unburned propellants ignited on impact, breaking the rocket in two, and the oscillograph film mechanism had failed, so there were no recorded measurements of Kreiselgeräte's control system, but it was a definite success: nearly two years after the devastating but informative A-3 failures, it was the first controlled flight of one of Ordnance's large rockets. Von Braun and Dornberger felt very relieved.[10]

A second vertical A-5 launch on 15 November was marred by a parachute failure and loss of the recorded data, but again the rocket appeared to work. It was time to try the tilt program, a clockwork mechanism that slowly rotated the stabilized platform, forcing the rocket's control system to tilt the vehicle in the desired direction of flight. After many more long delays the launch took place on 13 December. Out of desperation it was done through a low-hanging fog. The rocket quickly disappeared, but impact was spotted 3.6 km (2.2 mi) away. The oscillograph film was finally recovered and showed that the control system had more or less worked. While the results were far from completely satisfactory, von Braun's group had at last demonstrated the basic principles of simple ballistic missile trajectory. The next launches would not come until spring 1940, when the first Siemens and Rechlin systems would become available.[11]

Just before the last launch of 1939 a political shadow fell over the greatly accelerated rocket program. Hitler, still lukewarm about it, cut back its steel quotas in the face of shortages of critical munitions for the Western campaign, which he wanted to launch as soon as possible. Dornberger's Peenemünde rocket factory, then in the early construction phases, was heavily affected. A 20 November meeting between Becker and the Führer changed nothing; nor did Dornberger's subsequent memorandum arguing, on little evidence, that Germany was in a rocketry arms race with other countries. Von Braun's research and development side was not much impacted, but a bigger threat arose in January 1940: all Peenemünde construction could lose the designation "important for the war." That would not only lead to a massive exodus of construction workers from the factory and associated buildings, but also stop the construction of the new guidance and control laboratory and Test Stand VII—the massive A-4 launch site being started on the tip of Usedom, north of Test Stand I. (The Oie was deemed too difficult for the big rocket.) Even the university contracts could be lost.[12]

This potential disaster was fended off in large part by the intervention of

Albert Speer, who had taken a supervisory role over center construction at the outbreak of the war. Speer "liked mingling with this circle of non-political young scientists and inventors headed by Wernher von Braun—twenty-seven years old, purposeful, a man realistically at home in the future. It was extraordinary that so young and untried a team should be allowed to pursue a project costing hundreds of millions of marks." He found their objectives sometimes "utopian" but utterly fascinating. "It was like the planning of a miracle. . . . Whenever I visited Peenemünde I also felt, quite spontaneously, somehow akin to them." Von Braun was only seven years younger than Speer and like him had made a meteoric rise to take charge of gigantic, ambitious projects under the Nazis.[13]

Speer's intervention notwithstanding, the priority crisis would drag on for another year, creating an atmosphere of endless uncertainty. To make matters worse, on 8 April 1940, one day before Germany's lightning invasion of Denmark and Norway, General Karl Becker shot himself to death in Berlin. For months he had been under heavy criticism from Hitler and others due to shortfalls in munitions production. Becker found it humiliating that on 17 March the Führer had appointed Dr. Fritz Todt, the energetic builder of the autobahns and the West Wall fortifications, to accelerate production as the first minister for armaments and munitions. When Dornberger saw Becker for the last time, the Ordnance chief was uncharacteristically depressed. "I only hope that I have not been mistaken in my estimate of you and your work," he told an unnerved Dornberger. On hearing of Becker's suicide, he and von Braun were shocked that they had lost their old friend and chief protector, the man who had launched Ordnance into the rocket business. The very next day the two went to see Todt in his Berlin office. The new minister assured them of the rocket project's future but could not help with the shortage of construction workers. Luckily Becker's replacement, General Emil Leeb, turned out to be another artillerist as blindly enthusiastic as Becker about the ballistic missile.[14]

It was in the midst of this difficult period that the SS suddenly reappeared in Wernher von Braun's life. In 1947 he gave the U.S. War Department this account:

In spring 1940, one SS-Standartfuehrer (SS-colonel) Mueller from Greifswald, a bigger town in the vicinity of Peenemuende, looked me up in my office . . . and told me, that Reichsfuehrer SS Himmler had sent him with the order to urge me to join the SS. I told him I was so busy with my rocket work that I had no time to spare for any political activity. He then told me, that . . . the SS would cost me no time at all. I would be awarded the rank of a[n] "Untersturmfuehrer" (lieutenant) and it were [*sic*] a very definite desire of Himmler that I attend his invitation to join.

I asked Mueller to give me some time for reflection. He agreed.

Realizing, that the matter was of highly political significance for the relation between the SS and the Army, I called immediately on my military superior . . . , Dr. Dornberger. He informed me that the SS had for a long time been trying to get their "finger in the pie" of the rocket work. I asked him what to do. He replied on the spot that if I wanted to continue our mutual work, I had no alternative but to join. He added that he hoped our old cordial relation of confidence would avoid any future difficulties that could arise.

After receiving two letters of exhortation from Mueller, I finally wrote him my consent. Two weeks later, I received a letter . . . that Reichsfuehrer SS Himmler had approved my request . . . and had appointed me Untersturmfuehrer . . . in the staff of Obergruppenfuehrer Mazow [Mazuw], Stettin (whom I did not even know).

His SS record officially dates his "readmittance" (in view of his 1933–34 membership in the Reitersturm) to 1 May 1940; his sequential membership number was 185,068. Given the date, these events may well have taken place in April, the month of Becker's suicide.[15]

As with von Braun's party membership, we have no truly independent account of what happened, but his story is plausible. A loyal subordinate, Gerhard Reisig, asserted much later: "I remember very well when we were talking in a small circle with von Braun. He said, 'I just got the offer from Himmler to become an SS officer. Should I do it or should I not do it? Would it help me or would it be bad for me?' "[16] These words can be read as pure opportunism, but they are also compatible with von Braun's account that he reluctantly faced this choice. We know nothing about how he felt about his earlier experience in the Reitersturm, but his reluctance likely stemmed from the SS's association with Nazi ideological fervor, and less from its role in the secret police and the concentration camps, which loomed larger in later years, especially after the war. The timing was certainly bad, perhaps intentionally so on Himmler's part. Dornberger's pressure on von Braun must have been because of the political troubles of the rocket program, given his suspicion of SS meddling in rocketry.

In short, there is a lot to be said for von Braun's implied assertion that he felt trapped; he could refuse only at the cost of disobeying his superior and attracting a lot of unwanted attention to himself. Such an action was feasible if he was willing to make polite, apolitical excuses and stick to them, but that would have required strong, unspoken moral and political convictions and a willingness to damage his career. Since those were manifestly lacking, and only rocketry and spaceflight mattered to him, it is hard to see him doing anything else. But it was one more step in his deepening entanglement with the Third Reich's organs of political control and repression.

Afterward he was not ostentatious in his SS membership. He did not use his officer's rank on official correspondence and wore the black dress uniform with swastika armband only when he had to. Propulsion engineer Hartmut Küchen was astonished when he first saw the technical director in black. His jaw dropped; von Braun told him to shut his mouth and said: "*Es geht nicht anders.* [There was no way around it.]" In May 1942 von Braun was seen at a test stand wearing the uniform, a rarity; another time a Berlin researcher went into his office and saw it hanging on a hook on the wall. Presumably he had other reasons to wear it in those days. Ernst Kütbach, a worker at Peenemünde, has said that for monthly meetings of the local General SS unit, which von Braun attended perhaps half the time,

> ... he would come in uniform, we also had to come in uniform. You couldn't go there in civilian dress. He had the highest rank there, well the platoon leader was an Oberscharführer [sergeant] and he was an Untersturmführer [second lieutenant], wasn't he? And when the Doctor arrived, the platoon leader would announce: "*SS platoon 4-9,*" or whatever it was called, "*reporting for duty.*" And then he would sit down and listen to what the other one had to tell us about tactics and strategy.[17]

According to Kütbach, the unit leader highly prized von Braun for his marksmanship and would sometimes induce him to participate in shooting competitions with the local SA (Storm Troopers), NSKK (NS Drivers Corps), and NSFK (NS Flyers Corps). Still, "it was quite a surprise when he became an Untersturmführer, . . . well, he made the best of it, you know, he couldn't refuse." Despite his apparent lack of commitment, Himmler must nonetheless have received regular, favorable reports, as von Braun received promotions to Obersturmführer (first lieutenant) and Hauptsturmführer (captain) in November 1941 and November 1942, respectively.[18]

Shortly after von Braun rejoined the SS, the war situation was transformed. The long period of inactivity in the West, famously dubbed "the phony war" by an American reporter, was ended by the German onslaught that began on 10 May. Within a week Allied forces were collapsing; within two weeks Hitler's blitzkrieg had won a stunning victory. By mid-June

France was out of the war, and Britain appeared to be next. At no time in the history of the Third Reich was the Führer so popular as in the summer of 1940; most assumed the war was over.[19]

Between trips to the Oie to direct A-5 launches, of which there were eight in 1940, Wernher von Braun took advantage of Germany's new empire in the west. On 15 August he and Erich Warsitz flew to Paris in a modified two-engine He 111 bomber used for test flights; they stayed for three days. Perhaps inspection of French industry was the reason for the trip, but it was also a sort of vacation. On the eighteenth they flew to the coastal resort of Biarritz on the far southern French Atlantic coast, next to Spain, and returned to Paris the following day, before flying to Peenemünde on 20 August.[20]

The victory over France had remarkably little impact on the rocket program, however. Late in June the new Ordnance chief encouraged Dornberger to marshal the arguments for lifting the priority restrictions. But the effort went nowhere, as von Brauchitsch saw little reason to believe that Hitler had changed his mind. It was only in November, after the failure of the Luftwaffe to defeat the Royal Air Force in the Battle of Britain, that the dictator allowed the priority rating of the project to improve. The construction of the A-4 factory, on which Arthur Rudolph was chief engineer, was much delayed, but the impact on research and development was less. Von Braun's group had trouble getting corporate contractors to deliver on time, most notably in the guidance and control field, but contrary to Dornberger's later assertions there is simply no evidence that the actual development of the missile was delayed two years. More likely it was several months. The development of the big missile dragged on longer than expected for the simple reason that it was incredibly ambitious, a revolutionary breakthrough in rocket technology.[21]

In late October 1940 the very first nonflying A-4, Spritzaggregat 1 (Injection Aggregate 1), was completed in the assembly building at Peenemünde-East. Von Braun, whose few, sketchy memoirs are emotionally unrevealing in any case, has left us no record of his reaction, but it was undoubtedly one of immense excitement and pride. Although puny by later standards, the A-4 was a monster in its day. Fully 14 m (46 ft) tall and 3.5 m (11.6 ft) across the fins, it would weigh about 13 metric tons (28,500 lb) in its fully fueled launch configuration and would have a thrust of 25 tons (55,000 lb). To reach its projected range of 270 km (168 mi), it would have to accelerate to a velocity of 1600 m/sec (3,500 mph, Mach 4.5) and coast to an altitude of over 80 km (50 mi). As von Braun was acutely aware, it would be the first manmade object to reach the edge of space.

But to get to that day, many problems remained to be solved. Between 1937 and 1940 Walter Thiel's group, mostly at Kummersdorf, had produced a revolution in liquid-fuel rocket propulsion, drastically shortening the length of the combustion chamber by dropping the von Braun/Riedel/Rudolph engine design. Efficiency, mixing, and burning were improved, solving most of the cooling problems that had led to innumerable test stand failures. But the "eighteen-pot" engine, so called because it combined eighteen separate injectors to produce 25 tons of thrust, was deemed too complicated for mass production, and the steam generator and turbopump that supplied its propellants still needed much refinement to be reliable. In aerodynamics Rudolf Hermann's institute had demonstrated that Kurzweg's A-5 body and fin design could be used at subsonic and low supersonic velocities but was still trying to refine its wind tunnels so as to make them usable for higher supersonic speeds. Ernst Steinhoff's guidance and control laboratory had made much progress through the A-5 launches, and through aircraft tests of Helmut Hoelzer's guide beam, but there was a long way to go before a workable A-4 guidance system would be available. And Walter Riedel's design bureau had laid out the blueprints for the first A-4, but the very complex plumbing and electrical systems of the missile still needed to be extensively tested.[22]

The only person pulling all these disparate fields together was von Braun. The rocket project had grown up organically, based on the subject-area specializations of Thiel, Hermann, Riedel, Steinhoff, and others. The one division that logically integrated all parts of the A-4, Riedel's design bureau, left the gyroscopic, electrical, and electronic devices to Steinhoff's group, as Riedel's group lacked expertise. Nor were any techniques like systems engineering or project management available, as these were invented in the Cold War United States to get control over even larger and more complicated weapons systems. The later structures chief, Raithel, has said: "It's amazing. There was no systems integration group that was responsible for the whole thing [the A-4], and yet it worked, but I think that was only due to the intellect and the immense capacity of work of Wernher von Braun." In short, the systems integration group was inside von Braun's head.[23]

Yet he was no miracle worker. The great majority of the problems that arose with the first and subsequent A-4s had to be ironed out in innumerable tests and modifications, with many severe setbacks. That began when Spritzaggregat 1 was moved to Test Stand V at the end of October 1940. Final installation of the propulsion, valve, and electrical systems dragged on for two months; then testing lasted the entire first half of 1941. Even though the propellants were not burned, merely run through the pipes and dumped through the engine into a trench, there were welding problems, frozen valves, and difficulties in making the complex plumbing and electrical systems work correctly. Spritzaggregat 2 was completed only in July 1941, once reasonably functional systems had been worked out, but it nonetheless contained alternate, simplified systems. The third vehicle followed shortly thereafter, but all required further modifications and upgrades before being moved on to engine and guidance tests in the fall. Early A-4s would have versions of Fieber's Vertikant system improvised from available components.[24]

With the era of big rockets at last at hand, but the demands of mass production not yet dominating the center's agenda, dreaming about the future reached its apogee for von Braun and his associates during this period. Shortly before the beginning of the war, a designer in the (Future) Projects Office had proposed putting wings on the A-4 to extend its range through gliding. This idea fascinated von Braun, as it did others, because it seemed to be a cheap way to perhaps double the missile's reach, but also because it looked like a manned space plane. Spaceflight had absolutely nothing to do with why the German army funded Peenemünde—the whole point was to produce decisive, revolutionary weapons—but space played a useful psychological role at the center. Thanks to Dornberger's and von Braun's leadership, and the presence of two dozen members of the old rocket groups among the thousands who worked there, spaceflight dreams remained on the informal agenda. Von Braun was able to enthuse some of his leading subordinates, like Hermann, for the idea; he made them feel like pioneers in brave new territory. Early on, the Mardi Gras costume party for 1938 had a Mars theme; von Braun showed up as a professor in his seventies, figuring that that was how old he might be when he got to the red planet. An aerodynamicist also remembers him giving a lecture about his plan for a Moon rocket one evening when they were on the Oie. At its height in 1940–41 the leading engineers toyed with ideas of multistage launch vehicles, and Thiel and von Braun took an interest in the exotic topic of nuclear rockets for spaceflight as a result of their contacts with the German atomic bomb and reactor project, which Ordnance also directed until mid-1942.[25]

So fascinated was von Braun by the future possibilities of nuclear energy that he went to see Nobel Prize–winning atomic physicist Werner Heisenberg more than once, the last visit being in 1942. Unfortunately there are no written records of any of these encounters. Heisenberg is the scientist or engineer now most associated with the dilemmas of a Faustian bargain with the Nazis, but in comparison to von Braun's his compromises were modest.

Although a conservative nationalist too, he never joined the party and was more conflicted about building weapons for the Nazis, however little practical effect that had on the nuclear project, which never received top priority and failed to produce a bomb or even a working reactor. Von Braun thus was well aware of the possibility of a nuclear-armed ballistic missile, but he gave it little or no consideration because a German atomic bomb, especially one light enough to fit on a rocket, seemed a remote prospect. Still, it must be said: if von Braun had been asked to build a nuclear missile for Hitler, he doubtless would have done so as a patriotic duty.[26]

On 1 September 1941, in the midst of this period of unbridled technological enthusiasm, spaceflight theoretician Hermann Oberth came to Peenemünde. His two-year stay would not, however, be a happy one. Since 1938 the Air Ministry and Ordnance had employed him on make-work projects in Vienna and Dresden to keep him quiet and away from Peenemünde, but Dornberger and von Braun eventually reluctantly accepted the space pioneer when he became completely frustrated and threatened to quit. At the center he quickly showed his true colors by criticizing the A-4 for an inefficient design, on grounds that made theoretical sense but blithely ignored the practical engineering realities. Von Braun continued to honor Oberth as his inspiration and mentor but nonetheless could do little with him. He gave the theoretician a job investigating foreign patents that might be useful to the project, but once again it was make-work; the most useful thing that Oberth did was write a theoretical study of how to optimize the number and size of stages of multistage rockets.[27]

This study was relevant because the apogee of dreaming in 1940–42 also had a military dimension, one directly related to the apogee of the Nazi empire. The winged A-4, dubbed the A-9 in 1940, was made an important priority of the aerodynamics program in order to find possible wing and fin configurations. Someone then proposed putting it on top of the "100-ton [-thrust] device," now called the A-10. This two-stage missile, the Projects Office calculated in July 1940, could have a range of 2500 km (1,500 mi). As the possibility of an American entry into the war became more apparent in 1941, the A-9/A-10 concept was revised. A first-stage thrust of 180 tons (400,000 lb) might allow attacks on U.S. east coast cities from launch sites on the fringe of Nazi-occupied Europe. Some handwritten calculations from September 1941, probably by the chief of the Projects Office, Ludwig Roth, give the range from Brest (in Brittany), and from Lisbon, to New York, Pittsburgh, and Washington. The A-9/A-10 was, on paper, the world's first intercontinental ballistic missile (ICBM), but it was no more than a fantasy, as a hypersonic glider was far beyond Peenemünde's technological capability. It would also have been an absurdly expensive way to deliver a one-ton high-explosive bomb—the same warhead as the A-4, unless restrictions on chemical warfare were lifted or the atomic bomb project worked out. But the A-9/A-10 was potentially useful for currying favor with Hitler, who was looking for ways to attack the United States.[28]

In the spring of 1941 the army had at last succeeded in getting Peenemünde development, meaning essentially the A-4, restored to top priority, but not the production plant and its associated projects. As the concept of Dornberger and Ordnance was to mass-produce the missile as soon as it became available, this was unsatisfactory. Moreover, new threats to the program appeared at the time of Hitler's gigantic assault on the Soviet Union, which began without warning on 22 June. Grossly overconfident of the outcome of "Operation Barbarossa," the dictator had issued orders redirecting armaments production away from the army and toward the Luftwaffe and the navy for a renewed war against Britain. In addition, Armaments Minister Todt became more and more disgruntled with the extravagant construction at Peenemünde and threatened a cutback. In the midst of all this confusion, Army Commander in Chief von Brauchitsch was at last able to secure permission from Hitler for a briefing about the rocket program, which led to von Braun's fourth encounter with the Führer, on 20 August 1941.[29]

Hitler was now ensconced in his new headquarters, the Wolfsschanze (Wolf's Lair). Located in the Masurian lake district of East Prussia, it was perhaps 100 kilometers southeast of the ancestral von Braun estate of Neucken, which Fritz still farmed and which Magnus Sr. would soon inherit because both Fritz and Siegfried, the middle brother then serving in the Netherlands occupation force, died in 1942, after Fritz's son had been killed in the 1940 campaign. (In the spring of 1941 the war again impacted the family, this time more benignly, when the British interned Sigismund and his wife in Kenya after overrunning Addis Ababa.) With Steinhoff as primary pilot, Dornberger and von Braun flew east on 20 August and landed at Rastenburg, then were driven through a series of security barriers to get to the inner sanctum, a collection of bunkers and barracks well camouflaged in the forest. Few details are available, as neither Dornberger nor von Braun later mentioned this visit in their memoirs. They construed a very similar trip to the Wolfsschanze two years later as *the* breakthrough in Hitler's favor for the A-4 and found it difficult to fit this puzzling encounter into that framework. But at the time it was a dramatic, important event.[30]

Only two documents, both by Dornberger, give insight into what happened: an outline of his presentation to Hitler, dated 31 July, and a memo-

randum on the meeting, written the day after, 21 August. We do not even
know whether von Braun spoke at the Wolfsschanze meeting, although it
seems likely that he did, either during the A-4 and A-9/A-10 presentation,
or during the screening of a promotional movie about Peenemünde made in
late 1940. It showed the A-3s, A-5s, test stands, and facilities and ended with
an ominous warning of foreign competition in rocketry. Like the film shown
two years later, it was without sound, presumably so it could be narrated by
a speaker. In 1943 the speaker would be von Braun.[31]

Hitler's reaction to the presentation and film was stunning: "The Führer
emphasized that this development is of revolutionary importance for the
conduct of warfare in the whole world. The deployment of a few thousand
devices per year is therefore unwise. If it is deployed, hundreds of thousands
of devices per year must be manufactured and launched." He saw clearly
that small numbers of conventionally armed missiles were not going to be
decisive, and thus asked for hundreds of thousands, as if they were artillery
shells. Dornberger could only appeal for a complete reorganization of the
war economy in order to try to implement this ludicrous idea, yet Hitler
wisely refused to commit himself to mass production until the A-4 was
actually shown to work. The upshot of the meeting was that the Peenemünde rocket factory was upgraded to top priority and integrated into the
center, instead of being administered separately. Economic planning quickly
demonstrated the absurdity of the dictator's numbers; by late September,
Ordnance and the economic staff had settled on a preliminary output of five
thousand a year. Von Braun quickly found himself immersed in the first of
many attempts to prepare the A-4 for production at a time when the missile
had yet even to fly.[32]

Events that fall and winter were to demonstrate how far from ready it
was, leading to an unusual state of tension between Dornberger and von
Braun. Around the beginning of November explosions on Test Stands I and
VII damaged or destroyed two of the three nonflight A-4s. On the seventh
the chief of the rocket program sent the center a tongue-lashing. He was
appalled that "in the present life-and-death situation for HVP [Peenemünde-
East], young, inexperienced test engineers are left with the leadership of
tests." He demanded that von Braun, Thiel, or Walter Riedel be present for
the first thirty tests for each rocket and told them he was unsympathetic to
claims that development was being forced too quickly by orders from above.
"If the leading employees would pay more attention to what is actually of
burning importance to us, rather than wallowing in future dreams, then
deadlines might actually be met." Nor was he at all pleased when they went
off on "business trips for days on end" to talk to firms about equipment and

tools for A-4 production. "It is something out of a lunatic asylum, when individual Peenemünde-East employees believe that they can on their own tackle and solve a problem like mass production." He was obviously feeling severe pressure to produce results after all his promises, from the chief of Ordnance up to Hitler, to complete a weapon "that in a foreseeable period may decide the war."[33]

Another point of contention was the time spent meeting with the Air Ministry about the possibility of rocket interceptors or antiaircraft missiles. Ironically, Dornberger had started these discussions by passing along a request in May 1941 from flak (antiaircraft artillery) experts in the ministry to examine defensive missiles as a response to RAF night bomber attacks. Von Braun immediately revamped his July 1939 rocket fighter proposal, focusing, not surprisingly, more on the manned interceptor than on the unmanned missile. After a Peenemünde visit by the flak experts, the ministry started a feasibility study at the Fieseler aircraft company that ultimately went nowhere. Meanwhile the antiaircraft missile idea was shelved until 1942, when it came back to haunt Peenemünde. But in November 1941 Dornberger saw all such discussions as a distraction until the ministry came up with the personnel to do something. "I urgently request now that these totally useless meetings over future hopes stop and that you gentlemen alone concentrate on the <u>development</u> of the A-4."[34]

Six days later Dornberger issued another memorandum, indicating that he and von Braun had argued over what should follow the A-4. Fascinated by winged rocket vehicles, von Braun inevitably favored the A-9. But Dornberger felt that far too little was known about the aerodynamics and trajectory of the glider missile. He ordered Peenemünde to concentrate on the "pure rocket" in the shape of the A-5 and A-4, the only one proven so far to work. By this he meant the A-8, an idea for an improved A-4 using hypergolic (self-igniting) propellants. In early 1941 von Braun and Thiel had visited the rocket test facilities of BMW Aircraft Engines in Berlin-Spandau. There an Austrian engineer (and fanatical SS officer), Helmut von Zborowski, had been developing the combination of nitric acid and diesel oil for the Luftwaffe. Thiel, who had moved his group to Peenemünde in mid-1940, took up this combination with enthusiasm. The propulsion chief believed that it would be possible to develop a 30-metric-ton (66,000-lb) thrust nitric acid–diesel oil engine; with higher-density propellants, more could be put into the rocket, giving the A-8 a potential range of 450 km (280 mi) with a one-ton warhead. To Dornberger, this range was just adequate to be the A-4 follow-on, which he believed was needed to keep high-level support. Once again he ordered his Peenemünde engineers to give up their "future dreams" and concentrate on what was important. The A-8, however, would turn out to be abortive, as Hitler refused in the spring of 1942 to countenance a weapon that would make Germany's oil supply situation even worse. The single-stage A-9 resumed its role as the designated successor of the A-4, but soon it too would be eclipsed, as the production problems of the ballistic missile came to overwhelm everything else.[35]

Notwithstanding Dornberger's whip-cracking memoranda, it was impossible for von Braun to avoid involving himself in converting the missile to mass production, whether it be the vexed problem of eliminating scarce aluminum alloys, as Hitler demanded, or in finding industrial contractors. When the acting commandant, Major Gerhard Stegmaier, suggested the underutilized Zeppelin airship company for tank and middle-section production, von Braun was inevitably drawn in as chief technical expert. (Zanssen was away leading a solid-rocket battery in Operation Barbarossa.) He accompanied Stegmaier and Dornberger on visits to Zeppelin headquarters on Lake Constance and was thrilled to meet its leader, Hugo Eckener, the world-famous airship captain. In December 1941, just as the war took a worrying turn with the Soviet counterattack before Moscow and Hitler's declaration of war on the United States in support of Japan, the army decided to make Zeppelin the second A-4 assembly works. Ironically, Zeppelin's specialty was lightweight aluminum structures, just as Dornberger was pressuring von Braun to convert the propellant tanks to steel, a metal that could be very brittle at liquid-oxygen temperatures. Sitting in Berlin, exposed to the intense political pressures on the program, Dornberger saw von Braun's organization as too slow and too undisciplined. The latter charge, as we have seen, was not unjustified, but the missile was very technologically immature, as Dornberger well knew. No evidence survives as to how von Braun reacted to all this pressure and criticism, but throughout his life he generally handled such situations with tact and aplomb. He was loyal and obedient to authority and extremely resilient under stress. Whatever his short-term frustration and depression, his natural optimism and his enthusiasm for the work always won out.[36]

And work he would, as he had bigger problems that winter—above all, trying to get the A-4 into the air. The fall test stand explosions inevitably had set back the launch of the first flight model yet further. Now he hoped that it could be fired by late February 1942, but at the end of January the missile fell out of its "corset" on Test Stand I. Because of an oversight due to inexperience, no allowance had been made for the shrinkage of the rocket while tanked with liquid oxygen. Three of the four fins were severely bent. On 5 February Dornberger unleashed another tirade at the center leadership (he never seemed to target von Braun personally), blaming Peenemünde-East for poor organization and a Raketenflugplatz mentality of showmanship over substance, resulting in a lack of attention to the military necessities of producing a simple missile as soon as possible. The rocket was a "flying laboratory" that seemed to be designed "as if hundreds of people had the time to spend weeks going all over the rocket on the test stand, installing valves, doing assembly work, moving cables and generally fumbling around." He skewered the lack of cooperation between "Papa" Riedel's design bureau and Thiel's propulsion and test organization—a criticism that foreshadowed the end of Riedel's tenure in the job. By the summer von Braun would have to shunt his old right-hand man into another position, because "Papa" was in over his head and lacked sufficient engineering training. Another fault line in the organization is revealed in "the wish Dr. v. Braun presented to me on 4 February 1942, that if it comes to savings cutbacks, to shut down the VW [the production plant]" so that the development side could use the remaining engineers. Apparently he saw Dornberger's rocket production plant as a sinkhole for resources and people, which it was. In early 1942 it was far from complete; meanwhile whatever von Braun's genius for management, he was grappling with a vehicle that was being rushed into production even while it was seriously underdeveloped.[37]

The bad luck did not end. The first flight vehicle, now called Versuchsmuster 1 (Test Model 1, or V1, like an aircraft), was rescheduled for launch in late March, within a few days of von Braun's thirtieth birthday. But on the eighteenth, just before midnight, Thiel and his crew were running the third engine burn on Test Stand VII when an explosion blew out one side of the vehicle. A dangerous mixture of fuel and oxygen vapors had built up over the head of the motor due to vibration-induced cracking. That was the end of A-4/V1; it was cannibalized for parts. This time Dornberger seems to have passed on another outburst, recognizing as much as anyone that there were development problems beyond their control. It did not get easier with the second flight vehicle, which was damaged in April by a dimensional mismatch between the rocket and the new transporter used to raise it into position. It was mid-June 1942 before it was ready for launch.[38]

During this period von Braun was immersed in endless rounds of meetings not only about modifying and testing the A-4/V2 and subsequent vehicles but also about creating a mass-production infrastructure. On 3 March he fended off an attempt to split fabrication of the vehicle over many contractors for security reasons, arguing that the shortage of highly specialized welding machines and tooling needed for the missile meant that it could be assembled only in two or three places. Dornberger backed him up and specified that they would stay with Peenemünde and Zeppelin. Von Braun also suggested the necessity of creating a special organization in Peenemünde to take over the responsibility for production planning. The production draw- ings remained in a state of confusion, in part because too little was known, in part because the shortages of key aluminum alloys and special steels meant that the situation was constantly changing. Dornberger finally accepted the necessity of this reorganization in June, separating these functions from von Braun's development group.[39]

On the day of the first A-4 launch attempt, 13 June 1942, Dornberger sought help finding an industrial expert for production planning from the new armaments minister, Albert Speer. In another stroke of good fortune for the rocket program, Hitler had appointed Speer minister after the sudden death of Todt in a plane crash at the Wolfsschanze in February. Speer, who had supervised the construction of the Peenemünde production plant since 1940, eventually found a man with experience in the aircraft industry, but his organization was little more successful in mastering the problem of pro- duction planning.

For the launch of the A-4/V2 Ordnance had, in a fit of optimism, invited many VIPs. Speer headed a delegation of the armaments chiefs of the three services. As he attests, von Braun was in a state of great excitement and sus- pense over this groundbreaking event. Indeed, in a letter his father sent him after the first American satellite launch in 1958, Magnus von Braun sug- gested that it was the second great day in his son's life—after the launching of the world's first big rocket on 13 June 1942. He could have gotten that only from Wernher.[40]

Speer describes the launch:

> At the predetermined second, at first with a faltering motion but then with the roar of an unleashed giant, the rocket rose slowly from its pad, seemed to stand upon its jet of flame for a fraction of a second, then vanished with a howl into the low clouds. Wernher von Braun was beaming. For my part, I was thunderstruck at this technical miracle, at its precision and at the way it seemed to abolish the laws of gravity. . . .
>
> The technicians were just explaining the incredible distance the pro- jectile was covering when, a minute and a half after the start, a rapidly swelling howl indicated that the rocket was falling in the immediate vicinity. We all froze where we stood. It struck the ground only half a mile away.

Actually it crashed into the sea 600 m (2,000 ft) offshore. Roll control had failed immediately on liftoff, and the vehicle eventually tumbled, ripping the fins off. Dornberger's "consoling" remark to a crestfallen von Braun was: "Well, Doctor, it just isn't so simple to tickle a porcupine."[41]

It took two long months to prepare the next vehicle, as the guidance and control system obviously needed strengthening. On 29 July von Braun told Stegmaier, now his direct superior as head of the development works, that their guidance work would be simplified and the system's effectiveness improved if Hoelzer's analog computer was installed, even though it would cost two more weeks. It was a fundamental innovation that really made a mass-produced guidance system possible.[42]

The A-4/V3, painted like its predecessor in black and white patterns for better photography, lifted off on 16 August 1942 in front of a more restricted group of observers.

> In an elegant curve [von Braun later wrote], the bird picked up more and more speed and passed without the slightest fuss through the dreaded "sonic barrier," thus relieving us from a terrible nightmare— for many an aerodynamicist had sworn that the missile would be ripped to pieces by "transonic phenomena" which we all knew so little about in those days. But in the 45th second of flight, when we were confident that everything was going fine, the rocket showed signs of trouble. The trajectory began to oscillate, white steam emerged and the missile finally broke apart in mid-air.

It crashed into the Baltic 8.7 km (5.4 mi) away. Analysis of the film showed that acceleration had slowed after 36 seconds, probably due to some failure in the steam generator/turbopump combination, leading to a sudden shutdown at 45 seconds. The nose broke off as the missile began to stray, indicating that the forward fuselage also needed to be strengthened. The fact that the missile had flown so much longer seemed, however, to be a sign of progress; the later string of failures would indicate that it was more luck than anything else.[43]

As von Braun and his team rushed to modify the A-4/V4, Dornberger fought to protect the program in Berlin. Speer had announced on 13 June that the program would get a special super priority for the first twenty A-4s, but how long could the failures go on before top-level support dried up? On the eve of the next launch, on 29 September, Dornberger sent an urgent memorandum to Peenemünde-East outlining the seriousness of the situation. The Führer did not believe in the missile's guidance and control. Speer doubted the success of the ballistic missile too, and his doubts were being bolstered by his deputy Karl Otto Saur, and by Göring's deputy in the Air Ministry, Field Marshal Erhard Milch. (Milch had an ulterior

motive: the Luftwaffe had begun a competing program, Cherry Stone—
a pulse-jet-powered flying bomb later called the V-1). Equally disturbing
for Dornberger was that his own army superiors were beginning to doubt
his word. He appealed to the entire staff, not just the top managers, to work
day and night to fire as many A-4s as possible by the end of the year. Their
motto should be "launch, launch, launch."[44]

Yet von Braun could scarcely have worked any harder. He was committed
day and night, weekdays and weekends, and was constantly on the road or
flying to contractors and government offices. How heavy his workload was
can be gathered from a comment he made in a letter to his parents in fall
1956, when work on his American missile projects was building to a fever
pitch: "I can only say that work, in regard to the tempo and the hectic back-
and-forth, is more and more resembling conditions in Peenemünde."[45]
Although, as Dornberger well knew, he could lose focus and get carried away
by "future dreams" about intercontinental rockets and space travel, he had
proven himself on many levels to be a masterful leader of a huge engineering organization as well as a loyal subordinate and servant of Hitler's army
and Reich. In return for the tremendous opportunities and influence he had
been given at such a young age, little more was asked of him than that he
work hard, turn a blind eye to the regime's doings, and become a nominal
member of the party and the SS. But what would be the consequences of
success? Von Braun could scarcely contemplate that in the fall of 1942; all
that mattered was finally getting the A-4 to work.

CHAPTER SEVEN

A Pretty Hellish Environment

1942–44

The head forester does not want to see what might be embarrass-
ing for him, that is what makes him complicit, and in that he is
typical and representative of a huge stratum.
    —VICTOR KLEMPERER, diary entry, 10 August 1942[1]

It was a beautiful fall afternoon. Shortly before four p.m., Saturday, 3 October 1942, Wernher von Braun waited nervously atop Peenemünde's rocket
assembly building for the third A-4 launch attempt. With him were Lieutenant Colonel Gerhard Stegmaier, chief of the development works, and
Ernst Steinhoff, head of guidance and control. On the roof of the Measurement House nearby, Colonel Walter Dornberger, chief of Army Ordnance
rocket development, and his close friend Colonel Leo Zanssen, commander
of Peenemünde-East, stood alone, waiting, after Dornberger gave the order
to launch. Two kilometers to the north, a gleaming black-and-white rocket,
14 m (46 ft) tall and weighing 14 metric tons (31,000 lb), sat on its launch
table inside the massive oval earth wall of Test Stand VII. A stream of vapor
trailed off its side, as evaporating liquid oxygen streamed through the vent
valve. "X minus two" minutes: the launch warning siren sounded. All over
the complex thousands of people gathered outside the buildings listening to
loudspeakers.[2]

"X minus one." The vent valve closed, and the liquid-oxygen tank began
to pressurize. At ten seconds the test stand crew sounded the siren again and
shot off a smoke bomb. "X minus 10, 9, 8, 7, 6, 5, 4, 3, 2, 1, *Zündung eins*
[ignition]." "*Vorstufe* [preliminary stage]." A flame shot out of the A-4's
tail—one-third power, 8 metric tons (18,000 lb) of thrust, still not enough to
lift the missile off the table. "*Hauptstufe* (main stage)." The turbopump
spun up, the valves opened, and the ground power cable dropped. The rocket
lifted slowly, majestically into the air and began to accelerate.[3]

From the assembly building von Braun saw the vessel of all his hopes and dreams, the A-4/V4, rising in silence out of the dense trees surrounding Test Stand VII.

The flame darting from the stern was almost as long as the rocket itself [Dornberger later wrote]. The fiery jet of gas was clear-cut and self-contained. The rocket kept to its course as though running on rails; the first critical moment had passed. . . . The projectile was not spinning; the black and white surface markings facing us did not change.

"A sound like rolling thunder" reached their ears after traveling the 2000 m (6,500 ft) from the launch site, and it rapidly built into a "thunderous rumble." Four seconds after liftoff, the missile began its pitch-over to the east, curving over the cold, green Baltic waters. Through his binoculars von Braun could see the missile tilting, accelerating, getting smaller, staying on trajectory. Over the loudspeaker he could hear the Doppler tone climbing in pitch, giving in audible form the velocity measurement from the rocket's transponder, while the test stand announcer monotonously read off the seconds since launch. At 25 seconds the A-4 passed "sonic velocity," the "sound barrier." Fifteen seconds later, "A paralyzing shock! A trail of white appeared in the clear blue sky." There were shouts from the ground: "An explosion!" But it was only a contrail, soon distorted by upper atmosphere winds into a zigzag of "frozen lightning." On and on the missile flew; unlike the last it did not falter. Now it was just a glowing dot at the end of a white streak. Just before one minute, "*Brennschluss* [cut-off]" rang out from the loudspeaker, as the engine throttled back from 25 to 8 tons of thrust and then shut down entirely. Von Braun and his compatriots cheered, yelled, hugged; Dornberger and Zanssen cried and laughed for joy.[4]

The leaders rushed down to the street. After "much handshaking," Dornberger

bundled von Braun into the car and drove at reprehensible speed to Test Stand VII. As we shot through the open gate in the sand walls surrounding the great arena we beheld something like a popular riot. The test field crews had surrounded Dr. Thiel and the chief engineers. Everyone wanted to communicate his own particular observations and experiences.

Dornberger had to calm the celebration. There was one last milestone before the launch could be declared a complete success. After arcing nearly 90 km (56 mi) high, the rocket would plunge back into the atmosphere at

5000 km/h (3,100 mph); it must survive the searing heat of reentry. And it did. Just before 5 minutes' elapsed time the tone stopped. The missile had smashed into the Baltic about 190 km (118 mi) away. Von Braun and Steinhoff immediately rushed over to Peenemünde-West and took off to confirm the impact. They "found a large green stain in the sea" just in the spot predicted—the marker dye left by the A-4. They had done it! That night, at the celebratory dinner at the officers' club, "a deeply moved" Dornberger told his leading engineers, who were well on their way to getting completely drunk: "Do you realize what we accomplished today. . . . This afternoon the spaceship was born!" But he added to von Braun: "Lest you think that your headaches are over, I am telling you, they are just beginning!" The A-4, the new superweapon, must be put into production as soon as possible for the Führer and victory.[5]

The third of October 1942 was indeed a watershed: on that day the A-4 became the first man-made object to touch the edge of space, as Dornberger indicated and as von Braun and the Peenemünders liked to remember after the war. But this accomplishment had nothing to do with why the vehicle was funded, or its importance at the time—or, to a significant extent, afterward. It was the world's first successful ballistic missile, the harbinger of a new international arms race, and its launch was the success that the Ordnance rocket program so desperately needed to justify the huge sums the National Socialist state had already spent on Peenemünde. The summer of 1942 had seen new triumphs of German arms in southern Russia and North Africa, an Indian summer of conquests for Hitler's empire, but with the fall the war situation, like the weather, took an ominous turn. The lucky flight of 3 October 1942 arrived just in time—within weeks Allied victories would make the Führer receptive to "wonder weapons."

For von Braun, rushing the A-4 into production would force him into even deeper compromises with the Nazi system. As relentless pressure built up first from the Armaments Ministry and then from the SS, he would have to redirect his research and development team away from endless experimentation and incremental improvements and turn Peenemünde-East into a quasi-industrial organization. Simultaneously he would have to divert significant effort into developing an antiaircraft missile for the Luftwaffe as the Allied bomber offensive became ever more devastating. For the first time he would also have to think, however fleetingly, about what he was fighting for. The comfortable cocoon of Army Ordnance could no longer protect him; high Nazi authorities would intervene directly in a project now viewed as an urgent national priority. Ultimately he would have to come face-to-face with the apparatus of oppression, slavery, and murder at the heart of the government for which he so energetically labored.

Three days after the launch Zanssen ordered Stegmaier and von Braun to accelerate A-4 firings as much as possible, so as to speed up development and deployment. Von Braun immediately set about to survey the project to see how quickly missiles could be put through testing and brought to the launch pad. In the program he issued on the tenth, he laid out all of the major sections and components, and where the bottlenecks were, designating specific engineers as "commissars" for making these components available.[6]

In a cover memo to von Braun's program, Stegmaier made clear its assumptions and implications. The minimum time it would take to process a missile through Test Stand VII was eight days, and the objective would be to launch sixteen rockets by the end of February 1943. In order to carry this out, some activities were closed down altogether, at least until the end of that period. In fact his memo signaled a fundamental and long-lasting shift in Peenemünde-East's priorities. The A-9 glider missile would be put on the back burner, and the majority of the Projects Office would be dispersed into test and development branches. Only a vestige under Ludwig Roth would continue as the design bureau for a new antiaircraft missile to be built for the Air Ministry.[7]

Just a week before the successful A-4/V4 launch, von Braun had led a meeting in Peenemünde to discuss the implications of the new flak program reluctantly issued by Göring on 1 September. As a result of the energetic campaign of advocates in the antiaircraft branch, air defense missiles were put back on the agenda, after having been scratched in 1941. The increasing force of the British strategic bomber offensive, the prospect of an American one, and the apparent dead end of trying to design ever more powerful guns to knock down aircraft at ever higher altitudes were behind this decision. It was a reasonable long-term program, but as a short-term response to a worrying situation, it was quite unrealistic, based as it was on very optimistic assumptions about possible guidance technologies—optimistic assumptions that von Braun initially shared. The tactical demands of the Luftwaffe program led Dornberger's section to propose two missiles, a smaller solid-fuel one and a larger liquid-fuel rocket based on the hypergolic combination of nitric acid and a hydrocarbon, such as had been contemplated for the A-8. While the former project would soon be canceled in favor of an industrial contractor, the latter would become Wasserfall (Waterfall), von Braun's second major development project for the next two years.[8]

Just as this new interservice project was getting under way—the first major collaboration since the end of the rocket aircraft program—rivalry reappeared, showing how complicated army–air force relations were. On 9 October Dornberger ordered von Braun to report in one week on Cherry Stone, the Luftwaffe's cruise missile project. "Recently there have been repeated remarks from government offices, firms, etc., that the A-4 program no longer has the importance ascribed to it by its participants." Indeed, Cherry Stone might even overtake the ballistic missile project and make it "illusory"—assertions that obviously reflected hostility in the air force to the A-4, which some viewed as treading on their turf. After talking to friends and acquaintances in the Air Ministry and Peenemünde-West, von Braun sent an encouraging reply on the sixteenth: the flying bomb had every prospect of success, and would be cheaper, but its lesser velocity of impact, poorer accuracy, and vulnerability to conventional air defenses and to attacks on its fixed launch sites gave it no clear advantage. His memo did little to reassure Dornberger, but von Braun clearly thought the two missiles might be complementary rather than competitive.[9]

Under Speer's influence, Hitler had come to the same conclusion two or three days earlier. But he remained lukewarm to the two weapons, asserting that either should be deployed only if five thousand were available for a gigantic "mass attack," which was absurd on production and deployment grounds. It took the military setbacks of November to move him to start grasping at straws. Early in the month Rommel's army began to crumble and retreat at El Alamein; on the eighth Anglo-American troops landed in Morocco and Algeria; on the nineteenth the Red Army began its offensive around Stalingrad, leading quickly to an encirclement of the Sixth Army. On 22 November Speer had a long meeting with Hitler about armaments. The minister's summary states: "The Führer takes great interest in the production planning for A-4 and believes that—if the necessary numbers can be produced—one can make a very strong impression on England with this weapon." Hitler went on to suggest a couple of technically dubious improvements to the warhead and ordered big bunkers to be built on the Channel coast for A-4 deployment.[10]

This requirement set off "some hot debates" between the Peenemünde engineers and Dornberger. One day after receiving the order, von Braun described a preliminary design for a massive bunker with three platforms that could roll the missiles outside just before launch. He must have spent many hours sketching and planning with his old Raketenflugplatz friend Klaus Riedel, since 1940 his special assistant for planning military ground equipment. (Thiel had replaced Riedel as head of the test stands when he moved from Kummersdorf.) Von Braun argued that a bunker was better suited to the preparation of the technologically immature missile (i.e., much more like a test stand) than the mobile units, which could come later. Dornberger, on the other hand, a veteran of the heavy artillery, had always argued for the superiority of the ballistic missile over long-range guns because of lightweight equipment; he saw the bunkers as a serious mistake. Later, after they were bombed mercilessly, von Braun would have to admit he was right, but in the short run Dornberger had little choice but to go along, as building the bunkers was not one of those "Führer orders" that could be easily ignored.[11]

Why von Braun thought the A-4 too technically immature is easily understandable from the frustrating results of the launch program. The next five failed, each worse than the last, culminating in V10, which toppled over at liftoff in January 1943 and detonated with a tremendous explosion, damaging much of the launch equipment. The first rocket to exceed the 3 October distance was launched in mid-February; the first rocket to exceed the advertised range of 270 km was fired in mid-April, but it crashed on land 38 km (24 mi) to the right of the specified trajectory. Although the range was something to celebrate, the first really satisfactory launch took place in late May 1943.[12]

Notwithstanding the early failures, Albert Speer moved energetically in December 1942 to take control of A-4 production, just as he had other sectors of the war economy. He got Hitler to sign an order authorizing manufacturing, and on the twenty-second he met Dornberger, Ordnance chief Leeb, and others in his Berlin office to discuss preparations for the bunkers, road-mobile units, and production. It is not clear if von Braun was present. Speer introduced Dornberger to Gerhard Degenkolb, a engineering manager from heavy industry who had made a name for himself in 1942 as the "czar" of locomotives, shaking up production at a time when the Nazi empire was desperately short of transport.[13]

Heavyset, with a bull neck and completely bald head, Degenkolb was an old party member with a restless and dictatorial personality. Speer gave him the job of organizing Special Committee A-4, with the task of overhauling the production process, which was in a terrible state. An attempt to produce a complete set of production drawings in 1942 had been a total failure because of the ever-changing design of components and shortages of raw materials. When Degenkolb went to work in January 1943, he set up a system of subcommittees of engineers and industrial representatives on the Speer model. Von Braun was made the head of the Final Acceptance Subcommittee, "which made it my business," he later said, "to specify the requirements and test procedures for all component parts and . . . prevent inadequately manufactured parts from reaching the assembly line." Degenkolb's emphasis on quantity over quality guaranteed fiery confrontations with von Braun, who in later years remembered how they had "often and thoroughly battled" with each other.[14]

One problem was that von Braun and his organization saw every vehicle as a handcrafted experiment subject to endless improvement. Wilhelm Raithel, then chief of structures, recalls that sometime in 1943 he told von Braun of a design weakness in the instrument compartment that might be leading to failures. " 'Well,' he said, 'there's a missile sitting there that's going to be launched tomorrow morning, bright and early. Why don't you fix it up. It has already been checked out.' " Raithel was "squeamish" about doing that, because if it failed he might be blamed. Von Braun told him: "I can arrange it for you to meet the best welder we have here, and I'll tell the guard, whom I know personally, . . . and just the few of us will know." Raithel met the welder in the dead of night, they strengthened the instrument compartment, and the missile flew successfully the next day. This improvement was then introduced into later rockets, but such last-minute modifications, which were far from atypical, made proper documentation and a rational process of introducing new changes impossible. It was precisely what Dornberger had complained about a year previously, after the first accident with the A-4/V1. In defense of von Braun, the missile was far too experimental to have been rushed into production, but these sorts of habits had to be unlearned only through a painful process of coming to grips with industrial methods forced through by Degenkolb and the Armaments Ministry.[15]

As Speer's "muscle men" (as von Braun later called them) moved in on the A-4 program, the SS also became involved, at the invitation of Dornberger and Rudolph. On 11 December 1942 Reichsführer-SS Himmler made his first visit to Peenemünde in order to watch the launch of the A-4/V9, which crashed spectacularly after only four seconds. His purpose seems to have been entirely informational: to see the miracle weapon endorsed by the Führer less than three weeks before. We do not know if von Braun was present, although it seems very likely in view of the launch. (The later loss of his flight log for mid-1940 to mid-1943, along with most of his personal papers before 1945, makes it difficult to know his whereabouts.) Only five days later, SS-Gruppenführer (Major General) Gottlob Berger, one of Himmler's top deputies, sent his boss a letter. Lieutenant Colonel Stegmaier, an old friend and Nazi enthusiast, "who was happy as a small child about his special greeting from the Reichsführer SS," asked him to convey the following message: "The section chief, Col. *Dornberger* wishes to make an official presentation to the Führer, together with the developer [of the missile] Dr. *v. Braun*, in order to . . . hear the views and wishes of the Führer, especially regarding the deployment possibilities of the device."[16]

Dornberger was trying to make an end run around Speer in order to go directly to Hitler, perhaps to make a final appeal against the bunker idea. He got nowhere, as Himmler apparently did not approach Hitler for some time, and then was turned down. At the end of January 1943 Dornberger again used the Stegmaier-Berger connection to appeal to Himmler to intervene with the Führer for higher priorities for A-4 electronic equipment over radar, again without result. These letters give the lie to Dornberger's postwar memoirs, which, like so many others, use the SS as a scapegoat and alibi. Rather than Himmler moving in from the outset as a dark force looking to take over the project, Dornberger invited him in.[17]

Once there, however, Himmler did exploit the connection. At the end of March, when the Gestapo falsely reported that Zanssen had contact with a Catholic anti-Nazi group in the nearby city of Stettin, Himmler asked Berger to talk to Stegmaier. The development works chief visited Berger over the weekend and secretly stabbed his superior in the back, describing him as an alcoholic of dubious political opinions. Zanssen, who had apparently become alienated from the regime after his service on the Eastern Front, was temporarily removed from his position of commander (a title earlier upgraded from commandant, reflecting the center's massive growth). Dornberger spent the summer at Peenemünde, until Zanssen could be cleared and then return. Himmler thus lost this battle, but it was a foretaste of future interventions.[18]

Meanwhile the SS's involvement in the army rocket program had deepened considerably in April, with the decision to use concentration camp labor. The context was a national labor shortage, combined with the intense pressure from the regime to accelerate missile production at a time when the war was going badly. On 3 February the government announced the loss of the entire Sixth Army at Stalingrad, a setback so grave it could not be covered up. On the eighteenth Goebbels gave his infamous speech in Berlin calling for "total war" and began to emphasize the new miracle weapons that would be coming to reverse the tide. A campaign of vague hints and deliberately planted rumors soon stirred great hope in a large part of the population. In the interim Degenkolb rapidly escalated the production targets to levels von Braun and his associates found incredible. In early April he decided that output by December would be nine hundred A-4s per month—three hundred each from three factories: Peenemünde, Zeppelin/Friedrichshafen, and Rax-Werke in Wiener Neustadt, Austria, formerly a locomotive plant. Shortly thereafter Degenkolb accelerated this goal to September. To keep his people in line, von Braun was compelled to issue a circular order on 30 April that the new Degenkolb program was the only valid one. Always the loyal soldier once commanded to do something, he laid out various deadlines for the completion of drawing sets and parts lists that he knew full well were optimistic or even utopian.[19]

But where would the laborers come from? The Peenemünde plant was supposed to use many skilled workers, but that became unrealistic as the Eastern Front absorbed German men of fighting age. The year 1942 saw the accelerating conversion of the war economy to heavy dependence on foreign labor, first through the exploitation of surviving Soviet POWs (the Wehrmacht had allowed three million to die of disease and starvation in 1941–42), followed by the dragooning of large numbers of civilian laborers from the occupied countries, and then by a massive expansion in the employment of SS concentration camp prisoners outside the main camps. The construction site at Peenemünde had used small numbers of foreign workers since 1939, but in 1942 Speer's organization began to employ several thousand forced laborers, mostly Poles and Soviets, on the completion of the production plant, the new electrical power and liquid-oxygen facilities in Peenemünde village, and the electrical commuter rail system that began running in 1943. Earlier concerns about secrecy had to be relaxed, and the forced laborers became a source of leaks to British intelligence, but they worked under harsh racial rules and exploitative conditions typical of "Eastern workers." Von Braun was certainly aware of them but bore no direct responsibility for their conditions and likely paid no attention to them. Stegmaier's 10 October 1942 memo, however, mentioned that Soviet POWs would in the future be used in nonsecret areas of the development works, and indeed two small camps were set up, which did put him in the line of responsibility. Not surprisingly, when Arthur Rudolph outlined the labor plan for the Peenemünde factory in February 1943, A-4 production was now to be done primarily by "Russians."[20]

After the 8–9 April visit to Peenemünde of a Mr. Jaeger, responsible for labor supply in Special Committee A-4, Rudolph and his boss, Godomar Schubert, quickly accepted Jaeger's suggestion to use concentration camp laborers instead. On Monday the twelfth Rudolph visited the huge Oranienburg plant of Heinkel Aircraft, just north of Berlin, to view the exploitation of SS prisoners there. He came back with a ringing endorsement: "Provisions, clothing, sanitary arrangements, etc., guarding naturally above all, are carried out by the SS, so that the factory has only to be concerned with the labor supply." The system had "considerable advantages" over other forms of foreign labor not only because of that but also because it offered "greater protection of secrecy." He concluded: "Production in the F1 [main assembly building] can be carried out by prisoners."[21]

When Dornberger went on a Special Committee trip to Friedrichshafen and Wiener Neustadt a few days later, he participated in the decision to expand concentration camp labor to Rax-Werke; Zeppelin had already added SS prisoners to the POWs and forced laborers in its workforce. The Air Ministry then decided it wanted a concentration camp for Peenemünde-West, which was set up first, on 22 May, right by one of the main roads around the Luftwaffe facility. In preparation the SS had established new security checkpoints around the island a day earlier. That camp held at least five hundred male prisoners, all non-Jewish, shipped from Buchenwald, but it officially was a subcamp of the main women's camp of Ravensbrück. On 17 June two hundred more men, "half German, half Russian," arrived from Buchenwald for the Peenemünde production plant and were housed in the F1. Another four hundred, many of them French, followed on 11 July. The factory liaison to this camp, which also reported to Ravensbrück, was von Braun's close friend Arthur Rudolph.[22]

At the time the development works and the rocket factory were separate directorates reporting to the commander, so von Braun took no part in the decision to use slave labor and bore no official responsibility for it. Yet once again he must have been well informed about what was going on. After the war he avoided any mention of the existence of concentration camp labor in Peenemünde, knowing how damaging that information would be to his reputation and to the myth of the rocket center as a "clean" research facility insulated from the worst aspects of the Third Reich.[23] Thus we can say nothing definite about his reaction to the arrival of SS prisoners, but it is unlikely that he thought much about it at all, preoccupied as he was by the immense technical challenges of pushing the A-4 into production—not to mention Wasserfall, which had finally gathered momentum when the Air Ministry began to assign personnel to Peenemünde-East.

A political conformist and nationalist who had no previous contact with concentration camp prisoners, von Braun was also undoubtedly influenced by the regime's propaganda, which described the camps as sites of punishment and labor for dangerous opponents and antisocial elements. Indeed, Dornberger gave a speech describing the newly arriving camp inmates as "murderers, thieves, criminals." According to Dieter Huzel, an electrical engineer who arrived in the summer of 1943, it was only after he encountered a group of Peenemünde-West prisoners in mid-1944 that he had a "feeling of uneasiness" about the concentration camps. "What had started as a means of getting able-bodied prisoners to do useful work had apparently turned into a device for political persecution." In fact, the Nazis had created the camps in 1933 for the express purpose of destroying the left-wing opposition, then expanded them to take in other perceived enemy groups, including finally Jews simply as Jews rather than as members of other targeted categories. Contrary to later assertions by the German populace that "we didn't know," the camps were well publicized and praised in the illustrated press before 1939.[24]

Sometime after 1953, probably in the late 1960s or early 1970s, von Braun told space and science fiction author Arthur C. Clarke: "I never knew what was happening in the concentration camps. But I suspected it, and in my position I could have found out. I didn't and I despise myself for it." Knowing what we know now about his direct encounter with SS prisoners starting in mid-1943, the first sentence of this statement could be interpreted as a bald-faced lie. But more likely this unconvincing piece of self-criticism, which Clarke quotes without context, refers to the Holocaust rather than to slave labor in the rocket program.[25]

Von Braun seems to have modeled his statement on Albert Speer's late-1960s denials of knowledge of the genocide, now shown to be false. Recent research has demonstrated that the mass shootings of Jews in the East were widely known among the German populace, and a minority also heard about the general program of extermination from the BBC's German-language broadcasts. What was lacking was any understanding of the very secret, post-1941 gassing program at six camps in Poland, although the BBC broadcast details of Auschwitz back to Germany in 1944. Listening to foreign radio was certainly dangerous because of the possibility of denunciation to the Gestapo, and the horror stories sounded like enemy propaganda, yet millions listened anyway, and rumors circulated. Indeed, von Braun says in one memoir: "We heard rumors of concentration camp atrocities. They were unbelievable at first." But he could not have avoided hearing about the deportation of tens of thousands of Berlin Jews beginning in 1941, although he may have blinded himself as to their fate. From late 1943 on he also traveled frequently to Poland, where a new A-4 test range was set up. If he knew nothing about the Holocaust, it was only because he was working with feverish intensity on innumerable technical problems and just did not want to know.[26]

When Himmler came for his second visit to Peenemünde on the evening of 28 June 1943, he probably said little specific about the Jews, but von Braun did hear the Reichsführer-SS's long explanation of the necessity for a brutal racial policy toward the occupied Slavs. Although the rocket engineer never discussed this visit publicly, Dornberger devotes a whole chapter of his book to their conversation with Himmler late into the night in the Hearth Room of the officers' club, together with Stegmaier, Steinhoff, and others. Von Braun likely was sitting around the table in the black dress uniform of an SS-Hauptsturmführer (captain), because Dornberger ordered him to wear it for the Reichsführer-SS, and one photograph from the next day—the only so far known to exist—shows him, half hidden by Himmler, doing so. The program for the twenty-ninth featured two A-4 launches instead of one. The first rocket crashed embarrassingly on the Peenemünde-West airfield, creating a huge crater and destroying some aircraft, but the second worked well. Himmler was sufficiently impressed to give von Braun an early promotion to Sturmbannführer (major), dated to 28 June. Two weeks earlier Hitler had approved Dornberger's appointment to brigadier general.[27]

While in Peenemünde, Himmler might have asked von Braun about a personal matter: three months previously the young engineer had asked his office's permission to marry, which the SS strictly controlled to maintain racial and hereditary purity. On 25 March von Braun had sent the SS Race and Settlement Main Office a request for the proper paperwork. "As a result of the total loss that the parents of my fiancée suffered in the last big raid on Berlin, I would like to carry out the wedding as soon as possible, so I would be thankful for an acceleration of this matter. A hereditary pass for my fiancée is enclosed." The woman in question was Dorothee Brill, a Berlin physical education teacher; they had been engaged since January. He returned the preliminary application, on 5 April 1943, coincidentally her twenty-sixth birthday; he had just passed his thirty-first. This time the cover letter was properly addressed through Himmler, who was also head of that office. At the top of the typed letter on personal stationery, to which he added his SS rank, someone wrote "*Führer!* [Leader!]"—addressing Himmler in SS style. It may have been one of the Reichsführer's subordinates.[28]

What do we know about Dorothee Brill and her romance with Wernher von Braun? Very little, as the engagement quickly collapsed, the SS marriage file ends without explanation, no personal correspondence about the engagement is known to have survived the war, and he and his friends rarely talked about it afterward. Until von Braun's SS records came into the public domain in the 1980s, no one outside his personal circle even knew he tried to marry someone other than his later wife. The only possible hint at the length of the relationship comes from von Braun's close friend Erich Warsitz, the former test pilot. Forced to stop flying for health reasons in 1940–41, Warsitz had set up or taken over a firm in Nazi-occupied Amsterdam and began manufacturing components for Peenemünde. He filled out one of the two mandatory SS questionnaires about Brill, whom he had known "for many years." To the question of her political reliability, Warsitz, an early party member, wrote: "The fiancée and her family are certainly to be regarded as reliable defenders of the National Socialist worldview. The fiancée as a sports teacher has contributed personally and voluntarily to the physical training of youth." Born in the southwestern German university town of Tübingen, she had lived with her parents in the well-to-do Berlin suburb of Steglitz and came from an educated middle-class background. There is no indication that she had been at Peenemünde in the labor service, so they must have met through friends and seen each other during his frequent trips to the capital.[29]

Judging by the very traditional manner in which von Braun sought permission to marry from his parents in 1946, he would have consulted them, as he was expected to do. His parents had in fact obstructed a previous engagement of Sigismund, but they learned from the resulting conflict and stood aside when Sigis proposed to another, Hildegard Margis, before going back to Ethiopia in 1939. (In early January 1943, in a happy family event, the two returned from British internment in Kenya after a diplomatic exchange, bringing their new baby daughter, Carola, with them.) Magnus and Emmy von Braun did not stop Wernher's engagement either; they filled out the elaborate SS genealogical chart tracing his ancestors back through seven generations. But they never sent it in, as the relationship collapsed soon after their son's SS application. According to a former secretary, Dorothea "Dorette" Kersten Schlidt, his mother had intervened after all—there was something about Dorothee Brill she did not like.[30]

For von Braun, this setback was a stunning blow; another secretary reports that he had been very happy whenever he came back from visiting her in Berlin. She believes that he had looked forward to establishing a private life outside the nonstop pressures of his office. In the aftermath, von Braun—whom a British reporter later called "handsome enough to be a film star, and he knows it"—reverted to an earlier pattern of a string of less serious affairs.[31]

We know of one of these especially. In April 1963, in the midst of the race to the Moon, he received at his NASA office a letter from a Frenchwoman. In a five-page letter in French that he painstakingly translated into German, she wrote passionately of their 1943 affair in Paris, which he apparently visited several times as a result of A-4 deployment preparations in northeastern France. She had seen him on TV speaking in French, and wanted to write, "because for twenty years scarcely a day has gone by without you being the object of my secret thoughts." The letter paints a scene worthy of a Hollywood war film: "When you came to see me for the last time, at 50 Ponthieu Street in Paris in 1943, my mother told you that I was in prison, and asked that you do everything possible to get me out, and you promised that too." She was released at the beginning of 1944, but she had not yet reached her low point. In August 1944, after the liberation, she was one of the women persecuted and imprisoned for collaboration. She was questioned before the tribunal about their relationship but was in luck because no one could give his last name. "My cleaning lady and my concierge called you 'Monsieur Werner,' and another piece of luck for me was that I thought then that you headed a factory in Poland, and that is all." If they had really known who he was, she would "without a doubt have been sentenced to death and executed." After spending a year in prison in "indescribable circumstances," she was released and emigrated, penniless, to French Morocco.[32]

In 1957 she saw his picture in an illustrated magazine. It was "clear to me in that moment to what degree you had played a role in my misfortune, and why the Gestapo had gone to such lengths to separate us. In this situation it was also unbelievable that we tried to keep up a love affair in the middle of the war, in such difficult circumstances." She also attributed to the secret police the disappearance of all her letters to Peenemünde (although he perhaps merely did not answer them). After her 1957 discovery that he was alive and famous, she wanted at all costs to see him but eventually gave up the idea as impractical. A couple of years later she was forced to leave Morocco with the French departure and ended up in the Pyrenees. "Today I am still just as poor, with all of my wonderful memories and much bitterness in my heart." When she saw him on television that night before, "my heart began to pound. . . . You are my joy and my misfortune and I will always love you." In the end, she knew that perhaps all he could do would be to secretly send her some money to help her leave the backwater she was stranded in. As there is nothing further in von Braun's file, he apparently decided to leave the letter unanswered.[33]

Whatever the vicissitudes of his private life, in spring–summer 1943 von Braun devoted almost all of his waking hours to meetings or to flying around the country in an attempt to rush the ballistic missile into production, while pushing forward Wasserfall. The number of technical and organizational problems was simply overwhelming, and it was only due to his enormous energy, commitment, and optimism that he was able to master the stress. To take a few examples, in March von Braun told Degenkolb that the production of valves, which were so critical to the complicated propulsion system, had been neglected, and much needed to be done to get past this bottleneck. In May he sent a long memo to Dornberger about the problem of building up an engine test site at Rax-Werke in Austria—every engine and every turbopump had to be calibrated and then matched. Even though they were already completely overburdened in Peenemünde, he concluded from their experience with the Zeppelin test site that if they let Ordnance's procurement office try to build it on their own, "nothing intelligent would ever come of it." The same day von Braun chaired a meeting about the aerodynamic design of Wasserfall, and a week later he attended a higher-level gathering in which he and Dornberger told the Luftwaffe representative that if they really wanted to build five thousand missiles a month they would need an aircraft firm to produce them and thousands of workers—but the Air Ministry said there was no capacity in industry. In late June he sent a memo to Steinhoff and others about the numerous delays in electrical and guidance equipment; his former design bureau chief "Papa" Riedel was appointed his special assistant for tracking deadlines—yet another attempt to find something for him to do after failing both in his old job and in the creation of production drawings.[34]

In addition, a constant stream of Third Reich bigwigs like Himmler were now passing through Peenemünde, and von Braun had to be present. Dornberger counted on his masterful salesmanship and ability to speak to laymen. The most notable event was the so-called comparison shoot of 26 May, in which Speer brought Grand Admiral Karl Dönitz, Luftwaffe Field Marshal Erhard Milch, and Army Armaments chief General Fritz Fromm, among others, to the rocket center. There was to be a competition between the A-4 and the Fieseler Fi 103 cruise missile (earlier known as Cherry Stone). Even though the Fi 103 failed twice, versus one success and one partial success for the ballistic missile, the day appears to have been nothing but a political exercise organized by Speer, who wanted to build both—and that is what the meeting approved. Speer promised to grant the A-4 a "DE" superpriority until the end of the year, to try to clear out of the way remaining obstacles and bottlenecks toward the fulfillment of the Degenkolb program, and a week later it was done.[35]

The final seal of approval came on the morning of 7 July, when Dornberger suddenly received a call from Speer: the Führer wanted to hear an A-4 presentation that very day. He and von Braun must come to the Wolfsschanze at once. After hurriedly gathering the film that had been made about the 3 October 1942 launch, plus charts, graphs, and models of the launch bunker and of the road vehicles for the A-4 batteries, the two took off in a Heinkel 111 with Ernst Steinhoff as primary pilot. (Afterward Himmler forbade them to fly together again in case a crash hobbled the whole program.) A thick fog had settled over Peenemünde and the Baltic coast, but once they crossed the Vistula, the forests and lakes of East Prussia spread out before them. After landing in Rastenburg, they were told that the audience had been postponed to five in the afternoon, and they were taken to the army guesthouse.[36]

An hour before the talk von Braun, Dornberger, and Steinhoff began negotiating the gauntlet of security posts and fences to reach the innermost area of the Wolfsschanze, as they had on 20 August 1941. They arrived at the film projection room, put up their materials, and waited. The appointed hour was soon long past.

> Suddenly [Dornberger later wrote] the door opened and we heard someone call out, "The Führer!" Hitler appeared in the company of [Field Marshal] Keitel, [General] Jodl, [General] Buhle, Speer, and their personal aides. No visitors were allowed. I was shocked by the change in Hitler. A voluminous black cape covered his bowed, hunched shoulders and bent back. He wore a field-gray tunic and black trousers. He looked a tired man. Only the eyes retained their life. Staring from a face grown unhealthily pallid from living in huts and shelters, they seemed to be all pupils.

The Führer and his entourage quickly sat down in front, and after a few introductory remarks by Dornberger, the silent film began, with von Braun's narration. "For the first time," says Speer in his memoirs, "Hitler saw the majestic spectacle of a great rocket rising from its pad and disappearing into the stratosphere. Without a trace of timidity and with a boyish enthusiasm, von Braun explained his theory." When von Braun was asked afterward how he could speak so assuredly in front of great men, he said he imagined them all in their underwear.[37]

The film closed with the written motto: "*Wir haben es doch geschafft!* [We made it after all!]" "Von Braun ceased speaking. Silence. No one dared utter a word." Hitler appeared "moved" and "agitated." As Dornberger began further explanations, the dictator now seemed transfixed, jumping up to look at the table with the models on it, interjecting questions. What exactly happened next is unclear, as the various memoirs are inconsistent. Speer remembers only Hitler's unbridled enthusiasm. He was in a good mood; his last, ultimately futile offensive on the Eastern Front, at Kursk, had begun just two days earlier. Dornberger remembers asking Hitler not to believe that the ballistic missile was a "wonder weapon"—a hardly credible assertion from a man who had pushed the war-winning potential of the A-4 since 1939. In the general's telling, Hitler even exploded momentarily when

Dornberger explained that he could not have a bigger warhead or more rockets for some years. "A strange, fanatical light flared up in Hitler's eyes. . . . 'But what I want is annihilation—annihilating effect!'" Dornberger had to appease him. Yet he remembers Hitler twice apologizing for not having earlier believed in his work.[38]

Von Braun had his own curious encounter with the Führer. As he explained the greatly added impact energy of the supersonic rocket, doubling or tripling the explosive power of the one-ton warhead, Hitler interjected: "The contact fuse of normal bombs operates with such a large delay that, with the high impact velocity of the rocket, its warhead will penetrate too far into the earth. The explosion will mostly throw up a lot of dirt and the impact effect will be reduced." Von Braun listened respectfully but did not believe him, although in fact no one had ever worked out theoretically what would actually happen in a Mach 3 impact. Soon after getting back to Peenemünde he asked for an investigation, and it turned out Hitler was correct. Von Braun was quite impressed with the dictator's knowledge of weapons technology.[39]

As the Führer and his entourage prepared to leave at the end of the briefing, von Braun noticed Dornberger whispering to Speer, then Speer doing the same with the dictator. "A few moments later Hitler stepped up to me, reached for my hand and said: 'Professor, I would like to congratulate you on your success.' In this most unconventional way I received the title." In Germany it was and is possible to receive the title, normally given only to holders of senior academic chairs, as a high government honor; Hitler had earlier made professors of then-architect Albert Speer and aircraft designer Willy Messerschmitt. Dornberger had asked Speer on 26 May to give his protégé the honorific, and now the armaments minister had no problem delivering. Hitler told Speer: "Yes, arrange that at once with Meissner [one of his senior assistants], . . . I'll even sign the document in person." Afterward he pressed Speer: "Weren't you mistaken? You say this young man is thirty-one? I would have thought him even younger!" In future monologues Hitler often rambled on about how most people wasted the best years of their lives, mentioning Alexander the Great's conquests in his twenties and Napoleon's victories at age thirty. "In connection with this he would often allude, as if casually, to Wernher von Braun, who at so young an age had created a technical marvel at Peenemünde." Two weeks later Dornberger handed von Braun a large diploma with Hitler's crabbed, bizarre signature. He loved being called Professor and continued to accept it from his German subordinates well into the 1950s, until its dubious origins became an embarrassment.[40]

Hitler finally left the room, giving the rocketeers "an extremely cordial good-by." As they walked out with Speer, they ran into one of the minister's top economic managers, Hans Kehrl. Speer introduced von Braun, saying: "Congratulate the youngest professor of the Third Reich."

I congratulated him and we talked without Speer for half an hour, naturally only about rockets. Braun was in a euphoria over all the future possibilities. After the first tests in Peenemünde, the most difficult problem, the take-off from the ground, could be regarded as solved. Only with the "directional capability" were there still problems. Von Braun nonetheless enthused about how one day men would fly to the moon with the help of the rocket. That was too much for me! When I told my wife about this encounter, I began the conversation with the remark: "At headquarters today I met a real lunatic."[41]

In view of Kehrl's anecdote, how credible then is von Braun's statement that, at his last meeting with the dictator, "Hitler suddenly appeared to me as an irreligious man, a man who did not have the feeling of being responsible to a higher power, someone for whom there was no God. . . . He was completely unscrupulous." Obviously, as a memory of his immediate reaction to the meeting, it is not credible at all; moreover, his religious conversion experience did not occur until he was in Texas in 1946. Before then he was a nominal Lutheran, although he did not resign from the church and declare himself simply "*gottgläubig* [believer in God]," as good SS men were expected to do. Yet it is undoubtedly true that his alienation from the regime would increase in the next months, as it became apparent to him that exaggerated hopes were put on the missile, which could never reverse the catastrophic course of Hitler's war. Thus it is possible that one of the longer-term effects of the dictator's outbursts on 7 July was to initiate this process of disillusionment.[42]

One thing is certain: Hitler's blessing only magnified missile mania in the highest reaches of the regime. Speer's deputy for technical issues, the engineer Karl Otto Saur, converted from A-4 skeptic to rocket fanatic. He immediately set out to double the goal of the Degenkolb program to eighteen hundred A-4s per month and threatened prominent industrialists with Gestapo arrest for sabotage if they questioned the feasibility of this absurd objective—one of them being the liquid-oxygen-equipment manufacturer Paul Heylandt, who had supported Max Valier's primitive experiments only thirteen years previously. In early August Speer himself had to put the brakes on Saur by reinstating Degenkolb's production program, as least in the shorter run. Far from 7 July 1943 being the great breakthrough in

Hitler's approval, as Dornberger later pictured it in his memoirs, the second visit to the Wolfsschanze was merely the capstone and the reward for decisions made by Hitler and Speer dating back to November 1942; its effects were mostly counterproductive.[43]

Tuesday, 17 August 1943, was the last day of the old Peenemünde. It had been a hot summer's day, perfect for going to the beach—for the few who had the time. Dornberger remembers a heated meeting that afternoon in the commander's office, in which von Braun, among others, complained of the overwhelming problems of trying to meet the deadlines for A-4 production. That evening, however, they all relaxed and laughed over drinks at a gathering in the officers' club for the famous test pilot and favorite of Hitler's, Hanna Reitsch, who had taken glider training with von Braun so many years ago in the Silesian mountains. She had recently recovered from a serious crash in the Me 163 rocket fighter.[44]

Joining them at the party was von Braun's slim, boyish-looking, twenty-four-year-old brother Magnus Jr., who had arrived one month previously. Greatly influenced by his charismatic sibling, Magnus had pursued a chemical engineering degree at the Munich Institute of Technology, graduating with excellent grades in 1940. Like his brother, he had become an enthusiastic sailplane pilot, but because it was war, he was drafted into the Luftwaffe immediately upon graduation. Somehow avoiding frontline service, Magnus became an experienced night and instrument flying instructor at various schools, until Wernher initiated a transfer to Peenemünde in the spring of 1943 for the Wasserfall missile project. Magnus's education was certainly valuable to the propellant development section, his initial assignment, but the family also wanted him kept away from the front. In view of the casualty rate of Luftwaffe pilots, especially in the last two years of the war, this move probably saved his life.[45]

Around eleven p.m., as "the party broke up," von Braun escorted Reitsch to the car that was to take her to her quarters. He retired to his rooms nearby.

I had just fallen asleep when the sirens sounded. Upon hearing aircraft noises, I hastily dressed, went outside and walked over to the air raid alert and communications center to get a status report. . . . Waves of bombers coming from England were reported approaching across Denmark and Schleswig-Holstein. As this was a frequently traveled "minimum flak exposure route" to Berlin, the consensus . . . was that this was just another of those rather frequent raids on Berlin.

Radio reports that the night fighters had been dispatched to the capital "seemed to confirm that assessment. Confident that this was not 'our night,' " von Braun "strolled back" to his quarters with the idea of going to bed again. "As I walked I noticed that the artificial fog system enshrouding the Peenemünde facilities had been activated. Through the thin fog shone the pale reddish disk of a full moon. Suddenly I saw a flare lighting up through the fog, and within a minute the sky was covered with what we called 'Christmas trees.' "[46] These were the British red and green target-marking flares, already known from city raids; three weeks earlier, in a horrible catastrophe, the RAF had succeeded in starting a firestorm in Hamburg, destroying much of the city and killing forty thousand people, an event that had spread a wave of panic across the Reich.

It was about 1:10 a.m., on 18 August. As the flak guns opened up, von Braun proceeded to the main air raid bunker. Shortly thereafter, once the first bombs had already battered the bachelor quarters, Dornberger showed up half in uniform, half in pajamas. The attack was massive—about six hundred heavy bombers with 1,800 tons of bombs—and to the south devastating, although it was some time before von Braun and Dornberger had any picture of what was going on. The first wave of the RAF attack had the housing settlement as target, with the quite conscious objective of killing the center's engineering leadership—the brains behind the newly discovered, exotic weapons system that could threaten Britain. But due to the inherent difficulty of hitting a small target at night, even at full moon, some of the Pathfinders put their markers down two miles south of the settlement, with the result that the full weight of the bombs fell on the Trassenheide forced laborers' camp, with disastrous results. Trapped behind barbed wire and lacking any shelters, six hundred workers were killed. The settlement and the adjoining homes for women at Karlshagen beach were nonetheless hit with a hurricane force, a mixture of high-explosive bombs and incendiaries that demolished and burned almost everything. The slit trenches and shelters recently built for the settlement mostly worked, however, so that the only prominent loss was Walter Thiel and his whole family, whose trench took a direct hit. The attack then advanced up the island, with the production plant being the second objective and the development works the third. Many bombs from these waves also fell to the south, or in the Baltic, so the result was that the huge factory buildings were not much damaged, and the development works were hit hard but only in a scattered way. Some buildings, like the Aerodynamics Institute and all the test stands, were entirely untouched.[47]

Inside the shelter, according to Dornberger's adjutant,

we could feel shock waves through the ground of the nearby hits before we heard their explosions. We were all very anxious for the obvious danger to our lives but there was no panic. . . .

It eventually diminished and finally stopped altogether. We opened the door and found that there were no more aeroplane engines to be heard. We went out of the shelter and saw many of the surrounding buildings on fire. I shall always remember exactly what General Dornberger said: *"Mein schönes Peenemünde!"*—"My beautiful Peenemünde!"; he said it with great sadness.

It was about two in the morning. Dornberger left the shelter with his top people and sent von Braun off to organize the salvaging of Building 4, the development headquarters.[48]

Fire raged from the roof of one wing, and the other wing showed the first flames from incendiaries. Helped by one of Dornberger's officers, Kurt Bornträger, and by one of his secretaries, Dorette Kersten, von Braun plunged into the building to salvage secret documents and plans. Kersten Schlidt (she later married one of the engineers who came to the United States) wrote this account sometime later:

The Professor takes me by hand, quickly and carefully. It roars, crackles, and rattles. Feeling our way along the wall, we find ourselves in the hallway: one, two, three, four, five—yes, that is our door, we must get in! The doors are no longer there. Fire to the left of us and in front of us. We press ourselves flat against the still standing wall. The other half of the room has collapsed.

We are into the room. Open the safe and grab the stuff! I now know the still traversable way, run a few times downstairs loaded with secret files and come back up—until it is no longer possible. The Professor is still up there, along with a few other men. They throw out the window any furniture and things that can still be grabbed. I stay on alert downstairs, chuck everything into the safe, which was moved out the window and is now lying on its back.

This work went on until nearly dawn; characteristically, von Braun showed great physical courage. He and Bornträger would get the War Service Cross, First Class with Swords, for salvaging much of the building. So too would Hermann Oberth, who also rescued documents and materials from other burning structures. Shortly thereafter he finally left Peenemünde, transferring to a firm south of Berlin to work on a solid-fuel antiaircraft missile.[49]

As dawn broke, Dornberger walked south from the production plant buildings. He was stunned to see across an unrecognizable landscape of splintered trees and ruined buildings all the way to the settlement, which was in flames. The base housing was essentially gone. Around eight o'clock von Braun took him up in a Fieseler Storch to look at the damage. It was emotionally wrenching, yet reassuring to see that the test stands had been ignored by the RAF and that the development and production plants were mostly usable.[50]

The raid, which had killed about 135 Germans in addition to the forced laborers, had the effect, however, of scattering the native workforce to the four winds, as many left, or sent their families away, or sought their own local accommodation. Dornberger and von Braun had to rally those remaining. Dieter Huzel, who had had the good fortune to be on a trip, came back two days afterward and found von Braun near the military administration building, speaking through a loudspeaker system on a parked truck, displaying his usual self-possession and leadership skills: "Announcements came from him in a continuous flow, carried by a clear, determined voice, spiced by an occasional humorous remark."[51]

Finding housing was the other urgent need. The army commandeered hotels and houses on Usedom, sending the vacationers home once and for all. Staff members were also quartered on the local population; von Braun even had his favorite relatives, the von Quistorps in Bauer, house a few engineers, as the rocket center's divisions were dispersed across the island or even to the mainland. With his own rooms in Building 5 ruined, von Braun "moved out to one of those charming 'inns by the lagoon,' " the Inselhof (Island Court), in Zempin, south of Zinnowitz.[52]

He probably spent little time there, as he was sucked into a whirlwind of meetings and travel spawned by the raid, which came on top of earlier attacks on Zeppelin and Rax-Werke. At the Wolfsschanze, Himmler convinced Hitler to move A-4 production underground, "with increased use of workers from his concentration camps," and appointed the ruthless and energetic chief of SS construction, Brigadeführer (Brigadier General) Dr. Hans Kammler, to head that up. Albert Speer, who had flown into Peenemünde on the day of the raid, moved quickly to reassert the primacy of the Armaments Ministry in the production of the missile, in collaboration with the SS. On 24 or 25 August, Dornberger called from Berlin, asking his top staff to come to the capital for consultations on moving parts purchasing and rocket assembly away from Peenemünde.[53]

Before departing on 25 August, von Braun chaired a meeting at the center. According to the minutes—the first surviving document linking him to the concentration camp prisoners—he, his deputy Eberhard Rees, and five others discussed using "caves" near Saarbrücken in far western Germany. "The workers for the middle and center section manufacture previously planned for VW [pilot production plant] can be drawn from the prisoner camp F1. The German supervisory personnel will go along with them." That afternoon the group went down to Berlin in a Junkers Ju 52 trimotor piloted by Magnus von Braun, with Wernher as copilot. (He lacked the multiengine ticket necessary to command the airplane.) They returned the same evening. The following day Walter Dornberger met Speer, Kammler, and Degenkolb in the minister's office, where they decided instead to take over a large underground storage facility in north-central Germany near the small city of Nordhausen.[54]

After making another round-trip to Berlin on the twenty-seventh, the von Braun brothers again took off in the Ju 52 on Sunday morning, 29 August, this time heading for Saarbrücken with a stopover in Nordhausen, returning to that place at six p.m. on the thirtieth. Wernher spent three full days around Nordhausen, leaving only on the evening of 2 September. Who else was there and what he did is unknown, but he undoubtedly entered the huge Kohnstein tunnels for the first time through one of the northern entrances to main tunnels A and B, each large enough to accommodate two railroad trains. Less a mountain than a long ridgeline covered in trees, the Kohnstein was a southern extension of the Harz range. About 1.6 km in width, its southeastern end concealed a gigantic, ladderlike tunnel network bent into a gentle S-curve. There was nearly 1 million cu m (35 million cu ft) of space underground. A government company in Hermann Göring's empire had expanded an old anhydrite mine into a central petroleum reserve for the Reich. (Anhydrite rock could be converted to gypsum or used in the chemical industry.) Cross tunnels every 30 m (100 ft) or so contained giant storage tanks, at least up to the middle of the mountain. Beyond that, the tunnels were unfinished, and tunnel A had not yet broken through to the south side. On 28 August the SS had trucked the first 107 concentration camp prisoners from the relatively nearby Buchenwald camp, outside Weimar, and an identical number two days later; one task would be to finish the mining. With no barracks to sleep in, the prisoners of subcamp Dora were first put in tents by the south entrance to tunnel B. Von Braun may well have seen striped uniforms, but the tunnels were not yet the Dante's Inferno they would shortly become.[55]

Throughout the fall von Braun's frantic travel schedule continued, occasioned by the top-to-bottom reorganization of the A-4 production program.

On 9 September he was in Berlin again, reporting to Speer's high-level Long-Range Bombardment Commission: "The development of the A-4 device has practically been brought to a conclusion." It was an extremely optimistic statement in view of the missile's technical inadequacies. He and Dornberger were pressed on the dates for the readiness of the mobile launch units and the firing of missiles with live warheads, but they could not promise the former until December and the latter no earlier than 15 November. Four days after the meeting he and his brother flew for the first time to Mielec, Poland, 100 km (60 mi) east of Krakow, the access point for the SS artillery range at Blizna called Heidelager (Heather Camp). Armed missiles were to be fired northward from there into a thinly populated region to the northeast of Warsaw. Himmler had arranged for testing to be moved when he spoke to Hitler immediately after the raid; the resulting "Führer order" had also included the provision that a new underground development works to replace Peenemünde would be constructed nearby.[56]

That was not feasible, however, in the flat, forested terrain by the confluence of the San and Vistula Rivers, so a suitable location was found in the central Austrian Alps near the Ebensee, a scenic mountain lake. Around the same time, the Armaments Ministry had commandeered a nearby brewery, 55 km (35 mi) east of Salzburg, for an underground liquid-oxygen plant and aboveground engine-testing site to replace the one at Rax-Werke. Von Braun's first visit to the region took place on 16 October, but he was there only long enough to see the engine site code-named "Schlier." He spent a day in the same area later in November and must have also seen the tunneling project at Ebensee, now code-named "Zement." By then both sites had concentration camp laborers working in terrible conditions. In a lengthy memo in early October von Braun had opposed the whole idea of moving his staff underground, based on the future demands of the Wasserfall and A-9 programs and the extremely disruptive character of such an evacuation, but it was to no avail. His influence, and that of Dornberger, was declining as the Armaments Ministry and the SS exerted more and more control.[57]

As part of the postattack reorganization, General Fromm had taken Dornberger out of Army Ordnance as of 1 September and made him a direct subordinate with the title BzbV Heer (an acronym for army commissioner for special tasks). The aim was to make the rocket general supreme commander over the program and future operational commander of the missile, which proved to be impossible because of the rise of Speer's and Himmler's organizations, the opposition of operational officers, and the lack of support even from Hitler as the program fell into crisis that winter. Zanssen returned to

Peenemünde as commander and also took over Dornberger's Ordnance rocket section in Berlin. This double burden proved too much, however, and Ordnance soon split off the solid-fuel programs, then appointed an artillery general, Josef Rossmann, to command the liquid-fuel section. From von Braun's standpoint, all of these changes put Dornberger farther and farther away, both organizationally and geographically. (The general set up headquarters in Schwedt an der Oder, south of Stettin.) He would never again work directly in Dornberger's chain of command, although his father-son relationship with "Seppl," which had been at the heart of army rocket development since 1936, meant that he continued to see Dornberger as his de facto boss. The two were allies, but they now had to work in a much more complicated and nasty political environment, one in which they did not have the freedom Ordnance had once given them.[58]

No one embodied the dangerously politicized postraid environment more than SS-General Kammler. Dornberger's "first impression was of a virile, handsome, and captivating personality. He looked like some hero of the Renaissance, a *condottiere* of the period of the civil wars in northern Italy." He was forty-two and conveyed an air of energy and arrogance. Like Dornberger, von Braun soon came to despise him. In 1946 he told his parents: "Kammler is in fact the greatest rogue and adventurer that I have ever seen. Character acrobat, dynamic personality, actor, criminal, all in one person. A shining product of the atmosphere in which he became 'great.' " Neither man was inclined to give Kammler much credit for competence, even though he had a civil engineering doctorate and carried out his construction projects with speed and success—in large part by showing utter contempt for the lives of the concentration camp prisoners. Dornberger and von Braun knew nothing of Kammler's important role in the Holocaust, supervising the construction of the Auschwitz gas chambers, but they certainly picked up on his ruthlessness and ideological fanaticism. After the war, Kammler was a convenient scapegoat for the murderous treatment of slave labor in the rocket program.[59]

Nowhere were the effects of Kammler's methods so catastrophic as in the Mittelwerk (Central Works)—the name applied to the underground rocket assembly facility near Nordhausen, and to the government company set up by the Speer ministry to run it. By the time von Braun came for his next visit on 8–9 October, there were three to four thousand Dora prisoners living in the tunnels, mostly sleeping on straw or bare rock. Kammler put no priority on building the aboveground camp; bunk beds were constructed instead in cross tunnels 43 to 46 at the southern end of main tunnel A.

When von Braun returned around 26 November, ten thousand were living underground in the new sleeping quarters, including the prisoners evacuated from the F1 in Peenemünde in mid-October. None were Jewish, except for a few who had hidden their background; three-quarters came from the USSR, Poland, or France; and over 10 percent were German, many of them Communists or criminals in slightly more privileged leadership positions as record-keepers, Kapos, and foremen.[60]

The overcrowded, four-story wooden bunks of the so-called sleeping tunnels quickly became contaminated with excrement, lice, and fleas; there were no sanitary facilities for the prisoners, only oil barrels cut in half, and virtually no drinking water. The dimly lit tunnels were cold and damp, and the prisoners wore only thin uniforms that quickly became rags. The work pace was drastic, whether it consisted of disassembling the fuel tanks, unloading factory machinery and rocket parts shipped from the three original sites, or, worst of all, completing the tunneling in the southern end of the complex. Explosions went on day and night next to the sleeping quarters, and the dust created catastrophic lung problems, especially among the mining crew. By November epidemics of pneumonia, dysentery, and typhus raged among the prisoners, exacerbated by exhaustion and starvation. Survivor and French Resistance leader Jean Michel describes the horrifying result:

> Some deportees are too weak and collapse. They have dysentery. They foul their trousers. They no longer have the strength to sit over the barrels, even to get to them. The SS beat them. The blows are useless, they do not get up. They will suffer no more. Those who know in their hearts that they too are at the end of their tether watch in silence. Will they be victims tomorrow? Soon? . . . Woe betide the man who is turned away, not ill enough for the infirmary Kapo! His days are numbered. The Kapos in the tunnel will work him to death.

By December more than twenty prisoners were dying per day.[61]

What did Wernher von Braun know of these horrors? Only in the 1960s and 1970s did he say anything, after sufficient information had come into the public domain to make total silence about Dora no longer a feasible option. In a deposition he gave in 1969 for a West German war crimes trial, he admitted seeing the tunnel accommodations during the mining phase, before production started—that is, in the last months of 1943. "At that time some of the prisoners were housed in these tunnels. I went through these temporary accommodations with some of the observing visitor group." And to an American television interviewer in 1976, he said: "The working conditions there were absolutely horrible. I saw the [M]ittelwerk several times, once while these prisoners were blasting new tunnels in there and it was a pretty hellish environment. I'd never been in a mine before, but it was clearly worse than a mine." He denied, however, ever seeing a dead prisoner, a beating, or a killing, and we cannot prove otherwise, even though a number of survivors assert that he must have seen the pile of dead prisoners in the tunnel. It would not be surprising if representatives of the Mittelwerk like Arthur Rudolph, who had been transferred there in mid-September, avoided taking visitors past that horrific sight. Nor, it must be added, would a brief walk through the "sleeping tunnels" have provided more than an inkling of what it would be like to be a prisoner there. Nonetheless it is clear that he saw a lot.[62]

As to his reaction, we are left only with speculation, as there are no contemporary sources, and all his statements come from decades later, in self-defense. To Bernd Ruland, the author of a heroic German biography published at the time of the 1969 Moon landings, he said: "It naturally left on me an extraordinarily depressing impression each time that I went into the underground plant and had to see the prisoners at work. It is repulsive to be suddenly surrounded by prisoners. The whole atmosphere was unbearable." And in response to accusations by French survivors of Dora, he wrote in a letter to the magazine *Paris Match* in 1966: "I readily agree that the entire environment at Mittelwerk was repulsive, and that the treatment of the prisoners was humiliating. I felt ashamed that things like this were possible in Germany, even under a war situation where national survival was at stake." However, he denied specifically taking any part in hangings, beatings, or other such actions, as was claimed by some survivors, and he said he had not set foot in the aboveground camp to which all prisoners were moved by June 1944. As the inmate areas of concentration camps were off limits to all but a few permitted visitors, and the SS handled all executions and formal beatings, these assertions are almost certainly true, but the bottom line of these and all other statements always seems to be denial of personal responsibility: only the technical dimensions of the rocket program were in his bailiwick, he was based several hundred kilometers away at Peenemünde and came only for visits, and the treatment of prisoners was the sole charge of the SS.[63]

Whether or not von Braun's revulsion at the state of the prisoners in late 1943 was as strong as he later said it was, he likely pushed it quickly to the back of his mind. He could not imagine opposing or subverting the war effort, even when the cause was immoral. He later asserted, regarding the military use of his rocket: "But war is war, and because my country found itself at war, I had the conviction that I did not have the right to bring further moral viewpoints to bear. My duty was to help win the war, whether I had any sympathy for the government or not. I did not have any"—a rather dubious statement before 1944.[64] The ideology that science and technology were neutral and apolitical, which he had absorbed from his youth and education, gave him yet another reason to distance himself from the consequences of his actions; he was merely supplying his expertise to his government, as he was expected to do. Yet driving the ballistic missile program forward at high speed would, as a consequence, also drive many prisoners into an early grave—a result he might have understood but could not accept as a personal responsibility.

To be fair, his ability to help the prisoners was minimal or nonexistent. The SS set the viciously inhuman conditions of the concentration camps, and Kammler violated even those in his relentless drive to transform the tunnels into a ballistic missile factory within months—not to mention finishing the many other sites of the A-4 program in which he was now involved.[65] He and the National Socialist fanatics in the Armaments Ministry, like Degenkolb, Saur, and Kammler's closest ally in the tunnels, diploma engineer Albin Sawatzki (originally sent to Peenemünde to shape up the production plant), saw the A-4 as the salvation of the Reich. They would brook no opposition or delay. But von Braun had helped Dornberger sell the ballistic missile as a war-winning weapon and now had to live with the consequences.

For Wernher von Braun, the implicit bargain he had made with the Nazi regime had come due. If he wished to have money for rocketry, if he wished to have a career, if he wished even to keep himself out of danger from the apparatus of repression, he had to participate in stoking the fires of hell. And he did. The only question is whether he made even a symbolic gesture in favor of bettering prisoner conditions, at least at Dora—in fact, he encountered slave labor at a minimum of eight other sites. The sole evidence that he might have said something comes not from him but from Ernst Stuhlinger, a nuclear physicist sent to Peenemünde in May 1943 after having spent two years as a common soldier in the rear areas of the Eastern Front (a commentary on the low priority assigned to the atomic bomb project). Employed at first in the guidance field, Stuhlinger became von Braun's close friend and scientific adviser in America. In the biography he cowrote long after von Braun's death, Stuhlinger claims that von Braun went to an SS guard in the Mittelwerk to criticize the mistreatment and was crudely threatened with being put in a striped uniform too; later von Braun allegedly went to a higher SS officer and complained that the prisoners' bad health conditions contributed to poor workmanship in manufacturing. The problem is that Stuhlinger attributes an identical encounter with a guard to Arthur Rudolph, whose Nazi enthusiasm is in little doubt, and both von Braun stories are told decades after the fact solely from memory of conversations with him, and in the context of defending him against charges of complicity in the horrors of Dora. As historical evidence, these uncorroborated, second-hand anecdotes are highly dubious, although they cannot be ruled out as impossible.[66]

Any judgment of Wernher von Braun cannot rest, however, solely on unanswerable questions about how deeply he was disturbed by slave labor in the fall of 1943 and whether he made symbolic attempts to better conditions. He could not divorce himself from the administration of concentration camp labor, whether he liked it or not. On 1 November 1943 Kammler, Dornberger, Zanssen, Sawatzki, and others met at the Mittelwerk company headquarters, which was in a school in Ilfeld, a village about 10 km (6 mi) from the tunnels. As usual, manpower shortages and allocation were among the main topics. Sawatzki wanted more Germans from Peenemünde to supplement the 470 blue-collar and 220 white-collar workers so far transferred to the company. As Dornberger could not see how to give any more up, the only other possibility was to take German skilled labor and supervisors from the Schlier and Mitte engine test sites. (Kammler was constructing the latter for the Mittelwerk in a slate quarry in southern Thuringia.) Slave labor would be substituted, which meant that SS prisoners would provide not only the unskilled labor to build the sites but also part of the crew to operate them. Arthur Rudolph and a Mittelwerk director then came up to Peenemünde on 9 November to discuss the manpower question, which had become central to von Braun's management role at least since early 1943. Either before or after that meeting von Braun made detailed handwritten calculations about the allocation of labor throughout the program, including how many could be freed up through the use of slave labor in engine testing. On the twelfth he sent Degenkolb the final proposal, which stated: "You have now given permission that the Schlier and Mitte facilities be manned with prisoners. In view of the difficulty of the testing processes to be carried out there, the ratio of prisoners to German skilled workers for the foreseeable future cannot exceed 2:1." It was for him perhaps only a detail in a complex calculation, but by taking part in a decision to employ more slave labor, he may have been guilty of a "crime against humanity."[67]

Of course, from the point of view of his daily life and job, concentration camp labor *was* only one more detail; serious problems continued to haunt the technically immature A-4 program, particularly in the turbopump–steam generator system, the guidance and control equipment, the servo-motors to move the jet vanes and air vanes, and the production of vehicles for the mobile launch crews. Launch testing resumed at Peenemünde in October or November, and in November firings also began in Poland. A detailed 5 December report written for or by von Braun noted that, of thirty-nine A-4 firings so far since 1942, only fourteen had been successful; eleven had failed due to propulsion problems, and fourteen due to guidance or electrical flaws. Eight of those thirty-nine had recently been launched in Poland, but only one had worked. The Peenemünde raid had set back the production of guidance and electrical equipment in particular, as it had destroyed all the model devices for that sector. In addition, an Allied air attack had ruined the first A-4 bunker in northern France, forcing the modification of a second, nearby bunker begun as a rocket storage dump. Von Braun must have seen these bunkers himself, as he had landed in Brussels on 21 October and spent four days in the West. All in all, the report concluded, the rocket center could not see how the missile could be put into military service before 1 April 1944, and no measures to accelerate it would do any good.[68]

Buried in the midst of this report was a comment that the one successful launch from Heidelager had broken up during reentry into the atmosphere, but that was due only to an easily repairable break in the missile's structural framework. In fact, it was the harbinger of a frustrating "air burst" problem that would plague the program for the next year. But those difficulties were obscured in the short run by other manufacturing and management problems that spawned a new wave of crashes. Tail explosions and control failures at launch endangered the soldiers testing the new mobile equipment; von Braun joked that the purpose of the testing program was to make it more dangerous to be in the target area than in the launch crew.[69]

In a notice he circulated at the beginning of February 1944, he reported that some failures were caused by changes in components not implemented in spite of earlier agreements and decisions; he had decided to create a formal "change service." The changes to the missile numbered twenty-five per day because of substitution of materials and corrections to tolerances, according to the 5 December report, adding up to thousands per year—although this was not a figure unusual to the aircraft industry. The production drawing and parts lists also remained quite unsatisfactory well into 1944. If his task up to the summer of 1943 had been to build a guided-missile technological system, now it was to reorient his Peenemünde development organization to the demands of quantity industrial production even as that organization began to shrink. Not only was von Braun's staff, which peaked at around five thousand people, being bled off slowly to the production side, but he also lost Rudolf Hermann's Aerodynamics Institute altogether, after the two had "a serious tug-of-war" in the fall of 1943 over evacuating the wind tunnels to the Bavarian Alps. By mid-1944 all the tunnels were gone, and the institute was independent.[70]

At the beginning of 1944 the magnitude of the problems created by assembling missiles in unfinished tunnels housing dying slave laborers hit home. The Mittelwerk goal for December had been two hundred A-4s (test missiles were still being built at Peenemünde), but only four or five were artificially forced through to completion by New Year's Eve 1943–44; Rudolph cursed Sawatzki when he was dragged out of his little celebration that evening and sent to the factory to certify their loading. Those first Mittelwerk A-4s were immediately sent back for repair after the first of January because their quality was so poor.[71]

This terrible workmanship immediately raised the specter of "sabotage" by the prisoners—a special warning to that effect was issued by the company head and the camp commandant on 8 January. Seventeen days later von Braun again visited the Mittelwerk and met with Sawatzki, who was infamous among the prisoners for beating and kicking them—as was Rudolph's deputy Karl Seidenstücker, according to survivors. Thus when von Braun claimed in his 1969 court deposition that "I never received an oral or written report that a single suspected or proven case of sabotage had appeared," he was almost certainly lying. It is believable that he never received a formal sabotage report, as these were to be directed to the Mittelwerk security officer, a member of the SD (SS Security Service). But in his informal discussions with Sawatzki, Rudolph, and others, the topic scarcely could have been avoided, as it was on everyone's mind throughout the short history of the Mittelwerk, and prisoners have testified that actual sabotage did take place. The reason for this presumed lie can only be that he saw how damaging it was to admit that he had heard about alleged sabotage, as those unfortunate enough to be accused ended up being hanged with agonizing slowness on the roll-call square of the aboveground camp.[72]

Attempts to blame the victims could not distract, however, from how bad the output of the Mittelwerk was, or how far from functional was the combined production system of Peenemünde, Mittelwerk, and hundreds of industrial contractors. Parts were unreliable, assembly points on the missile did not match, and the jigs, fixtures, and methods of work in the tunnel caused further damage to the A-4s.[73] When combined with the launch failures and growing evidence that a large percentage of the ballistic missiles were breaking up on reentry, this production failure pushed the A-4 program into a severe political crisis in early 1944: the date of deployment of the missile to the front was receding every day. Intense pressure from the Armaments Ministry and the SS now issued into severe criticism of Dornberger, von Braun, and their closest associates for making false promises that development was almost finished. It was a dangerous moment, one that would lead to von Braun's most bizarre and threatening encounter with the Third Reich.

CHAPTER EIGHT

A Young Man, of Very Germanic Appearance

1944–45

"Twenty-five thousand in a year and a half," he said. He was seventeen years old, Polish . . . "Twenty-five thousand in a year and a half. And from each there is only so much." The boy cupped his hands together to show the measure. I followed his glance downward. We were standing at the edge of what had once been a large pit, about eight feet long, six feet wide, and I guessed at six feet deep. It was filled to overflowing with ashes from the furnaces—small chips of human bone—nothing else. Apparently bucketsful had been thrown from a distance, as one might get rid of the ashes in a coal scuttle on a rainy day.
—CHARLES A. LINDBERGH at Dora, May 1945[1]

For Wernher von Braun, the last year of World War II would be the most difficult and dangerous of his entire life. His privileged position in the National Socialist system, his technical leadership, his central role in the development of rocket technology, all of these continued—and all of them were under threat. If, during 1943, heavy-handed political intervention, slave labor, a demagogic dictator, and a war going bad caused him to glimpse for the first time the kind of regime he was serving, 1944 brought an even more disillusioning experience: he too became a target of its apparatus of repression. In the aftermath of his arrest, von Braun realized that not only the future of the army rocket program but also his personal survival might be at stake. Still a believer in Germany, still loyal to Dornberger and the army, and still committed to his organization and to the missiles it had developed, he could easily demonstrate his value to Hitler's government—but could he appear to be enough of a true believer for the fanatics? And if he did convince them, what about the war? Could he salvage his career, and his dreams of spaceflight, out of that government's total collapse?

At 7:10 p.m. on Monday, 21 February 1944, the von Braun brothers landed at Peenemünde-West, after flying in from Nordhausen. It is most likely on this evening that Wernher received an unwelcome phone message from his senior secretary, Mrs. Lewandowski: Reichsführer-SS Heinrich Himmler wished to see him immediately and alone at his field headquarters near the Wolfsschanze, in East Prussia. "I was as much disturbed as I was surprised," he later told his biographer Bernd Ruland. "What did Himmler want with me? I had stayed completely out of the political battles between the army and SS. I could not figure out what Himmler had in mind." But it was an order that could not be ignored, so the next morning he flew into Rasten-burg. Because he did not record this flight in his logbook, and because the Reichsführer did not note it in his desk calendar, the exact date will never be established. Nor do we know if von Braun showed up in SS uniform, which he may well have felt was unavoidable under the circumstances.[2]

Von Braun later remembered Himmler's Hochwald (High Forest) head-quarters as "a temporary type of thing (low, wooden buildings, a 'command train' parked on a ramp, everything well camouflaged)." He found the Reichsführer-SS sitting behind a plain wooden table. In his 1950 draft mem-oir article, von Braun gave this account:

> I must confess that I felt a bit jittery when I was shown into his office, but he greeted me politely and conveyed rather the impression of a country grammar school teacher than that horrible man who was said to wade knee-deep in blood.
>
> "I trust you realize that your A-4 rocket has ceased to be an engi-neer's toy," he spoke up, "and that the German people are eagerly wait-ing for it. I can well imagine what a pitiful position you are in: a poor inventor enmeshed by Army bureaucracy! Why don't you come to us? You know that the Fuehrer's door is open to me at any time, don't you? I shall be in a much better position to help you lick the remaining diffi-culties than that clumsy Army machine!"
>
> I replied coolly that in General Dornberger I had the best chief I could wish to have, and that it was technical trouble and not red tape that was holding things up. I ventured to compare the A-4 with a little flower that needs sunshine, fertile soil and some gardener's tending— and said that by pouring a big jet of liquid manure on that little flower, in order to have it grow faster, he might kill it.

In one of his more dramatic tellings of this tale, Himmler was said to have "smiled sardonically," but von Braun later told Ruland that the Reichsführer merely laughed and smiled, and the conversation ended pleasantly enough after some small talk. Nonetheless he had shown courage in rebuffing Himmler's initiative.[3]

What did the Reichsführer have in mind? Von Braun never did find out, but it must have had something to do with bringing the army side of Peenemünde into the orbit of the SS, perhaps by supporting a Führer order that Himmler would try to arrange. Certainly it would have meant von Braun aligning himself with Hans Kammler, who was using the crisis in the A-4 program to try to increase his influence beyond construction.[4]

It seems no coincidence that, at precisely this time, the top reaches of the Nazi regime were rife with conspiracies against a seriously ill Albert Speer. After going into the hospital on 18 January for a knee infection, he collapsed in his bed on February 10 with a pulmonary embolism and raging infection; it even appeared that he might not live. Himmler, Göring, and others tried to exploit this situation to grab parts of his empire. It is noteworthy that Speer had become one of von Braun's fans and protectors. If the two could not be friends because of the gap in status, they did have a bond of mutual recognition as wunderkind technocrats who had made great careers at early ages. Speer's absence from the scene thus provided the Reichsführer an opportunity to try to put parts of the army rocket program under the influence of the SS, which he thought was the most efficient and zealous organization for carrying out the Führer's orders.[5]

Von Braun returned to his grueling work and travel schedule, going to the Oie on 29 February to see the first, unsuccessful launch of the Wasserfall, and flying to Berlin, Nordhausen, and southwestern Germany in March. But a month after his visit to Hochwald, "the pay-off came—Himmler-style." At two or three in the morning three Gestapo agents banged on the door of his room at the Inselhof. The date was most likely 22 March 1944, the day before his thirty-second birthday. He gave this account to Ruland in 1969:

> The officials demanded that I accompany them to police headquarters in Stettin. They said that I had to make an important witness statement there. I protested energetically and said that they did not have to rouse me out of my sleep at this unusual hour for that. I had only come back home at midnight after a strenuous business trip and reacted quite sourly to this imposition. . . .
>
> As the Gestapo men began to cite their orders, the penny dropped. I questioned them: "You therefore want to arrest me? There must be a

misunderstanding!" Now one of the Gestapo men let the cat out of the bag: "By no means are we talking about arrest! Rather we have the express order to take you into protective custody."[6]

Perhaps this hair-splitting distinction sounded reassuring, because von Braun claims that he then dressed calmly and slowly, packed a small suitcase, and followed them outside, where two cars waited. The Gestapo then went to collect three others who had been arrested—his brother Magnus, Klaus Riedel, and Helmut Gröttrup, Steinhoff's liaison to Dornberger's staff—and proceeded in darkness to the Oder River port city of Stettin (now Szczecin, Poland), a good couple of hours away. The four were lodged in the holding cells on the top floor of police headquarters, possibly the very same building where Magnus von Braun Sr. had been temporary police chief during the revolutionary upheavals of 1919.[7]

The nominal cause for the arrests was remarks that von Braun, Riedel, and Gröttrup had made at a party in Zinnowitz early in March, when they apparently talked a little too frankly after getting drunk. (Von Braun had long been a heavy social drinker in his increasingly rare moments of relaxation.) The only substantive document we have on the whole affair comes from General Alfred Jodl, chief of operations in the Armed Forces High Command—by an odd coincidence, Jodl's wife was a childhood friend of von Braun's, as she came from an estate next door to Crenzow. During an 8 March briefing by Abwehr (counterintelligence) officers, Jodl wrote the following notes:

> Assertions that the war will turn out badly, and regarding their weapon. The main task is to create a spaceship. S.D. [SS Security Service] has assembled material. RF SS [Himmler] has been told, is putting extensive material together.
> Riedel II [Klaus Riedel] treasonous assertions, previously League for Human Rights. No murder instrument.
> Gröttrup Pan Europa under Soviet leadership. All three very close friends.
> Dornberger does not know anything yet.

The first report from Peenemünde to the local SD man went back to 17 October 1943. Von Braun, who was "very friendly with Frau Gröttrup," was in the "Inselhof." Jodl concluded: "Refined Communist cell. All secret commanders there. Certain. S.D. wants to know what will happen when all three are snapped up."[8]

These absurd accusations are a window on the totalitarian realities of the late Third Reich. Any comments about losing the war, or opposing the use of the rocket as a weapon, were treasonous in the National Socialist context and the speaker was subject to arrest, detention in a concentration camp, internment, or even execution, for "defeatism" and "undermining the will to fight [*Wehrkraftzersetzung*]." It is therefore possible that the arrests had nothing to do with Himmler's talk with von Braun and were based solely on the SD informer's report. But this scenario seems unlikely given the highly political nature of any move to arrest key leaders of the A-4 program—a concern clearly demonstrated by the last line: what would happen when they were snapped up? Moreover, Himmler would never have approved such a move without considering the fallout. Arresting von Braun in particular could only have alarmed Dornberger and delayed the development and production of the new "wonder weapon." The Reichsführer-SS must therefore have wanted to achieve some advantage for his organization by punishing von Braun as well as his friends.[9]

Early on the morning of the arrest, Dornberger's ringing phone woke him up in his quarters in Schwedt, near Stettin. It was General Buhle telling him to come see Field Marshal Wilhelm Keitel, head of the Armed Forces High Command and chief military adviser to Hitler, at once. The Führer and his entourage had pulled out of East Prussia in late February, as the Wolfs-schanze buildings were to be strengthened against air attack, and had moved to the Berghof (Mountain Court), his old, favorite quarters in the Bavarian Alps near Berchtesgaden. Dornberger and his driver spent the whole day making their way from north to south, delayed by icy roads, snow, and air-raid-disrupted cities. Arriving late in the afternoon, he met Buhle, who told him about the arrests. Dornberger was astounded. "Von Braun, my best man, . . . whose whole soul and energy, whose indefatigable toil by day and by night, were devoted to the A-4, arrested for sabotage! It was incredible." And Riedel too, "who had worked out the entire ground organization with untiring zeal and absolutely outstanding perception of military needs."[10]

After a "practically sleepless night" Dornberger got the full explanation from Keitel. "The charges were so serious," the field marshal said, "that arrest was bound to follow. The men are likely to lose their lives. How people in their position can indulge in such talk passes my understanding." By his own account, Dornberger immediately leaped to their defense and claimed that the three were absolutely indispensable to the program; Keitel, known as a weak personality, then tried to send him to Himmler. But the Reichsführer refused to see Dornberger, directing him to Ernst Kaltenbrunner, the head of the security police and SD, at SS headquarters in Berlin. Dornberger "drove back to Schwedt in a white heat of rage."[11]

At Peenemünde the news struck like a thunderbolt at a "board meeting" of von Braun's top associates. Word quickly spread. Von Braun told an associate in 1959 that "everybody in the field knew it. My parents, my relatives, my friend [girlfriend?]. They learned it through the grapevine, via telephone, mail, etc. It was definitely not a state secret." Meanwhile the four sat in their cells knowing nothing at all. Wernher's first thought on getting locked up, he later asserted, was "what a terrific chance to sleep," but he admitted to Ruland: "The first days in the Gestapo prison in Stettin were naturally very unpleasant, especially because I had absolutely no idea why they locked me up." On his birthday he heard a car horn below on the street and went to the window, where he saw his driver and one of his engineers waving. His jailers allowed the chauffeur to bring the flowers and birthday gifts into the cell, and he was glad to share some of the food packets with Magnus, Riedel, and Gröttrup, with whom he otherwise had no contact. From all this, it is clear that they were being treated cautiously and were not in a special Gestapo prison at all, just the Stettin holding cells: thus they experienced no torture, abuse, or even deprivation. Himmler clearly wanted to wait to see what the political fallout might be. The situation was nonetheless very dangerous.[12]

The day after Dornberger's return he went with his chief of staff to SS headquarters, a complex of bomb-damaged buildings only a few blocks south of the von Braun family's onetime residence at the Agriculture Ministry. Kaltenbrunner was away; he was sent to Heinrich Müller, head of the Gestapo. In Dornberger's dramatically told account, Müller fixed him in a cold stare and "gulped in a somewhat angry fashion" when the general told him that he did not see the difference between the SD and Gestapo or between arrest and "protective custody." Müller, raising "his hand a few inches above the table," threatened Dornberger with the "fat file" of evidence that the Gestapo had against him for holding up rocket development. In turn, the general gave an innocent spin on the remarks of his engineers and demanded their release as absolutely indispensable to the ballistic missile project. The meeting was inconclusive. Wernher and his compatriots were left to fret in their cells for several days as machinations went on behind the scenes; others who had been at the party were hauled in for questioning. Eventually Magnus was released with the explanation that it was all a "misunderstanding."[13]

The first time that Wernher heard anything about the charges against him was near the end of March. He was led into a room that felt like a courtroom, but he faced only three Gestapo officers in SS uniform. The chairman read out all the charges, from his plan to sabotage rocket development by diverting it into spaceflight, to his alleged plan to fly to England with all the plans for the A-4—why else did he maintain his pilot's license? Producing "evidence" that went all the way back to his schoolboy science fiction story "Lunetta" and that included "some political remarks I had made years before," his interrogators demonstrated that they had a "fat file" on him too—although it is noteworthy that complaints about the inhumanity of concentration camp labor were not in it, indicating that von Braun had been too indifferent or too circumspect to say anything, even though he knew the prisoners were dying in large numbers. "This process was grotesque and had a macabre unreality. As an engineer I dealt constantly with tangible facts and comprehensible problems. Here everything appeared as if in a hallucination. Quite obviously they wanted to inject fear into me. If the Gestapo wanted to convict me—how was I . . . supposed to prove my innocence?" He was reduced to insisting that treason was the furthest thing from his mind. Back in his cell, von Braun was naturally very disconcerted, but later he felt lucky that he was "not in the position to even intelligently judge my situation."[14]

Suddenly, on the second day of questioning, the proceedings "were interrupted by the spectacular entrance of Dornberger resplendent in the red trouser stripes" of an army general. Shooting a reassuring glance in von Braun's direction, he wordlessly put a document down in front of the chief interrogator: a conditional release for three months, signed at Führer headquarters. Aided by one of the Abwehr officers who had briefed General Jodl, Dornberger had fought determinedly for the release of von Braun and the others. The document did not spring him immediately, but soon thereafter Dornberger came to retrieve him, "armed with a big bottle of brandy," and took him to Schwedt. It was probably the weekend of 1–2 April. Shortly afterward Riedel and Gröttrup were given a provisional release to Schwedt as well.[15]

Unbeknownst to Dornberger, he had been aided by Albert Speer, who had spent several days resting at an Austrian palace near Berchtesgaden before moving on to a month's cure in the Italian Alps. When Hitler came to visit the minister for the last time on 23 March, Speer intervened on behalf of the arrested men. Later he remembered how "von Braun and his staff used to talk freely about their speculations, describing how in the distant future a rocket could be developed and used for mail service between the United States and Europe." In May, when Speer returned to full-time work, he found "Hitler still grumbling about the trouble he had gone to." The Führer promised that "as long as he [von Braun] is indispensable to me [Speer], he will be exempted from any punishment, however serious the resulting general consequences might be."[16]

As one might expect, the whole Kafkaesque affair greatly increased von Braun's alienation from the Nazi regime. Before his arrest, whatever his gradually growing disillusionment, he had remained largely oblivious to personal danger from that regime's security apparatus. The "scientist and engineer in a totalitarian state," he told a public symposium after the Soviet launch of Sputnik in fall 1957, worked with far less control than was imagined by most Americans. "As long as he is considered useful, he is even coddled to some extent, and has practically all the advantages and privileges he enjoys in a free country. But there is always the looming danger that a brick may suddenly fall on his head." Von Braun compared the threat of arrest to "people's attitudes toward traffic accidents. You read in the papers that on every Labor Day weekend so many people get killed in automobile crashes, and yet you don't cancel your plans for driving in the countryside on Labor Day weekend. You just accept the unavoidable risk, and enjoy life in the face of this risk."[17]

After his arrest, however, he realized that he had to be more careful about airing his spaceflight obsession and to be particularly cautious about the war. It was perfectly obvious to him that it was going badly, but saying so was dangerous. He was certainly not a liberal democrat like Klaus Riedel or Helmut Gröttrup, two of the most left-wing people at the rocket center; his conservative nationalist background remained influential. Yet his inner alienation grew. In 1968 von Braun told a British writer that it was not "until about a year before the war's end," that is about the time of his arrest, that he came "to the realization that I might be aiding an evil regime," but by that time "my country was engulfed in a worldwide war" and he had to do his duty. The aerodynamicist Peter Wegener, who knew him only in the last two years of the war, observed the subtle signs of this alienation: "Von Braun joked in small groups about meetings with government leaders, and he extended his attitude later to the SS. It became obvious to me that he disliked Hitler and all that Hitler did. But it was Hitler who supported his dream."[18]

Wegener's remark captures perfectly the Faustian bargain in which even von Braun now saw he was trapped. To survive the war, he knew that he had to demonstrate his total commitment to the Nazi system more than ever, but this did not prove that difficult, as he remained completely committed to rocket development on grounds of loyalty, duty, ambition, and love for the technology. Only ten days after his release he was at the Mittelwerk again, negotiating with Sawatzki to sustain his control over Peenemünde's production supervision organization in the factory. On 25 April he completed a long memorandum requested by Dornberger about the obstacles to completing the development of the A-4 and its ground equipment. This document is very revealing of the turf battles taking place within Ordnance itself, as criticism was heaped on the rocket program for the delays, apparently not without cause. Although the memorandum says nothing about the SS, it is revealing of von Braun's postarrest psychology: he shows no signs of intimidation.

Frustrated by the organizational infighting and confusion, he asked for clear-cut authority for development: "In the area given to me, I would like to have complete responsibility and freedom of action, and a clear delineation of command authority and jurisdiction." He threatened to quit if, as was beginning to be discussed, his development organization was turned into a government company headed by director Paul Storch of Siemens, who chaired the electrical devices subcommittee in the Special Committee A-4. It was, he thought, a personal devaluation of his work. "I therefore ask that in the case that this decision actually comes to pass, I would be given permission to serve with the troops at the front." Yet in the very next sentence he undercut that threat by allowing for the eventuality that he would not be allowed to go, in which case he wanted to continue with full responsibility for development and a clear chain of command. Essentially he wanted Dornberger to be once again in direct command of the whole program—a pipe dream—but failing that he would continue working anyway, as he could no more imagine giving it up than "Seppl" could imagine losing him.[19]

Von Braun's omission of the SS from the memorandum was clearly no coincidence. Strictly speaking, Himmler's organization had nothing to do with A-4 development but, especially in the aftermath of the arrest, von Braun and Dornberger would not put anything down on paper about pressure from that quarter anyway. Yet SS interference was only one of the political problems afflicting the program as a result of the missile's shortcomings and the increasingly catastrophic course of the war. In response to "Big Week," the U.S. Army Air Forces' aerial assault on German aircraft factories in late February, on 1 March Erhard Milch convinced Albert Speer to sign, in his hospital bed, an emergency decree creating the Fighter Staff, a joint organization of the Air and Armaments Ministries dedicated to increasing fighter production. Hans Kammler, now an SS-Gruppenführer (major general), received the assignment to massively expand underground factory capacity, with many of the new mining projects located in the Nordhausen region, spawning many new and terrible subcamps tied to Dora. Milch used the political vulnerability of the A-4 program—symbolized by Hitler's 5 March request to Saur to investigate numerous complaints about its wastefulness and expense—to push for a handover of the Mittelwerk tunnels for jet fighter production. At the same time Luftwaffe representatives criticized von Braun's organization for diversions of its personnel from Wasserfall to the A-4 and asserted the superiority of the Luftwaffe's Fi 103 cruise missile, soon to be deployed. In the end Junkers Aircraft got the northern half of the Mittelwerk tunnels for a jet and piston engine factory, forcing the consolidation of the A-4 assembly line into tunnels 23 to 42. The resulting disruption, reinforced by a Hitler-ordered cutback in A-4 production and by design changes necessitated by the launch failures and airbursts, caused missile output to drop from 437 in May to 132 in June and 86 in July.[20]

In the months after von Braun's arrest, the continuing struggle to introduce new technical specifications in an orderly manner, and refine A-4 assembly, quality control, and inspection, helped him complete his most important management task of the late-war period: changing the culture of his Peenemünde development group to match the rhythms of large-batch production. He had to push through the completion of a set of production drawings for A-4 Series B, as the first operational version was called; usher in an orderly process of change submissions through a "Drawing Change Service" and a system of forwarding changes in blocks; and refine the inspection and acceptance process in the tunnels through his Production Supervision organization and through the corps of uniformed army acceptance inspectors. These processes had begun long before there was a Mittelwerk, but only in the summer of 1944—after a long struggle to overcome an underdeveloped rocket, a production process disrupted by going underground, and a freewheeling organization unused to the discipline of industrial production—did von Braun get the interface between the factory and Peenemünde to function with reasonable smoothness.[21]

In the process of continuing to visit the Mittelwerk so frequently, he inevitably became further enmeshed in the inhuman exploitation of concentration camp workers. On 6 May he and Dornberger were at a conference at the company headquarters to mark the installation of a general director, Georg Rickhey, whose job was to reorganize management and, so he later claimed, "to push back the influence of the SS." At the outset Sawatzki mentioned that he had asked Kammler for eighteen hundred more slave laborers, and he later noted that, if French subcontractors had to be evacuated to the tunnels with their machinery, "deployment of French workers in the MW [Mittelwerk] is only possible in uniform"—that is, only if they became concentration camp prisoners. Von Braun, who spoke at length on the technical troubles of the ballistic missile, can scarcely be expected to have said anything against these manifestations of the criminality of the enterprise, especially while on a three-month conditional release, yet his mere presence necessarily implicated him in the system, whatever he was thinking at the time.[22]

When the prisoners in the "sleeping tunnels" were finally evacuated to the outdoor camp in the spring, and mining operations in the Mittelwerk were finished, the death rate in Dora dropped dramatically, something von Braun also knew. Yet a part of the drop was simply due to the SS camp administration dumping worn-out prisoners on Kammler's nearby, deadly Fighter Staff projects; the factory was an appallingly inhuman place even in its improved state. In June the company was forced to issue a secret decree to its employees: prisoners had been beaten or even "stabbed with sharp instruments," but physical abuse was the province of the SS.[23]

Could von Braun himself have made a minor contribution to such abuse? French survivor Georges Jouanin claims to have been slapped by him, possibly in May 1944. Jouanin's job was to install cabling to the servomotors that powered the jet and air vanes. Before the production process for the tail section was changed to horizontal assembly, he had to climb through the empty hole for the engine and stand on the servomotors, which were a major source of concern at the time. In 1997 Jouanin provided the following account:

> [S]omeone has noticed my wooden-heeled clog atop such a fragile organ, and I feel a hand pulling insistently on the end of my striped pants, thus forcing me out of the tail unit. "You, out of here, man, you're committing sabotage! You shouldn't step with your foot on this!" I get slapped in the face twice and my head bounces against the metal panels of the tail unit. Cap in hand, I find myself in front of a man in his 30s, rather well dressed, angry, to who I am not allowed to give an explanation. The seven or eight engineers or technicians in the group out of which he came seem disconcerted, astonished. . . .
>
> I went back to my work space and the incident seemed over, without consequences. My civilian foreman, MANGER is his name, returns from break and tells me . . . : "Our big boss boxed your ears! That was v[on] Braun." I answer him: "I do not know him, Master! I have only seen him once." I never saw him again.[24]

Jouanin later added that, before slapping him, von Braun had said: "What are you then? Ruski? Ach, Frenchman!" He also claimed to recognize von Braun's voice in a recent film about Dora. Unfortunately, there are no other survivors left to corroborate this account, and it could be a case of mistaken identity. But the details of dress and age, and the fact that the man in question did not turn Jouanin over to the SS for possibly fatal punishment, seem believable.[25]

Another mid-1944 story from a French prisoner is much better documented and provides an important and interesting contrast to the one by Jouanin—indeed, it reveals that he did intervene on behalf of at least one prisoner. Charles Sadron, a forty-two-year-old physicist arrested in 1943 for Resistance activities, was assigned to one of the most elite work units in the tunnels, Quality Control Scherer, named after its German foreman. Located in a special barrack in cross-tunnel 28, this group was responsible for the A-4's guidance equipment. In a 1947 memoir Sadron said this about Peenemünde-East's technical director:

> I must, however, in order to be truthful, point out one man who took an almost generous attitude towards me. That is Professor von Braun, a member of the technical general staff that developed the aerial torpedoes. He came to see me in the shop.
>
> He is a young man, of very Germanic appearance, who speaks perfect French. He expresses to me, in measured and courteous terms, his regret at seeing a French professor in such a state of misery, then proposes that I come work in his laboratory. To be sure, there is no question of accepting. I refuse him bluntly [brutalement]. Von Braun excused himself, smiling as he left. I will learn later that, despite my refusal, he tried several times to better my lot, but to no avail.[26]

Written only two years after the end of the war, this evidence is important because it is undimmed by the passage of time and unaffected by von Braun's later fame. The politeness with which he handled a concentration camp prisoner, even after being rebuffed "bluntly," is also significant. Von Braun apparently identified with Charles Sadron as a professional equal imprisoned through the misfortunes of war.

Can this story be reconciled with that of Georges Jouanin? Perhaps, if we take into account the difference in status between the two—an ordinary prisoner versus a distinguished professor—and the fact that Sadron was known to von Braun. How that was the case is explained in a 15 August 1944 letter he wrote to Sawatzki:

> During one of my last visits to the Mittelwerk you suggested utilizing the skilled technical background of various prisoners available to you and to Buchenwald to accomplish additional development work, as well as to construct smaller numbers of sample devices. You also pointed out a prisoner, a French physics professor who has so far worked in your mixing-computer quality control and who has the special qualifications needed for the technical leadership of such a workshop.

I immediately looked into your proposal by going to Buchenwald, together with Dr. Simon [responsible for the placement of technical workers in the Mittelwerk], to seek out more qualified detainees. I have arranged their transfer to the Mittelwerk with Standartenführer [SS Colonel] Pister [Buchenwald camp commandant], as per your proposal.

After a long discussion of the obstacles encountered in setting up the workshop for "ground vehicle test devices," he ended the letter by stating: "I also feel it is expedient that the intelligent French physics professor, within the framework of the existing circumstances, be given certain privileges (possibly by allowing him to wear civilian clothes) so that his readiness to perform independent work might be increased. Couldn't you perhaps suggest something like this to Sturmbannführer [Major] Förschner [Dora camp commandant]?"[27]

Ernst Stuhlinger has claimed, based on comments von Braun made during the war and afterward, that his boss designed the whole scheme solely to help Sadron and other imprisoned "scientists" by putting them into a laboratory in the tunnels, then moving them to Peenemünde. This claim ignores evidence in the letter that von Braun might indeed have wanted such a laboratory because it would speed A-4 deployment, but if Stuhlinger's story is even half true, it would demonstrate that von Braun was disturbed about the fate of the prisoners, in line with his own later statements. Yet the Sawatzki letter also reveals that he knew the Dora commandant personally and met the Buchenwald commandant, presumably in his office outside the fence around the prisoner camp. Von Braun's letter is fairly definitive on the transfer of slave labor: "I [went] . . . to Buchenwald . . . to seek out more qualified detainees. I have arranged their transfer to the Mittelwerk with Standartenführer Pister." He must have been to Buchenwald before 24 July, because on that evening he assigned an engineer in Peenemünde to go to the Mittelwerk and set up the special test workshop. The SS transferred 300 prisoners from Buchenwald to Dora on 25 July, and 336 on 2 August—the latter labeled "skilled workers for K[omman]do Sawatzki." While we cannot prove that one of the transports included skilled prisoners assigned to Dora because of von Braun's actions, his words are quite clear, and such a transfer would, like the November 1943 letter on the engine test sites, theoretically put von Braun in violation of the Nuremberg war crimes standard regarding forced labor later applied to Albert Speer. Thus the effort to help a prisoner, whatever his other motivations, ironically helped to enmesh him deeper in "crimes against humanity."[28]

On the very day that he visited the Buchenwald camp commandant, von

Braun made an emotional visit to his old Ettersburg school. Through a strange twist of fate, the SS had built the concentration camp in 1937 just out of sight from the school, on the same hill where Goethe had once wandered. Von Braun described his visit in a 1955 letter to a classmate:

> I visited Ettersburg for the last time in July 1944, as that appalling war was already visibly approaching its end. I came through Weimar on a business trip and slipped that evening onto the balcony of the chapel. Franz Windweh [one of his old teachers] heard the creaking in the timbers and interrupted his lecture. After I identified myself, he asked me to come down into the hall. As we said our farewells the next day, I had a premonition that I would never see Ettersburg again.

He had a powerful bond to the school, even though he had been an "impossible" pupil there, because that was where he discovered his life's work: "flight into space."[29] As to what else he was thinking in July 1944, we can only guess. He certainly believed that he had remained true to his goal by accomplishing great things in large-scale rocketry, but he had done it only by working on a weapon being built by slave labor for a country being dragged into a disastrous defeat by a dictator. Stalin's "eastern hordes"—the racially loaded term he used with an American interrogator in June 1945—were advancing inexorably on Germany.[30] Where and for whom might he be working in a year?

Just at this time the war was taking an even more dramatic turn. On 13 June—exactly one week after the D-Day landings in Normandy—the Luftwaffe had finally begun attacking London with its cruise missile, which the Propaganda Ministry soon melodramatically dubbed Vergeltungswaffe 1 (Vengeance Weapon 1). After many delays and a rough start, up to several hundred unnervingly noisy "buzz bombs," or "doodlebugs," as the British called them, were crossing the Channel every day. Hitler, in a state of euphoria, ordered a shift in resources from the A-4 to the V-1. Newspapers and radio proclaimed revenge for the aerial destruction of German cities and stoked fantasies in the populace about a reversal of the war's course through panic and collapse in the English capital—hopes that von Braun, with his inside knowledge, no longer shared. Although the V-1 did cause an exodus from London and anxiety in Winston Churchill's government, by July it became apparent that nothing had really changed. The Allies kept expanding their Normandy bridgehead, and the Soviets virtually annihilated Army Group Center in a massive offensive that began on Barbarossa's third anniversary, 22 June. Four weeks later, on 20 July, Colonel Claus Schenk von Stauffenberg unsuccessfully attempted to assassinate Hitler with a briefcase bomb at the Wolfsschanze. The military coup that followed quickly collapsed, taking down with it the remaining power of the army officer corps. A vicious repression spread across the land. Thousands were arrested, including Sigismund von Braun's mother-in-law, who had had contacts with a Communist resister and who subsequently died in prison. In the highest reaches of Hitler's government, last desperate hopes for the war shifted to the Messerschmitt Me 262 jet fighter and to the A-4, soon to be known as the V-2.[31]

All that spring and summer, as Wernher von Braun rushed from factories to launch sites to construction projects, he had kept his organization focused on mastering the technical difficulties standing in the way of deployment. Once Peenemünde had somewhat mastered the rash of launch failures, many of them by terribly manufactured Mittelwerk A-4s, "air bursts [*Luftzerleger*]" became the outstanding problem. There were so many possible explanations, and so little evidence with which to work. Was it the result of an overheating of the alcohol tank and explosion of fuel remnants, excessive pressurization of the liquid-oxygen tank due to the failure of the relief valve, aerodynamic-pressure- or heat-induced buckling of the forward fuselage, or fins breaking off? The fragments that fell to the ground said little, and the only telemetry transmitter available was inadequate in the number of channels and not very reliable. Some warhead sections broke off and reached the ground anyway, but an even more insensitive fuse would have to be used, worsening the problem of burrowing in before exploding that Hitler had pointed out a year earlier.[32]

By summer, this frustrating mystery led Dornberger and von Braun to authorize some unorthodox attempts to visually observe air bursts. A-4s were fired vertically from the Greifswalder Oie using a mobile launch set brought over by barge; in one case the missile penetrated fully into outer space, reaching 176 km (109 mi) in altitude, a thrill for the two of them. They saw at least one low-altitude burst, but it was inconclusive.[33]

Arguing that "the bull's eye is the safest spot on the map," Dornberger convinced von Braun to join him at the center of the target area in Poland. It must have been during von Braun's five-day stay in mid-July—just before his trip to Nordhausen and Weimar, and not long before the range was abandoned altogether due to the advancing Red Army—that the two had the most hair-raising rocket-testing experience of their lives. Up to the last day, "every explosion was at a safe distance, hurling up huge fountains of dirt." Once or twice they glimpsed the beginning of an air burst. For the very last rocket, von Braun "was standing in an open field, and knowing the accurate launching time from a warning sign displayed from an observation tower, I beheld the rocket coming out of the blue sky." To his horror, he realized it was pointed straight at them—it would be a direct hit. "I threw myself down to the ground, but a moment later a terrific explosion hurled me high into the air. I landed in a ditch and noted with some amazement that I . . . had not suffered as much as a scratch." When von Braun "got up and walked into our observation hut, the look on Dornberger's face was something to see. A true scientist to the end, he had watched that rocket until it exploded, with the result that his window . . . was draped around his neck like a burlesque necklace." They later often laughed over this story, but their dangerous enterprise had contributed little to solving the mystery. Only after repeated launches with different configurations were their engineers able to conclude that the best results came from reinforcing the middle section's front end, near the instrument compartment, because heat and aerodynamic forces tended to weaken the skin there, leading to a breakup in midair. By that time the missile was already being launched against England and newly liberated western Europe.[34]

On 1 August 1944 Wernher von Braun found himself, after eleven-plus years working for the civil service, effectively a senior vice president of a private, government-owned corporation, Elektromechanische Werke GmbH (Electromechanical Works, Ltd.). The privatization of his development group had gone ahead in spite of his April blustering to Dornberger; apparently the Speer ministry and a greatly weakened Army Ordnance together decided that the corporate form might be more efficient and provide better protection against an SS takeover. This move was in many ways a symbolic repudiation of Dornberger's original model of a large in-house civil service laboratory, but the actual day-to-day operation of Peenemünde-East changed little. If anything, privatization added to the confusion, as the military base functions were separated from corporate functions, complicating local organizational arrangements. Since Hans Kammler found Leo Zanssen to be of dubious political loyalty and thus personally unacceptable, Zanssen was sent to command a solid-fuel rocket unit at the front, and a colonel took over the reduced position of commander.[35]

Just as he had feared in April, von Braun was put under Siemens director Paul Storch, with whom he had battled over the production of A-4 electronic devices. Dieter Huzel, von Braun's special assistant from September 1944 on, describes Storch as "a man about 55 years of age, graying but well preserved, his round, healthy-looking face punctuated by a mustache. He spoke with a slow, subdued but very determined voice. He was unused to being disputed or questioned." Storch's authoritarian corporate style clashed with the boisterous outspokenness of the brash, young engineering organization. Von Braun, ever the diplomat and the loyal subordinate once he accepted a situation, made sure that conflicts were smoothed over, and he was ably assisted by his primary deputy, the unobtrusive but effective Eberhard Rees. On the organization chart at least, von Braun's responsibilities were reduced, as he was chief of development in parallel with the chiefs of industrial operations (Rees), testing (Martin Schilling, Thiel's replacement after the air raid), and administration. At the same time he and the other company directors received big salary increases to bring them to corporate levels, but money meant little, as there was little to buy and almost everything was rationed anyway. In reality, von Braun remained technical director and second in command, skillfully limiting the issues that came before Storch. His personality and his ability to orchestrate productive teamwork, while minimizing outward expressions of ego, meant that his subordinates continued to hold him in awe and respect. A short biographical sketch drafted by an unknown Peenemünde author at the end of 1943 shows that a heroic personality cult, such as followed him later in his career, was already in place.[36]

During the summer and fall of 1944 the situation at Peenemünde, as elsewhere in Germany, slowly deteriorated; food and fuel got scarcer and call-ups to the military increased. While the location still had its advantages—former Peenemünders noted the availability of fish from the sea and alcohol from rocket fuel—the dispersal of housing and work sites all over the island and neighboring areas had reduced efficiency. As the supply of gasoline and other fuels fell into crisis in the late spring of 1944, communication was further impeded. Distant travel was affected too: von Braun virtually stopped flying after mid-July, with the only trips in his logbook at the end of July, at the end of August, and in mid-November. He mostly traveled in a chauffeured car, obviously a privilege, but that meant many extra hours in transit, and he must occasionally have taken the train like his subordinates. Train travel was already extremely slow and crowded and only got worse; major cities like Berlin, which he often visited, were being reduced to rubble, and most nights there were spent in air raid shelters. Peenemünde itself was attacked again three times that summer, on 18 July, 2 August, and 25 August, after an eleven-month reprieve due to effective means of concealment. This time smaller groups of American daylight bombers damaged the test stands, killing a dozen to fifty people each time; von Braun was away in Poland for the first and has left us no account of any of them. He also suffered a hard personal loss when his old Raketenflugplatz friend and Stettin jailmate, Klaus Riedel, was killed when he fell asleep and ran his car into a tree early on the morning of 4 August.[37]

Two days later Himmler appointed Hans Kammler his special commissioner for accelerating A-4 deployment. In a calculated insult to the officer corps, Hitler had given the Reichsführer-SS the positions of commander of the Replacement Army and chief of Army Armaments on 20 July because Stauffenberg and others had planned the coup from those offices. General Fritz Fromm, the former officeholder and Dornberger's superior, was thrown in jail and later executed. Kammler used his new orders to move ruthlessly to shove Dornberger and the designated operational commanders out of the way and take control over the mobile launch units, then approaching readiness for operations. By early September he had succeeded in seizing command and had induced Dornberger's chief of staff to stab his superior in the back by reporting directly to him.[38]

"Seppl" was in despair; he drafted a request to be transferred to the front. Von Braun and Ernst Steinhoff showed up at his home one Sunday to talk him out of it. "They lectured me for hours, telling me I ought not to leave the undertaking in the lurch at this stage, with the main crisis just coming on. If we were one day to have a place in the history of technology and receive recognition from the world for our invention of the long-range rocket, I ought not to desert the ship now . . . I should even try to help Kammler."[39] Dornberger eventually agreed, and after a long struggle with the SS general, he salvaged his position as inspector of rocket troops and chief of supply and training at home, while Kammler had overall command. Although neither Dornberger nor von Braun reported directly to Kammler, he was now clearly in the dominant position. Not coincidentally, Speer's power in the A-4 program, and in the Reich generally, was fading.

On 8 September, Kammler's rocket troops in the Ardennes and Holland successfully launched one ballistic missile at recently liberated Paris in the morning, and two at London in the evening. Von Braun, who received the news by teletype or telephone, was apparently unhappy that his rocket had finally been used to kill people, although it is very hard now to separate truth from myth. Dorette Kersten Schlidt asserted in 1987: "Von Braun was completely devastated. In fact never before or afterwards have I seen him so sad, so thoroughly disturbed. 'This should never have happened,' he said. 'I always hoped the war would be over before they launched an A-4 against a live target. We built our rocket to pave the way to other worlds, not to raise havoc on earth.' " This story, which she interestingly links to the almost-forgotten Paris attack, bespeaks a memory altered by the later defense of his reputation; key details lack credibility. Von Braun knew from the outset that the A-4 was a military weapon, and he was intensively involved in the preparations for deployment. Moreover, Dieter Huzel remembered a much more measured von Braun statement, although he erroneously put it in the context of a newspaper headline announcing the V-2 attacks on London. That event did not happen until 8 November, when Goebbels's Propaganda Ministry finally revealed the existence of the missile; the minister had wanted to avoid the aftereffects on morale created by the exaggerated hopes placed on the V-1. Huzel remembers von Braun telling his "excited" engineers: "Let's not forget . . . that this is only the beginning of a new era, the era of rocket-powered flight. It seems that this is another demonstration of the sad fact that so often important new developments get nowhere until they are first applied as weapons."[40]

Huzel recalls thinking that von Braun chose his words with great care in view of their political implications. Such a sentiment was not inconsistent with the statements attributed to von Braun and his friends before their arrest, and he apparently said something similar in the presence of test stand engineer Karl Heimburg. In spite of later exaggerations, it is believable that he felt some regret, just as physicist Robert Oppenheimer's second reaction to the bombing of Hiroshima—after relief that the A-bomb had worked—was that he had blood on his hands. If von Braun had second thoughts, however, many others did not. One of his leading associates told space writer Erik Bergaust in the late 1950s: "Don't kid yourself—although von Braun may have had space dust in his eyes since childhood, most of us were pretty sore about the heavy bombing of Germany—the loss of German civilians, mothers, fathers, or relatives. When the first V-2 hit London, we had champagne. And why not? We were at war, and although we weren't Nazis [a dubious statement for some], we still had a Fatherland to fight for."[41]

Von Braun certainly shared the last sentiment but apparently did not share their bitterness toward the Western Allies, perhaps because his family was indeed lucky—and privileged. His parents were safely ensconced on their Silesian farm, although they did endure frightening air raids in Berlin. As for their three sons of fighting age, none served at the front, due to their social class, talent, luck, and choice of occupations. Short-term health problems had prevented Sigismund's call-up when he returned from British internment in early 1943. The Foreign Office sent him instead to the German embassy to the Vatican; he and his family were safely out of the war in June 1944 when the Allies liberated Rome, leaving them stranded inside the pope's neutral microstate. In the months beforehand Sigis had quietly signed documents to allow a number of people to hide from or escape the German and Italian secret police; his dislike of Hitler's anti-Semitism and his exposure to the United States in 1933–34 had something to do with why he turned out to be a low-key resister, while Wernher, blinded by the future of rocketry, became mired in the system. As for Magnus Jr., Wernher had used his power and influence to pull him away from possible service, then turned him into his pilot and special assistant. In September 1944 he sent Magnus to the Mittelwerk full-time to be his representative for the vane servomotors, which continued to be troubled; the subcontractors had been evacuated to the tunnels, and his younger brother would now supervise them. By sending Magnus there, however, Wernher was putting him in the midst of concentration camp labor, as he well knew. With the moral obtuseness that he brought to such matters in the Third Reich, he doubtlessly saw this move merely as a pragmatic engineering decision, putting in place someone he could trust.[42]

Once the V-2 campaign got properly under way in the fall and winter, Wernher von Braun more than once visited the front, making a show of loyalty to the SS and the Nazi system, even while downplaying the effectiveness of his missile. An officer from the operational units told his British captors in March 1945 that "Professor von BRAUN . . . , despite his Nazi convictions and the fact that he often appears in a uniform suggesting that he held some form of honorary S.S. rank, was not greatly enamoured of the operational possibilities of the A-4. He regarded it more as a medium for stratospheric meteorological research and as a necessary stepping-stone to bigger things." Just at this time, the fall and winter of 1944–45, Peenemünde was preparing to launch a special package of scientific instruments called the "Regener barrel," after its team leader, upper-atmospheric physicist Erich Regener. Von Braun had helped organize the project in 1942, excited as he was by the promise of reaching regions inaccessible to balloons, and receiving data useful both for science and for missile trajectory calculations. As for von Braun's skeptical view of the military value of his own weapon, the prisoner's comments are confirmed by one of Dornberger's staff officers, who told the British in the fall of 1945 that "only one man [was] completely open and honest, Prof. von Braun. He had repeatedly and insistently indicated that the [A-4] device only had limited possibilities and could never deliver what had been promised to the people and to the Führer."[43]

Other evidence confirms the impression that von Braun walked a fine line in the last months of 1944, doing his duty energetically for the Fatherland and acting like a true believer in the National Socialist system, yet remaining clear-eyed about the coming catastrophic end. Kammler had to be watched particularly carefully, which explains von Braun's appearance at frontline units in SS uniform. For months, Dornberger asserts, Kammler had "been labeling Professor von Braun as too young, too childish, too supercilious and too arrogant for his job." Von Braun privately returned the contempt. When the SS general demanded a means of determining missile impact points, the rocket engineer wrote sarcastically on the margins of the Dornberger memorandum mentioning it: "Trivial! The day after tomorrow!" As to the war, when the author of a monthly report about the troubled Wasserfall antiaircraft missile discussed the urgent necessity of deploying it in order to achieve "the overcoming of enemy air superiority and thus the achievement of victory," von Braun ironically penciled in small letters: "Final victory? Well, well!" "Final victory" was one of the many increasingly ludicrous slogans coming from Goebbels, whom von Braun briefed in September, along with German Labor Front leader Robert Ley. He certainly was not as honest with them about the A-4/V-2 as he was with his colleagues. The fact that he even met those two Nazi leaders is revealed in a heated exchange of letters he had with someone in the Air Ministry over rumors about what he said to Goebbels and what that person said to Kammler—an exchange symptomatic of the dangerous atmosphere of the dying Third Reich.[44]

The story of how von Braun got the Knight's Cross of the War Service Cross—a very high noncombat decoration equivalent to the Knight's Crosses awarded for valor—reveals his peculiar place in the Nazi system in its final months. At the end of September Himmler had gone to Hitler and suggested V-2 medals for Dornberger, Walther Riedel (the head of the Peenemünde design bureau—by sheer coincidence, he had almost the same name as his predecessor, Walter "Papa" Riedel), and Heinz Kunze, Degenkolb's representative on the Special Committee A-4. (Degenkolb had by this time virtually dropped out due to alcoholism.) The Reichsführer-SS's omission of von Braun was obviously intentional—he no longer trusted him after the February meeting and the arrest and never promoted him again. But by that time von Braun had sufficiently proved his worth and political reliability that his conditional release from arrest had been either renewed or dropped altogether. He certainly still had a supporter in Albert Speer. On 11 November, Speer telegraphed Himmler that he supported Rickhey (of the Mittelwerk), Kunze, and Dornberger, but also von Braun, as Dornberger's closest collaborator in the rocket program from the beginning. Kammler had argued that the professor title was enough, an excuse to give von Braun nothing more, but Speer did not agree. After another long delay, doubtlessly due to behind-the-scenes politics, the minister was finally able to get Hitler's approval in early December.[45]

On the ninth Speer awarded the four medals in a melodramatic ceremony in an old stone castle, Schloss Varlar, near Coesfeld, between Arnhem and Münster. From October the V-2 units had focused their campaign not only on London but also on the Belgian port of Antwerp, which Hitler wanted to interdict as it was a major supply center for the Allies. Taking that city was, moreover, the objective of the last, desperate counteroffensive the Führer was preparing to launch through the Ardennes, a campaign that would become famous as the Battle of the Bulge. Dornberger describes the Wagnerian setting of the ceremony, one worthy of *Götterdämmerung* over Germany:

> Around the castle in the dark forest were the launching positions of V-2 troops in operation against Antwerp. The dining room was darkened. Every time a V-2 was launched, a curtain toward the launching site was opened. After each launch, Speer decorated one of the recipients. It was a scene, the blackness of the night, the room suddenly lit with the flickering light of the rocket's exhaust and slightly shaken by the reverberations of its engine.

A week later, on 16 December, Peenemünde held its own small party in the officers' club for the winners. Photos show von Braun dressed in a tuxedo with the medal around his neck, toasting and reading a telegram of congratulations with Dornberger. Around the table were officers, engineers, and Nazi bigwigs in full uniform. Quite by accident, it was the first day of the Ardennes offensive, hailed with triumphal fanfares by Goebbels's media, but few of those present had illusions about the coming last-ditch struggle.[46]

All that fall von Braun had soldiered on with the improvement of the A-4, whose production at the Mittelwerk had finally hit stride in September at over six hundred missiles per month, all the while trying to keep the Wasserfall project going and bring yet another project on line: the A-4's promised successor, the winged version called the A-9. The project had restarted in June 1944 after the inner core of the old Projects Office centered around Ludwig Roth was taken off Wasserfall. But it was only in September that the A-9 became an urgent priority, likely stemming from the sudden loss of France and Belgium and the threat that the western Netherlands— the only place left for attacking London with the A-4/V-2—might be captured too. More range was needed, and putting wings on a modified A-4 was the only short-term possibility for getting it.[47]

In order to capture the priorities of the ballistic missile, the A-9 was renamed the A-4b in October, and in order to cut short the development phase, von Braun ordered that many preliminary stages be discarded. After visits from Rudolf Hermann and other members of his aerodynamics group, now at Kochel in the Bavarian Alps, von Braun decided that a straightforward swept-back wing reasonably well known from earlier wind tunnel experiments would simply be grafted onto an A-4 fuselage, at least in the short run. On 24 October he and his associates decided further that five missiles would be "Bastard" versions lacking even the advanced guidance and control systems needed for a functional glider missile; they would simply bolster the power of the servomotors so as to make some preliminary launch tests feasible. This desperate approach certainly conformed to the military situation and to the demands for instant results, but the A-4b program above all served a political function. The glider missile helped "to keep the group together" and "make the authorities believe, well, there is something coming," according to Werner Dahm, a junior aerodynamicist in Roth's group. Two days after Christmas 1944 the first "Bastard" A-4b, which looked to von Braun so much like the space plane of his dreams, lifted off its launch platform on the beach near Test Stand VII and promptly went out of control due to wind forces on the big wings. A second test on a snowy 24 January was more successful, but a wing broke off on the way down, sending the vehicle out of control. There was simply no possibility of making it work in the time left.[48]

As 1944 drew to a close, desperation spawned ever more illusory projects that von Braun was forced to accept. All sorts of ideas were floated, but the one the Luftwaffe decided to support was Taifun (Typhoon), a small, unguided antiaircraft rocket meant to be fired in massive numbers. The Electromechanical Works (EW) was now responsible for developing it too—by January in two versions, liquid and solid fuel. Another project was "Test Stand XII," the code name for a U-boat-towed canister for the A-4, an idea that went back to Klaus Riedel. The canister was to be righted by flooding, the top opened, and a missile launched at New York, somehow affecting the course of the war. Von Braun delegated authority to a few select subordinates, but it was one more management headache.[49]

During the intervening months, evacuation preparations had accelerated; Storch ordered the archiving of key documents on the mainland. As of 20 November von Braun still believed that they would be moving to "our dispersal site in the south"—the Zement tunnels dug by Kammler's slave laborers in Austria—but a couple of weeks later space there not already given over to a refinery was seized for another factory. Meanwhile last-ditch defense preparations were under way at Peenemünde as the Soviets approached. Men in the EW, which had 4,325 employees in early 1945, were given mandatory infantry training for the Volkssturm (Home Guard). It was obvious to von Braun, as it was to almost everyone, that higher authorities might soon impose on them either a futile and suicidal defense against the Red Army or an evacuation westward.[50]

Von Braun knew where he wanted to go. Near the end of 1944 he was strolling on a cold Baltic beach at Peenemünde with an Air Ministry engineer he had known since the Kummersdorf period. Confident of not being denounced—the engineer had told him of discussions at headquarters of going with the winners if the war was lost—von Braun said: "[W]e can talk frankly about this, I have already packed my trunks, with the documentation, the staff I need, and I will offer my services to the Americans. . . . And then I will build my space rocket." For someone with his technological ambition—and fear of Stalin's "eastern hordes"—the United States was the obvious place to go. But he had personal reasons as well, as he explained to his Hollywood producer in 1959. After Sigismund returned from his world trip in 1935, "he told me a lot about America and American ways, and repeatedly said 'America is the place for you to build your moon rockets.' His glowing stories about his experiences and adventures in America (he had travelled all over this country in his Model A Ford, and as a hitchhiker) greatly influenced me in my decision to 'go West' during those crucial weeks in early 1945." More opportunistically, von Braun also told *The New Yorker* in 1950: "My country had lost two wars in my young lifetime. . . . The next time, I wanted to be on the winning side."[51]

On 12 January the Red Army launched a massive winter offensive, shredding the German front in Poland. Soon artillery could be heard in the dim distance—the final decision was at hand. Rumors of tanks only several tens of miles away spread panic on the eighteenth: the scientific group preparing the Regener payload left hurriedly, ending the project before it was ever launched. All the while, demoralized, hungry, freezing crowds of refugees trekked westward across the island, bringing with them tales of rape, pillage, and murder by Soviet troops, who were seeking revenge for what the Germans had done in the East. Only weeks later did it become clear that the axis of the Red Army advance was directed primarily at Berlin, bypassing Usedom and northern Pomerania for three more months.[52]

It was probably at this time, near the end of January, that von Braun called a secret meeting of a handful of top subordinates at a farmhouse in Zempin, near where he lived. One of the few accounts we have of it comes from von Braun's ghostwritten 1958 memoir article "Space Man": " 'Germany has lost the war,' I said. 'But let us not forget that it was our team that first successfully reached outer space. We have never stopped believing in interplanetary travel.' " He allegedly went on to ask: " 'Each of the conquering powers will want our knowledge. The question we must answer is: To what country shall we entrust our heritage?' " He already had the answer. "There was not one dissenter. Our decision was unanimous. We would surrender, it was agreed, to the American army." Did he really place so much emphasis on spaceflight? We will never know, but the meeting was certainly treasonous by the standards of the Nazi state.[53]

A decision about where to go remained in the realm of wishful thinking, however, because von Braun had no authority to order an evacuation. He reported formally to Paul Storch, and informally to Generals Dornberger and Rossmann, but it was Hans Kammler who was really in command. Promoted to Obergruppenführer (lieutenant general) in the Waffen-SS, Kammler gathered new powers in late January and early February, including control of the Luftwaffe's V-1 batteries and antiaircraft missile projects. Albert Speer had created a "Working Staff Dornberger" to rationalize all rocket projects in mid-January; now Kammler simply appropriated Dornberger's new committee. The question was, what would Kammler do about Peenemünde? No later than the twenty-sixth von Braun must have guessed the answer, as Dornberger wired him that he would be evacuating to Bad Sachsa, not far north of Nordhausen. Von Braun was then ordered to appear again at Mittelwerk company headquarters for a meeting on the twenty-ninth or thirtieth; the subject was the creation of an umbrella organization to concentrate secret weapons projects in the Harz Mountain region, which was effectively under control of the SS.[54]

Kammler appointed as head of this new organization a scientist with Nazi credentials, Dr. Alfred Buch. Before the meeting, which the Obergruppenführer did not attend, Buch was told that von Braun was not to be trusted, that he might be in touch with Allied forces (a charge that likely went back to the arrest) and certainly was more interested in rocketry for personal reasons than for fighting the war. According to Buch:

> The air was loaded with tension as Wernher von Braun entered the room unaccompanied, dressed in the uniform of an SS-Sturmbannführer and wearing the Knight's Cross of the Service Cross, which Hitler had awarded him shortly before. His youthful face made a sympathetic impression on me. The description of his personality by various acquaintances, that he knew . . . how to win over people, seemed to be confirmed. . . . Von Braun appeared downcast and uninterested, and he answered the questions put to him only unwillingly. Irritated by this behavior, [Heinz] Kunze pointed out to him the seriousness of the situation and the necessary measures that had to be taken immediately.

Upon questioning about the Peenemünde situation, which to Buch sounded more like an interrogation than a conversation, von Braun made clear that he believed the center's fate was sealed and evacuation was unavoidable. A Dr. Wagner, representing the SS, then confronted him with three questions that he had to answer in three minutes, or there would be undefined consequences, which Buch thought meant arrest and trial. They were: (1) Was he ready to evacuate rocket development to the Harz immediately and with extraordinary effort? (2) Was he ready to give up the militarily hopeless Wasserfall and concentrate on small rockets (presumably Taifun)? and (3) Was he ready to focus EW personnel only on the development of small rockets? "Without hesitating, v. Braun declared himself willing to fulfill the demands put to him. The color had drained from his face and he appeared white as chalk. This exchange and v. Braun's immediate concession put me in a state of shock that lasted long afterward."[55]

Von Braun may have gotten his wish to evacuate, but as this frightening meeting revealed, he would not be in control—he would be in the power of the fanatics. He returned to the rocket center. At midday on 31 January, "a cold and cloudy Wednesday," according to Dieter Huzel, he called an emergency meeting. " 'Kammler has just ordered the relocation of all the most important defense projects into central Germany,' he said quietly. 'This is an order, not a proposal.' " He asked his top staff to report within hours on how many people would have to be moved, how much equipment was going with them, and what kind of transportation they needed. First priority would be A-4 and Taifun, with A-4b and Wasserfall second. (Contrary to Buch's account, the larger antiaircraft missile was not canceled.) Launch testing would remain for the moment at Peenemünde, as would a portion of the organization. The biggest challenge would be organizing a fleet of trucks and the necessary fuel, as well as securing rail, ship, and even horse transport, using the priority orders granted by Kammler and by Army Ordnance chief Leeb, who confirmed the evacuation order on the first of February.[56]

After the war von Braun always liked to emphasize one story about the decision to evacuate, a dramatic account in which he was confronted with completely contradictory orders and used the opportunity to arrange their escape. An oft-repeated version of his anecdote is also the most wildly exaggerated: "Ten orders lay on my desk. . . . Five threatened me with immediate execution if we moved ourselves from that spot, five stated that I would be shot if we did not move." More soberly, he told his biographer Bernd Ruland that he faced two stand-fast orders contradicting the one from Kammler— from the chief of staff of Army Group Vistula, technically under the leadership of Himmler, and from the Nazi Party leader for Pomerania as commander of the Volkssturm. He took Kammler's order as the only means to carry out the secret decision at Zempin to surrender to the Americans. Yet, as we have seen, he was not the one who could give the order, and he had little choice but to play along with Kammler, who could have trumped anyone's order by calling upon Himmler and Hitler to authorize the concentration of secret weapons projects in central Germany. In the process of developing his story after the war, von Braun's ego seems to have led him into romanticizing his role and freedom of action in this absolutely critical situation.[57]

While packing and organizing went on day and night, von Braun made sure to visit his von Quistorp relatives and his parents to see about their arrangements for escaping the Red Army. In the first long letter he was able to send to his mother and father after the war, he mentioned that the last time he saw them in Oberwiesenthal, "the Russian front [was] of course only about 20 km eastwards." Shortly thereafter the evacuation of Peenemünde took place—it "was a wild affair." As the first rail and truck convoys left on 17 February 1945, this visit probably took place early in the month. He begged them to come with him, but they refused to abandon their home. He also visited and phoned his mother's relatives on the nearby mainland; in the preceding years he had become especially close to Alexander and Theda von Quistorp's family in Bauer. He had often eaten Sunday dinners there and had become close to his beautiful cousin Maria, not yet seventeen at the beginning of 1945. They were planning to escape to an estate they had at Norden, near the Dutch border and Spiekeroog; von Braun secured space for his aunt on one of the ships that carried equipment to the Baltic port of Lübeck. The cargo was then transferred to river barges for movement to the Harz region, but much of it never arrived. Among the items stranded and lost were almost all of his personal effects.[58]

Von Braun led one early truck convoy south, as he always liked to tell the tale of his confrontation with an officer at a roadblock. In order to talk his way past the blockade of civilian movements in the army's rear area, he had to reveal the secret weapons character of the enterprise, even give it an impressively opaque acronym, VzbV, derived from Dornberger's title, to be posted on all vehicles. What von Braun did not say in public after the war is what he told the U.S. War Department in 1947: "The only time I made use of my SS rank was during the evacuation." The situation was so chaotic that he signed transportation orders as an SS-Sturmbannführer "in order to put more steam under these movements." Indeed, he told a trusted German correspondent in 1957, he had confronted the officer dressed in "SS uniform and decorations," that is, with the Knight's Cross around his neck.[59]

By Huzel's account, von Braun returned to the rocket center on 27 February and stayed a couple of days. It must have been a strange feeling as he drove away for the last time from the place in which he had invested so much hope, energy, and enthusiasm. Peenemünde had opened less than eight years before, and it had been tied from beginning to end to the meteoric rise and fall of the Third Reich. Von Braun knew there was very little chance that he would ever see it again.[60]

Returning to central Germany meant returning to an elaborate charade, working energetically to organize an array of guided-missile-related projects moving to the region in the name of emergency defense and "final victory." Nearly three thousand members of the EW would be evacuated, along with several thousand more from many other firms grouped into the umbrella organization, the Entwicklungsgemeinschaft (Development Cooperative) Mittelbau. Mittelbau (Central Construction) had become the operative term for the whole SS-dominated region around the Mittelwerk, but it was also the name given to the Dora concentration camp when it became a new main camp, independent of Buchenwald, in the fall of 1944. On paper, von Braun held a high position as head of the organization's planning office, the technical director of an enterprise that included many firms with Luftwaffe missile, guidance, and proximity-fuse projects not previously in his control. Headquarters for his new office, and for the rump EW, were in Bleicherode, a small town 16 km (10 mi) to the southwest of Nordhausen in more open, rolling landscape. While the housing situation for most of those evacuated was difficult—they were quartered on the local population already burdened with refugees, or in various confiscated buildings—von Braun roomed very comfortably in a beautiful, modern house of a Jewish factory owner who had left for South Africa when Hitler came to power.[61]

A handful of surviving documents from the first half of March show von Braun rushing around the region scouting and confiscating mines, underground facilities, factories, schools, brick works, whatever was available, for the various units and firms moving into the region. He laid out for Kammler and others the prospects for creating new test stands, launch ramps, factories, and the like, while not hiding the immediate difficulties. Reality was nonetheless much worse than pictured, as Huzel found out when he arrived in Bleicherode in mid-March: "Extremely primitive headquarters had been set up in a former agricultural school. There was not much sense of order. We couldn't just bodily lift a whole engineering plant, drop it two hundred miles away, and expect it to continue functioning without interruption." When von Braun took over the school on the sixth, he signed documents giving him responsibility for a number of school desks, chairs, lamps, closets, and so forth, along with three drills and "2 ventilation models for cow stalls." He had no illusions, but with the last-ditch fanatics in control, he had to keep up his guard.[62]

During this period von Braun visited the Mittelwerk at least once, and he must have encountered concentration camp labor in many other places. The underground sites in the region were being dug by workers from some of the forty-odd subcamps now tied to Mittelbau-Dora. Conditions in the camps were catastrophic, as the food supply became erratic and thousands of mostly Jewish, extremely malnourished prisoners were dumped on the Mittelbau system as a result of the evacuation of Auschwitz and Gross Rosen. So many of those arriving at Dora were already dead that the crematorium was overwhelmed; the SS resorted to burning the corpses on open pyres. In the main camp repression of the underground resistance organization and of the prisoners generally reached its horrifying maximum in March, when a revolt of Russian and Ukrainian prisoners led to a series of gruesome mass hangings. Two were even inside the Mittelwerk, using the overhead crane that lifted V-2s into the vertical position for testing. Arthur Rudolph witnessed at least one of the hangings of twenty to thirty prisoners, as did several other former Peenemünders well known to von Braun. His brother Magnus may no longer have been in the tunnels, however, as several documents seem to indicate that Wernher had brought him to Bleicherode to be his special assistant again. It is quite unlikely that Wernher von Braun witnessed any of the true horrors of the last two months, but he certainly knew something of what was going on. Moreover, at least one underground project laid out in his planning documents would have involved the exploitation of more slave labor to complete a tunnel.[63]

Early on the morning of 12 March von Braun's incessant travel for Kammler's empire of shadow projects came to a sudden and nearly fatal end. Because of the threat from roving Allied fighter-bombers, he had traveled long distances only at night and had not slept properly in weeks. As he explained to his parents in his first long postwar letter:

My driver, out of exhaustion after having driven through two nights, fell asleep at the wheel at a speed of about 100 km/h [60 mph]. It was on the autobahn in the vicinity of Weissenfels, on a trip from Thuringia to Berlin. The car ran to the right down the 12 meter [40 ft] high embankment, or rather it flew through the air, and landed after about a 40 meter [130 ft] flight. . . . I was sleeping and awoke only during the flight because the tire noise suddenly stopped.

The car smashed into the ground next to some railroad tracks. Just before the impact von Braun put up his arm to protect his head, with the result that his left shoulder was smashed and his arm was broken in two places. He and the driver lay unconscious, and they might have bled to death except that two Peenemünde colleagues, facilities engineer Bernhard Tessmann and architect Hannes Lührsen, were also traveling to Berlin that night and spotted the wrecked car. Tessmann retrieved an ambulance, and the two were delivered to a hospital, where von Braun received a cast and an arm sling. Within a day he was moved to the hospital in Bleicherode and stayed for about three weeks in a private room, with secretive men from his group coming and going. One year earlier he had been sitting in a jail in Stettin; now he lay seriously injured, hoping for a fortunate end to the war—namely, the rapid appearance of the Americans.[64]

In the following days, that end seemed to be very near. British, Canadian, and American troops began their final offensive across the Rhine on von Braun's thirty-third birthday, quickly breaking into eastern Holland and the German heartland. Kammler was forced to end V-1 and V-2 operations against London and Antwerp and converted his units into an infantry division. Dornberger gives the most vivid picture of the SS general in these dying days of the Reich. He "was on the move day and night. Conferences were called for 1 o'clock in the morning somewhere in the Harz Mountains, or we would meet at midnight somewhere on the Autobahn. . . . [I]f he got impatient and wanted to drive on, [he] would wake the slumbering officers of his suite with a burst from his tommy-gun. 'No need for *them* to sleep! I can't either!' "[65]

On Easter Sunday, the first of April, Dornberger got a most unwelcome order from Kammler: he and 450 or 500 of the top people from the V-2 project must move at once to Oberammergau in the Bavarian Alps, where a Messerschmitt aircraft group was located—Hitler had bestowed on Kammler his last and most absurd title: "Plenipotentiary for Jet Fighter Aircraft." Von Braun was no happier to leave than Dornberger, as they had every prospect of seeing the U.S. Army arrive within a week or two. But Dornberger's chief of staff, Lieutenant Colonel Herbert Axster, "emphasized to me at the transmission of the command that—in his opinion—such men who would refuse to follow Kammler's command would run the risk of being shot by the SS." Moreover, Axster told him "to keep a 'stiff upper lip' upon arrival in Bavaria, because Kammler intended to allow nobody to fall into American hands," which von Braun took to mean that they might all be killed. Perhaps, but it is much more likely that the SS general was keeping them as a bargaining chip for the Allies in order to save his own skin, as von Braun said himself on other occasions.[66]

The select group—at least those who would let themselves be found—left a few days later on the "Vengeance Express"—the ironic title given to the train of sleeping cars used for accommodations at Heidelager and Bleicherode. With them were a large number of SS guards but not von Braun. Because of his injury, he was given special dispensation to travel in a vehicle convoy, since it would be so difficult to jump off the train in case of air attack. According to a senior nurse at the hospital, he received a new, massive cast immobilizing his whole left arm and then was spirited away one night without any warning. Von Braun spent a week with Dornberger in Bad Sachsa and left on 9 April, only two days before the Americans overran the area.[67]

After he arrived in the beautiful mountain town (in)famous for its decadal anti-Semitic passion play, von Braun found his group at an army barracks, surrounded by guards and barbed wire. Kammler soon showed up too. Von Braun saw him for the last time at an Oberammergau hotel just before the SS general took off on another of his mad journeys to single-handedly win the war. He handed over command of the group to one of his officers. Nervous about their possible fate, von Braun and Steinhoff set out to convince this SS-Sturmbannführer to let them disperse to villages around the region. The excuse they used was the possibility of the Americans bombing the barracks: what if the whole project was devastated, and he was held responsible for it? They had trucks modified to run on alcohol rocket fuel, and priorities to grab whatever they needed from Wehrmacht depots, so they could transport and feed several hundred people. The Sturmbannführer paused for what seemed an eternity. As if perfectly timed, a flight of American fighters suddenly roared over Oberammergau. That did it; they would be allowed to disperse, but each little group would have its own SS guard detail.[68]

Wernher moved to Weilheim, a larger town closer to Munich, along with his brother Magnus and several others. But very soon it became clear that he needed further treatment for his broken arm and shoulder, which had slipped inside his cast as a result of the rough journey south. A surgeon in the town of Sonthofen, 50 km (30 mi) to the southwest at the foot of the mountains, had a private hospital specializing in sports injuries and was willing to take him. When a totally exhausted von Braun checked in on about 21 April, the surgeon told him that the fractures would have to broken and reset, with four days in traction in between. "In my bed I felt extremely uncomfortable. . . . Because the first operation was to be followed by a second, I lay there with my smashed-up arm not in a cast. The smallest movement caused considerable pain." To attend to him, Dornberger had sent Hannelore Bannasch, one of his former secretaries and girlfriends, and then Sawatzki's secretary in the Mittelwerk, but von Braun was difficult and impatient. When awake, he could hear bombs falling in the neighborhood, and he imagined an SS man appearing to shoot him rather than let him be captured. On the afternoon of the third day, when a man in uniform shook him out of a morphine-induced sleep, "at first I was completely frightened." But it was actually a soldier sent by Dornberger, ensconced in a hotel only a few kilometers away high atop the Oberjoch—then known, but not for much longer, as the Adolf Hitler Pass. The French army was only hours away; he had to hurry. Reluctantly, the surgeon made him another giant cast immobilizing his arm in a horizontal position and told him to rest for a month. Later that day von Braun was joyfully received by Dornberger, his brother, and others at Haus Ingeburg, which was a snowy 1180 m (3,850 ft) high on the old German-Austrian border.[69]

There was little to do but sit on the terrace and contemplate the white-capped Alpine peaks while the catastrophes of the last weeks of the war unfolded far below. The spring weather was glorious; the sky azure blue; the only worries were how to get the SS guards to surrender and which of the Allies might arrive first. "There I was living royally in a ski hotel on a mountain plateau," he told *New Yorker* writer Daniel Lang five years later, ". . . the French below us to the west, and the Americans to the south. But no one, of course, suspected we were there. So nothing happened. The most momentous events were being broadcast over the radio. Hitler was dead . . . and the hotel service was excellent." Not the first time in his life, Wernher von Braun found himself lucky, and privileged. While concentration camp prisoners expired by the thousands in the death marches and camp evacuations, or died of disease and malnutrition even after liberation, he partook of the hotel's gourmet kitchen and wine cellar.[70]

He had survived—survived the arrest by the Gestapo, the A-4 impact in Poland, the suspicions of the fanatics, the adventures of the evacuation, the terrible car accident. He had received enormous resources for rocketry, but not without cost—he had had to actively collaborate in the exploitation of slave labor and in the waging of a futile war for a demagogic dictator who was leading the nation to disaster. Having at last seen the true face of the regime in the Stettin prison, he had to put on a charade of Nazi fanaticism. And yet he had hardly changed. In his last days in Bleicherode hospital he was visited by his old radio operator, who had flown with him on so many business trips on the Ju 52. Jokingly, von Braun told him that he "would need me as onboard radio operator when [he] fairly soon 'would fly to the Moon.' "[71] Now he needed only a deus ex machina to complete his rescue. If the U.S. Army was not going to find them, it was time to find the U.S. Army.

CHAPTER NINE

Morning in the Desert

(1945–46)

Morning in the desert, when the impossible not only seems possible, but easy. —ROBERT GODDARD, Roswell, New Mexico, 1937[1]

At 10:26 p.m. on Tuesday, May Day 1945, German radio issued one of its last lies: the Führer had fallen that day in combat, fighting the Bolshevik hordes in the ruins of Berlin. He had, of course, shot himself in the bunker the previous day. On the Oberjoch, the weather had turned cold, cloudy, and snowy. Still weighed down by the massive cast holding up his left arm, Wernher von Braun decided to approach Walter Dornberger for the first time about surrendering to the Americans. Hitler's death released faithful soldiers of the Third Reich—of which Dornberger certainly was one—from their personal oath to the Führer, and this might have motivated von Braun's approach. Revealingly, fifteen months later he already remembered his initiative being occasioned by the announcement of German capitulation on May 8, presumably because that did not make him feel like a traitor. As it turned out, Dornberger was amenable to von Braun's idea—he too felt that it was time "to put our baby [the rocket] in the right hands."[2]

Not long after breakfast on 2 May their elected emissary, Wernher's younger brother Magnus, set off on a bicycle down the steep road to the Austrian side. Magnus spoke the best English of anyone in the group, and from whatever sources of intelligence they had, they knew that the U.S. Army was there, whereas the French were to the northwest in Bavaria. After he departed, there was nothing to do but wait; as hours passed, Wernher became worried. At last, around two in the afternoon, Magnus reappeared and, sitting on a hotel sofa, told the tale of his adventure. He had run into an antitank platoon of the Forty-fourth Infantry Division and had spent over a half hour, in German and English, trying to convince a German-American private that he was not "nuts" for claiming that the "inventors" of the V-2, including his brother, were up on the mountain and wanted to be immediately taken to "Ike"—General Dwight Eisenhower. Fred Schneikert, from Sheboygan, Wisconsin, eventually relented and escorted the younger von Braun to Counter Intelligence Corps (CIC) headquarters in the town of Reutte. There First Lieutenant Charles Stewart, suspicious of Magnus but knowing that von Braun and others were on the watch lists for interrogation, gave him safe conduct passes and told him to go back and produce the people he claimed were there.[3]

Dornberger and von Braun quickly decided to lead an advance party of seven. They would be joined by Magnus and by Herbert Axster, Dornberger's chief of staff; Hans Lindenberg, a specialist in V-2 engine production; Dieter Huzel, Wernher's special assistant; and Bernhard Tessmann, a designer of test facilities. The latter two engineers had carried out von Braun's order to hide Peenemünde's precious archive in a mine in the Harz Mountains before leaving central Germany. After hurriedly packing their luggage, the seven got into three staff cars: Magnus von Braun, Tessmann, and Dornberger in the lead, Wernher and Huzel in the second, and Axster and Lindenberg in the rear. A little after four, with the light fading and sleet beginning to fall, they started down the treacherous mountain road, lights blazing, an unpleasant surprise to the well-armed GIs waiting in two jeeps at the bottom. After their passes were reviewed, they were escorted to an Alpine-style mansion occupied by the CIC in Reutte. Inside Stewart sat in the main hall doing paperwork in a gloom lit by a single candle. The seven were led upstairs by flashlight to their rooms, but suddenly the power came on again. After cleaning themselves up, they were treated to a repast of scrambled fresh eggs, pure white bread, ample butter, and real—not ersatz—coffee. Von Braun later claimed not to have worried about his reception, telling Daniel Lang in 1950: "I didn't expect to be treated as [a war criminal]. No, it all made sense. The V-2 was something we had and you didn't have. Naturally, you wanted to know all about it." Yet he conveyed a trace of the tension of that time when he added with a laugh: "When we reached the C.I.C., I wasn't kicked in the teeth or anything. They immediately fried us some eggs."[4]

The next morning they were treated to a similarly luxurious breakfast, although the Germans were surprised to see GIs cutting open little cereal boxes and putting milk and sugar inside. They were soon led outside on a cold mountain morning, slushy snow on the ground, for photos with the press. Von Braun, ecstatic at his treatment and speaking passable English, was anything but restrained. One member of the Forty-fourth later said that "he treated our soldiers with the affable condescension of a visiting congressman. . . . [His cast] did not prevent him from posing for endless pic-

tures with individual GIs, in which he beamed, shook hands, pointed inquir-
ingly at medals and otherwise conducted himself as a celebrity rather than a
prisoner. He . . . quickly let the word out that he had not only worked at
Peenemünde but had been its founder and guiding spirit."[5]

The fact that this large, almost overweight, young-looking thirty-three-
year-old claimed to be who he was produced a lot of skepticism. One GI
cracked that "if we hadn't caught the biggest scientist in the Third Reich, we
had certainly caught the biggest liar!" So unguarded and egocentric was von
Braun that he boasted to a reporter for the Seventh Army's *Beachhead
News* "that if he had been given two more years, the V-2 bomb he invented
could have won the war for Germany. . . . If Germany had been able to produce 200 V-2s a day [ten times Mittelwerk's output, at a corresponding cost
in lives], it was conceivable the course of the war could have been changed."
With two more years he could also have improved its guidance to "pin-point
accuracy." Regret for the fate of the concentration camp workers or remorse
for anything Hitler's Germany had done were notably lacking.[6]

The third of May 1945 was day one of von Braun's fundamentally American celebrity. Famous (or infamous) only in a restricted circle of Third Reich
leaders, army officers, scientists, and engineers, he had worked for twelve
and a half years in the deepest secrecy. Now he was on the verge of becoming, if as yet only in a small way, a public name.

The third of May was also day one of his American rocketry career too.
Von Braun naively expected the United States to jump on the bandwagon of
full-scale rocket development, this time directed against the Soviets, but
with the ultimate objective of reaching the Moon and the planets. Inevitably
there would be many disappointments. But even if the facilities the U.S.
Army provided in the desert did not live up to his expectations, he would not
be diverted from his course. It was a new start in a new country—his compromises with the Nazis safely swept under the rug—bringing with it the
promise that all his spaceflight ambitions would be fulfilled.

Already on that same afternoon von Braun and his compatriots were taken
away to more suitable internment locations. He may have gone directly
with Dornberger to the recently occupied Bavarian ski resort of Garmisch-
Partenkirchen, site of the 1936 Winter Olympics. There, within a few days,
the U.S. Army assembled in a large, three-story military administration
building perhaps half of the 450 or so Peenemünders sent south from
Thuringia a month earlier. And there the internees encountered an array
of Allied interrogators from often-competing intelligence operations: the
Naval Technical Mission in Europe, the Army Air Forces' "Operation

Lusty" (Luftwaffe secret technology), and the Anglo-American Combined Intelligence Objectives Subcommittee (CIOS, nicknamed Chaos for its byzantine bureaucracy).[7]

Wernher von Braun's name had been known to British intelligence since at least the fall of 1943, when captured German generals in bugged rooms talked too freely about the long-range rocket program. From late 1944 on his name was on Western lists of targeted individuals, although he was only one of many on such lists. The Soviets too wanted to find him; his name was known to the NKVD as early as 1935, when a Gestapo officer who was a Soviet agent visited Kummersdorf, but the agent could not follow up inquiries about von Braun and was later caught and executed. Not until mid-1944, following the catastrophes of the purges and the German invasion, would Soviet interest in long-range rocketry be revived. The Red Army did not capture Peenemünde until 5 May 1945, as it had been off the main axis of advance, and the Mittelwerk was not at first accessible at all, because the Nordhausen area was overrun by American troops on 11 April. There elements of the Third Armored and 104th Infantry Divisions had quickly found the amazing underground plant, but also scenes of horror at Dora and especially at the Boelcke Kaserne subcamp in the city of Nordhausen, which had been used as a dumping ground for sick prisoners. Adding to the disaster, this camp had been inadvertently devastated by RAF night raids on the city on 3–4 April. Just at that time the SS forced the great majority of the prisoners onto rail cars and death marches that took an enormous toll; most of the survivors were liberated at Bergen-Belsen and elsewhere.[8]

Isolated in a picture-postcard Alpine town not reduced to smoking rubble, von Braun and his compatriots knew almost nothing about what had happened elsewhere. They had left several thousand of their group, and most of their families, in Thuringia, but the collapse of the Reich left no functioning post office, telephone, or transport system. Communications were thrown back to the Middle Ages; travelers going in the desired direction were asked to hand-carry letters. For the von Braun brothers, the fate of their parents would remain an agonizing mystery for nine months, and no direct contact was established for over a year. All they had to go by were horror stories of Soviet rape and pillage coming through the press and by word of mouth, soon followed by news of the mass expulsion of Germans living in Eastern Europe and a huge swath of eastern Germany to be handed over to Poland. Within a year, in a gigantic "ethnic cleansing," about twelve million Germans would be expelled from the East, and untold thousands died. It was the sort of catastrophe, piled on the already-existing catastrophes, that made

Germans all too willing to think of themselves only as victims of the war, not also as its perpetrators.[9]

The first objective of the Garmisch group's leadership, Dornberger and von Braun, was to get them to stick together in the belief that they could negotiate a package deal with the United States. Their exaggerated belief in their own importance was symbolized by their demand on the first day to be taken to "Ike," and their hope for such a deal was symbolized by their bringing Huzel and Tessmann along because they knew where the archive was buried. Since they were never taken to "Ike," they continued to withhold information about the archive. A junior American intelligence officer, Second Lieutenant Walter Jessel, reported on 12 June:

> Control was exercised by DORNBERGER in the course of technical CIOS investigations. His first instructions, probably under the impression of immediate transfer of the whole group to the United States, were to cooperate fully with investigators. Sometime later, he gave the word to hold back on information and say as little as possible. Informants who are dissatisfied with his continued authority, while not in great fear, believe they will be exposed to disciplinary action on the part of the group.

While von Braun became primary spokesman because he spoke some English, as a loyal subordinate of Dornberger he willingly submitted to the general's overall leadership.[10]

Jessel astutely judged the Garmisch internees as falling into three basic groups: the early rocket and space enthusiasts, the engineers and technicians who came into the program as it was growing, and the army personnel transferred to Peenemünde after 1941. The "few exceptional rebels" were found in the last group. The second he found "ideologically the least sympathetic." While few were National Socialist fanatics (one notable exception was Arthur Rudolph, who a U.S. interrogator rated as "100% Nazi, dangerous type . . . <u>Suggest internment</u>"), they were engineers who had profited from the armaments buildup and had been loyal to the Hitler regime.

> There is almost nowhere any realization that there was something basically wrong with Germany's war or the employment of V-weapons. There is recognition of Germany's defeat, but none whatsoever of Germany's guilt and responsibility. Almost to a man these people are convinced that war between the US and Russia is around the corner. They shake their heads in amazement and some contempt at our political

ignorance and are impatient at our slowness in recognising the true saviors of Western Civilization from Asia's hordes. Which does not prevent them from playing with the idea of selling out to Asia's hordes if such recognition is not soon extended.[11]

Although von Braun was clearly in the group of the early rocketeers, and Jessel rated him as one of those most likely to be adaptable "to American methods and ways of life" despite his "Nazi background," he had the same blinkered, racist perspective of the others. After a security screening on 10 June, Jessel typed on von Braun's sheet: "Attitude characterized by the following quote: 'I always was a German and still am.' Considers Germany dead as a nation. Only German hope: To cooperate with western Allies to act as bulwark against eastern hordes, and as beachhead for US and British forces in the coming struggle." While von Braun was not one of those who could contemplate selling out to the Russians, in part because he feared punishment for the murderous treatment of Soviet prisoners in Dora, according to Helmut Gröttrup's wife, if he had been captured by the Red Army it seems likely that he would have pragmatically decided to make another bargain with them rather than go to the Gulag. Beyond family and friends, rocketry and spaceflight were all that really mattered to him.[12]

He finally got to unleash his breathtakingly futuristic perspective in a 15 May 1945 memorandum he wrote for two British CIOS investigators. Translated as "Survey of Development of Liquid Rockets in Germany and Their Future Prospects," this document would have considerable impact on American guided missile and space efforts in the postwar years. Von Braun opened with the statement that the A-4/V-2 was "an intermediate solution conditioned by this war, . . . and which compares with future possibilities of the art about in the same way as a bomber plane of the last war [World War I] compares with a modern bomber or large passenger plane. We are convinced that a complete mastery of the art of rockets will change conditions in the world in much the same way as did the mastery of aeronautics." The impact will be in both "civilian and military" fields, but it will require "large sums of money" and will involve both "setbacks and sacrifices." He went on to give a short history of German army rocket development, emphasizing the technology aspects of the A series. The Wasserfall he gave merely a paragraph, although antiaircraft missiles were of potentially great interest to the Allies, so that he could move on to what really excited him: the A-9, or winged A-4, which had appeared late in the war only in the compromised form of the A-4b. It could be a glider missile of 500-km (311-mi) range, or with a pressurized cabin and landing gear, it could take a crew

600 km (373 mi) in 17 minutes. Its range could be extended by either launching it from a catapult or mounting it on a booster. The A-10, which "was to be equipped with air brakes and a special parachute," would be reusable after recovery from the water. Total A-9 gliding range would then be 5000 km (3,100 mi).[13]

His final two pages were even more fantastic, reaching realms that in 1945 most people would have considered worthy only of science fiction. Long-range rocket planes could carry passengers or bombs across the Atlantic in 40 minutes. "Multi-stage piloted rockets" could reach a speed of "7500 meters per second" and thus stay in orbit—a concept he felt he had to explain in several sentences. "The whole of the earth's surface could be continuously observed from such a rocket. The crew could be equipped with very powerful telescopes" and observe "ships, icebergs, troop movements, constructional work, etc.," or could carry out "physical and astronomical research." It would also be "possible later on to build a station especially for the purpose," which could be erected in space by men in "divers suits" equipped with "small rocket propulsion units." Next von Braun presented the idea of Hermann Oberth's space mirror, lightly constructed and "kilometers" in diameter, which could focus sunlight to modify the weather or destroy things on Earth. "When the art of rockets is developed further, it will be possible to go to other planets, first of all to the moon. The scientific importance of such trips is obvious. In this connection" it might be necessary to combine rocketry with "the work done all over the world in connection with the harnessing of atomic energy . . . , the consequence of which cannot yet be fully predicted." He meant the nuclear rocket, not the atomic bomb; three months before Hiroshima all he knew was that the German uranium project had not gotten very far in the latter direction. He ended his memorandum by noting: "A prophecy regarding the development of aviation, made in 1895 and covering the next 50 years, and corresponding to the actual facts, would have appeared at least as fantastic then as does the present forecast of the possibilities of rocket development." As was the case for aviation, however, these developments would require "the combined experience of many thousands of specialists." Here he spoke from his experience as an organizer and manager of a huge technological project.[14]

His interrogators did not record a reaction to this mind-boggling piece, and the questions they put to him on 15 May, and that other interviewers asked on subsequent dates, were mostly confined to narrow technical discussions of propulsion and guidance. But the advanced thinking that he and other Germans displayed, and their willingness to go over to the United States immediately, set the imaginations of some American officers, scientists, and engineers afire. The war had taught them that the future of military power lay in advanced technology. Now they had a chance to exploit the German rocketeers, both for shorter-run developments that might affect the Pacific war (then expected to last at least another year) and for the future. Already by 23 May the chief of the rocket branch of Army Ordnance research and development in Washington was seeking permission to move five V-2 specialists to the United States. They would aid a project to launch up to one hundred V-2s at a new test area in New Mexico as a part of Project Hermes, a guided-missile program that Ordnance had contracted to General Electric (GE) in late 1944 in response to the V-weapons. In Paris the request for a hundred V-2s had come in April to a spare, kindly-looking officer with wire-rimmed glasses, Colonel Holger Toftoy, chief of Ordnance technical intelligence in Europe. At the time Toftoy, an expert in submarine mines who had helped clear harbors in France, knew little of rockets. He asked two of his officers, Majors William Bromley and James Hamill, to carry out the order, not realizing it would change his whole career.[15]

Bromley and Hamill went to central Germany to salvage as many missiles as they could, under pressure because of the unwelcome news that U.S. forces would be withdrawing as early as 1 June to the occupation zone agreed to at Yalta; thus the rocket factory would be handed over to the Soviets. Although there were by no means a hundred complete V-2s available, in a herculean effort they organized U.S. soldiers and former camp workers to put partially completed rockets and major components into hastily requisitioned rail cars. From 22 to 31 May one freight train left Nordhausen each day for the port of Antwerp—and then they found out that the U.S. withdrawal was being put off for three weeks.[16]

Meanwhile another young Ordnance major in his twenties, Robert Staver, arrived on the scene in Nordhausen in late April as part of a CIOS team, and he rapidly became enthused by the possibilities for enlisting the Germans in the American cause. Scouting the region, Staver eventually found a large number of prominent former Peenemünders who had not gone south, notably Eberhard Rees, von Braun's deputy; Karl Otto Fleischer, an army business manager sent to the rocket center in 1944; and Walther Riedel, chief of design after 1942. Riedel he found in a jail in Saalfeld, where U.S. soldiers had knocked out his teeth while questioning him about his alleged development of a "bacteria bomb." Around 20 May Staver tricked Fleischer into giving up the location of the Peenemünde archive, which he had heard about from Huzel and Tessmann before they left. Near the end of the month U.S. Army trucks evacuated fourteen tons of documents from a mine north of the Harz Mountains just before the British began setting up

The von Quistorp estate house at Crenzow, West Pomerania, ca. 1900, the birthplace of Wernher von Braun's mother. She and her sons also lived there, 1917–19, while Magnus Sr. was working in Berlin, Stettin, or the East. *(Bernd Jordan)*

Sigismund and Wernher in summer 1914, ages three and two, probably in Wernher's birthplace of Wirsitz (now in Poland). *(C.-F. von Braun)*

Because of his poor grades, Wernher's parents sent him to the Lietz boarding school at Ettersburg, outside Weimar, in fall 1925. This picture may have been taken on the very day of his arrival. He is at right, turned toward the camera.

(Archiv der Lietz-Schulen)

The Lietz high school at Spiekeroog on the North Sea, was in his mother's words, "a happy time and place for him." He is shown here in white, behind the boy in white shorts, as part of the "family" of Alfred Andreesen (left, with walking stick), probably in summer 1928.

(Archiv der Lietz-Schulen)

After reading Hermann Oberth's first spaceflight book in 1926, von Braun became a enthusiast. He is shown here at age eighteen, second from right, after a July 1930 rocket test in Berlin. Oberth is standing next to the large rocket, in profile. Rudolf Nebel is on the far left, and in the white coat, holding the rocket, is Klaus Riedel, who was becoming a close friend of von Braun. *(NASM)*

Von Braun and his American student friend, Constantine Generales, made an adventurous trip from Switzerland to Greece and back to Germany in summer 1931. Here they are seen with Generales's car in the Gotthard Pass in the Alps.

(NASM)

Left: Magnus von Braun Sr. was Reich minister of agriculture in the last two Weimar cabinets immediately preceding Hitler's coming to power. He is standing left on the steps of the Reichstag on Constitution Day, 11 August 1932. Front and center, with the Iron Cross, is Chancellor Franz von Papen, whose reactionary government was, ironically, in the midst of undermining the Weimar constitution. *(Bundesarchiv)*

Right: The von Braun family at Oberwiesenthal for the parents' twenty-fifth wedding anniversary in July 1935. Sigis, just back from his world tour, is at left, Magnus Jr., age sixteen, is at center, and Wernher at right. *(Hans Schaller/Der Spiegel)*

The author in summer 2000 at the former von Braun house in Oberwiesenthal, Silesia, now Bystrzyca, Poland. Von Braun's parents bought it in 1930 and lived there full-time from mid-1934 until their expulsion in 1946. *(author's collection)*

On 22 June 1932, Rudolf Nebel's Berlin amateur rocket group made a demonstration launch for the army at the Kummersdorf firing range. Although the rocket was a failure, this day led to the Reichswehr's offer to Wernher von Braun (right) to carry out secret rocket research at Kummersdorf. *(NASM)*

An aviation enthusiast and avid pilot, von Braun got his first soaring license in 1931 and this motor-aircraft license in September 1933. He flew until 1944, then again in the United States after 1957, eventually earning an airline pilot's rating. *(NASM)*

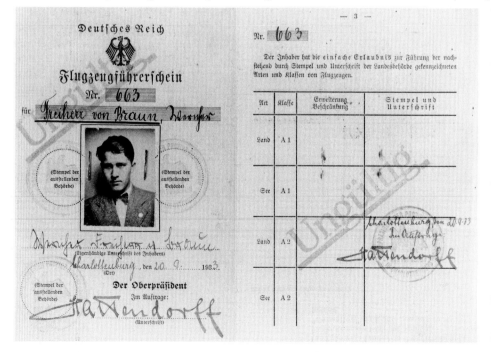

Von Braun saw Hitler five times; the second occasion was at Kummersdorf in early 1934. Von Braun is standing near the top, under the doorway of the Kummersdorf officer's club. At bottom, behind Hitler, are Rudolf Hess and Martin Bormann. Second from right, in the first row, is General Karl Becker, the moving force behind Army Ordnance's entry into rocketry. *(Wolfgang Fleischer)*

On a freezing December day in 1937, an A-3 rocket is prepared for launch on Greifswalder Oie, off-shore from the new Baltic rocket center at Peenemünde. Von Braun has his hand in his vest. The A-3 flights were a shocking failure. *(NASM)*

Several months after moving to Peenemünde in 1937, von Braun was told to join the National Socialist Party. In this August 1938 photo, he is wearing the swastika badge. Although not an ideological Nazi, the "Aryan"-looking, six-foot, blue-eyed blond was a loyal servant of Hitler's Reich. *(USSRC)*

An A-4 (V-2) ballistic missile is being prepared for launch in 1942–43. It was the technological accomplishment that made his career, but also drew him into deeper complicity with Nazi crimes. *(NASM)*

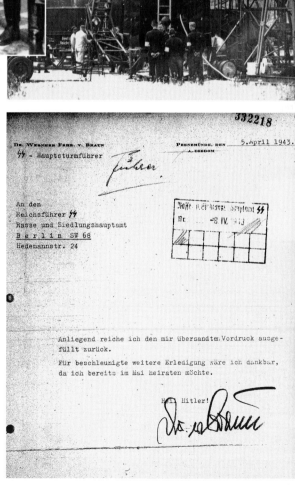

Reichsführer-SS Heinrich Himmler visited Peenemünde for the second time in June 1943. Left is von Braun's mentor and head of the Army rocket program, General Walter Dornberger. Half-hidden behind Himmler, in the black SS uniform, is almost certainly von Braun, in the only photo found thus far of him wearing it. He somewhat reluctantly became an SS officer in 1940.

Doris Dornberger/Sanford Greenburger Associates

In spring 1943 von Braun wished to marry a Berlin woman, Dorothee Brill. As an SS officer, he had to apply for permission to the Race and Settlement Office, headed by Himmler. In this cover letter to the Reichsführer-SS, von Braun gives his rank at the time, *Hauptsturmführer* (captain). The handwritten *Führer!* (Leader!) on top may come from a Himmler aide. But the engagement fell through, probably due to his mother's opposition. *(NARA)*

With the movement of A-4/V-2 production underground in August 1943, von Braun became much more directly implicated in concentration camp labor. The one prisoner he demonstrably tried to help was the French physicist Charles Sadron, shown here working in the quality control of guidance systems at the Mittelwerk.
(Ullstein Bilderdienst)

Despite the relatively privileged position of a few prisoners like Sadron, the Mittelwerk and the Mittelbau-Dora camp system were the scene of innumerable crimes and horrors. Shortly after liberation, French survivor Léon Delarbre sketched this picture of one of the mass hangings in Dora in March 1945.
(Musée de la Résistance et la Déportation)

Thanks in part to Albert Speer's intervention, von Braun not only survived his brief Gestapo arrest in 1944, he also was awarded the Knight's Cross of the War Service Cross by Hitler. At the celebratory party on 16 December at Peenemünde, he speaks to Special Committee A-4 head Gerhard Degenkolb. Guidance chief Ernst Steinhoff is at left.
(Deutsches Museum)

Wernher and Magnus von Braun Jr. in Reutte, Austria, on 3 May 1945, the morning after their surrender to the U.S. Army. Wernher had been in a near-fatal car crash seven weeks earlier. *(NASM*

Von Braun in Munich in June 1945. This picture was probably taken just minutes before the United States flew him to Nordhausen to help in the emergency evacuation of Peenemünders living in the zone to be given up to the Soviets. *(USSRC*

roadblocks in the new part of their zone. As with the rocket parts that went to Antwerp, Ordnance went out of its way not to share the documents with the British before shipment to the States. In hindsight, the American evacuation of matériel, documents, and personnel from the Nordhausen region in May–June 1945 looks like a precursor of the Cold War, but as these stories show, the primary objective was to seize as much German rocket and missile technology for the United States as possible, regardless of which allies it might offend.[17]

Meanwhile Staver set out to evacuate key Peenemünde personnel to the west before the Soviets moved in. After he made a quick round-trip to Paris to talk to Toftoy, the latter sent him a cable on 25 May, indicating that "Washington and Paris" were already in discussions about bringing the rocketeers to the United States and authorizing him to "remove the German Technicians and their families to an area under U.S. control." On the twenty-sixth, in his Nordhausen office, Staver wrote his superior officer in London that after discussing the matter with Riedel, he wanted to get "von Braun, [Ernst] Steinhoff, [Martin] Schilling and [Hans] Hüter" flown to Nordhausen to help search for equipment and people. Reports from Garmisch that they were too much under Dornberger's control provided an extra incentive to get them out of there. Nothing happened right away, but the postponed withdrawal gave him three extra weeks. On 8 June Steinhoff, Schilling, and Axster were sent north, but the head of the Garmisch CIOS team, a U.S. Army Air Forces (USAAF) lieutenant colonel, "withheld von Braun from plane trip to Nordhausen." The excuse given was that he still needed medical attention, but by that time he was wearing only a smaller cast in an arm sling. The CIOS team may have felt they still wanted to question him. An irritated Staver told Quinn: "Final list [of names of people to evacuate is] impossible without von Braun." Riedel had clearly sold him, sight unseen, on the Peenemünde technical director's leadership ability and knowledge of the whole organization.[18]

Relaxing with the others in Garmisch, von Braun knew little of what was going on. Other than dealing with GIs who were hostile or stole things, it was an easy life in which interrogations provided a welcome diversion. The rocketeers organized a camp orchestra, library, English lessons, technical lectures, and a theater group in which Magnus played a prominent part, and they sunned themselves while admiring the view of Germany's highest mountain. Von Braun and Dornberger were even allowed to give an interview to a British reporter from the London *Daily Express*, who met them in the general's "white-walled bed-sitting room" decorated with a framed quotation from Goethe: "He who wishes to create must be happy." The reporter described von Braun as "a tall, blond German with piercing blue eyes that make him look like a Nazi artist's picture of the 'Perfect Aryan' man." As on 3 May von Braun was jocular and charming but still insensitive as to how an Allied observer might view his work. "From the start of our talk he made it clear that his one passion in life was the success of his rockets. It was immaterial to him whether they were fired at the moon or on little homes in London so long as they could prove his invention worked efficiently. He feels no guilt at all. He talked to me in good English, with occasional interruptions in German from General Dornberger, a little rat-like man of the stiff German officer type."[19]

On Sunday, 17 June, not many days after giving this interview, von Braun was suddenly told that he should pack, as he would be leaving in an hour or two for Nordhausen; Staver had finally got his way. Along with a couple of other Germans and Dr. Richard Porter of General Electric, a thirty-two-year-old electrical engineer from Kansas who headed Project Hermes and had joined the CIOS team, von Braun got in a jeep headed to the bombed-out city of Munich and was flown north in a C-47 (DC-3) transport. The group already began planning for the evacuation on the plane, and once there, Porter later said, "we landed running." Staver had a card file of addresses, and he and Porter sent out teams with trucks, donkey carts, whatever was available, to roust the most desirable rocket engineers and technicians out of surrounding towns and villages and bring them to Nordhausen on short notice. Von Braun later said that he "sat day and night in American trucks" rounding up his people.[20]

This action was part of the United States' hasty evacuation of several thousand scientists, engineers, technicians, and their families westward to keep them out of Soviet hands. The Red Army, which had sent an inspection team to the Mittelwerk in late May, was still expected to advance on 21 June. That same night Porter commanded an overloaded train out of Nordhausen that brought the Peenemünders to two small towns just inside the new zonal boundary, Witzenhausen and Eschwege. Again the Soviet advance was postponed, this time to 1 July. On that date the Red Army finally began moving into Nordhausen, the Mittelwerk, and Bleicherode.[21]

For the better part of three months von Braun led the core group in Witzenhausen, which was about 25 km (15 mi) east of the wrecked industrial city of Kassel as the crow flies, but farther on the small, winding roads. Whereas the evacuees in Eschwege were quartered on the local population, in Witzenhausen eighty families were crammed into a two-story school called the Kollmannhaus. The food and hygiene situation was difficult. "Here we organized a 'communal kitchen,' " von Braun later said. "We built a sort of an emergency community, sent our men to the farmers, bought from them, for example, their entire bean harvest, and scraped other food-stuffs together with much luck and good words." In the school's main hall, beds were jammed wall to wall; men, women, children, and elderly relatives lived together with no privacy. Von Braun, on the other hand, either roomed elsewhere or had the rare privilege of his own room; he quickly acquired a new girlfriend.[22]

While waiting for word of a definite policy from Washington, he and his chief associates had long discussions with Porter and Staver about the appropriate size and composition of a group to go to the United States. Von Braun wanted a group of 520 to get a sufficiently broad range of expertise, a breathtakingly audacious proposal that reflected his continued belief in the unique value of his group. With difficulty the GE engineer talked him down to under 350 as more likely to be acceptable: "Von Braun was tearing his hair . . . it was like pulling teeth." Porter argued that GE could supply the draftsmen, clerks, and skilled craftsmen.[23]

For a project beyond the transfer of V-2 and Wasserfall experience, the two discussed the development of a ramjet missile. In Garmisch von Braun had already picked up on Porter's interest in the ramjet, which at its simplest is little more than a tube with constrictions for the intake and exhaust noz-zle, plus some kind of fuel injection and ignition system. Air is compressed in the inlet at high speeds and burned with the fuel, providing thrust, but a booster, usually a rocket, is needed to accelerate the vehicle to a high enough speed to make it work. German engineers and scientists connected to the Air Ministry had made progress in researching this exotic propulsion system. The appeal of the ramjet to American engineers and military officers, who were then becoming interested in all types of guided missiles, was its appar-ent greater efficiency as an air-breather (it did not have to carry its own oxi-dizer, as did a rocket), and the apparent greater ease of guiding a cruise missile operating like an aircraft at supersonic speeds in the upper atmo-sphere. The accurate inertial guidance of a ballistic missile over ranges of thousands of kilometers seemed difficult or impossible at the time; the V-2 had proven erratic in actual operations when fired over a distance of less than 320 km (200 mi). Moreover, no way was known to protect a ballistic missile warhead against the heat of reentry for ranges over about 960 km (600 mi).[24]

Because of Wernher von Braun's burning ambition, reinforced by favor-able images of America from his brother Sigismund and fear of the Soviets, he was unswerving in his desire to work for the United States, whatever the project. But the same could not be said for many of his subordinates, even though they too were young men who had hardly done anything else in their careers. In the absence of a concrete American contract offer, there were doubts about its length and possible terms, and whether families would be coming, or if left behind, how they would be cared for in a devastated country. Many of the engineers also simply had the stumbling block of German national identity and needed to decide whether to change sides, possibly even to emigrate permanently and become U.S. citizens.[25]

As the Soviets began building up their rocket program just across the zonal boundary, with one institute only 50 km (30 mi) away in Bleicherode, the Germans had the further temptation, all ideology aside, of defecting. Soviet radio broadcast offers of high salaries and good living conditions for German weapons experts, with promises that the work would remain in Germany. Specific invitations to von Braun, Steinhoff, and others were allegedly made too, via radio and loudspeakers across the border. According to Boris Chertok, a Soviet guidance engineer then living in the villa recently vacated by von Braun, his group even toyed with the idea of kidnapping the rocket engineer, but they were overruled because the intelligence services did not want to create an international incident. Ultimately only a handful went east, most notably Helmut Gröttrup, who had been arrested with von Braun in 1944. He was relatively left wing, he did not want to leave Germany, and he was at odds with members of the group. Gröttrup became the leader of the German group in Bleicherode and in the USSR, after they were forcibly deported in 1946. Anti-Slav racism notwithstanding, the Germans' fear of Stalinist duplicity turned out to be quite justified.[26]

At the end of July 1945 von Braun's group finally got word that the Joint Chiefs of Staff in Washington had approved a plan to bring the Germans to the United States. Under the secret "Project Overcast," 350 German specialists were to be sent, with the nominal rationale being assistance for the war against Japan, although its surrender four weeks later changed little. But with that news came a shock: this number did not encompass only Ordnance's Peenemünders. In fact Colonel Toftoy, who had been called back to Washington in late June to take over the rocket branch, was given a quota of one hundred; the USAAF and the navy had their own long lists of desirable specialists. Toftoy returned to Paris for meetings in late July and then visited Witzenhausen. He heard firsthand about the urgency of finding long-term family accommodations, especially as contracts were to be for a year only and family members were to stay behind. Ultimately, after another round of consultations with Staver, Porter, von Braun, and the leading Germans, Toftoy decided to accept about twenty extra, his orders notwithstanding.

The first version of "List I," as the Germans called it because they believed more would come later, had 124 names and was completed on 2 August. One of those names was Magnus von Braun, by then living in Eschwege.[27]

One of the complications in drawing up a list was that, after a behind-the-scenes tug-of-war, the British had succeeded in getting the U.S. Army to lend some of its rocketeers to "Operation Backfire." Based at the North Sea port of Cuxhaven, Backfire aimed to give the British Army experience with V-2 handling and launching. Dornberger was sent to Cuxhaven in mid-July, but he was soon shipped off to a POW camp in England for high-ranking generals, where he was threatened with a war crimes trial for the indiscriminate bombing of civilians. Hans Kammler was nowhere to be found and likely died near Prague at the end of the war, so Dornberger was the chosen scapegoat, but the whole idea ultimately foundered on its hypocrisy in the face of Hamburg, Dresden, Tokyo, Hiroshima, and so on. Neither the British nor the Americans connected Dornberger, von Braun, Rudolph, or any of the others to the horrors found at Dora and Nordhausen, however. Allied officers and specialists automatically assumed it was the sole responsibility of the SS and that there was a fundamental distinction between technical experts and Nazi war criminals. In his 17 June report to Ordnance in Washington, Staver described the rocketeers as "top-notch engineers" no different from Allied "scientists" in developing weapons of war.[28]

Wernher von Braun was on British lists as a desirable technical expert too, whether for Operation Backfire, for interrogation in England, or even for long-term employment. On 18 July the Backfire group asked the U.S. Army for the "apprehension" of von Braun, Rees, Schilling, and Steinhoff, "last reported as free civilians in area WITZENHAUSEN-ESCHWEGE." This request went nowhere. A month later Sir Alwyn Crow, who headed missile projects in the Ministry of Supply in London, asked more realistically for the loan of von Braun, Axster, Steinhoff, and Rees for one week. As of 23 August this request was still under discussion by U.S. representatives. On the twenty-eighth von Braun wrote from Witzenhausen advising Dieter Huzel to marry his fiancée so that she would qualify as a dependent when he went overseas, and Wernher and Magnus together wrote a letter in the blind to their parents, promising them full support if they came to the American zone. They spoke in code of going to the United States: "In the near future we will probably move to Ntino [Constantine Generales] and his people." Thus it appears that Wernher von Braun's pleasant interlude in London, his first since his Christmas 1934 trip, probably did not occur until the very end of August or the beginning of September 1945.[29]

He and the three others were flown to England and were interned in a special camp for German experts in Wimbledon, very near the famous tennis grounds. There he ran into Heinrich Klein, a leading designer of artillery and solid-fuel rockets for Rheinmetall-Borsig: "v. Braun, a little superior, let it be known that now the real work in the rocketry field could begin, as the land of unlimited possibilities was contemplating it." He went on about the A-9 as the "first intercontinental rocket," but it was only the initial step to a satellite that would orbit at 300 km (186 mi) altitude and 30,000 km/h (18,600 mph) velocity. Apparently nothing of the difficulties of the preceding months had dislodged him from his enthusiasm for, and rather unrealistic expectations of, working in the United States.[30]

He was a little more anxious about how the British would treat him, but he found that as soon as he met Sir Alwyn Crow, "I was hardly inside his office before we were engaged in friendly shop talk." Crow tried to get a list of people not going to the States whom von Braun might recommend to the British, and he may even have invited him to work for Britain—in both cases without success. One of the most memorable incidents of his London stay occurred during his morning ride between Wimbledon and the city center. The RAF driver silently pulled over and stopped in front of a building demolished by a rocket. "I was unable to tell the precise way in which the V-2 had done its damage, because the rubble had been cleared away," von Braun later said, never giving any indication that the sight affected him more deeply. Soon thereafter he and his compatriots were flown back to Germany, and he was told of his imminent departure for America. It was time for the great venture into the unknown to begin.[31]

Early on the morning of 12 September 1945 von Braun climbed into one of two jeeps in Witzenhausen. Traveling with him as the "advance guard" of the German rocketeers in the United States were Eberhard Rees and five middle-rank engineers chosen to process the Peenemünde document haul. The group's primary driver was First Lieutenant Morris Sipser, a young German-speaking intelligence officer. Like many such officers he was of European Jewish background, which did not make him any more inclined to like his charges. As they drove to Frankfurt, von Braun cracked a lot of jokes, perhaps unaware that Sipser understood the language, because Sipser found his jests smart-alecky and vaguely anti-American. After stopping for the night at a POW camp, and being given a medical examination, the seven and their two drivers set out for Paris in a bigger truck the next afternoon. Crossing the Saar River into France, von Braun said: "Well, take a good look at Germany, fellows. You may not see it for a long time to come."[32]

After a brief rest stop they finally reached the Paris suburbs at five a.m. on the fourteenth and a château near Versailles several hours later. It was a luxurious lockup for the interrogation of valued experts and former military leaders of the Third Reich—another sign that knowledge was becoming more important than crimes. Here von Braun signed his first formal contract with the U.S. War Department. Lasting six months and renewable for another six, it specified a salary of 31,200 marks a year paid into an account in Germany (in theory about $9,500, rapidly diminishing due to inflation), plus a per diem while on travel (including his whole stay in the United States) of six dollars a day. Project Overcast maintained the fiction that he and the other Germans were only on temporary duty and would soon return home.[33]

Late on the afternoon of 18 September the seven Peenemünders plus nine other Germans—aeronautical engineers and scientists destined for the army air forces' Wright Field in Dayton, Ohio—were driven to Orly Airport. After dinner at the officers' club, they got on a four-engine military C-54 airliner (DC-4) bound for America. By later standards it was an incredibly long, tedious, and exhausting trip, but in 1945 it was a privileged mode of transport across the Atlantic; the rest of the Germans would come on slow-moving troopships making rough crossings in the middle of the winter. The airplane took off at nine p.m., landing in the Azores for refueling around dawn, and flew ten more hours to Newfoundland for another refueling stop in the evening, finally making it to New Castle, Delaware, at two a.m. on the twentieth. After waiting another hour or two, the sixteen Germans were put on a two-engine C-47, where they proceeded to fly back over their previous course to reach Boston. Von Braun later told his parents: "[T]hey told us that the big four-motor transoceanic airplane could not land at the relatively small Boston airport." As day was breaking, they were put in army vans and finally on a ferry, because their destination was Fort Strong, a rather dismal old fortified island in Boston harbor. By mysterious bureaucratic fiat, it had been assigned as the processing point for Overcast.[34]

Here von Braun and the other fifteen filled out paperwork, and here "I became sick for the first time. It appeared to be jaundice, but later it turned out to be a liver infection. Nasty tongues naturally asserted that I had merely eaten myself sick." It was in fact hepatitis, presumably caused by the curable hepatitis A virus that he might have caught as a result of poor sanitary conditions back in Witzenhausen. Typical symptoms are jaundice, fatigue, abdominal pain, nausea, diarrhea, loss of appetite, and fever, but they developed slowly with von Braun, as he carried on for nearly three weeks with minimal treatment.[35]

At the beginning of October Major James Hamill appeared to collect the seven Peenemünders; Toftoy had assigned him responsibility for the rocket-ramjet project over Staver, as he knew Hamill better. Destined to be von Braun's boss for several years, Hamill was a clean-shaven, all-American-looking native of New York City in his late twenties who had earned a physics degree at Fordham before entering the army in 1940. He escorted the seven by train to Baltimore, where all but von Braun were sent on to Ordnance's Aberdeen Proving Grounds, north of the city, the location of the Peenemünde document cache. Hamill and his charge traveled on to Washington, D.C., for consultations with Toftoy and Ordnance leadership. On entering the Pentagon, von Braun "created quite a stir," as he was one of the first German scientists and engineers brought to the United States after the war: "People in the information booths stared in curiosity."[36]

Either in those meetings or beforehand from Hamill, von Braun first heard that his final destination was on the Rio Grande, opposite Ciudad Juárez, Mexico. "When I was first informed that I was going to be sent to El Paso I was intensely curious to see it. I knew it was a part of the great American 'Wild West.' " Like most Germans, he drew his impressions from the westerns of Karl May, a late-nineteenth-century German author who, without ever setting foot in America, wrote numerous novels about the German-American cowboy Old Shatterhand and the noble Mescalero Apache chief Winnetou. Lacking any other knowledge of a place so foreign to his European experience, von Braun half expected it to be the way it never was.[37]

Outside El Paso was his actual destination, Fort Bliss, the closest army base to the new White Sands Proving Ground in New Mexico. In 1944, even before Army Ordnance became involved with GE, it had sought a continental U.S. launch site for its nascent missile programs with the Jet Propulsion Laboratory (JPL) of the California Institute of Technology in Pasadena. The army chose the beautiful but desolate Tularosa Basin, over four thousand square miles of white gypsum sand dunes, lava flows, yucca, and cactus extending north-south in central New Mexico. JPL, which had its origins in a pioneering rocket group that had begun work at Caltech in the mid-1930s, first used it in the spring of 1945, before there even was a White Sands. In July Colonel Harold Turner showed up to create something from nothing. Early one morning shortly after he arrived there was a huge explosion on his territory—explained as a remote ammunition-dump accident, but actually the first A-bomb test—and he had not even been told about it. A month later he was informed that hundreds of boxcar loads of V-2 components had arrived from the port of New Orleans and were sitting in every rail yard for two hundred miles. He had to empty all those cars immediately. Turner pulled it off, but the parts were piled in crude warehouses or even outdoors in the new base area at the south end of the range, twenty-five miles over the Organ Mountains from Las Cruces, New Mexico, and fifty miles north of Fort Bliss—but eighty by road, as a direct route through the desert did not yet exist.[38]

On 6 October Hamill and von Braun set off for Texas by train. It was a long and memorable trip in Pullman convertible sleepers. Hamill was supposed to be with von Braun twenty-four hours a day; the presence of the German specialists in the United States was a secret, they were (not surprisingly) still being treated as security risks, and they were not even in the country as legal immigrants, the whole process having been bypassed when Overcast was set up. When the two reached St. Louis, Hamill found that they had been assigned to a car "full of ambulant wounded veterans of the 82nd and 101st Airborne Divisions" who had raised hell coming west. He had to do a lot of talking to get them reassigned; the only seats available were at opposite ends of a car.[39]

As the train approached Texarkana, Texas, Hamill noticed a "very animated conversation" between his charge and another man, ending at that stop with "much hand shaking and back slapping" as the other passenger got off.

> When I asked Wernher what had happened, he told me the following story. The man had asked him where he was from. Switzerland, he had replied. Upon inquiry as to what business Wernher was in, he replied, "the steel business." Well it turned out that this particular gentleman knew Switzerland like the back of his hand and was himself in the steel business. Further discussion led Wernher into the ball bearing business in which his section companion was an expert. Thank the Lord for the intervention of Texarkana at this particular time.

The man exited the train heartedly thanking von Braun, for "[i]f it wasn't for the help that you Swiss gave us, there is no telling as to whom might have won the war."[40]

Their welcome in El Paso on the evening of 8 October was not a warm one. The commanding general of Fort Bliss, to the north of the city, had no idea they were coming and was, moreover, a wounded veteran of both world wars. Hamill was relieved, however, not to have to spend every minute with von Braun now that they were on a military reservation, but he was awakened at eleven-thirty at night and told that he did have to share the German's room for security reasons. Someone kindly supplied a bottle of "Juarez rum," and they toasted their arrival at the base of their new operations. It had been four weeks since von Braun had left Witzenhausen.[41]

Jim Hamill was rescued from having to spend more of his "honeymoon" with von Braun, as he related it to Toftoy, as a result of the latter's worsening illness. Von Braun would spend the next eight weeks in the post hospital, and it was there that his hepatitis was finally diagnosed. It was a lonely and depressing period, as he found himself staying with wounded soldiers, thousands of miles from his family and comrades, with no means of contacting any of them. "Officials advised me to hide my identity, but I couldn't conceal my still broken English. The GI's sized me up with uncomfortable accuracy, and began calling me 'The Dutchman.' " They did, however, let him play poker with them. Later in October Eberhard Rees came out from Aberdeen to take over some of the duties von Braun could not handle. But out of the ward's windows von Braun saw the barren Franklin Mountains rising up west of the base and wondered if he could ever get used to this alien desert landscape.[42]

His emergence from the hospital was shortly followed by the most welcome arrival on 8 December of the first regular shipment of rocketeers, including his brother Magnus. On 3 November sixty-nine had left the Bavarian city of Landshut, 65 km (40 mi) northeast of Munich, not long after the U.S. Army had set up the family settlement there in a former military barracks. Sailing from Le Havre six days later, they spent a week on a troopship, followed by docking in New York and three weeks at Fort Strong, near Boston. Their departure for El Paso or Aberdeen was shortly followed by the arrival of twenty-one from the second group, including Arthur Rudolph. They did not reach El Paso until 15 January 1946, followed by a group of thirty that sailed in January and reached Fort Bliss on 20 February. Meanwhile most of the Aberdeen documents group, which had been supplemented by Ernst Steinhoff, Walther Riedel, and a few others from the first shipment, was sent to Texas by February. By one count, Ordnance brought over 127 German rocketeers in the first wave, but not all of them were ever in the West at the same time. In mid-February Hans Lindenberg suddenly died of diabetes, which he had neglected to treat, and another member of the group developed schizophrenia and was shipped back to Germany in December 1946.[43]

The surviving paperwork that ninety of them filled out at Fort Strong encompasses nearly three-quarters of von Braun's group at Fort Bliss. Almost all were in their thirties, with seven (including Magnus) in their mid- to late twenties and nine in their forties. Fourteen had doctorates (ten in engineering), twenty-nine were diploma engineers (equivalent to a master's), thirty-six were two-year engineers or had some engineering training, eight were foremen and skilled workers, one was a patent lawyer before the war (Axster), one a graphic artist, and one an administrator. Almost half had been members of the Nazi Party, although in several cases only for a short time, or rather late in the war, indicating low commitment; twenty-one had been in the SA (Storm Troopers), most of them the same people who had been party members; and two had been in the SS. Thus the term Americans often applied to them—"Nazi scientists"—was half right in the first instance and almost completely wrong in the second.[44]

In the first few months at Fort Bliss, von Braun faced several major leadership challenges. First, he had to initiate the supersonic ramjet project that the group would soon name "Comet"; its beginning can be dated to 10 December 1945, the day he started approximately forty pages of dense, handwritten calculations of the operation and efficiency of ramjet motors. At Peenemünde he and his group had never worked on this propulsion system, so it was a new topic for everyone, compounded by the fact that their facilities were primitive and they had no aerodynamicists: the U.S. Navy had shipped nine members of the Kochel institute and parts of the former Peenemünde wind tunnel to the outskirts of Washington, D.C., and the USAAF had grabbed Kochel's chief, Rudolf Hermann, much to the distress of Hamill. Early in 1946, in order to make some progress on the design, von Braun had to resort to sending questions by mail to Hermann at Wright Field and to Steinhoff and Riedel, still resident in Aberdeen, and waiting two weeks or more for the answers to wend their way back through the army system.[45]

Second, he assigned three dozen people to make the long bus commute to White Sands almost daily. There they would train GE Project Hermes personnel to assemble and launch V-2s. In Europe missile components had deteriorated so quickly that operational V-2s were fired within a few weeks of exiting the Mittelwerk. Now the Overcast and GE personnel had to reconstruct working rockets out of months-old, rusting, dried-out parts. "That job took eight months," von Braun later told Daniel Lang. "We seem to be expected to do it in two weeks." A particular burden was placed on American White Sands personnel. The first barracks and mess facilities were primitive, air-conditioning and heating were poor or nonexistent (the nights could be very cold), and potable water was in very short supply. One scientist who arrived in the heat of June, when outdoor temperatures often exceeded 100°F, declared the living conditions "intolerable."[46]

The barracks and mess situation at Bliss were a bit better, but von Braun and his deputies also faced a morale challenge there, especially in the early months of 1946. An unbearably long delay in establishing mail contact with the families in Landshut led to much discontent. Nothing at all was heard until the second shipment of hand-carried letters arrived in January, and regular letters took several weeks longer. Overcast personnel could write only to family members, and all correspondence went through censorship and took one to two months to reach its destination. Once contact was established, the men heard of a factional battle among the wives in Landshut over how the camp was being run, and they received letters describing how this or that spouse was creating trouble. Von Braun as leader was caught in the middle and eventually wrote to the leading wives on 20 May 1946 that "the impact of the tensions there tears at the nerves of the men here and also leads to friction among us." If the friction continued, he stated melodramatically, the whole project could be endangered and they would all be sent home.[47]

While the Landshut families were relatively privileged in the midst of the hunger and destitution of occupied Germany, their letters also mentioned the lack of nutritious foodstuffs, clothing, and everyday items. Family and friends not in "Camp Overcast" were much worse off and often on the verge of starving. The State Department forbade the mailing of packages, but after Colonel Toftoy, for one, pushed hard in Washington, permission to mail items was granted as of 1 June. The "prisoners of peace," as they ironically dubbed themselves, gladly spent part of their per diem buying things during their excursions to downtown El Paso, when five Germans would be escorted by one U.S. soldier for shopping, dinner, perhaps a movie. In the early days such excursions happened only monthly, but they became more frequent in the spring, as Hamill came to trust them and conceded the need for more outlets. Cooped up most of the time inside a fenced-off area on the base, the Germans organized more English lessons and gradually developed their own clubhouse and bar into a pleasant means of after-work escape, beginning with $100 that von Braun lent to the new club on 11 December 1945.[48]

As one might expect of a bunch of young men forced to live communally without families, fraternity house antics ensued. For a while there were frequent battles between barracks using fire extinguishers, pillows, and sandbags; once when von Braun was on the roof with his group, the leader of the opposing forces told him to surrender because he was outnumbered. A physicist by training, he retorted: "[Y]ou forget our higher potential energy; we're *up* here throwing *down* there." On 7 February, after a barracks inspection, Hamill felt compelled to complain to von Braun in a written memo: "Several rooms are in such a poor state of police as to make them almost uninhabitable by human beings. . . . The wall of Mr. Wiesemann's room has been broken through. This matter was not reported to this office. The pieces of the wall have evidently been distributed to various occupants of Barracks Number 1."[49]

In later years the Fort Bliss and White Sands veterans often remembered the pioneering period through a nostalgic haze, but other evidence indicates that von Braun really faced a crisis of morale in February. The most bizarre document from this period is the "black hand" manifesto of early that month, an anonymous letter in which the black hand was a rubber-stamped outstretched left hand that appeared in place of signature and self-identification. It could easily be dismissed as more barracks shenanigans except that it complains that "it is high time for our leadership, with a view to our self-respect and our future, to step forward more forcefully," especially in regard to mail, packages, infrequent trips off base, and condescending treatment from Hamill and other Americans. Those who wanted to go home should be supported to do so, the document concludes. At almost exactly the same time von Braun received a second long, anonymous letter of complaint.[50]

One factor in the morale problems was the realization, soon after arrival, that El Paso and White Sands were not the new Peenemünde. Von Braun told Lang in 1950: "Frankly, we were disappointed with what we found in this country in the first year or so. At Peenemünde we'd been coddled. Here you were counting pennies. Your armed forces were being demobilized and everybody wanted military expenditures curtailed." Primitive or aged wooden workshops were all that was available in the early months, and some of the engineers had to crawl under them to run their own cabling, wary of poisonous snakes and spiders. At White Sands the only launching equipment available at first was a mobile launch set from Germany, in the same condition as the rocket parts. Even when the new launch pad and blockhouse were finished during the summer, there were facilities to fire only a couple of V-2s per month.[51]

Other problems sprang from the peculiar status of those who had been brought over under Project Paperclip, as Overcast had been renamed in March 1946. Toftoy told the Ordnance Department Advisory Committee in June: "The Germans . . . are allowed no access to American classified projects and are not permitted to leave their designated area without a military escort." Thus it was difficult or impossible to have any real interchange with other missile and ramjet experimental groups in the United States—of which there were many in a postwar environment marked by pluralistic experimentation and interservice rivalry. Two rocket propulsion firms (Aerojet and Reaction Motors) had already been founded during World War II. The U.S. Army, Army Air Forces, and Navy were funding missile projects at a number of aircraft companies, such as Douglas and Martin, and the services had projects in their own laboratories and in university labs such as JPL and the Johns Hopkins Applied Physics Laboratory. While the United States was considerably behind Germany in rockets and missiles in 1945, within three or four years German technology was absorbed and surpassed, although budget cuts meant that most missile projects remained experimental.[52]

Von Braun and his leading men did willingly submit to a series of interviews with American scientists and engineers who came to Fort Bliss to pump them for their knowledge and experience. These exchanges could be stimulating, but they allowed for little knowledge to flow in the opposite direction and did not always go well. Especially noteworthy was a spring 1946 visit by Milton Rosen and Ernst Krause of the Naval Research Laboratory (NRL) in Washington, D.C. They were planning to build a large sounding rocket, later called Viking, that would incorporate innovations such as tanks integral to the fuselage (the V-2's tanks were hung inside the structure and were not load-bearing) and an engine that could be gimbaled—moved in two axes—for attitude control (the V-2 used jet vanes in the exhaust). Von Braun was skeptical, the long and difficult birth of the A-4/V-2 having made him and his associates very conservative rocket engineers. Rosen and Krause in turn perceived him as resistant to innovation. His conservative engineering style was to serve von Braun quite well in the future, but until the late 1950s he and his group were often not on the cutting edge of rocketry in the United States.[53]

In mid-1946, however, von Braun and his deputies still hoped that they would be allowed to fulfill their grandiose postsurrender plans, a hope encouraged by their American superiors. In July Hamill passed along Army Intelligence's questions about the A-9, A-10, and A-11 (a projected even larger booster for the other two). This inquiry was tied to questions about the potential of the Soviets to resume rapid rocket development in Germany. Von Braun's answers played up the Soviet threat, emphasizing the thousands of former Peenemünders available in Germany, plus the captured facilities at the rocket center, the Mittelwerk, and elsewhere. If the United States brought many more of his former colleagues from Germany and Britain, he argued, the A-9/A-10 program could be revived, and the three-stage orbital version with the A-11 could be ready by 1955. "The detail design of the A-10 was continued by the German group at Fort Bliss from December 1945 until March 1946," he noted, before it was "discontinued" because of "more important tasks." Presumably intended as the booster for a ramjet-powered A-9 (the winged V-2), the A-10 must have been the sizing factor for a massive test stand that Ordnance built on a mountainside at White Sands in 1946. Capable of holding down a rocket of half a million pounds (225 metric tons) of thrust, it was soon dubbed "the White Elephant" since there was nothing anywhere near that size to test.[54]

A clearer picture of what von Braun was planning that spring can be drawn from a 12 April memo entitled "Use of Atomic Warheads in Projected Missiles," sent to Toftoy by Hamill's executive officer, Major Walter Singles. Von Braun or his closest associates originally drafted it in German as a letter to Robert Oppenheimer, then head of the Los Alamos laboratory in northern New Mexico, after a visit by Ordnance leaders to El Paso. The draft letter and Singles's memo outline two versions of the ramjet. The "Small-Type Comet," to be launched on a modified V-2 booster, could have a warhead of 1,100 or 2,200 lb (500 or 1000 kg). The "Large-Type Comet," presumably based on the A-9/A-10, was to have a payload of 6,000 lb. Both missiles would have a flying time of 20–25 minutes, which indicates a range of under 1,000 mi (1600 km) at Mach 3.3 (about 2,000 mph), the nominal working velocity. Neither the Germans nor their U.S. Army superiors had the slightest conception of the size and weight of the Hiroshima and Nagasaki bombs, then a great secret, as the memo inquires whether it would be possible to fit an atomic warhead in the rather small spaces of the 1,100-lb version, or only to the 6,000-lb warhead "Large-Type Comet." The 1945 bombs were in fact in the neighborhood of 10,000 lb (4500 kg), and it was not until the late 1940s that momentum was regained in nuclear weapons design. Thus the inquiry was quite premature and nothing came of it.[55]

It must be said that von Braun did not invent the idea of combining the guided missile and A-bomb into a frightening superweapon. It was so obvious that the Western press discussed it immediately after Hiroshima and scientists in the Manhattan Project before that, as they wondered why the Germans would ever develop V-weapons armed only with relatively puny high-explosive charges. Thus, with or without him, nuclear warheads were coming. But in his July 1946 answers to the A-9/A-10/A-11 questions, von Braun first raised a specter central to his vision of rockets and space stations in the late 1940s and early 1950s: orbiting vehicles as atomic bombers able to rain down death from space. The "nation that first reaches this goal possesses an overwhelming military superiority over other nations," he asserted, with the clear implication that the United States had to beat the Soviet Union or face a dire threat. The roots of this vision lay in Oberth and in interwar German science fiction, where there was a fascination with the idea of the space platform or ballistic missile as the ultimate weapon for dominating the Earth.[56]

Despite all the frustrations inherent in the Fort Bliss situation, von Braun found other compensations in his work. During the spring, summer, and fall of 1946 the V-2 launch program began to gather momentum, and his wartime creation at last became a means for the scientific exploration of the upper atmosphere and near space. Back in Washington, Colonel Toftoy had been instrumental in rousing interest in navy, air forces, and university groups for the V-2's potential for increasing scientific knowledge, as the military also benefited from information about the environment through which missiles traveled. At White Sands the combined German-GE team launched the first rocket on 16 April. It spun out of control and crashed, but the next launch on 10 May reached an altitude of 70 mi (112 km), although no scientific results were returned. American scientific teams, lacking the resources to imitate Peenemünde's Regener Tonne project to parachute a sophisticated package of instruments from high altitude, went ahead and installed their experiments in heavy containers. When nothing could be recovered from the supersonic impacts, the Germans suggested explosives to blow off the warhead, so that the two parts tumbled more slowly to earth. Other teams slowly improved the return of data by telemetry. By the fall a couple of American groups obtained substantive scientific results. A V-2 rose to 107 mi (172 km) on 10 October carrying an NRL spectrograph that first imaged the Sun's spectrum in the ultraviolet, a feat possible only in space.[57]

While the Germans could play only consultative roles on vehicle engineering and were excluded from the science teams, von Braun was happy to see some scientific results from his work. The beauty of the desert and the pioneering atmosphere of White Sands also appealed to him; instead of taking the long, roundabout trip there by bus, he loved cutting across open country in a jeep. "It is such a romantic Karl May affair," he told his parents in August. His 31 July letter said simply: "[T]he work is a lot of fun."[58] He still had every hope that America would fulfill his dreams.

CHAPTER TEN

Mars Project

1946–49

From my earliest youth, I have despised the Greek proverb which claims that War is the father of Events. Nevertheless, my whole life has been one consecutive revelation of the core of truth which lies within that proverb. . . .

Do you believe that the thousands of scientists, engineers and craftsmen who labored for decades on rocket aircraft, guided missiles, and finally, on our great satellite vessels, envisaged in their loving work and ingenuity the diabolical ends to which their creations were often put? I tell you No, gentlemen! Those men were animated by secret visions of reaching into the heavens.

—GENERAL BRADEN in Wernher von Braun's "Mars Project"[1]

Just as the American intelligence officer had predicted in Garmisch, Wernher von Braun adapted fairly easily to American life, although he continued to show "a marked deference in the presence of a uniform," a British reporter said in 1948. Although he was disappointed that El Paso, then a city of 100,000, was not the Wild West, he was impressed that it was "a modern metropolis with traffic lights, airport, and skyscrapers. This change had come in less than two decades, which told me something about America's tremendous vitality." A true believer in science and technology, with a strong tendency to technological utopianism, he was most impressed by the contribution of machines of all kinds to the then-unrivaled U.S. standard of living. At the beginning of May 1946 he, Walther Riedel, Karl Heimburg, and Kurt Debus had taken a used car they had bought communally and gone on a five-day trip to Los Angeles and San Diego, accompanied by a sergeant sent along by Hamill. Von Braun loved the scenery of the Southwest but was even more impressed by southern California, its engineering achievements and its massive growth: "It is really fabulous with what optimism and entrepreneurial spirit this California is being built up," he told Klaus Riedel's widow in a letter. The one thing that really stuck in his mind afterward, however, was simply the freedom to travel thousands of miles without ever crossing a border or meeting a demand to produce his papers.[2]

But a demobilizing America was not yet ready to launch into a new arms race with the Soviet Union, with the result that the next three years would be a time of professional disappointment for von Braun and his Germans. Cutbacks during Fiscal Year (FY) 1947, which began on 1 July 1946, effectively killed the Large-Type Comet ramjet missile and reduced the V-2–launched Small-Type Comet to an experimental program. In January 1947 Ordnance renamed it Hermes II, symbolically attaching it to GE's Project Hermes, which included V-2 firings, the development of a Hermes A-1 derived from Wasserfall, and other missiles. General Electric supplied some manpower to Fort Bliss but never seems to have accepted the German project as its own.[3]

In January and May 1946 and January 1947 Hamill's rocket group also asked Washington to bring over 300 or 317 more Germans from "List II"— personnel who would be needed only if the ramjet project were greatly accelerated. Von Braun, while less and less optimistic, still thought in the fall of 1946 that they would get another "100 to 150," numbers that must have come from Hamill or Toftoy. Only after President Harry Truman made further cuts in military research and development in January 1947, in response to the decisive victory of conservative, budget-cutting Republicans in both houses in the November midterm elections, did von Braun begin more realistically to seek small numbers of specialists to fill particular gaps. Beginning that year, a few new Germans did arrive.[4]

Faced with a prolonged drought in the rocket business because of a lack of popular support, von Braun would turn to the idea of selling the American public on spaceflight. Since it obviously was not going to come about simply as a by-product of military development, he had to convince ordinary people that space travel was not a silly or utopian proposition. But the question was how? Sometime in 1947 he decided it could be done through the medium of a science fiction novel. At a time when his job was keeping him busy scarcely more than the regulation forty-hour week, writing a novel gave him an outlet for his creative energies. With renewed hope, he began creating the work that would lay a foundation for all his later successes in space advocacy.

The fallow years, 1946–49, were also fundamental in establishing a new life for himself in the United States. Like his work, that process was not without its frustrations. His formal immigration, and that of others in his group, would be repeatedly delayed by government red tape and by renewed questions about their service to the Nazis. Bringing family members across the ocean also proceeded slowly. Nonetheless, during this period his inner and outer life would be transformed in ways that marked the final maturation of his personality.

All through the first months in America, a shadow had hung over his life and that of his brother Magnus: the fate of their relatively elderly parents (Magnus Sr. was sixty-eight and Emmy nearly sixty). Only in late January or February 1946 had they heard any news at all: the two were still in their Silesian village, but in the pastor's house rather than in their own. This most welcome but isolated and puzzling piece of information came via a couple of routes, including through Sigismund, still sheltering in the neutral Vatican with his family. (In 1944 Sigis's wife had given birth to a second daughter in Rome, Christina, and at the end of 1945 a son, Christoph-Friedrich, in the Vatican itself.) Over the spring a few letters and postcards from the parents to others did get through to Wernher and Magnus, but there was no direct mail between the United States and Polish-run Silesia, and U.S. censors forbade the inclusion of letters for forwarding by others. Magnus Sr. and Emmy von Braun in turn had heard only on 26 November, from a neighbor who had been in Berlin, "the big sensation" that their sons were already in America. While the parents had avoided the worst disasters of a Red Army occupation followed quickly by an influx of Polish settlers, they had suffered multiple intrusions into and expulsions from their house, accompanied by theft, harassment, and wanton vandalism. The sons, reading "in the newspapers here such terrible things about conditions in Silesian Poland," were frightened that worse could befall them and knew that the Germans would likely be expelled. Deeply concerned about their survival, Wernher von Braun requested Army Intelligence to launch a special mission to bring them out. Nothing, however, came of it.[5]

On 12 July 1946, the baron and baroness's thirty-sixth wedding anniversary, their forced expulsion to the West began; a miserable trek to a terrible transit camp was followed by robbery of more of their goods, a multiday rail journey by cattle car to the British zone, another transit camp, and for a couple of days a private room. Somehow their presence was communicated to Landshut, and on 27 July an American officer and driver appeared to take them and their few belongings across Germany to the camp. They were warmly welcomed in the middle of the night. On 31 July Wernher opened a huge letter to his parents, cosigned by Magnus: "Hurra!!!!! Today the telegram came that you had arrived on the 27th, thus four days ago. You can't possibly imagine how much we have waited for this news." Magnus wrote the same day, "The joy was naturally huge." And when Wernher finished his letter on the first he mentioned "how much yesterday evening, after the arrival of the telegram, we were crying for joy."[6]

Immediately the two of them began to write many letters, in part to convince their parents to come to the United States when the movement of the families under Project Paperclip finally came through. Wernher could say only little in early August about this long-promised possibility. But in his 21 August letter he was able to tell them that he had received the news "that the conclusion of new contracts has been approved by all responsible American authorities." These agreements, he believed, would convert them from travel status to salary in U.S. dollars, would last three to six years, and would allow reunification of the families in the United States and legal immigration for the specialists, starting the five-year clock until they could actually be sworn in as citizens. Notwithstanding the salesmanship for El Paso that shines through in this and other letters, he makes a statement of his commitment that sounds anything but convenient or forced:

> We have both firmly decided . . . to remain here in America. It is a young, huge country with a great future; people are not at all unfriendly, and one also does not feel as if one is in a foreign country, because in contrast to other foreign countries there are so many Germans here. . . . The feeling of being a stranger in a strange land is something one has much less here than any other country I have ever seen.[7]

Their concern that their parents would find it difficult to abandon Germany was well founded, however, at least in the case of their father. On 2 September, after what seemed like an eternity, they got the first letters from Landshut. Their mother's account of the ordeal they had endured is lost or currently inaccessible, but we do have a letter to Wernher from his father, dated 29 July, thanking him first for his deep and sincere commitment to help them with letters, packages, and attempts to intervene on their behalf. Magnus Sr., however, mourned the loss of "my beautiful big library," the family heirlooms, the estates in Silesia and in East Prussia, and "the graves of my grandparents and great-grandparents." On top of this, both his sisters had died in 1945. Neucken, as he later found out, had been totally pillaged.[8]

It was symptomatic of a whole world going down in flames. The collapse of Hitler's Germany, and the triumph of Stalin's USSR, meant the end of the eastern European aristocracy as a landowning class, the radical redistribution of land at the barrel of a gun, and the ethnic cleansing of the entire region. For the patriarch of the von Braun family, whose life had been dedicated to that world, personally and politically, it was an indescribable loss. To come to America would mean total dependence on the two sons. But he had no place to go back to in Germany, no way to make a living, and no state to pay a pension. He and Emmy ultimately had little choice but to move.

One of the primary reasons Magnus Sr. wrote directly to Wernher on 29 July, however, was to tell him to end Magnus Jr.'s long-distance engagement to a woman whom his youngest son had met in Garmisch. The two had played the leading roles in the camp theater. She was four years older than Magnus (now twenty-seven) and separated from her husband but not yet divorced. These factors alone may have been sufficient to make her unacceptable to his old-fashioned parents, but something she apparently wrote in a letter to them made them even more convinced she was bad for him. So overwrought was his father's letter that he even equated the situation to the two brothers' Gestapo arrest in 1944. Once again Magnus Jr.'s "childish gullibility" would get him in trouble; Wernher "should avoid bringing his brother into such a precarious situation a second time." This ultimatum left him little choice but to show the letter to his brother, which eventually provoked Magnus to break off the engagement.[9]

Wernher sent his parents two letters in the fall that he kept from Magnus and that dealt, in whole or in part, with their close but problematic relationship. On 3 September he told his parents that he had not approved of Magnus's fiancée but did not want to burden their relationship by interfering. On 4 November he indicated that he held back in part because he had already intervened enough, having pulled Magnus into the rocket business in 1943 to keep him away from the front, then put him on the short list of people to go to America—he did not add that he had sent him to the Mittelwerk and that there were certainly more qualified candidates for America than Magnus. Although the youngest von Braun quickly settled in at Fort Bliss, where his excellent English allowed him to earn significant money tutoring others, it could not have been easy living in the shadow of his incredibly talented brother, especially in such close quarters.[10]

Their relationship was further tested in June 1946, when Magnus sold a platinum bar to an El Paso jeweler for $100, triggering a police and Justice Department investigation that revealed that he had smuggled it into the United States. Hamill succeeded in hushing up the story in the name of secrecy, but he later told the FBI, perhaps hyperbolically, that Wernher had given his brother a "severe physical beating" for endangering the project. Magnus's discomfort with his role at Fort Bliss became manifest in his Paperclip files, as people interrogated about him sometimes found him distant, conceited, and snobby about his aristocratic heritage, at least until they got to know him better. One American security officer took such a dislike to him that he ludicrously described Magnus in 1948–49 as "a worse threat to security than half a dozen discredited SS Generals."[11]

Magnus von Braun's gloom in the fall of 1946 over his failed engagement was not helped any by Wernher's ebullient mood. In the same 3 September letter that he did not show to Magnus, Wernher broached to his parents something else that had been "on my heart, and indeed something big."

> I have, since the time I was still in Pee[nemünde], developed a silent love for Maria [von] Quistorp and carried the idea with me since that time that she was the right woman for me. She knows nothing of this. In the last year before the war's end I did not give even the slightest indication of that, although in that period I was often in Bauer and had frequently seen and spoken to her. The situation for the future was then so uncertain that I did not want to allow a romance to develop that might all too easily have been destroyed by hard events.[12]

Perhaps he feared for his own survival, given the possibility of being caught in an Allied attack or being rearrested by the Gestapo.

Maria von Quistorp was of course a first cousin, the daughter of Emmy von Braun's brother Alexander, and was not much more than half his age, having turned eighteen only in June 1946. He mentioned both issues in his letter to his parents but expressed confidence that they liked her and her parents so well that it should not be a problem for them. He asked them if one or both could not make the difficult trek to the farm near Norden in far northwestern Germany to which Maria, her mother, and her siblings had escaped, or returned to, at the end of the war. (Her father, known to the von Brauns as "Uncle Allack," had been arrested by the Soviets in fall 1945 while trying to go back to Bauer; his fate was worrying and uncertain.) By a lucky coincidence, Maria was visiting the von Brauns in Landshut on the day the letter arrived in early October. Von Braun got this account from Maria by mail afterward: his "father dashed up waving a letter he had just received from me [W.]. 'I'm supposed to find out if you will marry Wernher,' he demanded. 'What shall I tell him?' 'I told him I'd never thought of marrying anyone else.' "[13]

For von Braun, however, it would be a long wait, as the minimum time for an answer would be seven or eight weeks. His intervening letters were filled with revealing details of everyday life at Fort Bliss. Classical music was important to him and the rest of the highly educated German group, and they organized "symphony concerts . . . on excellent records supplied by our music-enthusiast major, [and] broadcast by loudspeakers" wired up by their "first-class high-frequency specialists." He remembered fondly trying to play an arrangement of Schubert's *Unfinished Symphony* in a four-handed duet with his mother. (He had also occasionally played cello in a string quartet at Peenemünde.) The last time he had his hands on a piano was in the château near Versailles, and he was pleased when the clubhouse got one later in the fall, although his left arm still gave him trouble. On weekends they often went downtown to buy things for packages to Germany, but what really excited them was the freedom to sign out unescorted, starting on 13 September, one year after the first contracts were signed in Europe. The next day, a Saturday, Wernher relished being able to wander alone through the Mexican quarter of El Paso and take a bus to see the old town of Yleta, twenty miles away in the fertile Rio Grande valley.[14]

Magnus, although still urging his parents to come, was less inclined to give a sales pitch in his letters and noted the limitations of El Paso entertainment in a "dry" state with restrictive alcohol laws. In an earlier letter he mentioned the brutal summer heat, which made it impossible to go back into their barracks until midnight, as temperatures of up to 46°C (115°F) had been measured inside the rooms. Instead they would sit outside reading or hang out at the club. In order to make work in the offices tolerable, Hamill had gotten them an early form of air-conditioning: evaporative "swamp coolers."[15]

On 21 October Wernher von Braun's wait for an answer ended. The next day he wrote: "Yesterday came father's letter from 3 October! I am naturally in seventh heaven! Life has taken on a whole new meaning." On the thirtieth he wrote again, after receiving older letters from them and his aunt/mother-in-law-to-be, and the first letter from Maria in Landshut, "full of touching confusion and burning acceptance." The emotional impact on him was profound: "Tears came into my eyes—I am not normally like this—from emotion and joy." The feeling was at bottom religious in tone. He saw the timing of her visit as not accidental but divinely inspired. "The Texas sunshine up to now—by itself something to be reckoned with!—is like a weak little oil lamp in comparison to the sunshine that now spreads over me. Everything is so white on white that I almost feel uncomfortable. 'I shudder before the envy of the gods' or something like that."[16]

It was right around this time that he was "born again." Von Braun later spoke only reluctantly of his conversion experience, which he viewed as deeply personal, but he did once discuss it with a small religious magazine. One day in Fort Bliss "a neighbor called and asked if I'd like to go to church with him. I accepted, because I was anxious to see if an American church was just a religious country club, as I'd been led to expect." Instead he found a "small, white frame building . . . in the hot Texas sun on a browned-grass lot." A little while later the minister arrived in an "old, battered bus" that he had driven up to forty miles to retrieve parishioners who did not have cars. "Together these people made up a live, vibrant community. . . . This was the first time that I really understood that religion was not a cathedral inherited from the past, or a quick prayer at the last minute. To be effective, religion has to be backed up by discipline and effort." Although he had remained a perfunctory Lutheran in Germany, the old state-supported religion had not much emotional appeal for him; the welcoming inclusiveness of American evangelical Protestantism came to him just at a time when he felt both blessed by God and in need of acceptance in a new land.[17]

His conversion also helped him to deal with feelings coming from an unprecedented direction: fear of the human race's inability to deal with advanced technology, fear ultimately of the Bomb. Twice in a week at the beginning of September his letters expressed concern about worsening relations with the USSR over Germany. It is probably no coincidence that the entire 31 August issue of *The New Yorker* marked the first publication of John Hersey's *Hiroshima*. On 2 September von Braun wrote: "Today all of civilization is already in play. . . . Will man's intelligence keep up with his technology? If not, it will be the end of the human race and then maybe people such as we technicians will be at fault." And on the ninth he wrote: "My God, my need for war is so fundamentally satiated that I hope that it will all right itself somewhat. Poor Europe would of course suffer most." Immersed in a peacetime American context, his postsurrender belief in an imminent war with the Soviet Union had faded, and nuclear weapons—and the inevitability of his becoming mixed up in them—had made him more thoughtful.[18]

As he became, over the course of some weeks or months, more and more Christian in feeling, he came to see religion as the answer to the dilemmas of technology: only a religiously based ethical code could control the evil that humans could unleash with their own hard-won knowledge. It was something he deeply felt, but it was also a way to pacify his own conscience. One searches in vain, however, for any deeper sense of guilt over the Nazi period or the fate of the concentration camp prisoners. The sole reference he made to any of this in his fall 1946 letters was his characterization of Hans Kammler as a "rogue" and "criminal," presumably in response to a question by his father. Like many Germans, he seems to have accepted the maxim of not looking back. If the Third Reich's crimes could be blamed on Hitler and a handful of evil people around him, then so much the easier. Looking to the future was a reflex that came naturally to him.[19]

The very happy news of his engagement brought a new phase of waiting embedded in old issues: the new Paperclip contracts, the shipment of families to the United States, and housing for them. Further delays in Washington meant that the army did not present the new five-year contracts until later in November. When they finally did arrive, Wernher was satisfied with his annual salary of $9,975, then a substantial middle-class income. (Multiply by ten for approximate current dollars.) As for the housing problem, Toftoy and Hamill had once, while driving around the base, spotted the Annex to the William Beaumont Hospital, a fenced-in area on the northeastern perimeter of Fort Bliss. With the postwar cutbacks, the hospital director was happy to get rid of it. Rather than one building, the Annex was actually eighty separate buildings, almost all one-story wood-frame "wards." At the end of October, Magnus reported to his parents, "the long awaited and announced move has been finished. It was fairly difficult," but the work and living quarters were much better. The actual refitting of the old ward buildings into apartments was delayed repeatedly, however, so at first the housing was somewhat provisional. Both the contracts and the Annex nonetheless signaled a new permanence in their residence in the United States. In December the very first families arrived from Landshut.[20]

Because of uncertainties in when Maria might come over as a fiancée and when Sigis might return from Rome to Germany, and because of confusion generated by the endless delays in correspondence, von Braun decided to push his family back to number sixty-two in the shipment queue. In his 25 November letter he told his parents that he expected them to come in January but shortly thereafter reported more delays, throwing everything into uncertainty again. He also had as dependents Klaus Riedel's widow and three-year-old daughter, whom he generously supported at Landshut out of concern for their well-being and in honor of his close friendship with Klaus going back to the Raketenflugplatz. It was uncertain whether they would come or not, and whether their dependent status would be permitted under the new contracts. Eventually they were allowed to retain their status but they never came to the United States.[21]

Further uncertainty hung around Sigis's plans. From the Vatican he had earlier talked about emigrating to Australia, where his brother-in-law was, or going to America, an idea that Wernher and Magnus naturally greeted with enthusiasm. Nothing came of these plans, however, and in the fall of 1946 Sigis left his family behind and returned to Germany, where he was, against his expectations, immediately thrown in an American prison as a former official of the Third Reich. He was released only in November, whereupon he made his way to Landshut, future plans quite uncertain. As an able-bodied man, he could not go to the United States as a Paperclip dependent with family, so he had to seek his own way in a still prostrate Germany. Indeed, the winter of 1946–47 would turn out to be the rock bottom of the occupation, with terrible cold exacerbating food and coal shortages. Those in the Landshut camp were again the lucky ones, but even there things were difficult. Wernher and Magnus were upset in January to get letters saying that their mother's health and ability to travel were threatened by nutritional deficiencies.[22]

In the interim Wernher von Braun had achieved a new fame, as he proudly indicated to his parents on 8 December 1946. The War Department decided to confirm the presence of the Germans at Fort Bliss and Wright Field (the air force was not independent until the fall of 1947), following leaks and Soviet accusations of hypocrisy—their response to Western criticism of the sudden deportation to the USSR of Gröttrup's rocketeers and several thousand other German specialists and their families in late October. A couple of days after the Fort Bliss Germans got their contracts on 22 November, reporters came to the base, and von Braun and other leaders gave a two-and-a-half-hour interview. Because of military censorship, the news emerged everywhere on 4 December. The *El Paso Times* ran a banner headline: "118 Top German V-2 Experts Stationed in E.P.," accompanied by a picture of von Braun and Hamill. Other stories included "German Scientists Plan Re-fueling Station in Sky on Route to Moon," a product of the discussion of space ideas at the news conference, and a von Braun engagement announcement that falsely described Maria as a "second cousin," no doubt because an accurate description of their relationship would have raised too many eyebrows. Pictures of him also ran in *The New York Times*, *The Washington Post*, *Time*, and *Life*.[23]

Von Braun himself was in Washington and New York when these stories came out, on a trip with Ernst Steinhoff for meetings in the Pentagon and with a gyro contractor on Long Island. He was bowled over by New York, its skyscrapers and technological sophistication. The lifting of secrecy gave him a chance to hear from his old friend Dr. Constantine Generales, then in Arizona, and to look up Willy Ley in Queens, their first encounter since the Raketenflugplatz's dying days. Ley had fled to the United States in 1935 and had later written for the leftist New York tabloid *P.M.* They enthusiastically discussed the German project until 2:45 a.m. Ley told Herbert Schaefer, the only other Raketenflugplatz veteran to emigrate, "that I found no reason to regard v.B. as an outspoken anti-Nazi. But just as little, if not even less, did I find him to be a Nazi. In my opinion the man simply wanted to build rockets. Period." While this judgment contained a lot of truth, it would not be the last time that von Braun received a free pass on his Third Reich activities from his fellow space enthusiasts.[24]

After two more months of waiting for his parents and Maria von Quistorp, Wernher suddenly flew back to New York on 12 February 1947: he was to get married in Germany. Only two days earlier he had written to his parents, indicating that he still expected them. The very next day Toftoy sent a memo to the chief of Army Intelligence asking for special permission for von Braun to return to Landshut under the emergency clause of the Paperclip contract. His mother was ill and needed care in the United States, and fiancées had been ruled ineligible for travel as they were not legal dependents. The only solution was to send him over to get married and bring back all three with him; Toftoy stated that in view of his "outstanding value to the United States . . . it is requested that he be placed under direct military custody during his entire stay in Europe." The army was afraid of a Soviet kidnap attempt. By the fourteenth von Braun was on a ship to the North Sea port of Bremerhaven, and following a storm-delayed crossing he took trains to Munich and Landshut on the twenty-seventh, escorted at all times by American minders. En route he bought Maria flowers and presents using three cartons of cigarettes, which amounted to a small fortune in Germany, where paper marks were increasingly worthless. Forewarned by a telegram from New York, his father and Sigismund had hurriedly arranged for Maria and her mother to come to Landshut and had pulled together a ceremony. It was a joyous reunion on the platform; Wernher had not seen Maria or his parents for over two years, and Sigis for over three.[25]

On a cold and gray Saturday, 1 March, American MPs and Bavarian police ringed the main Lutheran church in the old center of the very Catholic city of Landshut; only the wedding party and guests were allowed inside the cordon. After the ceremony and reception, the happy couple repaired to a small apartment in the settlement for their honeymoon, escorted by numerous armed MPs. There they found "[t]wo military policemen had already established themselves in our quarters. 'Just pretend we're not here,' they said. 'If you need us, we'll be in the kitchen.' " They would shadow them every minute after they returned to the ship in Bremerhaven. Before von Braun was allowed to go, however, he was taken to U.S. military headquarters in Frankfurt and questioned for several hours on 8 March about the organization of the German rocket program and buried document caches, as Allied technical intelligence officers in Europe thought he had been less than perfectly frank. His own "evasive" answers to some questions that day only increased their suspicion. Because "many senior officers, especially in Army

Ordnance, hold him in high esteem and consider him invaluable in his work," the "interrogation" was, however, "conducted very informally and on cordial terms."[26]

Denied a proper honeymoon, Wernher and Maria hoped to have one on board ship instead. Alas, they found that only women got cabins. Emmy roomed with Maria, while Wernher and Magnus Sr. slept in large open bunk halls with the soldiers belowdecks. The crossing was even rougher than in the opposite direction and took fourteen days. They docked in New York on a misty 26 March morning, three days after Wernher's thirty-fifth birthday, but were soon treated to an astonishing view of "magnificent Manhattan with huge skyscrapers" (Emmy von Braun). After being held for a day on the ship, they traveled for three days and three nights by train. At the El Paso station, they received a "big reception. Schnick [Magnus's nickname; he later changed it to Mac] fetched us in his very chic 100 horsepower car (with a radio and all the bells and whistles!), and immediately drove us on a beautiful mountain road around the city." At Fort Bliss the five von Brauns— Wernher, Maria, Magnus Sr. and Jr., and Emmy—would live together for a couple of months in one of the provisionally refitted ward buildings before getting their own apartments. Starting over had its difficulties, such as the lack of basic household goods and the unavailability of servants for the parents, but after all the catastrophes of the preceding years, they were just happy to bring most of the family back together in a prosperous land that promised both security and stability.[27]

The dramatic changes that von Braun had undergone since the fall of 1946 had in many ways matured him. He found a new stability in his sincerely passionate love for his wife and the family to come, and in belief in God. Faith became important to him: "I began to pray daily, hourly. . . . I took long rides out into the desert where I could be alone at prayer. I prayed with my wife in the evening. As I tried to understand my problems I tried to find God's will in acting on them." The resolution of his parents' travails also ended two years of "nervous tension and insecurity" that colored his life; now he had a family to come home to at night.[28] The cutbacks in the Hermes II project provided another, unwanted form of stability. The next three years at Fort Bliss would be quiet ones, quite unlike the periods dominated by crash programs at Peenemünde and again in Huntsville. To fill his spare time he would turn once again to his first love, space. Many evenings and weekends from 1947 to 1949 would be spent planning his expedition to Mars and then writing a novel about it.

The first half of 1947 would provide an unwelcome reminder, however, that the Nazi issue had not gone away and could come back to haunt him. The public unveiling of Project Paperclip provoked a backlash among left-wing scientists, liberals, and Jewish groups, all of whom protested the employment of "Nazi scientists," as they were most typically labeled, on the grounds that they were morally and criminally compromised by their work for Hitler, carriers of race hatred and alien ideology, and/or mere engineers and technicians who were not real scientists. A fair amount of prejudice, some of it crudely anti-German, was thus mixed up with some telling critiques of the amorality of the U.S. military hiring those who had so recently designed weapons to be used against Allied populations. Certain damaging cases came to light, notably Herbert Axster and his wife, Ilse, who had been a leader in the Nazi women's organization and had allegedly abused forced laborers on their farm. In the end the Axsters were sent back to Germany, but only several years later. Von Braun was fortunate that his SS membership did not become public during the 1947 flap, and he and several others were equally fortunate that the Dora story remained buried, despite the Nordhausen war crimes trial that the U.S. Army staged at Dachau that fall.[29]

Preparations for the trial did produce some uncomfortable moments. Investigators looking for the Mittelwerk's general director, Georg Rickhey, found him in Dayton, writing reports on underground plants for the army air forces. He was sent back to Germany for trial, leading to a search for witnesses at Fort Bliss or White Sands. An AAF interrogator, Major Eugene Smith, turned up in El Paso in late May and interviewed Arthur Rudolph and several others; Magnus von Braun was away on temporary duty in Illinois. The Germans admitted that there had been problems at the Mittelwerk but offered a whitewashed picture of prisoner conditions and Rickhey's role. Von Braun's good friend Rudolph "impressed" Smith "as a very clever, shrewd individual. He did not wish to become involved in any investigations that might involve him in any way with illegal actions in the underground factory and as a result, was cautious of his answers."[30]

For unknown reasons Smith did not try to talk to Wernher von Braun. On 31 July 1947, however, the 7708th War Crimes Group requested his presence in Dachau as a defense witness for Rickhey, but Ordnance refused to allow him to travel to Germany "for security reasons," pointing instead to Karl Otto Fleischer, then being sent back to find other employment, or Walter Dornberger, recently released from a British POW camp but already designated by the AAF for Wright Field. As an alternative, Ordnance suggested sworn testimony in response to questions sent by Rickhey's attorney. Von Braun gave his answers on 14 October, showing detailed knowledge of conditions in the Mittelwerk, but he described Rickhey as a figurehead whom

Kammler had bypassed by going directly to Sawatzki. The latter was not around to be tried, as he had died mysteriously while in U.S. custody near Nordhausen at the beginning of May 1945. In the end Rickhey was acquitted. Only former camp guards and Kapos who had been prominent in physical abuse of prisoners were convicted; one was executed. The ending of the Dachau Nordhausen trial in December 1947 effectively closed the Dora issue for over twenty years; the American public found out nothing about the connection to the rocket engineers. Von Braun and his compatriots learned once again, however, that the best strategy was never to talk about it, except on occasion among themselves, and to omit it from their Peenemünde stories if at all possible. Their American military superiors fully agreed with those principles and used the secrecy that still surrounded Paperclip to keep damaging information buried in the files.[31]

Meanwhile the protest movement against Paperclip had petered out, as the public had other things to worry about, notably the growing "Red scare," which soon ended all debate about former Nazis. On 12 March 1947 President Truman made his speech to Congress asking for aid to Greece and Turkey against Communist subversion, a milestone in the emergence of the Cold War; three months later Secretary of State George C. Marshall announced an economic plan to aid Europe. The public debate over Paperclip had, however, made life at Fort Bliss less pleasant, as Hamill was forced to tighten restrictions on the Germans as a result of complaints in the press and a resulting military investigation. Public criticism also contributed to a continuing stalemate inside the U.S. government over clearing the Germans for immigration. Von Braun had repeatedly expected that formal immigration, ending their extralegal status, would come through in 1946, either with the new long-term contracts or with the arrival of the families. But it would be a very long wait.[32]

The fundamental issue was the security clearance of Germans tainted with memberships in Nazi organizations, notably von Braun, who was one of the most problematic cases because of his SS officer rank. At first the process seemed to go well. Ordnance listed him as number one for immigration from Fort Bliss in November 1946, and he filled out an application in February 1947, just before his sudden departure for Germany. As motivation, he gave the anti-Communist argument in quaint English: "I want to devote my future work to the progress and the strength of the Western Civilisation and I consider the United States as their [sic] bulwark." The first security report issued by the Office of Military Government U.S. (OMGUS) in Germany was perfunctory, declaring him "not a war criminal and . . . not an ardent Nazi." But as paper started to flow back and forth through the

Pentagon and European headquarters, red flags went up over his party and SS record. His "Revised Security Report" in September 1947 made things worse instead of better. Now it read: "Based on available records, subject is not a war criminal. He was an SS officer but no information is available to indicate he was an ardent Nazi. Subject is regarded as a potential security threat by the Military Governor." Meanwhile, to answer such questions, he had given a sworn affidavit on 18 June, from which we draw much of our information about his Nazi past and Gestapo arrest.[33]

Investigations produced more allegations. There were accusations that cronyism had led to the selection of Axster, Fleischer, and others of marginal qualifications—a charge with substance, but it is not clear who was to blame: von Braun, his deputies, or the Americans who approved the list. There was a claim that von Braun was striving to keep a former girlfriend away from Fort Bliss, and that he had withheld information regarding buried documents. His 8 March interrogation in Frankfurt had only made matters worse, because the ensuing investigation revealed that in Landshut Wernher had given Sigismund "location sketches" for a "tin" hidden under a tree stump in the Oberjoch, near Haus Ingeburg. It contained a manuscript of their father's memoirs, some silver belonging to Dornberger, and perhaps some notes about where other boxes were buried. The CIC in fact briefly arrested Sigis in June and questioned him about the tin. An AAF lieutenant colonel, after interrogating von Braun and five others at Fort Bliss about the matter, was so infuriated that on 23 July 1947 he asked that Axster, Fleischer, and von Braun be "returned to Germany for internment at Oberusel with additional interrogation in mind."[34]

Such a request went nowhere with Ordnance supporting him so strongly. From the standpoint of Toftoy and Hamill, he had been only responsible, cooperative, honest, and security conscious, not to mention a brilliant leader with extraordinary talent. As von Braun's access to classified information and knowledge of the U.S. missile scene grew, so did his "denial value" as well—he could not be allowed to leave the United States because no other power, notably the USSR, should get access to him. Yet his immigration still languished. In early 1948 he had to fill out OMGUS's denazification questionnaire, which he had previously avoided, and that organization issued yet another security report, stating: "Like the majority of [party] members, he may have been a mere opportunist. Subject has been in the United States more than two years and if, within this period, his conduct has been exemplary and he has committed no acts adverse to the interests of the United States, it is the opinion of the Military Governor, OMGUS, that he may not constitute a security threat to the United States." Even that did not do the

trick. The FBI was tasked with doing another round of background investigations, and Germans with easier records were processed instead, including
his brother, the platinum bar incident notwithstanding. Wernher von
Braun's immigration file was left on the back burner until May 1949, when
the rising anti-Communist tide finally made it possible to begin processing
the "problem cases."[35]

We do not know von Braun's reaction to this endless wait, punctuated by
periodic requests for more form-filling. Where we have any evidence at all it
is von Braun's frustration with the slow pace of the missile program in the
wake of the FY 1947 budget cutbacks. A GE employee told the FBI in 1960
that von Braun had been "hypercritical of the slowness" of U.S. rocket development in the late 1940s. And one former U.S. Army officer reports that, sitting alone with von Braun on the patio of a local Mexican restaurant in the
winter of 1946–47, the German told him "he was on the verge of deciding to
leave the organization and go to private industry." It seems highly improbable, however, that Ordnance would have allowed this, although it did send
Walther Riedel to North American Aviation (NAA) in Los Angeles at AAF
request—Riedel had propulsion experience that could aid NAA in copying
the V-2 engine and he was not well liked in El Paso. According to legend, von
Braun came into conflict with Hamill often enough to threaten to resign
multiple times, although the only written evidence we have is one resignation letter from January 1948. Angered over receiving no advance notice of
the transfer of guidance chief Ernst Steinhoff to the U.S. Air Force (now an
independent service) at Holloman Air Force Base in Alamogordo, New Mexico, von Braun asserted that he had been "bypassed for months in almost all
essential questions that concern this project [Hermes II]. . . . Time and again
orders and directives have been issued to the sections, without notifying me
at all." Hamill paid no attention to this outburst.[36]

From 1947 on Hermes II was indeed pretty much the only project, as GE
took over V-2 launches almost completely and the Germans traveled less to
White Sands. Von Braun and his associates did consult on a navy project to
launch a V-2 from an aircraft carrier, on the manufacture of V-2 parts by
American companies, and on Project Bumper, which involved puttting a
JPL-designed WAC Corporal sounding rocket on a V-2 nose to gain experience in staging. Von Braun was as thrilled as anyone when, after four failed
attempts, the fifth Bumper WAC reached a record altitude of 250 miles (400
km) and returned scientific data on 24 February 1949. But GE ran the program as part of Hermes, and contrary to many later accounts it had little to
do with the Germans.[37]

Hermes II had its own problems. The very first test launch, "Missile 0," famously crashed near a cemetery outside Juárez, Mexico, causing an international incident on 29 May 1947, although the fact that it was not an ordinary V-2 was covered up at the time and has been little known since. In the nose of the V-2 was the "organ," a series of openings to test different configurations of the diffuser—the ram-air inlet where the air was compressed. Immediately after the evening launch, as the rocket spectacularly ascended from dusk into gleaming sunlight, one American observer noted that it had tilted south instead of north as it was supposed to, but his warning was ignored by one of the Germans, who did not order radio cut-off of the engine. Everyone was very fortunate in that the missile missed the city and killed no one, and the commander of Fort Bliss exploited his good relations with his Mexican army counterpart in Juárez and issued an immediate apology.[38]

Aerodynamic data on the Hermes II design, which had stubby, rectangular wings containing the ramjets protruding from the short, tapered missile body that replaced the V-2 nose, also showed it to be aerodynamically unstable at almost all velocities, requiring much more work on guidance technologies. The Fort Bliss group began to perfect air-bearing gyros and other devices to improve control and accuracy, the most important technological legacy from this period. By 1947 it became clear that the inherent difficulties of the ramjet had been underestimated throughout the defense complex, and Hermes II in particular suffered from the shortage of aerodynamic talent in the Fort Bliss group. The Research and Development Board (RDB), tasked with coordinating the competing programs of the three services, asked why von Braun's Germans were working on something in which they had little experience. The growing rivalry with the air force over roles and missions in the missile field also led to a USAF recommendation in late 1947 that Hermes II be terminated, but the army stuck to its program, and the RDB was too weak to force any change. At Fort Bliss, meanwhile, von Braun's group built modest test facilities for combustion and high-altitude research and soldiered on. With the shortage of funds and all the design problems, the first launches of Hermes IIs with ramjet wings did not occur until January and October 1949, and both were failures due to unanticipated vibration, causing structural breakup. The Germans also produced a new study of a large booster rocket for use in long-range missiles and even satellite launchers in the spring of 1949. But in the stringent budget climate of that time, not to mention the climate of skepticism and even dismissal that often met spaceflight plans, it had no chance of finding support.[39]

As von Braun absorbed the democratic culture and political traditions of the United States and saw that the budget cutbacks of the late 1940s were fundamentally rooted in the public's desire to demobilize, he realized that it would no longer suffice to sell a program to a dictator or powerful military superior. Now he had to convince ordinary Americans before their leaders might take him seriously. "A bit reluctant at first," he began to search for a means to preach the gospel of space travel. His first public speech in the United States was to the El Paso Rotary Club on 16 January 1947, in the wake of the December unveiling of Paperclip. After discussing the basic principles of the rocket, he presented ideas much like those in his May 1945 memorandum, with more elaboration of his space station. Drawing on Oberth, on Noordung's 1929 book (presumably), and on fifteen years of private thinking, he described an inflatable wheel 150 feet in diameter that rotated to provide gravity. The station in turn could provide a "harbor" for spaceships that could travel to the Moon and planets; he specifically mentioned a circumlunar trip to see the still-hidden far side of the Moon. The speech won him a standing ovation but could not readily be repeated, as the army still restricted his movements and activities, notably after the spring 1947 public controversy over Paperclip.[40]

Neither did the space and rocket societies as yet provide much of an outlet. He did not join the American Rocket Society (ARS) until early 1950, when a Texas–New Mexico chapter came into existence. After the loosening of restrictions on his correspondence, von Braun got back in touch with German space advocates in 1948–49—notably Hermann Oberth, who was barely scraping by at his house near Nuremberg, and Eugen Sänger, who was working in France. He was particularly happy to be named an Honorary Fellow of the British Interplanetary Society in August 1949, as it lessened his isolation and signaled that "the grief . . . [I] and my associates [had] brought to the British people" had not stood in the way of a common enthusiasm for space. As with Ley, the V-2 breakthrough into the realm of high-powered rocketry covered a multitude of sins.[41]

Still, the question remained: how would he reach the American people? In 1947 he hit on the strategy of presenting an elaborate spaceflight feasibility study in the form of a science fiction novel. It was not an original idea—already in the 1920s Max Valier had published a few stories with the same intent, and the movie and book *Frau im Mond*, although conceived as entertainment, became a mechanism for popularizing Oberth's ideas. But the content of von Braun's novel would be highly original: a fully worked-out expedition to Mars based on chemical rocket technology. The choice of Mars is fascinating because, as he told Daniel Lang several years later with "an intensity he had not shown all evening: 'Personally, though, I'd rather go to the moon than to Mars.' " It was his goal and obsession, but as far as he was concerned—and this shows how far ahead he was of almost everyone—it was *too easy* to prove that humans could land on the Moon with extrapolations of existing technology. Mars, and all interplanetary travel, was, on the other hand, widely viewed even by space advocates only as a distant future possibility if atomic rockets could somehow be perfected.[42]

The calculations that undergirded his novel, "Mars Project," although rooted in his 1935 nighttime speculations with Arthur Rudolph in the Kummersdorf officers' club, were mostly made in 1948 and were done in his spare time with no tools other than a slide rule—the now-vanished approximating instrument of the engineer. Assisting him on occasion were half a dozen other Germans at Fort Bliss, most notably the space enthusiast Krafft Ehricke. These calculations were then drawn together in 1949 in a "Technical Appendix" of over 120 pages in typescript, and later formed the entire content of the book he published as *The Mars Project* in 1952 in German and in 1953 in English. The novel itself von Braun wrote in 1948–49, and after it was typed by his ex-secretary, Dorette Kersten Schlidt, it was a very substantial 482 pages in German. The manuscript was translated by an American acquaintance of his mother, Lieutenant Commander Henry J. White. Von Braun, a night owl by habit, spent many late evenings writing in the cramped quarters he shared with Maria and, after December 1948, with his newborn daughter Iris Careen, the first American in the family.[43]

The scale on which von Braun conceived his "Mars Project" was grand—or grandiose. For the very first expedition to the Red Planet, manned or unmanned, ten "space ships" would be assembled in Earth orbit to carry seventy men (literally—the novel is unthinkingly patriarchal, the only female characters being housewives or Martians). Each ship would weigh 3720 metric tons (about 8.2 million lb) with full fuel load. Three would carry "landing boats," large winged craft to glide down to the Martian surface, based on astronomers' estimates of atmospheric surface pressure that would later turn out to be much too high. The landing crews, after spending a year on the planet (dictated by the need to wait for the two planets to come into the alignment required for the return trajectory), would remove the wings and erect two of the boats vertically for launching from the surface. Forty men would stay in orbit with the seven ships for returning to Earth (analogous to the later "lunar orbit rendezvous" scheme with a mother ship and lander used in Apollo, but on a vastly larger scale). After a nearly three-year expedition, the voyagers would return to Earth orbit, to be fetched by ferry ships, as von Braun did not have a heat-shield technology for plunging directly into the atmosphere at interplanetary velocities.[44]

To launch 82 million lb into Earth orbit required a huge logistics operation that he developed at length. Each three-stage "ferry vessel" was 60 m (nearly 200 ft) high, weighed 6400 metric tons (14.1 million lb), and had a first-stage thrust of twice that. Compared to his later masterpiece, the giant Saturn V Moon rocket, this vehicle was shorter, fatter, weighed more than twice as much, and had more than three times the initial thrust. Behind these calculations stood quite conservative assumptions about rocket technology. He rejected liquid hydrogen and liquid oxygen, the near-ideal chemical propellant combination discussed by Oberth (and, unbeknownst to him, also by Goddard and Tsiolkovsky), based on logistics considerations and the evaporative losses of these supercold liquids over long periods. (He had a bias against liquid hydrogen, after experiments at Kummersdorf in 1937–38 that showed it to be very difficult to handle.) Instead he chose the less energetic but hypergolic (self-igniting) and easily storable combination of hydrazine and nitric acid. In the novel, building up the Mars ships requires 950 ferry launches in eight months, most of them to carry up fuel, but only 46 ferries are needed, as all stages are recoverable. The total cost of the Mars expedition he ventured at $2 billion in the novel, roughly equivalent to the Manhattan Project, if no allowance is made for inflation. In the introduction to the published calculations, he put the requirements more vaguely as "no greater than those for a minor military operation extending over a limited theater of war." These estimates are, needless to say, extremely optimistic, although hindsight makes it too easy to pick apart the predictions of any technological prophet.[45]

Perhaps most fascinating are the assumptions behind the "Mars Project," both the ones von Braun declared openly and the ones he took for granted. In his preface he stated that one of his fundamental points was to bring home the massive scale of organization and investment that would be required for spaceflight. He put it best in the introduction to the published version: the central figure of most science fiction tales was the "heroic inventor" and his "little band of faithful followers, [who] . . . secretly built a mysteriously streamlined space vessel in a remote back yard. Then, at the hour of midnight, he and his crew soared into the solar system to brave untold perils." In contrast to this naive view, interplanetary flight "can only be achieved by the coordinated might of scientists, technicians, and organizers belonging to very nearly every branch of modern science and industry. . . . We the space rocketeers of all nations (where permitted) have made it our business to rally this kind of talent around the standard of space travel, which in the nature of things, is synonymous with the future of rocketry."[46]

Curiously, this introduction, and its precursor, the novel's preface, leave out the fact that only through massive government funding could such a coordinated effort come about. Yet the novel itself reveals his understanding of those political realities. In order to get the $2 billion to mount the Mars expedition, the United Space Forces have to appeal to the president and Congress of the United States of Earth in the world capital of Greenwich, Connecticut. It was von Braun's projection of the American system over the whole globe.[47]

How the planet got to that state is outlined in the novel's fascinating prologue, "A.D. 1980": "The final catastrophic conflict was over. The great Eastern Bloc, after five of the most frightful years in the history of the world, had finally succumbed to the last despairing blows of the almost exhausted Western Powers. Of the great Asiatic mass had become a group of smaller states, slowly digging out from under the ruins of the war." The key to victory, after "the motorized forces of the Western Allies had ground to a solid stop in the vastness of the steppes of Asia," in "the dread winter of 1974/1975," had been the space station Lunetta—the name he still treasured from his teenage short story of 1930. It had served as a battle station for dominating Earth, dropping atomic bombs on Soviet industrial and military facilities until they were defeated—the vision he had presented to the army in July 1946. It is quite interesting that, while von Braun could be a visionary in technologies he really cared about, mostly spaceflight, for others he was unimaginative: he did not foresee thermonuclear weapons or the resultant escalation of destructive power to levels suicidal for the human race.[48]

Several interpretations could be imposed on von Braun's fantasy or nightmare of World War III. Was this a useful plot device to set up a unified Earth expedition to Mars, a prediction of an unavoidable hot war that must come out of the U.S.-Soviet confrontation, or a right-wing fantasy of a successful blitzkrieg? Certainly this vision was rooted in his anti-Communism, which had only been strengthened by the Soviet domination of Eastern Europe, the ordeal of his parents, the imprisonment of Maria's father in the Soviet zone of Germany, and the death of Hans and Hans-Ulrich von Quistorp, the owners of Crenzow and Bauer-Wehrland, in the same Soviet camps. The German catastrophe had forced him to abandon the German nationalist parts of a conservative worldview he had inherited from his father, but he remained conservative by instinct, now transferring his allegiance to the United States as the "bulwark" of Western culture. In the preface to the novel, von Braun wrote regarding the military implications of rocket development: "My most earnest hope is that the world may be spared another conflict, but if such a conflict should be inevitable, as appears at times, I want the homeland of my free choice, America, to hold the weapon of rocketry against her adversaries, whoever they may be."[49]

The Janus-faced character of the rocket, its fundamental duality as an instrument for both science and war, nonetheless left him feeling deeply ambivalent. Von Braun put his own feelings into the mouth of the commander of the Space Forces, General Braden, in his speech to the world Congress in favor of "Operation Mars." Finding his life an unwilling demonstration of the "Greek proverb" that "War is the father of Events," Braden proclaims that the rocket designers were and are "animated by secret visions of reaching into the heavens" but are often appalled by the military use of their technology.[50]

The Mars expedition is in fact sold to Congress with a rather dubious military rationale. The new 100-in (2.5-m) telescope in orbit near Lunetta has revealed that the Martian canals can only be the signs of an advanced civilization; if that civilization were to come and occupy Lunetta, then the whole world would be at the mercy of the Martians. Led by the novel's hero (and another of von Braun's alter egos), Colonel Gary Holt, the first landing boat, *Oberth*, lands on Mars's south polar cap and finds a Martian pumping station, proving that American astronomer Percival Lowell was correct in his turn-of-the-century vision of the Red Planet as the seat of an ancient civilization saving water through a global system of canals. Von Braun's novel actually contains several paeans to the wisdom of Lowell, although it is not clear if he was actually a fan of the astronomer's works or simply found them useful for constructing a plot. At any rate Holt and his crew are soon transported into the underground world of the Martians, who have constructed a whole civilization in pressurized cities connected by magnetic levitation trains. They are soon joined by the crews of the boats *Goddard* and *Ziolkowsky* (the German spelling for Tsiolkovsky) and spend a comfortable year living in a technological utopia, where the planet has been unified by the global necessity of survival in the face of declining atmospheric pressure and a decreasing water supply. The Martians themselves turn out to look much like us, and worship one God, because that is God's design for intelligent life (one of many references to religion in the book). The only disadvantages to this "age-weary" civilization turn out to be its bland sameness and loss of vitality—vitality that promises to be revived by an interchange with planet Earth. At the end of the novel the adventurers return with three Martian scientists, although Holt and his crew barely make it back alive after a failure in Mars orbit.[51]

From sketchy references in von Braun's correspondence, it is apparent that he completed the German draft of the novel by the summer of 1949 and received the completed English translation from Henry White a few months after that. (They were working in parallel.) Walter Dornberger saw it on his first visit to Fort Bliss in early August, for when he returned to Dayton, he wrote that he was sorry that he had forgotten the manuscript. (He also wrote, after seeing von Braun with his new wife and baby: "Doctor, Mensch, who would have thought that you would ever become such a complete married man. I had already given up all hope.") By November, Dornberger had read it and was very enthused, predicting a "best seller" for 1950. A note from an American rocketry colleague at White Sands, also in November 1949, was similarly enthused about the English manuscript. All that von Braun needed was the security clearance from Ordnance to publish the whole thing, including the technical appendix. It was his pride and joy, and he had every hope of finding a publisher, perhaps even a movie deal, out of his venture into science fiction.[52]

That fall he received further welcome signs of a secure future in America. Earlier in the year Army Ordnance had indicated that it was hoping to move the Germans to a new facility not so hemmed in by the limitations of Fort Bliss. Huntsville, Alabama, emerged as the most likely candidate, as two shuttered World War II arsenals were available outside town, making a concentrated army rocket and missile center possible. After considerable lobbying by Holger Toftoy in Washington, aided by a worsening world situation that culminated in the Chinese Communist victory and Truman's 23 September 1949 announcement of the detection of the first Soviet A-bomb test, Ordnance at last received word that it would get both arsenals. On 4 November the word became public in El Paso: the Germans and their rocket activities would be leaving in 1950.[53]

Two days earlier von Braun had passed his own milestone—he had at last legally entered the United States. Through the late summer and early fall he heard that his papers were moving in Washington. Now he could do the final step, one that his brother Magnus and many other German rocketeers had already completed. On Wednesday, 2 November, accompanied by an American officer in civilian clothes, he took the streetcar to Mexico. In Juárez they went to the American consulate and presented papers, chest X-rays, and eighteen dollars in cash. Von Braun received the requisite stamps, and they proceeded back to the border. Everything had been prearranged with the Mexican and American officers. When the streetcar returned over the Rio Grande, and the immigration officer on the American side asked him where he came from, he answered, as required: "Mexico." His papers were stamped; the five-year clock to apply for citizenship had at last begun. He was home.[54]

CHAPTER ELEVEN

Space Superiority

1950–54

Behind a black wall of secrecy, the U.S. is climbing slowly toward a new level of warfare. In every U.S. factory, every technical institute, and every electronics laboratory, the military phrase of the day is "guided missiles."
—JONATHAN NORTON, *Newsweek*, 21 May 1951[1]

Nineteen-fifty was a year of great hope, new beginnings, and not a little frustration. Early in February Wernher von Braun sent off his massive novel, with its equation-laden scientific appendix, to a New York agent. Several weeks later he wrote Ken Gatland of the British Interplanetary Society: "I am presently corresponding with several American [publishing] houses . . . and I think a final publication contract is just around the corner." Alas, it was not to be. Although he seems to have thrown away most of his rejection letters, a couple survive. On 24 March a Doubleday editor wrote his agent that "Mars Project" "is a perfectly fascinating book—but not, I'm afraid, from the standpoint of a potentially salable novel. As you warned me, there isn't much story there, and the mass of information is hardly useful for a collaborator to do much with." He added jocularly: "We're all agreed that we can't publish it, and the only thing I can think of that we might do with it is build a rocket ship. I assure you if we ever get to that point, I'll ask for it again as a reference." A Macmillan editor told his agent in May: "I know exactly what the Doubleday editor meant: somewhere in this pulpy mass are the seeds of a good piece of science fiction. But I'm darned if I can get at them." In the end something like eighteen publishers rejected "Mars Project." A few months later von Braun paraphrased their critique to Heinz Hermann Koelle, a German space enthusiast: " 'Who's interested in the Mars atmosphere or the initial thrust of a satellite ship? The story lacks a girl! Etc.' " His characters were wooden, and the didactic material inserted into the dialogue was a dead weight on the text. A couple of editors suggested instead that he write a popular science book laying out his ideas, but he was reluctant to let go of both the novel and its detailed mathematical proof.[2]

In the midst of this came the move to Huntsville, which began with his departure from El Paso on 10 April 1950, followed a few days later by Maria and sixteen-month-old Iris. Moving several hundred personnel, plus shops and test equipment, out of Fort Bliss and setting them up in converted buildings at Redstone Arsenal was a job that took six months. Von Braun complained to Koelle in mid-June: "I only moved to this pretty little city in Alabama six weeks ago, was scarcely here when I had to go to New York/Niagara Falls, then Texas/New Mexico, and I fritter away most of my existence in trains or airplanes." Barely had he settled in when he had "to move out of my house yet again and relocate inside Huntsville. The effort expended at the moment is huge, the productive work virtually zero."[3]

While he and his wife loved the first rental house they moved into, it had been promised to another German family for the long term, and the second was not nearly as appealing. So von Braun purchased a lot outside town for $900 and began negotiating with contractors and securing a mortgage to build his own house. In late August he and the family went back to El Paso for ten days to get Maria and his parents through the immigration formalities at Juárez, and to bring Emmy and Magnus Sr. to live in their own apartment in Huntsville. (Magnus Jr. came with the ramjet test group in September, not long after marrying the daughter of one of the other Germans.) In late November or December Wernher and Maria made their third household move. "No sooner did I settle down," von Braun told another correspondent in February, "[then] a new project hit us which again occupied all my time." But that new, secret project would at last provide a solid foundation for the Germans' work for the U.S. Army: the Redstone ballistic missile.[4]

While 1950 was a hectic and difficult year, it ushered in a four-year period during which von Braun's American career was well and truly launched— on the one hand, as engineering manager of a large and important missile program again, on the other as a space advocate in national magazines and even on radio and television. While "Mars Project" failed as a sci-fi novel, it would provide the basis for his campaign for space, one that made a fundamental breakthrough in early 1952.

For Wernher and Maria von Braun, and for almost all the other Germans who came with them, Huntsville quickly became home. For the first time they could live outside a fenced-in base and integrate themselves into

American daily life. Many, like von Braun, fell in love with "this pretty little city" near the Tennessee River and were happy to move from the desert to a green, hilly region that bore a resemblance to parts of Germany, the sticky summer climate notwithstanding. They made a cultural impact on the town by founding a Lutheran church, strongly supporting the library and local education, starting a chamber orchestra, and, under the active leadership of von Braun and Stuhlinger, launching an amateur astronomical association in 1954.[5]

The locals did not, however, universally herald the arrival of more than three hundred Germans (including wives and children) and several thousand native-born Americans, when the officers, enlisted men, civil service employees, corporate contractors, and families from all the army rocket and missile programs around the country were concentrated at Redstone Arsenal. Although Huntsville was promoted as the Watercress Capital of the World and the birthplace of movie star Tallulah Bankhead, it was really a small cotton town of sixteen thousand in 1950, dependent on the local farmers and the oft-shuttered textile mills in the city center. A World War II boom, when Ordnance and the Chemical Warfare Service opened two arsenals southwest of town to produce munitions, had been followed by a bust that left bitter feelings against the army. Twenty thousand workers had labored in the two arsenals at their height; at the end of the war almost all of them immediately lost their jobs. Would the new center, consolidated now into one arsenal, be another short-lived project? The conservative white southerners were also not always happy to see this influx of Yankees and foreigners disturbing their traditional way of life. The town was centered on its Confederate monument and was as segregated as any other place in the state. The Germans, already well acquainted with American race hierarchies from El Paso and the reluctantly desegregating army, quickly fit into local white culture, however, and were pleasantly surprised that they met so little resentment as recent enemies. After a few years in which the new boom continued without letup, and the city doubled and tripled in size, lingering resentments against the outsiders disappeared.[6]

Wernher von Braun's initial title was project director of the Ordnance Guided Missile Center, commanded by Major James Hamill, who was in charge of seven hundred of the nearly three thousand people employed at Redstone Arsenal at the end of 1950. A parallel Ordnance Rocket Center ran many other projects, mostly contracted to industry. During the initial months of move-in, the von Braun group's chief job remained Hermes II, the experimental Mach 3.3 ramjet cruise missile. In a January 1950 Pentagon meeting Colonel Toftoy all but admitted that it had become a make-work project for the Germans. Moving to Huntsville did not change that; in fact, in May the Defense Department reduced Hermes II to ramjet research with no planned missile application. Ordnance decided to transfer a Mach 4 ramjet project from GE to the von Braun group as a result, but it was even further in the future.[7]

What changed everything was the Korean War, which erupted without warning on 25 June. Badly prepared South Korean and American troops retreated in a near rout before the North Korean assault, seeming to confirm the rampant fear of a world Communist conspiracy on the march—World War III again appeared on the horizon. On 11 July von Braun closed a letter to his parents with "This Korea thing is damned hot, no? Let us pray that it does not become a world conflagration." Eighteen days later another letter mentioned holdups in his mortgage and contracting negotiations "because of the general hysteria." President Truman immediately secured a large supplemental budget increase for the Defense Department, and expenditures kept climbing thereafter. The true watershed in the creation of a large, permanent U.S. military establishment was Korea, not World War II; the defense budget quadrupled to $50 billion by fiscal 1953 and dipped to $40 billion only after the war, before increasing again.[8]

Especially in the winter of 1950–51, when Chinese intervention in Korea smashed the big gains made after the September Inchon landings, fear grew that the Korean War was only a precursor to Stalin's invasion of Western Europe, where the newly formed NATO forces were badly outnumbered by the Red Army. On 15 December 1950 Truman declared a state of national emergency to mobilize for Korea more effectively.[9] Deployable, surface-to-surface guided missile systems, possibly with nuclear warheads, thus seemed increasingly urgent in both Asia and Europe.

The Hermes ramjet projects were still years away from producing weapons; the American defense establishment's love affair with the ramjet was already waning in any case, as this propulsion system proved much more difficult to make work in practice than in theory. Ordnance therefore ordered the Jet Propulsion Laboratory in Pasadena to "weaponize" its Corporal short-range ballistic missile and transferred GE's Hermes C-1 study of a 500-mi (800-km) range rocket-powered missile to Huntsville in September 1950. Although von Braun and many of his people went back to White Sands in early November to fire Hermes II Missile 2A, which in its modified form was at last successful in staying together through the V-2 launch, it would prove to be the last time the test vehicle was ever fired—and the ramjet itself was never ignited in flight. The new ballistic missile project would have to be based on existing or easily developed technology.[10]

For von Braun's group, the obvious thing to do was to build a greatly improved super V-2. The engine, for one, could be taken directly from North American Aviation's rocket propulsion group (soon called Rocketdyne) in Los Angeles—a 75,000-lb (34,000-kg) thrust motor derived from the 55,000-lb (25,000-kg) thrust V-2 engine, using the same propellant combination of water alcohol and liquid oxygen, but much reduced in size and increased in efficiency. When NAA engineer Doug Hege came to Huntsville with a film of the engine tests at the company's Santa Susana site, von Braun exclaimed, "I'll buy it, I'll buy it, I'll buy it." He bonded with the NAA engineers under Sam Hoffman and enjoyed viewing engine firings at their complex in the dry, scrub-brush mountains above the San Fernando Valley that Hollywood had used to shoot westerns. Von Braun even got them a surplus army tank so that he could get close enough to the blast to observe the combustion patterns. The close alliance with NAA/Rocketdyne meant that von Braun did not have to build a new rocket engine development group at Huntsville.[11]

The same could not be said for guidance and control. A survey of the existing firms, von Braun told the Air War College in 1953, showed that "there was always something wrong. Either the principle was not suitable or expedient for our range, or it was still in too premature a development stage, or we found it too complicated or it didn't satisfy our stringent accuracy requirements." Those requirements had become especially stringent in February 1951, when K. T. Keller, chairman of the board of Chrysler Corporation and part-time director of guided missiles for the Defense Department, strongly endorsed the new missile project during a Huntsville visit but specified that it should be able to drop a 6,900-lb (3130-kg) atomic weapon within 1,000 yd (914 m) of its target. This warhead, which was more than twice as heavy as the vaguely defined "payloads" in the preliminary studies, reduced the range of the missile to 182 miles (293 km), but even at that range this accuracy requirement was a daunting prospect, considering how the V-2's operational accuracy had been ten or twenty *miles* at the same range. Later in 1951 the requirement was tightened again, to a "circular probable error" of 150 yd (137 m) (50 percent falling within a circle of that radius), an extremely difficult figure. Even Keller's earlier number, however, necessitated terminal guidance, that is, guidance during the descending phase of the trajectory, not just during powered ascent. In turn, terminal guidance strongly implied a separable warhead section, which would be smaller and more maneuverable, with its own aerodynamic control surfaces for adjusting its targeting during descent. Von Braun and his guidance deputies, Theodor Buchhold, Walter Haeussermann, and Fritz Mueller, decided that it would do just as well to modify the stabilized platform and air-bearing gyros developed for Hermes II rather than simply contracting out to a firm.[12]

The in-house design of the guidance, which Ford Instrument on Long Island would produce, complemented the approach chosen for the missile body. One of the few other innovations for the Redstone, as it was dubbed in 1952, was the adoption of an aluminum fuselage with integral tanks. (The missile's skin would serve as tank walls.) For ease of manufacturing, the main body would be cylindrical rather than the elegant tapered shape of its predecessor. Ordnance contracted with Reynolds Metal to produce the fuselage based on the Arsenal's design, with the intent that final assembly of the missile would be carried out in-house. Von Braun's group wanted to resurrect the "everything-under-one-roof," state-dominated model of Peenemünde, but the "arsenal system," as the U.S. Army called it, had a long American history as well. The Army Ordnance leadership, however, ordered Redstone Arsenal to find a prime contractor for the missile in April 1952, arguing that it should remain a research and development organization and not become an industrial concern too. A survey of the possible contractors proved problematic, as von Braun's organization ruled out the aircraft industry as being too close to the air force, which bitterly opposed any army role in long-range missiles. When Chrysler turned out to be almost the only viable candidate but was reluctant to take on Redstone, Keller had to go to the board with a direct appeal. In order not to delay the program, the auto firm would phase in missile assembly in the Detroit area but not before two dozen rockets were put together at the Arsenal.[13]

The construction of this in-house industrial capacity, along with cumulative army decisions to build substantial laboratories for guidance, computers, and other fields, gradually rebuilt von Braun's empire to dimensions not seen since Peenemünde. In mid-1952 he and the other Paperclip Germans were converted to regular civil service status; in January 1953 he became the civilian head of a division for the first time: the Guided Missile Development Division of the renamed Ordnance Missile Laboratories, now commanded by Holger Toftoy. As part of a decentralization of authority in Ordnance, Toftoy had been promoted to brigadier general and sent down from Washington, displacing, much to von Braun's relief, Hamill and his "regime of junior officers." By September 1954 von Braun had 950 employees; four years later that number had quadrupled to 3,925. Once again he proved to be a virtuoso in building and managing huge, complex, technically demanding programs.[14]

Even as the Redstone missile project began to take off in 1950–51 and von Braun dealt with the disruptive moves of his household, he struggled to find

spare time to promote "Mars Project" and his second career as a space advocate. For a time in the summer and fall of 1950 it seemed as if the leadership
of the American Rocket Society might be willing to publish his novel, but in
the end the idea failed for lack of funds. He was back to square one.[15]

While this was discouraging, true believers in space travel had signs of
hope. The V-2 and postwar rocketry had legitimized spaceflight ideas, at least
in part, slowly undoing the damage in the United States caused by the very
flourishing of Buck Rogers and the pulp science fiction genre since the
1920s, which had made the subject ridiculous for many. In late 1949 Willy
Ley's large-format book *The Conquest of Space* was a significant success,
mostly, as he admitted in a letter to von Braun, because of the beautiful
paintings of Chesley Bonestell. A former architect, Bonestell was making a
handsome living as a special effects artist in Hollywood, but his true enthusiasm was astronomical and space painting, for which he was already well
known. He did the backdrops for the lunar scenes in *Destination Moon*, a
groundbreaking, realistic space film that opened across North America in
the summer of 1950. At the end of September the first International Astronautical Congress met in Paris, a gathering of small European space societies
that led to the formation of the International Astronautical Federation (IAF)
in 1951. All these things were encouraging signs for the future growth of
"our cause," as von Braun sometimes called it. Yet he was still marginal to
space advocacy, although he was no doubt pleased to receive a message of
greetings and respect from the delegates to the 1950 Paris congress.[16]

The first small break came not from the United States but rather from
West Germany, which had been created in 1949 out of the Western occupation zones. In August von Braun had sent the German original of "Mars
Project" to H. H. Koelle, who was an engineering student in Stuttgart, a former Luftwaffe pilot, and a leader in the revived Society for Space Research
(GfW), one of several small German space societies. Koelle in turn passed it
along to a publisher, Otto Wolfgang Bechtle, another Luftwaffe veteran who
had inherited his father's publishing house in the industrial town of Esslingen, near Stuttgart. On 15 January 1951 Bechtle wrote Koelle that he was
very interested in von Braun's novel if it received a thorough rewrite by
Franz Ludwig Neher, a former Nazi propagandist who had ghostwritten several memoirs after the war. The costs for publishing the scientific appendix
were so high, however, that he hoped it would be separately published in the
United States—not knowing that von Braun had completely struck out on
that score.[17]

When von Braun got this letter via Koelle, he was "naturally very happy"
and wrote back on 2 February of his willingness to have the book rewritten.

He suggested that the GfW's journal publish the appendix separately as a multipart article. Above all, he was simply relieved to find any publishing outlet for "Mars Project" after a year of frustration; the fact that the three of them shared Luftwaffe flying experience (if only noncombat in von Braun's case) was an added bond. Von Braun signed a publishing contract with Bechtle on 23 March 1951, his thirty-ninth birthday. Bechtle got all rights, including selling the English-language manuscript and publishing the appendix in whatever manner could be found. When the publisher came for an extended trip to the United States in June and July to work on various book and movie deals, he met the engineer in Los Angeles, Huntsville, Chicago, and New York. They became fast friends.[18]

Meanwhile, von Braun found himself in another lively correspondence with members of the British Interplanetary Society (BIS), which was to host the Second Astronautical Congress in London in September 1951. He was pleased to accept their invitation to give a paper at the congress but thought the chances were "rather dim" that he could do it in person: "Old Joe [Stalin] from behind that [Iron] Curtain keeps us pretty busy and my personal finances aren't too rosy, either. A couple of months ago I broke ground for a new home and now I'm broke myself. But let's wait. It is still six months hence, so Old Joe may meanwhile become a monk and I may hit the jackpot. Who can tell?" Several of his letters in this period mention money problems; he was in conflict with his home builders over payments, and he had to help support his parents too. "Mars Project" had so far failed to pay off, although there was at least the prospect of splitting lesser German royalties with Neher.[19]

The BIS invitation spun off a revealing round of correspondence with A.V. "Val" Cleaver, an aeronautical engineer who had been one of the moving spirits of the British group since its 1933 origin. The subject was the IAF's formation and the GfW's utopian idea that the federation could become an international organization for carrying out space exploration, above governments and their militaries. Cleaver was more reluctant than von Braun to accept the inevitability of military control over the exploration of space. On 21 May 1951 von Braun replied:

We should stop bewailing the fact that our beloved space travel idea is being pulled into the capacious maw of the military. It is certainly deplorable that the world is faced with a grave new crisis, but we should eventually realize that this is beyond our control. The old idea of human flight is still alive notwithstanding the fact that the airplane has been abused for destructive purposes. . . .

You may say that my argumentation indicates a rather immoral opportunism. But I don't think it is. Weapons are not only something terrifying once a war is unleashed, but are also the most effective deterrents of war ever invented by man. They are certainly more effective deterrents than that sort of goody-goody pacifism to which so many people in their desperation take refuge in these troubled days. Why, I just don't believe that Uncle Joe will realize some day he is wrong and become a Roman Catholic![20]

A 20 June letter to Cleaver stated his position even more clearly:

It is perhaps due to some patriotic feeling toward my new home country that I am tempted to call "Pax Americana" what maintains peace today. The ethics of the Western World alone, or the general public desire for peace, just is not enough to keep the Communist tide in check. It is "The Bomb in Being," that does the trick.

In his 21 May missive von Braun argued that the way forward was to recruit young people to devote their lives to rocketry, build up the credibility of the "astronautical societies" as a "gold mine of talents for the military," conduct studies and experiments with military money, and cultivate international contacts only within the Western alliance, thereby not violating military security. The spaceflight idea would therefore be sown inside the military, the only likely funding source. Not surprisingly, he expected space travel to be carried out by a separate military service and missions of exploration and occupation to be military operations. But in that respect he was no different from prominent science fiction authors of his day such as Robert Heinlein.[21]

The paper von Braun wrote in April and May for the London IAF congress, "The Importance of the Satellite Vehicle as a Step towards Interplanetary Flight," not surprisingly described the outlines of his Mars expedition and his giant launch vehicle to loft the pieces into orbit. Bechtle printed up the talk as a small eight-page pamphlet for the congress; von Braun hoped that the scientific appendix would appear by then as a publication too so that he could demonstrate that his extraordinarily bold and elaborate proposals were based on something. But publication of calculations by September proved impossible, as the appendix was simply too long to be serialized in the GfW's little journal; eventually Bechtle and the publisher of that journal worked out a deal to print it as a supplement. It would finally appear in early 1952 as Das Marsprojekt (The Mars Project), a modest eighty-one-page paperback booklet but one that at last gave von Braun his first long publication stemming from all his evenings and weekends at Fort Bliss.[22]

Meanwhile the process of looking for someone to give the London paper brought him a new and valuable friend, Lieutenant Commander Frederick C. Durant III. Val Cleaver had offered to read it, but just at that time—May 1951—the ARS caught wind of his paper too and asked von Braun to present it as a society member. It would have been impolitic to say no, even though he was also an honorary member of both the BIS and the GfW, as he needed to demonstrate his loyalty to his new country. One of the people who the ARS suggested would be going to England was Fred Durant, who had recently moved to Washington from the navy's rocket center in New Jersey. In early August, not long before Durant sailed to Britain, he met von Braun in New York City and was an instant convert. The German's romantic ambition to be the Columbus of space inspired him, and von Braun brought with him not only his exuberant, magnetic personality but also the aura of real authority and accomplishment—whatever else he did, he could be credited with bringing the world-changing V-2 into existence. Von Braun himself was acutely aware of this accomplishment. He told Bechtle in March 1951: "I can with full right and authority call the V-2 my baby."[23]

The London speech delivered by Durant, together with von Braun's first American publication, created a small but significant burst of press attention in September and October. *The New York Times*, the newsmagazine *Time*, and various London papers reported on his proposed launch vehicle and Mars expedition. Almost simultaneously a talk he gave on the space station appeared in *Space Medicine*, the proceedings of a Chicago academic conference held in March 1950 at which von Braun had given his first high-profile speech in the United States. *Popular Science* and the *Huntsville Times* reprinted a space station diagram from the book, depicting a 200-ft-diameter bicycle-wheel-shaped station with many spokes; it would rotate to create artificial gravity and have a very large solar-concentrator mirror to generate electrical power. Awkward and ugly, this first visualization of von Braun's wheel space station would quickly vanish in favor of more artistically polished versions shortly to come. *Popular Science* ended its two-page spread with an ominous quote from von Braun's article: "the nation which first owns such a bomb-dropping space station might be in a position virtually to control the earth."[24]

In spite of his growing prominence, it is noteworthy that von Braun was not on the program for the First Annual Symposium on Space Travel, organized by Willy Ley and held in New York at the Hayden Planetarium, American Museum of Natural History, on Columbus Day, 12 October 1951. Perhaps he declined attendance in correspondence that is now lost, but it would certainly be the last one at which his attendance was not viewed as absolutely essential. In the audience were reporters for *Collier's*, one of the large-format, general magazines like *Life* and *The Saturday Evening Post*. *Collier's* had a circulation of over three million and an estimated readership in homes and barbershops of several times that, although it would be among the first of those magazines to succumb to television. Articles about the wonders of future technology were common in *Collier's*, so the intrigued editor sent an assistant editor, Cornelius Ryan, to a scientific conference in San Antonio, beginning on 6 November. Entitled "Medicine and Physics of the Upper Atmosphere," it was organized by the USAF School of Aviation Medicine at Randolph Field in San Antonio—the home of a number of German aerospace medicine experts under Hubertus Strughold. (The fact that Strughold and a few of his subordinates had firsthand knowledge of, even if no direct involvement in, gruesome experiments on concentration camp prisoners at Dachau was a fact well covered up by the Germans and their air force handlers.) Von Braun had been invited to attend the conference too but had not been asked to speak.[25]

Connie Ryan, a former war correspondent later famous for his D-Day book, *The Longest Day*, was less than thrilled by his assignment for *Collier's*. Von Braun ran into him, probably on the very first afternoon, as the rocketeer had to leave the next day.

> Leaving one of the sessions and stepping [up] to the bar of the hotel . . . I made the acquaintance of a good-looking Irishman who, gazing at the crystal highball between his hands, was sunk in a brown study. "They've sent me down here to find out what serious scientists think about the possibilities of flight into outer space," he growled. "But I don't know what these people are talking about. All I could find out so far is that lots of people get up there to the rostrum and cover a blackboard with mysterious signs."
>
> I volunteered to help. But when Mr. Ryan suggested that Collier's intended to bring a fifteen or twenty page cover story on space flight my enthusiasm faded a bit. I had visions, I must admit, of the kind of explosive journalism which, I felt would simply add to myriads of science fiction stories flooding the bookstands.[26]

This momentary reaction did not stop von Braun from trying to sell Ryan on the reality of spaceflight, and he was joined by two other prominent names at the conference: Joseph Kaplan, a leading upper-atmospheric physicist, and Fred Whipple, chairman of the Harvard astronomy department and a space enthusiast active in many military-financed programs investigating meteors. Whipple never forgot the ensuing "evening of cocktails, dinner, and impassioned long-into-the-night discussion" with Ryan, Kaplan, and von Braun ("certainly one of the best salesmen of the twentieth century"). "That evening he [Ryan] appeared to be highly skeptical about any possibility of artificial satellites or space travel. . . . The three of us worked hard at proselytizing Ryan and finally by midnight he was sold on the space program."[27]

In the aftermath of what von Braun called "our most inspiring discussions," he was still not clear what *Collier's* plans for him were. He sent Ryan copies of his London speech and a manuscript memoir of his Third Reich adventures, which he had written for Ken Gatland of the BIS in the spring of 1950 for a book that was never published. He also sent the London paper to Chesley Bonestell, who he had met for the first time in San Antonio too, thanks to *Collier's* paying the artist's way.[28]

The magazine's plans were indeed ambitious. By 1 December von Braun was writing his old friend Constantine Generales, now a general practitioner in New York, that he and Maria planned to fly in on the tenth and stay for several days, all at *Collier's* expense. Joining him were Whipple, Bonestell, Willy Ley, Dr. Heinz Haber of San Antonio (a Paperclip German and von Braun acquaintance who had spoken at both the Hayden and the air force symposia), and two successful illustrators and commercial artists in New York, Fred Freeman and Rolf Klep. Joseph Kaplan and Oscar Schachter, a top UN lawyer who had discussed space law at the Hayden Planetarium, would also write articles. After their first meeting in the magazine's offices on 11 December, von Braun was presented with a contract for his article and payment of $1,000—10 percent of his annual income. Only three months previously he had lamented to Haber that "with serious contributions, there's no money to be made from spaceflight these days. One has to write science fiction!"[29]

For von Braun, the New York meeting sparked a most fruitful collaboration with Ley and Ryan on the one hand and with the three artists on the other. The day after Christmas 1951 he mailed Ryan the first draft of his long article—over twenty pages—for the planned multiauthor "symposium" in *Collier's*. As published in March, his article was by far the longest and the one given top billing, because Ryan and his boss had bought into his conception of the space station as a superweapon in the Cold War. Ley and Ryan then gave the article a major overhaul in late January and early February 1952, along with the other articles. Ley spent days in the *Collier's* offices debating every point with Ryan and his staff so that the average reader could understand the physical laws and the technological principles involved in this still-exotic topic.[30]

As for the artists, von Braun sent Bonestell, Freeman, and Klep drawings on graph paper, showing his booster, space station, and various pieces of equipment. These they rendered into preliminary drawings that were sent back to him for critique on both technical and aesthetic grounds—his correspondence with Bonestell shows that, while he was ultimately responsible for factual accuracy, he also absorbed the artist's concern for aesthetics. Indeed, in order to make his original very fat and squat booster (220 ft tall, 65 ft in diameter) more elegant, he stretched it, or allowed Bonestell and Klep to stretch it, fudging the numbers that went into calculating the total area taken up by his gigantic engine clusters (fifty-one rocket motors in the first stage alone). In late January Fred Freeman showed up in Huntsville to gather more detail for the cutaway drawing of the space station and made a "brilliant impression" on von Braun.[31]

By the end of February the rocket engineer was already thrilled by plans for broadcast appearances in New York, which notably featured him and none of the other contributors. He wrote Ryan on the twenty-sixth: "I'm tickled to death about this TV and radio business: Space rockets are hitting the Bigtime [sic]!!!" And to his German publisher on 6 March, he called the upcoming PR "by far the greatest public advertising campaign for spaceflight and the artificial satellite . . . the world has ever seen." Four days later, after weathering a ridiculous military flap about the accidental omission of Redstone Arsenal from his byline, he left for Washington, where he saw Ordnance security and public relations people: even though the entire Redstone missile program was still classified, the army liked the publicity von Braun garnered, but he had to be constantly vigilant about what he said.[32]

The next day it was on to New York, for a rehearsal and filming session with NBC-TV. On Thursday, 13 March, at 7:45 p.m. Eastern, the night before the issue hit the newsstands, he appeared nationwide on *Camel News Caravan*, a pioneering network news show with an estimated audience of 5.5 million. *Collier's* provided big, table-sized models of his space station and launch vehicle, produced at its expense by the Huntsville Germans' graphic artist, Gerd de Beek. The same night von Braun made another TV appearance and two on radio. The next morning Dave Garroway interviewed him on NBC's *Today* show, and he was on CBS-TV in the midafternoon. He made several other appearances, ending with ABC's *Tom Corbett, Space Cadet* science fiction serial for children at 6:30 p.m.[33]

At the same time *Collier's* publicity director, Seth Moseley, unleashed a major public relations campaign, including twenty-eight hundred "press and radio kits" to be handed out by sales representatives; window displays on Fifth Avenue in New York and in downtown Philadelphia; and a flood of copies to be sent to senators, congressmen, and influential people. Von Braun did two more TV appearances the following week, gave two speeches, and ended his trip back in Washington on 19 March, where he spoke on "Let's Tackle the Space Ship" for the American Rocket Society. Held at the Naval Ordnance Laboratory in suburban White Oak, Maryland (to which the Peenemünde/Kochel wind tunnels had been evacuated in 1945), von Braun's appearance that evening caused an enormous traffic jam. Three thousand cars had to be turned away and five thousand people heard the lecture, many over loudspeakers outside the hall. Attendance exceeded his "wildest expectations," forcing him "to virtually fight my way into the building."[34]

The *Collier's* issue was spectacularly bold, with a beautiful Bonestell painting of von Braun's winged third-stage rocket on the cover, separating from its second stage at dawn over the Pacific Ocean. In the upper-right corner was the teaser: "Man Will Conquer Space <u>Soon</u>: Top Scientists Tell How in 15 Startling Pages." Inside, the space section opened with an editorial titled "What Are We Waiting For?," followed by the feature piece, von Braun's "Crossing the Last Frontier." Another Bonestell—a stunning two-page spread of the winged ship in orbit over Central America with the space station and space telescope—graced his article's opening. Other pieces included Ley on the station, Kaplan on the upper atmosphere, Whipple on space astronomy, Schachter on space law, and Haber on space medicine, plus a question-and-answer section designed by Ryan and his editors to cover issues deleted from the articles. Klep, Freeman, and Bonestell's illustrations were sprinkled throughout. It was a milestone in selling spaceflight and made von Braun's wheel the iconic space station for nearly two decades.[35]

Promotion of exploration and science certainly played a part in this first *Collier's* issue, but the predominant argument was Wernher von Braun's militant Cold War claim for the space station as a superweapon. "Crossing the Last Frontier" opened: "Within the next 10 or 15 years, the earth will have a new companion in the skies, a man-made satellite that could be either the greatest force for peace ever devised, or one of the most terrible weapons of war—depending on who makes and controls it." From its two-hour orbit at 1,075 mi (1730 km), the crew would employ "specially designed, powerful telescopes attached to large optical screens, radarscopes and cameras. . . . It will be almost impossible for any nation to hide warlike preparations for any length of time." Much later in von Braun's article, after elaborate descriptions of a trip into space on his three-stager, and of how the space station worked, he mentioned the station as "a terribly effective atomic bomb carrier," explaining how nuclear missiles could be deorbited from it. The magazine's editorial made his argument even more explicit: a new Manhattan

Project was needed, an estimated $4 billion expenditure to dominate space: "the U.S. must immediately embark on a long-range development program to secure for the West 'space superiority.' If we do not, somebody else will. That somebody else very probably would be the Soviet Union." Von Braun's speeches and media appearances sounded the same theme.[36]

He returned home via Nashville (airline service into Huntsville was still minimal), just in time to celebrate his fortieth birthday with his family. Maria was now over seven months pregnant with their second child and his parents were about to leave for West Germany, as Magnus Sr. had decided he wanted to free himself from dependence on his sons by applying for his pension rights as a former civil servant. On the day von Braun returned, Seth Moseley sent him a note thanking him for his "magnificent cooperation": "You are as successful as a salesman as you are a scientist." Von Braun replied six days later: "I am still trying to get my feet back on the ground after those thrilling, stimulating, hectic days in New York. Fan and crack[pot] letters keep on pouring in at a rate of 10 to 20 a day, but the tide is slowly receding." In fact the tide did not recede much, as the Collier's issue and subsequent press coverage provoked an explosion of interest among the public, including a number of lunatics with secret inventions and people volunteering for space missions. Most touching for von Braun was the enthusiasm of children and teenagers, who wrote in large numbers, many asking how they could get an education suitable for a space program. He did not mind answering these as much, but the volume of mail was so overwhelming that his letters to his parents complained constantly of a bursting mailbox and the impossibility of dealing with it. As far as the army was concerned, his space advocacy was a private activity, so he received no secretarial help to deal with his fame.[37]

April also brought the worst sinus infection he had ever suffered in his life—an old problem exacerbated by hay fever and exhaustion. He told a navy admiral on the last day of the month: "For the last three weeks, I have been pretty sick. Acute inflammation of all three sinuses at the right side, with resulting surgery and shock cures with some of those new anti-biotic drugs, forced me to stay in bed for ten days." Having gone back to work, he was now sick again, and his doctor told him to go on vacation.[38]

That he could not do right away, as Maria was about to give birth. On 8 May a healthy daughter arrived, Margrit Cecile. A week or so later he left for Florida with three-year-old Iris to give his wife a chance to deal with the new baby alone for two weeks. He told his parents afterward: "Iris was sweet, but totally shameless. She ruled me completely." The vacation was a "complete success," no doubt because he finally had rested. Although he possessed enormous physical energy, he had for months worked both a full schedule on the Redstone missile and evenings and weekends on the *Collier's* piece, the Bechtle-Neher matter, his correspondence with space advocates in the United States and Europe, and so on. Not long after he had come back, he also had to expand his magazine article for a book version of the *Collier's* issue, which was to be issued in the same format and by the same publisher as Ley and Bonestell's *Conquest of Space*.[39]

The most exciting but strictly secret by-product of the *Collier's* issue was the "A.V. Grosse action," as von Braun dubbed it. Aristid V. Grosse, president of the Temple University Research Institute in Philadelphia, was a German-trained atomic chemist and a member of President Roosevelt's first committee to investigate the A-bomb. He was also friends with President Truman's personal physician. The 22 March *Collier's* spurred Grosse to ask the doctor if he could query Truman about the need to investigate the space station and the possible Soviet threat. The beleaguered president, whose poll numbers were low because of the Korean stalemate, the apparent corruption in his administration, and the prevailing anti-Communist hysteria, had just announced that he would not run again. According to Grosse, Truman said: "Sure, Wallie [the physician's nickname], you go ahead and have him write a report for me." After making arrangements through senior army channels, Grosse then traveled to Huntsville in April to meet von Braun. The two immediately hit it off; von Braun found the visit "inspiring." Here was a chance to perhaps make his orbital battle station a reality, or at least get some money toward a less ambitious space project. With almost everything in the guided missile field shielded behind classification, and with Grosse's personal experience of the Manhattan Project's origins in a secret committee, it did not seem at all ludicrous to the two of them that this was exactly how a space program could start: as a secret, crash military project.[40]

Grosse had some intriguing ideas of his own; he focused on unmanned vehicles and the possibility of influencing the anti-Communist struggle in Asia with a satellite he called the "American Star," which could be a visible symbol of U.S. prowess or could perhaps even broadcast propaganda or jam signals from Red transmitters. Von Braun conveyed these ideas and news of the Grosse mission to one of the few people outside Huntsville to whom he felt he could talk about such potentially classified matters, Commander Robert Truax, a navy rocket specialist, longtime space enthusiast, and friend of Robert Goddard's during the latter's unproductive work for the navy in Annapolis during World War II. (Goddard had died the day after the Nagasaki bombing in August 1945, forty-one days before von Braun set foot in America.) Truax was also active in the American Rocket Society, which was increasingly divided between the space advocates and those who felt that it would bring practical rocket engineers into disrepute. During von Braun's June trip to NAA in California, he flew up to Monterey to see Truax and also talked to Karel "Charlie" Bossart, the Convair company's chief engineer for Atlas, the air force intercontinental ballistic missile (ICBM) project.[41]

As von Braun told Grosse in a long 21 June letter, they agreed that the beginning step was to form a committee of influential scientists and engineers and try to get several million government dollars for a study of programs and launch vehicles. Von Braun explained:

> To ask for hundreds of millions for a program that in many minds will [be] of rather dubious value (or at least nothing but an interesting technical and military gamble) would be tantamount to asking people to stick their neck way out. Nobody likes a thing like that. But to ask for a few millions to be invested in a modest program for the purpose of evaluating a new idea in the field of military science which is virtually "pregnant" with dreadful potentialities and could easily bring unpleasant surprises if some day a potential enemy should be discovered to have reached an orbit first,—isn't this really easing the burden of responsibility of policy makers, high-ranking officers and statesmen?[42]

Over the July Fourth weekend, while on a trip to Washington and New York, von Braun saw Grosse again at the resort town of Cape May, New Jersey; they agreed to invite several more insiders in the rocket and space business to participate in their committee. As von Braun told Maurice Zucrow of Purdue University: "Grosse is well aware of the fact that during an election year no dramatic action may be expected. But he also feels we should have our plans and strategy ready when and if a new administration, regardless of what brand, takes over." By this time the victory of General Dwight Eisenhower seemed likely, but there was still a possibility that Democratic nominee Adlai Stevenson could win. At any rate, there would be no quick decision from Truman, as von Braun may have hoped in April, but the presidential connection, as tenuous as it was, was tantalizing.[43]

In marked contrast to the *Collier's* campaign and the "A.V. Grosse action," von Braun's dealings with Germany had taken an increasingly annoying turn, dashing much of the hope he had invested in the Bechtle deal. First and foremost was Neher's rewrite of the novel, now titled *Menschen zwischen den Planeten* (Men Between the Planets), which Otto Bechtle had once hoped would be published by the end of 1951. But Neher kept none of his deadlines, and what he eventually provided exasperated von Braun no end. On 10 February 1952 he wrote Bechtle, after receiving pages 54–98 of the new version: "Unfortunately I must tell you, the prospect that further manuscript sections will be similar has put me in a thoroughly depressed mood." He found Neher long-winded and boring, but even more critically, Neher discussed political questions, including American policy in Germany, in ways that were embarrassing to him "as an employee of the U.S. Army." Worst of all, Neher had made technical and scientific mistakes "that would cause a physics student in his second semester to blush with embarrassment." To be listed as coauthor on such a book was "impossible." "I would ruin not only my scientific reputation, the whole matter would put me in an impossible situation with my American employer." Either the entire coauthorship arrangement had to be ditched as a failed experiment, or he (von Braun) had to take his name off the book, or Neher could completely revise his manuscript, which von Braun thought highly unlikely based on previous correspondence.[44]

Otto Bechtle would not be so easily discouraged and sought to calm his author down, telling him that of course he would have say over all technical things and asking him to please give Neher the chance to write more. Von Braun's translator-friend, Henry White, also offered to help by cutting the Neher manuscript and producing an English translation, although he had as low an opinion of it as von Braun. When copies of the *Das Marsprojekt* technical treatise arrived in April, von Braun was very happy—it was an encouraging sign that something good had come of the Bechtle deal. Moreover, the University of Illinois Press, which had published *Space Medicine*, was interested in printing an English translation of the booklet. But after he received the next segment of the Neher novel, his reaction was the same: he wanted to kill it off or at least take his name off it. White felt the same way and no longer was willing to translate. But Bechtle would not give up, so the whole situation continued into the summer of 1952.[45]

A second source of irritation in Germany was his old Raketenflugplatz mentor and intermittent troublemaker, Rudolf Nebel. He went around giving lectures in West Germany about how the V-2 was his invention and how von Braun and Dornberger had stolen it from him. Unlike the situation just a few years later, when von Braun was treated as a shining hero by space enthusiasts and the press in West Germany and the United States, he was far from untouchable in the early 1950s. Hermann Oberth complained to others that von Braun's arrogance and naked ambition had allegedly led to his (Oberth's) exile into minor positions in Third Reich rocket development. But Nebel's complaints were the ones that got into West German popular magazines and newspapers, leading von Braun to initiate a slander lawsuit against him in a Munich court, a matter that dragged on through 1952 and 1953 and ultimately produced nothing.[46]

If Nebel provoked von Braun's wrath, Oberth was another matter; von Braun still honored him as his true teacher and founder of spaceflight theory in the German world. Hearing that Oberth's future employment prospects were weak after a small rocket development job for the Italian navy came to an end, at the beginning of 1952 von Braun approached Ley about possibly bringing Oberth over under the successor program to Paperclip; he hoped Willy might be a good intermediary as Ley had been close to the cranky theorist. Just at this time von Braun's deputy Eberhard Rees went to West Germany for several months on a recruiting program for the Redstone project, as they had a hard time attracting sufficiently qualified American engineers to a small town in Alabama with a hot, humid climate and a severe housing shortage. But bureaucracy and security clearances would drag out the recruitment of Germans for years; Oberth would not reach the United States until mid-1955. But von Braun was at least able to win him over through correspondence and a job offer in the fall of 1952, convincing the theorist of his sincere interest in the older man's welfare.[47]

All the while von Braun was also corresponding energetically with German, British, and American space advocates about the next IAF congress, to be held in Stuttgart under GfW auspices at the beginning of September. Early in 1952 he was fairly optimistic that he would finally get to return to Germany, probably because of the *Collier's* money. He planned to travel with his wife but gradually became more and more skeptical of the trip's feasibility. He was very busy, and it was expensive; he had likely used part of his check to help pay for his parents' voyage, and Maria's mother was willing to come visit instead. What finished it was Walter Dornberger's tale of how U.S. agents had shadowed him every minute to prevent the Soviets from supposedly kidnapping him, with the result "that he could scarcely go to the bathroom alone." The army was promising the same treatment for von Braun. On 14 July he sent Koelle his definitive statement of nonappearance, regardless of his role as congress keynote speaker. Once again the solution was for Fred Durant, now ARS vice president, to read the speech. Von Braun may not have known then that Durant was a covert CIA officer who maintained a downtown Washington office as a front. He traveled to IAF congresses as a way to gather intelligence on foreign rocket programs and space advocates and even became the federation's president from 1953 to 1956.[48]

The speech Durant delivered for him, "Space Travel—Its Dependence upon International Scientific Cooperation," assured the space societies that there were studies that could be undertaken involving spaceflight, notwithstanding the fact that military secrecy cut them off from almost all money and knowledge derived from practical rocket projects. Von Braun adopted Robert Oppenheimer's claim that deadline-driven development programs exploited but did not produce new scientific knowledge. He was no doubt thinking of his situation, where he made a living managing the development of a weapon of mass destruction with a range of less than 200 mi (320 km), while dreaming of space projects for which there was no money. The assertion was nonetheless dubious, as almost all advances made in missiles, rockets, and spaceflight in the 1950s came from government investment in concrete engineering projects, not science.[49]

Two weeks after writing Koelle, von Braun told Otto Bechtle of his final, unalterable decision to take his name off Neher's rewrite after reading the last segment. At most he was willing to accept a weak credit on the title page as inspiration for the novel. Bechtle was already very frustrated by the situation. Emmy von Braun recounted in a letter the publisher's surprise visit to Landshut, where the U.S. Army was temporarily housing the elder von Brauns. (In the fall they moved to the Alpine village of Oberaudorf am Inn, on the Austrian border.) Having just visited Neher, Bechtle told Emmy of "wild battles" with the writer, "so sharp that Neher's wife got heart pains because of the raw tone of the negotiations. . . . For you [Wernher] he [Neher] has formed a kind of 'love-hate.'" When Bechtle got the rocket engineer's letter, he replied legalistically, describing how von Braun was violating the terms of the contract. Von Braun proposed a way out. He would try to eliminate as many of Neher's scientific and technical errors as possible; he would write a foreword that would allow Bechtle to put his increasingly famous name on the cover; he would give most of the royalties to Neher; and he would not try to publish the original novel in English—an idea he had briefly entertained when U.S. publishers showed renewed interest after the *Collier's* bombshell. This deal was acceptable to Bechtle. The publisher was also no doubt mollified by Dornberger's memoir *V-2*, which was a hit in Germany in late 1952. It had come about because von Braun had pointed out his former superior's unpublished manuscript. Neher had rewritten Dornberger's book too, but it was a much easier job and he received no public credit.[50]

In the summer of 1952 von Braun had even more on his plate. With the first *Collier's* issue a big success and the book on its way, Ryan and the magazine's leadership decided that they could proceed with the second "symposium" discussed the previous December, on the Moon trip (Mars being the third). At the same time Willy Ley and the Hayden Planetarium began to make plans for the Second Annual Symposium on Space Travel in October; this time von Braun's presence would be essential. For maximum publicity the two would be timed together, not long after the publication of the book derived from the first issue, *Across the Space Frontier*. On 6 July, the day after von Braun saw Grosse in Cape May, he was in New York to begin planning the Moon issue with Ryan, Ley, Klep, and Freeman. This issue—which soon became two—would have an even bigger payoff than the first, $1,500, money that von Braun used in August to finance a car trip to New York with the family to pick up Maria's mother. He spent several more days in the magazine's offices.[51]

In the meantime von Braun had to weather another exasperating military flap. On 14 July he sent Ryan a letter that opened: "Lest you think that I am a miserable, uncooperative, double-crossing stinker, I'll fill you in on a couple of details which caused me to assume such a constipated attitude in this clearance business. . . . Several days ago, there was an inquiry from the Central Intelligence Agency why a booklet called 'The Mars Project,' by Wernher von Braun, had been published in Germany." An agent had picked it up in a bookstore there, "and, impressed by the many formulae in connection with my name, must have thought that he had caught a flagrant case of a leak of military secrets." Unfortunately the original "Mars Project" manuscript with the DOD clearance stamps was in Germany, and the cover letter may have been at *Collier's*, which set off a flurry of phone calls. In the end von Braun was able to still the waters, but he would have to jump through more clearance hoops for the first *Collier's* book and the Moon issues. More seriously, he had to be cautious in the future about publishing things in Germany that were not translations of U.S. publications, as he still had to prove his loyalty to America.[52]

That loyalty was certainly on display on 17 September, when he spoke before a blue-ribbon audience in Washington on "Space Superiority as a Means for Achieving World Peace." It was the high-water mark in his campaign for a military space station. The Business Advisory Council of the Department of Commerce was loaded with leaders of giant corporations, and not coincidentally its executive director was the brother of his translator, Henry J. White. As he proudly told his parents afterward, his speech at the Mayflower Hotel was attended by numerous corporate chieftains, two cabinet members, the chief of naval operations, former ambassador Averell Harriman, and former German occupation governor General Lucius Clay.

Afterward he was up until two-thirty a.m. with Clay at a cocktail party hosted by the president of Standard Oil of California. It was almost exactly seven years since he had set foot on American soil as a quasi-prisoner.[53]

His speech repeated all the arguments of the 22 March *Collier's*, but most interesting was his discussion of the military superiority of the station and how it might defend itself against attack. In revising and extending his article for the first *Collier's* book, he had already elaborated his thoughts, perhaps in response to readers' letters. One objection was that an enemy could merely launch a cloud of shrapnel into an orbit that intersected the station, wrecking it; he thought the guidance challenges for such an attack so great that, when combined with the station's ability to maneuver, it would be possible for the station to easily avoid that threat. Dismissing the possibility of developing accurate, vertically launched nuclear missiles, he expected that the only real threat could come from armed, piloted space planes. His answer, as given in the speech, was radical: "The space station can destroy with absolute certainty an enemy space-craft prior to its launching." He hoped deterrence would work, but in essence he advocated preemptive (probably nuclear) strikes on the USSR as the last resort to protect the station's dominance of the skies—something he had already imagined in the opening to his ill-fated novel.[54]

He appealed again for a $4 billion Manhattan Project–type commitment to develop this "ultimate weapon" to enforce a *Pax Americana* on Earth. The air force's strategic bombers were doomed to failure in the face of the rapid development of Soviet jet fighters (remarks edited out of the published version in *Ordnance* magazine, no doubt because of the trouble they would have caused between the services), but if his launch vehicle and station system were developed before the Soviet ones, the USSR would have no answer. It is remarkable that he failed to see the imminent arrival of a world of intercontinental ballistic missiles, which would make orbital bombs a poor second choice, stuck as they were in predictable orbits that would pass over targets only once or twice a day. The space station as superweapon, a concept he took from Oberth and German science fiction, was clearly an idée fixe for von Braun; he advocated it as late as October 1956, his own participation in ballistic missile development notwithstanding.[55]

Von Braun told Grosse after his speech that he had made one clear convert, Juan Trippe, the famous head of Pan-American Airways, but it was hard to tell what the impact of "Space Superiority" might be. He and Grosse exchanged more letters and met in Philadelphia. They had longer exchanges with Walter Dornberger, now at Bell Aircraft in Buffalo (maker of the X-1 and X-2 rocket planes), and succeeded in winning over Dornberger's boss,

Larry Bell. After Eisenhower's election on 4 November, Grosse wrote him: "I have been busy on our problem since the elections, and have had some important discussions. Wise men, however, advise me to go slow for the next two months."[56]

In fact, it was virtually the end of the "A.V. Grosse action." In mid-1953 Grosse wrote his report, which discussed the unmanned satellite as a psychological weapon and a possible scientific or reconnaissance vehicle, while leaving aside von Braun's manned space station as too far in the future. Its most striking feature is Grosse's accurate prediction of the shock effect of a Soviet satellite triumph. But with the new Republican administration reorganizing the Department of Defense (DOD), it was September before he was able to hand the document over to Donald Quarles, the new assistant secretary of defense for research and development, whose bureau replaced the committee-ridden Research and Development Board. The Grosse report appears to have had no immediate impact on Eisenhower defense policy, although it might have influenced the first serious discussions of a satellite in 1954. Concerned by Soviet progress in ballistic missiles, Ike and his Defense officials decided instead to put urgent priority on the Atlas ICBM rather than on expensive space programs.[57]

Three weeks after the Washington speech von Braun flew back to New York for the second *Collier's* publicity blitz of 1952. Once again Seth Moseley distributed press releases, window displays, and press packets and lined up radio and TV interviews around the unveiling of the first Moon issue on 10 October. While the media interest was not quite as large the second time around, highlights included von Braun's interview on NBC's *Kate Smith Show*, which had "the largest daytime audience in America," a couple of other television appearances, plus several national radio interviews. The tour ended in Baltimore on the twentieth for an appearance on a science show that was broadcast on twenty-three TV stations.[58]

In the middle of this trip was the second Hayden Symposium, which ended with a quasi-debate: Milton Rosen, technical director of the Viking sounding rocket program at the Naval Research Laboratory, would present a more skeptical view of von Braun's space plans, followed by the man himself. While *Collier's* once again pushed the military space station as an urgent Cold War necessity in its press releases, this second publicity blitz initiated a new phase of von Braun's spaceflight campaign, shifting readers' attention from military dominance to lunar exploration, crew training, unmanned satellites, and human flights to Mars. As the Rosen critique revealed, von Braun also had to respond to a growing wave of criticism from within the ARS and the rocket engineering community, many of whom were very uncomfortable with his bold proposals.[59]

Von Braun's articles for the 18 and 25 October issues, "Man on the Moon: The Journey" and "Man on the Moon: The Exploration," were no less audacious than the first: he could imagine space exploration only on a gigantic scale. The very first human landing on that body would be a three-ship, fifty-man expedition, requiring six months of assembly in orbit next to the space station. "Each ship is 160 feet long (nine feet more than the height of the Statue of Liberty) and about 110 feet wide. Each has at its base a battery of 30 rocket motors, and each is topped by the sphere which houses the crew members, scientists and technicians on five floors." All three ships would descend directly to the lunar surface together. One was a one-way cargo vehicle that would be partially disassembled to build a temporary base to house the crew members, all men of course. As he described in the second article, credited jointly to Fred Whipple, the expedition also had several tracked vehicles to carry out its scientific work. In one case, ten men set off to explore a crater almost 200 mi (320 km) away. After six weeks on the surface, all fifty crew members would lift off from the Moon in the two remaining ships.[60]

In the expedition's scale one can see von Braun's underlying adolescent delight in simply imagining it. As he put it:

> After a day of excruciating meetings for the Redstone Project, with all these contractors, laboratory and shop workers, Army officers, designers, budget people, and test engineers, hammering out performance data, safety rules, flight-test programs, production quotas, contractor bonuses, acceptance criteria, and what-have-you, it is such an enjoyable relaxation to transpose yourself to the lunar surface and simply charge ahead with a colorful description of all the exciting adventures that you expect there. . . . I mix me some martinis, put a Brandenburg concerto on the record player and just write and write . . . until Maria gets out of bed and reminds me that I must be in the office two hours from now.[61]

As was typical of von Braun's visions, his Moon flight was marked by highly optimistic estimates of the cost (half a billion dollars, not counting the space station) and by a timetable that also seemed quite optimistic: within twenty-five years, that is, by 1977. Almost no one in 1952, except von Braun and his fellow enthusiasts, could have imagined that the manned lunar landing was only seventeen years away, but all would have been surprised that it involved only three astronauts and cost forty times as much (not allowing for inflation).

At the Hayden, von Braun presented the Moon expedition, but the symposium's real importance was the reaction of the press to his pairing with Milt Rosen. According to Rosen, Willy Ley wanted to stop him from giving his paper criticizing von Braun for "being too far out and being beyond what could be done, of using very optimistic numbers . . . there was no margin for error in any of his calculations." But von Braun "overruled" Ley. "He said, 'The more criticism we get from Rosen the better. If he agrees with us, it won't attract any attention at all.' And he was right about that." After the session, Rosen recalls saying to von Braun:

> "You know you don't really believe those calculations that you've done for this giant Orbiter around the Earth and all that."
>
> He said, "Listen, Milt, you're an American. You should know advertising is everything in America. . . . The way you're talking about space flight, it'll never come. The way I'm talking about it will get people interested in it, and you'll benefit from it as much as me."[62]

Von Braun did in fact believe his calculations, however much arm-waving was involved in some arguments when specific technical solutions did not yet exist. But as this anecdote shows, he was acutely aware that, notwithstanding public enthusiasm for the *Collier's* series, his first task was to sell space to a skeptical or indifferent majority.

As von Braun predicted, their opposing views did stimulate interest. The next morning *The New York Times* ran an article titled, "2 Rocket Experts Argue 'Moon' Plan." Seven weeks later, in early December, *Time* had a major story on spaceflight that pleased him less. The cover was graced with an illustrator's strange but striking interpretation of the theme, a robotic spacecraft with walking legs, a head, and TV cameras for eyes. The story featured technical skepticism from "practical missile men" like Rosen, and medical skepticism from San Antonio; Strughold stated that he was not sure humans could work effectively in weightlessness. But most irksome were the political critiques. Rosen saw von Braun's ambitious plans as prescriptions for jumping immediately into a major space project without preliminaries, damaging all guided missile research and thus U.S. national security. "An important missile expert" who would not be quoted by name was even harsher: "Look at this Von Braun! He is the man who lost the war for Hitler. His V-2 was a great engineering achievement, but it had almost no military effect. . . . Von Braun always wanted to be the Columbus of space. He was thinking of space flight, not weapons when he sold the V-2 to Hitler. He says so himself. He . . . is trying to sell the U.S. a space flight project disguised as a means of dominating the world."[63]

The anonymous critic's playing of the German card shows that von Braun could not escape his Nazi past even in an era of obsessive anti-Communism. Knowing this, he had gone along with the publication in September 1952 of a celebrity profile in the form of a ghostwritten memoir article that he did not like much, "Why I Chose America." It appeared in a women's magazine and, as he noted ironically to Dornberger in 1953, even won him an award for patriotic writing. Together with *The New Yorker* interview and the as-yet-unpublished memoir for the BIS, this article was one of his first attempts to create an official history of his experiences in the Third Reich, one that naturally played up his Gestapo arrest and surrender to U.S. forces and that omitted any mention of concentration camp prisoners or his SS membership. Yet even at *Collier's* in New York the shadows of that past never completely went away. One day when Ryan, von Braun, and Heinz Haber, the aerospace medicine specialist, were on the elevator, a mischievous staff member felt Haber's leather coat, saying: "Human skin, of course?"[64]

While the Nazi issue mostly stayed in the background, the same could not be said of the growing criticism of von Braun's space proposals. Among the wider public, skepticism, dismissal, and ridicule did not go away, even in Huntsville. When his longtime and indispensable executive secretary, Bonnie Holmes, first expressed interest in the job in 1952, her colleagues in the Arsenal post engineer's office said: "Surely you can't really want to work for 'those crazy Krauts.' There is no future for you in such a business." Among the rocket engineers Rosen's critique hit a nerve in part because of the way the ARS had minimized spaceflight since the mid-1930s to achieve respectability, and in part because of the way *Collier's* had presented von Braun's proposals as flat-out assertions with all qualifiers removed and with no discussion of intermediate steps. Military security prevented von Braun from talking about how the still-secret Redstone missile or other rockets might be adapted to launch a small satellite, although he or Grosse did mention the "American Star" idea to *Time*.[65]

Von Braun was particularly annoyed by *Time* writer Jonathan Leonard's dichotomy between space true believers and "practical missile men." He told an ARS meeting in Indiana in May 1953, after arriving and finding himself "the central figure in what seems to be a major controversy": "Being a hard-boiled development man, who [has] had his ample share of setbacks and disappointments, I am <u>not</u> recommending to go off half-cocked and immediately embark on a hard-ware development program involving a 7000-ton[,] 3 stage rocket." He went on to justify his plan for a nuclear-armed station in detail, coming back to the need to outstrip Soviet capabilities and not prop up the strategic bomber as a deterrent. It was the kind of performance that won him many new friends and adherents. Robert Kraemer, then a young engineer at NAA/Rocketdyne, remembers another von Braun speech to an ARS meeting in Los Angeles six months later. He went armed with various criticisms of the *Collier's* articles and came away a convert to von Braun's cause.[66]

A couple of months before the Indiana meeting, the magazine had published its third set of articles, in three consecutive issues from 28 February to 14 March, on what we would now call astronaut training and survival. (The term *astronaut* was not yet used for spacefarers; some journalists employed it to describe astronautics advocates like von Braun.) It is noteworthy that there were no more media extravaganzas and the articles had no bylines except Ryan as editor, although von Braun was listed as a contributor to the second and third issues.[67] Presumably because his role was diminished, there was no single concept to promote, and space was becoming routine even for *Collier's*, the magazine decided not to spend much money on publicity.

The series had come about because Connie Ryan and his staff had been impressed with the outpouring of public interest in how "space men" would be prepared for and survive their journeys. Von Braun had already begun to sketch his Mars landing craft for use by the artists in what would be the final issue or issues, but just before he came to New York for the Moon blitz in October 1952, *Collier's* had sent him a $4,000 contract for "an original article of approximately 5,000 words in length, various memoranda and blueprints dealing with The Men Who Will Conquer Space." (In fact, the new series did mention that women would go into space, although "not as pilots, perhaps.") As the new series evolved under Ryan's editorship, navy and air force doctors came to play a bigger role, and von Braun's contribution was eventually melded into the training and rescue articles—the first one having focused on spacesuits. Beyond drafting his contribution, von Braun's primary role during the winter of 1952–53 was to advise Ley, Haber, and the artists on the visualization of the centrifuge and other trainers, and to conceptualize the escape pod that would allow each crew member to eject from his winged, third-stage rocket. All of this was done in his spare time, of course. In parallel, von Braun also began working with Ley, Whipple, and Ryan on the considerable expansion of the October series into the second *Collier's* book, *Conquest of the Moon*. It appeared in the fall of 1953.[68]

Extending the series on preparations for the first human flights, in April the magazine asked von Braun to write about unmanned satellites for $2,500. What he came up with was the "Baby Space Station," a conical multipurpose scientific satellite carrying three rhesus monkeys in a relatively low orbit of 200 mi (320 km). Published in the 27 June issue, this time under his name, it was typically ambitious for what was advertised as the "First Step in the Conquest of Space." His small, three-stage expendable booster for the satellite was 150 ft (46 m) high and 30 ft (9 m) in diameter. In fact, he knew that the first satellite would be nowhere near this ambitious and might involve a passive object that merely was visible as it passed overhead, but he, and the magazine, felt a need to hype the new proposal.[69]

As an act of imagination, the "Baby Space Station" was fair enough, but the way this issue had arisen as an afterthought shows clearly where von Braun's mind had been all along: on human exploration. He and his fellow space pioneers had devoted little or no attention to the issue of robotic exploration; indeed, they had scarcely imagined it at all. The limitations on electronics of that day certainly seemed to dictate hands-on control, but for him and for the others, human exploration was the only purpose of space-flight. Von Braun gave it no deeper thought, assuming that space travel would open new vistas for humankind and its sciences, and went back to doing what he really wanted to do: imagining the hardware that might take him, or someone, into space.

At the time von Braun felt he lived a completely bifurcated professional existence. He told Hermann Oberth in December 1952 that his public activity might lead to the false impression that he was involved in planning future spaceflights. "My daily work is rooted, however, in very real short-term problems, and is not dissimilar to what it was in Peenemünde: completion under time pressure of a 'cobbled-together' bird, with worries about money, personnel, reductions in the failure rate, test stands, launch attempts," and so on. As frustrating as some of these might be, he was much happier under the leadership of Toftoy, who gave him more freedom and responsibility than Hamill had.[70]

The spring of 1953 also saw the hardware he was actually building, not imagining, take shape. The Arsenal shops assembled the first Redstone missile, the RS-1, for its maiden flight in August—a half year behind the original schedule because of routine development problems and a budget that was by no means extravagant. Indeed, lacking earmarked funds to build a test stand to static-test the missile (i.e., to run a live engine firing while the vehicle was held in place), his division had put one together out of scrap metal and old railroad tank cars for less than $25,000, thereby evading budget restrictions. Eisenhower's defense reorganization and cutback, and the further reduction in funds that followed the Korean armistice of 27 July, produced worrying money problems, but Redstone had a sufficiently high priority that it was not drastically affected by budget cuts, although there was a stretch-out of production in 1954. But these cuts did spell the end of the Hermes ramjet program, which had limped along as a secondary line of work for von Braun's division.[71]

As the result of phasing out the ramjet engine test stand, von Braun had to find a new job for his brother Magnus. He was fortunate that just at that time, June 1953, one became available as liaison to Chrysler for Redstone production. His younger brother was happy to change to a better-paying, white-collar occupation that was less in his brother's shadow, as it meant traveling often to Detroit. In the spring of 1955 of Magnus left the Arsenal's employ altogether to become a manager at Chrysler; six months later he turned down a lucrative offer from Wernher to return to Huntsville, telling his parents that he did not want to spend "my whole life stuck with the stigma of a protégé." His childless marriage broke up at about the same time. As for Sigismund, he had brought his family back from Rome in 1949, had held both government and corporate jobs in the Rhineland, and in late 1953 rejoined the diplomatic service, this time as an official of the West German embassy to London. He and his wife had two more daughters in 1952 and 1954.[72]

In the stifling heat of mid-August 1953, von Braun journeyed to Cape Canaveral, Florida, for the launch of RS-1. Conditions at the new national missile range run by the air force were scarcely less primitive than they had been for the first launches there, Bumpers 7 and 8 in July 1950. It is not clear if von Braun attended those, but when he and the launch team led by Kurt Debus came three years later, they had to stay thirty miles away in often dumpy, cockroach-infested motels in Melbourne or on the barrier island opposite; Cocoa Beach was not yet the missile-race boom town it would shortly become. The Cape itself was a wide spot in the barrier islands, a scrubland with mosquitoes, armadillos, and scorpions, alligators in the Banana River separating it from the mainland, and rednecks in areas not already taken by the government. The best observing post was on top of the historic Canaveral lighthouse, and von Braun was sometimes seen there during the early firings. Dieter Huzel, now working for Rocketdyne on the engine, was struck by the sense of déjà vu: the sand, the sea, and the rocket on the simple launch table all reminded him of Peenemünde, palm trees notwithstanding.[73]

After several delays Redstone RS-1 lifted off on the morning of 20 August 1953 and quickly disappeared into the overcast. All seemed normal, but then some observers heard the engine acting erratically and the missile crashed 7 mi (11 km) offshore. As investigators discovered later, problems in the control system had caused it to go off course and fly loops above the clouds before diving into the sea. But since only a substitute control system derived from the V-2 was in use, and the primary reason for the launch was to test the propulsion system and the integrity of the fuselage, von Braun and his group were quite satisfied with the launch—the thing had held together while doing powered loops.[74]

In the weeks before and after his trip to Florida, Mars again came to dominate von Braun's spare-time agenda. *Collier's* had put the Mars issue back on the front burner immediately after the "Baby Space Station" was wrapped up, aiming for one or two articles in October—perhaps for cost reasons the magazine had given up the idea of a more elaborate "symposium." Suddenly Connie Ryan needed the manuscript from von Braun. The engineer had earlier suggested to the editor that the whole expedition could be revolutionized if something Ernst Stuhlinger was studying, electrical or "ion" rocket engines, were used in place of traditional chemical rockets. But under the pressure of time, in August or September he drafted the article simply as a popularization of his original Mars Project, with its monumental ten-ship, seventy-man expedition. Meanwhile the University of Illinois Press edition of his calculations, entitled *The Mars Project*, was finally moving into production, entailing work on the cover drawings and page proofs; it came out in late September 1953. That same summer Neher's version of his "Mars Project" novel at last appeared in Germany, accompanied by von Braun's oddly distanced foreword describing the "difficult birth" of the book. He gave no indication that the book's basic plot, even the names of most of the characters, had originally come from him, however much the details had been embellished and altered.[75]

What von Braun found particularly perplexing were all the contractual complications arising from so many versions of his Mars ideas, which were complicated yet further because Willy Ley and Chesley Bonestell were inviting him to participate in a Mars book they had long planned for the close approaches of Mars to the Earth in 1954 or 1956. So far they had withheld that news from Connie Ryan, fearing accusations of betrayal. Von Braun kept mum, but before he would sign the $3,000 contract for the article that *Collier's* had sent him, he had to get his agent, Mike Watkins, to convince the magazine that publishing *The Mars Project* would not conflict with the article version of the same ideas. Just after he returned the contract in late September 1953, Bonestell almost blew up the whole deal when he fired off a nasty missive to Ryan over the Moon book, just published by Viking Press in the same format as *Conquest of Space* and *Across the Space Frontier;* he thought the color reproductions were inferior to the other two. "The Moon book has made me so damn mad I decided not to write you any more, so here goes." After discussing astronomers' meetings about Mars that he would like to attend, he mentioned the verbal agreement that he and Ley had with Viking for a Mars book, now put off until 1956—he wanted *Collier's* to renounce book rights to his paintings.[76]

This letter produced an explosion. On 9 October von Braun wrote Bonestell:

> Master,
> What hast thou done? I had a phone call from Connie Ryan today and he was all up in arms about the letter you wrote him. It had been my understanding that you had planned to stay mum about this book project because there was no rush about this whole thing anyway. That is at least what Willy wrote me. But now you let the cat out of the bag and all New York is on fire.

The artist replied four days later, using another jocular nickname no doubt stemming from von Braun's visits to his Pasadena studio:

> Dear Brushcleaner:
> Ain't we having fun! First, do not worry about Collier's not publishing the Mars article. It is scheduled for March or April of next year (I told you the deadline was a fraud) and since they sent me their check for $7,000.00 in the terms of my contract it is proof of acceptance, and since they are in that deep I doubt if they will cancel it to please Connie Ryan.[77]

Indeed the threat was an empty one. The project proceeded at the pace set by the artists, but relations with Ryan were never the same again. The magazine threatened to use the Mars issue and other contributions for its own book, making von Braun nervous about the other book plan, but that threat came to naught too, as did a plan to issue the spring 1953 training and "Baby Satellite" articles as a book. The Mars issue finally appeared on 30 April 1954 with a Bonestell cover and two articles, Fred Whipple's one-page "Is There Life on Mars?" and von Braun's longer "Can We Get to Mars?" The German engineer was not very happy with the result, feeling that his piece had been "edited to death" by Ryan to overemphasize the long trip to Mars and all the obstacles on the way, leaving only a truncated ending for his Mars landings. The issue was, however, illustrated with more superb color paintings by Bonestell and Freeman, making it a worthy conclusion to the series.[78]

The *Collier's* Mars issue marked the end of the first phase of von Braun's campaign for spaceflight, and it had a profound and lasting influence on both U.S. public perception and government policy. In late 1949 George Gallup conducted a poll of public expectations for scientific and technical advances by the year 2000. Eighty-eight percent foresaw a cure for cancer, and 63 percent atomic trains and airplanes, but only 15 percent thought "men in rockets will be able to reach the moon in the next 50 years." By 1955 that had gone up to 38 percent, in large part because of *Collier's*. As for public policy, the magazine series launched what one analyst has called the "von Braun paradigm"—a "logical" plan for spaceflight whose fundamental elements were a reusable space plane for transportation, a wheel-type space station as an orbital base, a landing on the Moon, and finally a Mars expedition, all of them of course with human crew. Robotic spacecraft were quite simply an adjunct and afterthought, something that von Braun knew would come first but that did not engage him very much. Human exploration would be its own reward; science would advance and, with it, human welfare. After the Soviet Sputnik triumph in 1957, the "von Braun paradigm" repeatedly influenced where NASA, the newly created civilian space agency, thought it should be going.[79]

Personally, the series was just as fundamental for von Braun. It vaulted him to a new fame, especially in the English-speaking world and in West Germany, where translations of the *Collier's* books were quickly published, and made him the Western world's chief prophet for spaceflight for the next two decades. Financially it was a godsend; all told he made about $12,000—roughly his annual salary—from writing and speaking in 1953. His Christmas letter to his parents that year mentioned that the family had given itself a twenty-five-foot used "cabin cruiser" with mahogany fittings, "4 beds, a pantry, a toilet, a big roofed cockpit and a 95-hp motor." It would be docked on Lake Guntersville, one of the TVA lakes on the Tennessee River, southeast of Huntsville. Four years earlier they had come to the little Alabama city always cash-strapped, between supporting his parents and building a house. Now Magnus and Emmy were independent and the von Brauns had a nice upper-middle-class lifestyle; he could take Maria to New York City for shopping and culture every year, as promised. He had no qualms about discarding his baronial title in the United States, he told his parents in 1953, but with the sophisticated tastes in music, food, and furnishings that he and his wife had absorbed from their aristocratic upbringing, they no doubt enjoyed having the money. When von Braun left the new Lutheran congregation in 1952 because of the overly "businesslike" approach of its pastor, he not only sought a more emotional religious experience, he also showed his usual, acute sense of social class, taking his wife and two little daughters into the Episcopalian Church, long associated with the upper strata in the eastern United States.[80]

By spring 1954 Wernher von Braun was also much more professionally secure, in part because of *Collier's* but mostly because of the Redstone project, which finally created a sound position for himself and his Germans in the American rocket and missile business. The RS-2 launch in January 1954 was a sterling success, and although the third blew up on the pad in May due to an engine problem, the fourth and subsequent launches would see many more partial and complete successes. By midyear he had nearly a thousand people under him, 85 percent of them native-born Americans. He told the president of ARS, Andrew Haley, in November: "Our development program here at Redstone Arsenal has tremendously gathered momentum and has turned into real big business"—so much so, in fact, that it forced him to cut back on his speaking engagements "for an orderly space flight program."[81] The challenges of the next three years would be to find ways not only to continue to sell space but actually to try to get into the business of entering it. There would be new triumphs and many frustrations along the way, but once again von Braun would find that the real money in his business came not from space travel but from the race for ever more devastating weapons.

CHAPTER TWELVE

We Could Do It!

1954–57

"With the Redstone, we could do it!" "Do what?" . . .
"Launch a satellite, of course!"
—VON BRAUN to Stuhlinger, c. 1953[1]

On 7 May 1954 Dien Bien Phu fell to the Vietnamese Communists, marking the effective end of the French phase of the Indochina war. In the aftermath Wernher von Braun found the world situation "more confusing and worrying than ever." He was not sure if the H-bomb would intimidate the Chinese, and he expected more small countries to fall to the Reds one by one, as President Eisenhower himself predicted. Ten days later the U.S. Supreme Court ordered the desegregation of the nation's schools. The relatively liberal Alabama governor, James "Big Jim" Folsom, announced that his state would obey the law—but of course that was not at all how things would turn out. On 27 May the loyalty board investigating leading Manhattan Project physicist J. Robert Oppenheimer revoked his security clearances, as it did not find him sufficiently trustworthy; von Braun would later denounce this outcome as unfair and anti-intellectual. As if in counterpoint to the Oppenheimer case, on 9 June Senator Joseph McCarthy finally "destroyed himself on national television" when his irresponsible and bizarre investigation into alleged Communists in the army provoked the service's special counsel to exclaim: "Have you no sense of decency, sir?" The hearings petered out eight days later. McCarthy was finished.[2]

Against this backdrop, on 25 June von Braun attended a small but exhilarating meeting in a shabby temporary building on the Mall in Washington, D.C. Lieutenant Commander George Hoover of Air Branch, Office of Naval Research (ONR), had called the conclave, he said, to initiate an Earth satellite program, rather than just talk about it.[3] It was the beginning of an on-again, off-again project that would be a continuing thread in von Braun's mid-1950s life. Even as Walt Disney's TV program made him yet more famous and army missile development intensified the demands on his time, the dream of launching the world's first satellite, and the fear that the Soviets would do it instead, was constantly on his mind.

Ever since von Braun's 15 May 1945 report to Allied interrogators on rocketry's future prospects, there had been repeated discussions of a satellite inside the American military. Spurred by the initial enthusiasm, a navy group had actually started such a project in the fall of 1945 and had approached the USAAF to collaborate, spurring the formation of RAND as an air force–affiliated think tank. RAND's first, historic, and secret report was the 2 May 1946 "Preliminary Design of an Experimental World-Circling Spaceship." (Whether von Braun was later allowed to see it is unknown.) The drastic budget cuts of 1947–48 killed off the first wave of enthusiasm, however. Interest in both satellites and long-range ballistic missiles began to revive only during and after the Korean War, mostly due to reports of Soviet advances in rocketry and, most alarmingly, in nuclear weapons: in August 1953 Moscow announced its first H-bomb test, only nine months after the United States exploded the gigantic, 10-megaton-yield "MIKE" device in the Pacific. Several early 1950s RAND reports for the air force quite sensibly focused on the robotic photoreconnaissance satellite as the ultimate answer to the near-impenetrability of the "iron curtain" to Western intelligence. Space applications still, however, seemed too much like Buck Rogers comic book material to most military leaders, despite or perhaps because of von Braun's campaigns for "space superiority" through a nuclear-armed space station.[4]

In the unclassified world, space advocates also circulated several proposals for small Earth satellites, the most prominent being S. Fred Singer's MOUSE (Minimum Orbital Unmanned Satellite of Earth). Singer was a young University of Maryland physicist who had been ONR liaison in London at the beginning of the 1950s, becoming friendly with the British Interplanetary Society leaders in the process. He promoted the idea of the small satellite as the ultimate extension of the pioneering sounding rocket research into the upper atmosphere and near space, which had begun at White Sands immediately after the war. For his efforts, Singer earned the reputation in scientific circles of a loose cannon.[5]

The stars began to align in 1954, however. First the marked progress of large American ballistic missiles raised the promise that satellite launchers were not so far away after all. Von Braun's Redstone flew a fully successful test in January 1954, and the air force Atlas ICBM project rapidly accelerated soon afterward. Fear of Soviet rocket advances, the Eisenhower administration's drive to replace expensive conventional forces with the threat of "massive [nuclear] retaliation," disillusionment with long-range cruise missiles (essentially unmanned jet aircraft that were inaccurate and vulnerable to air defenses), and technological breakthroughs in inertial guidance systems and in light and extremely powerful thermonuclear warheads, all made the ICBM suddenly an idea whose time had come. On 1 July 1954 Air Research and Development Command established a Western Development Division (WDD) in Los Angeles, commanded by a forty-three-year-old rising star, Brigadier General Bernard "Bennie" Schriever. The creation of WDD and the investment of billions in Atlas markedly shifted the balance of American rocket development toward the air force and its allies, the aircraft industry based predominantly on the West Coast.[6]

Satellite ideas also gained in credibility as a result of a secret study of the threat of surprise attack. After Eisenhower voiced his fear that Soviet weapons development and lack of good U.S. intelligence could lead to a "nuclear Pearl Harbor," he appointed James Killian, a scientist and president of the Massachusetts Institute of Technology (MIT), to head a Technological Capabilities Panel with unlimited secret access. The Killian panel saw the RAND reports on reconnaissance satellites and in the fall of 1954 supported the idea of a specialized, extremely high-altitude spy aircraft that would become the ultrasecret U-2. In the course of their study, Killian's group also hit upon the idea of developing a small scientific satellite as a "stalking horse" for the later intelligence spacecraft, because it could benignly demonstrate the principle of "freedom of space"—that is, that airspace stopped at the sensible limits of the atmosphere, as international lawyers had already argued, and that a spacecraft, unlike aircraft, could overfly another country with impunity.[7]

It may or may not be a coincidence that precisely during the same period the idea of a scientific satellite came on the agenda of the international scientific unions and the planning for the International Geophysical Year (actually eighteen months: 1 July 1957 to 31 December 1958). The IGY was to be a worldwide, coordinated period of research on the Earth and its environment, especially the polar regions, the ionosphere, and near space. A small geophysical satellite, such as Singer advocated, would obviously greatly increase knowledge of the realm several hundred miles above the Earth, which otherwise could only be briefly sampled in sounding rocket flights. But the upper atmospheric scientists needed to be convinced that a satellite project would not just take away all the Defense Department money devoted to sounding rockets. It took the lobbying of Singer and a prominent American scientific statesman with navy connections, Lloyd Berkner, to get the satellite on the agenda of the international scientific unions in the fall. Berkner, who sat on the international committee for the IGY, had the sort of connections that might have given him knowledge of the RAND reports or the Killian panel's considerations regarding "freedom of space." Or it might have been simply that the idea of a satellite came first for primarily scientific reasons, and then U.S. policymakers came to see it as valuable for intelligence reasons. In any case, the result was the same.[8]

All of these contexts would come into play in the story of Project Orbiter, as it was called after January 1955, but its origins lay specifically in von Braun's ambitions and how they meshed with those of ONR Air Branch. By Ernst Stuhlinger's recollection, sometime early in the history of the Redstone, likely 1952 or 1953, his boss had surprised him with the statement, "We could do it." By this he meant that a Redstone with smaller rockets as upper stages could boost a minimal payload up to orbital velocity and altitude, about 17,000 mph (7600 m/sec) horizontally at 150–200 mi (240–320 km).

In all probability von Braun was thinking from the outset of using clusters of Loki unguided antiaircraft rockets on top of the Redstone. The Loki was a small U.S. Army solid-fuel rocket only a few inches in diameter that had been directly derived from the Taifun, the late-war, emergency antiaircraft projectile begun in Peenemünde. The fact that all stages would be derived from German technology (the Redstone being effectively a super V-2) may indicate a hidden agenda, but it is also true that when von Braun looked around, he did not see any other rockets that would do the job without substantial additional money and development. It is noteworthy that he did not look deeply into adapting liquid-fuel sounding rockets, such as the smaller Aerobee or the larger Viking, as upper stages for Redstone, as they would have required much work and a new guidance system. Although he had warned Toftoy in January 1954 that a major new missile project was needed in Huntsville by late 1955 to sustain his large, in-house development organization, apparently von Braun saw the satellite not as that project, but rather as a quick way to beat the Soviets into orbit.[9]

From the beginning von Braun's launcher idea was the exact opposite of his grand *Mars Project* and *Collier's* schemes: it was to be simple, low-budget, and technologically conservative, highlighting the apparent contradictions of his character. On the one hand he was a dreamer, now perhaps the world's most famous dreamer of future human ventures in space, and on the other he was a working rocket engineer with a very conservative style. The Huntsville Germans were rapidly acquiring the reputation of building heavy, overengineered rocket structures, which, from their World

War II experience, they felt were necessary if missiles were to withstand launching and handling. But von Braun did not feel this contrast as a contradiction; he distinguished between short-term and long-term perspectives and believed that in order to sell space to the public, he had to go for the grand scale.[10]

No later than May 1954 he already had the Redstone/Loki cluster combination roughed out with the assistance of Stuhlinger and other members of his staff. After spending several days visiting von Braun in Huntsville, British engineer and BIS leader Val Cleaver wrote to Fred Singer on the twenty-sixth, obliquely indicating the German's idea by asking whether Singer would be willing to cut down "the MOUSE's weight to 20 (at most 40) lb., and building your instrumentation to stand 250 g." That is, the satellite would sustain an acceleration of 250 times the Earth's gravity, which would be the case because the Lokis' firing time was short, only two seconds, and three stages would fire one after the other quickly; much of the acceleration to orbital velocity would therefore occur in the last ten seconds. The number of Lokis in von Braun's proposal varied with the version, but the one he presented first at the 25 June meeting had nineteen in the second stage (Redstone being the first), seven in the third, and three Lokis as the fourth stage, carrying the satellite at their tip.[11]

In order to stabilize and guide the rocket cluster, it would have to be spun up to several hundred rpm on top of the Redstone, then lobbed to orbital altitude by the missile. A special nose section carrying the upper-stage cluster and satellite would separate from the body of the rocket and orient itself horizontally to the Earth's surface; just before the apex of the trajectory was reached, the Lokis would fire, separating themselves from the nose section. As the ability of this launcher to get a payload into orbit was marginal, the Redstone would also be a special elongated version, carrying more alcohol fuel and liquid oxygen. Two lengthened missiles, RS-27 and -29, had already been designed for high-speed reentry tests connected to a possible 500-mi (800-km) range follow-on to Redstone. As complicated, even Rube Goldbergish, as von Braun's satellite setup was, it did have the virtue of being relatively cheap and fast in execution.[12]

ONR Air Branch had funded giant balloons to reach the very top of the stratosphere, some manned, and it had ambitions to build a piloted rocket aircraft that would fly into space, building on an existing navy rocket plane. Understanding the environment it would pass through would be valuable. In the spring of 1954 Commander George Hoover of that branch decided that he would be able to free up about $100,000 in the FY 1955 budget for a satellite study that would pave the way to building actual hardware, although whether he made that decision before or after he heard of the German's idea is unknown. Hoover was acquainted with von Braun's friend Fred Durant, who was then finishing a covert tour of duty in the CIA's Office of Scientific Intelligence. Durant called von Braun: "I just had a very interesting talk with a man in the Office of Naval Research. . . . He wants to get rolling on a space vehicle. Do you want to meet him?" Von Braun was thrilled: "Did I want to meet him! Ever since boyhood I'd dreamed of building a rocket that could fly to the moon and on beyond into interplanetary space." On 17 June he phoned Hoover, and soon the meeting was set for the twenty-fifth.[13]

Attending in addition to von Braun, Hoover, and Durant were Singer, Alexander Satin (chief engineer of ONR Air Branch), Andrew Young of the rocket propulsion contractor Aerojet, and Fred Whipple of Harvard, who could provide expertise in optical tracking. Von Braun presented the Redstone/Loki combination, with a more conservative projection of 10 lb (4.4 kg) into an orbit around the equator to gain the maximum velocity from the Earth's rotation during launch. But he also mentioned the possibility of a super-Redstone with a revolutionary new rocket engine that Rocketdyne was developing in California: it would have 120,000 to 135,000 lb ((54,000 to 61,000 kg) of thrust for half the weight of the 75,000-lb (34,000-kg) Redstone engine. Instead of having a cooling jacket in which fuel circulated between inner and outer walls of the combustion chamber, the entire engine wall was made up of thin cooling tubes through which the fuel flowed. But this engine would not be available in production quantities until 1956 at least. The seven participants also discussed a wide variety of other rocket projects and how they might fit, but ultimately it was von Braun's cluster project that seemed the only one that promised an orbital vehicle in a hurry. Beating the Russians was the point, after all, at least in the minds of von Braun and Durant, who shared the opinion of Grosse and several others that the first superpower to launch a satellite would achieve a profound psychological victory—RAND had made the same prediction as far back as 1946. Hoover left the meeting determined to move the idea up to higher levels in the navy, and von Braun would have the same assignment in the army.[14]

Probably on that very same evening of 25 June, Durant and his wife entertained von Braun for dinner in suburban Washington. Also present were British author and space advocate Arthur C. Clarke, who von Braun had finally met the year before, and Erik Bergaust, an immigrant Norwegian space enthusiast and journalist. Both were quickly becoming close friends of von Braun. In the backyard after dinner Clarke regaled them with his enthusiasm for scuba diving, his planned expedition to the Australian Great Barrier Reef, and his thoughts of moving to Ceylon (now Sri Lanka). Von Braun became fascinated with the possibility of these undersea vistas, and according to Bergaust: "From that moment on, most of the conversation developed into a dialog between von Braun and Clarke. . . . Durant and I were actually witnessing how Clarke 'brainwashed' von Braun into taking up scuba diving." He could see how it "could turn into a rewarding pastime for him during his frequent visits to Cape Canaveral," where he was often stranded for days during extended countdowns. Von Braun was so enthralled by the idea that he was determined to try it during his weeklong sojourn to southern California in mid-July.[15]

During that business trip von Braun would spend several evenings at the Burbank studios of Walt Disney—the beginning of a new phase of space promotion that would vault him to even higher levels of fame. On 29 April, just after the *Collier's* Mars issue appeared on the newsstands, he had received an intriguing call from a Disney official: would he be interested in doing a couple of space shows for their new upcoming television series? That series had arisen when Walt Disney, seeking money for his new Disneyland theme park in Anaheim, had made a deal with ABC-TV to provide financing for the park in return for a weekly series structured around its four areas: Adventureland, Frontierland, Fantasyland, and Tomorrowland. Not having a clue what to do with the last, Disney had gone to one of his key creative talents, Ward Kimball, a boyish-looking free spirit known to wear wildly colored clothes just to shock people. Kimball mentioned that he had been following the *Collier's* series: "It was fascinating for me to realize that there were these reputable scientists who actually believed we were going out in space."[16]

Von Braun at first had to say no, as he had just signed up for a TV deal with Beverly Hills producer Marché Goddard in late March, during his most recent trip to Los Angeles. That series was to be thirty-nine weekly half-hour science-fact programs for CBS on the beginning phases of space travel. He had earlier been more interested in working with Hollywood producer George Pal, whose credits included *Destination Moon* in 1950, *When Worlds Collide* in 1951, and *War of the Worlds* in 1953, as Pal had optioned Ley and Bonestell's *Conquest of Space* book. The producer was making a movie of that name (ultimately and uncharacteristically a bomb) as a realistic tale of the first human trip to Mars. Through Bonestell, von Braun met Pal several times, and things were friendly, but nothing concrete ever seemed to come of it. Seeking a new outlet for his space travel crusade as well as new income to replace the *Collier's* money, von Braun signed up with Goddard.[17]

Disney did not give up so easily, largely because Willy Ley was its first hire, and he kept von Braun's name on the agenda as the ultimate salesman and idea man for spaceflight. After three more Disney inquiries in May and June, and several phone calls and letters between von Braun and Goddard over the failure of their series to materialize, von Braun finally forced the producer to give him his release on 18 June. The Disney deal was on. A week later, the day von Braun was in Washington, Ley wrote him a long letter from the Disney studios outlining their method of work and early ideas for the first program, which would include another *Collier's* collaborator, aerospace physician Heinz Haber. Disney would be building a *Collier's*-like space station model, as well as von Braun's monster three-stage launcher, except that the manned third stage would have a delta wing instead of the original swept wing, as "the artists" all felt that it would look "more modern."[18]

Von Braun had no problem with that. He told Ley that he was willing to go further in adapting his *Collier's* schemes, both to avoid copyright problems and to respond to criticisms of gigantomania from within the rocket-engineering profession. The "somewhat controversial size of the three-stager" could be reduced in all stages by creating two versions, one that had a smaller rocket plane for personnel only and one with a nonrecoverable cargo stage that "could be <u>unmanned</u>"—apparently a radical idea for him. It would be guided in orbit by remote control from a previously launched manned ship. (In fact, Disney and von Braun soon added a small stage for maneuvering the space plane in orbit, making the launcher a four-stager, further distinguishing it from the magazine version.) The individual bailout capsules could also be discarded in place of a recoverable crew capsule. This rethinking was not the first that von Braun had done. During the preceding months he had conducted a lively correspondence with Ley and Bonestell over the 1956 Mars book that had caused the blowup with Ryan. He and Bonestell worked out the ideas for a much-scaled-back ten-man, two-ship Mars expedition (one lander, one orbiter), and Bonestell painted several pictures that von Braun saw in Pasadena at the end of March. He wrote afterward: "As usual, those hours in your studio were an unforgettable experience. I feel almost at home on Mars now." The only problem he had with changing his vehicles came from his fan base, who often took his ideas for finished plans rather than fact-based speculations that he was quite willing to throw overboard when better ideas came along.[19]

On 10 July 1954 von Braun flew out to Los Angeles in order to talk to Ley over the weekend about the project, prior to visiting the Burbank studios after hours during the week. While there, he and his new Hollywood agent worked out a consulting contract with Disney that would pay him $5,500 (before the 10 percent agent's fee). After evening discussions with Kimball, Ley, and the crew, the whole project grew even bigger when the two forty-eight-minute shows (before commercials) expanded into three because there was so much potential material, starting with the origins of rocketry and going all the way to a Mars expedition. Von Braun, with his Moon obsession, was happy to support Kimball in his desire to add a middle program about the first human expedition to loop around that body, catching a view of the still-hidden far side, which no one in human history had yet seen. That trip also became the basis for the Rocket to the Moon ride at Disneyland, which opened in July 1955. But beyond glancing at the plans, von Braun had little impact on the ride, which posited a single-stage nuclear rocket carrying ordinary passengers—far more speculative than even his Moon vehicles. For the extensive consulting work on the lunar show, however, von Braun's agent got him an additional $1,000, much less than they had asked for, but Kimball said the project was already far more expensive than anticipated. In large part this cost was entailed by a thoroughness and drive for scientific accuracy that Walt Disney demanded and that von Braun greatly admired.[20]

While Kimball and his crew were charmed by Ley and his "music hall German accent" and enjoyed working with Haber, it was von Braun who really won them over. As always, his boundless enthusiasm, infectious good humor, and powerful charisma worked their magic, as did his ability to translate scientific and engineering material in a way that inspired the imagination of ordinary people. Disney and Kimball went out of their way to accommodate him on his working trips to Los Angeles in 1954–56. According to Charles Shows, a writer who had been hired to work on the project, during von Braun's visits they assigned a "top-salaried" artist "to do nothing but supply them with fresh, hot coffee all day. This beautiful young woman spent 12 hours a day making fresh coffee, cutting fancy cakes and feeding a stereo tape machine classical guitar music selections." It being the 1950s, no one asked her opinion of this use of her talents. No doubt von Braun appreciated it. He retained his eye for attractive women and his ability to charm them. But his happy marriage and religious belief made him resistant to the many opportunities for philandering that came his way on his incessant travels, although he later dropped hints that he had not been perfectly faithful.[21]

Kimball's crew was certainly astounded by his "enormous physical energy." During his eight days in southern California in July 1954, von Braun tried undersea spear fishing for the first time, telling his parents afterward that it was a "wonderful experience, unforgettable." Shows claims that on some of his trips to California, von Braun

> worked non-stop for 12 hours at the studio, then took a taxi from Hollywood to Long Beach, about 50 miles away. There he rented a speedboat and piloted it 22 miles across the water to Catalina Island. Once there, von Braun skindived all night, then piloted his speedboat back to Long Beach at dawn. He rode a taxi back to his hotel for a quick shower, then reported back to Disney Studio.

While this story is likely exaggerated, "iron man von Braun" really did go to Catalina for scuba diving and he put in long hours at the studios, usually after a day of army business at various contractors. On one occasion, after they had worked until nearly midnight, von Braun the night owl looked at his watch, announced that he had no appointments until seven a.m., and was willing to start on the next problem. Ley and Bill Bosché, Kimball's chief writer for the series, turned him down but predicted that with such ambition he "might make a name for himself yet."[22]

At least once Shows drove von Braun back to his hotel and later reported the following revealing anecdote, probably true in essence if not in details. After von Braun listed all the things he liked about America, Shows asked what he did not like: "Yes ... I don't like being treated like a foreign spy. ... Everywhere I go, the FBI has me followed. I can't even go to the bathroom without an FBI man tailing me." Claiming that the third car behind them was actually following them, he exclaimed: " 'They're always around. My telephone is bugged, and the FBI reads more of my mail than I do.' He sighed aloud. 'I hope someday they'll trust me—and leave me alone.' " Von Braun's FBI files do not reveal that he was tailed in Los Angeles at this time, but he certainly had been earlier, when his immigration and security clearances had been processed, and the experience had left him a little paranoid.[23]

One last story captures the power of von Braun's personality over Kimball and the Disney crew. In the summer of 1956, when they were working on the Mars show with von Braun and Ernst Stuhlinger, they had a last long, exhausting script session in the studio until the middle of the night. Kimball says:

> When he was through, he threw down his pencil and turned around to a piano and for ten minutes played Bach, wide open. I didn't even know he played the piano. He just rattled it off, flawless. He was a genius. He could do anything. Then he stopped, clapped his hands, and said, "Well,

Wahd," (that's the way he pronounced my name), "how about taking us back to the hotel?"[24]

After von Braun returned home in July 1954, his first task for Disney was to work out the various details regarding the launch vehicle and space station, with the result that he stayed up to midnight almost every night. The next task was to design the Moon trip that formed the second program—both the spacecraft and its trajectory—which he did in late August, after returning from two weeks in Florida centered on the successful launch of RS-4. (Maria, Iris, and Margrit often vacationed with him at a beach motel before, during, or after such trips.) The net result was an impressive thirteen-page, equation-laden, typed treatise, "Voyage from Space Station Around the Moon and Back," and a series of related sketches, all of which he mailed to Kimball near the end of August. Showing the sensitivity he had developed to the appeal of aesthetics to the common person, he sent Kimball one sketch of a Moon ship with a spherical crew section, such as appeared in *Collier's*, but commented: "Brother, ain't it ugly?" Instead, he adapted his fourth-stage space plane by taking off the wings and adding a ring of disposable fuel tanks, resulting in a much more streamlined spacecraft that he could rationalize as an improvisation for a preliminary loop around the Moon. As for spacecraft power, he sketched a big, awkward solar concentrator mirror but was quite willing to give way when the Disney crew wanted a much more compact and ultramodern-sounding nuclear reactor, reflecting Eisenhower's "Atoms for Peace" initiative and the fad for everything atomic in American culture.[25]

On 18 October von Braun flew from Birmingham, Alabama, to Los Angeles at Disney expense and took Maria along with him. Together with Ley and Haber, he did the live-action shooting of the first show. The Disney crew had long since decided that the space station would be put off to the second program, as too much time was needed to get in all three speakers and the animated and film segments. After introductions by Disney and Kimball, the segment would have five parts: a humorous look at rocket history using cartoons and movie footage; a section on the principles of the rocket and of orbits, narrated by Willy Ley; one on space medicine using amusing cartoon material, narrated by Heinz Haber; one on the design of the four-stage launcher, as told by von Braun; and a final animated dramatization of "man's first trip into outer space"—typically for von Braun, carrying ten "space men" at once. To a more media-savvy age, von Braun appears a bit stiff, but he always carried an air of authority. The writers gave him a line that well expressed his feelings: "if we were to start today on an organized and well-supported space program, I believe a practical passenger rocket could be built and tested within ten years."[26]

When "Man in Space" was finally broadcast on 9 March 1955, millions of Americans would hear for the first time his soft, rolling, and rather incongruously high-pitched German-accented English; his *Collier's* audiences had been much smaller. The Disney crew had in fact discussed whether it was a problem that all three experts were German. But their very accents fit an American cliché of scientific gravity, and as for the Nazi issue, Walt Disney was the quintessential conservative, midwestern middle American and seems to have given it little thought. Two weeks before broadcast Kimball sent him a reminder postcard: "Tell the boys at the plant that Mr. Mickey Mouse of V-2 fame will hold forth." Von Braun replied in a letter to Bill Bosché: "Brother, this is the only topic in our home! Has he really t[h]ought that I had forgotten?"[27]

The very next month, on 14 April, he was in the news again when he and 102 other Germans (including spouses) were sworn in as American citizens at Huntsville High. He was genuinely moved by this ceremony of loyalty to his new country, but he was not above spinning it politically to the gathered press:

> This is the happiest and most significant day in my life. I must say we all became American citizens in our hearts long ago. I have never regretted the decision to come to this country. As time goes by, I can see even more clearly that it was a moral decision we made that day at Peenemunde. . . . Somehow we sensed that the secret of rocketry should only get into the hands of a people who read the Bible.

To his parents, who he knew were less enthused, he reported it rather differently: "It was a terrible circus, with film crews, television, press people and the usual misquotations. . . . I escaped from this rather ticklish situation" by emphasizing the correctness of the choice between "West and East." But as with his appearance on Disney's TV show, this event fortified his position with the public as a loyal American and leading space advocate and helped neutralize the ever-lurking Nazi question. It also gave him access to a Top Secret clearance, with the result that by the fall he could see intelligence about the Soviet missile program previously barred to him. To his chagrin he found them much further along than he had expected from the reports of German rocketeers returning from the USSR.[28]

While the Disney enterprise was gaining momentum in the public domain, von Braun's satellite project was also picking up speed in the classified world, much to his delight. On 3 August 1954 George Hoover and another ONR officer went to Huntsville and talked to von Braun and Toftoy, now commanding general of Redstone Arsenal. Von Braun wrote White Sands optical tracking specialist E. P. Martz on the thirtieth: "Army and Navy see eye to eye on it and have promised each other fullest cooperation. It is intended, however, to get the Air Force in on it too, so it may really become a joint project."[29]

At the Arsenal, Gerhard Heller and two other German engineers were completing a design study. Von Braun's division issued the resulting report, "A Minimum Satellite Vehicle Based on Components from Missile Developments of the Army Ordnance Corps," on 15 September, under his name and with his editing. As the title was classified Confidential, the report also had an alternate, unclassified cover sheet: "A Minimum Proposal for Project Slug." "Slug," coined by George Hoover, stuck as a nickname inside the project group as it ironically represented the proposed satellite: an inert 5-lb (2.3-kg) metal object, probably a sphere. In the process of refining the proposal, von Braun and his subordinates had become even more conservative about what performance they were willing to promise from the Loki cluster, now redefined as 24 + 6 + 1—the last, single Loki being the orbital injection stage. In order to get the maximum boost from the Earth's rotation, as well as to maximize the possibilities for tracking the satellite, von Braun's report proposed launching it at the equator, from an island or a navy ship. If the satellite orbited exactly around the equator, it would also pass over the same tracking stations on every orbit rather than covering a much broader band of the Earth.[30]

From the outset, the problem of optical tracking had loomed large, which is why von Braun had brought Whipple and Martz into the project at an early stage. In Huntsville's limited experience with miniaturized electronics, 5 lb appeared to be too little for a radio transmitter and power source, not to mention any scientific instrumentation. Even if Slug were the projected 20-in (50-cm) sphere, it would be no brighter than a very faint naked-eye star, and it would be visible only at dawn and dusk, when the satellite was still illuminated by the Sun, while the Earth below was in darkness. It might reach orbit and no one would ever know. Without instrumentation, its scientific value rested entirely on the optical tracking, as the slight friction of the very tenuous outer reaches of the atmosphere gradually lowered the apogee (high point) of its initial orbit, projected at about 150 by 800 mi (240 by 1280 km), enabling a characterization of near space. Martz proposed, and the report mentioned, that the visibility of the satellite could perhaps be increased through a flashing light powered by solar energy accumulated during the daylight part of its orbit, but that remained a speculative idea until the technology was developed.[31]

Why then settle for such a limited project? Beyond the von Braun group's conservative engineering style, and their interest in keeping the launch vehicle entirely in the army for reasons of organizational simplicity and perhaps parochialism, the explanation must again lie in its Cold War objective of simply beating the Soviets as quickly as possible. Von Braun's report presented as its third rationale:

> The establishment of a man-made satellite, no matter how humble, would be a scientific achievement of tremendous impact. Since it is a project that could be realized within a few years with rocket and guided missile experience available <u>now</u>, it is only logical to assume that other countries could do the same. It would be a blow to U.S. prestige if we did not do it first.

It was an argument straight from the Grosse report of a year earlier, and it also reflected CIA concerns and the influence of Fred Durant, who was exiting the Agency for a job at a consulting firm in Cambridge, Massachusetts. Only a couple of weeks later, at the end of September or in early October, Allen Dulles, the director of central intelligence, received a briefing on this issue and on the state of the various satellite projects, including the ONR-army collaboration. Von Braun may not yet have known that his friend Durant was CIA, but he and the other leaders of the project certainly knew they had strong Agency backing.[32]

Over the fall and winter Slug only gained momentum. On 6 October von Braun flew to Washington, again with Stuhlinger and Heller, for a meeting with Hoover, Durant, and a representative of the Loki cluster contractor in California. Exactly two months later the Office of Naval Research staged a two-day conference in the capital attended by over fifty people, including all the principals, three CIA representatives, A. V. Grosse, and navy rocketeer Bob Truax. As always, von Braun spoke on the booster configuration and logistics of launching. To increase the odds of tracking, there had been some serious discussion of using a balloon, but there was fear that micrometeoroids would puncture and deflate it quickly, so the group leaned toward a structure that would deploy in a spherical shape, perhaps with metallic corner reflectors that would enable passive radar tracking. During the evening after the first day of the conference, von Braun, Stuhlinger, Heller, Durant, and others went back to the Statler Hotel and excitedly planned out a possible project timetable on Durant's yellow legal pad. Four satellite launching attempts are indicated in August–September 1957, just after the beginning of IGY, and under "Crash Program" Durant marked a date in late 1956. Slug seemed increasingly real. In January 1955 the army and navy forwarded the proposal for Project Orbiter, as it was finally dubbed, to the assistant secretary of defense for R&D, Donald Quarles.[33]

One unsolved political problem was the failure to interest the air force in the project. Only a junior officer from Air Research and Development Command (ARDC) attended ONR's conference. With Ordnance's approval, von Braun tried to work his connections, writing just before Christmas to a friend who headed the ARDC aeromedical division. Nothing came of it.[34]

Behind this unresponsiveness lay the USAF's parochial interest in protecting the reconnaissance satellite program that was just then emerging from the RAND study of spring 1954, as well as its general hostility to any long-range rocket development by the army and navy. At precisely the same time as the Orbiter initiative, late 1954 and early 1955, Army Ordnance approached the air force with the suggestion that von Braun's group build what the USAF was calling the tactical ballistic missile (TBM), with a projected range of 1,000 nautical mi (1,150 statute mi; 1,850 km). A year earlier Ordnance had approved Redstone Arsenal's plans to begin to look into a 500-mi (800-km) class missile using the new Rocketdyne engine, in line with von Braun's concern that his organization needed a major new project by the end of 1955. Toftoy and von Braun increased funding for research into reentry materials, as bare steel would no longer be sufficient to protect the warhead. Now it seemed, in the wake of the huge Atlas ICBM buildup, that the air force was the service with the mission and the money. But on 30 March 1955 the WDD chief, Brigadier General Schriever, wrote his superior, General Thomas Power, that he could not see how the USAF could manage and control an army program, and in any case "it would be naïve to think the Army would develop a weapon and turn it over to the Air Force to operate." He also saw no value in helping the scientific satellite project, which would "contribute little if anything to the ICBM program" or to "furthering a militarily useful satellite." If politics compelled the air force to take part in the scientific satellite, it should launch a competing proposal; such was Schriever's opposition to helping the army in any way. While this feeling was not shared by all air force officers, it certainly represented the attitude of the service's leadership.[35]

Air force opposition to Orbiter, however, manifested itself externally as sniping criticism and reluctance to participate, and the project seemed to gather speed through the spring. On 17 March von Braun was in Washington again for another Orbiter committee meeting and spoke on the most troublesome question about his launcher: whether all the Lokis would fire reliably; the failure of even one could cause a failure to reach orbit. Through quality control and testing, he thought that the new Loki IIA version could be made 99.9 percent reliable. A little over two months later the core Orbiter group, including George Hoover and other members of ONR, flew into Huntsville for a briefing on 24 May, then went on to Cape Canaveral, where they saw the successful launching of Redstone RS-10.[36]

Inside the top echelons of the Eisenhower administration a scientific satellite program for the IGY became official policy that May, thanks largely to an endorsement from the Killian panel. Killian and Ike were particularly persuaded by the argument that a scientific satellite would set a precedent of "overflight" over other countries, laying the ground for a later photorecon-naissance orbiter, but that argument was extremely closely held, such that von Braun and all others at his level had no knowledge of it. The satellite decision was itself still secret, but those in the rocket business heard through the grapevine that the Defense Department was moving toward funding an actual project. In April and May Milton Rosen's Viking group at the Naval Research Laboratory (NRL) and an air force group headed by von Braun's old Peenemünde guidance chief, Ernst Steinhoff, had floated competing ideas as a result. Yet neither of these schemes seemed very credible by com-parison. Von Braun and Hoover had every reason to be confident.[37]

Faced with three proposals, however, Quarles decided to constitute an expert committee of eight to pick a winner, six of whom would be nominated by the three services and two by his office. Chaired by Homer Joe Stewart, a leading engineer at Jet Propulsion Laboratory in Pasadena, the so-called Stewart Committee included two old acquaintances of von Braun's: Joseph Kaplan, chairman of the U.S. National Committee for the IGY, who had helped sell space to Connie Ryan and had participated in the first *Collier's* issue, and Richard Porter, head of General Electric's rocket programs, who had played a key role in the summer 1945 interrogations of the von Braun group. As it turned out, neither one would be in his camp. Indeed, Porter had a conflict of interest: his GE 27,000-lb (12,200-kg) thrust rocket engine was to power the scaled-up Viking that was the first stage of Rosen's three-stage launcher.[38]

Stewart had his own conflict of interest, which was not unusual in the rocket community, small and closely connected to the services as it was. JPL was effectively an army missile lab, although run by Caltech, and Stewart had been drawn into the analysis of Orbiter during the spring at the behest of JPL's director, William Pickering, a tall, balding, scholarly-looking New Zealander. Out of that interaction would come a close collaboration between Huntsville and Pasadena that would last nearly four years, as well as two ideas that would have direct impact on Orbiter and its later incarnations: (1) new, larger solid-propellant motors derived from JPL's Sergeant missile project in place of the Lokis, and (2) a miniaturized radio transmitter, dubbed Microlock, that could allow the satellite to be tracked by other than optical means. While the scaled-down Sergeants were incorporated as an option into the proposal that von Braun and the army presented to the Stewart Committee, Microlock was not, as JPL did not make its presentation on it until the middle of July. However, in response to the constant criticism of the feasibility of optical tracking, von Braun did mention the possible incorporation of a miniaturized transmitter from the NRL proposal or a small device from an army laboratory that would retransmit a signal from a ground radar. One other crucial difference in the Orbiter proposal was that it was indeed only army. Hoover's superiors in ONR forced him to withdraw, probably in June, when it became clear that NRL, a branch of the Office of Naval Research, actually had a viable proposal. No sources record von Braun's or Hoover's reaction to this sudden change, but in hindsight it was an omen.[39]

In July 1955 everything came to a head at once for von Braun, making it an extraordinarily busy month. On the seventh and eighth, respectively, he made two detailed pitches at the Pentagon, for Orbiter and for a Huntsville-designed tactical ballistic missile, an idea still in play because the USAF leadership could not openly declare that it refused to work with the army. On the ninth von Braun met the Stewart Committee again, after being surprised to find that Rosen was regarded as a serious competitor. Then he flew to the West Coast for live-action shooting for the Disney Moon program on the eleventh, twelfth, and thirteenth, followed by several more days of meetings on rocket engine development and Orbiter. In the midst of all this he greeted Hermann Oberth, who had finally reached Huntsville on the seventh through the successor program to Paperclip. (H. H. Koelle had arrived a few weeks earlier.) Von Braun and the family then went to a North Carolina mountain resort for the last week of July, except that he had to spend most of his vacation trying to finish his contribution to the 1956 Mars book, describing the scaled-back expedition to the Red Planet. He was not successful and mailed the manuscript to Willy Ley only later in August.[40]

While he was in North Carolina the White House suddenly announced on Friday, 29 July, that there would be a U.S. scientific satellite for the International Geophysical Year. The news flashed around the world as a milestone in spaceflight's transition from science fiction to reality. Insiders had expected it after a specific proposal had been selected, but the administration's timing was perhaps influenced by the sixth IAF congress in Copenhagen at the beginning of August, where the Soviets might announce a satellite program. Radio Moscow had in mid-April revealed the formation of a space committee in the USSR. Upon von Braun's return to work on Monday, press inquiries compelled him to issue a statement through Ordnance welcoming Eisenhower's announcement—it was released on 5 August. In the interim he was in Washington again, giving his standard Orbiter briefing to the Army Policy Council on the third, along with Colonel John C. Nickerson, the Ordnance officer at the Pentagon who had served as point man.[41]

Shortly before the report came out on the fourth, von Braun received shocking but still classified news: the majority of the Stewart Committee had recommended Milton Rosen's proposal. He was not prepared for this outcome. On 16 July he had spoken confidently in Pasadena about Orbiter, and Army Ordnance and JPL staff subsequently expressed complacency about winning.[42] Their proposal was the only one based on a well-developed vehicle, Rosen's launcher was a paper project for a virtually new rocket, and the air force Atlas–based one was too hypothetical to take seriously. How could Orbiter possibly lose?

In fact, of the seven committee members who participated actively, only two voted for the army proposal, Stewart and the other likely army nominee, Clifford Furnas; five picked the navy. From the outset Rosen had three solid votes, those of Kaplan, Porter, and Charles Lauritsen, a navy-affiliated Caltech rocket specialist, in large part because the NRL rocket, later called Vanguard, was more advanced in concept and promised to loft a much bigger, instrumented payload of 20 to 40 lb (9 to 18 kg) from Cape Canaveral—logistically much more convenient than an equatorial launch. It was a very efficient launch vehicle on paper, despite its underpowered first stage (one-third the thrust of Redstone), and the satellite promised real scientific capability and had an excellent radio transmitter and tracking system, nicknamed Minitrack. Von Braun's strategy, to produce a minimum vehicle with little payload in order to beat the Soviets, had come back to haunt him.[43]

A secondary concern of the majority was whether the army project would interfere with an ongoing missile program, Redstone, but this factor is stated so weakly in the report that it does not seem to have been a big factor. Kaplan, however, seems to have thought that the all-American, more civilian-looking NRL proposal (with no stages based on military missiles) might provide a better external image for the U.S. IGY program than a satellite project based on "German V-2 developments"—suggesting anti-German bias as well as inside knowledge of the overflight issue, which was not discussed in the committee. In the end the two likely air force nominees, George Clement and Barkley Rosser, voted with the majority unenthusiastically, and the one ill member, the astronomer-industrialist Robert McMath, sent a letter supporting Orbiter but had no influence over the proceedings. Perhaps if he had attended, the whole vote might have swung the other way. In any case, the final vote was a victory for science over engineering: among the majority, only Porter had rocket engineering experience, and he was supplying the first-stage motor to Rosen. Time would prove von Braun and Stewart right that the Vanguard launcher, consisting of highly modified Viking and Aerobee-Hi rockets topped with a new, solid-fuel third stage, would be much more difficult, expensive, and time-consuming to develop.[44]

The Stewart Committee's recommendation to Quarles, which was split between majority and minority reports, set off a scramble in Ordnance to overturn the decision. Teletypes flew back and forth among Washington, Huntsville, and Pasadena, and von Braun and his associates again had to revisit all their calculations and assumptions. Quarles's R&D Policy Council, with representatives of all three services, was to meet on 16 August. Out the window went von Braun's conservative strategy; now Ordnance was willing to promise a 162-lb (73-kg) satellite in August 1957 if the 135,000-lb (61,200-kg) thrust version of Rocketdyne's new engine was used; alternatively, an 18-lb (8-kg) payload was feasible by the end of 1956 if 1,700 lb (770 kg) of weight were cut out of the military Redstone.[45]

In the council, the army representative played up the Soviet announcement of a satellite program at the Copenhagen IAF meeting in response to Eisenhower, with a timetable of eighteen months being reported (falsely) by some newspapers. Only Orbiter could launch by late 1956, and the army was also willing to let NRL build the later, heavier satellites. These arguments swayed Quarles, and despite navy and air force votes in favor of the NRL proposal, he was able to potentially reverse the committee's recommendation. Stewart's group was to report in one week as to the feasibility of having the army build the lightweight Redstone and the navy build the satellite. In the aftermath Milton Rosen and several admirals above him were appalled—their upset victory looked as if it were about to be thrown out.[46]

On 23 August von Braun and Rosen once again appeared before the Stewart Committee in Washington. By Rosen's account, von Braun spoke first and "easily for three hours, just hammering away at the committee, talking down to them, as if how dare they question his authority on that subject. I felt he was making a mistake." Indeed, von Braun looked down his nose at the scientists on the panel, whom he felt lacked the engineering experience to see through Rosen's proposal, not to mention the wisdom to understand the reality of the Soviet threat. Apropos, he gave part of his time to ONR's Alexander Satin, a Russian émigré who thought the Soviets likely to meet the eighteen-month timetable. In the afternoon Rosen spoke less extensively, making the most of the engineering continuities between Viking and Aerobee-Hi and his launcher stages. He was able to brandish prime contractor Martin Aircraft's promise to produce a satellite vehicle in a year and a half, although he did not believe it and was glad when no one on the committee challenged it. That did it; the majority was not to be swayed, and anyway there was something vaguely desperate in the army's casting about for new ideas after its original proposal failed. The next day the R&D Policy Council, no longer chaired by Quarles as he had just become secretary of the air force, upheld the original recommendation. The game was up. Redstone Arsenal was out of the satellite business—for now.[47]

Afterward von Braun and Fred Singer had a revealing exchange of letters. Singer wrote how much Ike's satellite announcement had boosted the IAF in Copenhagen, but he was disturbed when he had talked to "members of the IGY group" in Washington upon his return. "I found rather antagonistic feelings expressed on the part of some people whenever I brought up your name, or even the name of Redstone." Von Braun replied on 9 September, apologizing for the delay caused by another Florida " 'event' ": "You know how close this whole subject [Orbiter] is to my heart." He gave four possible reasons for the antagonism: his space publications, his "German background," "professional jealousy," and interservice rivalry. These prejudices had influenced the committee's deliberations, von Braun believed. Singer agreed, replying that anti-German prejudice was not a major factor, but interservice rivalry certainly was. The votes in the committee bear out this point—while many factors led to the army's defeat, the votes fell out more or less along service lines.[48]

So convinced were Wernher von Braun, Homer Joe Stewart, and the Ordnance leadership that the NRL project would likely fail to meet its deadlines that they immediately set out to preserve the army's satellite capability in another guise. Encouraged by Nickerson, Stewart stopped in Huntsville on his way back to California on 26 August and discussed with von Braun and company how to circumvent the policy of his own committee. Orbiter would be refashioned as an RTV, for reentry test vehicle. Based on further analysis in Pasadena, a cluster of $11 + 3 + 1$ scaled-down Sergeants would be mounted on top of the long-tank Redstone in the satellite configuration. When used to test new reentry materials under development in Huntsville for nose cones, the last stage would be replaced by a model warhead instead.

On 8 September von Braun confirmed that projected reentry missiles RS-27 and -29 would be diverted to this program, along with three other Redstones. Ultimately, however, to justify the RTV program the army would probably need to win a role in future long-range missile development. Indeed, as he had warned a year and a half earlier, the long-term survival of his big development organization was at stake.[49]

In part because of the extended fight over the satellite decision, the Defense Department took two more months to make a decision on the intermediate-range ballistic missile (IRBM), as TBM was renamed. Behind the drive to add the IRBM to the ICBM was the Killian surprise-attack study once again. Intelligence indicated that the Soviets would soon have a ballistic missile that could threaten Western Europe and East Asia. Now a missile with a range of 1,500 nautical mi (1,725 statute mi, 2,760 km), deployable from overseas bases, seemed urgent as a political response and as a strategic stopgap until Atlas was ready, in around 1960. One obvious solution—and one that would have made much more sense for the United States than what actually happened—would have been for the air force to spare itself the extra burden and make Huntsville its contractor, as Ordnance had been advocating for a year. But giving the army any role was impossible for the air force generals to accept. At the same time the navy did not want to be left out and was looking for a new ballistic missile that could be deployed from ships and submarines, but it did not have an independent development capability. That opening allowed an interservice compromise that the Eisenhower administration found impossible to avoid because of the perceived Cold War emergency and the entrenched power of the services. The USAF would build "IRBM #1" based on components from the Atlas program, while the army in collaboration with the navy would develop "IRBM #2" with both a land-based and a sea-based capability. On 8 November 1955 Defense Secretary Charles Wilson, a former chief executive of General Motors, issued the order.[50]

For von Braun this news was naturally a great relief. With Nickerson's invaluable guidance, during September and October he had again made several trips to Washington to lobby, once in front of Wilson himself, and had to steer many technical studies of the 1,500-mi missile. Now he could write his parents: "after long battles [we] have landed a completely new project, which will lead to major increases in personnel, more than double the budget and much work for the future. It appears as if we will remain many more years in Huntsville after all."[51]

Even though corporate salaries were much higher than those of the civil service, leaving for industry was not something von Braun contemplated lightly. Twice before Walter Dornberger and Larry Bell had tried to lure him away to Bell Aircraft in Buffalo in the belief that their air force studies would lead within a few years to a manned space plane. This offer had caused him several "sleepless nights," he told Dornberger in November 1953, but ultimately he had to refuse because he had felt great personal responsibility for the Redstone project, which was then building up, and he could not just leave the army in the lurch. Fourteen months later he even called a sudden departure "immoral."[52] The mentality of state service he had inherited from his father remained influential; as much as he liked money, cashing in for personal gain or career enhancement was not something he could do if it conflicted with his basic loyalties. He felt a powerful personal responsibility to his Peenemünders; even as several left for industry, most remained and he was their leader. Short of a major setback that would drastically reduce funding in Huntsville, he would have found it extremely difficult to quit. But without the army-navy IRBM alliance, that indeed might have happened.

A "crash program" to build Jupiter, as the missile was soon called, brought with it more changes than just doubling the budget and personnel. The army agreed to create a new organization, the Army Ballistic Missile Agency (ABMA), that would cut the red tape of the traditional acquisition bureaucracy, paralleling the special arrangements now installed for the air force under General Schriever. As Toftoy was not viewed as tough enough, ABMA would arise on the territory of, but separate from, Redstone Arsenal and would be headed by Major General John Bruce Medaris, chief of Ordnance's Industrial Division. Medaris, a fifty-three-year-old World War II veteran, was a blunt, hard-charging leader. Von Braun was not entirely happy with his undiplomatic treatment of the gentlemanly and paternal Toftoy when the former arrived to take over command of von Braun's division on 1 February 1956. Medaris offended others with his obsession with correct uniforms and "spit and polish," but von Braun liked serving a decisive commander and Medaris certainly gave him that. They soon got along famously.[53]

ABMA's creation produced several advantages for von Braun. He finally could get a GS-17 "super grade," above the usual civil service cap of GS-15, meaning a salary increase of a couple of thousand dollars. A number of his top people would ascend into the super grades too, alleviating somewhat the problem of departures for better money and better school systems than those of Alabama. On the development side as well, money problems largely went away for a while. Von Braun told his parents in June that, whereas before some bureaucrat would complain that they were spending too much money on phone calls to missile contractor Chrysler in Detroit, which would also produce Jupiter, now the budget official would show up and arrange for a special dedicated line. Everything was "big time"—a morale-boosting vote of confidence from the U.S. government.[54]

Notwithstanding the heavy workload involved, especially in the early months of 1956, von Braun described himself in the same letter as very happy in his job and marriage. The mid-1950s were among the best years of the von Brauns' lives. They had their boat on Lake Guntersville, on which they spent most summer weekends, and as rigorous as his travel schedule was, he was home for many of them. He had enough free time to take up flying again, to go hunting with influential people from Huntsville, and to pursue his passion for scuba diving when near the ocean. In the spring of 1956 the von Brauns were able to welcome Maria's parents for an extended visit thanks to free transportation from Europe provided by Secretary of the Army Wilber Brucker. Alexander von Quistorp had been released on New Year's Eve after ten hard years in East German camps and prisons following his arrest by the Soviets in 1945 as a banker and landowner. Three days earlier, on 28 December 1955, Wernher von Braun had reappeared on national television as the primary star of Disney's "Man and the Moon."[55]

The expansion of von Braun's organization, now called the Development Operations Division, from sixteen hundred to nearly three thousand people by late 1956 once again demonstrated his superb talent for the construction and leadership of huge engineering enterprises. One von Braun management innovation from around this time was the system of Monday Notes. After Kurt Debus's Missile Firing Laboratory became permanently established in Florida because of the greatly increased firing rate of Redstones, von Braun asked Debus to send a weekly, one-page summary of all key activities. Seeing the value of that, he then asked all the laboratory directors and administrators two levels down (below his deputy, Eberhard Rees, and his technical director, Arthur Rudolph) to produce notes on Monday, which he would then guarantee to read and mark up before the end of the week—von Braun was celebrated for his pithy and sometimes humorous marginal comments. The notes were then copied and distributed to all those on the list, providing a unique system of horizontal as well as vertical communication.[56]

Another management mechanism was the Development Board, a body of almost exclusively German-born laboratory directors that had developed out of the Fort Bliss experience. The board was opened in the 1950s to include a few American-born budget and contract administrators from outside the technical divisions but at the same bureaucratic level. Visitors reported that the Germans maintained an obsessive concern for rank and hierarchy, which determined their exact placement around the table, but while they competed with one another, they never questioned von Braun's authority. Outside observers often found these and other meetings tediously long, as von Braun allowed discussion to go on and on, but realized afterward that what he had accomplished was to produce a consensus that all could live with, assuming he did not see external forces that compelled a particular technical or organizational solution.[57]

In the mid-1950s and after, his management rhetoric also emphasized "teamwork," "dirty-hands engineering," and "automatic responsibility." All were based on twenty years' rocket-building experience in Germany and the United States. The first helped weld together disparate in-house laboratories and contractors into a team; the second demanded that managers stay close to the actual hardware and not just push paper; and the last required that anyone who had anything to do with the functioning of a particular component or system had to take responsibility for its operation and integration and not hide behind "it's not my department." The result was an organization of very high morale and competence that could penetrate deeply into the workings of corporate contractors. Of course, von Braun was not a perfect manager. He did not like to discipline people, he could make too many promises that his organization found hard to deliver, and he could overspend. Rees played an essential role as his alter ego, enforcer, and budget man.[58]

Von Braun needed all the management tricks in his bag to deal with the design challenges of Jupiter. A single-stage, nuclear-armed 1,500-nautical-mi-missile had become feasible in 1955 because of several breakthroughs: a 1,500-lb (680-kg), megaton-class thermonuclear warhead; the lightweight Rocketdyne engine, now upgraded to 150,000 lb (68,000 kg) of thrust by increasing chamber pressure and burning RP-1 (highly refined jet fuel) instead of water alcohol with the liquid oxygen; and gimbaling the same engine so that it could swivel in two axes for guidance and control, eliminating the need for jet vanes in the exhaust and air vanes on the fins. Fins themselves became optional, as the missile no longer had to be aerodynamically stable because control was so sensitive. However, Huntsville's fall of 1955 preliminary design had to be thrown out because the navy needed Jupiter to be as short as possible to fit in a ship or submarine launch tube. At the cost of two months of work for the design team, the diameter was increased and the missile shortened to 58 ft (17.7 m), resulting in a fat, finless cylinder with a conical warhead and a single engine at the rear. And that was only the beginning. The problems of launching from a rolling ship, dealing with liquid propellants at sea, and creating a guidance system that would be reasonably accurate from a moving vessel were daunting. Von Braun and his designers dealt with a navy liaison group in Huntsville for such questions.[59]

To the development pressure was added pressure from Washington to fire a missile, any missile, over IRBM range as soon as possible. Apparently this idea originated in political considerations, such as reassuring allies that the United States was not falling behind the Soviets, who had plunged into ballistic missile development right after 1945. Neither Jupiter nor its air force competition, Thor, could be launched before 1957, and the same went for the reentry configuration of the Redstone/RTV, as more time was needed to select the reentry materials and design the subscale Jupiter warhead. But ABMA had a nearer-term capability because the satellite configuration was already well along in engineering. Thus von Braun's group proposed to fire the first such missile, RS-27, with a dummy fourth-stage rocket. It could be lobbed, still attached to the third stage, several thousand miles. Two weeks after ABMA came into existence Medaris met the secretaries of defense and the army, and they had underlined the urgency of doing that by September, the earliest von Braun could promise.[60]

This date was possible only because, as von Braun told a former Orbiter contractor on 17 February, "you know we have never lost a day in pursuing our project." He added: "And it looks like we are about to move it [the satellite version] back to official status, at least as a backup." Vanguard was months behind schedule because of long negotiations between NRL and its contractors, raising renewed prospects for the army. If RS-27 was successful, the backup vehicle, 29, could be used to orbit the pencil-shaped fourth stage with a small, 17-lb (8-kg) payload of transmitters in January 1957. This performance was achieved in part by stripping the Redstone of excess weight and fueling it with a higher-energy "hydyne" combination in place of water alcohol. Inducing permanent confusion in later observers, the Redstone/RTV stack would be called the Jupiter-C (for composite) to capture the priorities of the IRBM program. Redstone launches in support of Jupiter development would be labeled Jupiter-A.[61]

For almost three months in the spring of 1956, encouraged by the enthusiastic Medaris, von Braun once again hoped and dreamed that his satellite would become a reality. On 23 April he and Nickerson spoke one more time before the Stewart Committee, which had continued to serve as a satellite advisory board to the assistant secretary for R&D, now Clifford C. Furnas, the other pro-Orbiter vote on the original committee. Beforehand Medaris outlined very carefully how von Braun was to frame the talk, as it had two touchy aspects: not offending the navy and not admitting too openly that the army had circumvented national policy. But Vanguard had a lot of bureaucratic and political inertia. Stewart again lost to the committee majority, who could not see how a launch months before the beginning of IGY and by a separate program was compatible with Vanguard publicity. Moreover, any follow-on army satellites would delay Redstone and cost extra money at a time when the NRL project's estimated expense had already tripled from $20 million to $60 million. When the matter reached the National Security Council on 3 May, President Eisenhower agreed: he did not want to spend even more. As much as he and his advisers might have agreed that beating the Russians was important, they could not seem to take seriously the possibility or impact of a Soviet first. The army capability would remain in the wings as a kind of unofficial backup, and von Braun would remain frustrated.[62]

When RS-27 was being stacked in September, "a thrilling period for all of us," Medaris says, this prehistory worried officials in Washington. The Pentagon actually sent an inspector to the Cape in case the army was planning to launch a satellite "by accident." They need not have worried. Not only was the fourth stage loaded with sand and structural elements instead of solid propellant, the vehicle lacked the attitude-control system to fire the JPL-designed upper stages horizontally at orbital altitude after a long coast. Rather, the second and third stages would fire immediately after separating from the Redstone, maximizing range. As always von Braun, Medaris, and key Huntsville engineers joined Debus's crew for the tense launch preparations. In order to get visual observations of the later phases of the trajectory, the rocket would be fired at night. Rain ruined the countdown on the first attempt and the weather remained marginal the next evening. Finally at 1:47 a.m. on 20 September, after hours of holds, the Jupiter-C lifted off, with its cylindrical tub of rockets spinning on top. Radio signals showed that all worked well—before burning up on reentry, the last two stages set world records: a range of 3,355 statute mi (5400 km), an altitude of 682 mi (1098 km), and speed of 12,800 mph (20,600 km/h). In the blockhouse von Braun "danced with joy."[63]

Afterward ABMA was forbidden to tell anyone outside the classified world—perhaps the administration felt that RS-27 raised questions about Vanguard, stoked interservice rivalry, or was not a real IRBM anyway. Von Braun wrote his parents on the twenty-ninth: "Recently we did something at work that was fairly epochal, about which we are still not allowed to say anything more specific. Because the press suspects something and are already digging away energetically, I expect a public statement soon. (Stay calm: it is still no Orbiter.)" In fact the news only came out after a leak to the magazine Missiles and Rockets, recently founded by von Braun's friend Erik Bergaust. Medaris later thought it was Nickerson, who would soon be infamous for another leak. Von Braun is a less likely culprit, as he tended to be cautious about violations of secrecy.[64]

A month before that launch the army had asked Medaris to accelerate the Jupiter IRBM launch schedule yet further. Under the rubric "Operation Blast," von Braun's group proposed firing two missiles, IA and IB, with simplified control systems and preliminary engines, before missile I, still scheduled for May 1957. This move appears to have had more to do with beating the enemy near at hand, General Schriever's air force team, than it did the USSR. The Thor-Jupiter competition had only magnified the rivalry between the two services. Led by prime contractor Douglas Aircraft of Santa Monica, California, the Thor launch team was to fire its first from the Cape around the turn of the year. It seems less than coincidental that the target date for Jupiter IA was now January. In an early September board meeting von Braun conceded, however, that February was more likely.[65]

By the fall of 1956 storm clouds were gathering over the Jupiter IRBM program. The navy was showing more and more interest in a solid-fuel missile, as Jupiter's size and the hazards of liquid propellants seemed to make the IRBM completely impractical for submarines. The navy would have to build special surface ships. Army–air force rows over the IRBM and other issues, meanwhile, were publicly embarrassing to an Eisenhower administration that was then in the midst of a reelection campaign. Fairly soon a decision would be needed as to whether both IRBMs were wanted and, if so, who would deploy the land-based version of Jupiter—the army or the air force. The army was the stepchild of Ike's New Look policy, which slashed regular forces and equipment to pay for strategic nuclear systems. Jupiter was the service's one piece of that action, so achieving early launch success might determine whether it got to deploy the missile, or indeed whether it was allowed to build it at all.[66]

On 6 November Eisenhower won a landslide victory over Adlai Stevenson in the midst of one of the most frightening crises of the Cold War. Soviet armies were crushing a rebellious Hungary when Britain, France, and Israel invaded Egypt over its nationalization of the Suez Canal. The Soviet leadership issued a "thinly veiled threat" of launching its nuclear missiles against London and Paris. Eisenhower had to threaten the Russians with war if they intervened in the Middle East, while forcing the British and French to withdraw. It was a sobering reminder that all those missiles under development might one day destroy the world.[67]

On the twenty-sixth Secretary of Defense Wilson issued his settlement of the IRBM deployment issue: only the air force could operate any land-based ballistic missiles of a range greater than 200 mi (320 km). Twelve days later, on 8 December, came a second, demoralizing blow for ABMA: Wilson approved the navy's request to withdraw from Jupiter to focus on a smaller, two-stage, solid-propellant, submarine-launched missile called Polaris. Even before the first decision, Medaris and von Braun knew what was coming from the rumor mill and the press. On 20 November Medaris wired General James Gavin, army deputy chief of staff for R&D, that various disparaging comments by navy and Defense Department people that Jupiter was "as good as dead" were creating "an atmosphere threatening disintegration and dissolution" of "this priceless national asset" (the von Braun team). Medaris opened his staff meeting on the thirtieth by saying: "A bunch of people around this place are acting like children." Demoralization was rampant. He told everyone to get back to work and pointed out that the deployment decision had no bearing on whether Jupiter would be built. With the navy apparently pulling out, the only customer would be the air force, and they should make every effort to work with that service. Privately, he and von Braun felt that Thor would fall on its face, as Douglas and the air force's management contractor, Ramo-Wooldridge, were too inexperienced, but they knew full well that the air force would take Jupiter only if it were forced to. Although the chief of Ordnance quietly told Medaris of contingency plans for Huntsville in case of a Jupiter shutdown, the ABMA chief naturally maintained the same positive line even after the navy pullout, and von Braun transmitted this upbeat message to his organization. He seems to have believed it. In April 1957 he told his old associate Ludwig Roth, now in industry, that "in an all-out competitive struggle with some of our friends at the West Coast . . . we think we have a very good chance to win."[68]

Politically, the situation got even uglier on New Year's Day 1957. The army inspector general arrived in Huntsville on one day's notice, suspecting Medaris's involvement in a serious leak. Wilson and Army Secretary Brucker were furious. Someone had sent to columnist Jack Anderson, as well as Bergaust and several congressmen and senators, an incendiary, anti–air force document entitled "Considerations on the Wilson Decision." Attention quickly focused on Colonel Nickerson, who had transferred to Huntsville with General Medaris. The general had warned him to keep his extremely partisan service viewpoint in check. On the third, military police appeared outside Nickerson's house on Redstone Arsenal, and when they barged in, they found him burning documents. He was immediately arrested. Erik Bergaust arrived in town a day later and talked to von Braun, who asked the editor to protect his friend Nickerson as much as possible, as the memo did not contain any truly classified material. He added, with a "big smile": "And I think it is a damned good piece of literature." In this matter von Braun was less savvy than Medaris, who thought it disclosed many secrets and was a political disaster to boot. It certainly stiffened the resolve of Schriever's WDD to stonewall ABMA on deployment planning for Jupiter. When Nickerson's court-martial finally unfolded in the summer of 1957, von Braun testified on the colonel's behalf. Nickerson got off fairly lightly and was shipped to Panama with temporary reduction in pay and rank. Whether for reasons of von Braun's indispensability as a manager, his friendship with Nickerson, or his relatively tactful handling of the matter in public, Medaris does not seem to have held his actions against him.[69]

Notwithstanding the air of gnawing insecurity that now hung over the Jupiter program, the new year brought a further intensification of an already frantic effort. On 12 December von Braun issued a memo calling for holding modifications to a minimum in view of the "increased tempo of the firing schedule in 1957 in conjunction with a greater variety of individual missiles"—Jupiter, Jupiter-A/Redstone, and Jupiter-C. In January ABMA was given more work when the Defense Department secretly selected the reliable Redstone for Operation Hardtack—a project to detonate nuclear bombs at heights of 20 and 50 mi (32 and 80 km) above the Pacific island test range in 1958. At the same time, despite the Wilson decision, the army was becoming interested in a 500-mi (800-km)-range successor to Redstone, and Vanguard's continuing troubles kept the satellite question perpetually open. Eberhard Rees joked, according to Medaris, that planning for Jupiter cancellation was one thing—"Much vorse ve need an emergency plan in case ve should be told to go ahead vith more than half the bids ve have made."[70]

At the Cape the Thor-Jupiter race built to a feverish intensity; von Braun found himself traveling to Florida every few weeks for ABMA launches. On 25 January, Thor 101 rose 9 in off its pad, the engine cut off, and it fell back and blew up in an explosion heard miles away. Jupiter was next. Debus's group fired AM-1A, as it had been renamed, on the late afternoon of 1 March. It flew perfectly for 74 seconds and suddenly exploded. From telemetry, von Braun's team quickly diagnosed excessive tail heating caused by the expansion of the rocket exhaust in the thin upper atmosphere and a relative vacuum around the engine. The straightforward solution was a fiberglass blanket and modification of lines near the motor. On 19 April the air force/Douglas team fired Thor 102, which also flew perfectly for a while, then was blown up by the range safety officer, who thought it was heading for Orlando due to crossed wires in his console. He was shipped off to a remote tracking station in the South Atlantic. A week later ABMA launched

AM-1B, which flew for 93 seconds before again erupting in a spectacular fireball. This time the cause was spiral sloshing of the propellants due to the missile's large diameter and its steering motions during launch.[71]

In a solution that Medaris thought proved the value of their Arsenal organization, rather than writing a contract and waiting a long time for the result, the structural engineers built a simulator from a water tank and an old locomotive engine, then put together an interim fix—a net of floating metal cans, jokingly called the "beer can" solution. (Later missiles would have baffles inside the tanks.) On the last day of May the "beer can"–equipped AM-1 (in fact the third Jupiter) flew 1,319 statute mi (2123 km), the first successful IRBM launch. Ten days earlier Thor 103 had exploded on the pad five minutes before launch, and the first long-range flight of that missile would not come until September. Jupiter's early success was the most powerful argument that Medaris and von Braun had to keep their underdog program alive.[72]

Meanwhile Debus's crew had launched the second Jupiter-C, on 15 May, in the first test of the subscale Jupiter warhead. The missile went off course, and the nose cone was not recovered from the sea, but telemetry indicated that the so-called ablative heat shield had worked all the way down. Ablation was the process by which the plastic-fiberglass composite covering the shield sublimed directly from the solid to gaseous state under the tremendous frictional heat flux produced when the vehicle reentered the atmosphere at hypersonic speeds. Early in the 1950s aerodynamicists at the National Advisory Committee for Aeronautics (NACA), the federal research establishment for this area, had shown that a blunt heat shield would create shock waves ahead of it that would hold off a large fraction of the frictional heating. Still, a shield of some sort was essential for higher velocities. When the air force started the ICBM program, it bet on the "heat sink": heavy, flat, conical, polished copper shields that, if designed correctly, would reflect some heat and soak up the rest without melting.[73]

The Huntsville approach, which was the greatest single technological contribution made by von Braun's group to U.S. missile programs after the V-2, had evolved from their low-budget, empirical investigations into materials to replace the Redstone's graphite jet vanes. In 1953 his team observed that a particular plastic failed as a jet vane but eroded in a most interesting way: below the surface layer the material had remained largely intact. In 1954, in conjunction with studies for long-range missiles, von Braun had designated the old ramjet test stand for reentry work, employing a Hermes rocket engine as a crude analogue. Out of this came the phenolic resin, fiberglass, and asbestos heat shield of Jupiter. In 1956 and 1957 he and his associates presented these results to Defense scientists and engineers. The fundamental proof came on 8 August 1957, when the third Jupiter-C flew entirely successfully. The nose cone parachuted into the sea and was later shown by the president on TV and given to the Smithsonian. It was a proud success for von Braun and his group, and one that made them feel once again that they had one-upped the much-better-funded air force.[74]

Even before the Jupiter and Jupiter-C successes, Wernher von Braun received yet more signs of fame and recognition. On 20 April he and Maria were flown to Washington by special army plane for the presentation of a Distinguished Civilian Service Award by Defense Secretary Wilson. With his parents he could be unguarded, comparing it to the highest medal he had received from Hitler: "That is so to speak the 'Peacetime Knight's Cross of the War Service Cross.' In view of my relatively short stay in this country it is a fairly big deal. . . . Yes, it isn't so shabby as it was in Ft. Bliss." In the same letter he told them that he had been offered 100,000 Deutschmarks (about $24,000) by a Munich film company to cooperate in a movie about his life, a reflection of a growing hero worship in West Germany, where he was a symbol of the alliance with the United States: "Was too much to say no." He hoped that he might go to Munich as early as the summer to talk to the studio. In June he was able to confirm the trip, but it would all have to be carried out in secret; he would get military flights across the Atlantic and be accompanied at all times by a security officer to prevent him from being kidnapped by the Soviets—such was the continuing Cold War paranoia. Von Braun spent ten days in Germany in late July, his first visit since the 1947 wedding trip and the first chance to see his parents since they left in 1952. He was relieved to find his mother healthier than expected. The trip was a success, not least because the press never caught wind of it.[75]

The spring of 1957 also brought yet another false dawn for the satellite project. On 23 April von Braun wrote Fred Durant that "more and more people in important quarters are beginning to realize that it might be a good idea to get us back in." The causes were the same: more slippage in the Vanguard launch schedule, accompanied by major cost overruns, and more evidence that the Soviets were rapidly advancing. Homer Joe Stewart, who was closely involved with the RTV, once again pushed ABMA's capability onto his committee's agenda, ultimately with as little success as before. Meanwhile leading upper-atmospheric physicist James Van Allen called for Jupiter-C launches after the navy secretary announced that the first full-sized Vanguard satellite launch might not come until late 1958. Van Allen had made sure his cosmic-ray experiment would fit the ABMA rocket after Ernst Stuhlinger had quietly visited him in Iowa in November 1956, following the success of the RS-27 long-range shot. In April Stuhlinger drafted an elaborate report showing that ABMA/JPL thinking on the satellite had proceeded quite far, with layouts for a cylindrical payload on the end of the fourth-stage rocket. (The old spherical Orbiter design had been dropped a year earlier, thanks to the higher payload of Jupiter-C, the availability of miniature radio transmitters, and weight and balance considerations for the spinning cluster.) Stuhlinger's paper, combined with a leak to the press, however, created a flap that resulted in the Defense Department demanding to know if ABMA had gone too far in satellite development. In late June and again in July, Medaris issued decrees stopping all work on satellite configurations of the Jupiter-C and even upbraided von Braun for having let things go beyond his orders. Missile 29 was to be held ready to launch in four months from a go-ahead, and 24 in five, but assembly was to proceed no further.[76]

That summer Wernher von Braun shared the gnawing feeling of many inside the rocket business that the Soviet Union was about to pull off the triumph he had long feared. In late August Soviet dictator Nikita Khrushchev announced their first successful ICBM test, and the Academy of Sciences even published the satellite's frequencies in amateur radio periodicals. The press talked about it too, although none of it seems to have penetrated deeply into American public consciousness. Von Braun wrote to Krafft Ehricke on 6 September regarding an American Rocket Society proposal for a national space agency funded at $100 million per year:

> I am convinced that, should the Russians beat us to the satellite punch, this would have all kinds of severe psychological repercussions not only among the American public, but also among our allies. It would be simply construed as visible proof the Reds are ahead of us in the rocket game. The fact that people would be able to <u>see</u> a Red satellite going around above their heads would impress most people far more than any assurances that the equipment our Western satellite, once successful, will carry[,] will be more sophisticated and refined.

Despite this prescience, he nonetheless considered $100 million too high to be salable to the penny-pinching Eisenhower administration. Soon it would be far too little.[77]

CHAPTER THIRTEEN

The Seer of Space

1957–58

In spite of the sputnik cocktails being served (one part vodka, two parts sour grapes) the space age has now dawned. Your place in it is still at apogee. —LEY to von Braun, 6 November 1957[1]

Late on the afternoon of Friday, 4 October 1957—just fifteen years and one day after the first successful V-2 launch in Peenemünde—Wernher von Braun went back to his Huntsville office. There was to be a brief interlude before cocktails and dinner at the officers' club. Together with General Medaris, he had been showing the newly nominated defense secretary, Neil McElroy, and Army Secretary Brucker around Redstone Arsenal all afternoon. The phone rang; it was a British newspaperman calling from New York.

"What do you think of it," he asked.
"Think of what?"
"The Russian satellite. The one they just orbited."
I wasn't surprised. I'd long known that the Russians had a satellite capability. I was just disappointed, and a little bitter that we hadn't been allowed to do it before they did.[2]

When von Braun reached the party, he sought out McElroy and Medaris. As he recalled the moment a few months later, he exclaimed: "If you go back to Washington tomorrow, Mr. Secretary, and find that all hell has broken loose, remember this. We can get a satellite up in sixty days." Medaris's 1960 memoir is more dramatic, based as it is on a surprise announcement by his public relations chief, Gordon Harris, who was not even at the party. Perhaps the bearer of bad news was von Braun himself.

There was a moment of stunned silence. Then von Braun started to talk as if he had suddenly been vaccinated with a victrola needle. In his driving urgency to unburden his feelings, the words tumbled over one another. "We knew they were going to do it! Vanguard will never make it. We have the hardware on the shelf. For God's sake turn us loose and let us do something. We can put up the satellite in sixty days, Mr. McElroy! Just give us a green light and sixty days!"

Medaris finally interjected, "No, Wernher, ninety days."[3]

The launch of Sputnik (Russian for "satellite" or "fellow traveler") was one of the defining moments in Wernher von Braun's life and one of his greatest disappointments. It stirred in him a boiling mix of emotions: frustration at two years of official setbacks for his satellite project, annoyance and depression at the propaganda harvest reaped by Khrushchev, jubilation at the prospect of finally being released from restraints, and hope that Sputnik would shock the United States into pursuing an energetic space program. Quite suddenly the "Space Age"—as the press almost instantly dubbed it—had dawned, and von Braun was its prophet.[4] Within four months, after the launch of the first U.S. satellite, he was a bona fide American hero, the Western world's most prominent gladiator in a celestial contest with the Soviets.

Knowing Vanguard's slim chances of an early success, von Braun and Medaris expected a quick approval of their program. It was not forthcoming. President Eisenhower and his advisers professed themselves undisturbed by the Soviet first. They had good reasons based on highly secret intelligence, notably the dangerous and illegal U-2 flights over the USSR, not to be worried about the U.S. position in the nuclear arms race. Sputnik had, moreover, inadvertently established the principle that satellite "overflight" was not a violation of airspace, unlike aerial intrusions. But administration leaders could not talk about these deeply classified matters, so their equanimity just made them look clueless to their many critics.[5]

For von Braun, the lack of any affirmative news from Washington made the post-Sputnik period trying, an extension of the tense weeks immediately preceding the Soviet triumph. According to his wife, he had been making business trips out of nervousness and dejection even before that launch, and he continued them afterward in order to avoid the press. Washington had imposed a news blackout, probably after an anonymous Huntsville "scientist," who may well have been von Braun, told an Associated Press reporter how "angry and distressed" he was over the failure to get Orbiter approved in 1955. That story, in a limited and distorted form, had been in circulation since 1956 but gained new significance in the climate of finger-pointing that ensued in the capital and in the press. The fact that all the original proposal offered was a 5-lb (2.2-kg) inert object, or at most one with a small transmitter, was unknown or simply forgotten. The public and the media cared little about what the United States could have orbited, only about why it was second. Not only had the Soviet Union acquired enormous scientific and engineering prestige, but it had also suddenly made credible its August ICBM announcement. If the Reds could put a 185-lb (84-kg) "moon" into orbit, they must be able to drop an H-bomb on New York—or so the reasoning went.[6]

The president's 9 October news conference in particular irritated von Braun and his compatriots. Not only did Eisenhower downplay the Sputnik accomplishment as putting "one small ball in the air"; he asserted that the Soviets had triumphed because they had "captured all the German scientists." Soon thereafter a journalist filed a story from Huntsville in which a "top missile man whose name is nationally known" complained about Orbiter and pointed to earlier statements in print to get around the news blackout. During the same news conference Eisenhower also put ABMA on the spot when he indicated that the army would investigate whether it could help Vanguard. Von Braun and his leading specialists hurriedly studied how a regular 20-lb (9-kg) Vanguard satellite might be mounted on a Jupiter-C. It was a project of dubious feasibility, as was predictable, but they used it to propose that two of their satellites be launched first as "tests." That argument got nowhere. Medaris found himself further and further out on a limb, as he had authorized preliminary work on two Jupiter-C boosters without any budget authority to do so.[7]

Having received limited backing in the Pentagon to continue satellite planning, however, Medaris told von Braun and his Germans that they would *not* use the ABMA-developed radio-transmitter payload for the fourth-stage rocket. Rather, the Jet Propulsion Laboratory would be tasked with combining James Van Allen's cosmic-radiation experiment into the very first satellite, making the Pasadena laboratory responsible for the entire upper-stage cluster. JPL director Bill Pickering recalls that there was "dead silence in the room for quite a while" afterward. Medaris knew that if their rocket carried an official Vanguard experiment for the International Geophysical Year, which had begun on 1 July, it would increase their chances of approval in Washington. The same strictures did not apply to Vanguard: under pressure to produce results, the White House had already announced that 3.4-lb (1.5-kg) radio-only minisatellites would be installed on Vanguard test vehicles from the first orbital attempt in December. The larger satellites would follow on regular Vanguard launchers.[8]

If Sputnik had only increased the tension in ABMA over the satellite issue, there was at least minor relief for the Jupiter IRBM program. McElroy, after his installation as defense secretary, allowed the "weaponiza-tion" of both Thor and Jupiter to go forward, without as yet any clear deci-sion to put both into production for the USAF. Meanwhile Jupiter development and flight testing still dominated the workload in von Braun's Development Operations Division. On 22 October the fifth missile success-fully lobbed the first full-size ablative nose cone over a range of 1,100 mi (1770 km). Yet planning for operational equipment lagged far behind because of foot-dragging in General Schriever's renamed Ballistic Missile Division (BMD).[9]

It took the second, even more shocking Soviet triumph on 3 November to resolve many of these issues—eventually. Sputnik 2 weighed a stunning 1,118 lb (508 kg) and carried the first living being into orbit, the doomed canine Laika, just in time for the Red Square celebration of the fortieth anniversary of the Bolshevik Revolution. No one in the West knew that the feat was even more amazing than it appeared: the team led by the anony-mous chief designer, Sergei Pavlovich Korolev, had thrown Sputnik 2 together in less than four weeks to satisfy Nikita Khrushchev's desire for yet another propaganda victory. The climate of recrimination and hysteria in the United States rose to a fever pitch—the same 18 November *Life* mag-azine that carried von Braun on the cover included an opinion piece, "Argu-ing the Case for Being Panicky." The author asserted: "In short, unless we depart utterly from our present behavior, it is reasonable to expect that by no later than 1975 the United States will be a member of the Union of Soviet Socialist Republics."[10]

The public furor drove the administration to give in, slowly and reluc-tantly, on the issue of army satellites as a supplement to Vanguard. On 7 November Eisenhower went on national TV to reassure Americans about their nuclear deterrent, while promising a satellite by March. He showed off a Jupiter-C subscale nose cone recovered in August that proved the ablative heat shield concept, without ever crediting ABMA. The next day McElroy issued the satellite order to Brucker, but the wording instantly made Medaris furious rather than happy. It said they were to prepare to launch but did not actually authorize them to do so. Medaris called a colonel in the Pentagon and asked him "was this a backup deal"—meaning, if Vanguard was successful, would their launches be canceled? Answered in the affirma-tive, he said: "Dr. von Braun is going to blow his top." He called von Braun on the "squawk box" intercom and told him, "Let's go," but had to follow it up with an explanation. After seeing him in the late afternoon, along with Pickering, Medaris sent a teletype in which he stated that all three of them threatened to quit if they did not get a firm commitment to launch. It was an empty threat but one that served to get people's attention.[11]

Already in October Medaris and von Braun had decided that old number 29, which had been held in reserve as a satellite vehicle for two years, could be launched by the beginning of February 1958, and RS-26 (which had displaced 24 as the backup) about a month after that. But it took two months of dunning Washington before they finally got approval. In late November, with the encouragement of the chief of Ordnance, Medaris approved 29 January as a preliminary date for the first launch attempt, but formal permission from the Defense Department came only the day after Christmas. At JPL's suggestion the satellite version of the Jupiter-C was to be named Juno—wife of Jupiter in the Roman pantheon.[12]

The von Braun cover story in *Life,* the number-one picture magazine in the United States, was the high point in the early wave of publicity, even adulation, that was now fixed on him. The article, entitled "The Seer of Space," showed the "thoroughly Americanized German" in pictures with his family at home and with colleagues in the offices and workshops at Huntsville. It was not, however, the first article to anoint him as the once-ridiculed, now-vindicated prophet of astronautics. That title had already been conferred by *The New York Times* in its 20 October Sunday magazine piece, "Visit with a Prophet of the Space Age." The portrait was generally friendly but had little touches of skepticism, such as describing the "unruly wisps of curls jutting from his temples" that gave him the look of a "cherubic Mephistopheles," or noting that everyone in Huntsville called him "the Professor," a title "awarded to him by Hitler." (No doubt due to an intentional policy of the army, "Doctor" had already displaced "Professor" in official parlance.) Von Braun told some of his best stories about Hitler and Himmler and brought up his Gestapo arrest, which more than anything else provided him with cover for his Third Reich activities.[13]

Clearly the news blackout had not lasted very long under the pressure of press demands to talk to von Braun, and although he could not bring up the Orbiter-Vanguard decision again, it did not stop him from speaking out very bluntly about the race with the Soviets. His 9 November interview with the Associated Press in particular created political waves in Washington. He asserted that the main reason for the Soviet lead was "that the United States had no ballistic missile program worth mentioning between 1945 and 1951," years that were "irretrievably lost." These remarks became a political football, as Republicans seized on them to blame the satellite and missile lag on President Truman, who in turn questioned von Braun's credibility, as did the Democratic national chairman. Other comments irritated the Republican administration, however, notably those regarding cuts in ballistic missile funding in 1957 and on the need for an all-out, centralized space program to compete with the Soviets, something Eisenhower wanted to avoid because he viewed unconstrained deficit spending as a long-term threat to the national economy. By early 1958 a testy Ike was complaining to his aides about von Braun's outspokenness and "publicity-seeking."[14]

While von Braun was certainly now a loyal American, some of his remarks showed an impatience with aspects of democracy. He expressed exasperation at all the advisory boards and committees he had to talk to, many of them staffed by scientists with little or no engineering experience. He told *Life*: "I just wish someone had the authority to tell me, 'All right, we'll leave you alone for two years, but if you fail we're going to hang you.' " Although his Gestapo arrest had disillusioned him about totalitarianism, he warned the American public not to believe claims that only bad science and engineering came out of totalitarian systems, as technical experts were often coddled in them. He was especially worried by the rapid gains in Soviet science and technology and the perceived inadequacies of American scientific education.[15]

If von Braun inevitably became the most visible and vocal advocate of a space race, he took it for granted that "space weapons" would be part of it. "Ten or 15 years from now space superiority will have taken the place of today's air superiority," he told the AP reporter. Nuclear missiles in orbit were still the ultimate weapon, he thought, although he did not say so explicitly in the interview, presumably because that might have been too controversial. Not long after Sputnik 2, however, he again advocated orbital bombs in a draft article called "The Meaning of Space Superiority," although he conceded for the first time that a manned space station might be vulnerable to attack. But missiles launched from space planes would be much more accurate than any ICBM could ever be, he claimed. It was *Collier's* redux.[16]

Despite von Braun's long history of militant anti-Communist statements, it is an interesting aside that even key Soviet space scientists and engineers were obsessed with him. Already in the fall of 1956 Sergei Korolev had become convinced that the long-range Jupiter-C shot must have been a failed von Braun satellite attempt. When Ernst Stuhlinger came back from the International Astronautical Federation congress held in Barcelona just after Sputnik 1, he reported that Soviet delegate Leonid Sedov was surprised to hear that von Braun was not involved in the Vanguard program; he had expected the German-American to be at the center of everything.[17]

In the United States von Braun's profile was raised further when Senate majority leader Lyndon B. Johnson, a Texas Democrat, called him before one of the most important congressional hearings of the Cold War. Johnson's Inquiry into Satellite and Missile Programs, which opened on 25 November 1957, was transparently designed to embarrass the administration and boost his presidential chances in 1960. McElroy, at the outset of his testimony two days later, sought to neutralize at least one line of attack by announcing that both Thor and Jupiter IRBMs would go into production. One year after the Polaris and Wilson decisions, it felt like vindication.[18]

Wernher von Braun's turn to testify came up on 14 December, immediately following Medaris. In the meantime events had conspired to make him even more prominent. Ten days earlier the Mars show of the Disney space series had finally appeared on ABC-TV; it had been much delayed because Disney had agreed to make a Vanguard program that it canceled immediately after Sputnik. The Mars segment, which Ward Kimball had found the most difficult because it was the most speculative, was rushed to completion. In contrast to the first two, von Braun's role was limited. He and Stuhlinger were shown only with models of Stuhlinger's design for an umbrella-shaped, electric-rocket ship, voiced-over by a narrator. Two days later, on 6 December, the Vanguard TV-3 vehicle rose a few inches off the pad in Florida, cut off, fell back, and exploded in a spectacular fireball broadcast live on national television. This further national embarrassment—ridiculed as "Flopnik" and "Stayputnik" in the newspapers—did not guarantee that von Braun and the army would put up the first U.S. satellite, but it certainly increased their odds, and the enormous pressure and scrutiny that went with it.[19]

Von Braun's testimony to the Johnson subcommittee was, in the words of *The New York Times*, a "hit." "He drew many sympathetic laughs as he smilingly grappled with questions" from the committee counsel, Johnson, and other senators. "Dr. von Braun, blond, broad-shouldered and square-jawed, joined General Medaris in stressing the importance of developing a rocket carrying a man into space." *The Washington Post* summarized the pair's testimony with the page-one headline, "All-Out Push to Dominate Space Urged." Of the Soviets, von Braun said: "They consider control of space around the earth very much like, shall we say, as the great maritime powers considered control of the seas, in the 16th through the 18th century, and they say, 'If we want to control this planet, we have to control the space around it.' " Von Braun advocated a "National Space Agency," either inside or outside the Defense Department, that would carry out all military and civilian space programs; the American Rocket Society proposal for such an agency meanwhile had finally appeared and he was one of the signatories. He told the senators that all space activities should be under "one man," but he did not mention what at least some in Huntsville had said: it should be him or Medaris.[20]

In contrast to the hundred-million-dollar budget in the ARS's pre-Sputnik draft report, von Braun now thought the agency should get $1.5 billion per year. He was open to either a military or a civilian space agency and was also willing to consider transferring ICBM and IRBM development programs to it. He was certainly not as shortsightedly partisan as Medaris, who testified that all ballistic missiles should be army because they were just an extension of the artillery. Von Braun's extraordinary talent for explaining difficult concepts, his exotic background, and his image as the prophet of space and as the man who could have put up a satellite before the Soviets, all made him enormously appealing. He had, moreover, made statements that Johnson and the Democrats could use against the administration. The hearings launched von Braun on a long career as a popular congressional witness. Senators and congressmen began coming to the table to shake his hand; colleagues of von Braun, like Pickering, found themselves slighted in the process.[21]

Von Braun's $1.5 billion figure came from a classified proposal for "A National Integrated Missile and Space Development Program" that he and his closest associates had just completed. It laid out a family of launch vehicles, building on the rather primitive Jupiter-C/Juno I combination. The first obvious idea was to mount the same three-stage cluster on top of a lengthened Jupiter IRBM in place of a Redstone; this launcher was soon called Juno II and could be used to launch heavier scientific satellites or Moon probes, both of which the army had already proposed. The next step would be Juno III, with a more powerful and advanced cluster on a Jupiter, but it still lacked an actively guided upper stage or a fundamentally new booster. Using the 380,000-lb (172,000-kg) thrust E-1 engine that NAA/Rocketdyne was proposing, they could upgrade the Jupiter as a booster, or four E-1s could be clustered to produce a superlauncher of 1.5-million-lb (680,000-kg) thrust. The air force had also begun to fund development of a one-million-lb-thrust F-1 motor at Rocketdyne (later upgraded to 1.5 million), providing a basis for even larger rockets. As for what could be accomplished for that billion and a half per year, the program optimistically predicted a one- or two-man spacecraft by fall 1962, a manned Moon circumnavigation by fall 1963, a twenty-person space station by fall 1965, and a manned Moon landing by spring 1967, among other things. Naive or deliberately underbid proposals were the order of the day. In March 1958 the air force proposed a human spaceflight program leading to a manned lunar landing, the total price of which was $1.5 billion.[22]

Not surprisingly, and in marked contrast to his public flexibility, von Braun's program was as narrowly service-centric as anything coming out of the air force or navy, because it was part of a scramble for position inside the Defense Department. USAF space proponents and their allies in the aircraft industry were already energetically arguing that spaceflight was a natural extension of the air force mission, so it should control the space program, including, of course, any piloted spacecraft. Public relations people for the air service even invented the word *aerospace* to signify the unity of that mission.[23]

Proposals, advocacy, and fame aside, Wernher von Braun's plate was overloaded with urgent engineering management tasks in the winter of 1957–58. The first satellite attempt loomed, and ABMA found that it had to redesign the compressed-air jets that would orient the rotating cluster. Operation Hardtack was fast approaching too, with April set as the target for launching two Redstones from Johnson Island in the Pacific, armed with nuclear warheads to be exploded at the edge of space. In preparation, Kurt Debus's group fired two more Redstones from Cape Canaveral to test the special measurement pods that were to be jettisoned during ascent. ABMA was also in the midst of formulating the obsolescent Redstone's replacement, a 500-nautical-mi (925-km) missile called Pershing that Eisenhower had approved after lifting the 200-mi "Wilson decision" limit in August 1957. If all that was not enough, the Jupiter IRBM suddenly developed a serious engine problem. In November and December two in a row lost thrust during powered flight due to turbopump bearing failures. Von Braun put absolute top priority on the Rocketdyne-led redesign, but IRBM launches stopped for five months. And now that the Jupiter was going to be deployed, ABMA was finally able to talk directly to the user, the Strategic Air Command, but that meant ground equipment had to be finalized. While ABMA's massive in-house laboratories and its contractors worked each one of these tasks, von Braun spent long hours in meetings about every important technical decision.[24]

Despite the many distractions, his focus turned toward the anxiously awaited satellite launch. In mid-January he went to the Cape for two days to check on preparations. But before the army had its shot, Vanguard had another go. Four times the Naval Research Laboratory team counted down its next vehicle, and four times weather or technical problems scrubbed the attempt. Needing to stand down anyway to fix a damaged second-stage motor, the Vanguard team yielded to the army's launch window beginning on the twenty-ninth. The Cape and the tracking stations of the Atlantic Missile Range, both run by the air force as national facilities, could accommodate only one firing at a time.[25]

When the time came to count down RS-29 from the cramped Cape blockhouse, von Braun would not be there. "It was a severe personal blow," he wrote soon afterward, when Medaris told him that he had to be in Washington for a news conference in case of a success. To his father two days after the launch, he said: "when one has worked for 28 years on such a thing and now expects the culmination, it was a fairly bitter pill." But Medaris, the army, and the administration wanted to avoid the media circus that had prevailed before and after the Vanguard TV-3 fiasco. The air force general who ran the range made a deal with the press to give off-the-record briefings in return for holding all stories until after the launch. But to keep many journalists away, the National Academy of Sciences was to host a special news conference in case of success. Von Braun, Pickering, and Van Allen, representing ABMA, JPL, and the satellite's scientific package, were thus assigned to sweat it out in the national capital.[26]

The planned launch time was ten-thirty p.m. to permit photographic tracking of the upper-stage cluster firing, so von Braun did not have to leave for Washington until midday. But on the twenty-ninth he did not leave at all. Medaris, directing the operation in Florida himself, canceled the attempt in the morning as the jet stream had moved far south, right over Cape Canaveral. Weather balloons detected winds of 165 to 175 knots in the stratosphere, enough wind shear to destroy the rocket. The next day there was hope that the winds would die down, and von Braun flew north at noon, but again the countdown was canceled. Friday, 31 January, represented their last shot for a couple of weeks, as Medaris had dignitaries coming to Huntsville on 1 February for the second birthday party of ABMA, and they had to yield the Cape to the Vanguard team anyway.[27]

Much to everyone's relief, midday weather data on the thirty-first showed the winds down to a tolerable 120 knots, and optimism rose through the afternoon. At around eight or nine p.m. von Braun, Pickering, and Van Allen arrived at the Pentagon's army communications center. They were soon joined by Secretary Brucker, five generals, a host of colonels, lieutenant colonels, and lesser officers, and several civilians. Richard Porter of GE, who had interrogated von Braun in Germany in summer 1945, and voted against his Orbiter proposal in summer 1955, was there too, likely representing the National Academy of Sciences' IGY committee. There was no closed-circuit TV or continuous voice link to the Cape; the height of 1958 technology was the teletype machine, the printed words of which were projected onto a screen overhead. Supplementing it were a number of telephones. General J. Hinrichs of Army Ordnance describes the teletype "chattering, stuttering, silent, then starting up intermittently." A local radio station was on, conveying live updates from a reporter in Florida standing miles away with binoculars. Brucker, having come from a party, was in a tux; von Braun, in a dark suit, was "somewhat studiously calm, perhaps, but confident. Pickering under fair control at this time, but keyed up." At 9:49 there was a hold for a hydrogen peroxide leak, but that was quickly cleared up. The count resumed at "X" minus 45 minutes at 10:03.[28]

Fifteen minutes later, at X − 30, lights suddenly illuminated the 83-ft (25-m) tall black-and-white vehicle, a long, finned cylinder with a cylindrical tub sitting on top of the tapered nose, and on top of that, sticking out, a lone pencil—the combination fourth stage/satellite, which the army had secretly decided to name Explorer I if it orbited. On the booster's side were the letters UE, code for "29," from the letters in Huntsville. In Washington the teletype clattered out: "Eye witnesses say that the missile is a beautiful sight with the searchlights playing on it." At X − 10 the tub began to spin up, to reach 550 rpm before launch, only to be stepped up again to 750 during its ascent. Von Braun and the others stared at the screen or the teletype as it printed out:

X − 3 at 2245
X − 2 minutes—Liftoff is scheduled for 16 seconds after X − 0.
X − 1 minute—Final weight measurements being taken. Spinner still running smoothly.
X − 20 seconds
X − 10 seconds
Firing command
Mainstage
Liftoff
Program is starting.[29]

At the Cape, Medaris, Debus, and the others inside the blockhouse witnessed the ignition flame at 10:48 p.m. through thick, blast-proof windows; the vehicle quickly disappeared from their limited vision. Although von Braun missed this sight of his life, in the Pentagon the radio reporter's words rang out: "Slow rise, faster, faster! Straight up, found a hole in the clouds! Is beginning to tilt on course—Is apparently still on course, rising, and going away. It is out of sight, but it must be successful!" The teletype was by contrast laconic, typing out "Still going" and then the elapsed time every 10 or 20 seconds, although noting after 90: "Has passed thru the Jet Stream OK." At 156 seconds the first stage cut off, and the nose section with spinning tub separated and began to orient itself during the four-minute coast to the apex. Von Braun turned to Pickering: "Bill, it's yours now."[30]

In a building at the Cape, Ernst Stuhlinger now hurriedly looked at the data from three different tracking sources and fed them into a crude analog "apex predictor" computer that would send the signal to start the firing sequence for the upper stages. Just to be sure he had a manual backup button that he pushed at the predicted time. When the spinning cluster fired away from the tub, there were no more signals except that of the satellite. In Washington the teletype sputtered out: "Second stage ignition OK. Apex prediction came through and was given [as] approximately 403 seconds. Although it is too early to determine whether Satellite is in orbit the launching is successful." "For ABMA from Prof VonBraun: Did 3d and 4th stages fire?" Reply: "Do not know yet. Will let you know as soon as possible. Gen Medaris has arr[ive]d at the JPL bldg. Gen Medaris says have a cup of coffee, smoke a cigarette and sweat it out with us." A tense Pickering exclaimed to von Braun: "It <u>must</u> be in orbit!" The rejoinder: "I am sure it is, but we don't <u>know</u>."[31]

Minutes later some relief. Medaris and Jack Froehlich of JPL informed von Braun and Pickering via the teletype: "Things look good. Minitrack acquired. Antigua Doppler had not acquired, but they are examining tapes. During the period for nominal high speed stage operation cluster frequency shift was OK. . . . [Satellite] appeared over Antigua at the proper time." There followed a first estimate of the orbit: perigee 184 mi, apogee 1,230 mi, period 106 minutes. That would put Explorer I back over the West Coast at a bit past 12:30 a.m. Eastern Time.[32]

Von Braun and Pickering, pressed by army public relations to authorize the release of a statement by the president, urged waiting until it came around. That meant an excruciating hour and a half of "more cigarettes, more coffee, more doughnuts," according to Hinrichs. (Von Braun had given up smoking by this time but was known to mooch cigarettes on occasion.) An "enthusiastic and jovial" Brucker, a former Michigan governor, "made several good cracks. One—'Boys! This is just like waiting for the [election] precincts to come in!' Another—'Boys! Let me tell you about the night Lydia Grey went to the electric chair.' "[33]

With the time approaching, an impatient Pickering took off into the next room and phoned California, but as it was too early he spent the time making chitchat. Cradling several phones at once, he was soon in touch with all four JPL tracking stations, but the time came and went—nothing. Von Braun wrote his father two days later:

> The uplifted, optimistic feeling [in the Pentagon] . . . sank deeper and deeper, the faces became longer and longer. The public-information generals, who had pressed me for an hour-and-a-half to declare the shot

a success to the press, were now glad that they hadn't done it. . . . Then, suddenly, after 8 tortuous minutes of desperate waiting, all four stations on the west coast called within 30 seconds of each other to say that they had a clear, strong signal on both satellite transmitters. Tears ran down the face of old Brucker. . . . It was truly exciting.

In the room, "jubilation!" The predicted orbital period was several minutes off.[34]

Von Braun, Pickering, and Van Allen sped off across the Potomac in a chauffeured car. On their way to the National Academy building in downtown Washington, the JPL director remembers thinking, Who could possibly show up for a one a.m. press conference on a cold, rainy winter night? On the contrary, the auditorium held a huge crowd of reporters, plus live radio and television. The atmosphere was electric—U.S. national honor had been saved. They kept the trio on the podium talking until three a.m., and as they talked, reports from around the globe came in that Explorer's signals had been heard. Someone suggested the three hoist the full-size model of the slim, cylindrical rocket over their heads. It was the iconic picture of the night, and it became one of the iconic pictures of the space age. In Huntsville a spontaneous crowd had its own celebration: it burned former Defense Secretary Wilson in effigy on the courthouse square.[35]

Three days after returning home to a hero's welcome, von Braun was back in Washington: he and his wife had been hastily invited to a White House state dinner for the scientific community on the fourth, their first encounter with a president. Maria wore a beautiful brocade evening gown that he had given to her for Christmas in anticipation of such an event. At the time she thought his optimism bordered on cheekiness—when would she ever wear such a thing in Huntsville? As the dinner was "white tie" and he did not have one with his rented tux, Wernher managed to borrow one from the White House usher. When Eisenhower appeared, the president said little except to apologize for being late because of a fruitless search for his white tie.[36]

Further signs of von Braun's status as a national and international hero quickly followed. By the end of the week two *Time* reporters were in his office. The newsmagazine's 17 February issue carried a cover painting of "Missileman Von Braun"—in 1958 there were few greater signs of celebrity in America than being on the front of *Time*. Von Braun also graced the cover of its West German equivalent, *Der Spiegel*, which cropped Van Allen and Pickering out of the news conference photo and trumpeted the alleged

centrality of German rocketeers to both the Soviet and the American triumphs. Von Braun had been on the front of that magazine once before, at
the end of 1955, feeding a hero worship in West Germany that now rose to a
frenzy. His father wrote him that various groups of expellees from the
East—East Prussians, West Prussians, and others—were arguing over who
could lay claim to his origins.[37]

Both the *Time* and *Der Spiegel* profiles included a clean version of his
Third Reich career in which his Gestapo arrest was mentioned prominently,
but not his party membership. As for concentration camp horrors or his SS
officer status, the journalists knew nothing. A decade of U.S. secrecy about
Project Paperclip, von Braun and Dornberger's omission of damaging facts
from their memoirs and interviews, and the Western press's Cold War–
driven disinterest in investigating further, had ensured that reality. By 1958
a quasi-official version of von Braun's biography was already in place. His
original 1950 memoir had finally appeared in the *Journal of the British
Interplanetary Society* in 1956, and although few read it there, he gave it to
journalists during interviews and it was reprinted in a book. In the summer
of 1958 *The American Weekly*, a Sunday newspaper supplement with a circulation of ten million, issued a new memoir in three installments, "Space
Man—The Story of My Life," which a writer constructed out of interviews
and materials, with von Braun's editing. "Space Man" cemented in the public mind the official history of his German adventures already available elsewhere in print.[38]

Fame brought money too, and the army was in general happy to let him
accept it, as he was their greatest asset in the missile and space race. *The
American Weekly* paid him $5,000 for "Space Man." A rival Sunday supple-
ment with an even bigger circulation, *This Week*, had already given the
same figure for an Orbiter/Explorer memoir. (He split these fees with his "as
told to" coauthors.) *This Week* was so happy with the result of that article,
which came out in April, that the weekly established a consulting relationship with von Braun, resulting in a couple of articles per year over the next
few years, mostly about space, but also short essays on religion such as
"Why I Believe in Immortality." The religious pieces were often reprinted
elsewhere, making von Braun into a force for the promotion of deistic belief
in the United States.[39]

His celebrity even allowed him to realize his frustrated ambitions as a science fiction writer. In fall 1958 and spring 1959 *This Week* published his
novella, *First Men to the Moon*, in four parts, detailing a two-man expedition using a huge rocket and direct ascent from Earth—no station and no
assembly in space, in contrast to his earlier visions. Such a scenario certainly

excited his abundant imagination, and the story was skillfully illustrated by one of his *Collier's* collaborators, Fred Freeman. Padded with popular science material on spaceflight, it appeared as a short book in 1960. That same year *This Week* issued a three-part science fiction story based on his old *Mars Project* novel, using modified excerpts from his spacefarers' encounter with the Martians. Von Braun noted the ironies of fame—a decade earlier no American publisher would touch it.[40]

In the meantime he had signed up with a speaker's bureau and could earn up to $2,500 for a single evening in the spring of 1958, minus a 30 percent commission. (In 1959 his salary was an upper-middle-class $19,000 per year, although he could have earned many times that in industry, giving him a sense of entitlement.) He was an extraordinarily good speaker, funny, entertaining, and often with something profound or topical to say. The army gave him freedom to speak on very broad and philosophical topics, usually involving meeting the Cold War threat of Communist science and technology. But immediately following Explorer I, Medaris warned him that he was overburdening himself and told him to cut back to no more than two speeches per month. Von Braun's letters often bemoaned his frantic life, but he could not seem to resist the temptations of money and celebrity. The big fees began to embarrass the army. By the beginning of September 1958 Medaris told Brigadier General Chester Clifton of Army Public Information that "he had a touchy situation—all this business has gone to [von Braun's] head."[41]

The most lucrative deal at all was the movie about his life, for which the German producers had originally promised 100,000 Deutschmarks ($24,000). After Sputnik and Explorer it became a German-American coproduction that was potentially even more lucrative. Columbia Pictures was first off the mark, registering its interest in a von Braun picture with the Defense Department a mere three days after Explorer reached orbit. In April the rocket engineer told a German producer that Columbia was offering an additional $25,000 plus 7 percent of the net profits. He said, with no lack of ego: "I agree with these conditions and in view of my increased 'publicity value' see them as fair." Actually nailing down the complicated deal between German and U.S. film companies proved difficult, however, and the contract was not finished until early 1959. Placating the feuding armed services inside the Defense Department was a further problem, and as Medaris put it to Clifton in June 1958, "beginning the story in Germany is, of course, hazardous." A few days later von Braun's most trusted producer from Germany, Friedrich Mainz, wrote from Hollywood about the process of formulating a story treatment: "As you know, they are anxiously trying to show that you were no Nazi, although you were a member of the Party and built the V-2 for Hitler." Thus began the tortured process by which the script for a heroic "biopic" was to be created out of a mixture of fact, fiction, and multiple interventions by multiple parties.[42]

The money funded pleasant increases in the von Brauns' lifestyle. The first installment of nearly $6,000 that he received from Germany in 1957 probably went into the down payment on a new, larger, split-level home that the von Brauns occupied in May 1958. The next month he traded his older American car for a new white Mercedes-Benz. It was his treasured possession, but according to his friends he continued to be as reckless a driver as in his youth, speeding and running stop signs while reading paperwork.[43]

But fame had its costs. Maria, by nature a retiring and private person, hated the rush of publicity after Explorer, especially when it extended to her, Iris, and Margrit. And as the result of all his travel, he spent less and less time with the family, to the point where his daughters asked him to quit rocketry and buy a drugstore so that he would come home every day. On the road Wernher found himself subjected to "some bitter experiences in out-of-the-way places." He told a correspondent in June 1958: "On some occasions I had hardly left the airplane when I found myself confronted with a murderous schedule of cocktail parties, off-the-cuff speeches, luncheons, invitations by private individuals, press and TV conferences, etc." He had to get better control over his schedule, in large part by depending ever more on his staff. In order to fend off some of the onslaught of autograph seekers and fans, they often made hotel reservations and air tickets under an assumed name, and von Braun and his assistants became experts at seeking out the dark corners and rear exits of bars and restaurants. He became accustomed to traveling with an entourage and almost never carried any money.[44]

Long gone were the days when he had one secretary and answered his space-advocacy mail at home. Especially after the arrival of Medaris and the greatly increased money for the IRBM project, he got more help. His extremely capable executive secretary, Bonnie Holmes, was the center of his office staff, but now he also had a military aide as his assistant at work and on travel. In 1956 von Braun brought in a young engineer and space enthusiast as well, Frederick I. Ordway III, to help him with writing and planning projects. Ordway, his aide, or the public relations staff increasingly drafted most of his speeches and articles. When Explorer produced a huge crush of foreign congratulatory and inquiry mail, mostly in German, von Braun hired Ruth von Saurma, the multilingual widow of one of his Peenemünders, to handle much of it. Still, most of the correspondence had to be dealt with through form letters, and only a select minority got more than passing attention from him. This extraordinarily loyal office staff, motivated by hero worship and the thoughtful way he treated them, became the engine that produced the vast array of letters, speeches, and articles that issued from his office between 1957 and 1970 under the name "Wernher von Braun."[45]

After Explorer I von Braun's situation was as hectic professionally as it was personally, a continuation and even amplification of the situation following Sputnik I. Explorer achieved a sterling scientific success that ironically disrupted his immediate plans. At the same time American space policy was in a state of flux, leading the administration to form both military and civilian space agencies to try to control the interservice free-for-all. Von Braun, Medaris, and the army naturally threw in several bids for new programs, expecting to play a central role in the space race against the Soviets.

For the second satellite attempt on 5 March, von Braun could watch from the blockhouse, but the fourth stage failed to fire and burned up over the South Atlantic. Three weeks later he was back again for the successful firing of Explorer III. This satellite carried a miniature tape recorder as part of Van Allen's cosmic radiation experiment, allowing a better understanding of anomalous readings from Explorer I. That satellite could transmit only real-time data; now it was possible to play back information received over entire circuits. By April it became clear that the Earth's magnetic field was trapping a belt of charged particles from the Sun, leading to a heavy radiation belt at altitudes over 600 mi (1,000 km), soon named the Van Allen Belt. The Iowa physicist also ended up on the cover of *Time*, but the scientific success redounded to the credit of von Braun and the army too. Meanwhile the NRL team finally had luck as well, orbiting Vanguard I on 17 March. The Soviets followed on 15 May with their huge geophysical satellite Sputnik 3, weighing 2,919 lb (1327 kg), nearly one hundred times the Explorers (with empty fourth-stage rocket motor) and almost one thousand times the Vanguard minisatellite, which Khrushchev had ridiculed as a "grapefruit."[46]

The Explorer data on trapped radiation meanwhile had set off turmoil inside the Defense Department. Shortly after Sputnik a University of California physicist, Nicholas Christofilos, had proposed that nuclear bombs exploded in space could produce a trapped radiation belt, perhaps one so strong it might damage intercontinental ballistic missiles that passed through it on their way to their targets. The Explorer results seemed to confirm the Christofilos effect and even set off paranoid suspicions that the Soviets had conducted secret bomb tests in space. Medaris observed on 25 April that "the panic over ARGUS has almost gotten out of hand." He was referring to the theory and to the project Eisenhower had approved to test it:

air force solid-fuel rockets would secretly launch small atomic bombs to an altitude of 500 mi (800 km) from a ship in the South Atlantic.[47]

Argus doubly impacted Huntsville and with it von Braun's workload as the leader of the ABMA engineering team. First, the Defense Department decided at the last minute to postpone the April Hardtack Redstone launches from Johnson Island, which were to explode megaton-class warheads at lower altitudes. Ultimately these tests would immediately precede Argus in late summer. This change was very disruptive to Kurt Debus's launch team, which was in the midst of moving a crew to the Pacific, and it also derailed von Braun's plan to take his wife to Hawaii for a vacation later in the month, while using it as a staging ground for trips to watch the two launches. (They went to Jamaica instead, where von Braun scuba-dived to a depth of 165 ft [50 m].) The second impact was a Defense authorization for two further Explorers, IV and V. Publicly they would extend IGY scientific efforts, but covertly they were tied to the Argus and Hardtack experiments. The timing of those bomb tests was in fact determined by the dates when ABMA and JPL could launch new Jupiter-Cs, late July and late August, carrying satellites with improved Van Allen experiments to directly measure the aftereffects of the bomb tests on the Earth's magnetosphere.[48]

The Argus project was being funded and coordinated by a new Defense organization, the Advanced Research Projects Agency (ARPA), which Eisenhower had established on 7 February as a holding company for military space programs until more permanent solutions could be found. The army as an underdog to the air force was inclined to cooperate with ARPA, but first it had to fend off an attempt to give the new agency direct command of von Braun's organization from Washington. Once Medaris and Ordnance had succeeded in that, ARPA became a contracting body that farmed out projects to the services, and its chief, former GE executive Roy Johnson, established friendly relations with Medaris and von Braun.[49]

Among the very first projects ARPA funded was one that certainly sparked von Braun's enthusiasm, an attempt to launch two probes to the vicinity of the Moon. That idea had arisen in October, reflecting the first urgent attempts in Pasadena and Huntsville to come up with some propaganda triumph to beat the Soviets. The launch vehicle would be the Juno II, the Jupiter IRBM with spinning cluster. A parallel proposal came out of the air force and its contractors, putting the Vanguard rocket's upper stages atop the Thor. The administration caved in to space-race pressure: soon after ARPA came into effective operation in March, it authorized both army and air force lunar attempts in late 1958. The program would be called by one name, Pioneer, in a futile attempt to mask the race between the rival services.[50]

Von Braun was also enthused by another idea that came out of his organization: firing a man 150 mi (240 km) into space on a ballistic trajectory, using the long-tank Redstone as a booster. The Jupiter IRBM nose cone would serve as the basis for a capsule. The project's first name in January 1958 was Man Very High, a proposed extension to the air force Man High program that had carried pilots in balloons to 100,000 ft (30 km). Von Braun was able to work his friendly relations with the navy and air force aerospace medicine people to gain their informal agreement to cooperate. Not surprisingly, the air force soon officially nixed participation, as it was working up its own urgent human spaceflight project; it went by the unintentionally funny acronym MISS (Man in Space Soonest). It was the second such project the air force had started, as it had already begun developing the X-20 Dyna-Soar (for dynamic soaring), an ambitious winged space plane. But to beat the Soviets, such efforts would have to take a backseat to "human cannonball" approaches, using ballistic missiles and blunt-body reentry vehicles derived from the same programs—a development not anticipated by von Braun and other space visionaries before Sputnik.[51]

The army renamed its project Adam, for "first man." Knowing that support in ARPA was lacking, however, ABMA justified the project in a 17 April proposal as a precursor to the transport of army soldiers and equipment by ballistic missiles, a bizarre idea that Medaris and General James Gavin, Army R&D chief and famous World War II paratroop commander, came to believe in fervently. But that was not von Braun's motivation—he wanted to beat the Russians to putting the first human in space. He had already forwarded a summary of Adam to his old friend Fred Durant, in order to, as Durant put it, "find a channel" to "whatever national body was charged with the consideration of the psycho-political aspects." Von Braun must have known by then that Durant was connected to the CIA.[52]

Adam never had a chance of approval in Washington, as it offered no development capability beyond a couple of ballistic shots. Nonetheless, as with Orbiter, von Braun found it hard to understand why using a bare minimum approach to one-up the Soviets was not an absolute priority. He told a congressional space committee in mid-April that "this program has not received official approval yet. I do not know why." Hugh Dryden, the chairman of NACA and a distinguished aerodynamicist, dismissed Adam in the same hearing as having "about the same technical value as the circus stunt of shooting the young lady from the gun." It was a biting comment that undercut both the project and Dryden's own chances of becoming the first chief of the civilian space agency that the administration and Congress were building on the foundation of NACA. Several congressmen felt that Dryden's comments showed too little imagination to run the new National Aeronautics and Space Administration (NASA). As for von Braun, despite serving on a special NACA spaceflight committee formed after Sputnik, he had little faith in the old aeronautical research establishment's ability to become the basis for a decisive new agency to lead an all-out space race with the USSR.[53]

Beyond Adam, Pioneer, Explorer/Argus/Hardtack, and Juno II, von Braun juggled several more major projects that spring. On 18 May Jupiter IRBM launches resumed, and for the first time ABMA recovered the full-scale reentry vehicle. Future monkey flights were planned for the winter of 1958–59, presumably in preparation for Adam. There was also enormous pressure to produce a deployable squadron of nuclear-armed Jupiters by the end of 1958. ABMA had been pushing for a television-based reconnaissance satellite too, based on talks with electronics giant RCA going back to October 1956, after the corporation lost out in the air force spy satellite competition. When the Defense Department finally made it clear in early 1958 that space reconnaissance was an air force mission, a typically inventive von Braun told an RCA engineer: "Let's look at clouds!" The army/RCA proposal evolved into a weather satellite project that later went to NASA as Tiros.[54]

In addition, the Pershing medium-range ballistic missile came to fruition in the first half of 1958. Medaris, momentarily complacent about the army's role in U.S. space exploration, expected many new jobs to be assigned. He decided that this missile would be contracted to an aerospace firm (ultimately Martin), although von Braun's Germans would have preferred sticking to in-house development. Pershing would also be solid-propellant, a backhanded admission that liquid-fuel missiles like Redstone and Jupiter were becoming obsolete as the technology of giant solid rockets matured. If the von Braun group was to have a future, it would have to be in large, liquid-propellant launch vehicles, as space applications favored the highest-energy propulsion systems, in contrast to military applications, where quick reaction time and ease of use were paramount.[55]

The proliferation of projects strained the management structure of von Braun's Development Operations Division, forcing a transition "from a single project to a multi-project organization," as he put it. Ever since Peenemünde, one program—V-2, Hermes II, Redstone, or Jupiter—had usually predominated in succession, which worked fine with traditional functional divisions between the so-called laboratories (Aeroballistics, Guidance and Control, and so on). But beginning in January 1958, von Braun created project managers for Pershing, Redstone, and Jupiter, who reported directly to him through Eberhard Rees, cutting across the divisions. Arthur Rudolph took over Pershing and Redstone, and Konrad Dannenberg Jupiter. But von

Braun found he had to keep defending their prerogatives against the lab chiefs, who felt they took orders only from him or Rees.[56]

As spring turned into summer in 1958, Medaris and von Braun received the first signs that the army's future in space was not simply ensured by Explorer I. Space race or no, Eisenhower and McElroy struggled to cap the explosive growth of missile and space programs, which meant that the Advanced Research Projects Agency had to make some tough choices in FY 1959 (which began 1 July 1958) and FY 1960. With the USAF offering more capable future launch vehicles based on Thor and Atlas, at what the army viewed as artificially low prices because of costs subsumed in ballistic missile development budgets, it was hard to support Huntsville's most expensive ideas. In May ABMA and JPL discarded Juno III as too backward compared to air force proposals and moved on to Juno IV, which foresaw JPL developing two liquid-fuel upper stages for Jupiter. ARPA funded it briefly but canceled it in October. A couple of weeks later von Braun told a Pasadena meeting that it had been a "mistake" to recommend "developing new vehicles which are already available at much less cost."[57]

Beyond the commitment to launch eight Juno IIs for lunar probes and Earth satellite missions, Huntsville had really only one launch vehicle project left: the proposed 1.5-million-lb-thrust Juno V superbooster. At least Saturn, as it was soon named, was unique: much bigger and more powerful than boosters based on air force ICBMs, it promised to finally give the United States a shot at equaling the Soviets' obvious and embarrassing heavy-lift capability. A "quick and dirty" fix seemed urgent, and ABMA needed a new project to keep it going. On 15 August ARPA chief Johnson ordered Medaris to proceed with the booster "based on a cluster of available rocket engines." Rocketdyne promised to develop the H-1, a simplified version of its Jupiter-Thor engine with thrust increased to 188,000 lb (85,000 kg)—eight would equal 1.5 million lb (680,000 kg). After several engineering studies of the rocket, someone in Huntsville had a crucial insight: eight cylindrical tanks of Redstone diameter, 70 in (177 cm), would fit around one center tank of Jupiter diameter, 105 in (267 cm), which would enable ABMA's big "Fab Lab" (Fabrication Laboratory) and its booster contractor, Chrysler, to use existing tooling for handling, riveting, and welding fuselages. The center tank and four in the outer ring would carry liquid oxygen (lox), the other four the refined kerosene called RP-1. It was the quintessence of Huntsville conservative engineering: structurally heavy yet innovative, and relatively fast and cheap too. ABMA promised ARPA a static firing by the end of 1959. It was the kind of big space project that inflamed Wernher von Braun's imagination.[58]

It had a been a busy and exciting summer, one dominated by the secret Hardtack/Argus experiments. In early July, after his wife and daughters had sailed to Europe to visit the grandparents, von Braun made a trek to Johnson Island to check on preparations, on the way finding the Hawaiian Islands "simply paradise." He was back at the Cape on 26 July for the successful launch of Explorer IV and immediately flew to the Pacific again. On the thirty-first he witnessed the launch of the first U.S. ballistic missile to carry a live nuclear warhead, under worrying safety conditions. At ten minutes before midnight the H-bomb exploded at an altitude in excess of 43 mi (70 km) in a test code-named "Teak." It was, he said in a 1959 speech,

> by far the most spectacular ever fired by this country. . . . Teak produced a bright fireball which grew rapidly and started to rise at a rate of approximately one-half mile to one mile per second. An aurora developed from the bottom of the fireball and spread rapidly to the North. The fireball reached a diameter of approximately 11 miles in three-tenths of a second and a diameter of more than 18 miles in three and a half seconds. The fireball continued to grow brightly for about five minutes.[59]

If the destructive power of the bomb frightened him, he never gave any indication. He left for Huntsville immediately without seeing the second successful Redstone nuclear shot on 11 August. Although Explorer V failed to reach orbit two weeks later, it had been a summer of success for his organization, one that still seemed to promise the army a central place in U.S. space programs.

CHAPTER FOURTEEN

I Aim at the Stars

1958–60

Some people regard von Braun's unwavering dedication to the grand dream of space flight as heroic and farsighted. Others cannot overlook the grotesque means and unprincipled behavior he used to realize his dreams. I am among the latter, but in this instance I was glad to exploit his willingness to go, without argument, wherever the money was.　　—HERBERT YORK[1]

Sputnik and Explorer had at last established Wernher von Braun's indispensability to American space efforts. But based, as he was, in a military service whose core mission was supposed to be ground combat, that position could not guarantee him a secure existence. The years 1958–59 would once again put Huntsville's survival as a major rocket center into question, confronting him once more with the possibility of having to leave for a job in industry. When his group was integrated into the new civilian agency in 1960, however, he was, after twenty-eight years, finally able to get out of the weapons business and devote himself exclusively to the exploration of space.

Sputnik and Explorer had also made him a hero and an icon. Indeed, von Braun was never more famous than he was between 1958 and 1960. That celebrity allowed him to sell spaceflight to the public and the media, along with a sanitized version of his National Socialist past. But it also led him into an act of hubris: collaborating in a motion picture about his life that unavoidably brought to light questions about his relationship with the Nazis.

Toward the end of August 1958 von Braun finally was able to attend an IAF congress, this time in Amsterdam, followed by another visit with his parents. A couple of weeks after his return, the question of Huntsville's relationship to the new NASA suddenly came to a head; by mid-October it was a full-blown national controversy in which he was a central figure. The agency would officially start operation on the first of that month, but its chief, Dr. T. Keith Glennan, president of the Case Institute of Technology in Cleveland, Ohio, was already on the job as administrator. On 18 September Glennan arrived in Huntsville accompanied by NACA chief Hugh Dryden, who would stay on as his deputy. The two wanted to talk to Medaris about the future relationship between NASA and the army's space and missile programs, but their not-so-hidden agenda was to size up those programs for acquisition. Although the incoming NASA heads said they did not want to break up ABMA, one of Medaris's officers claimed that "Glennan must have said to him at least 8 or 10 times things like 'What the hell is the Army doing in this business; what are you in the space and satellite business for?' "[2]

The NASA Administrator quickly recognized that ABMA and JPL were the prime assets available to build his agency, as the air force needed its organizations for military space programs and contracted out most work anyway. Beyond inheriting NACA's three research laboratories—Langley in tidewater Virginia, Lewis in Cleveland, and Ames in the San Francisco Bay area—NASA had so far been promised only the navy's Vanguard group, which would become the core of a new space center outside Washington, D.C., later named for Robert Goddard. In addition, NASA was assigned ARPA's budget authority over the Explorer scientific satellites, the Pioneer Moon probes, and the F-1 engine project, as well as responsibility for the "Man in Space" project, soon dubbed Project Mercury. Eisenhower and his advisers found the interservice battle over human spaceflight distasteful and could see no compelling military rationale for what was primarily a prestige program versus the Soviets. A primary motivation for creating NASA in the first place had been the belief, shared by Dwight Eisenhower and Lyndon Johnson, that the United States needed separate civilian and scientific space programs for reasons of international image. But it was not at all clear that the agency would become a major player in the space business. Many expected the air force to dominate in the end, as it continued to run most national security space projects and fly piloted space planes too. In any scenario, there did not appear to be a secure place in space for the army.[3]

Glennan knew immediately that he wanted JPL as a center for electronics and deep space probes, but ABMA was so big and expensive, with its massive in-house development and manufacturing capability, that he commissioned a study from his new chief for spaceflight operations, Dr. Abraham (Abe) Silverstein, a brilliant, combative engineer from the Lewis Research Center. Silverstein had been among the small group there who had worked on advanced rocket concepts such as liquid hydrogen as a propulsion fuel. He immediately recommended taking about half of von Braun's division, around two thousand people.[4]

Glennan lined up support from the president and his chief science adviser, James Killian. Feeling he was on the verge of winning, on 10 October he went to see Deputy Defense Secretary Donald Quarles, and Quarles asked him to go down the hall to meet Secretary of the Army Brucker. Glennan details what happened next:

> I began, in a halting fashion, to discuss the situation and finally made the proposal that we take over a substantial portion of von Braun's operation and the Jet Propulsion Laboratory. It immediately became apparent that "fools rush in where angels fear to tread."
>
> Brucker became irate, and while stating the desire of the Army to be helpful, said he could not countenance . . . "breaking up the von Braun team." To an extent, this was a proper characterization. I had not realized how much of a pet of the Army's von Braun and his operation had become. He was its one avenue to fame in the space business. . . . I finally left with my tail between my legs.[5]

To Brucker, von Braun, and Medaris, Glennan's proposal looked like a recipe for disaster. Von Braun's division then had 3,925 employees, and the rest of ABMA had 1,081 mostly administrative personnel, for a total of 5,006. Separating out 2,100 or 2,200, the figure NASA finally specified, would have been long, messy, and expensive. Von Braun explained his view in a November letter to his parents:

> Because NASA was tasked quite officially from the President and Congress with taking over all spaceflight projects, it is plain that we would be all too pleased to work for them. The trouble was only that NASA's (for us very flattering) wish to take over the whole thing was impossible for lack of money, and thus someone had the genial idea to slice through the shop and take only half. The question was then: Which half? Only the brains, so that the brains wouldn't have any hands with which to build? Or only half of the pyramid, sliced from top to bottom? How could one then have dealt with a test stand with its crew or a guidance laboratory? On top of that, we had urgent military projects, above all Jupiter, to finish, and a radical internal reorganization would have seriously delayed these jobs.[6]

Medaris, trying to derail what appeared to be a fast-moving express train, responded with an old Washington trick: the anonymous leak. While in the national capital on 14 October, he met with a friend, the *Baltimore Sun's* military correspondent. The next morning, under a front-page headline, the *Sun* carried his story that the Huntsville "scientists," led by von Braun, were opposed to "breaking up" his team, which would have serious consequences for army missile development. Glennan was furious. ABMA followed it up by releasing a statement from von Braun that day: "It would seem something less than prudent to risk the dissolution of such an asset at a time when the national security and prestige demand a unified effort to achieve and maintain supremacy in rocket and space technology." By "dissolution" von Braun was alluding to the real possibility that he and his top managers would disperse to much-better-paying industry jobs, rather than accept the transfer. This statement by "America's No. 1 space scientist" (*Baltimore Sun*) was quoted in newspapers from coast to coast and probably more than anything else made it politically impossible for Glennan to win.[7]

The NASA Administrator clearly had made a fundamental mistake in asking for half of von Braun's shop, but he was operating within the budget-conscious constraints of Ike's space policy. Von Braun and company did not feel comfortable until November, but it gradually became apparent that Glennan had lost the public relations battle. On 3 December 1958 the army and NASA concluded a peace treaty, a cooperative agreement in which ABMA would work on contract. Glennan won, however, on the issue of JPL, which was transferred to NASA the same day. The Caltech trustees and the JPL scientists and engineers were more than happy to get the laboratory away from military dominance and into NASA as the center for lunar and planetary exploration. That meant the eventual end of the close alliance between Huntsville and Pasadena that had prevailed since 1955.[8]

Just before the public crisis erupted, ABMA had become involved with the agency in another way. A small delegation from NASA's new Space Task Group (STG), based at the Langley center in Hampton, Virginia, came to Huntsville on 6 October to talk about their "Man in Space" project. Over the summer the army had continued to push Adam in Washington, to no avail, in spite of CIA support for the project's propaganda aspect. Von Braun himself had far from given up; when the space agency delegation sat down with them, the STG's Paul Purser reported that "von Braun expounded at length on the merits of ADAM, future possibilities, etc. Finally I interrupted, graciously, I hope," and explained that his group had the full backing of ARPA and NASA to do the human spaceflight mission, and that suborbital missions on the Redstone were a sensible precursor to launching into orbit on the Atlas ICBM. "With the air thus cleared we got down to business." Huntsville was to work up a proposal for ten Redstones and three Jupiter IRBMs, the latter to test the Space Task Group's bell-shaped capsule in higher-speed reentries. It may not have been von Braun's spacecraft, but at least it would be part of the program that would put the first American into space; it did not even occur to him to launch a woman.[9]

From the first von Braun's public image was very much tied up with the touchy relationship between his team and the Space Task Group, which started with only forty-five people but would rapidly evolve into the NASA human spaceflight center in Houston, Texas—a counterpart and rival to Huntsville. The head of the STG and later of Houston, Robert R. (Bob) Gilruth, was a forty-five-year-old aeronautical engineer who had started at Langley just before World War II. Like many of his contemporaries, he could not quite forgive von Braun's work for the Nazis, but von Braun's opportunism made him even more uncomfortable. Gilruth, a reticent Minnesotan whose completely bald pate made him look older than his years, summed up his attitude in the spring of 1959: "Von Braun doesn't care what flag he fights for." He made this remark to Christopher Columbus Kraft, Jr., the subordinate who was in the process of inventing Mission Control.[10]

Later that year Chris Kraft would have a run-in with von Braun at a party in Dallas that put on display the tensions between the two organizations. "Von Braun's notoriety and fame made him the only person in the room whom everybody knew or recognized. He was accustomed to being the center of attention. It didn't take him long to tell me that our mission control center concept was all wrong." As Kraft notes, von Braun was "an experienced pilot" going back to Germany and saw the Mercury capsule as just another "flying machine." (Indeed, von Braun had begun flying again in 1957, ultimately to achieve a multiengine airline pilot rating in 1968.) Moreover, "Wernher had a Teutonic arrogance that he'd honed to a fine edge. He saw himself as the number one expert in the world on rockets and space travel and had polished that self-image with magazine articles, books, lectures and technical papers." In his contributions to *Collier's*, Disney, and elsewhere, one might add, von Braun had never foreseen a mission control that kept his space travelers on a short leash. He was not about to back off from his point of view, but then neither was Kraft. The two got into an argument that became increasingly loud until Maria von Braun skillfully interrupted her husband and led him away.[11]

While cooperation between Huntsville and STG in Project Mercury went well overall, for the simple reason that Redstone was already a sound vehicle, the original plan for Mercury-Redstone launches by the end of 1959 or early 1960 soon fell by the wayside. The capsule was a much more complex problem than expected, but von Braun and his associates, in the name of reliability, also introduced more testing and more changes to the Redstone—the kind of changes that produced grumbling about German overengineering. Moreover, as guided missile people the ABMA engineers wanted a completely automated abort sensing system to signal when the escape rockets on top of the capsule should fire to yank it away from a failing booster, leading to longer debates about the role of man in the control loop.[12]

Still, as a frustrated space traveler von Braun bonded completely with the seven new Mercury astronauts when they visited Huntsville in June 1959. He told Bill Pickering:

> They are the most wonderful bunch of people you've ever seen. No daredevils by a long shot, but serious, sober, dedicated and balanced individuals . . .
>
> You immediately feel that these men are thrilled by the challenge of their assignment, but they deeply resent the suggestion that they are human guinea pigs rather than engineering test pilots.

The astronauts in turn were pleasantly surprised to find that von Braun did not embody some authoritarian Teutonic stereotype but rather was multi-talented and charming, with interests far beyond science and engineering.[13]

In December 1958 von Braun expanded his team's role in Mercury when he successfully talked STG into using the Jupiter instead of the Thor for long-range, unmanned tests, as it would not require dealing with yet another contractor. He promised that ABMA would match the prices and delivery dates of the air force for Thor. But when Huntsville had to raise its overhead charge in the summer of 1959 because of financial troubles in the ABMA budget, NASA eliminated the Mercury-Jupiter flights altogether.[14]

Huntsville's problems were a sign of a deeper malaise that set in at the end of 1958. The Jupiter IRBM program, after being incredibly urgent since the beginning, suddenly was cut back because diplomatic troubles delayed deployment to Europe. In the end there would be only forty-five Jupiters in Italy and Turkey, and these were not deployed until 1960–61. With that program passing its development peak and the air force certain never to assign another ballistic missile project to Huntsville, and with the Pershing missile contracted to Martin, it was clear that almost all future work to sustain ABMA's expensive, in-house capability would have to come from ARPA or NASA. But ARPA did not have enough money to fund the Saturn project adequately because of Eisenhower administration budget limits for FY 1960, leading von Braun to make a public plea in January 1959 for an extra $50 million to $60 million for the big rocket. He did not get it. The question of transferring them to NASA thus might well come up again.[15]

On 16 January 1959 von Braun wrote a fascinating "Personal—Confidential" memo to Medaris revealing what he and his German lab directors thought about the civilian space agency. Entitled "Team Stability," it was based on discussions with his key managers over Christmas and presented an alarmist picture of "the very imminent danger of loss of a number of our key scientists and engineers" due to "highly attractive and lucrative offers from industry." Such offers were "not new," but "frustration is . . . rather widespread."[16]

Based on his discussions with his deputies, von Braun instead proposed that "rather than becoming attached to another government agency . . . where we would again have to operate under all the handicaps" of the civil service, "such a transfer would be the logical moment to convert our organization from a government agency to a company-operated industrial plant."

> The reason for this is <u>not</u> lack of confidence in NASA as such, or in Dr. Glennan's leadership. It is rather the fear of all our accomplishments with the Army, won over so many years of struggle, to adapt to Civil Service procedures at least half-ways to our unusual needs, would be lost if we were suddenly (and as an orphan child adopted into an existing family!) confronted with the old, well-entrenched NACA bureaucracy wherein most of our administrative accomplishments and streamlined procedures are unknown. In other words, the aspect of "having to fight the war all over again" would be so depressing to our lab chiefs that they would prefer to take a less worrysome [sic], less frustrating and better-paying job with some existing missile contractor.[17]

Von Braun did not mention that his proposed conversion to an industrial firm was essentially what had happened to the Peenemünde group in 1944, when the German army and the Speer ministry had turned von Braun's development group into a government corporation to keep it out of direct control by Himmler's SS. Medaris apparently did not respond in writing to the memo, but in the months afterward subordinates of von Braun's informally discussed an industrial takeover with Raytheon and with Solar Aircraft in California "to rescue them from NASA."[18] The idea was fundamentally unrealistic, however, reflecting among other things von Braun's lifelong naiveté about national politics, whatever nation he was in. There was little likelihood of the U.S. government privatizing a major civil service agency in 1959, even though transfers from the military to civilian agencies were on the table. Eisenhower may have wanted to restrain federal budget growth based on a traditional conservative ideology, but he was not dealing with a Republican right that wanted to privatize government services.

Despite the anxiety that hung over Huntsville in the winter of 1958–59, the JPL-built lunar probes Pioneer III and IV brought yet more glory and fame to Wernher von Braun. The country had already held its breath through three air force Moon shots, one unnamed, but of these only Pioneer I was even partially satisfactory. It fell just short of the required escape velocity on 11 October, ascending over 71,000 mi (114,000 km) before falling back to Earth. To the world press, that still seemed like a marvelous achievement when no man-made object had ever gone higher than a couple of thousand miles.[19]

For Pioneer III on 6 December, the arrangements for von Braun were much the same as Explorer I: he and Pickering were told to wait out the firing in the Pentagon, thus missing the first Juno II launch. Afterward the two went to another news conference on the graveyard shift—this time 3:15 a.m. at NASA, which had taken title to the Moon program. The results were much like Pioneer I. The Juno II, already marginal for the job, had small shortfalls in performance that resulted in a failure to reach escape velocity. The tiny 13-lb (5.9-kg) probe rose to 63,500 mi (102,200 km) and fell back but broadcast much better radiation data than Pioneer I, clearly showing that there were two Van Allen belts, not just one. As von Braun told the panel on the national TV program *Meet the Press* on Sunday the seventh, the failure was actually advantageous, as the scientists got two cross-sections of the belts, one going up and one coming down.[20]

The second attempt would not come for three months due to changes in the launch vehicle and spacecraft. In the meantime the Soviets once again had another stirring and worrying triumph. On 2 January 1959 Sergei Korolev's team sent off Luna 1 (the Western press insisted on calling it Lunik) after two earlier, secret launch failures. Luna weighed an impressive 800 lb (360 kg) and in two days flew by the Moon, the first human object to escape the Earth. Korolev had been aiming to hit the lunar surface, but the rocket's guidance system was not quite good enough. No one in the West knew that, and in the USSR few cared but him. For Khrushchev, it was a new propaganda coup that produced yet more Western hand-wringing; *Time* said that the space race "may decide whether freedom has any future."[21]

ABMA's answer came on 3 March. This time von Braun watched in the blockhouse as Pioneer IV was sent on its way. Juno II performed perfectly, and JPL's gold-plated cone sailed past the Moon eighty-two hours later at a distance of 37,000 mi (60,000 km), the first U.S. spacecraft to go into orbit around the Sun. Returning home the next day, he got another hero's welcome. He reported to his parents: "Huntsville has been turned upside down. Victory parade in a column of cars through the decorated city, with a band in front. Iris and Margrit sat beside me on the backseat of the open car and were completely astonished by the cheers and hoopla." The rapidly growing boom town, which styled itself "Rocket City U.S.A." and then "Space Capital of the Universe," had long since abandoned any skepticism about von Braun, the Germans, or the army.[22]

The spring and summer of 1959 saw von Braun's usual frantic round of activities, including the successful recovery of a Jupiter IRBM nose cone with monkeys Able and Baker inside in May, but no issue seemed quite as consequential as the Saturn project, on which the future of his team depended. Money was short, but there were heartening signs of progress too: Rocketdyne sent the first H-1 engine to ABMA for testing in late April, and with Jupiter missile production handed off to Chrysler, the Fab Lab began to build the first huge, non-flying Saturn test booster, SA-T, in June. In May, after several systems studies and many presentations by von Braun, ARPA ordered that the Saturn's second stage be based on the air force's Titan ICBM, being constructed by the Martin company outside Denver. But that reckoned without ABMA's old nemesis, General Schriever's Ballistic Missile Division, which threw up roadblocks to direct communication with Denver on the ground that it might interfere in urgent ICBM development. While that issue dragged on, ARPA also tried to induce the air force to consider launching its Dyna-Soar space glider on Saturn, but BMD put together an alternate, cheaper proposal for bundled Titans called Titan-C. The problem was that Saturn lacked any clear mission beyond launching a twenty-four-hour-orbit communications satellite that the Army Signal Corps was to build for the Defense Department. The air force wanted no part of it because it was army; NASA could take only a secondary interest because it was not the agency's responsibility. Saturn's fate would stand at the heart of the second crisis over the disposition of von Braun's Development Operations Division, one that would erupt at the end of August.[23]

The key actor was a rising star, the young nuclear-bomb physicist Herbert York, who had spent nearly a year as chief scientist at ARPA on his way to becoming the first director of defense research and engineering in late 1958—another administration attempt to control the fractious services. Agreeing with critics who thought that the army was becoming too distracted from its core combat mission, York set out to rationalize the military space program by pushing Saturn, followed by most of ABMA, into NASA, leaving the air force with the dominant position in military space applications. But he must have felt that he had to proceed in a rather Machiavellian fashion, because what he appeared to do was try to cancel the superbooster altogether.[24]

The first warning signs came early in August 1959, with inquiries from York about Saturn's increasing costs, combined with NASA inquiries about what overhead it was going to be charged if other programs were eliminated—this just after the cancellation of Mercury-Jupiter. Medaris also heard the first rumors of a reordering of military space missions as a result of a long secret debate inside the Joint Chiefs of Staff, the upshot of which was a recommendation to Defense Secretary McElroy, over the objections of the army and navy, that the air force take control over military space launches and most satellites. ARPA would lose its role as the Defense space agency. The news got worse. On 29 August, while von Braun was in Germany for meetings on his movie and two major speeches, Medaris heard that York was about to try to cancel Saturn in favor of Titan-C, which was supposed to be less capable but a lot cheaper. Two days later Army Secretary Brucker sent Medaris a long series of questions to be answered immediately, the gist of which was, what would happen to ABMA if Saturn was canceled? The answer was pretty clear: within two years three-quarters of the staff would have to be laid off, and the von Braun team would probably break up.[25]

During an emergency Sunday morning gathering in Huntsville that included Eberhard Rees and other leading engineers, "several of our people felt that we should ally ourselves with Dr. Glennan[,] who had the real valid requirement for SATURN." Clearly the prospect of NASA no longer seemed so bad under the circumstances. But when the administrator arrived at ABMA on 3 September for a meeting, Glennan said that "NASA alone cannot . . . support" all of ABMA and had the budget for only twenty-five hundred man-years—about half, the same as in 1958. He definitely wanted Saturn but "believe[d] that the necessary situation could be achieved by ABMA becoming a Department of Defense agency, either singly or within the framework of a joint command." He had been badly burned by the 1958 battle and had promised Medaris not to try again.[26]

NASA's support for Saturn nonetheless helped save it, as did Cold War arguments about the need to catch up with the USSR's big lead in boosters. Just after von Braun returned from Europe, Sergei Korolev obliged by launching Luna 2, which became the first human object to hit the Moon—or any heavenly body—on 14 September. That day von Braun was in Washington to make Saturn presentations to a launch vehicles committee convened by York, but already in the morning Medaris phoned Brucker that the big booster was safe, partly as a result of the Russians.[27]

Brucker, however, was pessimistic about the draft directive giving the air force dominance over military space missions, and von Braun was already discussing jumping ship, much to the secretary's annoyance. Brucker called

Medaris again later on the fourteenth and told him that von Braun "had said . . . [that] he would go with who[m]ever had the money." For the first time Brucker questioned von Braun's loyalty to the army; Medaris defended him but asserted that "Dr. von Braun has said if this whole business did go to the Air Force, this would be the best solution—for them to go too." On the other hand, von Braun told York that "all I really want is a rich uncle"—an expression that he had used in the press as early as January 1959. It was a bald statement of opportunism that rather repelled the physicist.[28]

Wernher von Braun's first concern was keeping his organization intact, however, and not simply what was good for his space ambitions, and for that objective he thought the air force looked like a safer bet to come up with the funds. He also got encouragement from the air force that was unprecedented in view of Schriever's earlier opposition. During the York launcher committee meetings the air force assistant secretary for R&D, Joseph Charyk, approached von Braun with an offer. As Medaris described it in a highly restricted message for the chief of Ordnance, "Charyk told him that the Air Force would welcome ABMA. He said Schriever wanted the team and that the Air Force was in urgent need of creating a substitute for STL." STL was the Space Technologies Laboratories, the systems manager for Schriever's ICBM and space programs. The air force was getting considerable criticism at this time from contractors and congressmen about that company's privileged relationship with the air force even though it was a private contractor. Charyk told von Braun further that "the idea was that ABMA would be assigned the entire space field as the primary technical authority of the Air Force," while STL would retain missiles. "Charyk went on to say however that there was a considerable difference between the Defense Department and NASA as to which should have the responsibility for big boosters. He said this difference would be answered in the [National Aeronautics and] Space Council [a body chaired by the president]. . . . NASA was making a strong pitch for the booster responsibility."[29]

When von Braun asked Charyk about the opinion of Richard Horner of NASA, the prior holder of Charyk's job, von Braun found himself meeting Horner and Glennan at the latter's apartment to hear NASA's side. Medaris continues: "Wernher says he brought up the budget necessary for NASA to support big booster development. Glennan answered that he was sure that the money would go with this assignment, that NASA expected to present the matter to the Space Council for decision . . . , that he was reluctant to deal with any single service for his hardware and felt that the situation would be much better resolved with the assignment in NASA hands." In the end von Braun used a variant of his jocular but truthful line on Glennan:

"Look, all we want is a very rich and very benevolent uncle"—to which the administrator's later comment was "What a personality!" But based on his conversation with von Braun, Medaris thought that "Wernher was obviously most uncomfortable about the whole situation and attempted to make it clear that he had gotten sucked into these conversations just by 'trying to be polite.' He . . . did not want to operate in that field and hoped to stay away from the whole business until some decision was reached." Medaris in turn told von Braun that they would have to wait, but if "the decision went to NASA . . . for the big booster, the invitation to join up with NASA would then be open as representing the logical method for carrying out the situation." Indeed, by the time Medaris had written this memo, on 21 September 1959, McElroy had already signed the directive giving the air force dominance in military space, and Medaris had already told Brucker that it would be better for the army if NASA got the heart of ABMA, not the air force. Fed up, Medaris had also decided to retire in early 1960 but withheld that news from the press until the transfer decision was complete.[30]

For Glennan to have promised von Braun that he would have the budget to support Saturn and ABMA was a fundamental change. He must have received encouragement from Herbert York and others, because his statements differed markedly from those he made in Huntsville only two weeks previously. Right up to the final public announcement on 21 October, however, the press presented the matter as a battle to be decided by the president. But the cards were already stacked in favor of NASA. On the seventh, York, Glennan, presidential science adviser George Kistiakowsky, and General Andrew Goodpaster, Ike's close aide, discussed a draft directive to transfer the Development Operations Division to the civilian space agency. A few days later the Soviets one-upped the United States in the space race yet again: Korolev's Luna 3 returned the first, fuzzy photos of the far side of the Moon, a second lunar triumph in less than a month. Finally the president authorized a press release approving the transfer. After a year of on-again, off-again struggles, Glennan got what he wanted, and more than he originally thought he could afford: all of von Braun's division, instead of half.[31]

Von Braun himself may have remained dubious about NASA until the last minute. In a 4 October letter to his parents, he presented himself as happy that Saturn was safe but said that his group was "in the position of a beautiful young girl who has two suitors, and must be on alert that she marries honorably, and is not dishonorably led astray." Richard Horner later said that he and Glennan had to meet von Braun in a "Washington hotel room" the night before the 21 October announcement to counter von Braun's considerable misgivings about the plan. Although Horner might have been misremembering the meeting in Glennan's apartment a month earlier, von Braun did tell him that "the new baby agency wasn't really going to command . . . long-term support" and "that his long-term interest lay with the Air Force."[32]

Thus von Braun greeted the president's announcement with no little nostalgia for the army, but his overall reaction, and that of his colleagues, was one of relief and restrained enthusiasm. On the twenty-sixth he wrote Walt Wiesman (formerly Wiesemann), a Peenemünder who was representing him during the shooting of his movie in Munich:

> We hadn't asked for a divorce from the Army because our relationship had been quite happy, but after all this tug-of-war and uncertainty, we are all very happy that the President has made a clear decision and we now know where we belong. We have great confidence in Dr. Glennan, head of NASA, personally, and we know that the enthusiasm with which he accepted us in his fold is genuine. We think in the long run the NASA decision is right. Moreover, the very idea behind NASA's formation was to have an organization that pursues space flight for space flight's sake, and not because of some temporary military objectives connected with outer space.

The downside, he thought, was the agency's lack of experience in managing and contracting huge sums of money, but that problem would likely soon be overcome.[33]

The transfer to NASA almost immediately produced a fundamental technological decision for the Saturn program. During a series of Washington meetings in November and December 1959 to better define the new launcher, space operations chief Abe Silverstein pressed von Braun to convert all upper stages (i.e., all stages mounted on top of the clustered booster) to high-energy liquid hydrogen (LH_2) fuel; liquid oxygen (lox) would remain the oxidizer. Although von Braun had earlier accepted a smaller, air force–funded, liquid-hydrogen-fueled rocket called Centaur as a potential third stage, Silverstein wanted to go further, to a big LH_2 second stage. Von Braun, who had long been skeptical about this extremely cold (−423° F) and difficult-to-handle propellant, was worried about this leap, and he even went home to consult with his equally conservative engineers. But Silverstein and his compatriots were able to show that the rocket could lift almost as much payload if they put the Centaur third stage directly on top of the Saturn first stage as when they put a kerosene-fueled second stage in. Von Braun reluctantly conceded the point and accepted the change.[34]

In January 1960 any lingering reservations he and his compatriots had about NASA disappeared when Saturn truly became a national priority. The agency saw the big rocket as a heavy booster for robotic probes and satellites but above all as the future of the human spaceflight program, once the first tentative steps of Mercury had been taken. That gave Saturn a clear purpose and direction. After Senator Lyndon Johnson publicly supported the idea of giving von Braun another $100 million for the rocket, President Eisenhower reluctantly accepted the necessity of accelerating the project because of the space race's effect on American prestige around the world. He asked that the FY 1961 Saturn budget be raised from $140 million to $230 million and approved a top national priority rating.[35]

As the Senate majority leader's support indicates, von Braun had reached an enviable position in Congress, thanks to his visionary image and relentless advocacy for a space race, combined with the growing conviction that Saturn was the answer to catching up with the Soviets. The acerbic syndicated columnist Mary McGrory wrote after watching a February House hearing: "Only [FBI director] J. Edgar Hoover has a comparably dissolving effect on congressmen. . . . The hardest thing the German-born scientist has to do is to say 'down, boy' as eager congressmen press additional millions on him and beg him to tell them if he isn't treated right."[36]

As for the actual transfer to NASA, that would take many months of careful planning, and a huge amount of administrative work on von Braun's part, so that the Development Operations Division could operate independently from Redstone Arsenal and the rump of ABMA. The reconstruction of support services, plus the acceleration of Saturn and NASA's assignment of various launch vehicle and engine projects to manage, gave him room not only to protect the status quo but even to ask for manpower increases— more than Glennan wanted to provide, but he recognized von Braun's independent power on Capitol Hill. The new George C. Marshall Space Flight Center would come into business on 1 July 1960, still on the territory of Redstone Arsenal, with 5,500 civil servants and 1,189 on-site contractors, the largest NASA center by far. For the first time in his career, von Braun would not be the technical director: he would be in command of his own facility.[37]

Just as the battle over the future of von Braun's team moved to a crescendo in the fall of 1959, his movie, now titled *I Aim at the Stars*, began production. But it had not been easy. A year earlier his German producer, Friedrich Mainz, had already told him "that no film project had brought me anywhere near as many difficulties and unexpected events as our film." The complexity of generating a story treatment and script from a German-American coproduction in which Hollywood had the upper hand was one problem, as was the necessity of getting U.S. Defense Department and army clearances for those documents. Afterward there was always a list of comments to be incorporated, due to sensitivities about how to portray the army, General Toftoy, or General Medaris in a favorable light while not insulting the air force, the navy, and the Vanguard project. In question was primarily the American part of von Braun's career, up to its climactic conclusion with Explorer I. The military took little interest in the Third Reich segment of the story, because it did not touch on service concerns about image but also because the whole movie was predicated on a depiction of von Braun as a space dreamer persecuted by the Nazis and given a second chance by the United States.[38]

It was in the German scenes that the movie most departed from reality. Right from the first Hollywood story treatment in mid-1958, screenwriter George Froeschel, ironically a 1933 refugee from the Nazis, introduced purely fictional elements in the name of making the story palatable to an American audience: von Braun's secretary at Peenemünde became an Allied spy, romantically mixed up with an equally fictional Anton Reger, his best friend since the early rocket days. But Froeschel's treatment was weak and his plan to put von Braun into a love triangle with those two was thrown out in the first script draft by another writer, Jay Dratler, because it would hurt the family of the movie's main subject. Maria von Braun gained at least ten years so that she could become his fiancée even in the Peenemünde years, when she was just a young girl. Hermann Oberth became a constant presence as von Braun's mentor, although they had rarely been together, while no other key associates except Dornberger appeared under their real names. Whereas von Braun had argued that huge military-industrial teams were needed to carry out rocket development and space exploration, his movie group was effectively reduced to half a dozen people on the argument that Americans could not keep track of all those characters. Von Braun's true forte, the engineering management of giant enterprises, thus disappeared, to be replaced with a clichéd picture of the inventor-scientist.[39]

Most insidious was the screenwriters' depiction of von Braun as a blatant anti-Nazi forced to join the party to complete his work. The villains of course were the jackbooted SS, headed by a renamed caricature of General Kammler. The movie von Braun was given heavy-handed anti-Hitler and antiparty lines that would have been suicidal and, moreover, falsified his true feelings at any time before 1943–44. Although the real von Braun would later forswear much responsibility for how the script came out, saying he was the captive of Hollywood pressures, he in fact wrote two multipage commentaries that, for all their suggested changes, explicitly approved or silently accepted both the fictional elements and the unconscious falsifications that arose from the screenwriters' attempts to turn his quasi-official biography into a dramatic film.[40] As his later, clear memory of events at Mittelbau-Dora shows, he had not forgotten all the scandals omitted from that biography, but he certainly seems to have begun to believe in his own mythology, or at least its power over other people; otherwise he would not have risked the chance of exposure that critical scrutiny might bring.

For all the efforts of the screenwriters and producers to depict von Braun as a noble dreamer, the final script shows that they were discomfited by having to explain away his working for the Nazis and then so easily changing sides. Dratler's April 1959 first draft introduced an American character, a major who lost his family in a V-2 attack on London. He becomes a hectoring presence after the war as an intelligence officer and then as a journalist who keeps hounding von Braun with hostile, Germanophobic questions about why he shouldn't be hanged at Nuremberg and why "scientists" like him would serve any master who supplies them with funds. Von Braun himself approved of this clumsy plot device, saying it was necessary to embody the criticism of him in one of the characters. The film also explicitly raises the issue of the Faustian bargain. When his movie mother urges him not to join the party, von Braun insists on its necessity for staying at Peenemünde. She comments: "Long ago, they said witches made a pact with the devil, so they could fly on broomsticks." He replies: "My broomsticks fly without the devil's help. But if they didn't—I guess I'd be willing to sign with him." This line was obviously meant to underline his single-mindedness about space travel; for once this willfully inaccurate movie hit a vein of truth.[41]

To play von Braun, Columbia Pictures and the chief American producer Charles Schneer insisted on using Curd Jürgens (which the studio often anglicized as Curt Jurgens), the only German actor with a reputation as a leading man in Hollywood. Jürgens even looked like von Braun; he had the same massive football-player physique, and he was even taller than the man he played. But as Mainz pointed out, he was much too old to be von Braun in Germany, and was too stolid and uninteresting an actor. As for the director, Schneer hired J. Lee Thompson, an up-and-coming Englishman who would be best known for his next movie, *The Guns of Navarone*. Apparently it was a conscious choice to answer potential critics by using someone whose nationality did not suggest sympathy for the V-2's architect.

When Thompson and von Braun met in Munich at the beginning of September 1959, that choice was revealed as a fiasco. On their way to visit the German producer, Mainz, the two immediately started arguing in the car about whether von Braun was a "traitor," leading to an "18-hour, non-stop row" over the script. At least that was the perhaps hyperbolic account that Royal Air Force veteran Thompson gave the London *Daily Express* two weeks later, in a move hardly inclined to create favorable publicity for the film he was about to direct. Thompson's view, much like that of Bob Gilruth at NASA, was that von Braun had changed sides much too easily, betraying his country. As von Braun himself pointed out, it was a rather simplistic Anglo-American view of the morality of the situation—would it have been better to be loyal to Hitler to the bitter end? Would it have made more sense to allow themselves to be captured by the Soviets?[42]

While the encounter with Thompson in Munich boded ill for the movie project, the rest of von Braun's German trip underlined his heroic status in West Germany; the Communist East was another matter. He gave a closed speech at the Bonn Defense Ministry, and President Theodor Heuss presented the Great Service Cross of the German Order of Merit, a recognition of von Braun's impact on American and world opinion of Germans. Sigismund, now protocol chief of the Foreign Office in Bonn, was present, along with his family. Two days later, on 6 September 1959, Wernher gave a very high-profile speech in Frankfurt at St. Paul's Church, a symbol of German democracy as the seat of the ill-fated parliament of the 1848 revolution. His report on the present and future of space exploration, made for the fiftieth anniversary of an historic aviation exhibition, could not avoid the topic of the Janus-faced rocket as an instrument of both science and war. He ultimately declared it "unfair" to blame scientists and engineers for the weapons they create, as they were caught up in larger social and political forces.[43]

The fact that his parents were able to attend the speech, and that he had visited them beforehand in Munich, was a highlight of the trip. A month or so later Magnus and Emmy von Braun were given a royal tour of the movie sets outside Munich, meeting the principal actors. These occasions became a comfort to him, as his mother died not long thereafter. She was rushed into the hospital for an emergency colon cancer operation just before her seventy-third birthday on 3 November. According to Sigismund's son, when Emmy was unable to sleep, she demonstrated her astonishing memory by citing thousands of lines of Goethe's *Faust Parts One* and *Two* by heart. She never left the hospital, dying shortly after Christmas. Her death was a hard personal blow for Wernher, as his mother was the one who had particularly encouraged his space dreams. To escape with his thoughts, he spent a long night observing the stars alone with the 16-in (41-cm) reflector of the local astronomical club he headed. Due to short notice and lack of time, he was unable to attend her funeral, but he told his father that he had wanted to stay away anyway because his presence might have turned it into a media circus.[44]

Von Braun hoped to make a quick visit to his mother's grave in January 1960, appended to a London trip to review the first cut of the film. That idea was canceled, however, when the American producer, Charles Schneer, decided that he had to have a screening in Washington for Pentagon officials as part of the clearance process. When von Braun viewed the film on 18 February, he was satisfied with it, telling his father that is was "quite gripping. . . . It has no dull moments, is full of tempo and style and the human conflicts are believable and clear." He did not tell him that they did have some substantive complaints about lines in the movie that touched directly on the issue of opportunism. He and others in the screening room objected to the embittered major, Taggert, saying sarcastically about the United States using the German rocketeers: "When Judas kissed Jesus that was expediency." And Maria von Braun, who had also attended, objected to this comment put in her husband's mouth: "The main thing is we are all now on the victorious side." That to her sounded too much "like unscrupulous expediency." These changes set off a long-distance battle with the director, Lee Thompson, who hated these interventions in his film, whereas von Braun felt the director was trying to undermine him, although these lines were in the final approved script. Since von Braun was insistent and the Pentagon held ultimate approval over the movie, he got his way. The lines were removed or voiced over.[45]

In the meantime Maria von Braun took advantage of the new transatlantic jet service to fly to Berlin and visit her parents in January. She accelerated the date of her trip because of a very pleasant surprise: she was pregnant again, seven years after the birth of Margrit. The baby arrived at the beginning of June 1960, a huge (9 lb, 22 in) son they named Peter Constantine, for her brother Pieter and his old friend Constantine Generales. Wernher told his father that "he was completely overjoyed." At last there was a boy to carry on the family name.[46]

Three weeks later came the next event for *I Aim at the Stars*, a congressional preview sponsored by Alabama senators John Sparkman and Lister Hill; needless to say, von Braun had cultivated good relations with these southern Democrats, especially Sparkman, who came from the Huntsville area. On second viewing his misgivings increased, but that was not something he would ever admit in public. He told his father that "it had some noticeable weaknesses . . . , but it was clearly not so easy to cram 30 years into 1½ hours." But the audience was pleased. Afterward he was surrounded by women who told a reporter that they found him younger and better-looking than the movie star who played him.[47]

After von Braun nixed the idea of a formal premiere in Stockholm for the IAF congress in August because it might offend Soviet-bloc delegates, the producers decided on Munich. He was skeptical of that place too, not knowing how the Germans would react to the movie, but eventually gave in. On 23 July he and Maria flew to Zürich for a three-week vacation in Switzerland. (Peter was left with a nurse, Margrit with neighbors, and Iris was already in Europe with relatives.) During that time he got to see his father. Afterward he flew to Stockholm, then back to Munich for the event on 19 August.[48]

His earlier concern turned out to be justified. "Film on Von Braun Has a Stormy Bow," said *The New York Times* the next day. Despite his departure to NASA, the U.S. Army saw the movie as advertising and put on a massive show in front of the movie theater in downtown Munich: three unarmed tactical nuclear missiles were lined up on the street, an army band played for the huge crowd, and several generals showed up in full uniform. Fifty policemen were needed to hold back the crush, which was dominated by people who just wanted to catch a glimpse of von Braun and Jürgens. But in that era of nuclear fear, with Khrushchev provoking episodic crises over isolated West Berlin, a hundred or so pacifist, ban-the-bomb demonstrators made their presence felt, and the army's pompous show only provoked them further. The demonstrators handed out leaflets demanding that von Braun quit work on weapons that "could help cause the grisly deaths of millions of people"—perhaps they did not know that he for the most part already had, although not for reasons of conscience. (Marshall Space Flight Center did have a temporary military division to complete development work on Jupiter and Pershing.) At a news conference before the premiere, von Braun, accompanied by Jürgens, had to answer "critics, mostly British, who complained that the film whitewashed and made a hero of a man who helped to make the Nazi V-2 bombs that hit Britain in World War II." He replied: "I have very deep and sincere regret for the victims of the V-2 rockets, but there were victims on both sides. . . . A war is a war, and when my country is at war, my duty is to help win that war."[49]

The Munich premiere was only the first of several incidents. When Lee Thompson showed the movie at the Edinburgh Film Festival a few days later, he told the press: "Von Braun and I disliked each other on sight. After a time, I grew almost to like him—almost, but not quite." Antwerp, the forgotten target of more V-weapons than London, forbade the showing of *I Aim at the Stars*, a fact reported in the world press. In New York the October opening was picketed by ban-the-bomb demonstrators, but a few signs also denounced von Braun as a Nazi. In London the December British premiere attracted protests with a local flavor. Demonstrators inside the theater showered down leaflets denouncing the film as "a mockery of the tributes to our fallen dead." Two men unfurled a banner reading, "Nazi Braun's V-2 Rockets Killed and Maimed 9,000 Londoners." The U.S. premiere, by contrast, was completely tame. The movie opened on 28 September in Washington, D.C., with a benefit for army wives, and von Braun escorted the First Lady, Mamie Eisenhower, into the theater. As always, he defended the film as substantially accurate, but what he really thought of it is revealed by his friend, the aerospace journalist Erik Bergaust. On a prearranged signal he escaped the reception afterward and went home with the Bergausts, telling them in the car that he did not like the movie very much.[50]

The protests were colorful, but that was not what did the movie in. Although *I Aim at the Stars* gathered some positive reviews, influential outlets panned the film and the public stayed away. *The New York Times* reviewer called it "poorly written" and a "sluggish and plot-logged affair." The reviewer for *Time* denounced it for "platitudes about the moral dereliction of the scientific community—personified in Von Braun. The moviemakers . . . have leaned over backward to stress his war guilt, with the unhappy result that the hero comes off as a jolly accomplice in mass murder. . . . Von Braun possibly has grounds for a libel suit, but then he might do better to ignore the picture. So might everybody else." The rocket engineer, who professed himself to be thick-skinned, claimed not to have been bothered by hostile reviews, which never seemed to criticize him anyway, in contrast to the actors, producers, or director. But by the beginning of 1961 it became obvious that the movie was a bomb at the box office, which also meant that his share of the net profit would be zero.[51]

In the larger scheme of things, *I Aim at the Stars* was at most a minor setback in his career, a momentary distraction overshadowed by the rise of Saturn and his new space center. Between the Munich and Washington premieres, the president had come to Huntsville on 8 September to dedicate the facility to his old mentor General Marshall, the only army general to win a Nobel Peace Prize. Von Braun basked in this new presidential encounter, riding around in an open car with Ike and showing him the giant new Saturn first stage in the Fab Lab. Eisenhower went away happy and wrote a nice personal thank you to von Braun, but he still resented the rocket engineer for relentlessly campaigning for more space money. A couple of years later Herbert York asked Eisenhower about his famous January 1961 farewell address. Who did he have in mind when he warned about "public policy" becoming "captive of a scientific-technological elite"? Eisenhower replied unhesitantly: "(Edward) Teller and (Wernher) von Braun."[52]

But the movie was not without impact, if only because it saddled von Braun with one of the most famous put-downs of his career. The sardonic comic Mort Sahl joked that *I Aim at the Stars* should have been subtitled *But Sometimes I Hit London*, a line that has been repeated ever since. Von Braun, intoxicated by his fame and how it might be used to promote his space goals, and tempted by the money, had encouraged a project that could not avoid raising uncomfortable questions about his Nazi collaboration and his opportunism. He was lucky that the Western press had so little interest in digging further, although a hostile article in the sensationalist magazine *Confidential* did discuss "the slaves in the underground factory at Nordhausen [who] sweated and died to put together the V-2 parts."[53] Certainly Wernher von Braun was in over his head in a movie business that he knew nothing about, but in the end he went along willingly with this falsification of his past. And although it raised his profile in the short run, it also marked the beginning of the slow downward curve of his celebrity, which had risen so high after Sputnik and Explorer I. As a symbol of the Cold War battle with the Communists in space, he would gradually be displaced by others, most notably the astronauts. But all this scarcely mattered to him. The dream project of his life was within reach: the first human trip to the Moon.

CHAPTER FIFTEEN

Before This Decade Is Out

1960–63

Of course, the Moon [had] a romantic connotation for me as a young guy, but I must confess, that as soon as President Kennedy announced we were going to land there within this decade, I began to identify it [the Moon in the sky] more and more with the target in space and time. . . . It was a constant reminder, "We'll get you before this decade is out." —WERNHER VON BRAUN[1]

At nine a.m. on 21 November 1960 von Braun watched from the old Redstone blockhouse as the first unmanned Mercury-Redstone was about to lift off. What unfolded, however, was a comic fiasco, as the vehicle rose a few inches, fell back on the launch ring, and tottered precariously in place, unconnected to any ground power or command systems. The Mercury capsule's automatic systems, meanwhile, thinking the launch was over, jettisoned the escape tower, which went roaring off in a cloud of smoke. The parachutes followed, popping out of the capsule and hanging limply over the side. If the wind picked up, they could fill, toppling the fueled rocket and provoking a fiery explosion.[2]

Inside the armored blockhouse, one of the ex-Peenemünders, Albert Zeiler, suggested getting a rifle and shooting holes in the liquid-oxygen tank to relieve pressurization. Von Braun must have supported the idea; otherwise Zeiler never would have discussed it on the open circuits. But a few miles away in Mercury Control, flight director Chris Kraft and his colleagues were appalled at this bizarre suggestion. In the end, they decided to do nothing. The winds were supposed to remain calm, so if the booster was left alone, the batteries would eventually run down, the liquid-oxygen tank valve would pop open, and the oxygen would evaporate. The next morning workers were able to disarm the vehicle and empty the alcohol fuel. They found a ground power plug with one prong shorter than the other because a worker had filed it to make it fit, and when the plug pulled out during launch, as it was supposed to, the difference in disconnection time triggered a cut-off signal to the engine. It was a lesson in the need to document every change in hardware.[3]

The infamous "four-inch flight" would mark the nadir of morale in Project Mercury, following as it did launch failures with the big Atlas and with the small Little Joe used for tests of the escape tower. When von Braun told the press that the escape tower firing was only "a little mishap," he earned an unusual amount of skepticism, even ridicule. Certainly any hope for putting the first astronaut into space on MR-3 in January 1961 was gone, and with it a good chance of beating the Soviets. But more important, it made NASA's human spaceflight program look bumbling and possibly disastrous at a very sensitive time.[4]

Thirteen days earlier Senator John F. Kennedy had narrowly beaten Vice President Richard Nixon in the presidential election. Many in NASA pinned hopes on Kennedy for a more energetic space program. Von Braun was one of them. We do not know how he voted in 1956, or whether he registered Democrat or Republican, but from a letter from his wife, we do know that they voted for Kennedy in 1960. Von Braun had actually met the then-very-young senator in New York at the end of 1953, when both were on a TV program, and came away so impressed that he told his wife that Kennedy could be president one day. By the end of the 1950s, thoroughly fed up with Eisenhower's moderately paced space program, von Braun eagerly accepted JFK's calls for more missile and space money and a more militant Cold War stance.[5]

He and other NASA leaders particularly hoped that Kennedy's budget would include Project Apollo, a program to send three astronauts around the Moon, announced, with unfortunate timing, on 29 July 1960, the very day that Mercury-Atlas 1 (MA-1) had exploded in flight. In the fall Eisenhower pointedly excluded Apollo from his last budget, saying there was no obvious justification for human spaceflight beyond the Mercury experiment. Despite Kennedy's rhetoric, and the presence on the ticket of his prospace running mate, Lyndon Johnson, there was no guarantee that the Kennedy administration would support a new, expensive program either. Kennedy's designated science adviser, Dr. Jerome Wiesner, proved to be a skeptic who led an ad hoc transition committee in writing an unfriendly report about the Mercury program. He did not think the new president should closely associate himself with something that might well lead to killing an astronaut on national television.[6]

From these rather unpromising beginnings, and with as yet no human spaceflight experience at all, NASA would find itself telling Kennedy and Johnson in April 1961 that it could land a man on the Moon, perhaps as early as 1967. It was a monumental challenge, potentially one of the greatest engineering feats in human history, and the culmination of von Braun's boyhood dream. But just figuring out how to accomplish and manage such a gigantic undertaking would be a major hurdle. During the years 1961–63 the Kennedy administration and NASA leadership would make three fundamental decisions for the Apollo program: committing to a lunar landing, then deciding how it would be done, and finally figuring out how to manage the lunar landing program and its launch vehicles. Von Braun would be centrally involved in each one of those decisions. In the process, he would be forced to transform the management structure of the Marshall Space Flight Center, and with it the culture of his center, in order to integrate it into a national effort far larger than the self-contained arsenal-system approach of Peenemünde and Huntsville.

Nothing more clearly indicates the impact of Soviet space accomplishments on American aerospace engineers than this rush to go to the Moon. Like many other space enthusiasts, von Braun was all too happy to postpone the winged space shuttle and the space station—the elaborate infrastructure he had claimed was needed for any deep space forays—in favor of a shortcut to a manned lunar landing. In truth, he simply wanted to go there, but realizing that he was getting too old to be in the first human lunar expedition, he at least wanted to play a central part in a historic enterprise that also had a good chance of beating the Soviets.[7] But if von Braun had been allowed to put the first satellite in orbit in 1956–57, the space race would have taken an entirely different course and the American public and its leaders would likely never have funded such a hugely expensive project. Now it appeared to be one of the few big, prestigious space programs that the United States had a good chance of winning, if only because the technological leap was so large that it potentially canceled out the Russian advantage in big boosters.

Von Braun first outlined a lunar shortcut back in late 1958. His novella *First Men to the Moon*, published in *This Week*, used what NASA would call the "direct ascent" approach to a lunar landing: a giant rocket would launch a smaller human craft directly at the Earth's only natural satellite. Turning around as it approached the Moon, the spacecraft would ignite a landing stage to alight directly on the lunar surface without going into orbit; that stage would provide the launch platform for the reentry vehicle to propel itself back to Earth. In actual practice, however, von Braun and his advanced missions people at ABMA, Ernst Stuhlinger and H. H. Koelle, tended to favor what NASA would call the "Earth-orbit rendezvous" method, that is, assembling and fueling the lunar landing vehicle in orbit around the home planet. The rest of the mission would be the same as direct ascent. The huge vehicle, which NASA would call Nova, could thereby be avoided, and more powerful versions of the giant but manageable Saturn could launch multiple payloads into orbit for assembly. This was the conservative approach that von Braun advocated to NASA at the end of 1958 when trying to sell Saturn, and it came up again in Project Horizon, an ABMA lunar base study carried out in 1959, and in an early 1960 proposal derived from it, "A Lunar Exploration Program Based upon Saturn-Boosted Systems"—this just after Saturn's acceleration and the announcement of transfer to NASA. Von Braun thus already had a considerable track record of trying to sell a fast lunar landing program before 1961.[8]

As NASA began to formulate its post-Mercury human spaceflight program in 1959, many others felt the same way. A study committee in midyear picked the lunar goal, which bolstered the space agency's interest in Saturn just as the fate of ABMA again came into play. Later in 1959 Milton Rosen, who had come from Vanguard to work in the launch vehicles office at NASA headquarters, pushed direct ascent and the use of liquid hydrogen in all upper stages, but that would still require a Nova first stage of at least 9 million lb (4 million kg) of thrust, grouping six of the 1.5-million-lb thrust F-1 liquid-oxygen/kerosene engines that Rocketdyne was developing. Later analyses indicated that his spacecraft weights were too low, however, so Nova (as it was vaguely conceived in 1960–61) was usually based on an initial thrust of 12 million lb (5.4 million kg), which would require a gargantuan first stage 50 ft (15 m) in diameter.[9]

The alternative that von Braun presented was multiple launches of the Saturn C-2, which would be a souped-up version of the basic Saturn, now called the C-1. The eight-engine first stage, labeled the S-I, would be increased from 1.5-million-lb thrust in the C-1 to 2 million, and liquid-hydrogen upper stages would be added. As the direct result of the Silverstein committee that made the fundamental decision at the end of 1959 to use this exotic, supercold propellant, von Braun initiated two projects. First, for the C-1, a contractor would develop a liquid-hydrogen/liquid-oxygen second stage confusingly called the S-IV. (Under the building block concept, it would move up to be a third or fourth stage in C-2 and later versions.) Von Braun and his Germans disliked handing over responsibility to a corporation instead of following the arsenal system of in-house development and corporate production, but Glennan gave them no choice; in May 1960 Douglas Aircraft of Santa Monica, the famed airliner company but also prime contractor for the Thor IRBM, won the S-IV competition.[10]

The second project was a liquid-hydrogen engine of up to 200,000 lb (90,000 kg) of thrust, ultimately dubbed the J-2, which Rocketdyne had already been working on. Up to this point the only liquid-hydrogen rocket engine under development was the small RL-10, at famed aero-engine manufacturer Pratt & Whitney; two were to be used in the Centaur upper stage for Atlas. The S-IV ultimately got six RL-10s for 90,000 lb (40,000 kg) of thrust, but the much bigger J-2 engine was needed for the projected S-II and S-III stages in C-2 and later, bigger Saturns.[11]

Of course, this alphabet soup of designations was bewildering for anyone on the outside at the time, let alone for later observers, but the bottom line for von Braun was that he would much rather contemplate the C-2 or larger versions of Saturn than jump to the truly monstrous Nova. NASA headquarters and the STG had meanwhile concluded that the Nova was still a distant prospect, and the Eisenhower administration was not going to fund a lunar landing anyway, so Apollo was announced in July 1960 as an Earth orbit and circumlunar undertaking with the potential to become a Moon landing vehicle in the 1970s. The boosters would be the Saturn C-1 and C-2. But Eisenhower would not fund Apollo at all, so there was also no money for the J-2-powered S-II stage, which was the first item von Braun needed to make C-2 feasible in the mid-1960s.[12]

Ultimately, for the incoming Kennedy administration to take NASA's ambitious Moon plans seriously, the agency could suffer no major setbacks with Mercury. On 19 December von Braun and NASA got a welcome Christmas present when a replacement booster lobbed the refurbished MR-1 capsule to an altitude of 131 mi (211 km). Everything worked normally. It was thus a nasty surprise when Kurt Debus's crew sent a second Mercury-Redstone aloft on 31 January 1961 with the chimpanzee named Ham aboard as a medical test subject, something the doctors required before the first astronaut could fly. Ham got a rough ride. Vibration created inaccuracies in the guidance system, and the Redstone's engine ran hot, burning through its propellant load quickly. Since the rocket burned out seconds earlier than expected, the capsule's automatic programmer declared an abort and fired the escape tower, sending the chimp 157 miles high instead of the planned 115 and subjecting him to punishing acceleration loads. The Redstone had been nicknamed "Old Reliable" in comparison to all the other missiles then blowing up at the Cape, but this performance, although far from catastrophic, was a further embarrassment for Huntsville.[13]

Key members of von Braun's team quickly decided that they wanted another booster test before a man could fly, and he did not overrule them, a decision that likely cost the United States the distinction of putting the first human in space. It certainly provoked more bad feelings between Marshall and the Space Task Group precisely because of that possibility. The previous August the Soviets had recovered two dogs from orbit in what was transparently a test of their manned spacecraft, but in December another craft failed to leave orbit properly and self-destructed, killing two more canines. America still had a chance to win. Bob Gilruth and his group did not want to derail a March launch of an astronaut for what they viewed as relatively fixable booster problems, but they ran into a brick wall in Huntsville. After Gilruth and the STG delegation visited Marshall on 14 February, von Braun told air force general Don Ostrander, launch vehicles chief at NASA headquarters: "Their feelings are quite bitter and feel that we are letting them down and that MSFC is chickening out, etc." To Ostrander, von Braun fudged his position, repeating Marshall's technical arguments but allowing an opening for headquarters to overrule. In the end Ostrander and the top NASA leadership agreed with von Braun and the MSFC, against the recommendation of Gilruth and Silverstein. It was, at bottom, a political decision: NASA was more afraid of the consequences of an accident than those of coming in second.[14]

In order to put the onus on Marshall and on von Braun, whom many in STG blamed for the decision, Gilruth's group refused to use a production-line Mercury capsule or even to give the extra mission a regular number. They called it MR-BD for "Booster Development." On 24 March the Redstone, topped by a crude "boilerplate" capsule, performed perfectly. But astronaut Alan Shepard, who had been secretly chosen for the first flight, was angry with von Braun because that could have been his launch. Meanwhile, in the USSR, Sergei Korolev's group had orbited a new spacecraft on 9 March, recovering a dog, and they did it again on the day after the American test. Given earlier failures and the need to qualify modified systems, Korolev apparently did not want to fly a cosmonaut without two successful tests, so it appears that the extra flight did indeed cost the United States the prize of putting the first man in space. He had instructed staffers to draw up a statement arguing that the American suborbital hop was not a real spaceflight in contrast to going into orbit, the only objective of the Soviet program, but he did not have to ask Khrushchev to release it. On 12 April 1961 Major Yuri Gagarin made a single orbit in Vostok (Dawn or East), then parachuted back to the Russian steppes after ejecting from his capsule. It was an internationally acclaimed triumph that outdid the 1959 lunar successes and almost equaled the Sputnik shock of 1957.[15]

Von Braun was not surprised; he released a statement congratulating the USSR on its achievement. It is unknown whether he had advance knowledge from intelligence sources beyond the rumors that had circulated in the world press, but he and other top NASA officials did have Top Secret clearances and access to reconnaissance photos as presented by the CIA. According to a former Marshall staffer, von Braun had also been cleared to inspect images of Soviet launch sites taken by the U-2 high-altitude aircraft before pilot Gary Powers was shot down on May Day 1960. That put him in a very select group.[16]

For President Kennedy, challenging the Soviet Union to a Moon race was already on the table as a possible response. In late March he and Vice President Johnson had met with the new NASA Administrator, James E. Webb. (Glennan had departed with the outgoing administration.) Webb, an ex-marine pilot, lawyer, and Washington insider with a North Carolina drawl, had been Truman's Budget Bureau director and undersecretary of state. He also had the backing of Johnson and his close ally Senator Robert Kerr of Oklahoma. Webb discussed Apollo with Kennedy on 22 March, along with Deputy Administrator Hugh Dryden and Associate Administrator Robert C. Seamans, an electrical engineer from RCA who had been NASA's general manager since September 1960. The three met JFK again on 14 April, two days after Gagarin's mission. While the president had earlier approved extra money for Saturn, allowing the S-II stage to go forward, he was still reluctant to commit to a Moon landing that might cost $40 billion—this at a time when NASA's whole budget was less than a billion a year.[17]

The Soviet triumph proved to be only the first of two humiliating blows. On the seventeenth CIA-trained and -supported Cuban exile forces landed at the Bay of Pigs, and within two days Fidel Castro's army smashed them. Kennedy, who had refused appeals for direct U.S. air strikes as too provocative, suddenly looked weak and inexperienced, after having received enthusiastic early press notices. On the nineteenth, after a day of devastating news from Cuba, the president called in Lyndon Johnson to talk about space again. At LBJ's request, he gave him a formal memorandum the next day. Its key paragraph: "Do we have a chance of beating the Soviets by putting a laboratory in space, or by a trip around the moon, or by a rocket to land on the moon, or by a rocket to go to the moon and back with a man. Is there any other space program which promises dramatic results in which we could win?" The memo was, in the words of historian Michael Beschloss, "redolent of presidential panic."[18]

First thing on Friday the twenty-first, before the notorious late-riser von Braun reached the office, his secretary Bonnie Holmes got a call from Washington telling her that her boss was to show up Monday at Johnson's command. The vice president had decided to hold an informal roundtable of experts, supplementing his meetings with top Defense and NASA officials. Also attending would be General Schriever, the admiral in charge of navy R&D, and several industrialists. Intriguingly, von Braun would be informally representing the army he had so recently left, not NASA; whether the army leadership was asked for its recommendation is unknown. It certainly was a great compliment to von Braun to be treated at the same level as generals, admirals, and corporate chieftains. His friendly relationship with Johnson since his testimony to the preparedness hearings in December 1957 was no doubt a factor, as was his image as America's most famous rocket engineer.[19]

Late on Friday afternoon the MSFC director had a long conversation with the headquarters man he dealt with most directly, launch vehicles chief Don Ostrander. (As center director he reported institutionally to Associate Administrator Seamans, but almost all of his money and program assignments came from Ostrander, who was under Abe Silverstein, head of the Office of Space Flight Programs.) Ostrander briefed von Braun on the president's memo, a copy of which had arrived at NASA headquarters, and asked him to come up on Sunday afternoon to discuss the matter over dinner at his house. A central question was how much Saturn could be sped up. In that connection von Braun mentioned a new first stage with two F-1s (3 million lb, or 1,400,000 kg of thrust) that Koelle had proposed—soon designated as the basis for a C-3. Ostrander was pleased, because the C-2 was looking increasingly marginal as the Apollo spacecraft concept got heavier and heavier on paper. The two also conversed about huge solid rockets, an idea the air force was pushing, but von Braun felt that it would create a lot of safety problems at the Cape, as he thought they would have to be treated as explosives. In fact, as a liquid-fuel man since the beginning of his career, he was biased against solids.[20]

The meeting itself took place at ten a.m., on 24 April, around a long conference table in the Old Executive Office Building, next to the White House. Webb and Dryden were there too. No minutes were taken and the session was not recorded, so we know nothing about what Wernher von Braun said. Willis Shapley, an examiner for defense and space in the Budget Bureau and a man not well disposed to von Braun, remembers that the latter was caught speechless when Johnson asked him to explain the value of the space program; Webb apologized for him. If that indeed happened, the high-level gathering gave the talkative and self-confident von Braun a rare case of nerves. Presumably, however, he must have said something along the lines of the letter he sent to the vice president on 29 April.[21]

In that letter von Braun discussed the weight-lifting capability of Soviet boosters based on payloads launched, and he estimated that, as a result, "we do not have a good chance of beating the Soviets to a manned 'laboratory in space.' " The United States had a "sporting chance" of soft-landing a probe on the Moon first and of sending "a 3-men [sic] crew around the moon ahead of the Soviets (1965/66)" but it might be possible that they could send one cosmonaut around the Moon with minimal safety provisions as early as 1962–63. His key recommendation was:

> We have an excellent chance of beating the Soviets to the first landing of a crew on the moon (including return capability, of course). The reason is that a performance jump by a factor [of] 10 over their present rockets is necessary to accomplish this feat. While today we do not have such a rocket, it is unlikely that the Soviets have it. Therefore, we would not have to enter the race toward this next obvious goal in space exploration against hopeless odds favoring the Soviets. With an all-out crash program I think we could accomplish this objective in 1967/68.

He went on to answer the president's other questions, asserting that the above program could cost as much as an extra billion dollars per year. He advocated funding all propulsion systems including large solid rockets and nuclear rocket engines, which would use a reactor to heat liquid hydrogen to very high temperatures, resulting in efficiencies much exceeding chemical rockets.[22]

Whether this letter had much impact on the Apollo decision is doubtful, as one day earlier LBJ had already sent Kennedy a memo saying more or less the same thing. Of course, the Johnson memo did not by any means finalize that decision, which went on for another couple of weeks as Johnson and Kennedy lobbied key congressional leaders. It is marginally possible that von Braun's letter had influence after the fact. But the similarity of Johnson's conclusions to those of von Braun proves little about the rocket engineer's influence, as von Braun's opinions were essentially those of NASA, notwithstanding a disclaimer in his letter. On 22 April, space agency leaders had already given the vice president the same basic estimate of the likelihood of beating the Soviets to the various goals outlined by the president.[23]

Ultimately what von Braun contributed most to the Apollo decision was credibility on the question of Soviet and American booster capability. He was the recognized chief U.S. expert on that topic, and if he said that sending humans to the Moon and back would require a tenfold jump in rocket power, that carried weight. His space advocacy activities in the 1950s had also helped legitimize the idea of going to the Moon in the 1960s. Only a decade before, a mere 15 percent of the American public felt it was even possible by the year 2000. Now it seemed entirely possible, if still mind-bogglingly expensive and difficult.[24]

Before anything of these discussions became public, however, NASA had to pass a very important test: it had to safely launch an astronaut. Wernher and Maria von Braun were at the Cape for the first attempt to launch MR-3 on Tuesday, 2 May, but after several hours of waiting bad weather washed it out. In the process the public and the press learned that Alan Shepard was the designated crewman. On the fifth NASA tried again. Von Braun spent hours in the blockhouse, as one technical problem after another delayed the ignition. He later said:

> I think all of us awaiting the countdown were in a state of utmost suspense. For the first time, an astronaut's life depended on the reliability of our veteran Redstone and the Mercury spacecraft. We were also aware that to a considerable degree the future of our entire manned space flight program hinged on the success of this flight.
>
> I talked through the intercom system to Alan Shepard after he had entered his spacecraft and was waiting for the blast-off. I had the definite impression that he was far less excited about the launch than I.

When the countdown went into another hold with less than three minutes to go, Shepard famously shook up the blockhouse crew by saying: "Why don't you fix your little problem . . . and light this candle." At 9:34 a.m. the Redstone rose slowly off the pad and with ever-quickening speed disappeared into the sky; 15 minutes and 20 seconds later Shepard plopped down in the Atlantic over 300 mi (480 km) away. Von Braun got another chance to talk to him, this time by phone to the recovery ship. It had been an exciting morning.[25]

One week later von Braun was in the capital again, to talk to Ostrander and others about the maximum speedup of Saturn and Apollo. In another two weeks he was back for a Webb briefing. By then he was fully apprised of the Kennedy administration's decision to go all out for the Moon. Early drafts of the speech the president gave on 25 May even set a target date of 1967, and Webb had to ask the White House to substitute the vaguer goal of decade's end to give the agency more breathing space. The year 1967 was NASA's and von Braun's best estimate of when a landing was first possible; it was also the fiftieth anniversary of the Bolshevik Revolution, an obvious Soviet target should they choose to join in the race.[26]

On the morning of the twenty-fifth von Braun and his Development Board listened in the conference room at Marshall as President Kennedy, toward the end of a long address to Congress about civil defense, foreign aid, and other matters, at last came to the space section.

> First, I believe this Nation should commit itself to achieving the goal, before this decade is out, of landing a man on the moon and returning him safely to the earth. No single space project in this period will be more exciting, or more impressive to mankind, or more important for the long-range exploration of space, and none will be so difficult or expensive to accomplish.

When the speech was over, the board meeting in Huntsville broke up with joyous cries of "Yeah!" and "Let's go!" Von Braun immediately took off for Tulsa, where Senator Kerr was hosting a space conference.[27]

If he withheld public comments in Tulsa on Kennedy's proposal, it was no doubt because Webb told him to, in order to give Congress time to deliberate—but it scarcely did. In 1961 at least, neither politicians nor the public had any trouble with the idea of spending billions to land on the Moon, so frustrated were they by the ongoing Soviet space firsts. As for von Braun, as the reality sank in, he became increasingly excited by the challenge. In a note to his public relations chief, he put his first priority simply: "We're going to the Moon!"

Deciding to land on the Moon was one thing; figuring out how to do it was another. It would take a full year to make all the necessary decisions on the launch vehicles, the spacecraft, and the landing method—much longer than anyone wanted or expected, to the point where the presidential goal was under threat. But the immediate reaction to the Kennedy decision inside NASA was that an all-out, crash program meant the revival of the giant Nova booster and direct ascent. That was certainly the conclusion of the first, emergency study committee organized at headquarters in early May, but it would prove to be only the first of many study committees. Webb and Dryden, in their news conference on the afternoon of the presidential speech, went so far as to announce that Nova would be the launch vehicle for the lunar landing program.[28]

In Huntsville, von Braun unleashed a blizzard of studies to plan for Nova and Saturn C-3, the launch site, and the production plant, even as all assumptions were thrown into the air. He told his father on 22 June, apologizing for the belated letter: "Ever since Kennedy declared his intent to go to the Moon, all hell has broken loose here. At the moment, we are working on plans which put in the shade everything we have done before and against which even our 'Saturn' [C-1] pales." The Nova, if it had the 12-million-lb (5.5-million-kg) thrust first stage, would not only be about 50 ft (15 m) in diameter, it would be around 400 ft (125 m) tall and would create so much noise during static testing and launch, and such a blast danger if it blew up, that it was dubious if it could even be tested or launched at Cape Canaveral. Perhaps they would have to go to some uninhabited island or offshore platform.[29]

Then there was the manufacturing problem. Any plant would have to have a "hook height" for overhead cranes higher than the 50-ft stage lying on its side, which meant the factory space would have to be taller than that. Yet already in May MSFC had begun looking into an enormous, empty, government-owned factory at Michoud in eastern New Orleans that had been built to assemble landing craft in World War II but had been used for aircraft, tank engines, and other military equipment. Its hook height was not nearly high enough for Nova without a major reconstruction project. By June von Braun and his bosses had already decided that Michoud was too good a deal to turn down, especially as it was conveniently located for barge traffic of rocket stages, in one direction to Huntsville via the Mississippi, Ohio, and Tennessee Rivers, in the other to the Cape via the sea. As von Braun also pointed out several times, crash program or no, NASA also did not have the resources to develop the C-3 and Nova simultaneously. Over the summer and fall, practical considerations thus piled up against Nova until it began fading as an option. This result suited von Braun and his associates, whose conservative engineering philosophy led them to believe it was too big a technological jump.[30]

As Nova and direct ascent faded in popularity, Earth-orbit rendezvous (EOR) made a comeback, much to their relief. Two more study committees at headquarters in June and July, to which Marshall sent representatives, looked at the rendezvous problem, which on the surface seemed intimidating and complicated. How were they going to bring two or more large vehicles together in space and gently link them up to form the lunar landing vehicle and its Earth departure stage? But the second committee concluded, in the words of notes that von Braun took: "Rendezvous less formidable than lunar landing." It was not the "pacing item" and could certainly be solved, although overall it looked simpler to just link up modules (later called "connecting mode") rather than transferring propellants from one vehicle to another (later called "tanking mode"). This group also recommended a Saturn C-4, with four F-1s totaling 6 million lb (2.7 million kg) of thrust in the first stage, double the C-3, as it could halve the number of vehicles to meet in Earth orbit from four to two. Every extra launch, in those days of frequent spectacular rocket failures, increased the odds that the whole lunar landing would be derailed by one failed firing.[31]

But von Braun remained loyal to the C-3 concept for far too long, perhaps because of the perceived difficulties of building an even bigger, more complicated vehicle, but also likely because the constantly changing picture made Saturn management a headache. It certainly made the S-II competition messy, because the diameter of the stage kept growing along with the first stage on which it would sit. At the outset, the S-II was to be 260 in (660 cm) in diameter for the C-2. In June von Braun told Harrison "Stormy" Storms, president of North American Aviation's new space division, the leading candidate for the S-II contract, to base their design on a 320-in-diameter stage (813 cm), and explain how they would cope with an increase to 360 in (914 cm). By the time Storms and NAA won the contract in September, von Braun was telling him: Plan for 360, but it could get bigger. The S-II, and the first stage underneath it soon called S-IC, would end up at an imposing 396 in (10 m), almost six times the diameter of the Redstone and just big enough to fit under the roof at Michoud.[32]

Managing the huge lunar-landing program, which would quintuple NASA's budget to over $5 billion per year in the mid-1960s, posed unprecedented management challenges for NASA. The triumvirate who ran the agency—Webb, Dryden, and Seamans—decided in July that they needed to reorganize and strengthen the leadership of the human spaceflight program at headquarters. At that point the impressive title of director of manned spaceflight was held by a very talented but junior engineer in his mid-thirties, George Low, who had come with Abe Silverstein from Lewis Center in Cleveland. He reported to Silverstein and saw himself as the Washington representative of the Space Task Group, which was run by the true head of the program, Bob Gilruth. STG obviously was going to expand massively and go somewhere, although not Huntsville, as the idea of subordinating the group to Marshall had already, wisely, been ruled out. In September Webb announced that that "somewhere" would be a cow pasture outside Houston, an obeisance to the power of Vice President Johnson and powerful Texas congressmen who sat on appropriations committees. STG became the Manned Spacecraft Center (MSC, renamed Johnson Space Center after the ex-president's death in 1973). But the Apollo program was much bigger than the one center, involving the coordination of Marshall, Gilruth's group, the launch site at the Cape, corporate contractors from coast to coast, and more. The triumvirate decided to create an Office of Manned Space Flight cut out of Silverstein's Office of Space Flight Programs. Having struck out

Von Braun with his American superiors, Major James Hamill (left) and Colonel Holger Toftoy, at Fort Bliss, outside El Paso, Texas, probably in 1945–46. *(NASM)*

The Hermes II ramjet missile, launched on a modified V-2, was the primary project for the Fort Bliss Germans in the late 1940s. Because it was severely underfunded, it had few successes and was later forgotten. *(NASM)*

The von Braun Paperclip group at Fort Bliss in 1946. Seventh from left, in the short white jacket, is Arthur Rudolph. Sixth from right in the first row, next to von Braun, is Ernst Stuhlinger. *(NASM)*

Von Braun's marriage to first cousin Maria von Quistorp on 1 March, 1947, in Landshut, Germany, was guarded by American MPs, who feared a Soviet kidnap attempt. On the steps behind Maria is Sigismund von Braun. The von Braun parents are to the right. *(Picture Press)*

After several years of frustration, von Braun's breakthrough in his campaign for spaceflight came in 1952 with the *Collier's* magazine series. Here he is standing in front of a copy of one of Chesley Bonestell's paintings, holding a Disney version of his giant booster rocket. This U.S. Army photo was taken in 1955. *(NASM)*

The *Collier's* articles helped spark the creation of space series on Walt Disney's new TV program. Von Braun appeared on-camera as well as shaping the content. From left, in Burbank, California, in October 1954: Willy Ley, Heinz Haber, Disney, Mrs. Haber(?), and Maria and Wernher von Braun.

(NASM)

The Orbiter group tours the Redstone block-house at the Cape in May 1955. Third from left is space advocate and CIA officer Fred Durant, and behind von Braun is Harvard astronomer Fred Whipple. Navy Lieutenant Commander George Hoover is in front with tie undone, and at far right is von Braun's Florida launch chief, Kurt Debus. Von Braun gave up smoking shortly after this time.

(NASM)

Right: JPL Director William Pickering, Iowa physicist James Van Allen, and ABMA project director Wernher von Braun triumphantly hold aloft a full-scale model of Explorer I early on the morning of 1 February 1958. After Orbiter project lost to the Navy Vanguard group in 1955, and after two Soviet Sputnik triumphs and a humiliating Vanguard failure in 1957, von Braun's U.S. Army team fired the first American satellite after all. *(NASM)*

Explorer I's Jupiter-C launch vehicle is prepared for launch on the night of 31 January 1958. The first stage was a Redstone missile. On top was the rotating tub of solid-fuel upper stages, with fourth stage/satellite sticking out on top.

(Desind/NASM)

General J. B. Medaris, von Braun's Army boss in Huntsville, Alabama, 1956-60, with him and Debus during the launch of Pioneer IV in March 1959. It was the first U.S. spacecraft to escape Earth's gravitational field, pass the Moon and go into solar orbit. *(NASM)*

The actor Curd Jürgens and von Braun's father meet him at the airport in Munich for the August 1960 premiere of the heroic biopic *I Aim at the Stars*. Jürgens played von Braun in the movie, which bombed and sparked a lot of protest. *(NASM)*

Von Braun met President Eisenhower several times, the last being Ike's September 1960 dedication of von Braun's new NASA Marshall Space Flight Center in Huntsville. T. Keith Glennan, the first NASA Administrator, is at left. Eisenhower resented von Braun, however, for relentlessly promoting more space and missile expenditure. *(NASM)*

The Saturn family of launch vehicles: the Saturn I (originally C-1) for unmanned Apollo Earth orbital launches, the Saturn IB (C-1B) for manned orbital missions, and the gigantic Saturn V (C-5) for lunar missions. Von Braun's masterly leadership of his huge rocket-engineering teams culminated in the perfect launch record of the Saturn series. *(Desind/NASM)*

Six days before President Kennedy was assassinated in November 1963, he visited the Cape launch site of first two-stage Saturn I. Von Braun explains the vehicle as Kennedy (in dark glasses) looks elsewhere. NASA Administrator James Webb is at far right. The older man to von Braun's left is Deputy Administrator Hugh Dryden. *(NASM)*

Von Braun and human spaceflight chief George Mueller watch in May 1966 as the first, non-flying Saturn V is rolled out of the assembly building in Florida. The rocket alone was thirty-six stories tall. *(NASA/NASM)*

The von Brauns after the Smithsonian gave him the Langley Medal in June 1967. Margrit, age fifteen, is at left and Iris, eighteen, at right. Peter had just turned seven. *(NASM)*

In January 1967, Max Faget and Robert Gilruth of the NASA center in Houston (left) and von Braun (center) and Ernst Stuhlinger (far right) of Huntsville made a visit to Antarctica to look for lessons for later space explorers. Houston and Huntsville were often at odds over their respective roles in human spaceflight. *(NASM)*

Von Braun was ecstatic at experiencing weightlessness in the Air Force zero-G training aircraft in August 1968. It was the closest he was to get to his lifelong dream of flying in space. *(NASM)*

Following the splashdown of the Apollo 11 astronauts in the Pacific on 20 July 1969, signaling the accomplishment of President Kennedy's moon-landing goal, von Braun was hoisted aloft by well-wishers in downtown Huntsville. *(NASM)*

Left: NASA Acting Administrator George Low and Deputy Associate Administrator Wernher von Braun during the Apollo 14 launch countdown in January 1971. Although the two were friendly, Low did not see von Braun's planning job at headquarters as particularly useful. Von Braun's two years in that position were a depressing time, as the NASA budget plummeted along with public support. *(NASM)*

Von Braun escaped to become a vice president of Fairchild, an aerospace firm based outside Washington, D.C. He was already a good friend and hunting buddy of its president and CEO, Edward G. Uhl, right. *(Fairchild/NASM)*

When von Braun visited the new, not-yet-finished National Air and Space Museum building in April 1976, he was already visibly declining from the effects of his second, ultimately fatal bout with kidney and colon cancer. *(NASM*

with some desirable external candidates, the only internal options appeared to be Wernher von Braun and Abe Silverstein. But Silverstein was too domineering and undiplomatic to get along with key actors in the much-expanded program. Rather than accept a reduced role, he returned to Lewis Center in the fall of 1961 as its director.[33]

In his memoirs Bob Seamans tells the best story about what happened next:

> What about bringing von Braun into headquarters and having him run it? One rather late night Jim Webb and I got talking about this possibility. Why couldn't he run Apollo? After all, he had had considerable success at Peenemünde. . . . The more we talked, the more infatuated we got with the idea.
>
> The next morning Hugh Dryden got together with us. Jim turned to me and said, "Bob, why don't you tell Hugh about our recent thinking on running Apollo?" Hugh sat there for what seemed like an eternity (probably five seconds) and said, "Well, if you and Jim want von Braun, that's fine with me. I'll take early retirement." That was the end of our thinking on that possibility.[34]

The problem with this story is that Seamans implies that the idea was dispatched in the course of an evening and a morning; but there is no doubt that in August 1961 von Braun went to Washington to talk about the job. On Monday the twenty-first a senior staffer at headquarters asked him to come in two days to talk to the associate administrator about "the organizational problem"; he might also see Dryden and Webb on Thursday. Either before or after those meetings, the Marshall director wrote two pages of notes titled "<u>Requirements</u>" that included: "Pick my own staff," "Resources control (vis-à-vis Wyatt and other Seamans staff members)," and "Have my own control office." He concluded with: "<u>At first:</u> Leave of absence status, assigned to HQ duty." These notes are filed with seven detailed pages in Eberhard Rees's handwriting, advising him on what to demand and how his local staff would react. ("They will feel honored by your assignment" but will conclude that "you can not afford to risk your name and reputation without having <u>an honest chance</u>.")[35]

In a 1968 interview Seamans told a different version of his story, one more compatible with these documents. He called the MSFC director in "on a Saturday and Dryden was out of town, and Webb took him over to the Metropolitan Club for lunch. And when he came back, you could sort of tell that they had hit it off well together, and Webb said, 'Well, Wernher is prepared to come right in here to Washington and feels that the management of

Huntsville can continue without him and be effective.' " So Seamans talked to von Braun for a long time that afternoon and promised to get back to him early in the week. On Monday morning they had their meeting with Dryden, and in this version of the story he said: "Well, . . . you and Jim can bring anybody you want in here to run this thing, but don't expect the whole organization to fall into line with you, including myself."[36]

Dryden and von Braun had had many friendly encounters before and after Marshall joined NASA, notwithstanding the former's dismissal of Adam as a "circus stunt" in the spring of 1958, so what was the origin of his resentment? It can only have been the general distaste among the veterans of the former NACA for what they viewed as von Braun's big-spending and self-promoting ways, plus his salesmanship for monumental space schemes in *Collier's* and on Disney's program, which were so at odds with the good, gray, low-profile research of NACA. Nor could agency veterans quite forgive him for his refusal to join NASA in the fall of 1958, since they did not understand how disruptive Glennan's attempt to take only half of von Braun's organization would have been. Then there was the Nazi question, which lurked in the background, although it had been fairly effectively neutralized. Recent attempts to see the friction between von Braun and Silverstein or Low as a German-Jewish issue (both were Jewish in background) do not seem to be based on much evidence, but Gilruth, who was not Jewish, used to get drunk and complain to others about "that damned Nazi" even after they had begun working closely together, according to one NASA insider. Finally, there was no little envy of von Braun's fame, which was completely out of proportion to his role as one of a half dozen center directors, two or three levels down from the top. Seamans said in a 1987 interview that von Braun was "our big celebrity. Nobody had ever heard of Gilruth at this time" (1961); nor for that matter did anyone but insiders know Webb. In the United States and around the world, many assumed that von Braun was the head of the space program. The MSFC director was acutely aware of this image problem and always tried to show proper deference to his Washington bosses.[37]

Since the idea of coming to the capital was so short-lived, von Braun probably discussed the matter with very few people besides his wife and Rees, his likely successor. But he must have been excited about running the Moon-landing program, his childhood dream, and it appealed to his considerable ego. Not only would he have run up against the resentment of Gilruth and other key players, however; he probably would have had the same problems that ultimately undermined the man who did take the job, Dr. Brainerd Holmes of RCA. Both he and Holmes lacked familiarity with systems engineering as developed by the air force, a skill set that would prove essential to Apollo's ultimate success as a coherent program. Nor would a paper-pushing job at headquarters have suited him, as evidenced by his experience there from 1970 to 1972. Although his job at Marshall was overwhelmingly administrative, that did not stop him from being a "dirty hands" engineer deeply immersed in the hardware that his center was building. One can only conclude that, when Dryden nixed the idea that would have changed his whole life, von Braun got lucky.[38]

A couple of months after these events, von Braun found himself the subject of a new intervention from headquarters, this time over the big speaker fees the MSFC director was earning. On 31 August Webb had signed a new NASA instruction on "outside employment." When von Braun sent in his speech list for approval, it showed fifteen different engagements between October and April, of which only three were "official" NASA events without honoraria. He anticipated making nearly $12,000 in six months after travel expenses, at a time when his government salary was $21,000 a year. Webb finally talked to him about it on 15 November. Accepting von Braun's offer to cut back if it was an "embarrassment" to NASA, he instructed Marshall's director three weeks later to accept only a "limited" number of paid speeches a year, which in practice turned out to be four.[39] That was four more than any civil servant would be allowed to make two decades later from job-related talks, but it was a significant reduction for von Braun.

The restriction does not seem to have had that much effect on his brutal travel and speaking schedule, however, as he was in constant demand as a lecturer, notably from congressmen. Nor does it seem to have had much effect on his subject matter. In the late 1950s the army had given him a lot of freedom, but even before he joined NASA he realized that the agency was unusually sensitive about public image. His advocacy for nuclear bombs in orbit quietly vanished. From 1960 on his speeches became nothing but salesmanship for Saturn, Apollo, and other agency programs. That makes them boring to read now, but his audiences were transfixed by his explication of the space exploration wonders to come.

Webb certainly appreciated that talent for salesmanship.

He [von Braun] had the instinct and intuition of an animal. I mean, he could sense danger. You know [when] an animal pricks up his ears, says, "what's going on here, the wind's bringing me a new scent?" Wernher had a remarkable sense of what his audience wanted to hear. And after all, I wasn't trying to control him, because if he said something that caused any trouble we would just withdraw our support from that. I don't think anyone had really put Wernher in a position where he had to think about how high the fence on the corral was before he did anything. Up to then, he'd done something, and somebody would have to stop him if they wanted to. I told him the limits with which he should go.

Around the same time, he sent his legislative director to von Braun to tell him that he had to stop acting so independently with Congress. Twice the new administrator reminded him, not so subtly, who was boss.[40]

Von Braun did not have a problem with that, as he venerated Webb. Early in 1961 he had favored a technical expert as administrator, but he quickly grasped Webb's political savvy and insider status in a Washington run by New Frontier and New Deal Democrats. He admired Webb's success with Apollo and accepted his authority and superior wisdom in political matters, which became especially important as the civil rights battle gained momentum in Alabama. Although a conservative anti-Communist by upbringing and instinct, von Braun as always was most comfortable operating as an apolitical technocrat. Finding that his closest allies in the 1960s were Cold War liberal Democrats, he readily adapted to the situation.

But it was the Saturn program that most preoccupied von Braun in the fall of 1961. On the morning of 27 October the first Saturn C-1 (later called Saturn I) thundered away from its new pad in Florida. The TV networks thought it important enough to carry it live, as it was the biggest and most powerful rocket ever launched at 162 ft (49 m) tall, 460 tons in weight, and 1.3 million lb (590,000 kg) of thrust. Watching from the spacious new Saturn blockhouse, von Braun and his Germans were not disappointed. The S-I first-stage cluster of nine tanks and eight engines, carrying two water-filled dummy stages, powered through "max Q," when aerodynamic forces were at their peak, and kept on going, setting off wild celebrations in the blockhouse. The vehicle reached a peak altitude of 95 mi (154 km) and dropped into the Atlantic. The perfect flight on the first try astonished the Marshall crew. It was also a propaganda triumph at a terrifying moment of the Cold War: Soviet and American tanks were gun barrel to gun barrel across the newly constructed Berlin Wall, causing von Braun to worry about Maria's father in West Berlin and about the possibility of nuclear war.[41]

Ironically, even as the C-1 scored its spectacular success, it was already being orphaned as a launch vehicle. The heavier the Apollo spacecraft became on paper, the more inadequate it appeared for even Earth orbital operations. Soon NASA would decide to build a more powerful version called C-1B (Saturn IB). Meanwhile the air force wanted its own heavy rocket and did not want to depend on NASA, so it came up with a proposal for a Titan III, strapping two huge solid-propellant rockets on the side of a two-stage Titan II ICBM, which produced a cheaper vehicle with the lifting power of a C-1.[42]

To add insult to injury, Gilruth's Manned Spacecraft Center, then preparing to move to Houston, picked the Titan II to lift its two-astronaut Mercury Mark II spacecraft (soon to be called Gemini). The lunar objective made it urgent that there be a gap-filler between Mercury and Apollo, one that would give human experience in rendezvous and docking. Von Braun, however, was furious because MSC had initiated a rendezvous program without any consultation with Marshall, which was studying the topic for the lunar mission. He was also annoyed that MSC had not considered Saturn as a booster, but it was really too big for what was supposed to be a scaled-up Mercury. Von Braun told Gilruth that he would take no responsibility for Titan II if it got into trouble. Gilruth was fine with leaving Marshall out, as he was already contracting directly with the air force for Atlas boosters. He had terminated Mercury-Redstone after the second manned suborbital hop by Virgil I. "Gus" Grissom in July in order to concentrate on orbiting a man, ending what little influence von Braun had on Project Mercury. Relations between the two centers were at their nadir.[43]

November and December 1961 at least brought the resolution of one central issue for the lunar landing project: the choice of the large launch vehicle. All through the fall von Braun had wavered between the C-3 and C-4, 3 versus 6 million lb of initial thrust. The answer would turn out to be neither. Milt Rosen, now heading the launch vehicles section of the new Office of Manned Spaceflight under Brainerd Holmes, came down to Huntsville to discuss the situation. (Ostrander had returned to the air force.) Rosen spent several days convincing von Braun and his associates that any of the rendezvous scenarios for Apollo needed the biggest rocket possible short of Nova. On paper the C-4's first stage could easily accommodate a fifth engine in the center, making it a C-5. In fact, the "hole" in the middle of the C-4 might well lead to tail-heating problems, and thanks to MSFC's conservative structural design, there was a big crossbeam there that could easily absorb the thrust of another F-1. Von Braun became a convert, even telling Holmes at the first meeting of the Manned Spaceflight Management Council in December that "the hole in the center was crying out for another engine." The final configuration chosen was: (1) the S-IC, a five F-1 first stage with 7.5 million lb (3.4 million kg) of thrust, to be built by Boeing; (2) the S-II, a five-J-2-engine, liquid-hydrogen second stage totaling 1 million lb (450,000 kg) of thrust, to be assembled by North American; and (3) the S-IVB, a single J-2-powered third stage with 200,000 lb (90,000 kg) of thrust, to be derived by Douglas from the S-IV. Later known as the Saturn V, the C-5 was really a small Nova, a monster that would be 363 ft (111 m) tall with the spacecraft on top, weighing over 6 million lb (2700 metric tons)—the displacement of a small warship. Von Braun had backed into a much larger vehicle than he had originally wanted to build.[44]

At this point the MSFC director just assumed that Apollo would have to be done by Earth-orbit rendezvous, as his many speeches attest. Headquarters felt pretty much the same way—no other scenario seemed very credible except direct ascent, which most NASA leaders had already ruled out for booster reasons. But a new and surprising contender arose in late 1961: lunar-orbit rendezvous (LOR). It was in fact not so new. A Langley Center aeronautical engineer, John C. Houbolt, had been championing the idea since at least 1960 on behalf of a small group there. He pointed out the fundamental physics. Whether you went direct or by EOR, and whether you went into lunar orbit first or not, the entire vehicle descended to the lunar surface. That meant that you had to carry a lot of propellants to get the big vehicle down, plus all the propellants needed to lift the Apollo spacecraft off the surface and back to Earth. Why not leave the propellants needed to get back to Earth in lunar orbit, and for that matter the whole main spacecraft, and descend to the Moon in a light vehicle designed simply for that job? It was not an original idea; von Braun himself had used landing craft and mother ships in his hypothetical Mars expeditions. But neither he nor almost anyone else had applied this concept to the Moon because it lacked an atmosphere. Going straight in just seemed intuitively obvious, and that was how he had proposed to do it in *Collier's*.[45]

Houbolt did not do himself a favor, however, by outlining lunar landers of unrealistically low weights, from under 15,000 lb (6800 kg) for a pressurized lunar module down to 2,500 lb (1140 kg) for an open platform in which one astronaut would descend in his pressure suit. Someone joked the astronaut should wrap an aviator's silk scarf around his neck. When Houbolt had presented these ideas at headquarters a year earlier, in December 1960, Gilruth's design genius Max Faget had apparently jumped up and exclaimed: "His figures lie." Von Braun was present. As the MSFC director later said regarding Houbolt's most elaborate proposal, the only one anyone took seriously: "[I]f . . . you have to have one extra crew compartment, pressurized, and two additional guidance systems, and the electrical power supply for all that gear, . . . will you still be on the plus side of your trade-off?"[46]

Moreover, Faget and almost everyone else had the instinctive reaction that the method was inherently more dangerous, because if the lander astronaut(s) failed to make the rendezvous with the mother ship, he or they were dead. In Earth orbit, if the rendezvous failed, then the astronauts would simply come home in their reentry vehicle. At this point no American had yet been in orbit, and no one had ever done a rendezvous. So Houbolt found he could get little respect from most of the committees that met in 1961; LOR was rated at or near the bottom in their reports. Out of frustration, Houbolt violated all channels by sending two long letters directly to Bob Seamans in 1961, one in May and one in November.[47]

The accounts of the principals diverge at this point as to how important Houbolt's November letter was in getting lunar-orbit rendezvous taken seriously. Von Braun, for one, later agreed with Gilruth and Faget that they were already coming around without Houbolt's new intervention. Supporting that contention is a rather tense phone conversation that von Braun and Gilruth had on 24 November, mostly about Gemini-Titan II. The MSFC director mentioned the fifth-engine idea for C-4 that had just come up in the Rosen visit. Gilruth said: "If you can go to lunar rendezvous then you can go direct with C-4 and with C-3 you couldn't." So he, Faget, and the MSC people had obviously run the weight calculation and concluded that even with a bigger lander, Houbolt was not far wrong. The weight savings were potentially so large that one could launch the whole spacecraft on one big booster, whereas Earth-orbit rendezvous required two of them. Von Braun did not react. He later claimed that "I had never committed myself to EOR," and that is true in the narrow sense that he never made a final decision and formally recommended it to Washington. But from the fall of 1961 until the spring of 1962 he had acted as if it were the way to go.[48]

During the Christmas holidays and beyond, von Braun got a welcome respite from the pressures of the "mode decision," as it came to be called. He set off on one of the most memorable trips of his life, exercising his new freedom to travel away from constant army surveillance. In January 1962 he had a NASA lecture tour in Australia and wanted to see his eighty-five-year-old father in Germany beforehand. His friend Carsbie Adams, an Atlanta industrialist on whose country plantation the von Brauns had often relaxed, suggested the two make a round-the-world trip to see India and the Himalayas, places von Braun had always dreamed of seeing. After passing through London and Munich, the two landed in New Delhi on New Year's Eve and spent six hectic days touring Nepal, the Taj Mahal, and other highlights before stopping briefly in Bangkok on the way to Australia. Maria von Braun may have indulged him this trip because of his upcoming fiftieth birthday in March. He certainly was away a lot. He told his old pilot friend

Erich Warsitz that he had spent over two hundred days on the road in 1961.[49]

The relentless, exhausting pace of the Apollo-Saturn program continued in 1962. Manned spaceflight chief Brainerd Holmes had hired a brilliant thirty-five-year-old engineer from New York City, Dr. Joseph Shea, to be his deputy for systems engineering. He was to pull together the mode decision. Touring the centers early in the year, he found that NASA was still more an agglomeration of organizations than an integrated agency. In particular, "you almost can't imagine the animosity" between MSC and MSFC, Shea later said, especially from Gilruth's side. Holmes organized dinners to accompany the Management Council meetings, and Shea found himself sitting at "some of the most strained tables I've ever been at." Moreover, EOR concepts at the two centers were fundamentally incompatible. "It was all booster oriented when Marshall presented it; and it was all spacecraft oriented when Houston did." He tried to get each side to analyze parts of the other. He also asked for assistance and found Huntsville markedly more cooperative than Manned Spacecraft Center (then in the middle of its move to Texas). Von Braun, always the gentleman and good soldier, volunteered the services of Arthur Rudolph, recently transferred from the army, and ten to fifteen other engineers to help Shea's systems analysis, if they could remain at MSFC. Faget, on the other hand, told Shea to get lost, and Gilruth backed him up.[50]

After Shea had toured the manned spaceflight centers in January, he came away "impressed with the overall competence" of von Braun's organization, but "MSFC has not paid any attention to LOR and was not in a good position to comment on the mode. Their instinctive reaction, however, was negative. This is to be expected, since use of LOR would lessen the MSFC role in the manned lunar program significantly." By this he meant that Marshall would no longer have a piece of rendezvous operations in Earth orbit. Shea's statement pretty much captures von Braun's attitude, so the question as to when and why he really began to take lunar-orbit rendezvous seriously is important but difficult to determine. He was exposed to the strongly pro-LOR presentation by Houbolt of Langley and Charles Matthews of MSC in the Manned Spaceflight Management Council meeting on 6 February, but that was not the first such talk he had heard.[51]

For many, including von Braun, it was the spacecraft design argument that finally decided the issue. Faget and his people were never able to satisfactorily solve the problem of how to land the big EOR vehicle on the Moon. Originally it was something like 90 ft (27 m) long. On 20 February the Mercury team had at last succeeded in launching John Glenn on his three-orbit trip around the world, yet here they were trying to figure out how to back a vehicle the size of the entire Mercury-Atlas rocket down to the lunar surface. To reduce the lander's size, Faget and his designers proposed a separable "lunar crasher" stage—a module under the Apollo Command and Service Modules (CSM) that would contain enough propellant to slow the spacecraft into lunar orbit, then lower it from lunar orbit down to near the surface, before being jettisoned in a hair-raising, low-altitude separation. Even with a smaller vehicle, in which the cylindrical Service Module would have legs and a base for landing and launch, the designers still faced a very difficult problem in giving the astronauts any kind of visibility. The Command Module was a flat conical reentry vehicle in which the crew would lie on its back for landing. Faget and company tried putting a "porch" on it or some other arrangement to allow the commander to stand up and see the surface as the vehicle came in, but they never found an adequate solution. Another proposal was for the vehicle to land on its side, but that meant launching from the Moon's surface almost horizontally, a dangerous proposition. Long before that time MSC leaders were all LOR converts.[52]

At the 27 March Management Council meeting von Braun asked Gilruth to present their arguments at a briefing in Huntsville, perhaps impressed by what he had heard. On 16 April Marshall got the full, all-day viewgraph presentation, nicknamed "Charlie Frick's Road Show," after the Apollo spacecraft project manager who organized it. A large Houston group, including Gilruth, Faget, Frick, and two Mercury heroes, Alan Shepard and John Glenn, were present. A Langley engineer who arrived immediately afterward states: "Apparently the presentation was well received by von Braun, since he made several favorable comments." Frick remembers von Braun making "a very gracious speech thanking us and saying he understood the advantages of the system." Max Faget came away with the even stronger impression of the MSFC director "very generously throwing in the towel."[53]

It seems that they were misled by von Braun's gift for diplomacy, as 16 April was by no means his unambiguous moment of conversion. In early May, in the midst of his usual round of travels to Washington, to the Cape, and to speeches around the country, he became infatuated with a proposal for "C-5 Direct" from TRW Space Technology Laboratories. A Saturn C-5 would launch a two-man spacecraft to land directly on the Moon. A "mission module" incorporating windows would be mounted on top of a small reentry vehicle. But that required throwing out the existing Apollo CSM, already contracted to Storms's division of North American Aviation, and using liquid hydrogen in the Moon-landing vehicle to gain higher rocket efficiencies, which was technologically risky. The idea really was a non-starter, although with Shea's support Marshall did briefly study it.[54]

By this time even manned spaceflight chief Holmes was pretty much a convert to lunar-orbit rendezvous after hearing the "road show" in Washington on 3 May. According to Shea, Holmes told him to feel out von Braun regarding a quid pro quo for accepting LOR. Houston would get another spacecraft, the Lunar Module (LM) as it was later called, while Marshall would lose all its tanker and orbital rendezvous work. Lacking any other projects, Huntsville faced its perennial problem of dependence on developing new, large rockets to keep the place going. While von Braun later denied that he made any deal, Shea insists that they had a frank conversation in his office. It could only have occurred on 15 May, when von Braun was in the capital again. Shea had already pushed the idea of a "lunar logistics vehicle," a one-way robotic lander to deliver a load of supplies to the Moon for use in later, longer-duration stays of astronauts or a lunar base. From what happened immediately afterward, it is clear that giving Marshall the dominant role in that became the basis for a deal. Von Braun's conversion to LOR may have been sincere, but he was a canny bureaucratic politician when it came to defending the interests of his organization.[55]

The moment at which one can definitely verify his decision to accept LOR is May 31, the first day in the office after the Management Council met in Huntsville on the twenty-ninth. Right after he got in, "Dr. von Braun called Tom Markley—MSC, requesting that someone from MSC come to Huntsville to see if some method can be devised to insert the MSC in-house bug into the Saturn." The "bug" was the Lunar Module's nickname because of the insectlike appearance of this oddly shaped vehicle with legs. "If this can be done it will save total vehicle weight and length, and make more payload available than if the bug has to ride on top." He was searching for a way to put the LM inside the shell-like adapter that joined the Apollo CSM to the "guidance slice"; Marshall had recently decided to put the guidance system for the whole rocket into a separate ring, later called the Instrument Unit (IU), mounted atop the S-IVB. Curiously, von Braun had not given the "bug" problem any thought, although its position had already been discussed in a Shea-organized LOR review in Washington. But he had not been there.[56]

Von Braun's formal coming-out was on 7 June 1962, at the end of a long day in Huntsville presenting Marshall's mostly pro-EOR studies to Joe Shea. It is a date justly remembered as one of the most critical in the history of Apollo. Apparently the shock in the room was palpable as von Braun got up and said, by Shea's account, "Well, gentlemen, I have listened to the arguments; I'm proud of the work you have done. Now I'll tell you the position of the center." The question is why anyone at MSFC should have been surprised. The previous three days had witnessed a grueling set of reviews. On Monday the fourth there had been an all-day practice session for the seventh, followed on the fifth and sixth by visits from the President's Science Advisory Committee and a delegation of congressional staffers. To the latter committees Marshall presented broader surveys that included Saturn, Nova, and the launch complex at the Cape. Von Braun later plausibly speculated that, as NASA had not formally made a mode decision, he and his staff withheld any conclusions in presentations to outsiders. As for the earlier dress rehearsal, he apparently did not reveal his decision to his chief EOR analyst, Ernst Geissler, or anyone else at that meeting, perhaps because he had not quite decided whether to suddenly end the debate. Although von Braun normally operated by consensus with his inner German-dominated group, apparently 7 June was one of those rare occasions when he decided that a decision was so urgent, he had to lead.[57]

We do not have the original transcript or notes, but we do have a polished version that von Braun dictated on the Saturday after. He began by listing MSFC's preferences in order: (1) LOR, preferably with "the development of an unmanned, fully automatic, one-way C-5 [lunar] logistics vehicle"; (2) EOR (tanking mode); (3) C-5 Direct; (4) Nova Direct. He preferred LOR because it had "the highest confidence factor of successful accomplishment within this decade," "an adequate performance margin" based on conventional, storable propellants in the Apollo spacecraft, and the ability to separate the reentry vehicle from the lunar landing vehicle—Houston's spacecraft design argument. Moreover, LOR offered "the cleanest managerial interfaces." "There are already a frightening number of interfaces in existence in our Manned Lunar Landing Program" necessitating too many "coordination meetings, integration groups, working panels, ad-hoc committees, etc." He concluded this section by noting that "John Houbolt of Langley" had been the first advocate. "Against this background it can, therefore, be concluded that the issue of 'invented here' versus 'not invented here' does not apply to either" MSFC or MSC as "both Centers have embraced a scheme suggested by a third source." This latter argument appears to be aimed at the pro-EOR people in his own center who may have found his conclusions a sellout to Houston. Indeed, he faced a "storm" of criticism at the next board meeting, according to Stuhlinger.[58]

As for EOR, von Braun noted that all the studies had concluded that "tanking mode," in which one C-5 would launch a liquid-oxygen tanker to fuel the Earth departure stage of the spacecraft, had a much bigger performance margin than "connecting mode," where the spacecraft and stage would link up. But even then EOR would require two launches, raising costs and lowering the probability of success, while making the interface between the centers more complicated. Finally there was simply the design problem: the present CM was "simply unsuited for lunar landing because of the poor visibility conditions and the undesirable supine position of the astronauts during landing."[59]

Von Braun went on to discuss the two versions of direct ascent in a part of the speech that is all but forgotten now. He showed himself still enamored of "C-5 Direct," but the marginal weight factors and the need to develop a "high energy" (liquid-hydrogen) propulsion system for the lunar spacecraft made it impossible to do it "within this decade"—Kennedy's all-important deadline. As for the Nova, the time factors for development were even worse; it would be completely disruptive to the current plans for the Michoud factory and the Saturn C-5 program. He hoped instead it would later become an even more gigantic "Supernova" successor vehicle for launching a lunar base or manned interplanetary program. He concluded by recommending LOR, a logistics vehicle, and the Saturn C-IB launcher, which Houston needed for Apollo rendezvous tests in Earth orbit.[60]

Von Braun's 7 June remarks were fundamental in closing the long, drawn-out "mode decision," which was threatening NASA's ability to meet the president's objective. In formal bureaucratic terms, the decision would go on until Holmes sold it to the Webb-Dryden-Seamans triumvirate later in June, but the unity of the manned space centers and von Braun's convincing arguments made that pretty much a foregone conclusion. His speech had another salutary effect: it improved Houston-Huntsville relations. There would be no bitter battle at headquarters over competing modes, and the booster-spacecraft interface would be straightforward. According to Shea, von Braun's talk was no less than "a major element in the consolidation of NASA, really."[61] Now would come a challenge that von Braun and his colleagues anticipated but still could not quite fathom: how to manage such a gigantic program successfully. In the process von Braun would be forced to reorganize his center and the Saturn program in ways that broke with the traditional arsenal approach. But first he would have to master several other management problems at Marshall.

Even as the mode decision moved toward its climax, von Braun came under public and congressional criticism because of an embarrassing launch failure. On 8 May the Atlas-Centaur vehicle carrying the world's first liquid-hydrogen upper stage, Centaur, broke up and exploded. Due to a fundamental design flaw, one of the insulation panels around the hydrogen tank tore off, leading to structural failure. A week later von Braun was in Washington testifying in front of a House subcommittee, along with other NASA leaders. He had to admit that MSFC had managed Centaur in a rather cavalier fashion as a result of the project's peculiar history. The whole story makes an instructive comparison with Saturn, which was already on its way to an astounding record of no catastrophic launch failures in fourteen years of service. Less than three weeks earlier, on 25 April, von Braun had watched as SA-2, the second Saturn C-1, repeated the sterling performance of the first, ending with the spectacular intentional explosion of the dummy upper stages, dumping "95 tons of tap water" into near space in an experiment of dubious scientific value but no little public relations effect.[62]

Centaur had originated in the fertile mind of one of von Braun's Peenemünders, Krafft Ehricke, who had departed Huntsville in the early 1950s, frustrated at its apparent lack of a space future. After spending a couple of years with Walter Dornberger at Bell Aircraft, he went to Convair (soon part of General Dynamics) in San Diego just as the Atlas ICBM became a crash program. Shortly after Sputnik Ehricke proposed a liquid-hydrogen upper stage based on Atlas's radical, lightweight, stainless-steel "balloon" design: the rocket always had to be pressurized or it would collapse. ARPA funded this USAF project, but in mid-1959 NASA took over Centaur, as it would launch mostly civilian payloads. When the von Braun group became the agency's primary rocket center a year later, it seemed natural for MSFC to take it on, along with the NASA version of Agena, another Atlas-launched stage of air force origin. But NASA had kept Centaur's air force project managers in Los Angeles, where a small number of officers administered the contracts. Von Braun found himself managing this cutting-edge enterprise at long distance with thin communications and very little "penetration" of the contractor—Huntsville jargon for on-site inspectors and close technical supervision. Preoccupied like everyone else at his center by Saturn, he seems to have allowed MSFC to neglect Centaur. Keith Glennan once remarked that for Marshall "Saturn was a dream; Centaur was a job."[63]

To make matters worse, every technical decision Convair made was contrary to Huntsville's conservative way of doing things. The clash of engineering cultures started with the balloon structure of chief designer Charlie Bossart, who in turn dismissed what he called Marshall's "bridge" construction. When he and MSFC's structures chief, Willi Mrazek, got into a whispering argument during the first Centaur review in San Diego, von Braun sent the two outside. There Bossart invited Mrazek to whack a pressurized Centaur stage with a special sledgehammer to demonstrate that such a structure would indeed hold up. The hammer bounced off violently and whizzed by Mrazek's head, knocking off his glasses and almost killing him. The Centaur had nary a dent, while Mrazek marched off in a huff. But in 1961–62 the combination of risk-taking design choices, poor organization at General Dynamics, Ehricke's weak leadership, and hands-off management by the air force and Marshall produced a major crisis for Centaur, delaying the ill-fated first launch by the better part of a year. When it was delayed again in February 1962 because of bad wiring, an already exasperated von Braun scribbled a note to Kurt Debus: "I'm about ready to suggest to blow up the whole darn project. How long is this kind of thing going to continue?"[64]

As a result of the technical crises, NASA had given Marshall direct management of Centaur in January. In place of eight air force officers as the technical staff, von Braun deployed 140 engineers and managers to "penetrate" the contractor. That set off a whole series of disputes over the rocket and especially the guidance system, which von Braun's experts wrote off as hopelessly flawed. After the launch disaster, relations with the contractors only worsened. Von Braun predicted that Centaur would never meet the performance goals needed for its most important mission, launching the Surveyor soft-landing probes to the Moon. By August he did want to blow it up. John Naugle, an official in the NASA space science office, recalls that "Wernher leaned across the table, beat on the table and said you should cancel Centaur right now." As an alternative, the MSFC director suggested a monstrosity, an Agena atop a C-1. The next month the NASA leadership finally gave Centaur to Abe Silverstein's Lewis Research Center in Cleveland, which had pioneered liquid-hydrogen technology in the 1950s. Von Braun also tried to kill off the technically troubled Atlas-Agena target vehicle for Gemini, which was to orbit Agenas as docking targets for the all-important rendezvous tests by the two-astronaut spacecraft. In December 1962 headquarters sent that program to Lewis as well.[65]

Both von Braun cancellation attempts were wrongheaded, and both programs ultimately succeeded. To be fair, he and Marshall were handed problem cases after they were already well along—von Braun compared the Centaur situation to "adopting a ten year old child." But it is also true that his center could not easily adapt to methods or projects other than its own. Von Braun, in a private communication to his managers, admitted that there was a lot of truth to the criticism. He wrote in February 1963 regarding a new project, Pegasus, to put micrometeoroid detection wings on orbiting S-IV stages: "No Centaur project. This time it is our design (NIH = Not Invented Here does not apply) and our concept. Please no passive resistance in [the] divisions."[66]

Clearing the decks of most other rocket projects in 1962 did have the salu-tary effect of clarifying Marshall's role in NASA: it was not the booster cen-ter for everyone; it was, overwhelmingly, the Saturn center for Apollo. An earlier 1962 reorganization had already taken a major step in that direction when Kurt Debus's Canaveral operation became an independent Launch Operations Center on 1 July. (President Johnson renamed it Kennedy Space Center after JFK's assassination in November 1963.)

Von Braun himself advocated giving away part of his empire when it became clear in 1961 that Debus would never be able to establish a central NASA launch facility for all centers if his organization remained part of one of them. JFK's Moon decision had impelled a massive expansion of NASA activity in Florida, resulting in the purchase of Merritt Island, north of the air force range for a new, gigantic Launch Complex 39 for Saturn C-5. No longer would Debus's ex-army organization be just one more government entity operating on USAF territory, as it still did for C-1 and older rockets; now it would also be the owner of land and buildings. But other NASA cen-ters continued to launch on the air force side too, notably MSC, which cut Marshall completely out of the loop on Mercury-Atlas and Gemini-Titan. Von Braun had great confidence in Debus, who he once thought could be his successor, and backed him on centralizing Cape operations into a separate center. Debus thus became the second ex-German NASA center director (and unbeknown to almost everyone, also the second one to have been a member of the SS).[67]

Wernher von Braun parted with the Cape fairly easily, no doubt because his own center was growing immensely, fortifying its position as the largest NASA unit. In addition to Huntsville and the Michoud factory in New Orleans, which was extensively refurbished so that Chrysler and Boeing could assemble first stages for C-1/1B and C-5 respectively, Marshall acquired mosquito-infested swamplands in Mississippi, thirty-five miles north of Michoud, for a rocket test facility. The 7.5-million-lb thrust S-IC and the 1-million-lb thrust S-II, which would arrive by barge from Califor-nia, created so much noise and blast danger that an isolated testing zone was best. Webb's expectation, as well as von Braun's, was that Saturns would be launched by the dozens, if not hundreds, as they would become the infra-structure for U.S. space exploration. If so, a test facility was needed to process these big stages on an industrial scale. If they had known that only fifteen Saturn Vs would ever be built, they probably would have tested them all in Huntsville.[68]

As it was, a humongous 406-ft (124-m) tall S-IC test stand arose at the southern end of Marshall, near the Tennessee River, because the development program could not wait for the Mississippi Test Facility (MTF). Von Braun was also building a new headquarters complex that included a gleaming ten-story office tower. When it opened in mid-1963, employees accustomed to drab army-owned quarters quickly dubbed it the "Von Braun Hilton," much to his annoyance. MSFC peaked in 1966 at 7,740 civil servants, over 20 percent of NASA, plus about fifteen thousand contractors. Von Braun administered a center budget that nearly tripled to a billion dollars per year by FY 1963—most of it going to the stage and engine contracts with North American, Boeing, Douglas, and Chrysler. For all the bureaucratic aggravation that running such a gigantic operation entailed, he loved it. He was building his own space empire and was part of going to the Moon.[69]

In September 1962 von Braun was drawn into an uncomfortable spotlight, however, when Kennedy took a tour of the manned space centers. Although NASA thought it had made a final decision for lunar-orbit rendezvous, it had to fight a rearguard action against presidential science adviser Jerome Wiesner. At Huntsville, while von Braun was showing off an entire Saturn C-1 in the assembly building, the president alluded to this argument and drew Wiesner into the discussion, putting von Braun on the spot to defend LOR. Webb quickly joined in. A *Time* magazine reporter overheard much of it and published an embarrassing account of the public spat. But Kennedy trusted Webb, so Wiesner was ultimately rebuffed. The tour nonetheless reinforced von Braun's glowing admiration for Kennedy. He was impressed by the president's visionary, prospace speech at a stadium in Houston and by his coolness and self-possession in the blistering heat. The next month came the Cuban Missile Crisis, which was fostered in part by the United States placing von Braun's Jupiter IRBMs in Turkey. The crisis further bolstered Kennedy's reputation but frightened everyone thoroughly. Von Braun's daily lunch meeting on 25 October, when the possibility of nuclear war seemed all too real, discussed civil defense measures and not causing "a panic in town." Afterward he had an underground fallout shelter built behind his house.[70]

Four weeks after the crisis Kennedy met Webb, Dryden, Seamans, and Holmes about rapidly growing manned spaceflight cost overruns, which were becoming a source of conflict inside and outside the agency. Holmes wanted to submit a huge supplemental budget request for an additional $400 million in FY 1963, but this was very hard to sell to the president or Congress. Contradicting his own rhetoric, Kennedy asserted: "I'm not that interested in space." What he wanted was to beat the Soviets to the Moon for political purposes. Seeing that Webb did not believe the supplemental would accelerate Apollo that much and that it would be unpopular in Congress, Kennedy had little desire to submit it. Webb accepted that reality, but Holmes did not and even went to the press with complaints about Webb's unwillingness to cut other programs to support Apollo. Ultimately it cost Holmes his job in June 1963, as the administrator could not tolerate his insubordination any longer. Making matters worse, in the summer of 1963 the American public was no longer as enamored of the Moon race as it had been after Gagarin's flight, leading to congressional discussions of budget cutbacks, exacerbated by an apparent Soviet disinterest in the competition. Von Braun was so worried that he or his staff drafted an opinion piece defending Apollo, but it never appeared, probably because headquarters nixed it.[71]

The money shortfall affected Marshall in several important ways. The lunar logistics vehicle and the Nova faded away as funds were diverted to Saturn and Apollo. Technical problems, such as the worrying tendency of the giant F-1 engine to blow up because of combustion instability, cost more money and added to a growing slippage in projected launch dates. Landing on the Moon in 1969, let alone 1967, looked increasingly difficult, but von Braun held to MSFC's ultraconservative, step-by-step approach. He told Shea in January 1963 that expecting anything less than six unmanned flights of the Saturn V (as it was renamed in mid-1963) was "very, very optimistic." He took it for granted that they would fly one live stage at a time, as they were doing in Saturn I. Indeed, because of the relatively late start of the S-IV in 1960, Marshall would launch that vehicle with dummy upper stages no less than four times, which looked increasingly pointless when none failed.[72]

The year after the mode decision von Braun was also centrally involved in a constant, often bitter battle with headquarters over how to manage the Apollo program. Early in 1962 he had sold the NASA leadership on the idea of an Apollo systems integration contractor after hearing a pitch from Dr. George Mueller (pronounced Miller), a vice president at TRW Space Technologies Laboratories hailing from German-American stock in St. Louis. Webb then awarded the contract to General Electric instead. Von Braun, Gilruth, and Debus all thought GE was arrogant and unqualified for the job and resisted giving the company any significant role. In reality, the field centers did not want headquarters to closely manage them anyway, figuring they could do it all with intercenter panels and committees. In August 1963 Shea told Webb that the GE contract had been "the Berlin in NASA's Cold War"—that is, the central place of confrontation in a deeper struggle over how the agency was to be run. The role of Joe Shea as Holmes's deputy and systems manager was a point of conflict in itself. Von Braun complained constantly about him. Right after hearing of Holmes's forced resignation (he would stay on until a replacement was found), von Braun called Gilruth on 22 June to talk about the pending reorganization and Shea's role. Von Braun complained about "the size of the engineering staff in Washington. . . . My reply to this whole problem is . . . to cut them down from 400 to 1 and we'll be in good shape." Gilruth agreed, but was reluctant to go along with von Braun in cooking up a conspiracy against headquarters.[73]

Von Braun's fundamental problem was the mentality that he brought from his record of success: a go-it-alone attitude and a feeling of superiority derived from thirty years of groundbreaking technological accomplishments with an arsenal organization that had enough capability to do most of the job itself. Mueller, who took over Holmes's job as the head of the Office of Manned Space Flight in the fall of 1963, later called von Braun his most difficult center director as he "couldn't stand these unwashed overlords from Washington." Webb noted that the MSFC director was "very impatient of paperwork." After Kennedy witnessed a big Saturn rocket test where Webb was present—almost certainly the September 1962 tour—the president was very impressed and asked von Braun what he needed. "Wernher said right away, 'Just give us the money and cut out all this red tape and we'll get the job done.' " Webb, as a former Budget Bureau director, reminded him that there was a legal process to be followed. But von Braun's attitude was, in Webb's summary: "Get out of our way, we'll do the whole job and we know more than anybody else. We're Mr. Space of the United States." But Apollo was a much, much bigger program than any that von Braun's organization had ever done, requiring coast-to-coast coordination of multiple government centers and corporate contractors.[74]

By the summer of 1963 human spaceflight was already projected to be $600 million over budget, including a Gemini program that was going to cost double the original estimates and fly a year behind schedule. In the case of Marshall, the Douglas S-IV stage for Saturn I had already gone up 60 percent in cost, and the NAA S-II stage for Saturn V was becoming the biggest technical and management headache of the entire Saturn program. Storms's division of North American had won the Apollo CSM contract in a controversial award just a couple of months after getting the S-II contract in the fall of 1961. That meant a huge expansion of employment for NAA, mostly in southern California, with the consequence that a lot of people were hired with inadequate experience for the job, with ripple effects on the S-II project. Storms, a "slightly built, wiry" man with the "look of an accountant," was actually a hard-drinking, flyboy type—that is, a man after von Braun's heart. But his "behavior"—including excessive spending, hot-tempered out-bursts, and management by intimidation, hence the nickname "Stormy"—was already raising questions. Von Braun got caught in the middle that spring when NASA headquarters, in his words, "crawled all over him" for big cost overruns, delays, and bad management in the construction of Storms's S-II assembly plant at Seal Beach, near Long Beach, California. On top of that there was simply the enormous technological challenge of that 33-ft (10-m) diameter stage, the biggest liquid-hydrogen vehicle ever built to that point, yet so thin-walled and light that its closest natural analogy was the egg.[75]

Worried by the cost and schedule crisis, Webb instigated a revolution-from-above that began in June with Holmes's firing; he immediately extended it to von Braun's domain. At the Manned Spaceflight Management Council meeting in Houston on the twenty-fifth, Webb, who did not nor-mally attend Holmes's event, put von Braun and Rees under pressure for exploding costs. On his way home the next day the administrator stopped in Huntsville and ordered von Braun to reorganize Marshall's management structure and hire someone from industry because they did not know how to manage contractors. A year earlier, in August 1962, the MSFC director had issued a "Management Policy Number 1" reemphasizing the impor-tance of the project managers, who were responsible for contract adminis-tration. It was not a new problem, but the entrenched culture of the highly competent "labs" (Computation, Aeroballistics, and so on) was that they did much of the work in-house and reported directly to Rees and von Braun. The decree thus had had little effect, and the problem of the lab directors bypassing the project managers continued.[76]

The day after Webb passed through, von Braun held a long meeting with his key deputies. He decided to split the center in two: he would group the labs into Research and Development Operations and build an entirely new Industrial Operations organization out of the project and systems engineer-ing offices, plus Michoud and Mississippi. The former would employ the great bulk of Marshall's civil service workforce, but the latter would control the 90 percent of the vastly expanded MSFC budget that went to contrac-tors. With Webb's intervention and help, von Braun then hired Robert Young from rocket engine maker Aerojet to head Industrial Operations. He was only able to begin in November and stay a year, but he was at least able to start the process by which contract management gained the upper hand at Marshall.[77]

Just at this time Webb also began turning up the heat on von Braun over civil rights. Already at the end of 1961 he had asked him to hire more

"Negroes" at Marshall, which was overwhelmingly white because of entrenched discrimination and the workforce's highly skilled character. That proved difficult, in part because black engineers understandably did not want to move to Alabama. The climate had only worsened in November 1962, when George Wallace was elected governor. His inaugural address threw down the gauntlet to the Kennedy administration with the cry "Segregation now, segregation tomorrow, segregation forever." Wallace was unpopular in Huntsville, where the presence of a large number of "Yankees" from the rocket boom, plus dependence on federal employment, caused him to get the lowest vote percentage of any city in the state. Although Huntsville was no racial paradise, peaceful civil rights boycotts in 1962 had quickly toppled segregation in its stores and public facilities. The same was not true in Birmingham, only ninety miles south, where the resistance of the local establishment, Wallace, and the Ku Klux Klan to Martin Luther King's campaign culminated in the infamous May 1963 attack on demonstrators with fire hoses and dogs, revulsing the country and accelerating segregation's demise.[78]

Von Braun's natural inclination was to duck, as he was neither notably prejudiced nor particularly interested in creating trouble for himself by speaking out against prejudice. But he could not avoid the issue any longer when Wallace promised to "stand in the school house door" to prevent the integration of the University of Alabama that summer. Test cases loomed at the main campus in Tuscaloosa and at the small branch in Huntsville, where a black MSFC mathematician wished to enroll. Von Braun issued a declaration supporting his employee's rights. Wallace staged his melodramatic stand in Tuscaloosa, however, letting the Huntsville case go quietly. But Webb, impelled by Lyndon Johnson's concern about the continuing lack of opportunity for African-Americans in Huntsville, sent von Braun a letter on 24 June 1963 instructing him to apply pressure on local contractors for more hiring. It was only the beginning of two years of episodic discomfort for von Braun over the civil rights issue.[79]

In the larger scheme of things, integration was only a passing distraction, quickly overshadowed by part two of the revolution-from-above, which began when Webb hired George Mueller to take over the Office of Manned Spaceflight. Von Braun knew Mueller, who had a prominent nose and black-framed glasses, as a friendly competitor at STL. During the month of August he met privately with the MSFC director and other key players in the manned program. One lesson he drew was: "Changes must not erode or drastically change the role of Debus, Gilruth, or von Braun. They must not be such as to cause any of the Directors to have a legitimate reason for complaint either to Congress or the press." But nonetheless something had to be done as, Shea told him, "there is no 'morality' in the centers on the maintenance of either milestones or costs. The point of view of both Marshall and the Manned Spacecraft Center are that R&D programs cannot be scheduled or priced." Moreover, "Marshall . . . is too weak to exert adequate control over contractors" and "there is no center/contractor relationship which is without trouble." Communications among the centers and with HQ were poor. "They would lose the program and also lose the respect of the country unless they did something different," Mueller later said.[80]

His answer was to institute systems management as developed by STL and the air force for the ICBM program. He introduced much more rigorous, paperwork-heavy mechanisms for program control over costs and schedule. He also centralized Apollo management in a headquarters office that would communicate directly with corresponding offices in the centers on a daily basis.[81]

Von Braun was at first quite upset by the direct communication, as it seemed to undercut the role of center director. After nearly thirty years working for the military, he felt most compatible with a linear organization, although he was already experimenting locally with "matrix management," in which middle managers reported to more than one boss to deal with the overlapping responsibilities of labs and projects. On one of Mueller's early visits to Huntsville, "Wernher gave one of his impassioned speeches about how you can't change the basic organization of Marshall. I listened to that and told him and them [the Development Board] that Marshall was going to have to change." The Marshall director needed to strengthen Industrial Operations, if possible by reassigning talented technical people from the labs. Mueller also reduced the Management Council to himself and the three center directors (he inherited direct supervision of the centers from Holmes, who got that authority in the fall of 1962) and made it oversee the program offices. After several months of turmoil at headquarters and the centers, it began to work, and von Braun eventually came around to seeing the virtue of this arrangement. He used a corporate analogy in a 1971 interview: the council had acted as a board of directors, while the program managers were the operating presidents of their divisions.[82]

After initiating the reorganization process in September, Mueller moved on to salvaging Kennedy's end-of-the-decade goal, which was ambiguous enough to mean 1969 or 1970—but no one really wanted to argue for the latter. Internal studies showed that the existing spacecraft and booster schedules already made 1969 impossible. The only way to catch up was to eliminate missions. Mueller started by deleting all four manned flights on

Saturn I, which would terminate after ten tests without ever launching an operational payload. Von Braun accepted that fairly well because it saved money and allowed a slight speed-up of Saturn IB. But the next move could cause rather more consternation in Huntsville. It went by the name of the "all-up decision."[83]

Von Braun first heard about it in Washington on 29 October, directly upon returning with his wife from a visit to Argentina and Brazil. Mueller emphasized "the importance of a philosophical approach to meeting schedules which minimizes 'dead-end' testing, and maximizes 'all-up' systems flight tests." In short, that meant launching the very first vehicle with all live stages, such as had been done with the USAF Minuteman solid-fuel ICBM. It also meant flying Houston's Apollo CSM in operational versions on the very first Saturn IBs and Vs. Mueller followed this up with a message to his three center directors telexed on 1 November. It proposed that humans fly as early as the third mission on each booster, if there were two successful tests. Officially the first manned flight would be the seventh, while the third through sixth would be listed as "man-rating" missions. But the objective of getting astronauts up as soon as possible was clear. It was a bold proposal.[84]

Von Braun did not actually have to deal with it until Monday, 4 November. He had gone directly from Washington to a NASA management conference in California and did not get home until the weekend. Somewhere along the way, in Washington or California, Mueller had given him his argument. As von Braun later summarized it: water in dummy stages gave the vehicle different dynamic characteristics from real propellants, so would it not be more realistic to put lox and LH_2 in the tanks anyway? He conceded the point. Now, if you have real engines instead of dummies would that not give a better simulation of performance? Okay, sure, he said. Then why not go ahead and light the engines—what have you got to lose? Von Braun: "I said, George, your logic is perfect. And . . . then that whole stack sits there, and when finally somebody pushes the button, we shall have our reputations go riding on it." It was risky, but he had to admit he did not have a strong argument against it.[85]

The reaction at Marshall was, however, as one might expect: "management has lost its mind," von Braun later said. Key individuals like his structures and propulsion chief, Willi Mrazek, were appalled—it completely contradicted Huntsville's tradition of exhaustive testing. But Mueller's letter essentially said: show me with technical arguments why this is impossible, or I am going ahead. Von Braun scheduled a briefing for Wednesday and a board meeting for Friday. His managers gave a number of reasons why Mueller's proposal was crazy, but von Braun would not accept most of them, since they amounted to the same old conservatism. There were sound technical reasons why the Saturn IB's performance would not be adequate for a manned mission until the fourth launch instead of the third, and early Saturn Vs would be below performance, and there was only one acceptable mission profile for a lunar-velocity reentry test of the Apollo Command Module on the very first flight, as Mueller wanted. Just as in the case of the LOR decision, von Braun made up his mind that the interests of the program overrode the parochial Huntsville viewpoint, especially as the technical arguments lined up against them. On Friday morning he called Mueller and told him of Marshall's acceptance, with the provisos. Needless to say, his boss was relieved.[86]

Mueller's management revolution would go on—by the end of 1963 he appointed Samuel Phillips, the air force general who had headed Minuteman, as Apollo program manager, and he sent Shea to take over the Apollo spacecraft office in Houston and George Low to be deputy director under Gilruth. But with the "all-up" decision, it can be fairly said that all the key early decisions of the lunar landing program were complete. NASA had convinced Kennedy that the United States could go to the Moon "before this decade is out" and had picked the launch vehicles, the landing mode, the management structure, and the schedule that would at least make that goal feasible. In every case Wernher von Braun had been a central player, although in almost every case he had not been the innovator and had often resisted—out of technological or organizational conservatism—what turned out to be the best course. There had been a useful creative tension in that: it helped ensure that NASA avoided fundamental technical mistakes, but when necessary, von Braun was willing to consolidate a consensus among the agency leadership by overruling his own people. If he had not done that, the program might have been a failure.

Apollo had gone through a rough patch in 1963, not only internally at the space agency but also in public questioning of the goal and of NASA's rising budget. When Kennedy spoke to the United Nations on 20 September, offering to go to the Moon jointly with the Soviets, it threw everyone in the agency for a loop, as he had not cleared it with Webb. The USSR inevitably rejected the idea, but as much of a propaganda exercise as it may have been for Kennedy, it also reflected his doubts about the huge expenditure he was undertaking. As if to reassure himself, eight weeks later, on 16 November, he made another trip to the Cape. At the Saturn I complex, where SA-5 was sitting on pad 37 with the first functional S-IV liquid-hydrogen stage, von Braun again briefed him and again came away deeply impressed with the president.[87]

Six days later von Braun was on a plane coming back from yet another congressional hearing when he heard the shocking news from Dallas. On Monday the twenty-fifth he and Maria were to attend their first state dinner with the Kennedys; it became a national day of mourning instead. Von Braun did paperwork in the office with only a couple of assistants, the funeral playing on television in the background. His secretary says that it was the only time she saw him cry. But the assassination had an ironic effect: Apollo became one of the Kennedy legacies that could not be easily questioned and one that President Johnson was determined to carry out. A month later LBJ invited von Braun to his Texas ranch to meet the new West German chancellor, Ludwig Erhard. The president gave von Braun one of his trademark cowboy hats, telling him he wanted to see that hat on the Moon. Von Braun was thrilled. But it would be five and a half long, grueling years, filled with many new technical, management, and political challenges, before the first astronauts would land there.[88]

CHAPTER SIXTEEN

You're an Optimist, but Then, So Am I

1963–67

We can lick gravity, but sometimes the paperwork is over-whelming. —WERNHER VON BRAUN[1]

The mid-1960s were years of nonstop management challenges for Wernher von Braun, as the Apollo deadline loomed over everyone who felt responsible for the promise made to Kennedy. Sometimes the end-of-decade objective seemed like an exciting challenge, the first step toward a wonderful space future, but often and increasingly the Moon seemed to be a clock in the sky, inexorably ticking away as problem after problem threatened to derail the program schedule. Having adapted to the requirements and decisions that headquarters imposed on him between 1961 and 1963, von Braun grew further as an engineering manager, skillfully reshaping his organization to meet Apollo's strenuous demands. Although he was only one of about ten top leaders of that program, the ultimate and stunning success of the Saturn vehicles, and thus of the Moon landing itself, is difficult to imagine without him.

At the same time the mid-1960s were years in which he was forced once again, as in the 1950s, to grapple with his center's organizational survival. The buoyant optimism that NASA and he had felt in the early 1960s gradually declined as rising national problems—riots in the streets, burning cities, a slowing economy, and a worsening Vietnam war—undercut support for space exploration. There were no more large launch vehicles on the horizon, and NASA's post-Apollo human spaceflight program floundered in uncertainty and disarray, as further expensive initiatives were politically infeasible. Von Braun decided that keeping Marshall viable must be his primary mission, once Apollo's requirements were satisfied. That meant bidding for new types of programs, notably in astronomy and the space sciences, that would force MSFC to alter its engineering-dominated approach. It is a testimony to his efforts that in the 1970s, long after he had left Huntsville, a now-more-diverse Marshall survived the complete shutdown of the Saturn program. Even so, he presided over a painful downsizing of his center beginning in 1966.

The mid-1960s were years, finally, in which von Braun coasted on his fame, although there were worrying signs that his image might be damaged by growing skepticism about his National Socialist past. He appeared in the media less as attention shifted to Houston and the astronauts, but that did not bother him much—he was tired of the personal publicity but remained an iconic figure, the one rocket engineer and NASA official whom most people knew by name. Yet as the Cold War consensus in American society eroded, his celebrity made him a target for further criticism and parody by avant-garde artists. While these new attacks episodically annoyed him, they were not a major problem in comparison to the slow trickling out of information about his SS membership and the horrors of Mittelbau-Dora. Thanks to an East German smear campaign with echoes throughout the Soviet bloc, damaging information about his compromises with the Third Reich began to seep into the Western media. He knew that this information could become a public relations disaster that would undermine his career and perhaps even the space program itself. To his relief, however, the story would always go away.

On 29 January 1964 the Kennedy and Marshall Space Center crews finally got the first two-stage Saturn I, SA-5, off the pad after two months of agonizing delays. It put the largest payload in history into orbit—the empty liquid-hydrogen/oxygen S-IV stage weighing over 37,000 lb (16,800 kg). An hour afterward President Johnson called von Braun in the Launch Complex 37 blockhouse and asked him if the cowboy hat he gave him at the ranch still fit—in other words, was the Marshall director getting a swelled head? Von Braun delightedly reported the story to his father, because it revealed his friendly relationship with LBJ, closer than with any American president. It was also one more milestone in the Saturn program, which was going from success to success. Perhaps the Moon was not so far away after all.[2]

Still, there were more demands from headquarters. In early 1964 von Braun found himself confronted with phase two of George Mueller's management revolution. Sam Phillips, a tall, lean officer in his forties, officially took office as Apollo program director on 1 January and immediately began pushing for a system of "configuration control," or "configuration management." Coming out of the air force ICBM experience, Phillips knew that without strict controls over the endless engineering changes that went into rocket and spacecraft development, costs would spiral, schedules would stretch, and failures would multiply. He pushed for rigorous systems of documentation at all levels and approval only by change boards. That meant a further, onerous increase in the amount of paper circulating among NASA and corporate engineers.[3]

At a June 1964 meeting of the Apollo Executives, an organization Mueller had formed to bring the top corporate leaders in the program together to facilitate cooperation, von Braun led the charge against configuration management. "This whole thing has a tendency of moving the real decisions up . . . from the guy on the line to someone else," he said. The president of Boeing countered that that was just good management. Von Braun argued that producing a small number of development vehicles was different from mass-producing a military weapon; "we have to retain a little more flexibility." Still accustomed to his organization operating as a self-contained unit with excellent internal communications, he did not see the point of yet more paperwork, an attitude well entrenched at Marshall.[4]

Mueller ended the discussion by pointing out that it was simply about documenting the configuration of the vehicle, creating orderly processes for deciding when to change, and then systematically telling everyone what was changing. Although Houston was even more resistant, Mueller and Phillips were not about to be moved. By 1965 von Braun himself was telling his people to implement the air force general's configuration manual. Just as was the case with the 1963 reorganization, he began to see its value in a huge national project. Phillips, when later asked about the MSFC director being a good team player, made the interesting observation that he "*became* a good team player."[5]

Phillips came into the job expecting to dislike von Braun. He had been closely associated with General Schriever's organization when rivalry with the army was at its height, and as a World War II fighter pilot, he had even flown escort on one of the 1944 American daylight raids against Peenemünde. Yet "after weeks and then months of interaction, Wernher and I became close friends. And remained so." Even though the MSFC director was energetic in defending his center's interests and was always trying to sell some idea or other, "he had that rare gift of giving his undivided attention to whomever he was talking to. He could make a person feel personally important to him and that their ideas were of great value."[6] His charm and genuine personal warmth disarmed Phillips, like so many others. Although von Braun resisted changing his organization's way of doing business, when he came to see the other side or when given a clear order, he was an effective advocate to his own people.

This advocacy turned out to be needed, for judging by the internal speeches and pep talks that von Braun gave to Marshall audiences in the mid-1960s, he faced ongoing tensions within his organization, especially over the 1963 split between Industrial Operations (contract managers) and Research and Development Operations (the "labs"). In June 1964 George Mueller was still disturbed by the R&DO laboratories circumventing the IO program offices and giving "technical direction" (engineering changes) to contractors while ignoring "normal contractual procedures." Presumably he or Phillips spoke privately about it to von Braun. The Marshall director, at an internal retreat for his managers six months later, emphasized: "IO is carrying the ball to manage the entire Saturn program" and the "role of R&DO is strictly one of support to IO." This scheme did not sit well with the proud labs, which traced their heritage back to Peenemünde. They still wanted to run projects on an arsenal-system basis.[7]

In fact, of the Saturn stages, about half were being done in a quasi-arsenal fashion anyway. Chrysler inherited the S-IB first stage for Saturn IB, with its nine tanks and eight engines, as it was essentially just an uprated S-I, which Marshall had mostly assembled in-house. Out of ten S-Is, the auto company built only two at the Michoud facility in New Orleans before switching to S-IBs. The monumental S-IC first stage for Saturn V, 33 ft (10 m) in diameter, NASA contracted to Boeing. But before Michoud could be tooled and equipped to produce flight stages, Marshall constructed three test stages and the first two flight stages in Huntsville. Hundreds of Boeing personnel came to work at MSFC to learn how to build the S-IC, to the point where the line between the company and the center was so blurred, Marshall could not blame the contractor when S-IC fell behind schedule in 1964–65. Another case was the Instrument Unit (IU), the guidance, control, and computing "brain" of the Saturn IB and V, isolated into a separate ring to effectively manage changes. It began as an in-house project of Walter Haeussermann's guidance lab. After NASA awarded the production contract to computer giant IBM, von Braun had to insist in that December 1964 retreat that the lab treat the company as a stage contractor through Industrial Operations, not as its sidekick. IBM decided it was best to construct its plant in Huntsville anyway, so that production remained strongly intertwined with MSFC. Only North American's S-II (Saturn V second stage), plus Douglas's S-IV (Saturn I second stage) and S-IVB (Saturn IB second stage and V third stage), were entirely contractor-designed and -built, all in southern California. The S-II in particular became the problem child of the whole program, which Marshallites blamed in part on the labs' difficulty in "penetrating" the contractor.[8]

With so much weight now placed on Industrial Operations' control over a billion-dollar-per-year Saturn budget, von Braun found that he needed strong managers as top administrators. In 1963 he had put his old friend and former Mittelwerk production chief Arthur Rudolph in charge of Saturn V, and an army colonel with long experience in Huntsville, Lee James, in as Saturn I/IB project manager. They were Sam Phillips's counterparts in his decentralized Apollo program office. Rudolph had already acquired considerable project management experience in the late 1950s and proved to be an excellent choice for what was Marshall's cornerstone project, the launch vehicle for the Moon landing. When James Webb viewed his elaborate, illuminated-chart Saturn V Control Room at Marshall in September 1965, he called it "one of the most sophisticated forms of human effort that I have ever seen anywhere."[9]

In 1964, von Braun still had the problem of replacing Rudolph's boss, IO director Bob Young, who was going back to Aerojet after his one-year stint. The answer came from Sam Phillips's determination to bring many more air force officers into the Apollo program to bolster the systems engineering and systems management capability of the whole organization. Phillips found Colonel (soon Brigadier General) Edmund O'Connor for von Braun, an experienced missile program manager, and O'Connor worked out so well that he stayed past the Moon landing. He was the first of about a dozen air force officers at Marshall, which must have been interesting for them, situated as they were in the middle of Redstone Arsenal and right next door to Army Missile Command. The fact that MSFC culture had a military heritage may have been a source of comfort, however. Phillips later recalled that, just as was the case for him in the air force, everyone at a Marshall meeting stood up when von Braun entered the room.[10]

Finding military officers to fill senior and midlevel slots was helpful, because Alabama's legacy of poverty and segregation made it difficult to attract industry managers to Huntsville. Young would not stay mostly because his family refused to move in the face of mediocre schools and the state's reputation for bigotry and violence—in September 1963 Klansmen had killed four schoolgirls in the bombing of a Birmingham black church. The difficulty of keeping Young seems to have been a primary cause behind Webb's outburst during the 1964 presidential election, one that again put von Braun in the middle of the crossfire between Washington and Governor George Wallace. During an October visit to Alabama, Webb lashed out against the racial climate, saying it hindered Marshall recruitment. He called the state the least appreciative for all the federal space dollars being poured into the Southeast. Hale Boggs, an influential Louisiana congressman, then released an announcement, based on a misunderstood conversation with Webb, that hundreds of top MSFC people, including von Braun, might move to Michoud. Webb did not exactly deny it, saying "Huntsville and Alabama don't have any monopoly on Dr. von Braun."[11]

Worried about the impact of the civil rights struggle on Marshall and under pressure from Webb, for about six months in 1964–65 von Braun became a cautious but important voice for integration and racial moderation in Alabama. When the Webb-Boggs imbroglio had a short-term disruptive impact on Huntsville's economy, von Braun reassured the local Chamber of Commerce in December 1964 about the city's future, but he asked them to conform to the equal opportunity provisions of the Civil Rights Act recently passed in Congress. In March 1965 Wallace's state police attacked a peaceful voting rights march in Selma. The next month von Braun spoke in favor of black voting rights to the Rotary District Convention, drawing both praise and scorn from local letter writers, some of them staunch white racists. He made at least one more such speech in May, attracting favorable attention from liberal newspapers outside the South. *The New York Times* ran a story, "Von Braun Fights Alabama Racism," on 14 June, which came in the wake of Wallace's stop in Huntsville on the eighth, part of a press tour of Alabama he organized to counteract the state's terrible image.[12]

Wallace's stop provoked a flurry of consultation between NASA headquarters and Marshall, including direct discussions between von Braun and Webb. When Wallace showed up with the press and members of the legislature, Webb appeared too. They were treated to the deafening, visceral power of a firing of the first S-IC test booster, 7.5 million lb of thrust. Von Braun gave a speech obliquely opposing segregation, saying Alabama had to "shed the shackles of the past." Afterward he asked Wallace if he would like to be the first person on the Moon, to which the governor joked: "Well, better not. You fellows might not bring me back."[13]

An interesting question is whether von Braun's relative outspokenness had any deeper connection to his Nazi past. James T. Shepherd, one of his special assistants in the 1960s, recalls that he, von Braun, and Harry Gorman, the MSFC deputy director for administration (paralleling Rees for technical issues), were waiting for a flight or a meeting in Washington, probably at exactly this time. Gorman worried that the Klan would burn a cross on von Braun's lawn. The Marshall director replied that he remembered those who had asked him, when he got to America, what he had done "when people were disappearing" in Nazi Germany. He said, Shepherd claims,

"That's not going to happen again. . . . I am not going sit quiet on a major issue like segregation." In fact, there is no indication that it bothered him until the early 1960s and ample evidence that Webb was pressuring him, often in a fairly condescending way. Marshall's record on integration under his leadership was also modest; the overwhelmingly white character of the workforce did not change much in spite of his honest efforts to recruit African-Americans. Still, he had ended up on the right side of a human rights issue for once.[14]

Just as in 1963, the civil rights crisis soon passed. The years 1965–66 were good ones for NASA and Marshall, marked by a string of successes that finally seemed to signal parity with the Soviets in the space race. Von Braun watched from the blockhouse on 23 March 1965, his fifty-third birthday, as Gus Grissom and John Young took off on the first piloted mission of the Gemini spacecraft. Although there were problems and emergencies in that program, NASA launched ten flights by November 1966 and tested many key technologies for Apollo. Marshall had nothing to do with Gemini, but it pulled off its own unbroken record of Saturn firings during this period. In 1964–65 five more Saturn Is orbited dummy Apollo command modules, the last three also deploying big Pegasus micrometeoroid detection wings from the empty S-IV stages. These payloads showed that the meteor danger to spacecraft was lower than expected. In 1966 Kennedy Space Center (KSC) launched three Marshall Saturn IBs with the new S-IVB upper stage. Two of the rockets lofted functional Apollo spacecraft on reentry tests and one carried out a liquid-hydrogen experiment. Von Braun basked in Saturn's string of successes. Another triumph was the May 1966 rollout at the Cape of the first, nonflying version of the gigantic Saturn V. By the end of that year, an optimistic von Braun told a newsmagazine that the Moon landing might be feasible in 1968.[15]

Out of the public eye, however, the mid-1960s were not years of complacency and ease for him or for the other key Apollo managers. Technical problems delayed the first Saturn IB launch and the Saturn V rollout by months. Serious design problems with the Saturn V launch tower's "swing arms," which were to pull quickly back from the vehicle at liftoff, forced von Braun and Kurt Debus to build a test facility, called the "arm farm," at the Cape in 1966. By late 1964 engineers had finally solved the combustion instability problem in the giant F-1 engine, but other engines and stages went through teething problems too. Douglas even blew up an S-IV in 1964 and an S-IVB in 1967, both due to procedural errors at its Sacramento, California, test facility. Yet nothing worried von Braun more than the S-II.[16]

The contractor was of course the same as for the Apollo Command and

Service Modules, Harrison Storms's space division of North American Aviation. Worry about NAA's management competence began as early as 1962.
In July 1964 von Braun and Gilruth sent a joint letter to Storms outlining
their concern about excessive manpower and large cost overruns. During a
September 1964 board meeting, "Dr. von Braun emphasized that the S-II is
the most important single problem confronting MSFC, and therefore carries
the overriding priority." Problems emerged with the external insulation, the
common bulkhead separating the oxygen and hydrogen tanks, and the welding of the thin aluminum walls of the stage. Everything was made tougher
by NASA pressure to reduce weight to increase Saturn V performance. In
the last, most refined version of the stage, structure constituted only *8 percent* of its fueled weight: it was one of the most lightweight rocket vehicles
ever built. The constant delays and new problems meant that von Braun had
to spend much time on the phone talking to Storms, or flying to the West
Coast for meetings, or participating in program reviews in Huntsville or
Washington.[17]

The worst crisis of the S-II program erupted, literally, late one night in
September 1965. NAA destroyed a test stage at its plant in Seal Beach, California, during structural testing with a load of water. It was lucky no one was
killed when the fragile structure collapsed and tons of water came crashing
out. At the same time the revision of North American's contracts revealed
huge cost overruns in the offing. Ed O'Connor told von Braun in a memo
that the "S-II program is out of control." He wrote it for the forthcoming
visit of Lee Atwood, the scholarly NAA chairman of the board, who came
without Storms, who was then in the hospital from a stress-induced heart
attack. Von Braun impressed on Atwood the need for urgent change and
gave him notice that a "tiger team" would be coming to California to review
both the S-II and the CSM.[18]

Rees, already harshly critical of Storms and his managers, was a key
member. After a multiday inspection trip in late November 1965, he wrote
von Braun in a very closely held memo: "It is not entirely impossible that
the first manned lunar landing may slip out of this decade" because of the
S-II. At headquarters Sam Phillips gathered together all the reports and
wrote a cover memo to George Mueller, later known as the "Phillips
Report," that indicated almost zero confidence in North American. He
wanted Storms fired. Mueller, feeling perhaps that this was further than the
government was allowed to go with a private contractor, left that out of his
letter to Atwood, but it was still harshly critical.[19]

Wernher von Braun and Eberhard Rees already had a well-honed, good-
cop/bad-cop routine for handling problems, and that is how, in general, the

Marshall director treated the S-II crisis. To NAA managers he sounded relatively sympathetic, at least in comparison to the infuriated Rees. Still, according to one Marshall insider, von Braun himself demanded Storms's resignation to his face in a company meeting. "There was dead silence [except for] a lot of gasping. That was a monumental thing . . . the most courageous thing he ever did." On another occasion in 1966, James Shepherd witnessed him telling Atwood: "Lee, Stormy has got to go." Atwood would not budge, and that was where the matter rested until the following year.[20]

The travails of the S-II program were not over. On 28 May 1966 Maria von Braun took a call at home from Storms. Her husband had already gone to Lake Guntersville, where they had a houseboat and a cabin cruiser, for the Memorial Day weekend. In a "tear choked voice," Storms told her that his crews had just blown up a test stage after a firing at the Mississippi Test Facility. Five were slightly injured. This failure was procedural and not the result of a fundamental design flaw, but it naturally caused more delays and more special reports.[21]

The bulk of key systems testing now fell on the first flight stage, the S-II-1, which was to fly with the first Saturn V, perhaps as early as the spring of 1967. But because of all the necessary repairs and fixes, it stayed in Mississippi through much of the fall. On 30 November 1966 von Braun was at last able to fly down for its first ignition test, leaving after work and not getting home until four a.m. When he came in the next afternoon, he told his secretaries "that the S-II-1 firing was a success; and that it was about time." The Saturn program might finally be in the clear.[22]

The same could not be said of post-Apollo human spaceflight. In the mid- to late 1960s the management problem that most preoccupied him, after the Moon landing, was keeping Marshall Space Flight Center in business after Kennedy's goal was achieved. By 1965 it became obvious to von Braun that the only project on the horizon capable of propping up employment at MSFC was the Apollo Applications Program (AAP), a stopgap project to use Apollo hardware for both Earth orbital and lunar missions.

Earlier in the decade von Braun had not worried much about the future of either spaceflight or the center, as it seemed obvious that the United States and the human race were heading toward a glorious future of space stations, Moon bases, and Mars expeditions. When in August 1963 Hermann Koelle wrote him that the production of fifty Saturn IBs and a hundred Saturn Vs "seem[s] virtually to be assured," he scribbled in the margin: "HHK You're an optimist, but then, so am I."[23] It just seemed unimaginable to him, and to other space enthusiasts, that the United States would throw away the elaborate spacefaring infrastructure created for Apollo. That was true even though the Moon and LOR decisions of 1961–62 effectively ended any possibility of starting a new large program like a space station. Landing a human on the lunar surface by decade's end was such a huge challenge that it left no room in the manned spaceflight budget to do anything else, a reality confirmed by the money and management crises of 1963.

The lack of any major program funding did not keep Marshall out of advanced technology development for space exploration, notably the nuclear rocket, a subject of great interest to von Braun. The Atomic Energy Commission's joint project with NASA, called Rover and later NERVA, was developing nuclear reactors that would heat liquid hydrogen up to exhaust velocities nearly twice that of liquid-hydrogen/liquid-oxygen combustion. From 1960 to 1963 Marshall managed a program to put a nuclear third stage on a Saturn V by 1967–68, but it was canceled at the end of 1963 because of major problems with the Rover engine. Von Braun also supported the even more exotic Project Orion, which aimed to create a massive spaceship propelled by exploding a string of small nuclear bombs underneath a pusher plate. As the air force lost interest, NASA and Marshall began to help funding, but headquarters cut it off in mid-1964 as too futuristic and too expensive.[24]

As a by-product of MSFC's work on landing payloads on the Moon for astronaut use, von Braun's center also funded lunar roving vehicles in the 1960s. Contractors even built experimental prototypes of Moon buggies and mobile laboratories and drove them around sites at Marshall. Moreover, Huntsville carried out several studies of human missions to Mars and Venus, beginning with a 1962 effort dubbed EMPIRE. With his personal history going back to *The Mars Project* and to his youth, von Braun was naturally fascinated by the prospect of humans visiting the Red Planet. He was often convinced that the space station would be more politically salable as the successor program to Apollo, but the dream of a Mars expedition was there as the ultimate objective of his life's work.[25]

Once George Mueller had succeeded in imposing systems management on the manned space program, however, he became more concerned in 1964 with a short-term program for using leftover Saturn boosters and Apollo spacecraft. James Webb, who had sold Congress on the need for an initial run of twelve Saturn IBs and fifteen Saturn Vs to accomplish Kennedy's goal, shared his concern that under the "all-up" schedule, several might be unused. In addition von Braun, Mueller, and Webb all expected that the Apollo production lines and test facilities could continue to spit out more boosters and spacecraft at a rate of up to six Saturn IBs, six Saturn Vs, and eight CSMs per year. It seemed like a waste to throw away this expensive national capability by ending production, but something would have to be done with all that hardware. Thus arose Mueller's idea for AAP.[26]

It proved so troubled, however, that some wag suggested the acronym stood for "Almost a Program." One reason was George Mueller's conception of AAP as a grab bag of missions designed to use Apollo hardware to prove the capability of humans in space. He and much of the NASA leadership, including at times von Braun, defined Apollo as Kennedy's goal of landing a man on the Moon and bringing him back: a couple of successes and it was over. Extended lunar exploration, including missions that might use Marshall's lunar rovers, were thus part of AAP. Also in the program were a variety of potential Earth orbital missions involving imaging of Earth resources, long-duration weightlessness experiments, and astronomy from orbit. Von Braun was conscious of the disjointed impression that this left, which made it difficult to sell to politicians or the populace. In April 1966 he told a top corporate executive that "we have never had a program with a poorer definition—AAP still tries to be a lot of things to a lot of people."[27]

Some of this was definitely Mueller's fault: his brilliant talent for operational management was not matched by one for long-term planning. But his hands were also tied by NASA's political dilemma of not being able to offer another ambitious manned program. Moreover, the agency had developed a bureaucratic self-interest in preserving the facilities and employment built up in the Apollo boom; otherwise the politically savvy Webb would never have supported AAP.[28]

Marshall's own survival certainly became von Braun's primary interest in the program, however aware he was of its failings. By 1964–65 it was clear that Marshall would have a problem maintaining its massive workforce, which peaked at over 7,700 civil servants and 15,000 contractors in 1966. As the Saturn launch vehicles had to be ready first so that test launches could be made, MSFC was already going to pass its peak with no new launch vehicles or large projects on the horizon. The contractor workforce could shrink dramatically, as much of it was constructing test stands and buildings at MSFC, MTF, and Michoud, but Marshall's in-house capability needed new development projects or it would face its own decline—a renewal on an even bigger scale of von Braun's dilemma of 1954–55 and 1958–59. In early 1965 he told Ernst Geissler, head of his Aero-Astrodynamics Laboratory, that "I am convinced that MSFC not only can, but will 'survive' in spite of the pressures and conditions you mentioned, and it is to this end I have dedicated myself."[29]

Out of the profusion of ideas for AAP came two fairly solid possibilities for Marshall: an improvised space station soon dubbed the Orbital Workshop (to distinguish it from a "real" station) and a human-operated solar observatory called the Apollo Telescope Mount (ATM). NASA would eventually launch these together in a cluster known as Skylab, but they started as two entirely separate projects.

The former began in "spent stage" ideas that went back to the beginning of the space race: if the last stage of the launch vehicle goes into orbit with the payload, could that big, empty piece of "space junk" not be utilized to create a makeshift station? Von Braun and his key people had earlier considered the feasibility of using the S-IV or S-II stages for this purpose. As AAP got started in 1964, he had his future projects office focus on the S-IVB launched as the second stage of the Saturn IB, as it offered more room and payload than the S-IV; Saturn I was being phased out anyway. Moreover, he was searching for a way to keep the IB in business beyond the early Earth orbital missions for Apollo. With the Orbital Workshop idea, not only was that rocket needed to launch its S-IVB, but others were needed to orbit the crews who would experiment in outfitting the stage's empty liquid-hydrogen tank as a living space. An airlock module and docking adapter would be fitted on the front of the tank to provide access and a place for key controls and equipment. Under von Braun's direction, Marshall studied the concept in 1965, culminating in selling it at the end of that year to George Mueller and to Bob Seamans, deputy administrator since the recent death of Hugh Dryden.[30]

The ATM solar astronomy payload began in 1965, when the NASA space science budget took a cut because Congress capped agency funds at around $5 billion per year and Apollo had to be protected. One canceled project was a sophisticated solar satellite. Now Homer Newell's space sciences office had a bunch of experiments with no way to launch them, while Mueller's manned spaceflight office was casting about for AAP ideas. Mueller favored mounting the experiment package on a Lunar Module ascent stage, which would provide the crew cabin for operating the solar telescopes. The astronauts would rendezvous with the ATM in an Apollo spacecraft and transfer two astronauts over to work the instruments while separated. This idea provoked stubborn opposition in Houston as the LM was unsuitable for living for any length of time. In any case the proposal threatened to complicate the module's development for lunar landing—it was already way behind schedule. The objections of Gilruth's center were only somewhat pacified in late 1966 when Mueller's office accepted the "cluster concept" of docking the

Apollo Telescope Mount to the Orbital Workshop, which would be upgraded to habitability on an earlier mission.[31]

Well before that time, at the end of July 1966, von Braun got the heartening news that Marshall would be assigned the ATM, fruit borne of what he called his " 'hard sell' policy in the AAP field." Huntsville beat out Goddard Space Flight Center, outside Washington, which was NASA's primary facility for astronomy and space science satellites but had no experience integrating big manned payloads. Moreover, it might pave the way for even bigger human-tended observatories, such as the later Hubble Space Telescope, which would better suit Marshall as well. Von Braun was well aware that MSFC's entry into science missions, even though it was overwhelmingly an engineering center, might require the center to lay off engineers and hire scientists over the long haul, but he just wanted to "plant a new flag in Marshall in some new field" to keep the place in business.[32]

At least in astronomy he did not face opposition from Gilruth's Manned Spacecraft Center, which was perturbed from the outset by the role in human space operations that Marshall was carving out with the Orbital Workshop. The LOR decision in 1962 had lessened tension between Houston and Huntsville by simplifying the Apollo interface: above MSC's spacecraft, below MSFC's booster. Now the turf battles began all over again, exacerbated by the confusing array of proposed missions for AAP in Earth and in lunar orbit, the great majority of which never materialized. A minor press flap broke out in the fall of 1965 when *The Houston Post* complained that von Braun's center was intruding on MSC's sacred astronaut turf. Another erupted a year later, and both provoked congressional inquiries. A further source of tension was MSC's opposition to the LM/ATM concept and to the challenges posed by refitting a spent-stage Workshop in weightlessness, as well as its reluctance to complicate Apollo's operational demands with AAP missions immediately after, or even before, lunar flights. Von Braun was very conscious of the fact that Marshall had to be constantly on its best behavior vis-à-vis Houston.[33]

The tension was such that in August 1966 George Mueller organized a retreat for human spaceflight leaders at Lake Logan, a North Carolina resort, in order to negotiate what amounted to a peace treaty between Huntsville and Houston. Von Braun and Rees attended, as did Bob Gilruth and his deputy George Low. They hammered out the "Lake Logan agreements," outlining a rather arcane division of responsibilities for a projected post-Apollo space station—AAP was only a stopgap. MSC would get the "Command Post," while MSFC would be responsible for the "Mission Module" where crews lived and worked. "Experiment Modules" could be made by either, with Houston controlling life sciences and Earth resources and Huntsville astronomy. The Workshop and the ATM missions were defined in such a way as to respect this turf division. Mueller also specified that Houston would get all lunar surface activities, forcing Marshall to give up most of its Moon projects by the end of the year.[34]

While all this was happening, AAP only limped along in NASA's budgets, undercut not only by its lack of a convincing mission and purpose but above all by the country's growing problems. In March 1965 President Johnson sent the first combat troops into Vietnam, ostensibly to prop up the South Vietnamese army and its American advisers, but the intervention rapidly escalated. By the end of the year 184,000 American soldiers were "in country." In August the Los Angeles ghetto of Watts erupted in rioting, leaving thirty-four dead and millions of dollars in damages; it was a precursor to more summer upheavals in American cities. Late in 1965 von Braun began to note both urban problems and the war in his public speeches and in talks to Marshall employees, indicating that NASA could expect no budget increases in the foreseeable future. As 1966 wore on, the situation became even more worrying. In October he told his board "that the President hasn't forgotten the space program and that our reverses have been a direct result of the war in Viet Nam." Both Webb and Johnson were committed to Kennedy's goal, and that act of political will kept Apollo on track, but only at the expense of any potential successors to it. The prospects for the FY 1968 budget did not look any better. It would turn out to be a very bad year indeed.[35]

If Apollo/Saturn and its aftermath dominated von Braun's working life, problems created by his fame episodically intruded upon his agenda. The most worrying of these were revelations about his National Socialist past that began to leak out in 1962–63. Shortly before Christmas 1963 Webb wrote von Braun: "Dryden, Seamans, and I have discussed the subject matter of our conference on December 17th, namely, the series or articles and book published in East Germany by a Communist writer which represent your activities in Germany in the past and now in the U.S. as militaristic and bloodthirsty." Von Braun had particularly sought his counsel regarding "the letter that you had received from Peter L. Krohn of Easton, Pennsylvania, referring to a radio broadcast repeating some of the East German allegations."[36]

These "allegations," which included the explosive facts of his SS officer rank and the horrors of Mittelbau-Dora, were in fact not so new. A year earlier West German correspondents had alerted the Marshall director to an East German magazine series that turned out to be excerpts from Julius Mader's forthcoming book, *Geheimnis von Huntsville: Die wahre Karriere des Raketenbarons Wernher von Braun* (Secret of Huntsville: The True Career of Rocket Baron Wernher von Braun).[37]

Appearing in mid-1963, that book threatened to become von Braun's worst nightmare. On the dust jacket was an accurate drawing of him in a black SS-Sturmbannführer's uniform, skull and crossbones on his cap and Knight's Cross around his neck. Inside was a long discussion of the Mittel-werk and the Dora camp. The U.S. news media had not picked up the story, likely because the West German press, which idolized him even more than its American counterpart, had resolutely ignored it. No doubt that was because Mader's works resembled East German attempts to smear West German politicians with their Nazi pasts, notably Heinrich Lübke, president of the Federal Republic (a largely ceremonial position) since 1959—he had been an official in Speer's Peenemünde construction group. Moreover, Mader's von Braun publications were crudely propagandistic in tone, mix-ing wild charges and completely fabricated scenes with damaging facts, which made it hard to determine what the truth about von Braun actually was. Especially after the creation of the Berlin Wall in August 1961, which ended the East German population's mass exodus and underlined the regime's totalitarian character, it was easy to write off everything coming from the other side as Communist lies and propaganda.[38]

But the implication of Krohn's letter, that the story could break out in America, obviously disconcerted the rocket engineer: for the first time he felt compelled to bring it to Webb's attention. Webb counseled him not to respond unless publicly questioned, in which case he was to answer that "everything related to my past activity in Germany . . . is well known to the U.S. Government." He had become a citizen and therefore was "not disposed to enter into discussion of events of many years ago."[39]

Thanks to the Western media's lack of interest, the story went nowhere in 1964 outside the Soviet bloc. A rare exception was a very short, unrevealing, and inaccurate *Washington Post* report in August that the Moscow newspa-per *Izvestia* had attacked him for the treatment of prisoners in an "under-ground Nazi rocket base in Poland." This charge was likely connected to the translation of Mader's work into Russian. In the United States and much of the world, von Braun's heroic quasi-official biography remained intact; indeed, several books about Peenemünde and Operation Paperclip in the 1960s only reinforced it. If he had concerns in mid-decade, they mostly related to skeptical treatments of his image in movies, popular music, and other venues susceptible to the influence of liberal intellectuals. These treatments were signs of the loosening of the anti-Communist Cold War consensus that had stifled dissent in the 1950s.[40]

One such treatment was Stanley Kubrick's brilliant film parody, *Dr. Strangelove, or: How I Learned to Stop Worrying and Love the Bomb*, which reached theaters early in 1964. The editors of a new liberal periodical, *The New York Review of Books*, sent von Braun a copy of its rapturous review of the movie, no doubt with a certain Schadenfreude. The reviewer speculated that the title character, the mad, ex-German nuclear scientist and strategist, was "a composite portrait of Edward Teller, Werner [*sic*] von Braun, and Herman Kahn." There is no evidence that von Braun's public affairs chief, Bart Slattery, ever showed it to him. A year later von Braun told Arthur C. Clarke, who was working on Kubrick's next movie, *2001: A Space Odyssey*, that he had "never got around to seeing it [*Strangelove*]." Clarke relates: "Stanley Kubrick once said to me: 'Tell Wernher I wasn't getting at him.' I never did, because (a) I didn't believe it (b) even if Stanley wasn't, Peter Sellers certainly was." Kahn, whose *On Thermonuclear War* was a best seller in 1960, was likely Kubrick's primary target, but Kahn, Teller, and another perennial favorite, Henry Kissinger, were all Jewish. As von Braun was by far the most prominent ex-Nazi technical expert, Strangelove's outburst to the president in the war room—"Mein Führer, I can walk!"—can only have been a parody of him.[41]

If that movie launched an eternal guessing game about its namesake character, no one could be in doubt about Tom Lehrer's song "Wernher von Braun," recorded live in July 1965 for his album *That Was the Year That Was.* Lehrer, a mathematician who had parlayed an incisive wit and talent for rhyme into a lucrative second career as a performer and recording artist, first wrote the tune in the early 1960s and played it on Harvard student radio. An inspiration may well have been Mort Sahl's joke about *I Aim at the Stars*, "but sometimes I hit London," until then the most famous put-down of von Braun's career. Lehrer's von Braun is "a man whose allegiance is ruled by expedience." "Don't say he's hypocritical/Say rather he's apolitical/Once the rockets are up, who cares where they come down?'/That's not my department, says Wernher von Braun."[42]

Lehrer tapped into the left-wing and Jewish undercurrent of skepticism about the rocket engineer, one that got little representation in the mainstream media but that nonetheless began to spread in the more open culture of the 1960s. Knowing nothing of von Braun's SS membership or role in the exploitation of concentration camp labor, facts unavailable to him because the Western press had ignored Mader, Lehrer pictured the engineer simply as an unscrupulous opportunist, willing to work for anybody, including the Chinese. It would long reign as the negative counterimage of von Braun.

This time it was an ordinary person who sent Lehrer's record to Marshall before it was intercepted by Slattery, who huffily replied that "when the so-called humor strikes at the very roots of a man's beliefs, it ceases to be funny." He refused to play it for his boss. (Italian journalist Oriana Fallaci memorably portrays Slattery in her impressionistic space book, *When the Sun Dies,* as a complete sycophant.) However, von Braun could not completely avoid it, for Clarke was once at a party where his friend's "great sense of humor" was "tested to the breaking point . . . when some tactless person played Tom Lehrer's brilliant song."[43]

Von Braun paid most attention to the third and most obscure of the unfriendly artistic representations in the mid-1960s, Jean-Luc Godard's avant-garde science fiction film *Alphaville.* An article in French or German alerted him to the French movie, for in August 1965 his translator, Ruth von Saurma, passed along the clipping and a translation to MSFC Security, which launched an investigation. *Alphaville* reached U.S. theaters in the fall. One American reviewer described the central plot: the newspaper "Figaro-Pravda" assigns "star reporter-photographer and super-hero Lemmy Caution to destroy the Orwellian dictator-scientist, Dr. Von Braun. Von Braun's computer-state, Alphaville, is preparing to wage total war on the outlander states where love still is known as a human condition." Caution, a stock character of French detective B-movies played by the American actor Eddie Constantine, succeeds in his task, rescuing the only person worth saving from the computer dystopia, the scientist's daughter. Perhaps to avoid a libel suit, Godard named his character Leonard Vonbraun (spelling the last name as one word). In September NASA's director of security sent to Marshall a large collection of newspaper clippings and even assigned someone to sit through the movie and file a report. Nothing further came of it. The film never made it out of the art house and festival circuit in the United States.[44]

At almost exactly the same time, the fall of 1965, *Operation Crossbow,* a British war movie named for the Allied offensive against the V-weapons, appeared in theaters. While the British scenes bear some resemblance to the discovery of the V-2 in 1943, the German scenes go off into territory even more fictional than *I Aim at the Stars,* with British agents successfully infiltrating the project. The producers made no attempt to represent Wernher von Braun, Walter Dornberger, or the rest of the Peenemünde leadership, likely to avoid seeking clearance for using their names. Curiously, the Mittelwerk does make an appearance near the end, but as a secret underground base where an intercontinental missile is being prepared to attack New York.

Just as the doors in the roof open to launch the missile, British bombers drop bombs through the hole to destroy the facility. The Paris edition of the *New York Herald-Tribune* wrote: "About the only person who shouldn't enjoy 'Operation Crossbow' is maybe Wernher von Braun, but then he's already had the last laugh."[45]

By far the most ambitious attempt to make a film out of the Peenemünde and Mittelwerk story came from East Germany. *Die gefrorenen Blitze* (Frozen Lightning—the name given to jagged, white rocket contrails at the Baltic center) was in production for years but was not released in East Berlin until April 1967. Inspired by Julius Mader's book, this high-priority project of the official GDR film studio DEFA set out to answer *I Aim at the Stars,* a primary purpose for *Geheimnis von Huntsville* as well. As such it represented the second East German attempt "to smash the myth of the fascist rocket baron Wernher von Braun."[46]

As the ambitious film evolved, however, *Die gefrorenen Blitze* lost its tight focus on von Braun in an attempt to create a war epic that could also be exported to the West. The director hired British, French, and Russian actors to do scenes in their native languages, got East German and Soviet military to help reconstruct scenes from Peenemünde and Mittelbau-Dora, and in line with East German official ideology greatly inflated the role of the Communist underground in Nazi Germany and in the Dora camp. The film budget grew to over five million East German marks, a very large sum in that economy, and the final product was nearly three hours long. To avoid being sued for slander in the West, DEFA decided to omit von Braun's name—he is referred to only as the "Raketenbaron" in the finished film—but even this was not enough for export. Instead, a bowdlerized version omitted many of the scenes involving him, notably one in which he witnesses an execution of prisoners at Dora, which was a slanderous invention of the screenwriter. *Die gefrorenen Blitze* became two different movies in Eastern and Western Europe, the Western one gutted of much of its anti–von Braun content. Even a broadcast of the shortened version on French TV was scotched in 1969 when the new West German ambassador to Paris, Sigismund von Braun, was called in to review it. In the end the film perhaps bolstered Mader's work in the Soviet bloc but had little impact in Western Europe and none at all in the United States, where it went unseen. Wernher von Braun may only have heard of it when he and his brother corresponded about the French television incident.[47]

Meanwhile, another, more serious threat to expose the Mittelbau-Dora issue arose in France in 1966, in response to *Paris Match* magazine's enthusiastic profile of von Braun and Marshall the previous October. French Dora survivors wrote protest letters detailing abuses they had suffered, including eyewitness reports accusing von Braun of participation in beatings and executions. If excerpts of these letters were printed in the *Life* magazine of France, it could be a public relations disaster. *Paris Match* passed along copies to him in April 1966, and he or his staff drafted a lengthy reply. "As much as I understand their bitterness," he wrote, "I am appalled at their false accusations aimed at me. I know and appreciate how they have been wronged; but doing me a wrong in this way will certainly not erase the ignominious treatment they have suffered." After a lengthy explanation of his position during the war, he came to the topic of the Mittelwerk.

> Each visit lasted only hours, sometimes one or two days, and was solely concerned with quality control problems. I would like to state emphatically that during my visits to the Mittelwerk I never saw a dead prisoner, I never saw a man beaten, I never saw a man hanged or otherwise killed, and I never participated in any acts of violence or physical mistreatment of prisoners. Nor have I ever called upon anyone else to perform such acts. Any testimony to the contrary can only be the result of mistaken identity.

This letter achieved its purpose. *Paris Match*'s editors forwarded it to the Dora-Ellrich survivors association and printed nothing about the whole affair.[48]

Although it is not known how he felt about the Dora story in the years after World War II, his self-confident promotion of a selective, quasi-official history in the 1950s does not bespeak someone burdened with a guilty conscience. With pressure increasing in the 1960s, however, he does seem to have expressed more guilt—but not very much. He always denied any personal responsibility for what happened to the prisoners. More than anything else, he was concerned for his own reputation if Mittelbau-Dora's horrors, and even more so the fact of his SS officer status, became public knowledge; he knew what it was like to live with skeletons in the closet. And yet these issues would always go away.

Certainly it was reassuring that the United States and the Federal Republic showered him with yet more honors in the mid-1960s. Early in 1963 von Braun made his first trip to Berlin since the dying days of the Third Reich when his original alma mater, the Technical University of Berlin (the former Institute of Technology), gave him an honorary doctorate, along with Hermann Oberth. Mader protested in the East German press—to no effect. In 1965 the (West) German Society of Inventors gave him its Diesel Medal in gold for his role in rocketry; in 1967 the venerable nature magazine *Kosmos*, which he had read in his youth, named him a recipient of its Wilhelm Bölsche Prize for public understanding of science and technology, presented by the federal minister for scientific research in person. At home, not only did he continue to collect honorary doctorates from various universities, but the Smithsonian Institution awarded him its Langley Medal in June 1967, an elite aeronautical honor restricted to great American pioneers, including the Wright Brothers, Charles Lindbergh, and Robert Goddard.[49]

Especially in West Germany the hero worship reached the point where even von Braun was fed up. When several West German radio stations wanted to do a personal profile of him in September 1964, he scribbled to his staff: "Hell NO. They try to get another 'BUNTE' thing started"—a reference to a fawning profile in the women's magazine Bunte that had provoked a new avalanche of mail and media interview requests. His instructions to Bart Slattery were "I'll be glad to talk about our work, but if he wants to talk about myself, he can save himself the trip. I'm eager to get out of this personal publicity bit and simply won't cooperate." Earlier in the month he had signed a staff-written letter to the publisher of Quick, another German mass-market magazine, giving the same answer. He noted the amount of work Bunte's article created for him and his staff and the negative impact of "personal publicity" on his relations with his peers: "Because I am, so to speak, only one gearwheel in the NASA machinery and the successful functioning of our extremely complex and wide-ranging project hangs on a frictionless and untroubled cooperation among a large number of quite outstanding personalities, . . . I cannot afford" to always be the center of attention.[50]

Because of the lack of truly historic space accomplishments in the mid-1960s attached to his name, his name did appear in print less, a fact noted with exasperation by his elderly, widowed father. Magnus Sr.'s early 1950s memoirs do not seem to accord any special pride of place to his middle son, in contrast to the supplement he added for the third edition in 1965. By that time he had decided that Wernher really was the Columbus of space. In a September 1966 letter to Maria, he compared her husband to the discoverer of the Americas: "The Jewish background of Columbus, his egotism, and other things distinguish the two very much. But the solid, unshakable belief in their personal mission are present in both."[51]

Thanks to international jet travel, congresses, and awards from West German organizations, Wernher managed to see his father almost once a year and was devoted to him. From 1962 to 1968 he saw Sigismund even more, as his eldest brother was West Germany's ambassador to the United Nations and resided on New York's Upper East Side. (Since neither Germany was yet in the UN due to a Cold War stalemate, technically he was only an observer.) The two got along well and treated each other as equals, since they both had outstandingly successful careers in entirely separate fields. Maria liked Sigis less; she felt he carried the patriarchal role of eldest son/heir too obtrusively. He certainly did not drop the baronial title, which was not only part of the family tradition but also useful in the upper-class and diplomatic circles he moved in.[52]

Magnus Jr. was, as always, the odd man out. Although relations with his eldest brother were friendly, Sigis's daughter Christina von Braun feels that her father treated him with "a certain underlying contempt." The same attitude appears between the lines of Magnus Sr.'s 1965 memoir addition; his youngest son's career simply did not measure up to those of his brothers. Yet Magnus was a successful executive at Chrysler in Detroit, better paid than either of his civil servant brothers, and happy after marrying again in 1957; Natalie Woodruff had two children, and they had three more of their own. His relations with Wernher, who had so dominated his life from 1943 to 1955, were ambivalent too. In 1968 he wrote his father: "I spoke to Wernher on the telephone a couple of days ago, but I have not seen him in person in ages. I have nothing to do with Huntsville, also very little with Florida, and he never comes here. And since we never see each other, naturally we get along very well."[53]

As for Wernher's family, the 1960s were happy years, although marred by his absence half the time. In August 1966, in a letter to Klaus Riedel's widow, he said: "I am so often on the road that Maria and the children will soon find my short stays at home no better than the visit of a guest. The prospects for improvement meanwhile seem poor" because of the onward march of the Saturn V program. Maria had long since learned to be self-reliant around the house; much to his surprise, she had acquired a box of hand tools and knew how to use them. As for his two daughters, they were also away more as the decade wore on. In a silent commentary on Huntsville's high schools, he and Maria sent them to elite boarding institutions, Iris in Washington, D.C., and Margrit in Atlanta, extending the highbrow and cultured upbringing they had received at home. Iris went to Oberlin College in 1967 to study history and music, while Margrit, who was more like her father, later became an engineer. During these years Peter was only reaching elementary school age. To try to establish some kind of family togetherness, Werhner tried to be home many weekends and school holidays, and he taught them how to swim and water-ski at the lake. He also arranged for a family trip to the Bahamas or a West Indian resort almost every year.[54]

Thanks to NASA buying a small fleet of Gulfstream I two-engine turboprops (Webb viewed jets as too ostentatious for Congress), he did not have to fly commercially on many business trips. It certainly made feasible his presence in Washington about every other week. He made the best of the situation by piling up more piloting hours, technically speaking in the right-hand seat, but he often took over, as that was his domineering nature. He was not a timid pilot; Marshall veterans relate flying *below* the rim of the Grand Canyon while von Braun gave a travelogue: "Look *up* and to your right to see the Indian village." Another time he buzzed Mount Rushmore's presidential faces to give his passengers a better look. And once near National Airport in Washington he maneuvered the aircraft "like an expert fighter pilot" when the NASA plane had a frightening near miss with a commercial airliner due to an air traffic controller's error. To keep flying the agency's aircraft, he upgraded to an Airline Transport Rating by 1968; he could have had a career flying airliners. Traveling companions also reported that he remained as much a night owl as ever and often near impossible to get up the next day. He often half-jokingly asserted that nothing important in world history had ever been "accomplished before ten-thirty or eleven in the morning!"[55]

In truth, von Braun liked his travel and his fame, as much as they inconvenienced him. They kept him away and wore him out, but he delighted in seeing new parts of the world. His celebrity was often irritating in its side effects, but he loved being the center of attention at parties and retained his taste for alcohol. His inclination toward manly diversions also drew him away from home. In the spring of 1964 he went on a panther hunt in the Yucatán with Fairchild corporation executive Edward Uhl (the contractor for the Pegasus micrometeoroid experiments) and a Florida congressman—and found that half-illiterate boys in the Central American jungle knew who he was. He went on hunting and fishing trips with other congressmen in Canada and in various parts of the United States. Sometimes the enforced camaraderie was a bit much; told that a powerful Texas representative wanted to meet again for dinner in the French Quarter of New Orleans, he asked if there was a serious purpose or if this was just another "getting drunk affair." Congressional requests certainly added to his heavy speaking schedule, often to his irritation. He cleared about $7,000 from his four paid speeches a year but made several times that many for NASA, invariably salesmanship for Apollo and agency programs. When it came to public promotion, he knew that he was one of NASA's biggest assets—James Webb had told him so.[56]

During the mid-1960s he also regained a role in popular writing about spaceflight when he accepted an offer from *Popular Science* to begin a monthly column in early 1963. The editor heralded it as the greatest event in the history of the magazine. These articles he wrote in longhand on nights and weekends and turned them over to his secretaries to straighten out. With the permission of headquarters, he earned $5,000 a year from this arrangement. A publisher gathered this material into a book, which appeared in 1967 as *Space Frontier* and was translated into several languages. That same year the large-format *History of Rocketry and Space Travel* came out with his name as first author, along with that of Fred Ordway, who wrote much of it while on leave as a technical adviser to Stanley Kubrick's *2001*. Von Braun collected 60 percent of the royalties for correcting the galleys. Thus he rejoined the ranks of popular authors while working sixty-plus hours a week as MSFC director.[57]

In short, von Braun continued to live his life at "full bore," as he liked to say, as driven as ever by his incredible physical energy and optimism. Whatever worries he had about his image and about his past, he pushed them aside and moved on to the next problem.

CHAPTER SEVENTEEN

A Pretty Emotional Moment

1967–69

[H]e can hardly by any organizational measure be the Boss, but to the public sense of these affairs, to the Press, and to the corps of space workers, he is the real engineer, the spiritual leader, the inventor, the force, the philosopher, the genius! of America's Space Program. Such is his legend in the street. That is the positive side of his reputation; it is enormous, say, rather it is immense. Yet he has that variety of glamor usually described as fascinating, which is to say, the evocation of his name is attractive and repellent at once, because no one forgets for an instant that he once worked on the V-2 rockets . . . and so was implicated on one occasion by giving an orientation lecture to the Leader himself.
—NORMAN MAILER at the Cape, July 1969[1]

On the day after Christmas 1966 Wernher von Braun left for the most thrilling trip of his life, an expedition to Antarctica and the South Pole. It had originated in his interest, and that of Ernst Stuhlinger, in lunar roving vehicles and the establishment of base camps in hostile environments. When the National Science Foundation invited him to spend a week in Antarctica with Stuhlinger at the height of the southern summer, his "first reaction was an emphatic 'YES.'" It was precisely the sort of exotic travel that excited him. By the fall of 1966 Mueller or Webb had added Bob Gilruth and Max Faget of the Manned Spacecraft Center, because the trip's purpose, to look at Antarctica as a learning experience for lunar bases and Mars colonization, was too much in their bailiwick. Mueller in fact thought it would be a good idea to put von Braun and Gilruth together "in close association for several days" so they might have "a closer understanding of each other[']s problems."[2]

Von Braun and Stuhlinger did not take the most direct approach to Christchurch, New Zealand, the staging base for U.S. Antarctic operations, but made overnight stops in Hawaii, Tahiti, Bora-Bora, and Fiji, apparently as a kind of minivacation. Either in Fiji or on arrival in Christchurch on New Year's Day 1967, they rendezvoused with Gilruth and Faget. Two days later the four left in a navy four-engine Constellation; von Braun promptly talked his way into the copilot's seat and flew most of the way to McMurdo Station near the Ross Ice Shelf. Once in the southern continent, they went to the dry valleys and magnificent mountain ranges, saw the original hut of Ernest Shackleton, and visited the various U.S. stations. At the South Pole they participated in the macho ritual of running around the world in three seconds clad only in shoes and a towel: the outside temperature was −18° F (−28° C). On the tenth the group left McMurdo, and von Braun arrived back in Huntsville three days later. He told his father: "Antarctica was a fabulous experience! The landscape was much more majestic and spectacular than I had imagined. Have you seen a glacier 60 km <u>wide</u> and 300 km long, that moves over 4 meters <u>per day</u>?" He felt they had also learned much about the logistics and the problems of scientific exploration in a dangerous and difficult environment.[3]

The trip itself was symbolic of a NASA optimism about its future that was increasingly out of step with reality. By early 1967 the war in Vietnam had killed 25,000 American soldiers and consumed over $20 billion annually. As NASA went through each budget cycle, AAP was the loser, but soon other programs would be cut as well. And while Apollo was relatively protected, it was about to suffer a severe technical setback. The glorious future of the United States and the human race in space seemed to be slipping away in the late 1960s, only to be revived with the Apollo triumphs of late 1968 and 1969. It was a revival that led to a false hope.

On Friday evening, 27 January, exactly two weeks after he arrived home, von Braun was at a dinner for Gemini and Apollo corporate leaders at the International Club in Washington. Gemini had just concluded, and Apollo was about to begin launching astronauts: Gus Grissom, Edward White, and Roger Chaffee were in training for a multiday test of the Command and Service Modules in Earth orbit, to be launched on a Saturn IB in late February. As he was standing around at cocktail hour with Lee Atwood, Jim Webb, Bob Gilruth, Kurt Debus, and Sam Phillips, Atwood was called to the bar for an urgent phone call. Ashen-faced, he turned to Gilruth, who was nearest: "Bob, we've had a tragedy." It was Harrison Storms calling—a fire in the spacecraft at the Cape had killed all three astronauts just after 6:31 p.m. Von Braun and Debus came up, followed by others. Webb took charge, and Phillips, Mueller, and Gilruth flew to the Cape. Atwood soon headed that way too. Von Braun was left to share a depressing dinner with the others. According to Willis Shapley, whom Webb had brought from the Budget Bureau in 1965 to be his legislative and budget adviser, several corporate executives got very drunk, because they were so upset. After a truncated meeting the next day, von Braun went home on Saturday afternoon.[4]

The fire set off the biggest crisis in NASA history, at least until the Space Shuttle *Challenger* accident nineteen years later. It forced a massive overhaul of the Apollo program, delaying the first manned launch until late 1968, although that was certainly not the expectation immediately afterward. But that was before NASA's leadership grasped how problem-plagued the Apollo spacecraft was. The space agency was allowed to investigate itself, as it was not in the two later shuttle accidents, but the fire inevitably attracted a lot of intrusive media and congressional attention, exposing how troubled the North American contract had been, both for the S-II and for the CSM. When Senator Walter Mondale ambushed Webb with a leaked copy of the December 1965 "Phillips Report" a few weeks afterward, it had far-reaching effects. Webb never trusted Seamans or Mueller again, feeling that they had hidden the true dimensions of the North American problem from him. Seamans announced his resignation in the fall. In April Webb finally forced Atwood to yank Storms out of the Space Division and let Mueller pull Joe Shea, who seemed to be working himself to exhaustion and falling apart, from his job heading the Apollo Spacecraft Program Office in Houston. Shea became Mueller's deputy, but when he found out how empty the job was, he left within months.[5]

Through all this turmoil Huntsville sailed essentially unscathed. The spacecraft, not the booster, had been the problem, and the S-II crisis already seemed to be largely under control, despite new concerns about the stage's structural integrity. After Mondale's surprise, von Braun was most concerned that Rees's very harsh, private, fall 1965 memoranda about Storms's division be held in confidence, and Phillips promised they would. Von Braun may have shared the widespread guilt feeling in NASA about the failure to see the fire danger of using high-pressure oxygen on the pad, something done since Mercury. A stress indicator may be that he asked for more sleeping pills from the Marshall medical office a month after the fire, but it may also reflect only what Ernst Stuhlinger has called his "strange predilection for pills" as an answer to a variety of minor ailments. He certainly underlined to his subordinates the need to review the fire danger in AAP, as there was some concern that a micrometeoroid strike could ignite the insulation on the inside of the S-IVB Workshop. As for Apollo, his biggest sacrifice was to lend Eberhard Rees as an expert adviser at the North American spacecraft plant in California in October 1967, in response to a Webb appeal to find some way to help Houston.[6]

The fire's psychological impact aside, von Braun and his center had every reason in the first half of 1967 to look forward with renewed confidence: Webb had just given Marshall an unprecedented role in the Voyager program to land several robotic spacecraft on Mars. These large, ambitious landers were to be equipped with laboratories to search for the possibility of microscopic life and were to be launched in pairs on the Saturn V. Marshall would thus provide the launch vehicles, but Webb upped the ante in mid-January 1967, when he decided to also give Huntsville the main vehicle that would stay in orbit around Mars. This decision would put von Braun's center in the robotic planetary spacecraft business. Worried about the deteriorating budget climate, Webb "wanted to link the Voyager to Dr. von Braun's name and to a proven management team—this should be soon in order to sell to Congress." Webb in fact asked him a week before the fire "to move to Washington for three months," but von Braun said that he would rather commute up two or three days a week and install an assistant at headquarters to be his local organizer. The accident made that moot.[7]

All of von Braun's hopes for this new major project were dashed, however, during the summer budget debates in Congress. The administration's budget request for NASA was $5.1 billion; but the appropriations bill Congress passed in the fall was half a billion less. The fire made NASA politically vulnerable, even as the Vietnam War escalated further and, along with it, the national debt. The kicker was the summer race riots, notably in Newark and Detroit, which left dozens of dead and inner-city slums burned to the ground. Liberal Democrats and Republican fiscal conservatives ganged up to slash the space program; Voyager was zeroed out. (The name was later used for two outer-planet missions in the 1970s.)[8]

One reason was that NASA planners had sometimes linked the "unmanned Voyager" to a "manned Voyager," that is, human flybys that were part of its planetary mission studies. The majority in Congress wanted to have nothing to do with astronomically expensive human Mars programs. Another casualty, inevitably, was AAP, which lost one-third of its $454 million request. No missions before 1970 were possible any longer. But most fundamental was the axing of Voyager Mars, which ended all Marshall's possibilities in robotic planetary spacecraft and their boosters. The NASA space science directorate had to revamp its planetary program, going to smaller spacecraft and the air force Titan III, the cheaper rival to the Saturn IB. These were bitter pills for von Braun to swallow.[9]

In the context of steadily deteriorating political prospects and an Apollo program still reeling from the fire, the first Saturn V launch, Apollo-Saturn 501 (AS-501), loomed as absolutely critical for Marshall and for the whole project; a catastrophic failure might derail Kennedy's timetable. In 1966 von Braun had expected the flight in the first quarter of 1967. By the end of that year it had retreated to the second quarter, and the fire only accelerated the slippage. Crews at the Cape took apart the Block I Command Module for the mission, the same type that had killed Grissom, White, and Chaffee, and found over fourteen hundred factory errors in wiring and other systems. The rocket's stages and all the pad systems and software also were full of problems. In June, after the vehicle was already stacked in the monumental assembly building of Launch Complex 39, concern about the quality of S-II welds forced the Kennedy Space Center crew to unstack the spacecraft and upper stages. To help Debus's KSC, von Braun decreed that a number of Marshallites would go to Florida on temporary duty assignments. Success was "a necessity."[10]

"501," as it was universally known to the Huntsville and Kennedy crews, was reconstructed in August and finally rolled out to the pad on the giant crawler vehicle on the twenty-sixth. NASA had meanwhile decided to call the mission Apollo 4, retroactively but never officially counting the three Saturn IBs launched in 1966, while leaving open the Apollo 1 designation that Grissom, White, and Chaffee had wanted to use for their ill-fated mission. Once at the pad, 501/Apollo 4 proved no less troublesome. The all-important Countdown Demonstration Test, which went all the way down to fourteen seconds before launch, began after many delays on 27 September. It was to last four days; it took seventeen, including several complete halts as the launch and pad crews neared total exhaustion. Von Braun flew down to the Cape more than once to sit through portions of this ordeal. Debus's launch director, Rocco Petrone, a former West Point football star and army officer at Redstone Arsenal in the 1950s, later considered the practice countdown a trial by fire that welded together the launch crew in a way essential to Apollo's success. But it often seemed like the damned thing would never leave the ground—yet more problems followed, further delaying the launch.[11]

At last, on 9 November 1967, launch day arrived. It was Saturn V project manager Arthur Rudolph's sixty-first birthday. Liftoff was scheduled for seven a.m. Eastern Time, so von Braun took his place in the mission manager row of the Launch Control Center's Firing Room very early, along with Rudolph, Debus, Mueller, and others. It was astounding how far they had come. Only a decade had passed since the shock of Sputniks 1 and 2. Six and a half years earlier von Braun and Debus's crews had launched Alan Shepard from a simple launch ring only a few hundred yards from a small armored blockhouse, which had to be close enough to the pad for the analog instrumentation to give proper readings. Now there were 450 engineers in a control center over three miles away monitoring everything through digital computers. The Redstone had only 1 percent of the initial thrust of the Saturn V, a vehicle taller than the Statue of Liberty and weighing more than a navy destroyer. During the launch the first stage's five engines would burn 200,000 gal (725,000 l) of propellants per minute, generating the equivalent of 160 million horsepower. *Fortune* magazine noted that the vehicle had the orbital payload capacity equivalent to 1,500 Sputniks, 9,000 Explorer Is, or 42 Gemini spacecraft. It was several times more powerful than any rocket that had ever been launched.[12]

That morning nothing went wrong. Without a single hold, the countdown proceeded to zero. Just seconds before liftoff, with the computers now completely in control, von Braun and the top managers swiveled around in their chairs and trained binoculars on the pad: they, plus the VIPs, were the only ones high enough to look out the windows. The F-1s ignited 8.9 seconds before liftoff, a glowing mass of flame erupting in total silence, since it took 15 seconds for the sound wave to reach observers inside and outside the Launch Control Center. When it did, 501 was already climbing majestically away from the launch tower, and von Braun was yelling, "Go, baby, go!" from manager row. Everyone outside was stunned by the visceral power of the vibration, which was not merely deafening; the low-frequency rumble shook one's whole body from the inside out. In the TV trailer where CBS anchor Walter Cronkite was giving his live broadcast, debris began falling from the ceiling, and he and a technician held the window, as they were afraid it would break. And the rocket kept going. Each stage worked nearly perfectly; after 11.5 minutes, the Apollo 4 spacecraft and its S-IVB were in orbit. The third stage reignited three hours later in a test of the parking orbit and lunar launch sequence, throwing the CSM into a high orbit. The Service Module engine fired to lift it even higher, to 11,000 mi (18,000 km), and then ignited again to accelerate the Command Module back into the atmosphere, achieving lunar-return velocity in a heat shield test. Almost nine hours after liftoff, it splashed down in the Pacific near the recovery ship.[13]

Hours earlier von Braun participated in an elated postlaunch news conference: "No single event since the formation of the Marshall Center in 1960 equals today's launch in significance [and] I regard this happy day as one of the three or four highlights of my professional life—to be surpassed only by the manned lunar landing." He could scarcely believe that this all-up test, which George Mueller had pushed on Marshall in 1963, and which he and many others had accepted with reservations, had actually worked. Rudolph's weekly note the next Monday summed up MSFC's sense of relief and disbelief about 501: "Gone—but never, never to be forgotten."[14]

That same week also produced what Stuhlinger called, in his weekly note, "the strangest dichotomy we have ever experienced at this Center: jubilation over the wonderful success of our first big Saturn, and gloom over the reduction-in-force which threatens our capability to develop payloads for the Saturn." A little over two weeks earlier von Braun had to issue a memorandum to all employees warning of a possible reduction-in-force (RIF, in government jargon) of 700 to 889 civil service positions because of the huge hit NASA had just taken in its FY 1968 budget. The very day of 501 headquarters confirmed seven hundred layoffs. Speaking in the main auditorium and via closed-circuit TV three weeks later, von Braun told his employees that attrition might reduce that by almost 10 percent, but the RIF would set off further disruptions through "bumping"; those with higher seniority could retreat to lower-grade positions, displacing others. Marshall had already been shrinking due to attrition and support contractor layoffs, producing unemployment in Huntsville as early as the fall of 1966, but now the real pain began. Just before it went into force in January 1968, the civil service unions halted it in court. Action was postponed until the end of March, by which time much of the layoff had been made moot by retirements and transfers. Nonetheless the effect was to accelerate the workforce's aging and to produce "grave and serious imbalances" in its composition. In September 1968 von Braun told Mueller that MSFC was just emerging "from the shattering experience" of the RIF.[15]

Meanwhile, Marshall carried on with the two projects that kept the place in business: Saturn and AAP. On 22 January 1968 the Saturn IB upon which the fatal fire had occurred, AS-204, launched the first Lunar Module in an unpiloted orbital test called Apollo 5; it was a solid success. Design and development continued on the Orbital Workshop and Apollo Telescope Mount, but von Braun and Marshall kept meeting resistance from Houston, which still was very skeptical of the Lunar Module ATM cabin and the "wet" Workshop—that is, a Saturn-IB-launched version in which astronauts refitted the S-IVB's liquid-hydrogen tank. MSC pushed a "dry" Workshop, an already-equipped engineless S-IVB launched by a Saturn V with only two active stages. Von Braun thought it a very logical successor that would help keep MSFC in business, but he stuck stubbornly to the "wet" version. His motivations seem to include genuine interest in what could be learned from such an exercise in orbital construction, and a desire to sustain Marshall's "can do" reputation, plus concern that the program would be seriously altered and postponed by going "dry." It might make it even more vulnerable to cancellation. The astronomers were meanwhile getting impatient with the expense and delays of human spaceflight, as ATM had been designed originally for the peak of solar activity around 1969, a date that was already impossible. A "dry" Workshop would push the flight into 1972. Mueller and Webb supported von Braun's position, so in 1967–68 the "wet" version remained on the program. In fact the Workshop/ATM cluster was the program; nothing else in AAP was funded any longer.[16]

Despite the latest Huntsville-Houston battle over the Workshop, intercenter relations began to improve in 1967–68. Mueller later attributed this to the beneficial effects of the Antarctic trip on von Braun and Gilruth's relationship, but it was driven mostly by the way that Apollo and the fire drew the two centers together. The successes of Saturn and the need to work closely on missions helped, as did Rees's seven months at North American as a special adviser to MSC. In the spring Gilruth even voluntarily gave Marshall the management of all remaining components of the cluster, citing Houston's overwhelming workload in preparing for a rush of Apollo flights, once the postfire modifications were finished. For his part von Braun enforced a policy of discretion when it came to publicly acknowledging steps on Houston's turf. That did not stop him from building a big water tank at Marshall so that technicians in scuba gear or spacesuits could experiment in simulated weightlessness with the construction of the "wet" Workshop, but he promised Houston that it was not for astronaut training—a restriction later dropped when no one cared any longer. In a maneuver reminiscent of his past, he had built the tank even when denied construction money and was later slapped on the wrist for misuse of funds. In the meantime he kept it secret from the press so that it would not be the cause of any further trouble with Houston.[17]

In the spring of 1968 Marshall had troubles enough already when the second Saturn V, AS-502/Apollo 6, proved to be no repetition of the first. With von Braun again in his Firing Room perch, it lifted off at seven a.m. on 4 April 1968.

Around the 125th second of flight [he later wrote] some slight excitement arose in the launch control center when someone pointed out that the telemetered signals from several accelerometers indicated an apparently mild "Pogo" vibration,—a longitudinal oscillation which makes a space vehicle lengthen and shorten several times a second like a concertina.

Seven seconds later the "Pogo" disappeared and the S-IC burned out and was discarded at around 150 seconds. The S-II seemed to work perfectly for 263 more seconds, but suddenly engine No. 2 of its five J-2s shut down, followed one second later by engine No. 3. Now the rocket's guidance system struggled to achieve the necessary velocity and altitude with only 60 percent thrust. Mission Control in Houston could have aborted the mission but decided not to after the vehicle stayed in control. Following an extralong burn, the S-II dropped off and the S-IVB powered Apollo 6 into a lopsided orbit, but not without all kinds of crazy maneuvers in a futile attempt to get to the right parameters. Two and a half hours later the S-IVB's single J-2 would not restart. Houston attempted it multiple times, and nothing happened. Eventually Mission Control separated the CSM and used the Service Module's big engine to put it in a high orbit for the repeat of the lunar reentry test and a successful recovery.[18]

This embarrassing series of failures was completely overshadowed by Martin Luther King's tragic assassination that very afternoon. Riots broke out in black districts all over the United States. Just four days earlier, on 31 March, President Johnson had announced that he would not run again in 1968 after barely beating Senator Eugene McCarthy in the New Hampshire Democratic primary. The rising tide of antiwar opinion, powered by the Vietnamese Communists' spectacular, if failed, Tet Offensive in February, had energized McCarthy's campaign. Senator Robert Kennedy, who had jumped into the race soon after New Hampshire, was murdered himself in early June. The year 1968 was quickly becoming one of the most troubled in American history. That left NASA in peace to deal with the 502 failures, but further budget cuts were inevitable.

Marshall and its major engine contractor, Rocketdyne, immediately plunged into an emergency analysis of 502. By the following Monday von Braun's subordinates were already able to pick out the possible problems. For one thing, telemetry made it obvious that North American had inadvertently cross-wired S-II engine three with two, so that the latter's shutdown cut off the former, although nothing was wrong with it. As for "Pogo," that was not a new problem in rocketry, but von Braun had assumed that his team had eliminated it in Saturn. On 502 the "apparently mild" vibration would actually have shaken up astronauts rather severely. The solutions were, however, straightforward: adjust the frequencies of the F-1 engines and inject helium into spaces around their liquid-oxygen valves, providing "shock absorbers" to dampen vibration. Von Braun was most in admiration of the detective work regarding the J-2 failures. The S-II No. 2 engine shutdown and the S-IVB restart failure turned out to have the same cause, a break in a small igniter line that fed liquid-hydrogen to a "pilot flame" in the engine. In firing tests on the ground, air liquefied around the line, preventing vibration failures in the bellows section that allowed the tubing to expand and contract. When the same engine test was performed in a vacuum, the line failed. The solution required only a redesign of the line.[19]

The rapidity by which these fixes were isolated allowed von Braun and NASA to make the bold decision to "man" AS-503, in line with the "all-up" philosophy. On 11 April he told Mueller that if he had to make a decision that day, it would be unmanned, but if Mueller gave them a couple of weeks they might be able to nail the whole thing down. Indeed by the end of the month Marshall was already fairly confident of the solutions, provided that testing confirmed expectations. Seven years previously von Braun's center had forced an extra Mercury-Redstone booster test under similar circumstances, much to the bitterness of Gilruth's group. Now, after so many Saturn successes, Marshall's technological conservatism did not undermine its confidence in the soundness of its program. If all went well, 503 could be manned. This outcome naturally pleased Mueller and Gilruth. If AS-205/Apollo 7, the first piloted flight in the new Block II CSM, was a success in October, the third Saturn V would carry a crew with both the Command and Service Modules and the Lunar Module in December.[20]

In August the Apollo leadership made an even bolder decision: why not send 503/Apollo 8 all the way to the Moon? George Low, who had taken a demotion from MSC deputy director to assume Joe Shea's all-important Apollo spacecraft job, was the moving force behind this idea. As the summer wore on, the LM for Apollo 8 continued to fall behind schedule. Waiting for it might mean no flight until February, putting the assumed Kennedy deadline of 1969 in even more jeopardy. ("Before this decade is out" could technically mean 1970, but no one in NASA wanted to argue that until they already knew they were going to miss 1969.) In the back of his mind Low already had begun to consider the possibility of sending the Apollo 8 CSM to lunar orbit alone as a way of advancing the program. After coming back from vacation on 5 August, he found the LM in worse shape than ever. He decided to act. He asked the head of mission operations, Chris Kraft, to look very quietly into the feasibility of reaching the Moon in only four months' time.[21]

The first von Braun heard of it was at about ten a.m. on 9 August, when Gilruth called him with a hint of the startling plan. Low had just told him at 8:45; at 9:30 Low had come back with Kraft and chief astronaut Deke Slayton, who backed the idea. Could the Houston group come to Marshall that same afternoon? The two set up a meeting for 2:30 in von Braun's office.

Low called the Cape, where he had just seen Apollo program head Sam Phillips the day before. Phillips would come with Debus and Petrone of KSC on another aircraft. When all were present in Huntsville, Low quickly outlined the advantages of jumping ahead to lunar orbit rather than waiting for the LM. They would need to find a substitute mass model so that the dynamics of the Saturn V were not changed, but all indications were that this exciting mission, potentially the first human venture beyond low Earth orbit, was feasible. Von Braun was as enthused as the others. He said something to the effect that, since they already had decided they probably could man 503, why not? Once you fired up the Saturn V, it did not matter how far it went. The heavy hitters of the Apollo program agreed to classify the whole thing as Secret and to meet again in Washington on the fourteenth. Webb and Mueller were in Vienna for a space conference, so someone would have to brief them if they decided to proceed. As the relatively new deputy administrator, Thomas O. Paine, was holding down the fort, Phillips would talk to him.[22]

An unanswered question is the impact of secret intelligence about the Soviet lunar program on all concerned. The NASA leadership, including von Braun, was cleared for Top Secret–compartmented data, notably photographs from Corona reconnaissance satellites. Because of budget cuts, Webb had been warning Congress and the public about a coming Soviet Saturn V–class launch vehicle, although he could not show anyone evidence of its existence. Ridiculed by some as "Webb's giant," the N-1 (a designation known only after the end of the Cold War) was in the later stages of preparation for its ill-fated first flight. The Soviets were also preparing a smaller Proton (Saturn IB–class) launch vehicle to send a two-man spacecraft to loop around the Moon; it was not capable of orbiting it. They made one partially successful unmanned test in early 1968 and two more in the fall under the rubric Zond (Probe). The CIA was predicting human circumlunar missions as a possible near-term Soviet achievement. Beyond that, how much Low, von Braun, and their compatriots knew of the Soviet program is unclear, but they were certainly aware that they were in a race.[23]

Von Braun, for one, sounded quite pessimistic about the American position in a September interview with *U.S. News & World Report*—in hindsight, with post–Cold War knowledge, almost absurdly so. "All our information indicates clearly that the Russian program is richer than ours. . . . I'm convinced that, unless something dramatic happens, the Russians are going to fly rings around us in space in a period of five years." He lashed out at the continuous downsizing of Saturn test facilities and production plants:

It may surprise you to hear this, but for the last two years my main effort at the Marshall Center has been following orders to scrub the industrial structure that we had built up at great expense to the taxpayer, to tear it down again. The sole purpose seems to be to make certain in 1972 nothing of our capability is left. That's my main job at the moment. And we haven't even put a man on the moon yet.

He was certainly a bit hyperbolic about how much time he was spending on planning for phasing out test stands and factory complexes in Louisiana, Mississippi, and other places, but it was nonetheless a major preoccupation. As each budget cycle went by, the long-term prospects for Saturn IB or V looked bleaker and bleaker; by the fall of 1968 it appeared that they had no future, as indeed turned out to be the case. Earlier, in the spring, he had warned a congressional hearing that the United States would go the way of Britain if it kept dissipating its technological lead. His characteristic optimism was fading as the space program steadily lost its political support.[24]

A couple of letters from this period also betray exhaustion with the relentless pace of the program and with the inexorable character of the Kennedy timetable. On the day after the secret August meeting in his office, he wrote his father that the Moon in the sky had turned into a "deadline display device" for him, but he was happy that he had finally secured a solid budget commitment for the Orbital Workshop and ATM; he had spent two weeks defending the latter to Webb, who had accepted another massive cut in the AAP budget to keep Apollo on track. Six months later, in early 1969, von Braun told his brother Magnus: "for over 30 years I have been lurching from crisis to crisis and have finally had enough." Magnus speculated that he was contemplating leaving NASA after the Moon landing.[25]

Still, there was much to look forward to in the immediate future. Although the Apollo leadership had some difficulty convincing Mueller and Webb of the wisdom of a very risky lunar mission on a Saturn V that had not even launched astronauts yet, the combination of Soviet competition and the program logic of the Apollo 8 flight was enough to keep the option open, if 7 worked. And it did. Von Braun took his usual observing position at the periscopes in the big, old-fashioned blockhouse of Saturn IB Launch Complex 34 when the first manned Apollo flight lifted off on 11 October. Astronauts Wally Schirra, Donn Eisele, and Walter Cunningham spent eleven days in space testing the revamped CSM, which worked perfectly.[26]

For this mission Webb was no longer in place as administrator. He had gone to President Johnson in mid-September to speak about an orderly transition in view of the upcoming election of either Vice President Hubert

Humphrey or former vice president Richard Nixon. It would be good to put Tom Paine in a position where he might continue as administrator, thus depoliticizing Apollo at its most critical stage. LBJ thought it was an excellent idea and suggested that Webb retire in three weeks on his sixty-second birthday, 7 October. Half in shock, Webb found himself in front of the White House press corps before he even had a chance to phone his wife. He used the opportunity to lash out about the Soviets gaining a lead.[27]

Paine was thus quite suddenly acting administrator and the man on the spot for the key Apollo missions. An engineer with a Ph.D. in metallurgy, he was a longtime General Electric executive and a former submariner in World War II. As von Braun noted after his first visit to MSFC in April, he was also "an enthusiastic space supporter including manned space flight."[28] But unlike Webb, Paine had little Washington insider experience, a factor that would play a crucial role in von Braun's post-Apollo life.

Planning for that rapidly approaching day was certainly on his mind in late 1968. Headquarters pressed him to revamp Marshall in view of the personnel imbalances caused by downsizing. He decided to push through another structural reorganization, one that would embed systems engineering methods more deeply within the center's culture while giving science a bigger role in what was still, overwhelmingly, an engineering organization. In particular, the AAP cluster (the later Skylab) required MSFC to integrate a complicated collection of systems and scientific instruments from heterogeneous origins. Already in early 1967 he had said: "MSFC must posture itself to 'move out' and do a major cluster systems engineering job." When Webb finally gave the go-ahead for the Workshop and telescope mount in August 1968, the administrator also underlined Marshall's enhanced systems responsibility. That month von Braun's special assistant, J. T. Shepherd, echoed R&DO director Hermann Weidner's comment that the "strong lab concept" made it "extremely difficult for a systems engineer located outside of a lab to talk to a subsystem engineer within that lab. . . . As a result of this problem we are systems engineering from the bottom up rather than the top down." Von Braun agreed. The labs were still the heart of Marshall, and as the AAP budget shrank, he depended on them even more to build things in-house, but they still acted too much as independent fiefdoms.[29]

Von Braun had always had a profound talent for building and managing huge technological systems, but the reorganization he finalized in January 1969 again demonstrated his capacity for growth. In the early 1960s he knew how to operate his organization only as an arsenal with "strong labs" and changed only because of Webb's ultimatum. This time, although headquarters pressure was again a factor, the energy to push through the restructuring came more from him. He reorganized the dualistic structure of the center into four directorates. The R&DO labs became Science and Engineering with a systems engineering group headed by Walter Haeussermann. Industrial Operations was renamed Program Management. The administrative offices were raised to an Administration directorate. Finally, to secure MSFC's future, he created Program Development, headed by the first non-German to be designated as a possible center director, William Lucas, whom he called his "vice-president for sales." He also elevated Ernst Stuhlinger to associate director for science within his office to underline the importance of space science missions in Marshall's future. It was, moreover, a good moment to consolidate the Saturn program offices under Lee James, following Arthur Rudolph's retirement.[30]

While he was finalizing the details of this reorganization, von Braun participated in all the decisions leading up to the spectacularly successful Apollo 8 mission over Christmas 1968. Phillips had mentioned the lunar possibility to the press in late August but buried it under obfuscation. Not until after Apollo 7's success did NASA endorse the idea publicly. At a special review Paine chaired on 11 November, von Braun and James represented the Saturn V and, like the others, saw no technical reasons to derail the exciting plan. Racing the Russians was not a formal factor, but just at that moment the USSR launched Zond 6, which looped around the Moon on the twelfth and returned to Soviet territory two days later—but unbeknownst to the West it crashed, making any cosmonaut attempt in December too dangerous. It was just one of several secret disasters that completely took the Soviets out of the manned Moon race.[31]

On 21 December, at 7:51 a.m., von Braun again observed from the Launch Control Center as AS-503 sent the Apollo 8 crew—Frank Borman, James Lovell, and William Anders—to the Moon. The launch vehicle worked perfectly. He then went on vacation, a long-scheduled family trip to the Bahamas over Christmas and New Year's. Especially with the two daughters away at school, such trips were his only chance to spend prolonged time with his wife and children, so he did not observe key parts of the flight from Houston Mission Control. For him, landing on the lunar surface was the ultimate objective. He presumably watched the astronauts' historic Christmas Eve broadcast from lunar orbit on television in the Bahamas.[32]

In the aftermath the triumphal celebrations brought him to the White House twice, on top of a visit to the LBJ ranch in November to fête the Apollo 7 crew and Jim Webb. He sent his father a picture of a crater the astronauts had unofficially named "Von Braun" and told him how happy he was that they could give President Johnson this great achievement before he left office. Incoming President

> Nixon now has the situation that, if he does not <u>also</u> support the space program well, history will say about him: as soon as the Republicans came to power, spaceflight went downhill. This he simply cannot afford, however, in view of the renewed popularity of flights into space. I am therefore confident about the future.[33]

Perhaps the era of budget cuts was finally over. It was an illusion widely shared in the NASA leadership.

During the preparations for Apollo 8, von Braun had received an unpleasant surprise, however: the Dora story again resurfaced. In an airmail letter dated 6 November 1968 a West German court in Essen, an industrial city in the Ruhr, informed him that he had been called as a witness in the trial of three former SS men from the Mittelwerk. He was offered dates immediately before Christmas or after New Year's to testify. If he could not come to Essen, his testimony could be taken through the help of an American court. Behind this request stood the East Berlin lawyer for the Soviet bloc survivors of Dora, Prof. Dr. Friedrich Kaul. He had previously advised the producers of *Die gefrorenen Blitze* on libel law regarding the movie's depiction of von Braun. Kaul's motion to testify thus represented the third major East German attempt to broadcast the connection between the rocket engineer, the SS, and the concentration camps.[34]

The NASA general counsel at the time, Paul Dembling, relates that von Braun was "troubled" by this letter, "certainly didn't want to go back to Germany," and was "afraid they were going to do something to him." He was particularly worried about the impact on U.S. public opinion regarding the postwar use of ex-Nazis. Concern about the fallout for NASA's programs certainly was also on von Braun's mind. When he finally answered the judge on 22 November, he declared that he could not come to Germany because of his obligations to the U.S. space program. Moreover, he had nothing to do with the running of the Mittelwerk or of the Mittelbau-Dora camp, only visited the former on several occasions, and had little to offer as a witness. If they still thought he was useful, however, the court should contact the MSFC chief counsel.[35]

A series of negotiations began. Dembling recalls getting an angry call from someone in Essen about von Braun not coming—perhaps it was Kaul. In conjunction with the State Department, NASA then proposed that the testimony be taken at the West German consulate in New Orleans. That site was chosen, according to Arthur Konopka, the German-speaking headquarters lawyer whom Dembling assigned to the case, precisely because it was off the beaten track of the U.S. media. Despite their efforts, on 4 January 1969 a UPI wire service report from Essen revealed that the court had called von Braun as a witness, an item that appeared in newspapers across the country. Two days later the Marshall lawyer offered the court the date of 6 February in New Orleans, later postponed to the seventh because of a conflict in von Braun's schedule. A week beforehand the State Department denied Kaul a visa, thus keeping the East German from joining the judge and prosecutors on the trip.[36]

By the time Konopka accompanied von Braun to the consulate, he felt that the Marshall director was no longer worried, but he clearly did not like answering questions about the mistreatment of prisoners, feeling that this was not his responsibility. Von Braun's 7 February testimony, which was not made available to the press, shows a very clear memory of the Mittelwerk and of the key people involved, but not only did he deny any personal involvement, he also denied ever having received a report of prisoner sabotage—although he cleverly phrased it as an *official* report of sabotage, so as to leave the false impression that he had hardly heard of sabotage at all. Afterward he gave a short statement on the consulate steps in which he declared that he had "nothing to hide, and I am not implicated." In the West German press, the line that was repeated was that he had a "clear conscience." Most of the American media either ignored the statement or never even heard of it, as neither NASA nor the State Department had informed them about the testimony. But in answering questions on the steps, he explicitly lied: he denied there had been any concentration camp prisoners at all in Peenemünde—a story that indeed did not come out for decades. Afterward, according to Dembling, he was pleased that the whole matter had turned out so well. Certainly they had controlled the publicity problem. Ten months later von Braun wrote Walter Dornberger: "In regard to the testimony, fortunately I too have heard nothing more." Dornberger, now retired, had been questioned right after him in Mexico, where he had begun spending his winters.[37]

The Dora story thus once again seemed to vanish; the spring of 1969 was a period of new triumphs for Apollo and greater optimism in NASA about the future. The Apollo 8 success and the resolution of the LM's troubles allowed MSC to lay out a clear plan leading up to a landing attempt on Apollo 11, probably in July. In early March the Apollo 9 crew tested the CSM and LM in Earth orbit, and all went well. A little over two months later, in mid-May, Apollo 10's astronauts carried out a full dress rehearsal in orbit around the Moon. Nixon meanwhile confirmed Tom Paine, a New Deal Democrat, as NASA Administrator for lack of a suitable Republican to take responsibility in case the landing was a disaster. Nixon also formed a Space Task Group under Vice President Spiro Agnew to look into post-Apollo plans. Naively overestimating Agnew's influence, Paine encouraged the agency's leaders to dream of permanent space stations, a reusable space shuttle, and even human expeditions to Mars. In early July he confidentially asked von Braun to draft a ten-year plan for the space agency.[38]

For the first time NASA also issued a clear postlanding plan for Apollo, which could carry out four additional expeditions, Apollos 12 to 15, plus the potential to do five more if all fifteen Saturn Vs were used. As recently as June 1968 von Braun had said that "he didn't think the taxpayers would stand for more than one trip after the successful landing . . . [because] right now there's just nothing in the program to make lunar visits meaningful." He later credited Sam Phillips for convincing NASA's leadership after Apollo 8 that it would be a waste not to use all the rockets and spacecraft in the pipeline for lunar surface science. Based on Huntsville's ability to extract more performance out of later Saturn Vs, a fact much appreciated in Houston, it would be possible to launch a heavier three-day-endurance Lunar Module for extended geological exploration. After a 21 May meeting at MSC during Apollo 10, George Mueller authorized MSFC to develop a small Lunar Roving Vehicle as well, a sort of dune buggy that could be folded up on the side of the LM and used for the extended missions starting in April 1971—a very short timetable. Notwithstanding the original Lake Logan agreements of 1966, von Braun's center had kept studying lunar rovers. Given Houston's heavy workload flying so many missions, it was logical to give the job to MSFC, which naturally pleased von Braun.[39]

That same May meeting led to another decision of great consequence for the post-Apollo schedule and for Huntsville: Mueller changed the AAP Orbital Workshop from "wet" to "dry." That eased many of the technical problems and weight limitations of the "wet" approach: having the astronauts refit an empty S-IVB that had just fired itself into orbit atop a Saturn IB. Von Braun himself became a convert at this time, recognizing that using a Saturn V to launch an already outfitted Workshop would be technically more straightforward, although it delayed the launches into 1972. With the seeming inevitable success of Apollo, he, Mueller, and the others were also more willing to consider using a big booster for that purpose. Since they were going to delay the cluster anyway, Mueller also decided to mount the Apollo Telescope Mount on the Workshop itself, getting rid of the Lunar Module cabin. During the Apollo 11 landing mission in July he made these decisions final. That eliminated Apollo 20, if no further boosters were built, but finally gave the troubled AAP program a configuration that all could agree on. Skylab—as NASA christened it in early 1970—had at last assumed its final configuration.[40]

As Apollo 11 approached, von Braun felt so comfortable with the Saturn V that he went on a trip to Europe with his wife and two daughters. (Iris was already in France as a counselor at a summer camp.) Using assumed names, he, Maria, Iris, and Margrit cruised the Greek islands and visited the shrine of Apollo at Delphi. He then flew to Germany to see his father and attend the seventy-fifth birthday celebration of Hermann Oberth at Salzburg, Austria, on 25 June, sponsored by the German spaceflight society. Unfortunately a pall was cast over the proceedings when they received a telegram that Willy Ley, a heavy cigar smoker, had died suddenly from a heart attack at his home in New York, three weeks short of seeing that dream of the Weimar rocketeers, the launch of a Moon landing expedition.[41]

Soon it was time to go to the Cape. The 16 July launch of Neil Armstrong, Michael Collins, and Buzz Aldrin marked the apogee of von Braun's life. He and Maria flew down from Huntsville on Sunday the thirteenth and stayed at the Cocoa Beach Holiday Inn. Around one million people descended on the region, with the result that there were gigantic traffic jams; people camped on every beach and green space with a hope of catching sight of the launch. NASA rented helicopters to ferry von Braun and its other top leaders over the gridlocked traffic. He had a long and burdensome list of obligations: the Apollo Executives meeting, management meetings on launch preparations, news conferences, plus celebrities and friends to greet. Ley would be much missed (von Braun had gotten him a VIP seat for Apollo 8), but Oberth and the leader of the Raketenflugplatz, Rudolf Nebel, attended the launch, along with Nebel's old nemesis Dornberger. Von Braun was regularly accompanied by a friend from *Collier's* days, Cornelius Ryan, now an editor of *Reader's Digest*, who was writing a piece about him in conjunction with von Braun's projected article on space travel after Apollo.[42]

But it was Norman Mailer in his Apollo 11 book, *Of a Fire on the Moon*, who penned the most unforgettable portrait of von Braun at the Cape. During the prelaunch press conference, the Marshall director stole the show from Mueller, Debus, and the others when he issued the most quotable line of the afternoon. "When asked how he evaluated the importance of the act of putting a man on the moon, Von Braun answered, 'I think it is equal in importance to that moment in evolution when aquatic life came crawling up on land.' It drew a hand of applause. . . . Some of the Press literally stood up." But Mailer noted von Braun's bearing at the beginning: "A press conference, no matter how many he had, was a putative den of menace. So his eyes flew left and right as he answered a question, flicking back and forth in their attention with the speed of eyes watching a Ping-Pong game." The writer was fascinated by the contrast between the "big, burly squared-off bulk of a body" with his "relatively small voice, darting eyes and semaphoric presentations of lip [that] made it obvious he was a man of opposites. He revealed a confusing aura of strength and vulnerability, of calm and agitation, cruelty and concern, phlegm and sensitivity, which would have given fine play to the talents of so virtuoso an actor as Mr. Rod Steiger."[43]

The night before the launch Mailer attended publisher Time-Life's gala dinner at the Titusville Country Club for corporate leaders, astronauts, and other VIPs. Von Braun, the keynote speaker, arrived by helicopter, dropping in like "the *deus ex machina* of the big boosters." When Mailer met him during cocktail hour, von Braun revealed that he was far from completely convinced that NASA's ambitious post-Apollo plans would sell: "You must help us give a *shove* to the program. . . . Yes, we are in trouble. You must help us." Mailer replied, "Who are you kidding? . . . You're going to get everything you want." "His eyes gleamed with sudden funds of pleasure at the remark [but] he quickly looked discomposed," and as quickly vanished without a reply. During the host's biographical introduction to the speech, "tension spread" across the room as von Braun's German career was briefly touched. "There was an uneasy silence, an embarrassed pall at the unmentioned word of Nazi." After the speaker moved on expeditiously to his naturalization and American career, however, the crowd erupted into a standing ovation.[44]

Von Braun got little sleep that night; due to a mix-up, the hotel clerk called even earlier than expected at three a.m. He soon got dressed, and when he kissed his wife goodbye, he said: "Pray"; she said, "Bye & good luck." First on the agenda was a 4:30 a.m. helicopter ride with three subordinates to Melbourne, about twenty-five miles away, to greet a group of French business and government leaders who came on a plane chartered by *Paris Match*. The West German ambassador to France—Sigismund—had to back out at the last minute, but he sent his only son, Christoph-Friedrich von Braun, then twenty-three. Christoph remembered the sweltering heat and humidity—it was in the upper eighties before dawn—but his uncle, who gave a short speech in French, looked perfectly composed and cool in a dark suit. His bearing, Christoph thought, exuded the thought "This is my day"—he may even have said it. After an abbreviated breakfast with the French, von Braun then departed for Launch Complex 39 by helicopter, even taking over the controls himself. Below them stretched miles of cars, bumper to bumper along all the highways leading to the Cape. The launch was scheduled for 9:32 a.m.[45]

Von Braun took his usual position in the mission manager row of the Launch Control Center, put on his headphones, and tuned in to four different circuits. The countdown chatter back and forth was routine; there was no need for him or Mueller and Phillips, on his left, or Rees and James, on his right, to intervene. Shortly before the liftoff he bowed his head and silently recited the Lord's Prayer. Apollo 11 made its fiery ascent on time and as routinely as ever. Three hours later, after translunar injection, Armstrong, Collins, and Aldrin were on their way to the Moon, and following the usual postlaunch news conference, he was free. He, Maria, and Peter spent two additional days at the Cape, mostly seeing old friends, relaxing, and catching up on their sleep.[46]

For the rest of the Apollo 11 mission, his job was to watch. Only in the case of a prolonged and severe crisis in space would the NASA management be called in to make a decision. Otherwise Mission Control ruled the roost. On Sunday morning, 20 July 1969—landing day—he flew down to Houston with a select group from his inner circle to observe the climactic moments of the mission from the VIP room overlooking the controllers. The seventy-some seats there were doled out to the privileged few. At the end of Armstrong and Aldrin's extremely tense, alarm-ridden, and prolonged descent in the Lunar Module came the commander's breathtaking words: "Houston, Tranquility Base here, the *Eagle* has landed." In the hubbub of the viewing room congratulations, von Braun graciously leaned over to thank John Houbolt, whose advocacy of lunar-orbit rendezvous a seeming eternity ago had been one of the factors that got them to that day. Several hours later, as Armstrong descended the ladder of the LM, he pulled on the cord to start the TV. The sight of that first leg coming into view was, von Braun later said, "a pretty emotional moment."[47] Although it was not his own leg on the ladder, a forty-year dream, the "romantic urge" of his youth, had been realized, and he had played a central role in it.

CHAPTER EIGHTEEN

For Him, a World Was Falling Apart

1969–72

In this world there are only two tragedies. One is not getting what one wants and the other is getting it. —OSCAR WILDE[1]

Four days after the Moon landing Huntsville city leaders hoisted Wernher von Braun on their shoulders and carried him up the courthouse steps as a conquering hero. Thousands jammed the city's downtown streets on that steamy Alabama afternoon, summoned by a cacophony of air-raid sirens, fire sirens, and church bells. The "spontaneous" demonstration, organized weeks in advance to attract media attention to "Rocket City U.S.A." at a time when Houston dominated the news of Apollo, followed the successful splashdown of the astronauts in the Pacific. Von Braun, accompanied by his nine-year-old son, Peter, told the crowd: "The ultimate destiny of man is no longer confined to earth. . . . Maybe one of these days we'll even have a man on Mars."[2]

The Red Planet was much on his mind. A day earlier he had begun preparing, at NASA Administrator Tom Paine's request, a presentation on just such a Mars expedition. Von Braun was to speak on 4 August to the Space Task Group, Vice President Spiro Agnew's committee to examine NASA's post-Apollo future. (It is not to be confused with the first STG, which became Gilruth's Houston center.) Agnew had already endorsed Mars as the next big goal in a Cape press conference after Apollo 11's launch—and had sparked an immediate controversy in Congress. Even the STG itself was split between Agnew and Paine on the one side and Bob Seamans, now secretary of the air force, and Lee DuBridge, Caltech president and science adviser to Nixon, on the other. The latter two were more skeptical of huge, expensive human spaceflight programs at a time of federal budgets strained by Vietnam, urban upheavals, and growing inflation. The president himself stressed austerity in the wake of Democratic Party deficit spending.[3]

Paine probably first asked von Braun to pull together a detailed Mars expedition in May 1969, following George Mueller's presentation of an integrated plan for human spaceflight. That ambitious plan, which Mueller had worked up independently of the centers, included continued use of the Saturn V as a heavy-lift vehicle, a winged "space shuttle" to ferry astronauts and smaller payloads to low Earth orbit, a "space tug" to move larger payloads between orbits, and a "nuclear shuttle" to cycle back and forth from Earth to lunar orbit, using the 75,000-lb-thrust NERVA (Nuclear Engine for Rocket Vehicle Application) that the Atomic Energy Commission was developing with NASA. This transportation infrastructure was to service Earth and lunar orbit space stations and lunar surface bases, a vision that owed much to the "von Braun paradigm" of the *Collier's* era. A year later von Braun's own assessment was that it was "fine and good" as a hardware program, but "the question of what are we going to do with it once we get there . . . was a weak point." In short Mueller had done little to explain to the American people why they should spend billions and billions on human spaceflight.[4]

Paine, who wanted to exploit Apollo's successes to get the maximum out of the political system, felt only one thing was missing, however: human planetary missions, the subject of many studies in the 1960s, including some at Marshall. Using the elements of the Mueller plan, von Braun's Future Projects Office then worked up feasible scenarios for two-year expeditions to Mars in the 1980s, using a Venus gravity-assist in one direction or the other, and employing the nuclear shuttle stages as basic propulsion. Two six-man crews would travel in parallel vehicles, in case one failed, with the first landing as early as 1982. Von Braun had at least the outlines of such a plan by early June, when he talked to a reporter about it.[5]

How much the erstwhile author of *The Mars Project* really believed in the Red Planet as a post-Apollo goal will forever remain a question. In late August 1970, when the future looked much less bright, he told a young political scientist, John Logsdon, that "I have never in the last two or three years strongly promoted a manned Mars project. . . . People . . . have tried to cast me in the image . . . of the Mars or bust guy in this agency, which I am definitely not." Lending credence to this assertion is the fact that, before mid-1969, he had left manned Mars expeditions out of his advocacy, not because he did not want to go, but because he did not see how to sell such an expensive proposition. "I, for one, have always felt that it would be a good idea to read the signs of the times and respond to what the country really wants, rather than trying to cram a bill of goodies down somebody's throat for which the time is not ripe or ready," he said in the same interview. All of this is an implicit critique of Mueller and Paine's approach to the post-Apollo problem, but a lot of it may be hindsight. There is no denying von Braun's personal rapport with Paine, nor his excitement in 1969 with the tantalizing possibility that all of his dreams might just come true. The NASA Administrator certainly admired von Braun as a "visionary" and saw his deployment to sell Mars as "wheeling up the NASA big guns."[6]

Von Braun put on a slick, three-screen, illustrated presentation for the Space Task Group on 4 August; it was so convincing that Agnew arranged for a repeat in front of the Senate Space Committee the next day. Willis Shapley, NASA associate deputy administrator responsible for political aspects of the agency's program, remembered the "gasp" from the audience that met von Braun's remark that the two ships would depart for Mars on precisely "the 12th of November 1981": "that was one of the most amazing congressional moments in the congressional hearings that I have ever been at." In order to calculate a mission all the way through, MSFC's planners had picked exact dates for every event from Earth departure until return, lending an air of finality to this rather hypothetical scenario. Shapley found it an impressive talk but never once believed that Paine's "bold, bold, bold" sales approach would work. During the question period the issue of cost inevitably came up, and nobody had a good number, but von Braun thought NASA's budget would have to rise to $7 billion a year (it was then about $4 billion), and Paine added that he thought it would be more like $9 billion.[7]

For von Braun, these talks were only two of the events that made the weeks after Apollo 11 nearly as hectic and exciting as the mission itself. On 30 July he had flown to Houston and participated in a fascinating debriefing with the astronauts, who were quarantined behind glass because of the remote possibility of lunar germs. He had gone on to JPL in Pasadena with Paine to observe the robotic Mariner 6 spacecraft's flyby of the Red Planet. There the two refined the STG talk, and Paine prepped for a couple of trial-balloon Mars speeches. Returning home for the weekend, von Braun then spent a week in Washington for the Mars presentations, Mueller's Management Council meeting, and a White House state dinner for West German chancellor Kurt Kiesinger. Six days after that gala he and Maria attended a second Nixon-hosted dinner, this time in Los Angeles on 13 August, for Armstrong, Collins, and Aldrin, just out of quarantine. This party for more than fourteen hundred was studded with celebrities; von Braun declared it "a thrilling evening." But outside left-wing demonstrators gave an indication of the realities NASA faced. According to Hans Mark, then director of the Ames Research Center in northern California: "A major feature of the demonstration was a huge sign with the legend 'Fuck Mars' printed on it in large letters that the demonstrators had somehow been able to hang along the upper floors of one of the office buildings across the street from the Century Plaza." The opinion of a majority of the American public, although less crude, was scarcely more enthused for a human Mars expedition, a poll taken at that time showed. Nor was Congress signaling its acceptance. Liberal Democrats, under siege from both left and right, had largely abandoned big space programs in favor of urban and social issues, while most of the Republicans leaned toward fiscal austerity as the war continued to grind up American soldiers and resources.[8]

Intoxicated by his relationship with Agnew, however, Paine continued to push the Space Task Group, which finally hammered out a compromise report in September. Unable to agree on a single proposal, the four voting members approved three options: level I had a space station and space shuttle by 1976, a fifty-man station and a lunar base by 1980, and a Mars expedition in 1983 instead of 1981. Levels II and III slipped the station and shuttle to 1977 and the other goals further into the 1980s; the only difference between the two was that level II had a 1986 Mars expedition (the next launch window), whereas III left the Mars goal open as a long-term objective. All levels included the space tug and nuclear-powered cislunar shuttle too. Nixon accepted the report but did not publicly endorse something that was already politically unpopular. Through the fall and winter Paine continued to believe that it provided the basis for the administration's space policy; only gradually did it become clear that the president and his staff supported none of the options. Paine was obtuse and naive, but it is also true that Nixon's behavior toward the space program in 1969–70 was disingenuous. He was quick to associate himself with the astronauts and the triumphs of Apollo when it was politically convenient, and he was equally quick to slash the budget of NASA when choices had to be made between agencies.[9]

If von Braun had doubts about Paine's approach that he expressed later, he certainly kept quiet about them in 1969; there was always hope that some part of it would come true anyway. But it is clear, especially in hindsight, how much NASA was headed for a fall, taking von Braun's career with it. Over the next three years the agency's future human spaceflight programs would shrivel until the space shuttle was virtually the only thing left. Von Braun himself would be lured to Washington by Paine, only to leave NASA a little over two years later. For thirty-seven of his fifty-seven years, from the Reichswehr's 1932 offer until the day Apollo 11 returned, he had ridden the wave of state interest in rocket development, first for weapons systems, then for space. Suddenly it was over.

For all the relief that the Moon landing brought—a success on the first attempt and within the Kennedy deadline—von Braun's job as Marshall director did not let up in the fall of 1969. In addition to his heavy responsibilities selling Mars and the NASA program, the strongest hurricane ever to hit the U.S. mainland, Camille, smashed through the center's Mississippi Test Facility on 17–18 August, leading him to organize relief for homeless and destitute workers. Saturn V operations continued at an only slightly less hurried pace, with Apollo 12 scheduled for November. Among future programs Paine had pushed the space station early in 1969, but by spring it was the space shuttle that came to the fore, because NASA had to make key technological decisions and investments to prepare for a reusable, winged space plane, such as a new high-efficiency engine. To keep Marshall in business beyond the Saturn and Skylab, von Braun strived to get the center pieces of both the shuttle and the station.[10]

At least in the case of the shuttle, a division of labor with Houston seemed immediately at hand. The baseline configuration that von Braun, Gilruth, and Mueller all accepted was a two-stage, fully reusable vehicle. The booster would be a huge, piloted rocket plane the size of a Boeing 747 airliner that would carry the orbiter nearly halfway to space before breaking away and returning to the launch site. The orbiter would be a 707-size winged spacecraft, making it even larger than the final design that emerged in 1971–72. Based on the Apollo model, the obvious deal was Huntsville managing the booster and Houston the orbiter, an idea the Marshall director pushed although it encroached upon MSC's sacred astronaut turf. It was a very ambitious project, its risks only magnified by the very high expectations that Mueller, the shuttle's chief champion since 1968, but also von Braun, had for it. The reusable booster was to bring about a revolution in the cost of spaceflight, lowering launch costs from $500 a pound to orbit to $50, allowing "airline-type" operations. Although there were technical reasons why Mueller and von Braun, but also Gilruth and his chief designer, Max Faget, believed in the feasibility of this revolutionary project, there was also a fair amount of Apollo hubris: if they could land a human on the Moon in only eight years, why couldn't they radically alter the economics of spaceflight?[11]

Von Braun had personal reasons for supporting the space shuttle as well, although they were not the deciding factors in his willingness to advocate the idea. He hoped it would be the means for him to achieve the unrealized part of his dream, that of flying into space himself. In 1968 he had used his connections to fly weightless parabolas in an air force training plane and to simulate zero-G in a spacesuit in Marshall's new water tank, bringing him about as close to the spaceflight experience as he could get. If putting his boot down on the Moon seemed less and less likely, seeing the beautiful Earth from orbit did not seem at all improbable with the shuttle. "There are flying grandfathers. I expect to be an orbiting grandfather," he told a reporter during Apollo 11. He was to get neither wish.[12]

At the end of his August 1969 Mars presentations, he raised an even more radical idea, evidence of his faith in NASA's ability to build a revolutionary vehicle that would make spaceflight "routine": why not orbit the president for the 1976 U.S. Bicentennial? When his testimony became public in September, this idea earned some respect and some ridicule. *The Washington Post* ran a satirical editorial: "But why wait? . . . Orbit Nixon Now should be the slogan of every sensation-seeking citizen. . . . On alternate Tuesdays, von Braun and the crowd down at Huntsville could orbit the cabinet for a conference on the war."[13]

Despite such reactions, the space shuttle was one of the few things that had political traction, thanks to NASA's promise that it would dramatically lower the cost of spaceflight. The air force was interested too. By contrast, the humans-to-Mars goal was virtually dead on arrival; indeed the Paine–von Braun initiative had done harm by associating all human spaceflight with something the majority of the public saw as unaffordable and unjustified. The space station remained closely linked to the shuttle in the minds of NASA leaders, but the agency had yet to provide either the politicians or the populace any compelling reason to support it. As for Moon exploration after Apollo ended in 1974 (the then-projected date), the details remained exceedingly vague, although the NERVA-powered nuclear shuttle was still on the official agenda. But to launch the nuclear stage or large station modules, NASA would need to keep the Saturn V in low-level production, which was entirely dependent on the Nixon administration's fiscal 1971 budget (beginning 1 July 1970). It loomed as a make-or-break test for Paine's ambitions, with the first budget numbers due in November 1969. He was in for a shock.

For some time Paine had discussed with von Braun the possibility of coming to NASA headquarters to help him sell the program. Willis Shapley told an interviewer in early 1970: "Paine has been wanting von Braun up here a year, and von Braun made noises last fall about being willing to do something except direct a center."[14] The Marshall director had told family members that he was burned out with his job. The question was, in what capacity could he best serve in the capital?

It is instructive to consider the positions for which Paine did not nominate him. Ever since Paine's confirmation as administrator in March 1969, his deputy administrator position had been vacant. Paine the liberal Democrat had searched for a Republican who was technically qualified but had no luck, so he decided to offer the apolitical George Low, Apollo spacecraft manager in Houston, a big promotion after Apollo 11. Paine said a year later: "I had a feeling that when you give a person in his forties an opportunity to run something like NASA you really bring out the best in NASA and the best in the guy. If you go and get a retired fellow who is in his sixties, late fifties, and ask him to do it, well, he's already got his reputation made and all he can do is lose and so he's going to be a little too cautious." His latter description, consciously or not, fit von Braun to a T. Graying at the temples and some-times wearing reading glasses, he was no longer the wunderkind.[15]

Of course, he had another problem: there was very little chance that the Washington political establishment would allow an ex-Nazi to serve as NASA Administrator, even in an acting capacity. Paine knew he was likely to be "a bird of passage" in the job, so he wanted to put a technically qualified person in place who could be acting administrator while Nixon's staff looked for a competent Republican. Paine did not worry about von Braun's past haunting the agency, unlike Webb in his later years as administrator, but he certainly was aware of the problem.[16]

Six weeks after Paine forwarded Low's name to Nixon in September 1969, human spaceflight chief George Mueller decided to quit, one of several who saw the accomplishment of Kennedy's goal as a good moment to return to their roots in industry or the military. Low pushed for, and Paine hired, Dale Myers, one of the engineering managers who had turned around North American Rockwell (as the company was now known) after the Apollo fire. Myers was very distinctive for always wearing a black patch over his blind left eye. If the administrator had simply promoted von Braun one step up the ladder, to head of the Office of Manned Space Flight, it probably would not have gone down well in Houston. An outsider had a better chance of being an arbiter between the rival centers.[17]

There was another unfilled slot at headquarters, however, called deputy associate administrator—or Associate Administrator Homer Newell's dep-uty. In 1967 Webb had named Newell, from 1963 to 1967 head of the Space Sciences office, to NASA's number-three position in order to bring a promi-nent scientist to the top; resentment in the scientific community had been growing over the agency's domination by engineers. Rather than giving Newell the "general manager" role once held by Seamans, Webb and later Paine had assigned him the long-range planning task of preparing for post-

Apollo. What came out of "Newell's monumentally bureaucratic planning process," to use Shapley's words, was, however, a pile of committee reports. Hence Paine and Mueller had initiated their own efforts in the spring of 1969, but there still seemed to be no coherent plan for the whole agency, one that took account of budget realities. The in-house planning staff was adrift as well. Thus Paine came to the idea, in discussions with von Braun and Low, of placing the MSFC director into the empty slot and giving him the job of putting "some imagination back into the future plans for the agency."[18]

On 1 December, after Apollo 12's successful conclusion, Paine called von Braun in Huntsville and asked him if he was coming up anytime soon, as he would like to discuss "some of the things we have been putting off for a while." In fact, von Braun would be in Washington at the end of the week. The context of the administrator's call was the worrying state of the FY 1971 budget. Paine had requested $4.5 billion, a significant increase over the previous year, but the Budget Bureau came back on 13 November with a figure of a billion less. His protests got him only an extra $200 million, for a total of $3.7 billion, which he still considered unacceptable. Saturn V production would end for good, and there would be no new money for the shuttle or the station in that year. Paine intended to appeal his case all the way to Nixon if necessary. He certainly felt he needed help, both in selling Congress and the American people and in planning for the intelligent use of a budget that was obviously going to be worse than expected. At their meeting on the fifth von Braun and Paine came to a deal: when von Braun returned from a nearly two-month vacation in the Bahamas that was to start in a few days, they would decide when to go through with his appointment as deputy associate administrator. He would be more than a planner; his role would be something like chief architect and salesman for the future program. On 8 December, his last day in the office before his vacation, von Braun held a "sensitive" meeting with his inner circle. He may have hinted at his possible departure, but he certainly gave them an inside look at the worrying budget situation.[19]

Von Braun's decision to leave Huntsville and his "rocket team" was a monumental one for the local community and for Marshall, as he well knew, but also for himself. But beyond his feelings of burnout and the need for change, family considerations came into play too: Maria was very much in favor of heading to the capital, as Paine knew. She had never particularly enjoyed being "first lady" of the Huntsville German group and felt constrained by the provincial city, although its population had grown by a factor of ten since they had moved there in 1950. Like her husband, she grew up in a very cultured aristocratic family that had lived mostly in worldly

Berlin. With her children maturing, she looked forward both to a more anonymous existence in the big city and to greater cultural and educational offerings for herself and the family. Iris had already gone to the National Cathedral School in the District of Columbia.[20]

But all that could be dealt with later. Wernher, Maria, and Peter von Braun took off for Grand Bahama Island and the longest vacation he had ever taken in his life, a post-Moon-landing reward for all of them. Iris and Margrit joined them during school vacations. They swam, relaxed, island-hopped by airplane, scuba-dived, and spent a week sailing. A month in, Paine called him to finalize the plan early, so he left for four days in Washington. He told Paine and Low on 13 January 1970 that, in Low's words, he "would be most interested in undertaking this assignment." The deputy associate administrator slot was a "Schedule C" political appointment, so Paine required clearance to put even a nonpolitical technical expert in the job, as was the case with Low.[21]

Paine and von Braun's plan for a carefully staged postvacation announcement was disrupted, however, when somebody on Capitol Hill leaked the news on the twenty-sixth. Facing the possibility of headlines the next day, Paine rushed his appointment letter to the White House, called Eberhard Rees to tell him that he would be the new center director, and flew down to Huntsville for a hurried press conference with Rees on the twenty-seventh. Throughout it all von Braun remained holed up in the Bahamas. He slipped home quietly with his family at the end of the week, not yet ready to face his German colleagues and Marshall employees. In the city the hero worship was such that many felt Huntsville was doomed without him; all kinds of rumors circulated as to his reasons. He gave his reassuring speech on his first official day back in the office, 2 February, resplendent in a full beard that he was about to shave off. "The exact timing of the final approval of the plan," he said, "was as much of a surprise to me, as it was to you." But he was looking forward to working with "a brilliant, capable scientist" like Homer Newell, and the new position, which would begin 1 March, offered a "challenge." The 1960s "ended with a blaze of glory for the space program. . . . The second decade of space exploration has gotten off to a sluggish start, to put it mildly. Now it is time to consolidate our gains, and to apply our space technology for the maximum possible returns," notably satellites to survey Earth resources and global environmental damage, topics that had long interested him.[22]

In the interim the agency's money situation had become even grimmer, as he well knew from his Washington trip. Nixon had rejected out of hand Paine's appeals for a budget higher than $3.7 billion, then allowed it to be cut twice more as deficit projections worsened. The final time, during von Braun's visit, Paine was entering a ballroom for some event when "the loud-speaker boomed out that I was to call the White House. . . . And I went with sinking heart knowing damned well they weren't calling to say that we had more money." The final, shocking figure was a $3.33 billion of new budget authority—at least that was the amount to be proposed to Congress, which could cut further. Even before that last reduction Paine had already announced the closing of the Electronics Research Center in Massachusetts, the ending of Saturn V after the fifteenth vehicle, and the delay of the Viking probe launches to Mars (which had replaced the old Voyager program) from 1973 to 1975. If von Braun had any reservations about what he was getting into, Paine no doubt appealed to him as someone uniquely qualified to sell the program in Washington. It did not hurt that the job included a promotion from $33,495 to $36,000 per year (equivalent to $180,000 in 2006). To the press, NASA also described the deputy associate administrator as the number-four position in the agency, although Willis Shapley, associate deputy administrator, privately quibbled with that.[23]

With less than four weeks to go before he began the new job, February became a harried month of back-and-forth between Huntsville and Washington, on top of already scheduled speaking obligations. He and Maria looked at fifty houses before picking a beautiful redbrick home on a secluded green cul-de-sac in Alexandria, Virginia, only fifteen minutes by freeway from NASA headquarters on a good day. But they could not move into it until the beginning of April, so he would have to spend March alone in temporary quarters. Tuesday, 24 February, was Wernher von Braun Day in Huntsville, and he and the family were paraded through the streets once again and witnessed the unveiling of a granite marker honoring him in the middle of downtown. On Friday, his last day in the office, he participated in yet another meeting to discuss how to handle the enormous intake of mail, speech and autograph requests, gifts, and so on that would continue to pour into his office at Marshall. At 5:45 he cleared out his closet and desk and took a look around, saying to his executive secretary, Bonnie Holmes: "Well, this is it. We've had fun in this office. I'll see you at the plane Sunday."[24]

She would in fact come up for a couple of weeks to help von Braun's new secretary, Julia Kertes, cope with the load. Kertes later estimated that he got more mail than Paine, Low, Newell, and Shapley put together—a sign once again of how much his celebrity was out of proportion to his job title.[25] Another problem was his German correspondence, some of which would have to be diverted back to Huntsville to answer. At MSFC he had had a well-oiled publicity, speech-writing, and correspondence machine, staffed by intensely loyal people who knew what he wanted to say. He would never have anything like that again.

The first months at NASA headquarters were overwhelming and some-times frustrating but also seemed to hold a lot of promise. He and Newell soon moved into a suite near Paine's office on the sixth floor of a seven-story federal office building near the Mall, opposite where the National Air and Space Museum now stands. A conference room was converted into the elab-orate Planning Control Room he wanted, with multiple projection screens and charts operated by a contractor staff of seven. Paine, Low, and Newell accepted von Braun's plan for an executive Planning Council chaired by him that included the chiefs of the three main program offices: Manned Space-flight (Dale Myers), Space Science and Applications (John Naugle), and Advanced Research and Technology (Oran Nicks). Paine took him to one of the Sunday morning TV talk shows to discuss the NASA program and Nixon's recent, rather bland space policy statement, a visible sign of the weight Paine put both on his planning effort and on his ability to communi-cate with the public. Von Braun told a press conference a couple of weeks later that he felt a bit like an admiral who had "to give up his beloved battle-ship and trade it for a desk in the Pentagon," but the new job was "intellec-tually a great challenge," and it was "a very exciting experience" to be so close to the centers of power.[26]

Socially he and Maria were inundated by invitations from the Washing-ton elite, many more than they could possibly cope with. He had certainly not lost his ability to charm the opposite sex. The *Washington Star* society columnist, Betty Beale, gushed about him in the paper: "One of the most fascinating men in the world has just moved to town. . . . The rocket genius is a brilliant conversationalist, extremely handsome and socially charm-ing. . . . His lucid conversation covers everything from the atom to God, who he believes in deeply." In April the von Brauns attended yet another glittering White House state dinner for a West German chancellor, this time the recently elected Willy Brandt. Von Braun then accompanied Brandt and Vice President Agnew to the launch of Apollo 13. They certainly talked about Sigismund, who was about to be called from Paris to Bonn to serve as one of the deputy ministers of the Foreign Ministry.[27]

Some of von Braun's problems in his early months at headquarters were harbingers, however, of more difficult days ahead. He told his father in April that his role as "chief architect" entailed building "a somewhat Spartan space program" without spectacular goals like the Moon landing, which would require him "to propose and push through unpopular things too." In the next letter he said: "My job was in the beginning somewhat difficult, because NASA has never had a central planning office and the different offices had developed their own programs fairly independently of one another."[28]

He also had problems with his bosses. Low, backed by Paine, rejected his first proposal for a top-heavy planning organization of forty people dominated by expensive "supergrade" civil servants. He cut von Braun's initial allotment back to thirty with fewer high-grade employees. In late March Low wrote in his "Personal Notes," a private journal he began keeping as deputy administrator: "During this time period I also became somewhat concerned about von Braun's understanding of what both Tom Paine and I are trying to tell him." They had asked for "an overall plan" for all studies that had to be undertaken to prepare for FY 1972, and von Braun came back "with one study in one area only," presumably the shuttle. Just before Low and Paine hurriedly left for Houston because of Apollo 13's near-fatal accident, they also told him that he could not take sides on shuttle questions. Apparently he had—not without reason—become skeptical of the expense and technical difficulty of developing a gigantic, piloted, winged booster and had begun advocating an interim, throwaway first stage. They told him his job was to present alternatives, not (as in the past) to be an advocate and a decision maker. "This perhaps will be one of the most difficult things for von Braun to understand to do, yet it is, of course, essential if he is to run a viable planning organization."[29]

As for the often unrealistic foundation on which NASA's planning was still based, there was plenty of blame to go around. Even as Paine, Low, von Braun, and Myers discussed short-term budget fixes such as canceling more Apollo lunar landings and postponing the space station until sometime after shuttle spending peaked, they still believed that the big FY 1971 cutback was only a temporary phenomenon. Low told von Braun that his baseline plan should be an agency budget rising to $4 billion in 1972 and $5 billion by 1975. He should also develop a contingency plan that remained level at $3.5 billion, but Paine subsequently discouraged von Braun from pursuing this unpleasant idea.[30]

In mid-June 1970 von Braun organized an advanced planning retreat at the agency's Atlantic coast station at Wallops Island, Virginia, so that the NASA leadership could look forward to the year 2000. Science fiction author, space advocate, and von Braun friend Arthur C. Clarke was the keynote speaker. With Paine's enthusiastic backing, it was Space Task Group 1969 all over again. Moon bases, human planetary missions, and technocratic fantasies of fixing all the world's problems through science and technology formed the substance of the weekend. Although NASA's leaders had begun to understand that the Soviet specter no longer worked very well as a sales argument, nobody really wanted to grapple with the fact that most Americans saw Apollo as an exercise in beating the Russians to the Moon and, once that was accomplished, had largely lost interest. Instead, von Braun, Clarke, and Paine all expounded on why "man" must explore.[31]

The Wallops attendees, von Braun notably included, were certainly out of touch with the public mood regarding technocratic solutions to social and political programs. Environmentalism was in the ascendant; the radical and countercultural left had largely turned against science and technology as the source of all the Earth's ills, while the rising conservative movement was blaming "big government" and Kennedy-Johnson social programs, among other things, for taking the United States so far off the track. The American popular mood was pessimistic, introspective, and antielitist yet bitterly divided over the Vietnam War and social policies. Nixon's invasion of Cambodia that spring had sparked renewed antiwar demonstrations. The Wallops conference, which von Braun thoroughly enjoyed, proved to be the last gasp of NASA's space dreams of the 1960s and also of Paine's leadership.[32]

Early in July Paine tried to get an appointment with Nixon to explain to him all the wonders of the future revealed at Wallops, but he got nowhere. Shortly thereafter he received an offer to return to General Electric that he thought was too good to turn down, even though he had promised not to leave NASA so soon. It was clear to him in any case that his political capital inside the administration was exhausted. Paine's surprise announcement that he would leave in September, which became public on 28 July, was greeted with relief in the Budget Bureau and White House staff, who viewed him as obstructionist.[33]

Although we do not know when and how von Braun got the news, he was "just devastated" by Paine's departure, his secretary Julia Kertes later said. Paine had brought him to Washington to plan the program, and now the future of that activity was unclear. Paine advised him to quit too, asserts von Braun's last special assistant in Huntsville, but even if that is true, he had just bought a new house and committed himself and his family to staying in the capital, so leaving would have been very inconvenient.[34]

Before Paine left office on September 15, von Braun participated in one of his last important decisions: whether to eliminate two more Apollo lunar landings, a matter of obvious symbolism for NASA. According to the official schedule, there would be a nearly two-year gap between Apollo 17 in mid-1972 and Apollos 18 and 19 in 1974, filled by the launching of the Skylab orbital workshop and three Saturn IB boosters carrying crews to it.

Although the FY 1971 budget expected from Congress was only slightly worse than the Nixon administration had requested, the outcome was a foregone conclusion: the last two landings were gone, less for the short-term savings than the almost $800 million that the agency expected to spare in future years by shutting down the Apollo program and Saturn V launches two years early. (Skylab would be the last launch of the giant booster, then expected in late 1972.) At the key 24 August meeting von Braun said little, but one can imagine his feelings: profound disappointment at the loss of the science and the adventure of two more explorations balanced against pragmatic considerations of cost and safety; as Apollo 13 underlined, these missions were dangerous. Increasingly, circumstances compelled von Braun's well-developed pragmatic side to come to the fore. Future dreams were all very well, but how were they going to pay for them?[35]

As he told political scientist Logsdon the next day, it was a question of "how bullish can you get in a bear market."

> I have been a space man ever since I was a child, and I think I would be betraying my profession if I were to tell you that we should not send a man to Mars. I think we should and we will, and I am all for the finest and most energetic space program we can imagine. I am convinced it will pay off very handsomely.

But the time was not right; the country was not in the mood to fund such a program. Nonetheless a lot of people in the agency lived in a world of illusions.

> I believe there may be too many people in NASA who at the moment are waiting for a miracle, just waiting for another man on a white horse to come and offer us another planet, like President Kennedy. . . . The legacy of Apollo has spoiled a few people at NASA. They believe we are entitled to this kind of a thing forever, which I gravely doubt.

In another interview he did the same morning, he was more inclined to blame the public. He summarized its attitude as: "These goddam[n] Apollo guys have had their day in court, they had all the fun, but now that we have landed on the moon, let's quit."[36]

For much of September 1970 von Braun escaped to Europe for an air show in Britain, reindeer hunting in Norway, and a visit to his father in the Bavarian Alps, so it was not until afterward that he encountered how depressing things were in a post-Paine agency. According to Kertes, he soon found that "the one-on-one informal sessions with the administrator ended and appointments with the acting administrator to discuss our programs became more difficult to set up as time went by." George Low was more reserved than Paine and, although on cordial terms with von Braun, simply was not his personal friend. Von Braun's nominal superior, Homer Newell, was not in Low's inner circle either, so he could do little to help him. The former Apollo program chief General Sam Phillips has said: "Planning offices are generally not effective as such. They are effective only, if at all, if they are an arm of the boss." Paine had brought von Braun in to plan NASA's future program, but as political support sank further in 1970–71, there was less and less of a future to plan. Low's major objective became salvaging whatever he could until the White House got around to finding a new administrator. Since that was not a high priority and it was difficult to find someone to take the job, Low would head the agency for eight months.[37]

Afterward many of von Braun's Huntsville colleagues blamed Low personally for the shipwreck of their former leader's hopes at headquarters. Even uglier, some ascribed it to a "Jewish Mafia" in Washington, an expression of an anti-Semitic undercurrent in the northern Alabama city. Low was a Jewish or half-Jewish Austrian refugee from Hitler's 1938 Anschluss; as a boy, Low, his mother, and a brother had escaped, aided by money from a factory she owned as a widow. After coming to the United States in 1940, they pursued a not-uncommon strategy of complete assimilation, Anglicizing their name and obscuring their Jewish background. If George Low had any feelings regarding von Braun's Nazi past, he buried them very deep, as there is no evidence that he voiced them. His closest ties were with Houston, and insofar as he ever expressed resentment, it was because he felt that Gilruth got shortchanged in the credit for the human spaceflight program in comparison with von Braun. Yet in February 1971, after von Braun and his associate Frank Williams briefed Low in Houston during Apollo 14, he wrote that he was "quite pleased" with their long-range plan as a basis for FY 1972 budget decisions. Low was not always that happy with von Braun's planning activity, but the assertion that his personal animus led to the rocket engineer's unhappy fate in Washington is unproven. If anyone was at fault, it was Paine for bringing him in to sell unrealistic goals, then abandoning him.[38]

Von Braun did have enemies at headquarters, inspired in part by the Nazi issue and in part by jealousy over his celebrity. The head of NASA public relations, Julian Scheer, resented him, telling a journalist that von Braun "is one of the most naïve men I've ever met." He pointed toward Albert Speer's recently published Third Reich memoirs as evidence. Scheer saw von Braun primarily as a promoter, dismissing his achievements as an engineering manager: "there are probably dozens of men in Huntsville who know more about the Saturn V." Soon thereafter Low fired Scheer for ineffectiveness in pushing NASA's agenda. Willis Shapley also saw von Braun as hopelessly naive. When, in a congressional hearing, NASA's planning chief argued against canceling the remaining lunar landings by saying that the pilots who trained for them would be very disappointed, a congressman slapped him down: pilots were being killed every day over Vietnam—who cared about the disappointment of a few astronauts? Afterward von Braun turned to Shapley, perplexed: "Did I say something wrong?" In fact, his magic touch with Congress was declining in direct proportion to the space program's fall in popularity. He could no longer automatically expect a friendly audience, with the result that NASA leaders sent him to Capitol Hill less often.[39]

While von Braun's troubles were primarily a function of the larger forces making space advocacy out of step with American society, the Cold War's eroding grip on American culture opened the way to further discussions of his past as well. On Dick Cavett's TV talk show the host embarrassed him in October 1970 with questions about the V-2's impact on British civilians and von Braun's compromises with the Third Reich. NASA had asked him to go on to sell the space program—against his better judgment, as he was "eager to get out of the show biz." Other incidents can be traced to a rising consciousness of the Holocaust, an almost taboo topic in America before 1960: in the fall of 1969 and in late 1972 Jewish groups protested von Braun speaking engagements by linking him to Nazi crimes. In West Germany the Dora war crimes trial at Essen and Speer's memoirs began to open up the prisoners' role in the V-2 program as well.[40]

Still, the press in neither country was willing to pursue the topic very far. When the columnist Drew Pearson revealed that von Braun had been an SS member in a column otherwise praising him during Apollo 11, that fact remained unmentioned in subsequent media accounts. One likely reason is that Pearson had no documents to prove it, since von Braun's Paperclip files remained secret. Once again the public relations nightmare he had feared since the early 1960s had failed to materialize.[41]

What he could not dodge was his growing isolation at headquarters, a product of the marginalization of his planning office and his unpopular stance on space shuttle funding and design. Earlier in 1970 Paine and Low had sidelined his questions about the expense and difficulty of the fully reusable, two-stage shuttle. In the winter of 1970–71 all of his concerns resurfaced. The Office of Management and Budget (OMB), as it was now called, confirmed previous warnings that NASA would get no more than the current fiscal year—$3.2 billion and change. With accelerating inflation, the budget was actually shrinking in real-dollar terms. While there would be money for shuttle studies and a new engine, there would be no formal go-ahead for the space plane in FY 1972 either. As for the rapidly fading space station, it was reduced to token study contracts. A fully reusable shuttle had an estimated development cost of $10 billion, which led to a big bump in NASA expenditures in the mid-1970s, but future-year fiscal prospects looked flat at best. Von Braun, as the one who had to make future planning fit the budget, could see no way to do it.[42]

The first break came in early 1971, when contractor studies showed that the orbiter's size could be significantly reduced if the bulky liquid-hydrogen propellant for the engines was put into a throwaway drop tank or tanks; taking the liquid oxygen out made the orbiter smaller still. Nonreusable tanks increased cost per flight but made the space plane technically less challenging and thus less expensive to develop. As for the giant winged booster, von Braun went back to his earlier arguments: it could be replaced with an expendable stage or even a cluster of large solid-fuel rockets, at least as an interim solution until the budget permitted funding a reusable booster. His "crusading" for a cheaper, less "grandiose" shuttle did not go down well, however, especially in Dale Myers's Office of Manned Spaceflight, which was fighting a rearguard action for a bigger human spaceflight program. Von Braun told his friend Ernst Stuhlinger: "I tell you, this is a thankless job. You don't make any friends being a Cassandra."[43]

When James Fletcher became NASA Administrator in May 1971, it temporarily improved the climate for von Braun. Fletcher, a Utah Republican engineer with experience in the aerospace industry and science policy, admired him, his *Collier's*-era visions, and his ability to communicate with the public. He told him so and listened to von Braun's thoughts on the shuttle. But Fletcher had an office that was responsible for its design—Myers's OMSF—and no more needed a "chief architect" and planner than did George Low. He had to spend much of his time grappling with near-term budget crises instead.[44]

That year was one long free fall for NASA. The grandiose visions of 1969 finally collapsed as more and more programs fell off the table. Right in the middle of Apollo 15 in late July and early August, as its crew beamed back spectacular color pictures of a mountainous landscape from Marshall's first Lunar Roving Vehicle, the head of the OMB told Fletcher that his FY 1973 budget might be $2.8 billion—another half-billion-dollar cut. Although Low had earlier saved Apollo 17 by cutting a secret political deal with the White House to postpone it until after the November 1972 presidential election, its survival once again became questionable. For a time Fletcher, Low, and von Braun also gave up hope for a powered shuttle. They resigned themselves to a "glider" launched by an enlarged, throwaway Titan III; the winged space plane would have a smaller payload capacity and no main engines. Von Braun outlined a "balanced low option plan" for level annual NASA budgets of $2.8 billion to $3 billion per year, but this prospect certainly did not make him happy. The only human spaceflight program that could be salvaged was the "glider" or something scarcely more ambitious. Spurred by attacks on the shuttle from scientists such as von Braun's old colleague James Van Allen, key Nixon administration officials even debated whether the United States needed a human spaceflight program. They decided that national prestige impelled the United States to keep flying people in space, especially if the Soviet Union was still doing so; otherwise it would look as if the country's best days were behind it. Since NASA wanted a space plane, by default it became the future of U.S. human spaceflight, but its shape had yet to be determined.[45]

Meanwhile the NERVA nuclear rocket was on its last legs. The cancellation of Saturn V deprived the nuclear stage of the heavy-lift vehicle needed to get it into orbit; the collapse of human Mars ideas, or even realistic plans for returning to the Moon, deprived it of missions. For some time the nuclear rocket stayed alive only due to the patronage of powerful Democratic senators from New Mexico and Nevada, where it was being developed. But the FY 1972 and 1973 budget cycles marked the end: NERVA died a slow death by budget starvation. NASA announced its cancellation in January 1972.[46]

Von Braun had earlier said that, if forced to choose, he would prefer to dump NERVA for lack of missions rather than lose another keystone NASA program, the "Grand Tour" of the outer planets. The orbital positions of Jupiter, Saturn, Uranus, Neptune, and Pluto in the late 1970s allowed robotic spacecraft to visit several in a row. Reminiscent of the Voyager Mars program, the agency developed plans for a huge and heavy spacecraft with advanced capabilities, making it too expensive and ambitious and creating dissent in the scientific community. Facing yet more budget restrictions in FY 1973, Fletcher and Low killed the program just before Christmas 1971. Revived as a smaller Jupiter-Saturn mission in 1972 that ultimately took the name Voyager, one of the probes eventually salvaged much of the "Tour" by visiting Uranus and Neptune too in the 1980s. Still, for von Braun in 1971, here was yet more proof that the country and its leadership lacked vision.[47]

Maria von Braun later told Stuhlinger: "On many evenings we walked around the block for hours and hours while he talked and poured out his soul . . . all I could do was just listen . . . he was so deeply depressed; for him, a world was falling apart." Although friends and colleagues report that von

Braun remained gentlemanly, funny, and considerate at work, never saying a bad word about his bosses, the usual spark in his eyes was dim. He began to tell his Huntsville friends that his talents were "wasted" in his paper-shuffling job. He missed hands-on experience with hardware, his genius for engineering management was lying fallow, he was isolated on the job, and he did not have anything very important to do. When a senior Marshall manager, John Goodrum Sr., ran into him in a downtown Washington bar, an unhappy-looking von Braun told him: "Well, John, . . . I've found out up here I'm just another guy with a funny accent."[48]

In speeches scripted for him by NASA, he lashed out against the nation's "anti-science mood" and the "irrational hostility" to science and technology manifested by many, notably the social critics and historians Lewis Mumford and Arnold Toynbee. He found particularly irritating the "Limits to Growth" studies of a loose grouping of scholars called the Club of Rome, who predicted a bleak future for humanity if it did not begin to regiment and restrict its use of rapidly depleting natural resources. Not without reason, he thought that these studies ignored both space resources and the potential of science and engineering to solve problems. But when it came to prospace advocacy, von Braun found himself hemmed in by NASA's difficult political situation and by the absence of responsible space groups with mass memberships.[49]

Symptomatic of that situation, after he met members of a small new club, the Committee for the Future, in fall 1970, he told its organizer, Barbara Hubbard: "Surrounded as I am in my new Washington job by a majority who appraise future programs only in terms of cost effectiveness and the like, it was a wonderful experience to spend an evening among idealists who defend our objectives with philosophical if not religious zeal." But then Hubbard's group cooked up a utopian plan to revive Apollos 18 and 19 as private missions funded by the sale of Moon rocks, advertising, and other such devices. In 1971 von Braun became Low's point man for killing this public initiative through behind-the-scenes pressure. He may well have agreed that the idea was ridiculous, but as with shuttle design and the NASA budget, he was again put in the ironic position of being the one who had to shoot down dreams.[50]

In truth, von Braun's days as chief American space visionary were almost over. Since 1960 he had turned himself into NASA's top salesman on the speaking circuit and had not had a really new idea in years. Any future visions he had offered of space stations, Mars expeditions, and the like were produced by Marshall's future programs people, other centers, or corporations on contract to the agency. During his little more than two years at headquarters, he continued his relentless speechmaking and his monthly column in *Popular Science*, now focusing largely on the prosaic things that the agency was trying to push: technological spin-offs from space, Earth-resources satellites, the space shuttle as a means to transform spaceflight into a "routine" low-cost activity, and so on. As a fervent believer in the beneficial effects of every kind of space activity, this sort of advocacy was no problem for him, but other than the (faint) hope that he might fly into orbit on the shuttle one day, his personal dreams were either fulfilled or dead.[51]

So depressed was he by NASA's budget situation that he was not even convinced that the space plane would come to pass. He also had grave—and justified—doubts about the realism of the cost estimates and economic models used to justify the shuttle. At the end of October 1971, Low wrote in his "Personal Notes":

> The one negative thing that came out of our in-house meetings on the Shuttle is that apparently von Braun is not a supporter . . . , and in fact may be an opponent. He expressed this quite clearly during a meeting with Fletcher and me last week. The reasons for the opposition are that he believes the Shuttle will cost much more than our current estimates . . . and that NASA cannot afford to proceed with development. To use his words, if we were given a Shuttle for a Christmas present, we would certainly use it, but, according to him, we cannot afford [it].

Low thought he might still support the "glider." But since the booster for it would be entirely expendable, it would do little to lower launch costs.[52]

Against von Braun's expectations, the Nixon administration did give NASA the shuttle as a Christmas present, but only after a long, chaotic design process driven by contractor studies and agency-OMB negotiations that fall. Nixon and his advisers wanted to help the depressed California aerospace industry in an election year, but they also accepted NASA's argument that the shuttle would revolutionize the cost of spaceflight. It was, moreover, crucial that the agency come up with a new design that at least partly answered von Braun's development-cost concerns. This "1½ stage" configuration is now familiar to all shuttle watchers: the delta-winged orbiter would be mounted on the side of a huge expendable tank, to which would be attached two reusable booster rockets. All engines in the orbiter and boosters would ignite at ground level, but the boosters would drop off partway to space. Its fundamental advantages were that NASA would not need to develop a big booster stage, reusable or expendable, and that the orbiter, although still large, could be kept as small as possible by putting all its propellants in a separable tank. Von Braun had discussed this configuration in meetings with Fletcher and Low as early as May 1971, but the studies that conclusively showed its technical and budget advantages had not yet been done.[53]

Nixon's announcement on 5 January 1972 of the shuttle as a "new start" in the FY 1973 budget, subject to approval by Congress, helped put NASA's budget back where it had been for the last couple of years, $3.2 billion to $3.3 billion. Fletcher and Low had also managed to protect the last two lunar landings, Apollos 16 and 17. This good news helped balance out the cancellation of the Grand Tour and NERVA. Also positive were the negotiations with the Soviets to stage some kind of human rendezvous in space, which were just coming to fruition in 1971–72 in conjunction with Nixon's détente policy toward the USSR. George Low played a prominent part in these talks, which ultimately led to the Apollo-Soyuz Test Project in 1975, a "gap filler" between Skylab and the shuttle. Thus, all was not bleak at the space agency as 1972 began—perhaps the bottom had been reached. But it was also clear that NASA would have to live during the 1970s with lean budgets and only one ambitious goal: attempting to build a revolutionary space plane on the cheap.[54]

Throughout all these consequential negotiations Wernher von Braun remained on the sidelines. He was not responsible for shuttle design or near-term budget questions, except for their impact on later years; nor did he have much of a role in international affairs. His lack of influence on shuttle decisions was underlined in March 1972, when Fletcher chose solid-propellant boosters over pressurized liquids. The latter idea was pushed by people at Marshall: instead of turbopumps, these boosters would use high-pressure gas, like von Braun's 1930s rockets but on a grand scale, to force the propellants from the tanks. The fact that these tanks would have to be heavier to hold the pressure was an advantage when the aim was to parachute them into the sea and recover them. Moreover, liquid-fuel engines could be shut down in a flight emergency, unlike solids, which made them safer for human spaceflight, as von Braun and his Huntsville associates had long argued. The 1986 *Challenger* accident, caused by a solid booster, would bear this out. But a solid-fuel booster was cheaper to develop, was based on known technology, and had a heavy casing more easily adapted to sea recovery. On 14 March a NASA historian recorded the following incident: in Newell's morning staff meeting von Braun was still defending the liquid-fuel booster as no more expensive than solids. He then left to attend a congressional hearing. At four p.m. the solid-propellant decision was announced on the radio.[55]

Von Braun's sixtieth birthday was coming up nine days later, on 23 March 1972. His wife had encouraged him to make the ocean sailing trip he wanted, knowing he would dread the celebratory, and hypocritical, cocktail party at NASA headquarters. He certainly enjoyed his escapes from the office, which provided some of the happiest times in those years. In the spring of 1971 he had lectured in Japan and been feted as a space hero, and in the fall he had inspected an Italian launch platform off the Kenyan coast, adding to it visits to a game preserve and a hunting ranch. As he told his friend Ed Uhl, CEO of the aerospace firm Fairchild Industries, he had "bagged one Elan, one Impala, one Mt. Kenya Hartebeest, one warthog, and one Thompson gazelle. Not bad for a 'little' white hunter, I thought."[56]

The southern Caribbean sailing trip turned out to be a minor adventure. An avid sailor since the late 1920s, von Braun had been a crew member in races with Hans Mark, the director of Ames. Mark, the only one with ocean sailing experience, unfortunately had to back out at the last minute, along with his wife. To replace them, von Braun recruited Ian Dodds from his office, along with his wife, to join himself and Frank Williams, another member of the planning staff. Maria would stay home, wanting neither to intrude on her husband's escape nor to work the boat as a crew member. Fortified with a case of rum, the four sailed from Grenada to St. Vincent and back in ten days beginning on his birthday. Showing he had not lost his spirit, he played a joke on his secretary, planting a note in a bottle with an acquaintance in the islands:

> Dear Julie:
> Had a rough trip. Down to one torn sail and two bottles of rum in bond. Whales to port, sharks to starboard and reefs ahead. Sun merciless. Twenty minute turns on the pumps. One crew member dying of tetanus. Scurvy rampant. Skipper delirious. Finishing our last days with the two remaining bottles of rum—and drifting into the sunset.
> Ruthie Wernher Frank Ian
> P.S. Please answer by return bottle: Is Nixon still running?[57]

Not long after getting back, he decided to quit NASA. He asked Ed Uhl to lunch, probably later in April, and indicated that he was indeed interested in the senior position that Uhl had offered him informally for years and more formally in 1971—he would not have to move, as Fairchild headquarters were in the outer Washington suburbs, in Germantown, Maryland. Earlier talks with NASA's leaders about what else he could do had gone nowhere, Low reveals in a note written after the announcement of von Braun's departure:

> [I]t had become quite apparent to Fletcher and me that von Braun was not contributing a great deal in the planning job, was not particularly good at it, and appeared to be very unhappy in it. Because of this, I had suggested to Fletcher [a] considerable time ago that he should start some discussions with von Braun to determine what he would like to do within NASA so that we could find the proper slot for him. The only things we could really suggest were in the semi-public relations area because he's so very good in that area. Specifically, we had tried to work something out wherein he would be the contact with the technical community that was not directly involved in technical or scientific projects with NASA.

By this they meant the Environmental Protection Agency, Arthur C. Clarke, and television oceanographer Jacques Cousteau, whom von Braun had met the previous fall. But this fairly insubstantial idea had not worked out, so "von Braun decided to take up an option that he had started working on almost a year ago with Fairchild."[58]

After he and Uhl had worked out a preliminary deal, he confidentially told the agency's top three that he was "retiring": at age sixty, he had enough years in the U.S. civil service to exit by that route. Newell wrote a memorandum on 10 May outlining for Fletcher and Low a much smaller planning office reporting directly to the administrator, in order to lessen the problem of isolation and lack of political clout. On 6 June Fletcher, however, "decided to abolish the entire Planning Organization; it was his feeling that we had accomplished our mission"; Newell added that von Braun's "office had done an outstanding job." Nice words could not conceal the obvious: whatever central planning had accomplished in 1970–71, it had become almost irrelevant by 1972. The remaining twenty-five or so employees of the office, which had been downsized at least twice in two years, were redistributed throughout headquarters.[59]

On Wednesday, 24 May, von Braun met Fletcher to confirm his decision to retire. On Friday morning, when he was out of the building, NASA sent out the press release announcing his departure on 30 June. Predictably, it set off a storm of press interest and much commentary on "the end of an era" in spaceflight. He was uninterested in talking, however, and refused all interviews, no doubt because he did not want to dance around the reasons for his unhappiness with the agency.[60]

As he would be away on vacation for much of the last half of June, NASA headquarters held its official farewell party for him on the eighth. Four years later, on his deathbed, von Braun told Ernst Stuhlinger that at that party Low had thanked him profusely, in the name of all NASA, for fighting for a "smaller and cheaper" shuttle. Low apparently said: "We were not at all pleased by your warning words, but finally we accepted your advice. . . . If you had not raised the red flag at that time, I'm certain the entire shuttle project would be dead by now." With tears in his eyes, von Braun later added: "That was the happiest moment during my time at headquarters."[61]

CHAPTER NINETEEN

The Heavens Declare the Glory of God

1972–77

It's not in my makeup to lead a quiet life. . . . I had, perhaps naively, thought that when I left the space program things would slow down a little. Not so. Not so at all.

—WERNHER VON BRAUN, 1975[1]

One might well ask why it took Wernher von Braun so long to join the corporate world. Friends indicate that he got in the neighborhood of $200,000 to $250,000 annually at Fairchild (the equivalent of at least a million per year in the early twenty-first century). Although his surviving papers give no information on corporate offers after Bell Aircraft in the early 1950s, one story is that General Motors or another giant corporation promised him half a million dollars a year in the early 1960s. Informal offers from corporate chieftains to consider their companies if he ever wanted to leave government, like those he received from Uhl, must have been fairly frequent.[2]

As long as he stayed in Huntsville, however, he felt a strong sense of personal responsibility to his Germans, his "team," his employers, and his rocket projects. Any portrayal of him as willing to do anything to advance his self-interest or ambition is simply incompatible with the fact that he regarded loyalty as more important than financial gain. Precisely those years when he was most famous were his best opportunity to cash in, and while he did energetically pursue money from speeches, writing, and movie rights, his Prussian civil service mentality meant that he thought government was a higher calling than the corporate world. He also saw the state—first German, then American—as the primary vessel for realizing his dream to be the Columbus of space. Corporations, depending on their competence and luck, might or might not have a part in such a project, but only nation-states had the resources to finance and direct huge guided-missile and space programs. In that sense, von Braun both foresaw the need for and was ideally suited to leadership of state-dominated military-industrial enterprises.

Leaving Huntsville at what he thought was an opportune moment, after the Moon landing and Marshall's reorganization, removed one major obstacle to leaving government. But he was still not ready, especially as Paine had promised him a position as quasi–"chief architect" of the post-Apollo future. Sticking with NASA appeared to be the safe path and the one that maintained continuity with his past. It took less than a year to show him how wrong that was. Yet he still did not quit in 1971; he probably felt some responsibility to the shuttle and other programs as long as their shape was unclear. Once the fundamental decisions had been made in early 1972, all of that evaporated.

Having decided to quit, why did von Braun go to a relatively weak aerospace firm, at least in comparison to Boeing and the other giants? Even Ed Uhl was a bit surprised at this choice. When Uhl had taken the CEO job in 1961, his first task had been to rescue a nearly bankrupt company started in the 1920s by aviation and aerial photography pioneer Sherman Fairchild. He got the contract for the Pegasus micrometeoroid wings from von Braun's MSFC and soon acquired Hiller Helicopters in California (an alliance that proved short-lived) and fighter jet manufacturer Republic Aircraft on Long Island. This success allowed him to open a new headquarters and a new space and electronics plant in 1966, both in Germantown, closer to Washington than the old factory at Hagerstown, Maryland. With Republic's F-105 fighter-bomber program winding down, however, the corporation's survival hung on winning another large airplane contract from the Pentagon. At the time von Braun joined as vice president for engineering and development in July 1972, Fairchild was in a fly-off competition for a heavily armored, close-air-support fighter-bomber. While Uhl and his company had faith in their A-10 prototype, the outcome had not yet been decided.[3]

For von Braun, the two obvious factors for his decision were Fairchild's proximity to Washington and his friendship with Uhl. The von Brauns loved their Alexandria house, which included a swimming pool they had built for his daily laps. In the spring of 1972 he was, moreover, in the midst of installing a backyard observatory dome and an 8-in telescope that his wealthy friends had given him as a sixtieth-birthday present. The daily trip to and from Germantown, which then took about an hour, seemed tolerable, especially as Uhl promised von Braun a corporate car and driver. Von Braun had first met Uhl, a U.S. Army Ordnance officer who had codeveloped the bazooka antitank rocket, in 1945, but he really got to know him as a result of Pegasus. Afterward they became hunting friends and saw each other more often after von Braun moved to the capital. Uhl was a "dynamic" corporate leader, but he was also gentlemanly and reserved. Von Braun felt he could trust him.[4]

A third factor was Fairchild's contentious win of the Applications Technology Satellite-F (ATS-F) contract in 1970–71, after successfully appealing and overturning NASA's original award to GE. This satellite, which had a 30-ft-diameter unfolding dish, was to be the first experimental test of "direct broadcast" of TV from a twenty-four-hour geostationary orbit to small receivers. At the time all communications satellites depended on central ground stations with huge antennas. ATS-F included demonstration projects with Appalachian states, Alaska, and India to highlight the educational value of satellite broadcasts for the poor and for remote locations. Von Braun had already praised the satellite in his speeches and articles for its potential to demonstrate the value of the space program for the underprivileged and the Third World. Immediately before NASA announced his exit, he showed an unusual interest in the state of the ATS-F, which was to be launched in 1974. Whatever else he had to do for Uhl at Fairchild, he had this one big space project to watch over.[5]

Von Braun left NASA headquarters with a sense of relief but also a little trepidation. With the exception of eight pseudocorporate months when his Peenemünde development organization became a government company in 1944–45, he had seen the capitalist world only from the other end of the contracting system. The money certainly helped, in part because Maria was just forty-four and Peter was six years away from entering college, eighteen months after Wernher would reach the then-almost-mandatory retirement age of sixty-five. That gave him a half decade to accumulate a bigger retirement fund.[6] But leaving NASA also meant leaving behind the remnants of his dream. While the corporate life was not his ideal, the Fairchild years would demonstrate his great ability to enjoy that life. As it turned out, however, these years would also be punctuated and then cut short by illness.

Just before he left NASA, at the end of his two-week vacation in June 1972, von Braun got a taste of the well-heeled executive life when he attended a Fairchild Industries retreat at a resort in Freeport, the Bahamas. The announcement of his hiring had already sent Fairchild's stock price up 31 percent in the first week. People inside the company thought Uhl had pulled off quite a coup, but there was some uncertainty as to what von Braun would actually do. His first Fairchild secretary, Patricia Webb, feared that he would be some kind of authoritarian martinet—an American stereotype of Germans. She found him to be exactly the opposite, the very epitome of a considerate boss. He also fit easily into the corporate world. In the executive lunchroom and on the road, he retained his unique appeal; here was a man who had shaken the hand of Eisenhower, Kennedy, Johnson, and Nixon—but also Hitler, Himmler, Göring, and Goebbels.[7]

Von Braun's first challenge, beyond learning a lot of names and faces, was understanding what his job as vice president for engineering and development actually entailed. Uhl made the engineering chiefs of all the subsidiary companies report to him, which quickly provided the welcome feeling of being back in touch with hardware. That meant the A-10 and the ATS-F above all, but the corporation was also involved in business and commuter aircraft, military drones, electronics, aircraft seats, and aerospace components. Uhl gave him the task of corporate strategic planning too—that is, recommending what businesses Fairchild should be involved in over the long haul. If his overall job did not fully employ his talents as a maestro of huge engineering projects, it was still varied and demanding enough to be satisfying.[8]

One of his early accomplishments was to use his knowledge of the space shuttle program to get a small piece of the action in late 1972: manufacturing the orbiter's vertical stabilizer for prime contractor North American Rockwell. Fairchild already made tail components for the F-4 and F-14 fighters, but this proved to be a difficult design job because of the extreme temperature stresses that the shuttle tail would endure. As the result of his close look at the shuttle program, von Braun quietly met Fletcher and Low in early 1973 to tell them that he thought that systems engineering did not meet Apollo standards; Low was inclined to agree with him.[9]

Von Braun focused even more attention on the communications satellite business that Fairchild hoped to develop out of its ATS-F experience. Federal telecommunications policy had focused on satellites for international traffic, but von Braun was an advocate of domestic comsats (in aerospace jargon) and praised Canada, the first Western nation to possess such a system. Uhl launched a subsidiary for domestic communications satellites, and von Braun lobbied NASA to upgrade its Delta booster to make it more suitable for that purpose, but ultimately Fairchild would find that it could not compete with companies with a stronger foothold in that field. But that would be some years in the future, and with the ATS satellite being built next door to corporate headquarters, he told a correspondent in mid-1974, "the interface between Space and Electronics Systems has become my bread and butter."[10]

Engineering oversight of the A-10 Thunderbolt II program also had him flying up to the old Republic plant on Long Island quite frequently. In mid-January 1973 Fairchild learned that it had indeed won the competition, providing the much-needed, long-term financial stability of a production contract for hundreds of aircraft. Von Braun's nephew Christoph, then looking for a way to study the communications satellite business, attended the company's celebratory party. He thought Wernher's smile was "not his smile"— in other words, his uncle's characteristic ebullience was missing. That may indeed be true, as von Braun had nothing to do with the A-10's fundamental design, although he was quite interested in its technological detail. The aircraft was, in any case, outside his main area of enthusiasm. When Ed Uhl and Tom Turner, Fairchild's marketing vice president, asked him to try to sell A-10s to Spain and Iran in 1974, two dictatorships, they found von Braun reluctant to hawk weapons. Ironically for someone who had designed ballistic missiles and advocated nuclear bombs in orbit, he had been in the civilian spaceflight business too long and was too invested in his public image as a benevolent space pioneer to want to play that role anymore. But Uhl and Turner valued his door-opening abilities too much to let him off the hook— von Braun's name got Fairchild into offices that might otherwise be closed to the company.[11]

There were perhaps other reasons not to feel quite the same joy during the Fairchild years: he had to watch silently as most of the remaining Peenemünders at Marshall were forced out in 1973 by a post-Apollo and post-Skylab downsizing. He was gratified that the latter program (the ultimate incarnation of his AAP workshop) was a success in 1973–74, but the country was preoccupied with a political crisis over Watergate and an energy crisis over oil. NASA limped along with budgets no higher than when he left, and the prospects for improvement seemed dim. In a spring 1974 letter to Tom Paine, he bemoaned "these days of general public lethargy about anything involving space."[12]

He also sometimes acted as if, with the Moon race over, he had expected all the annoying aspects of his celebrity to vanish. In spring 1974 he told Carsbie Adams that in the wake of Apollo and Skylab he was "a natural target for all sorts of peripheral activities, speaking engagements, special dinners etc. In this dilemma I simply have no other choice but to decline all these things." But in reality he often did not. A year later he told a German correspondent that he wanted "no press and TV coverage at all" of a forthcoming lecture.

> Ever since the Apollo moon landing program, whenever I showed up in
> Germany I became the target of several hundred letters of "old friends"
> or autograph hunters and I simply do not have the time (nor any
> German-language clerical help) to cope with this sort of thing. . . . I

hope you understand my predicament and give me as much protection of my privacy as possible. I have come to a point where I hate any form of publicity.

With his second Fairchild secretary, Kayren Redman Governale, he settled on a system where she simply threw away the over 80 percent of his mail that came from autograph and picture collectors, fans, crackpots, and the like.[13]

Still, his work was much more satisfying than during his time at headquarters. In 1974 he told Jim Hamill, his old boss from the El Paso days:

[F]or a guy who spent all his life disbursing lavish amounts of taxpayers' money on his beloved firecrackers, the world of profit-and-loss statements is definitely a new experience. More often than not, the question of new corporate initiatives and involvements is not what is worthwhile or what is feasible, but what is profitable and doable within the framework of existing company facilities and skills. But I must frankly say that it would have left a major gap in my education had I never spent some time in this productivity-obsessed environment.[14]

The job also had many perks. Company business, often involving the attempt to sell more educational satellite projects, took him on the foreign trips he relished, always on first-class tickets, an executive privilege at Fairchild. He went to Brazil and India in 1973 and to Spain, Iran, and Venezuela in 1974. Thanks to his name, he got to see Prime Minister Indira Gandhi, Spanish crown prince Juan Carlos (General Francisco Franco's designated successor), and the shah of Iran.[15]

These trips were in addition to numerous other visits to Europe, where he had frequent chances to see his brothers. Magnus had taken a leading position in Chrysler's London office in 1970–71, and Sigismund returned from Bonn to Paris in the fall of 1972 to serve again as ambassador to France until retirement. Wernher did not see his father after June 1972, as the ninety-four-year-old died two months later. In one of his last letters, Magnus Sr. compared him to "Kepler, Galileo und Copernicus" in historical importance; the old man had lived from the reign of Kaiser Wilhelm I to the age of lunar exploration. Wernher decided, as in the case of his mother, to skip the funeral, as he felt the press hoopla would be too disruptive. He visited the grave a little over a month later while on a speaking trip to Austria.[16]

At home, his marriage remained happy and his children were doing well. Iris taught after finishing her Oberlin degree in 1972, then went to New Delhi as a German instructor at the Goethe Institute and married a wealthy

Indian. Margrit transferred out of Oberlin to go to UCLA and finally Georgia Tech, where she ended up in "bio-engineering." (Her father's somewhat mystified comment: "The girls do the darnedest things these days, don't they?") She wed a composer and became a professor at the University of Idaho. Peter later studied history.[17]

Another source of joy was his new hobby of sailplane soaring. Toward the end of his time at NASA, he took up gliders for the first time since his lessons in the Silesian mountains in 1931–32. He trained at Elmira, New York, and then began soaring at Cumberland, Maryland, in the Fairchild years, buying a part-interest in a high-performance German sailplane. With his usual competitive nature, he set out to earn a prestigious badge, the Silver C, which entailed staying up for at least five hours after two tows aloft, plus going 50 km (32 mi) cross-country on a different attempt, obviously without any motor. He was to earn it in August 1974.[18]

His gliding was interrupted for several months in mid-1973, however, by "a shock and a surprise." To renew his FAA pilot's license, he needed once again to have a complete physical, something Ed Uhl also urged. For many years von Braun had been friends with a prominent Dallas physician, Jim Maxfield, and had his annual checkups done there. In June 1973 X-rays taken by Maxfield showed some kind of shadow around his left kidney. He had had no symptoms except, he said, "for some occasional minor backache (which Maria blamed on overweight)." In denial, perhaps because he felt healthy and had led a charmed life so far, surviving several near-fatal incidents, von Braun procrastinated before going to see a renal specialist at the Johns Hopkins University Hospital in Baltimore at the end of July. Told he urgently needed surgery, he canceled a family sailing trip. On 22 August the Hopkins surgical team removed the kidney, along with a large cancerous growth.[19]

Von Braun recovered quite quickly, being in excellent physical condition. After ten days in the hospital he went home and was much better by the end of September, when he began to spend abbreviated hours in the office. He had to cancel his foreign trips for a while but was pretty much back to normal by late in the year. In 1974, against the warnings of his doctors, he lapsed back into his life of constant business trips, speaking, and writing, interspersed with energetic vacations and soaring.[20]

That year would prove to be especially hectic because of the successful launch of ATS-F (which became ATS-6) on 30 May and his subsequent attempts to sell the backup spacecraft. Under the program financed by NASA, the satellite would participate in educational and medical direct-broadcast experiments to the Appalachian states and Alaska for one year before drifting in its twenty-four-hour orbit to a new position over the Indian Ocean. The special project with India, broadcasting educational programs to village receivers, would then last a year from July 1975. If the satellite was still functioning after that, it would be possible to bring ATS-6 back over the Americas. While von Braun's March 1974 trip to Spain was probably primarily about selling the A-10, the main purpose for his two visits to Iran in June and October was to try to induce the shah's government to fund its own direct broadcast experiments, either during the period of the Indian experiment or afterward. The best-case scenario would be for Shah Reza Pahlavi to buy the backup spacecraft and its launch outright, a proposition that would cost up to $50 million—but then, he was spending billions in oil money on new technological projects. After von Braun's "45-min[ute]" audience with the shah in mid-June, he pronounced him "a remarkable man indeed. Very confident, serious and unpretentious and clearly a 'man with a mission.' " The rocketeer had no more inkling than others that the monarch's relentless modernization campaign was to lead to his violent overthrow in less than five years.[21]

Between the two Iranian trips, von Braun suggested and participated in his most enjoyable excursion during his time at Fairchild, ten days in Alaska in September 1974. Its ostensible purpose was to witness the impact of ATS-6 broadcasts in small and remote settlements, including two-way medical communications with specialists in larger cities. But von Braun and Uhl also hoped to sell Alaska's political leadership on refitting the backup spacecraft to be ATS-7, so that the state would have direct broadcast capability over the long haul. As electronics giant RCA was already offering a communications satellite to Alaska with which Fairchild could not compete, von Braun and Uhl focused their pitch only on educational and medical aspects. Von Braun hired his old friend Erik Bergaust, the space writer and fellow hunter, to act as organizer and "advance man." In typically manic von Braun fashion, the three (plus aides) spent the first weekend big-game hunting (von Braun bagged a bull moose), jumped around the state in Fairchild's business aircraft, talked to politicians, visited villages involved in ATS-6, and saw the new Prudhoe Bay oil field on the Arctic Ocean. They ended the expedition with a fishing trip in the bush. Somewhere in the midst of all this he found time to pass his seaplane certification, which he called "really the ultimate in fun flying."[22]

Von Braun "loved" the ATS satellite project, Uhl later said: here was a concrete demonstration of the power of spaceflight to improve life on Earth. It provided direct benefits to the poor and to remote communities in the United States and promised to do the same for India. In the latter case it could, in his words, "break the stranglehold of illiteracy, which still retards the progress and well-being of a substantial part of mankind." But his attempts to set up further foreign demonstration projects and to sell the backup spacecraft in 1974–75 were met with frustration. He traveled twice to Venezuela, an oil-rich country like Iran, but nothing ever took hold there; nor did the second Iranian trip nail down a sale. As for Alaska, the new satellite was too expensive for the state alone to support. He and Uhl also tried to go back to NASA but were turned down. Von Braun told one of the ex-astronauts in the spring of 1975 that he was "dismayed by the complete lack of any systematic follow-on planning on the part of the government. NASA says 'we've demonstrated the technical feasibility, but there's nothing in our charter which says we are to help nurses in remote areas or educate little Indians.' " The backup spacecraft would never be completed or launched. Although ATS-6 was a sterling success, von Braun's follow-on communications satellite projects were going nowhere by summer.[23]

In the midst of all the demands of the spring of 1974 came the prospect of yet another publicity-generating imposition on his time: his boss and friends asked him to be the public face of a new space advocacy organization. According to Ordway and Stuhlinger, his first reaction surprised them: just "another talking club," he said dismissively. Such organizations that existed were either professional engineering societies like the American Institute of Aeronautics and Astronautics (into which the American Rocket Society had merged in 1962) or were small, insider organizations like the National Space Club, which brought together a few hundred prospace lawmakers, journalists, corporate lobbyists, NASA officials, and military officers in the Washington, D.C., area. No mass-membership space organizations existed, as from Sputnik to the Moon landings, such a thing seemed unnecessary when the government took the initiative for big-time space spending and elite opinion ran ahead of public support. Then in the early 1970s came the shocker for space advocates: the glorious post-Apollo future shriveled to little more than the space shuttle, and few seemed to care very much.[24]

Given "the general public lethargy about anything involving space," it is perhaps unsurprising that the National Space Association (its first name) did not arise from the grass roots. It began as a quiet initiative of Jim Fletcher and George Low to create the prospace mass support that NASA lacked, one not influenced by the Committee for the Future and other fringe groups. In mid-1973 Low noted that he had tried to get the agency public-affairs chief to organize the "space buffs" for some time, but nothing came of it. Another NASA official then suggested the Navy League as a model, an organization with tens of thousands of members. Perhaps the National Space Club could become the foundation for such a nationwide organization. It was not a new idea, but it never seemed to go anywhere as the club was too cozy the way it was. Early in 1974 the NASA Administrator approached Uhl for help in starting a new society. Why Fairchild? Fletcher clearly must have wanted to enlist Wernher von Braun as its public face.[25]

Uhl agreed to go along with the idea and assigned his marketing vice president, Tom Turner, to spend six months drawing up a plan for such an organization. Turner and von Braun met on this topic, probably for the first time, on 4 March—perhaps it was after this that he made his dismissive remark. On 30 May Turner and five local space advocates quietly incorporated the National Space Association as a nonprofit society in Washington, D.C., and began to draw up an organizational structure and plan. Von Braun soon became enthusiastic, as they convinced him that a space society with regional chapters and a hundred thousand members was feasible. But he could do little until late fall because of his hectic schedule. It was not until August that they formally asked von Braun to become chairman (later changed to president); he attended his first meeting on the twenty-second. Only at the end of the year did he really begin to participate. He told one of his soaring friends that he could not try for a gold or diamond badge in the near future as "this new job will require extensive traveling during the first months of 1975 to solicit the necessary support from industry."[26]

Here again was the initiative's fundamental contradiction: the attempt to create a mass-membership society from the top down. Not only did NASA start it, but its construction depended on the largesse of big aerospace corporations. The association hired an executive director, Charles C. "Chuck" Hewitt, and needed an office, and if possible a magazine, in order to solicit membership. At Fairchild's expense, von Braun and Hewitt began a series of trips early in the new year, to Boeing, McDonnell-Douglas, and others, seeking pledges of tens of thousands of dollars. They had some success, although it was scarcely overwhelming. They also got the message from their corporate counterparts that "association" sounded too much like just another Washington trade lobby. In April 1975 von Braun and the executive committee changed the name to National Space Institute (NSI). They planned a public announcement and membership solicitation in Florida for the 15 July launch of the Apollo craft that would rendezvous with the Soviet Soyuz. It would be the first U.S. human spaceflight in nearly two years and the last, as it would turn out, for almost six.[27]

Without von Braun's name, NSA/NSI would certainly not have gotten in the door of various corporate suites. His appeals also generated a large list of politicians and celebrities who agreed to serve on a largely symbolic "board of governors," although this unintentionally reinforced the impression that it was not a grassroots organization. The mere fact that Wernher von Braun was NSI's public face was a significant asset for attracting many space buffs too.

But he was also increasingly a face from the past. In 1974 the "visionary" torch was passed when Princeton physics professor Gerard K. O'Neill dropped a bombshell in the space advocacy community. He proposed huge, cylindrical colonies in space, orbiting at the "Lagrangian points" where the gravity of the Moon and the Earth balanced out. Von Braun, although still enamored of the idea of bases on planetary surfaces, was intrigued by these concepts but recognized that they were highly optimistic. The Cornell astronomer Carl Sagan was another rising star of space promotion—indeed, he was destined to be von Braun's successor in that role—but he soon refused to support the NSI because it was so tilted toward the space shuttle and human spaceflight. In 1979–80 he would help found a competing organization, the Planetary Society, that focused on supporting NASA's increasingly impressive robotic exploration of the solar system. Sagan and von Braun had known each other since the late 1950s, and the older man had a high opinion of the astronomer's popular writing, but the liberal, Jewish Sagan grew skeptical of von Braun because of questions about his Nazi past and his opportunism.[28]

By the spring of 1975 von Braun had high hopes for the NSI, but that was only one of the matters that was driving his unbelievable travel schedule. In mid-May he went to Berlin and then Stuttgart, where he met Werner Heisenberg, then gave a speech and joined the board of the Daimler-Benz automobile corporation. He followed it with soaring at the historic Wasserkuppe site in central Germany, then went on to London, where he gave another speech and met Queen Elizabeth, and finally to the Paris Air Show. Being friendly with the chief French test pilot for the new Concorde supersonic airliner, he canceled his return reservations and took a Mach 2 demonstration flight from Paris to Rio de Janeiro and came home from there. After another couple of short trips to Williamsburg, Virginia, and to Houston and Huntsville, he and the family vacationed in Ontario in mid-June. A day after he got back it was California and Illinois. Following the July Fourth weekend, he held a press conference to introduce the NSI in Washington and on the eleventh took off for San Francisco and a weekend at the Bohemian Grove, a famous superelite Republican men's club whose summer retreats he episodically attended. Then it was on to Florida, via private jet and commercial flight, for the institute's kickoff event for the Apollo launch. On the seventeenth he passed through Washington for six hours to make a TV appearance and then flew to Germany to attend a Daimler-Benz board meeting, afterward soaring at the Wasserkuppe again. He returned to work for a few days, then flew to Alaska for a week with the family at Glacier Bay and Juneau. He arrived home in time to attend a two-day Fairchild general management meeting on 4–5 August in Germantown.[29]

While on vacation in Canada, von Braun had noticed a little rectal bleeding. Again not wanting to deal with medical news that might derail his plans, he ignored it until the bleeding reappeared in Alaska. On 6 August 1975 he went for a "40-minute routine checkup" at the Johns Hopkins Hospital in Baltimore and was told he could not go home. Two days later the surgeons took out a large section of his colon with an aggressive tumor. Dr. Maxfield in Dallas had wanted to remove polyps in the colon years before, but von Braun had put it off; whether the 1973 kidney cancer was ultimately rooted in undiagnosed colon cancer, the disease that killed his mother, is a good question. Due to his robust constitution he was reading books only two days later, but this time was not to be the same. He developed a "pretty high fever," so the doctors decided to open him up again to clean up abscesses from the first surgery. The second operation took place on 30 August, which, he later told an astronaut friend, "really knocked me out for a while. . . . [R]eopening any area of your body that has been subjected to recent surgery is like pouring a jar of liquid oxygen into an open fireplace." He ended up spending almost the entire month of September in the hospital and lost a lot of strength and weight.[30]

After a few weeks at home under the expert care of Maria and his visiting daughters, he began to go to the office for a few hours a day. By November and December he was up to six hours daily but was ordered to cancel almost all travel. As in 1973 it was a disconcerting experience; suddenly his life was not one long string of short-term deadlines and long-term plans. Although told from the outset that his prognosis was poor, any illusions he might have had were soon dashed when his condition began to deteriorate again. The cancer was spreading. When Fred Ordway, with whom he was collaborating on two books, saw him in January 1976, he was moving slowly. By the time of his sixty-fourth birthday two months later, von Braun needed a cane and looked significantly worse.[31]

With mortality drawing near, his thoughts turned toward the comforts of religion, although nothing had really changed in his profound Christian belief since his 1946 conversion experience in El Paso. Over the winter of 1975–76 he wrote his intellectual testament, an eighty-two-page paper entitled "Responsible Scientific Investigation and Application." An Episcopalian for a quarter century, he was to give it to a Lutheran Church conference in late 1976, but it was expected at the printers in February. From the title one expects a philosophical treatise, but von Braun realized he was no theologian or philosopher. After ten pages of observations about the general problem of science and technology being value-neutral and thus requiring an external moral framework, his paper becomes a compilation of recent space advocacy speeches. It is imbued with the cultural pessimism of the 1970s, a decade overshadowed by oil and environmental crises and the continuing threat of nuclear war. He outlines how space activity can contribute to human "survival" in five realms: resources, environment, nuclear, spiritual, and scientific. He ended his paper with thoughts on science and religion, including a critique of fundamentalism. Although he had made public statements supporting "design" in the creation of the world and the human mind, he sought, like other mainstream believers, to integrate Darwin, big bang cosmology, and God. His thoughts along those lines were neither original nor profound, but he certainly was not about to forsake the science that pointed to a Universe and life-forms evolving for aeons, albeit subject to divine intervention.[32]

In mid-May 1976 he suddenly collapsed and was admitted to Alexandria Hospital, much closer to his home than Johns Hopkins. His internal hemorrhaging was getting much worse. Some of his distress he manifested in a letter to NSI director Chuck Hewitt that he dictated in mid-June, concerned by some statement that NSI claimed authorization to speak for him. Feeling hounded by media interest in his illness, he and his family made a pact with the hospital administrator, concealing when he was in and when he went home. His family (read Maria) was urging him to cut off the NSI if it did not cooperate in this policy; otherwise reporters would show up at the house or the hospital. He was furthermore concerned by a plan to build a Wernher von Braun library and conference center based on a possible contribution of land from a donor, as he did not want it to appear that he had started the NSI just to create his own monument. Hewitt reported in July that membership had risen to about twenty-five hundred and the trend was up, but it was still a long way from a hundred thousand. Von Braun's illness had inevitably hurt both fund-raising and visibility. His death would throw the NSI into a deeper crisis, and although it would survive and eventually thrive in the 1980s, it would be dwarfed by Sagan's Planetary Society.[33]

Wernher von Braun's dying was prolonged. Until October he moved back and forth between home and the hospital in Alexandria, before spending the final eight months in the latter. His daughters came home again for longer periods, Iris all the way from India, and it was a novel experience to have the family around him constantly after spending half his life on the road. When he felt well enough, he read and worked on his last book with Ordway, one on the solar system.[34]

Friends report him still the joker, but he made some intriguing comments about his past. As reported by his friends Ernst Stuhlinger and Fred Ordway, he asked several times whether he had chosen the right path in leading the United States toward spending so much on space. They of course reassured him that he had. Whether he had any second thoughts about his compromises with the Third Reich, we do not know. Either he did not talk about it or his friends would not report it if he had. But a month before his spring 1976 collapse, he made a filmed interview for the NSI with television personality Hugh Downs, a space buff who would succeed him as its president. It was then that, in the process of talking about his darkest days late in the war, he called the Mittelwerk "absolutely horrible" and "a pretty hellish environment." But when the NSI produced a transcript of the interview, it suppressed this section. The topic was still too dangerous.[35]

As 1976 moved toward its end, his terminal condition motivated a new behind-the-scenes effort to get him a presidential award. Earlier attempts had failed, notably in 1970 or 1971, when Nixon did not act on his nomination for the National Medal of Science. With his new cancer in 1975, his well-connected friends began another attempt to secure him a presidential honor, and it took on new urgency when he collapsed in May 1976. Now they tried to get him the Presidential Medal of Freedom, a possibility discussed inside the Gerald R. Ford White House until presidential adviser David Gergen scribbled a note in July: "Sorry, but I can't support the idea of giving [the] medal of freedom to [a] former Nazi whose V-2 was fired into over 3000 British and Belgian cities [sic]. He has given valuable service to the US since, but frankly he has gotten as good as he has given." Two days before Christmas, in view of von Braun's apparently imminent death, NASA Administrator Fletcher appealed again for an award from the outgoing White House. (Ford had lost the election to Jimmy Carter.) That worked. The president, who had known von Braun while a congressman, approved a special award of the Medal of Science as one of his last acts.[36]

Determined as ever to maintain their privacy, Maria von Braun wanted no publicity at all and no ceremony; the doctors would not allow a group in to see him anyway. The Carter White House handed the medal and certificate over to Ed Uhl, who visited von Braun sometime in February or March 1977, during an interlude of relative improvement. His appearance was shocking: "Did you ever see a skeleton with skin and bones?" Uhl later said. At the presentation von Braun was moved to tears of gratitude for this recognition from his adopted country. During his illness he had made several expressions of his patriotic feeling for the United States, which had taken him in and given him so much.[37]

Yet he had not lost his attachment to his native country either. When Albert Speer sent him a copy of his *Spandau Diaries,* an account of his twenty years of imprisonment, von Braun wrote back in November 1975, following his first, long hospitalization, that for the foreseeable future he would not be able to contemplate "a visit to my beloved Germany." He also told Speer: "How often I thought of you during those twenty long years when so much was happening in my life."[38] Here was the heart of his Third Reich problem: however much he had come to hate Hitler and regret what had happened in the camps, he could not divorce himself from his friends and allies then, even convicted war criminals. Nor could he repudiate his actions. The V-2 was his "baby" and was the foundation for his ambitions. He simply could not accept any deeper personal responsibility for the crimes connected to his program, as it would bring into question his whole life's work.

The last few months of Wernher von Braun's life were spent in constant pain and heavily drugged, with Maria always by his side. He finally passed at three a.m. on Thursday, 16 June 1977. In line with her intense dislike for publicity, he was buried the next day in Ivy Hill Cemetery in Alexandria, Virginia, in the presence of a small group of family and friends. The media heard of his death only after the simple ceremony. The grave marker soon placed there was equally unadorned, a plaque with three lines:

WERNHER VON BRAUN

1912–1977

PSALMS 19:1.

It referred to one of his favorite biblical passages: "The heavens declare the glory of God; and the firmament showeth His handiwork."[39]

A Faustian Shadow

*A kind of Faustian shadow may be discerned in—or imposed on—
the fascinating career of Wernher von Braun: A man so possessed
of a vision, of an intellectual hunger, that any accommodation
may be justified in its pursuit.*
                    —*Washington Star* editorial, 20 June 1977[1]

The announcement of von Braun's death produced an outpouring of obituaries, appreciations, and editorials. President Carter released a statement: "To millions of Americans, Wernher von Braun's name was inextricably linked to our exploration of space and to the creative application of technology. Not just the people of our nation, but all the people of the world have profited from his work. We will continue to profit from his example." The U.S. media's tone was similar; obituaries hewed closely to his quasi-official biography and, with a couple of exceptions, celebrated his life as a space visionary who had pursued his boyhood dream and helped put America on the Moon. Most remarkably, his Nazi Party membership was almost never mentioned, and the Mittelwerk and his SS status not at all.[2]

The British stories were a bit more pointed, at least the ones in the London tabloid press, noting the "terror" inflicted on civilians by his V-2s, along with von Braun's decisive contribution to exploring space. Only the *Daily Mail* mentioned "the starving slave workers of the rocket factories" in passing. The leading West German papers mirrored the American ones, producing appreciations and hero worship; one limited exception was the left-wing *Frankfurter Rundschau*, which brought up the Mittelwerk and the moral issues of building long-range missiles but largely as asides. As for East Germany, its official press printed only a one-paragraph item announcing his death. Around 1970 the Communist state had given up its campaign against von Braun, primarily because of a general retreat from the tactic of smearing ex-Nazis in the West, but also presumably because, outside the East Bloc and Dora survivor groups in the West, its campaign had failed to make an impression and had become increasingly irrelevant after the Moon landing.[3]

In Washington his friends and admirers wanted the public celebration of his life denied them by the quick burial. They organized a memorial service at the National Cathedral, an Episcopalian church, on the twenty-second. The West German ambassador brought an official wreath from his government and read scriptural passages; Ernst Stuhlinger, former NASA Administrator James Fletcher, and National Air and Space Museum director Michael Collins, the Apollo 11 astronaut, eulogized him in soaring rhetoric. Quoting the Hebrew prophet Joel, Fletcher called von Braun one of the "few men [who] arise in each century who 'see visions' and 'dream dreams' that give hope and spiritual nourishment to us all. . . . Such men cling to this vision despite all efforts to destroy it."[4]

Still, Wernher von Braun did not entirely escape posthumous moral critiques—in the U.S. capital's two major newspapers, of all places. A *Washington Star* editorial explicitly opened with the Faustian bargain, but after making that pointed statement, the editorial writer waffled. *The Washington Post* began its editorial with a variant of the old Mort Sahl gibe about aiming for the stars but sometimes hitting London. It followed with: "For most Americans, and others, it has never been possible to hear mention of the name of Wernher von Braun, space pioneer, without thinking, uncomfortably, of Wernher von Braun, rocket builder by appointment to Adolf Hitler." Friends wrote letters in protest. But the *Star* printed only one missive supporting von Braun and two attacking him; one correspondent declared him "unambiguously a Nazi and a war criminal."[5]

The totality of responses to von Braun's death accurately mirrored his bifurcated reputation. The media, major books, and government institutions continued to offer the heroic Cold War biography. Many, however, mostly on the left, disliked or even hated him but had little on which to base their critique but the official account of his Nazi years and the satires of Sahl and Lehrer. That situation finally began to change, at least in the English-speaking world, with the 1979 publication of French Resistance fighter Jean Michel's memoir, *Dora*, in translation. It shed light on the still virtually unknown horrors of the V-2 program.[6]

Michel's book was less important for its direct effects than for the U.S. government investigation it almost accidentally launched. Early in 1980 a Harvard Law student in his final year, Eli M. Rosenbaum, came upon the work in a Cambridge bookstore. The previous summer he had interned at the new Office of Special Investigations (OSI) of the U.S. Department of Justice, which had been set up by congressional amendment in 1979 to discover and deport former war criminals in the United States. Days later

Rosenbaum found another new book, *The Rocket Team*, by Fred Ordway and an MSFC writer, Mitchell Sharpe, an insider history of the von Braun group that had been under way for years. That book, which had received much more press attention than Michel's *Dora*, had a chapter on V-2 production that in hindsight reads like an apologia but at the time offered new information. When Rosenbaum went back to OSI full-time as a lawyer in the fall of 1980, he got permission to pursue the subject, in spite of skepticism from Deputy Director Neal Sher that any of the old Paperclip cases were worth pursuing. What did succeed was the case against Arthur Rudolph, whom Rosenbaum and Sher interrogated in 1982 and 1983, using classified documents from army security files, plus the records of the 1947 Nordhausen trial. These brought to light Rudolph's early Nazi enthusiasm and his role as the Mittelwerk's production chief. In the end the former Saturn V project director, worried that he might forfeit his civil service pension if he lost a court battle over his immigration, reluctantly signed a voluntary agreement with OSI to go back to Germany and renounce his U.S. citizenship. He departed with his wife for Hamburg in March 1984. In October the Justice Department issued its press release, provoking front-page stories around the world.[7]

"We're lucky von Braun isn't alive," the OSI investigators had said among themselves, as he might have been able to call the conservative Ronald Reagan White House and have the investigation quashed. (One might equally say that he was lucky not to be alive to endure what would follow.) Not only was Rudolph his good friend, it would have been obvious that the investigation could lead back to him. And indeed it did. The case opened the door to all the damaging information that von Braun and NASA had worked to contain in the 1960s. Investigative journalists armed with the Freedom of Information Act ferreted out new documents and wrote sensational narratives. Among the things that emerged in 1985, as a result of journalist Linda Hunt's work, were von Braun's SS and party record, his explanations to the War Department, and the bureaucratic battle over his security reports and immigration in 1947–49. His posthumous reputation was greatly damaged.[8]

In the aftermath the anti–von Braun camp shifted from picturing him as a pure opportunist to picturing him as an opportunistic Nazi war criminal. His defenders too were forced to grapple with these disturbing revelations about his past.[9] Nonetheless many in the latter community still say that "he only wanted to go into space," obviating the moral compromises he made en route. Driven by a hunger for exploration, adventure, and fame, von Braun certainly was single-minded in his space ambitions, but like Goethe's Dr. Faust, he made a bargain with the devil to carry out vast engineering projects, rationalizing them as being for the greater good of mankind.

All evidence suggests, however, that he was not even aware that he had made such a bargain until rather late in the war. His conservative nationalist upbringing and inclination toward apolitical opportunism made it easy to work for the Nazi regime, which asked for little at first beyond keeping quiet. Gradually, through seduction and pressure, he was drawn deeper into the system. In the end he had to accept the brutal exploitation of concentration camp laborers, and he had to play his part in administering that exploitation, implicating him in crimes against humanity. However much, like Goethe's Faust, he divorced himself from personal responsibility, after he toured the Mittelwerk tunnels in late 1943 he could have had no illusions about what that meant for the prisoners. His Gestapo arrest a few months later was the final straw; he finally and belatedly understood that he was "aiding an evil regime."[10]

Having survived the end of the Third Reich by both cunning and luck, von Braun was fortunate that the United States was happy to take him, motivated by equally amoral considerations of the national good. But the early promise of a technologically superior America proved somewhat illusory for him, as the populace was more interested in demobilizing after World War II. What money there was would go to military missile development, and even that was limited before the Korean War. Despite von Braun's influential efforts to sell spaceflight in the 1950s, it was not until after Sputnik—that is, after he already had been in the rocket business for a quarter century—that he had any money to build space hardware.

Before then the true foundation of his career had not been space but rather the interest of nation-states in the revolutionary strategic potential of the ballistic missile. What he had to offer was not his space plans but rather his "indisputable genius" for the management of huge military-industrial engineering projects. As a designer of nuts-and-bolts rocket technology, he was no better than many others, but as a manager he had few peers. He had a vision of how to build a giant engineering organization for producing such a radical new technology.

Without him, it is hard to imagine that the German army's liquid-fuel rocket project would ever have succeeded in producing the V-2. Although the V-2 was a profound military failure, that vehicle paved the way for the intercontinental ballistic missile, which when combined with a nuclear warhead finally lived up to the expectations German Army Ordnance had placed on rocketry. Von Braun's "baby" went on to influence missile technology in the United States, the USSR, France, Britain, and China, accelerating the arrival of the ICBM and the space launch vehicle by perhaps a decade. Nothing von Braun did in his life was ever as influential as that.

Nonetheless, he still managed to produce three more fundamental contributions as a U.S. immigrant and citizen: making spaceflight a reality to the public, leading the team that launched the first American satellite in 1958, and managing the development of the gigantic launch vehicles that sent humans to the Moon. The Saturns were his masterworks; astonishingly, not one failed catastrophically in flight.

The sum total of his accomplishments makes von Braun the most influential rocket engineer and spaceflight advocate of the twentieth century. Others—above all Tsiolkovsky, Oberth, and Goddard—proved that spaceflight was technically feasible. Goddard went further, developing the world's first liquid-fuel rocket, but he was a poor engineer and one constitutionally unsuited to leading a larger group. It fell to the second generation of rocket and space enthusiasts—chief among them being von Braun and Korolev—to realize the founders' vision by serving their governments as engineering managers in the development of ballistic missiles, then by selling those governments on the idea of spaceflight. In terms of firsts, Korolev's achievements undoubtedly exceeded von Braun's. His team launched the world's first ICBM, the first satellite, the first object to escape the Earth, the first object to hit the Moon, and the first man and the first woman in space. But his postwar accomplishments were founded on German technology: by Stalin's order, he started over in 1945–46 by copying the V-2.[11]

Five hundred years from now humans may remember little of the twentieth century except for the nuclear bomb, industrialized mass murder, the discovery of global warming, the emergence of computer networks, the achievement of powered flight, and the first steps into space. Assuming that we do not ruin the Earth through our environmental impact, actually leaving the cradle of all terrestrial life to establish a foothold in space may, in evolutionary terms, rank among the most important. In those terms, at least, Wernher von Braun deserves to be remembered as one of the seminal engineers and scientists of the twentieth century. His life is, simultaneously, a symbol of the temptations of engineers and scientists in that century and beyond: the temptation to work on weapons of mass destruction in the name of duty to one's nation, the temptation to work with an evil regime in return for the resources to carry out the research closest to one's heart. He truly was a twentieth-century Faust.

NOTES

Dates below are given in German form: day.month.year. A table of Significant Abbreviations Used in the Notes follows this section. Full bibliographic citations for published works and explanations of archival collections are given in the Bibliography and Archival Sources section.

PROLOGUE

1. Lang, "A Romantic Urge," 180. Reprinted with the permission of Simon & Schuster Adult Publishing Group, from *From Hiroshima to the Moon: Chronicle of Life in the Atomic Age* by Daniel Lang. Copyright © 1959 by Daniel Lang. Copyright © renewed 1987 by Margaret Lang, Helen Lang, Frances Laberee, Cecily Lang. "A Romantic Urge" originally published in *The New Yorker*. All rights reserved.

2. Ibid., 181.

3. Ibid., 182. The 1958 book version dates the visit to October, but it was probably a little later because the von Brauns only moved, after some delays, "shortly before Christmas": WvB to Lang, 29.12.1950, in WvBP-LC, Box 44, Publications . . . 1949–53. The article first appeared in the 21.4.1951 issue.

4. Ibid., 183.

5. WvB, "Behind the Scenes of Rocket Development in Germany 1928 through 1945," ms., 1950, 10 (quote), in WvBP-H, file 702-20; later published in modified form as "Reminiscences of German Rocketry"; Lang, "A Romantic Urge," 84–85. The words are so close that Lang may have lifted them from the ms., which WvB lent him.

6. See Mader, *Geheimnis von Huntsville*; Hunt, "U.S. Coverup" and *Secret Agenda*; Bower, *The Paperclip Conspiracy*; Eisfeld, *Mondsüchtig*; Neufeld, *The Rocket* and "Wernher von Braun, the SS. . . ."

7. Goethe, *Faust: A Tragedy*, translated by Walter Arndt, Part II, Act V, and commentary by Stuart Atkins, 580–81, and Marshall Berman, 718–26. Thanks to my friend Arnd Bohm for stimulating these thoughts and for providing expert advice on Goethe. Very late in the writing of this book, I discovered that the great historian of technology Thomas Parke Hughes also discusses Goethe's Faust as engineer in *Human-Built World*, 18–20.

8. See Goethe, *Faust: Part One*, 68. For the nineteenth-century Bayard Taylor translation used as epigram to this book, I used the dual-language-edition page provided by WvB and attached to Durant to WvB, 26.10.1970 (regarding WvB's reading of same in Huntsville), in NASM, WvB bio. file. The same quote is used in a slightly modified Bayard translation as the epigram to the English translation of von Braun's novel, "Mars Project: A Technical Tale," ms., Fort Bliss, Texas, 1950, WvBP-H, file 205-1. That may be the idea of his translator, Henry J. White. In my book, *The Rocket*, 264, I argue for a conservative estimate of ten thousand deaths among prisoners connected only to the V-2 program in the main camp, Mittelbau-Dora. Total V-2–related deaths in all camps may be twice that or more.

9. "System builder" comes from Hughes; for a definition, see his *Rescuing Prometheus*, 7–8. I have not elaborated on the concept in this book, but it has influenced my interpretation.

CHAPTER 1

1. MvB, *Weg*, 76.

2. S&O, *WvB* (Amer. ed.), 15 (quote); Ward, *WvB Anekdotisch*, 13.

3. MvB, *Die Freiherren*, 8–9, 13–17.

4. Ibid., 39–42; MvB, *Weg*, 1–12.

5. MvB, *Weg*, 1–2, 19–20, 35–36, and *Die Freiherren*, 50–55; WvB to MvB, 10.8.1968, in BAK, N1085/86.

6. MvB, *Die Freiherren*, 51, 54.

7. MvB, *Weg*, 21–25, 30; interview with C.-F. vB, Munich, 29.3.2001.

8. MvB, *Weg*, 23–48.

9. Ibid., 48–79; MvB civil service exam records, 1905, in GstA, I. HA, Rep. 125, Nr. 713. A draft of his letter proposing to Emmy still exists: MvB to Emmy von Quistorp, 9.2.1910, MvB Papers in possession of C.-F. vB, file 2.

10. Schnepel, "Die Quistorps"; von Quistorp, *Geschichte*, 302–5; 1877 will and testament in Landesarchiv Greifswald, Rep. 77, Nr. 3993. The oft-repeated assertion that the name is Swedish appears to be false.

11. MvB, *Die Freiherren*, 57, and *Weg*, 79.

12. MvB, *Weg*, 458 (quote); EvB, "Personal History Statement," 26.11.1947, NACP, RG319, IRR PNF WvB, Box 657A; Grigoleit, "Die Ahnen," 261–71, esp. 265.

13. B. Jordan interview by MJN, Lassan, 7.1999, and excerpt from *Gothaer Adelskalendar*, courtesy of same.

14. Pruss. Int. Ministry to MvB, 15.3.1911, GStA, I. HA, Rep. 77, Nr. 4548, and MvB to Reg.-Präs. Bromberg, 16.7.1912, in GstA, XVI. HA, Rep. 30 I, Nr. 719, Bd. 2; MvB, *Weg*, 80–87.

15. Reg.-Präs. Bromberg to Interior Minister, 9.10.1911, in GStA, I. HA, Rep. 77, Nr. 4548; MvB, *Weg*, 80–81; MvB, *Die Freiherren*, genealogical tables, 29–30; Caroline Garst, quoting EvB, to Maria and WvB, 6.6.1960, WvBP-LC, Box 9, 1963 B.

16. Peter Rehak, "Bored Von Braun Flunked Ninth Grade, Father Says," *Washington Evening Star*, 10.10.62, A5; Gerd Kleinfeld, "Aus unserer Zeit . . . In Memoriam Werner von Braun," *Kleine Weichselzeitung* (Celle), 1.2.1996, 10–11; SvB, "Memoiren," ms. c. 1990s, courtesy Christina vB, 8, 11. MvB's book unfortunately says little about his family; it is essentially a political memoir.

17. MvB, *Weg*, 88–90; MvB to "Mein Lieb," 28.7.1914, file 8, MvB Papers in possession of C.-F. vB, Munich.

18. MvB, *Weg*, 91–96; MvB Reich personnel records, 1915–17, BABL, R43I, Nr. 2881 and 2882, esp. MvB to Unterstaatssekretär in Reichskanzlei, 14.12.1917, in Nr. 2882.

19. MvB, *Weg*, 133–56; MvB Reich personnel records, 1915–17, BABL, R43I, Nr. 2881 and 2882; "Notiz," 8.7.1918, GStA, I. HA, Rep. 77, Nr. 4548; EvB, "Personal History Statement," 26.11.1947, NACP, RG319, IRR PNF WvB, Box 657A; SvB, "Memoiren," ms. c. 1990s, courtesy Christina vB, 12.

20. MvB, *Weg*, 156–72, and *Die Freiherren*, genealogical tables, 30; MvB, 26.8.1918, re: "Herrschaft Raudany," Historical Central Archive of Lithuania, Vilnius, 641-1-697a, Aug.–Nov. 1918, folio 27, note kindly supplied by Jürgen Matthäus.

21. Clipping, *Vossische Zeitung*, 23.9.1919, BABL, R43I, Nr. 2882; MvB, *Weg*, 173–76; SvB, "Memoiren," ms. c. 1990s, courtesy Christina vB, 12.

22. MvB, *Weg*, 177–79; Pruss. Int. Ministry Kapp Putsch records, 20.3.–6.12.1920, GStA, I. HA, Rep. 90a, D I 1, Nr. 30, Bd. 1, Bl. 4–5, 10, 12, 17, 208–9, 220–24; SvB, "Memoiren," ms. c. 1990s, courtesy Christina vB, 9 (quote). MvB's letter of 19.10.20 in GStA, I. HA, Rep. 90a, D I 1, Nr. 30, Bd. 1, Bl. 222, already has the Tiergartenstr. 20 address, so the family must already have moved by then.

23. Large, *Berlin*, 170–210; *Berlin und Umgebung* (1931 travel guide).

24. SvB, "Memoiren," ms. c. 1990s, courtesy Christina vB, 12–13; MvB, *Weg*, 180–88, 195; "Aufsichtsrat der Deutschen Rentenbank . . . ," ?.10.1923, BABL, R8034 II, Nr. 5064, S. 25–26; Large, *Berlin*, 175; MvB and EvB, "Personal History Statements," 26.11.1947, NACP, RG319, IRR PNF WvB, Box 657A. The office was at Schöneberger Ufer 36a.

25. Velder, *300 Jahre*, 478, 498, 504, 507; Frank, *Collège Français/Französisches Gymnasium*, 108; Frank and Rosemarie Eyck, interview, 24.5.2001, Bragg Creek, Alberta; telephone interview with M. L. Meyer, London, 20.2.2000; SvB, "Memoiren," ms. c. 1990s, courtesy Christina vB, 3–4.

26. Velder, *300 Jahre*, 498; telephone interviews with Kenneth G. Frazier (Friedländer), Florida, 24.11.1999, and with M. L. Meyer, London, 20.2.2000; Meyer to MJN, 21.3.2000; MvB, *Weg*, 70, 72, 102, 179, 358; WvB, "Space Man," 8–9; Weber to WvB, 1.12.1954, in WvBP-H, file 412-6, mentioning Privat-Turnverein-Concordia.

27. WvB, "Space Man," 20.7.1958, 8; Bergaust, WvB, 35; Beach Conger to WvB, 17.12.1952, in WvBP-LC, Box 1, 1952 A to Z, and same, 8.12.1964, in WvBP-H, file 403-1. Conger was in 1964 a leading editor at the *New York Herald-Tribune*.

28. MvB, *Weg*, 458.

29. Ibid.; C.-F. vB interview, Munich, 29.3.2001.

30. EvB quoted in S&O, *WvB* (Amer. ed.), 11. Note that the quote is presumably an Ernst Stuhlinger paraphrase based on conversations with her between 1947 and 1959.

CHAPTER 2

1. WvB, "Space Man," 20.7.1958, 8.

2. Ibid.; S&O, *WvB* (Amer. ed.), 10 (EvB quote). A typical beginner's instrument, a 60-mm brass-tube refractor with tripod, cost 300 or 400 marks in the late 1920s, a substantial sum. This is based on ads in the German nature magazine *Kosmos*, plus a survey of 1920s amateur astronomy periodicals at the U.S. Naval Observatory, including *Die Sterne*, *Sirius*, and *Himmelswelt*.

3. WvB, "Space Man," 20.7.1958, 8–9; S&O, *WvB* (Amer. ed.), 15; Eleonore vB to MvB, 14.6.1925, file 8, MvB Papers in possession of C.-F. vB, Munich; "Bored Von Braun Flunked Ninth Grade, Father Says," *Washington Evening Star*, 10.10.62, A5; Mosse, *Crisis*, 160–62.

4. Reisig OHI, by MJN, 1989, 3; Mosse, *Crisis*, 160–66; Koerrenz, *Hermann Lietz*, and same, *Landeserziehungsheime*.

5. Printed class lists, 1926–29, courtesy Archiv der Lietz-Schulen; Mosse, *Crisis*, 165–67; Koerrenz, *Hermann Lietz*, 21, and *Landeserziehungsheime*, 99–100, 147–48.

6. Interviews with Dr. Hartmut Henke and Mr. Heye Deepen, Spiekeroog, 27.3.2001; Mosse, *Crisis*, 163–64.

7. WvB, "Space Man," 20.7.1958, 9. It should be noted that this quote, like the article, is ghostwritten by the interviewer, Curtis Mitchell, but is one of the earliest versions of

this oft-told anecdote and one of the closest to the source. As to the original mention of Oberth, WvB asserted in an interview with *Kosmos* that he had spotted it in an astronomical supplement, *Das Himmelsjahr* (The Year in the Heavens), to *Kosmos*, but I was not able to verify that the magazine issued such a supplement. See Interview with Zeithammer/*Kosmos*, 25.8.1966, WvBP-H, file 227-10.

8. Oberth, *Die Rakete*; Barth, *Hermann Oberth*, 73–78.

9. Ley, *Rockets, Missiles*, 98–113; Neufeld, "Weimar Culture"; Crouch, *Aiming*, 41–44; Winter, *Prelude*, 21–30.

10. Georg Schulz to WvB, 9.4.1958, Archiv der Lietz-Schulen, WvB file (quote); Stucke notes on telephone interview with Wilhelm Theodor Schmieding, 20.10.1998, courtesy of Frank Stucke.

11. SvB quoted in Steinhoff, Pechel, and Showalter, *Voices*, 39; Bergaust, *WvB*, 35; MvB and EvB quoted in S&O, *WvB* (Amer. ed.), 10–11. SvB in his "Memoiren," ms. c. 1990s, courtesy Christina vB, 9, remembers the first experiments as being in the Beethovenstrasse, a short street off In den Zelten, and the cauliflower/broken glass incident being a shopwindow, not a greenhouse.

12. Eleonore vB to MvB, 14.1.1926, file 8, MvB Papers in possession of C.-F. vB; EvB to WvB and Maria vB, 4.11.1955, BAK, N1085/84; Hedwig Oeste filmed interview by Mausbach/Loopfilm, c. 2004, courtesy ZDF ("lazy").

13. WvB, "Space Man," 20.7.1958, 8; sheet music, WvBP-H, file 700-4; S&O, *WvB* (Amer. ed.), 10–11; Bullmann, Rathert, and Schenk, eds., *Paul Hindemith in Berlin*. Hindemith moved to Berlin in the spring of 1927 and was a professor at the Hochschule für Musik in Charlottenburg, where he taught university-level classes. Thus the lessons must have been private and there probably were not many of them.

14. "Sigismund von Braun," in Velder, *300 Jahre*, 498–503; Sulloway, *Born to Rebel*, 21, 55, 67–79; quote from MvB in S&O, *WvB* (Amer. ed.), 10 (paraphrase by Stuhlinger); "baffled" from WvB to Schneer, 2.1.1959, in WvBP-H, file 208-2, p. 8.

15. Quote from "Karlchen" in Gerd von Below to WvB, 2.2.1958, WvBP-H, file 412-11; MvB, *Weg*, 82.

16. Mercury transit drawing in WvBP-H, file 700-1; notes on telephone interviews with Karl Wagner, 4.12.1998, and Hilde Loch, 4.11.98, courtesy Frank Stucke.

17. Astronomy notebook and R. von Saurma's summary of same in WvBP-H, files 700-11, and 700-11a; WvB to MvB, 10.7.1947, BAK, N1085/84.

18. Space mirror notebook and Ruth von Saurma's summary in WvBP-H, files 700-2, 700-3; Franz Windweh to WvB, 13.8.1956, WvBP-H, file 412-8; notes on telephone interview with Joachim Rusche, 19.11.1998, courtesy Frank Stucke.

19. See Neufeld, "Weimar Culture," and Winter, *Prelude*, and the sources cited therein.

20. Ibid.; Ley, *Rockets, Missiles*, 119–24.

21. WvB to Schneer, 2.1.1959, in WvBP-H, file 208-2; WvB, "Space Man," 20.7.1958, 8 (block quote); Ruland, *WvB*, 49, 51 ("house arrest"). In various versions of this anecdote, WvB (or his ghostwriter) gives himself ages from twelve to sixteen, but in the cited versions WvB clearly links it to the Opel/Valier rocket stunts of 1928. It is possible that von Braun saw the 23 May test if the Pentecost holiday from school had begun early enough—the twenty-seventh was Pentecost Sunday. More likely it was later. "Space Man" gives the street as "Tiergarten Allee," but there was no such street in Berlin; it might be Tiergartenstrasse.

22. *60 Jahre*, 29–63; interviews with Hartmut Henke and Heye Deepen, Spiekeroog, 27.3.2001.

23. Ibid.; lifesaving certificate, 23.4.1928, in WvBP-H, file 704-13; EvB quoted in S&O, *WvB* (Amer. ed.), 16.

24. Dieter Pohl to WvB, 29.7.1969, in WvBP-LC, Box 60, 1969 Foreign Corr.; interviews with Dr. Hartmut Henke (shower story) and Mr. Heye Deepen, Spiekeroog, 27.3.2001. See also Kutzer, "WvB," 6–8.

25. WvB, "Die Sternwarte," 173; WvB to H. Andreesen, 7.4.1970, in WvBP-H, file 435-7. The objective has been lost, but the Hermann-Lietz-Schule Spiekeroog kept the telescope tube and a rough wooden tripod stand, which are now in the Deutsches Technikmuseum Berlin. The hut is long gone.

26. WvB, "Die Sternwarte," 173; Kathi Schesmer in *60 Jahre*, 52–55.

27. Kutzer, "WvB," 6–7.

28. WvB, "Zur Theorie der Fernrakete," ms. c. 1929, NASM, FE727c, original in the Deutsches Museum Munich (hastily scribbled notes on the back, perhaps in another hand, have 1929 dates in them); Oberth, *Wege*, 199–200.

29. Andreesen and WvB, "Die gegenwärtige Situation," 134–40.

30. Baranowski, *Sanctity*, 6–7; MvB, *Weg*, passim.

31. Kutzer, "WvB," 6–7; Heye Deepen interview, Spiekeroog, 27.3.2001; WvB, "Space Man," 20.7.1958, 9 (quote); S&O, *WvB* (Amer. ed.), 16.

32. Ley, "Count von Braun," 154; Ley, "How It All Began," 51; "Quittungen," *Die Rakete* 2 (15 Sept. 1928), 143.

33. WvB, "Briefe als Vorwort," 154.

34. Kutzer, "WvB," 7–8.

35. Ibid., 8; "Zeugnis der Reife" for WvB, 3.4.1930, copy courtesy of Dr. Hartmut Henke, Hermann-Lietz-Schule Spiekeroog; on the *Reifeprüfung (Abitur)*, see *60 Jahre*, 45.

36. WvB to Schneer, 2.1.1959, in WvBP-H, file 208-2; WvB postcard (in French) to Jean Moser, 13.7.1930, copy obtained from HORM; WvB, "Erinnerungen an den Sommer 1930," ms. for *Berliner Morgenpost* seventy-fifth anniversary edition, 11.6.1973, DM, Pers. 00022 (block quote).

37. Ley, *Rockets, Missiles*, 124–30; Rohrwild, *Geschichte der UFA-Rakete*; Günzel, *Die fliegenden Flüssigkeitsraketen*, 20–23; Horeis, *Rolf Engel*, 9–11; Rolf Engel interview, 1.8.1991; Ruland, *WvB*, 55; Ley to Fritz Lang, 4.7.1958, NASM, Willy Ley Coll., Box 2701, folder 200.

38. Ley, *Rockets, Missiles*, 131–32, 135; Nebel, *Narren*, 70–76; Rohrwild, *Geschichte der UFA-Rakete*, 13–18; *Mitteilungen: Verein für Raumschiffahrt E.V. Geschäftsstelle Berlin*, no. 1 (April 1930), and Nebel-Oberth correspondence, early 1930, copies from Oberth Nachlass and other sources courtesy of Karlheinz Rohrwild, HORM; R. Hess for Hitler to Nebel, 18.2.1930, NARA, T-175/R155/2685593. For the military context, see Neufeld, *The Rocket*, chap. 1, and "The Reichswehr."

39. Ley, *Rockets, Missiles*, plate IX, 135–36; Horeis, *Rolf Engel*, 9; WvB postcard to Jean Moser, 13.7.1930, copy obtained from HORM; WvB, "Space Man," 20.7.1958, 9; WvB foreword, 4.1969, to Alfred Fritz, *Der Weltraumprofessor*, in WvBP-H, file 430-8; VfR *Mitteilungen*, Extrablatt (May 1930), copy of scrapbook 1 in WvBP-LC, Box 53. Engel asserts that they met at a Berlin VfR meeting in the fall of 1928, but there were none there until early 1930.

40. Barth, *Oberth*, 155; Ley, *Rockets, Missiles*, 133–34.

41. WvB, "Behind the Scenes of Rocket Development in Germany 1928 through 1945," ms., c. 1950, WvBP-H, file 702-20 (block quote); Ley, *Rockets, Missiles*, 134;

"Raketenversuch in der Jungfernheide," *Berlin am Morgen,* 24.7.1930, newspaper clipping with the picture, WvBP-LC, Box 53, scrapbook 1.

42. WvB, "Lunetta," English translation in NASM, WvB bio. file; Noordung, *Das Problem der Befahrung des Weltraums* (translated as *The Problem of Space Travel*).

43. WvB, "Lunetta," 91; Johannes Weyer, *Wernher von Braun,* 7–8. I am indebted to Weyer's interpretation here.

44. Ley, *Rockets, Missiles,* 136–39; Nebel, *Narren,* 84–93; Günzel, *Die fliegenden Flüssigkeitsraketen,* 27–55. The site was buried under bomb rubble after World War II, when the French built an airfield that later became the Berlin-Tegel airport. The bunkers were near the location of the modern terminal.

45. Ley, *Rockets, Missiles,* 136; Nebel, *Narren,* 93–98.

46. WvB, "Behind the Scenes," 4–5, WvBP-H, file 702-20; Horeis, *Rolf Engel,* 18; Engel interview, 1.8.1991, Munich; Klemperer, *I Will Bear Witness,* 1:423; Jan Gympel, "The Jazz Singer," *Der Tagesspiegel* (Berlin), 21.12.2000, lyric from www.warnerchappel.com. S&O, *WvB* (Amer. ed.), 11, quote Rolf Engel, spelling it "sunny boy," but this is almost certainly incorrect, given that the song was famous in Germany, and the movie appeared there in 1929 or 1930 as one of the very first sound films.

47. Ley, "Count von Braun," 155; Horeis, *Rolf Engel,* 18.

48. WvB, "Behind the Scenes," 4–5, WvBP-H, file 702-20; Ley, *Rockets, Missiles,* 140–45; Winter, *Prelude,* 41–42.

49. WvB Grunau Flugbuch, 1931–32, in WvBP-H, file 700-16, and M. Sharpe questionnaire with WvB answers on pilot experience, 1971, in file 607-13 ("money").

50. MvB Oberwiesenthal docs. in BAK, N1085/2; SvB, "Memoiren," ms. c. 1990s, courtesy Christina vB, 14–15; MvB, *Weg,* 291. Oberwiesenthal is now Bystrzyca, Poland, near Wleń (German: Lähn).

51. WvB, "Anmeldung zur Aufnahme als Studierender," 14.3.1931, ETH Rektorat, Matrikelakt, copy courtesy of ETH archives; Ley, "Count von Braun," 155; WvB to Paganini, 21.9.1954, in WvBP-H, file 412-6; Generales, "Recollections," 75.

52. Generales, "Recollections," 75; for a slightly different version see his "Selected Events," 1310. The Einstein Papers Project has no such letter, but the staff has informed me that Einstein was not good at making copies of outgoing correspondence.

53. "Harvard Class of 1929," 1979 brochure in NASM, Constantine Generales bio. file; Generales, "Recollections," 76–78; DeVorkin, *Race,* chap. 1 and passim. For von Braun's version of the mouse story see WvB, "Behind the Scenes," p. 7 insert, WvBP-H, file 702-20. The published, edited version, "Reminiscences," 128, launched the oft-repeated but erroneous detail of "a ring of mouse blood" on the room's walls.

54. WvB to Rektorat der ETH, 15.7.1931, and Matrikel for WvB, 1931, ETH Rektorat, Matrikelakt, copy courtesy of ETH archives; Generales, "Recollections," 77–78; C. Generales, letter to editor, *New York State Journal of Medicine* (Nov. 1977), 2174–75; S&O, *WvB* (Amer. ed.), 20 ("girls"); Georg Schulz to WvB, 9.4.1958, WvB file, Archiv der Lietz-Schulen (Ettersburg story).

55. WvB foreword to Lasswitz, 1969, in WNRC, RG255, 73A-732, Box 7, Articles/Dr. von Braun, 1971; VfR "Mitteilungen," Feb., Mar., and Dec. 1931, mimeographed newsletters, copies courtesy of Herbert P. Raabe (statistics from Dec.); Ley, *Rockets, Missiles,* 145–52; Winter, *Prelude,* 42–44; Horeis, *Rolf Engel,* 21–22.

56. WvB, "Behind the Scenes," 7, WvBP-H, file 702-20; Horeis, *Rolf Engel,* 18; WvB, "Die Grundlagen des Berechnungsganges einer Flüssigkeitsrakete," ms., 28.2.1932, NASM, FE727c; WvB, "Das Geheimnis"; Nebel, *Raketenflug.*

57. WvB Grunau Flugbuch, 1931–32, in WvBP-H, file 700-17, Segelflugschule

Grunau, "Prüfungs-Bescheinigung" for WvB, 17.5.1932, in file 700-16, Reitsch to WvB, 7.12.1959, in file 600-2; Lomax, *Hanna Reitsch,* 12–13; S&O, *WvB* (Amer. ed.), 17–18. WvB sometimes recalled their meeting during the 1931 course, but 1932 appears more likely from the dates of her biography kindly supplied to me by Evelyn Zegenhagen.

CHAPTER 3

1. "Reminiscences," 95–96.

2. WvB, "Behind the Scenes," 8, WvBP-H, file 702-20, and "Space Man," 20.7.1958, 22; Nebel, *Narren,* 133–35. The "three liter" designation is the tank volume of the Repulsor, which various sources also call the Mirak 2 or Mirak 3.

3. Wimmer to Becker, 6.5.31, and reply, 12.5.31, in IWM, MI 14/801(V) (latter also in BA/MA, RH8/v.1226); Ley, *Rockets, Missiles,* 155.

4. "Sitzungsbericht vom 17.12.1930 über die Raketenfrage," in BA/MA, RH8/v.991a (microfilm copy in IWM, MI 14/820(V), Neufeld, "The Reichswehr."

5. On Versailles, see Dornberger, *V-2,* 19, and the critique and sources cited in Neufeld, "The Reichswehr." Since that article was published I have discovered one document that mentions the legality issue: Wa Prw 2 II to R. Tiling, 28.10.1929, in DM, Tiling Papers. Presumably it was quickly discovered that rocketry was not in the treaty, and the issue became moot.

6. "Sitzungsbericht," 17.12.1930, BA/MA, RH8/v.991a; "Sitzungsbericht vom 30.1.1932," in IWM, MI 14/820(V); WD army personnel file, NACP, RG242, German army officers, reel 135; Winter and Neufeld, "Heylandt's Rocket Cars," 55; Becker to AG für Industriegasverwertung, 16.10. and 9.11.1931, in NASM, FE724a; docs. on Wilhelm Belz, 1931–32, in NASM, FE366/3.

7. Becker to Nebel, 23.4.1932, pictured in Nebel, *Narren,* 134–35. As Nebel is unmentioned in the Ordnance rocket meeting of 30.1.1932, it likely developed as the result of a February visit, leading to Nebel's letter of 3.3.1932, and to another visit in mid-March or mid-April. (WvB was away from 23.3. to 10.4. at glider school.)

8. WvB quoted in Ley to H. Schaefer, 8.12.1946, NASM, Ley Collection, Box 5, file 165; Ley, *Rockets, Missiles,* 155–56; Nebel, *Narren,* 135–36; Wa Prw I to Schiessplatzkommando Z, 6.6.1932, in IWM, MI 14/801(V); Generales, "Recollections," 78; quote from WvB, "Behind the Scenes," 8, WvBP-H, file 702-20 (published version, "Reminiscences," 129).

9. Schneider report on 22.6.1932 launch, and Schumann note, 1.7.1932, in IWM, MI 14/801(V); WvB, "Behind the Scenes," 8; Nebel, *Narren,* 136–37.

10. WvB, "Behind the Scenes," 8–9, WvBP-H, file 702-20; WD, *V-2,* 27, 32; von Horstig to WvB, 16.3.1969, in WvBP-H, file 424-3.

11. WvB, "Behind the Scenes," 9, WvBP-H, file 702-20.

12. WvB, "Story of the V-2 Rocket," ms., c. 1950, WvBP-LC, Box 49, Speeches and Writings Undated. This appears to the first outline for the memoir article.

13. WvB, "Behind the Scenes," 10, WvBP-H, file 702-20. Compare this 1950 manuscript version to what was eventually published in "Reminiscences," 130, and to the version from Lang, "A Romantic Urge," quoted in the Prologue.

14. Horeis, *Rolf Engel,* 17–18, 24–25; Rahkmanin and Sternin, *Odnazhdy i navzegda,* 404–5, reference and translated passage kindly supplied by A. Siddiqi; Harrison, "Soviet Market," 22; Neufeld, "The Excluded"; Petzold, *Franz von Papen,* 66. The new information about Engel came after I published "Rolf Engel," and changes the interpretation of his 1933 arrest (discussed later in this chapter).

15. Horeis, _Rolf Engel,_ 24; Ley, "Count von Braun," 155.

16. WvB, "Behind the Scenes," 11; Sitzungsbericht, 17.12.30, 28; Hoffmann, "Die Physik an der Berliner Universität," 14–18; Becker and Schumann records in Humboldt University Archive, Phil. Fak. 1440 and 1479, and Universitätskurator, Personalia B118 and Sch 334; Reichswehr contract with WvB, 27.11.1932, in WvBP-H, file 702-2.

17. Petzold, _Franz von Papen,_ 63–66; Turner, _Hitler's 30 Days to Power,_ 6–12, 40–42; MvB, _Weg,_ 205–6. The house behind Wilhelmstrasse 72 was torn down and replaced in the mid-1930s by a showier house built for Propaganda Minister Josef Goebbels. That was destroyed in 1945, along with the ministry. The site became part of the "death strip" behind the Berlin Wall from 1961 to 1989 and is now part of the terrain of the new Memorial for the Murdered Jews of Europe—such are the layers of history on one Berlin site. See www.holocaust-mahnmal.de.

18. MvB, _Weg,_ 205; Petzold, _Franz von Papen,_ 74–75, 91–99; Kershaw, _Hitler 1889–1936,_ 367–75; MvB to Walther Darré, 9.8.1932, Bundesanstalt für Landwirtschaft und Ernährung, Reichsnährstand records, reference courtesy Rainer Eisfeld.

19. Generales to WvB, 6.10.1958, WvBP-H, file 400-01; W. Pantenius to WvB, 8.5.1952, WvBP-H, file 412-4 ("das Volk"); S&O, _WvB_ (Amer. ed.), 12 (Engel quote).

20. _Raketenflug,_ no. 6 (Sept. 1932), NACP, T-175/R155/2685604-05; _Raketenflug,_ no. 7 (Dec. 1932), personal papers of H. P. Raabe; Ley, "Count von Braun," 155–56. The news of WvB's election reached the American Interplanetary Society in New York. See Ley, "Around European Rocketry," late 1932, in Princeton University Library, Pendray Papers, copy in NASM, Ley bio. file.

21. MvB to Generales, 30.9.1932, copy in NASM, Generales bio. file; WvB, TH Berlin Vorprüfungszeugnis, 3.11.1932, NSS files, Washington, D.C.; Becker officer file, BA/MA, Pers 6/76; Reichswehr contract with WvB, 27.11.1932, in WvBP-H, file 702-2.

22. WvB's Protokoll of Gestapo interview, 16.7.1934, IWM, MI 14/801(V), gives 1.12.1932 as his starting date; his memoirs say 1.11., but this document is much closer in time.

23. WvB, "Behind the Scenes," 11 (quote), WvBP-H, file 702-20, and "Story of the V-2 Rocket," 6, WvBP-LC, Box 49.

24. Ley, _Rockets,_ 2nd ed. (1947), 214 (compare to first edition, 1944, p. 152); Ley to Schaefer, 8.12.1946, NASM, Ley Collection, Box 5, file 165.

25. WvB, "Behind the Scenes," 11; Grünow to WvB, 4.3.1956, WvBP-H, file 412-8; WvB, "Konstruktive, theoretische und experimentelle Beiträge," 4–6, 29–30; WD, _V-2,_ 23–26. In the latter Dornberger gives a spectacular description of an explosion, but it was not the first test; nor was it 21.12.1932; nor was Walter Riedel present. Riedel was not even hired until Jan. 1934. Dornberger's memoirs are invaluable but not very reliable.

26. On the car see Ruland, _WvB,_ 77. The family moved to Potsdamer Privatstrasse 121G, which is the only one of their former buildings to survive World War II. The street is now called In der Bissingzeile. (Thanks to Frank Stucke for this information.)

27. MvB, _Weg,_ 232 (quote); Turner, _Hitler's 30 Days;_ Kershaw, _Hitler 1889–1936,_ 391–427; WvB, "Why I Chose America," 111.

28. WvB to Schneer, 2.1.1959, in WvBP-H, file 208-2.

29. Schumann records, Humboldt University archive, Phil. Fak. 1440 and Universitätskurator, Personalia, Sch 334; Schumann NSDAP file card, BDC records; Hoffmann, "Die Physik an der Berliner Universität," 17–18, and "Das Physikalische Institut der Berliner Universität"; Sime, _Lise Meitner,_ chap. 6.

30. WvB, "Why I Chose America," 111 ("too wrapped up"); WvB, "Konstruktive, the-

oretische und experimentelle Beiträge," esp. 30; WvB, "Behind the Scenes," 11 ("Solidly"); Ley to Schaefer, 8.12.1946, NASM, Ley Collection, Box 5, file 165; docs. on aluminum, 1932–33, in NASM, FE744.

31. WvB, "Behind the Scenes," 11–12 (quote), WvBP-H, file 702-20; WvB, "Konstruktive, theoretische und experimentelle Beiträge," 29–37; Walter H. J. Riedel, "Raketenentwicklung mit flüssigen Treibstoffe" (ms., 1950; IWM, German Misc. 148), 25; WvB, "Die bisherige Entwicklung . . . der Flüssigkeitsrakete," 14.12.1933, in FE727c. For a more detailed description of the technology, see Neufeld, *Rocket*, 32–37.

32. WvB pilot logs and licenses in WvBP-H, files 700-16, 700-17, 704-12; WvB, "Biographical and Professional Data" form, 10.2.1947, NACP, RG330, Acc. 70A4398; Babs Riedel quoted in Günzel, *Die fliegenden Flüssigkeitsraketen*, 104; Lang, "A Romantic Urge," 181 ("startlingly handsome").

33. "Affidavit of Membership in NSDAP of Prof. Dr. Wernher von Braun," 18.6.1947, NACP, RG330, Accession 70A4398; "SS-Stammrollenblatt" for WvB, 28.2.1934, BA Dallwitz-Hoppegarten (may now be BABL); Wilson, *Himmler's Cavalry*, 9–10, 13–27, 51, 66, 117–18.

34. Photo in Ruland, *WvB*, 52; Steinberg, *Sabers and Brown Shirts*, 146–48; Wilson, *Himmler's Cavalry*, 13–27, 32–36.

35. WvB quoted in Ward, *Wernher von Braun Anekdotisch*, 28; photos in Fleischer, *Heeresversuchsstelle Kummersdorf*, 46–47. On another occasion he did remember the 1933 visit—see Ruland, *WvB*, 99.

36. Neufeld, "Rolf Engel"; Horeis, *Rolf Engel*, 47–48; Anhaltisches Amtsgericht release from jail, 18.5.1933, Rolf Engel Papers, EADS archive Ottobrünn; Engel interview, 1.8.1991. The pro-Soviet actions cited in a previous note confirm other evidence that Engel falsified his own past numerous times in documents, memoirs, and interviews, not always consistently.

37. Rietz, *Die Magdeburger Pilotenrakete*; WvB, "Behind the Scenes," 19–20, WvBP-H, file 702-20; Winter, *Prelude*, 44–48.

38. See Neufeld, *The Rocket*, 23–30, and "Rolf Engel," 57–58, and the sources cited therein.

39. WvB, "Protokoll" of Gestapo interview re: Nebel, 16.7.1934, IWM, MI 14/801(V).

40. Ibid.; Neufeld, *The Rocket*, 28.

41. WvB, "Die bisherige Entwicklung und der augenblickliche Stand der Arbeiten an der Flüssigkeitsrakete," 14.12.1933, NASM, FE727c; WvB, "Konstruktive, theoretische und experimentelle Beiträge," 31–36; Winter and Neufeld, "Heylandt's Rocket Cars."

42. WvB, "Behind the Scenes," 12–13 (block quote), WvBP-H, file 702-20; WD, *V-2*, 27–28.

43. WvB, "Konstruktive, theoretische und experimentelle Beiträge" (1960 reprint), original typescript in WvBP-H, file 700-19; WvB doctoral graduation records, 1934, Humboldt University Archive, Phil. Fak. PN 4 Bd. 559; Ruland, *WvB*, 87.

44. Promotionsprüfung, 7.6.1934, and Schumann note of 4.6.1934, Humboldt University Archive, Phil. Fak. PN 4 Bd. 559.

45. Reichswehr contract, 4.4.1933, WvBP-H, file 702-2; WvB, "Space Man" (20 July 1958), 23 (quotes); Kershaw, *Hitler 1889–1936*, 505–26.

46. MvB, *Weg*, 232–41 (quote 236–37), 266–73, 291–94. Wernher von Braun's apartment was at Nürnberger Strasse 16. On his postwar Paperclip documents he gives May 1933 as the date he moved there, but it may be a mistake for 1934. His "Biographical and Professional Data" form, 10.2.1947, NACP, RG330, Acc. 70A4398, gives 1933 but also

says he lived about two and a half years there, moving out in 1935, yet he did not move to the Kummersdorf area until 1936.

47. WvB to Schneer, 2.1.1959, in WvBP-H, file 208-2 ("bitterly"); SvB datebook entries, 26.6. and 24.7.35, AA/PA, Nachlass SvB, Nr. 20; SvB NSDAP file card, BDC records; Ley-Pendray correspondence, 1934–35, in NASM, Ley bio. file, and P. E. Cleator to G. E. Pendray, 30.10.1934, in NASM, Cleator bio. file (originals in Pendray Papers, Princeton University Library); "Affidavit of Membership in NSDAP of Magnus v. Braun," 2.6.1947, NACP, RG330, JIOA Case Files, MvB Jr. file. For SvB's U.S. stay and world trip, see his memoir, *Flüchtige Gäste;* a deeper discussion of his attitudes, his diplomatic career, and his anti-Nazi activities is found in his "Memoiren," courtesy Christina vB.

48. "Versuchsprogramm Nr. 7," c. 1935, USSRC, Huzel Papers, DH-4.8.1; Ruland, *WvB*, 80–82; WD, *V-2*, 29; Schneider report on 22.6.1932 launch, in IWM, MI 14/801(V).

49. WD, *V-2*, 36 (quote); Rielau, *Geschichte der Nebeltruppe*, 30, 142–46. Rudolf Nebel's later assertions that the *Nebelwerfer* were named after him are completely untrue.

50. Schneider order, and Becker to Marine-Waffenamt, et al., both 30.11.1934, in BA/MA, RH8/v.1945.

51. WvB to "Herr Hauptmann," 12.12.1934, ibid.

52. See ibid., Borkum expedition file, esp. WvB report, 28.1.1935.

53. Quoted in Ruland, *WvB*, 89.

54. Lang, "A Romantic Urge," 188; Gordon Young, "V-2 Inventor Reveals His Secrets," *Daily Express* (London), 18.6.1945, copy in NASM, Ley Collection, Box 5, file 165.

CHAPTER 4

1. WD, *V-2*, 38–39.

2. WvB, "Denkschrift," 18.1.1935, in NASM, FE727a.

3. Ley to Schaefer, 8.12.1946, in NASM, Ley Collection, Box 5, file 165; Oberth, *Wege*, 99–100.

4. Von Horstig to Becker, 4.2.1935, in BA/MA, RH8/v.1260; WD "Beurteilung" of WvB, 11.9.1937, in WvBP-H, file 702-2; Neufeld, *The Rocket*, 285.

5. Ordnance-Pietsch contract, 15.5.1933, in BA/MA, RH8/v.1225; WD, *V-2*, 30 ("lean . . ."); WvB, Rudolph test document, 18.8.1935, in NASM, FE727c; Rudolph NSDAP file card, BDC records; Rudolph OHI, 24–26.

6. Rudolph OHI, 46 (quote); WvB to Schneer, 2.1.1959, in WvBP-H, file 208-2 (on K. Riedel).

7. See Neufeld, *The Rocket*, 64–66, for more technical detail; WvB, "Behind the Scenes," 14 (quote), WvBP-H, file 702-20.

8. Von Richthofen to Ordnance, 6.2.1935, in BA/MA, RH8/v.1221; for a full description of the army-Luftwaffe alliance see Neufeld, "Rocket Aircraft."

9. Schneider marginal note on von Richthofen to Ordnance, 6.2.1935, and Zanssen (WvB) report, 16.2.1935, in BA/MA, RH8/v.1221; Zanssen/WvB report on Schmidt, 23.3.1935, in DM, Peenemünde binders.

10. Zanssen to von Richthofen, 22.5.1935, and related documents, in NASM, FE746.

11. Minutes of meeting, 27.6.1935, WvB draft agreement, Ordnance-RLM-Junkers-Heinkel, 4.9.1935, and minutes of 16.10.1935 meeting, ibid.

12. WvB pilot log, 1933–40, in WvBP-H, file 700-17; Riedel, "Raketenentwicklung,"

IWM, German. Misc. 148, p. 35; WvB, "Stellungnahme," (quotes) and minutes of meeting, 27.6.1935, and WvB, "Kostenaufstellung," 24.10.1935, in NASM, FE746.

13. Rudolph OHI, 31; WvB, "Reminiscences," 135 (block quote). The corresponding page is missing from the ms. version, "Behind the Scenes," and this version is rewritten by an editor. The date of these events is likely after 23.11., as von Braun wrote an overview memorandum on that date that does not mention a new rocket center: WvB to von Horstig (draft), in NASM, FE727a. On Bäumker, see Trischler, *Luft- und Raumfahrtforschung*, 208–19.

14. WvB, "Behind the Scenes," 18 (quotes), WvBP-H, file 702-20; WD, *V-2*, 27, 40; map, 18.1.1936, and "Organisations-Schema," 8.2.1936, in BA/MA, RH8/v.1945. Sigismund's datebook entries, 24.12. and 30.12.35, AA/PA, Nachlass SvB, Nr. 20, show that he and Wernher went to Wiesenthal on Christmas Eve and were still there on the thirtieth, when they visited Hanna Reitsch. A 1941 Luftwaffe construction office source cited by Zache in Erichsen and Hoppe, *Peenemünde*, 58–59, asserts that there was a Dec. 1935 survey, so it possible that someone had looked at the location before Christmas. Indeed, WvB's father later recalled the Peenemünde conversation taking place at Emmy vB's birthday celebration on 3.11.1935, which would fit that evidence better. MvB to WvB, 10.1.1953, in N1085/84. However, WvB always stuck to Christmas in his memoirs, thus I use it here. Stüwe's story in *Peenemünde-West*, 59, apparently coming from Erich Warsitz, that WvB surveyed the coast with Warsitz in a Junkers Junior in December 1935 is definitely fictional. WvB's pilot log, 1933–40, in WvBP-H, file 700-17, shows no such flights and all indications are that he did not meet Warsitz until a year later.

15. WD, *V-2*, 38–39; WD, "The German V-2," 397 ("military value").

16. WD, *V-2*, 39–41; von Richthofen report on 1.4.1936 meeting with Kesselring in NACP, T-971/73/no frame nos.; Wolgast-RLM contract, 2.4.1936, Landesarchiv Greifswald, Rep. 386 Wlg, Nr. 2773, courtesy Arthur Behn. Other documents Mr. Behn has given me show that the actual purchase of land took three months longer than Dornberger states in *V-2*.

17. WvB, "Behind the Scenes," 22, WvBP-H, file 702-20; WD, *V-2*, 47–48 ("Paris Gun"); Neufeld, *The Rocket*, 16–17, 51–53.

18. WvB, "Behind the Scenes," 20 (block quote), WvBP-H, file 702-20; WvB, "Re: Profile on Dr. Walter Dornberger to be published in Missiles and Rockets," 17.4.1959, DM, Pers. 00019 ("fatherly friend"); von Horstig, "Beurteilung," 19.2.1936, in BA/MA, RH8/v.1941; WD, "Beurteilungsbericht," 11.9.1937, WvBP-H, file 702-2.

19. Warsitz quoted in Ward, *Wernher von Braun Anekdotisch*, 8–9; on Junkers Junior, WvB to Lorenz, 24.4.1936, in NASM, FE746; Riedel, "Raketenentwicklung" (ms., 1950), IWM, German Misc. 148, p. 35. Von Braun states that Warsitz will be the test pilot in "Aktenvermerk," 1.3.1937, of monthly Ordnance-RLM meeting, NASM, FE746. Warsitz's visit must thus have been in February or earlier.

20. Ward, *Wernher von Braun Anekdotisch*, 9–11.

21. Ibid., 11–12.

22. WvB pilot log, 1933–40, in WvBP-H, file 700-17; WvB Wehrpass, 1936, in NACP, RG330, Acc. 70A4398; Kershaw, *Hitler 1936–1945*, 6–9.

23. WvB, "Versuchsvorbereitung," 10.8.1936, USSRC, Huzel Papers, doc. DH 4.9; Patent, 1.5.1936, NASM, FE190; WvB, "Stand der Entwicklung und laufende Arbeiten am 1.5.36," 28.4.1936, BA/MA, RH8/v.1260.

24. WD, *V-2*, 50–53. See Neufeld, *The Rocket*, 74–78, for more technical detail.

25. WvB, "Behind the Scenes," 18 (on Hermann), WvBP-H, file 702-20; WD, *V-2*, 53–54; Neufeld, *The Rocket*, 85–87.

26. WvB, "Gutachten" for Oberth, 7.5.1937, Schneider and Zanssen, "Grundsätzliche Stellungnahme," 28.2.1935, and related documents in BA/MA, RH8/v.1226; Neufeld, "The Excluded."

27. Wiemer to Zanssen, 6.9.1935 ("Ariernachweis"), and Wiemer to Becker, 17.10.1935, and related documents in BA/MA, RH8/v.1224.

28. WvB Aktenvermerk, 27.4.1936, and Chef Wa Prüf (WvB draft) to Abwehr, 29.4.1938, and related documents ibid.

29. Nebel, *Narren*, 142–47 (contract, 2.7.1937, pictured on 143–46); Günzel, *Die fliegenden Flüssigkeitsraketen*, 87–94; WvB to Rudolf Merta, 12.1.1955, WvBP-H, file 412-7; Neufeld, "The Excluded," 23–24.

CHAPTER 5

1. WD, *V-2*, 139.

2. For a description and many photos of Peenemünde, see Bode and Kaiser, *Raketenspuren*, 24–41; for construction, see Stüwe, *Peenemünde-West*, 63–80.

3. WvB to Schneer, 2.1.1959, in WvBP-H, file 208-2, WvB to Bergaust, 2.3.1952, in file 400-9, and Gretelill Fries to WvB, 6.2.1958, in file 413-2. (She became an Oslo actress; her letter includes her picture, about which von Braun wrote the enthused marginal comment.)

4. WvB to Schneer, 2.1.1959, in WvBP-H, file 208-2; WvB, "Biographical and Professional Data," 10.2.1947, NACP, RG330, Acc. 70A3498.

5. Ibid.; *Landwirtschaftliches Adressbuch der Provinz Pommern* (1939), 69–70, in Landesarchiv Greifswald; Bernd Jordan interview, Lassan, 4.8.1999, and excerpt from the *Gothaer Adelskalendar* supplied by same; Werner Jagenow interview, Bauer, 15.7.2000, and "Werner Jagenow erinnert sich an Wernher von Braun," *Ostsee-Zeitung* (Greifswald edition?), 12.12.1992, 11. The nickname "Uncle Allack" comes from WvB's postwar correspondence with his parents in BAK, N1079 (the MvB Papers); its origin is unknown to me.

6. Bode and Kaiser, *Raketenspuren*, 38–41. WvB's Zinnowitz address was Kirchstrasse 7, as shown in various personal documents. The building at this address in 2002 is probably the same.

7. H. Ranft (née Bannasch) interview excerpts, USSRC, Ordway Collection. Uhl, *Stalins V-2*, 32–34, 44, mentions that a Gestapo counterintelligence officer who was a Soviet spy, Willy Lehmann, code-named "Breitenbach," passed along information about Kummersdorf rocket engine tests and WvB in 1935. Further information might have leaked through the Soviet spy ring in the Air Ministry later called the "Red Orchestra." More famous is the "Oslo report," which someone mysteriously sent to the British naval attaché in Oslo in the fall of 1939. It included a small amount of garbled information about rocket development, but at first British intelligence did not take it very seriously. Hinsley, *British Intelligence*, 1:99–100, 508–12 (text).

8. Wegener, *Peenemünde Wind Tunnels*, 47–48.

9. Reisig OHI, 5.-7.6.1989, 18–19; Dannenberg OHI, 7.11.1989, NASM; Hoelzer OHI, 10.11.1989, NASM; Sherrod note to WvB, and reply, 30.4.1971 (champagne incident), NASA/HD, HRC 13254; von Tiesenhausen OHI, 22.1.1990, 10.

10. Kütbach interview, 13.12.1998, courtesy of BBC Television; Auguste Friede phone

interview, 26.8.2002; O&S, *Rocket Team*, 38; "Abteilungsfest Wa Prüf 11," 16.–17.7.38, WvBP-H, file 702-3; R. Hermann quoted in S&O, *WvB*, 34 ("never alone"). See also Ruth Kraft's East German novel about Peenemünde, *Insel ohne Leuchtfeuer*. She had been one of the labor service women. WvB is not a central character and is identified only as "the Doctor" but is nonetheless vividly depicted as an charismatic, obsessed dreamer and as a "moderner Dr. Faust." In one or two places he is also made out to be a male chauvinist.

11. WD, *V-2*, 139–40; Rudolph OHI (quote), NASM; "Abteilungsfest Wa Prüf 11," 16.–17.7.38, WvBP-H, file 702-3; Bergaust, *WvB*, 66–67 ("an elderly lady . . ."); Rees OHI, NASM.

12. WvB to WD, 20?.10.1937, and WD, "Notiz . . . ," 28.10.1937, in NASM, FE348; Rudolph OHI, 4.8.1989, 32–36; WvB to parents, 21.3.1938, MvB Papers in possession of C.-F. vB, Munich.

13. WvB to Schneer, 2.1.1959, in WvBP-H, file 208-2.

14. "Affidavit of Membership in NSDAP of Prof. Dr. Wernher von Braun," 18.6.1947, NACP, RG330, Accession 70A4398; WvB and Walter H. J. Riedel NSDAP file cards, former BDC records, now BABL, microfilm in NACP; for photos, S&O, *Wernher von Braun: An Illustrated Memoir*, 19, 20, 25. No picture clearly shows the swastika, but it is apparent what the button is in one or two cases.

15. WvB, "Why I Chose America," 111 ("fared"); Ward, *WvB Anekdotisch*, 28 (see full quote on Hitler in chap. 3).

16. WvB, "Why I Chose America," 111 ("warned me"); SvB datebook entry, 22.3.36, AA/PA, Nachlass SvB, Nr. 20 (MvB: "Chancen Wehrdiktatur nicht besser als Ns, da Probleme 'Arbeitslosigkeit' "); WvB, "Vorwort zu 'V2, Der Schuss ins Weltall,' " attached to WvB to WD, 29.4.1953, in WvBP-H, file 430-5—a foreword for French edition of *V-2* not actually used in WD, *L'arme secrète*.

17. WvB to Alan Fox, 22.1.1971, and Fox to WvB, 11.1.1971, in WvBP-H, file 405-7. The WvB letter is reprinted in full in Ward, *Dr. Space*, 227–29, albeit uncritically.

18. Rigg, *Hitler's Jewish Soldiers*; Kershaw, *Hitler 1936–1945*, 136–43. In WvB's pilot log, 1933–40, WvBP-H, file 700-17, entries for 9.11.1938 show a round-trip to Marienehe (the Heinkel works near Rostock) returning to P. at 16:23. Kristallnacht began that night. On SvB, see Hürter, et al., *Biographisches Handbuch*, 1:263–64; Hildegard vB (wife of Sigismund) to MvB and Emmy vB, 27.9.1946, in BAK, N1085/78; SvB, "Memoiren," ms., courtesy Christina vB, 29–36. According to SvB's "Memoiren," the assassinated Ernst von Rath was his successor, thus the transfer saved his life. Perhaps, but the teenager wanted to kill the ambassador but instead shot the first official he ran into.

19. Kershaw, *Popular Opinion*, 277.

20. Bode and Kaiser, *Raketenspuren*, 42; Wegener, *Peenemünde Wind Tunnels*, 44, 80–82, 105 (on Hermann's Nazi enthusiasm); Hermann questionnaire, 5.12.1945, in NACP, E.179, Box 703, file "Boston"; WvB to Schneer, 2.1.1959, in WvBP-H, file 208-2 (on Riedel and on "Nazis" at P.); Raithel OHI, 22.4.1993, NASM.

21. See Neufeld, *The Rocket*, 60–61, and "Rocket Aircraft," 215–19, for details and references.

22. Pauls, Künzel, Warsitz, and WvB, flight report, 3.6.1937, in NASM, FE746; Neufeld, "Rocket Aircraft," 219.

23. Pauls memo, 8.7.1938, and WvB marginal comment, 16.8.1938, in NASM, FE746.

24. Neufeld, "Rocket Aircraft," 214–15; WvB draft (signed by von Horstig) to Wa Prw 3, 2.10.1935, and WvB to WD, 9.2.1937, in BA/MA, RH8/v.1225; WvB to Grover Heiman Jr., 13.8.1962, WvBP-H, file 403-3 ("first manned space flight").

25. Neufeld, "Rocket Aircraft," 211, 219; Ordnance-Walter correspondence, 1934–36, in NASM, FE724/b.

26. WvB pilot log, 1933–40, WvBP-H, file 700-17; Mueller OHI, 6–8.11.1989, 19.

27. WD order, 1.9.1937, NASM, FE367; Reisig OHI, 5–7.6.1989, NASM; WD, *V-2*, 42–45; WvB, "Vorschlag . . . ," 10.10.1938, NASM, FE747.

28. WvB, "Das Aggregat III," 29.11.1937, with appended launch report (WvB cover memo, 6.7.1938), in DM, Peenemünde collection.

29. WD, *V-2*, 44–45; WvB, "Erfahrungs- und Versuchsbericht," 15.1.1938, NASM, FE747.

30. WvB, "Behind the Scenes," ms. 1950, WvBP-H, file 702-20; WvB, launch report, c. 7.1938, appended to "Das Aggregat III" (see above).

31. WD, *V-2*, 55; WD telegram to Woike, 6.11.37, NASM, FE367; WvB, launch report, c. 7.1938, appended to "Das Aggregat III."

32. WvB, launch report, c. 7.1938, appended to "Das Aggregat III" (quote); WvB to Haas/KG, 17.12.1937, in NASM, FE74/b; WD to Becker, "Vortragsnotiz" and longer draft, 29.12.1937, in NASM, FE367.

33. WvB, "Das Aggregat III," 29.11.1937, DM; WvB to WD, 8.1., and minutes of meetings with KG, 10.–20.1.1938, in NASM, FE119; Reisig OHI, 5.–7.6.1989, NASM. The minutes of the 20.1. meeting at Peenemünde contain a clear reference to this test.

34. WvB, launch report, c. 7.1938, appended to "Das Aggregat III"; WvB, "Behind the Scenes," ms. 1950, WvBP-H, file 702-20.

35. WvB, "Erfahrungs- und Versuchsbericht," 15.1.1938, NASM, FE747 (p. 5 has a reference to "Aggr.5"); WD, *V-2*, 56; WvB, "Behind the Scenes," ms. 1950, WvBP-H, file 702-20. For details on Kurzweg and the fins, see Neufeld, *The Rocket*, 89–90, and the sources cited therein.

36. Minutes of meetings with Siemens, 9.11.1937 and 24.1.1938, and with KG, 10.–20.1.1938, in NASM, FE119.

37. Rudolph OHI, 4.8.1989, 72; WvB, "Das Aggregat III," 29.11.1937 (A-4 references on pp. 5 and 55–56), DM. On the "everything under one roof" philosophy, see the more elaborate treatment in Neufeld, *The Rocket*, 73–74, 112–13.

38. Minutes of meeting with Siemens, 24.1.1938, Heitzer/KG to Peenemünde, 22.10.1938, in NASM, FE119.

39. Corr. re: Askania and Möller, 26.11.1938–6.8.1939, ibid.

40. K. W. Fieber, "Zur Geschichte der deutschen Raketensteuerung," ms., 1965, 25–26, copy deposited in the Siemens Archive Munich.

41. Fieber, "Zur Geschichte," 12–13.

42. Rudolph OHI, 4.8.1989, 68–69; interrog. of Schröder, report dated 4.9.1945, NACP, RG165, G-2 Library "P" file 1940–45, Box 431, folder "Captured Personnel Material 13800-826"; WvB, "Behind the Scenes," ms. 1950, WvBP-H, file 702-20; WD, *V-2*, 15.

43. Reisig, *Raketenforschung in Deutschland*, 283; WvB, "Vorschlag," 10.10.38, and Leuchtfeuer II documents, 19.7.–20.9.1939, and in NASM, FE747.

44. Von Brauchitsch order to Becker, 21.11.1938, in NASM, FE357.

45. The Bergaust and Ruland biographies, presumably based on WvB interviews, report that this visit took place exactly on 23.3.: Bergaust, *WvB*, 55; Ruland, *WvB*, 97–99. This appears impossible, as Hitler went to the newly annexed territory of Memelland that day, just after he had blackmailed Lithuania into giving back land lost in 1919. Kershaw, *Hitler 1936–1945*, 176. One possibility could be the morning of 22 Mar., before Hitler and Goebbels departed for Memel.

46. WD, *V-2*, 64; Bergaust, *WvB*, 55; Kershaw, *Hitler 1936–1945*, 168–75. See also preceding note.

47. Bergaust, *WvB*, 55–56; Ruland, *WvB*, 97; Rudolph OHI, 4.8.1989, 40.

48. WD, *V-2*, 64–65; Bergaust, *WvB*, 55–57; Ruland, *WvB*, 99–105.

49. Bergaust, *WvB*, 55–57; WvB quoted in Ruland, *WvB*, 105.

50. WD, *V-2*, 66–67; WvB quoted in Ruland, *WvB*, 108.

51. WD, *V-2*, 66–67; Speer, *Inside*, 366.

52. Neufeld, "Rocket Aircraft," 220–22; rocket aircraft correspondence, 1938–39, in NASM, FE746.

53. WvB pilot log, 1933–40, WvBP-H, file 700-17, and Heinkel to WvB, 28.12.1951, in WvBP-LC, Box 43, Correspondence, GfW 1950–52; Peenemünde rocket aircraft correspondence, 1938–39, in NASM, FE746.

54. See Neufeld, "Rocket Aircraft," 222–26, for details and references. WvB pilot log, 1933–40, WvBP-H, file 700-17, shows him returning to P. on 14.6.1939 from Kiel and making a day trip to Rechlin on the sixteenth.

55. WvB, "Proposal for the Development of an Interceptor Plane with Rocket Propulsion," 6.7.1939 (translation 29.4.1946), Redstone Scientific Information Center, Huntsville, Ala., FE595.

CHAPTER 6

1. Speer, *Inside*, 367, referring to the first A-4 launch on 13 June 1942.

2. WvB pilot log, 1933–40, WvBP-H, file 700-17; Kershaw, *Hitler 1936–1945*, 200–11. He did not decide on total extermination of the Jews until 1941, hence the qualification.

3. Kershaw, *Hitler 1936–1945*, 211–23.

4. WvB "Rundschreiben," 30.8.1939, in NASM, FE750. Note that it does not cover Thiel's group at Kummersdorf, which reported directly to Dornberger.

5. Von Brauchitsch order, 5.9.1939, WD to W Stab, 13.9.1939, and WD to Leeb, chronology of 24.9.1940, all in NASM, FE342; WvB to Schneer, 2.1.1959, in WvBP-H, file 208-2 (quote).

6. "Werdegang . . . der Prof. Dr. von Braun," c. late 1943, in NASM, FE341; Neufeld, *The Rocket*, 82–83; WvB, "Behind the Scenes," ms. 1950, WvBP-H, file 702-20.

7. WvB, "Behind the Scenes," ms. 1950, WvBP-H, file 702-20.

8. Hoelzer OHI, 10.11.1989, 7–10.

9. WD, *V-2*, 60–61; Bode and Kaiser, *Raketenspuren*, 46; Steinhoff, A-5 launch report, 19.3.1940, NASM, PGM, Peenemünde Archive Report 78/2; WvB pilot log, 1933–40, WvBP-H, file 700-17.

10. WvB, "Behind the Scenes," ms. 1950, WvBP-H, file 702-20; Steinhoff, A-5 launch report, 19.3.1940, NASM, PGM, P. Archive Report 78/2; WD, *V-2*, 61–63.

11. Steinhoff, A-5 launch report, 19.3.1940, NASM, PGM, P. Archive Report 78/2.

12. Heereswaffenamt Aktenvermerk, 21.11.1939, and WD Vortrag for Becker on 9.1.1940, in NASM, FE342, and WD Vortragsnotiz, 14.12.1939, in NASM, FE349. For secondary accounts of the priority battle, see Neufeld, *The Rocket*, 121–33, or Hölsken, *Die V-Waffen*, 20–30.

13. Speer, *Inside the Third Reich*, 366.

14. Neufeld, *The Rocket*, 126–27; WD, *V-2*, 70 (quote); Schubert chronicle, entry of 9.4.1940, in BA/MA, RH8/v.1207; WD Aktenvermerk, 24.6.1940, in NASM, FE342.

15. "Affidavit . . . ," 18.6.1947, NACP, RG330, Accession 70A4398; SS file card for WvB, former BDC records, BABL (also on microfilm, NACP); the latter says "W.A." referring to "Wiederaufnahme," i.e., "readmittance."

16. Reisig OHI, 5.–7.6.1989, 86.

17. Küchen in *Peenemünde: Schatten eines Mythos,* a film for the HTI Peenemünde by M. J. Blockwitz and A. Walter, 1999 version; Bode and Kaiser, *Raketenspuren,* 46; H. Raabe OHI, 15.4.1993, 20; Kütbach interview by BBC-TV, 1998, translated transcription kindly supplied by the BBC (block quote).

18. Kütbach interview by BBC-TV, 1998; WvB SS file card, former BDC records, BABL.

19. Kershaw, *Hitler 1936–1945,* 286–310.

20. Steinhoff report for 1940, 10.1.1941, in NASM, FE769; WvB pilot log, 1933–40, WvBP-H, file 700-17.

21. WD Aktenvermerk, 24.6.1940, in NASM, FE342; Keitel to von Brauchitsch, 19.11.1940, in NASM, FE349; Neufeld, *The Rocket,* 130–33.

22. For a much more detailed discussion of key technologies, see Neufeld, *The Rocket,* chap. 3.

23. Raithel OHI, 22.4.1993, 9.

24. WvB, "Kurze Übersicht," 24.4.1941, WvB minutes, 4.8.1941, and Thiel, Vortragsnotiz, 15.9.1941, in BA/MA, RH8/v.1260 (=FE733).

25. Patt glider-missile proposal, 16.6.1939, NASM, PGM, P. Archive Report 71/1; sketch of manned glider missile, 1941?, in DM, Peenemünde records; "The Memoirs of Rudolf Hermann," ms., c. 1989, 18–19, courtesy of Mrs. R. Hermann; Wegener, *Peenemünde Wind Tunnels,* 41–42; WvB minutes of meeting, 25.2.1941, in NASM, FE728f, re: Bothe's cyclotron; and Thiel to Schumann, 31.8.1941, in BA/MA, RH8/v.1260, requesting permission to attend monthly meetings of the nuclear group with WvB. (There is no evidence they actually did.) Ernst Stuhlinger claims that von Braun successfully diverted fifteen tons of steel to Bothe's cyclotron: Stuhlinger OHI by Tatarewicz, 2. and 5.4.1984, NASM. In the fall of 1942 Thiel let a study contract to the Forschungsanstalt der deutschen Reichspost that included nuclear rockets as a topic; see Thiel to Gerwig, 16.9.42, in FE692f; Ordnance contract, 15.10.1942, in FE331.

26. Zwicky interrogation of WvB, 22.5.1945, in U.S. Army Ordnance, *Story of Peenemünde,* 255 ("Braun was [saw?] Heisenberg in 1942 the last time."); S&O, *WvB* (Amer. ed.), 144. On Heisenberg and the German bomb project there is huge literature; see esp. Cassidy, *Uncertainty;* Walker, *German National Socialism* and *Nazi Science;* for extreme pro- and anti-Heisenberg views, see Powers, *Heisenberg's War,* and Rose, *Heisenberg and the Nazi Atomic Bomb Project,* respectively. In the 1970s WvB told the intelligence historian David Kahn that "German nuclear physicists with whom I talked in the 1943/44 time frame, told me that a bomb could probably be built if a large isotope separation plant were [*sic*] constructed. But they felt that even if the building of such a plant was attempted as a high-priority project it probably could not be completed in view of the incessant Allied bombings." WvB to Kahn, c. summer 1974, handwritten draft in WvBP-H, file 411-16.

27. For detailed information on Oberth and the Third Reich, see Neufeld, "The Excluded."

28. Graupe, "Berechnung . . . ," 29.7.1940, TA/Proj., "Entwicklungsstand der Gleiteraggregate," 21.1.1941, Roth? calculations, 9.9.1941, and Roth, "Zweistufenaggregat," c. 9.1941, in DM, Peenemünde archive; WD, *V-2,* 141–43.

29. For details and references, see Neufeld, *The Rocket,* 135–39.

30. MvB, *Die Freiherren*, 53–54, 56; von Thadden/Aus. Amt to MvB, 23.7.1941, and "Kurzer Bericht nach den Erzählungen von Sigismund und Hilde seit der Besetzung von Addis Abeba durch die Engländer," n.d. (early 1943), in MvB Papers in possession of C.-F. vB; on the Wolfsschanze, see Kershaw, *Hitler 1936–1945*, 395–96. The only opaque reference in Dornberger's memoir to this visit appears to be WD, *V-2*, 71.

31. WD, Vortragsnotiz, 31.7.1941, in NASM, 342, and Aktennotiz, 21.8.1941, in NASM, FE341; film scripts in NASM, FE338.

32. WD, Aktennotiz, 21.8.1941, in NASM, FE341; Neufeld, *The Rocket*, 140–43; WvB? report, c. 10.12.1941, BA/MA, RH8/v.1955.

33. WD to HVP, 7.11.1941, in BA/MA, RH8/v.1260 (initialed by WvB, 11.11.1941). A little more on the explosions is found in the minutes of the 1.11.1941 meeting, ibid., and Thiel, "Zündung A 4" report, 7.11.1941, in NASM, FE728e.

34. WD to HVP, 7.11.1941, in BA/MA, RH8/v.1260 (quote); WvB, "Einsatzmöglichkeiten des Strahlantriebs zur Bekämpfung feindlicher Nachtangriffe," 27.5.1941, NASM, PGM, P. Archive Report 58/1; v. Zborowski NSDAP and SS records in former BDC records, now BABL, microfilm in NACP; Neufeld, *The Rocket*, 150–53.

35. WD to HVP, 13.11.1941, in NASM, FE342.

36. Stegmaier minutes of 3.–4.9.1941 meeting at LZ, in NASM, FE728b; WvB to Stegmaier, 3.10.1941, in BA/MA, RH8/v.1260; WvB minutes of meeting, 16.12.1941, in NASM, FE728f; WD to HVP, 23.12.1941, in NASM, FE728e.

37. WD to Peenemünde, 5.2.1942, in NASM, file "Peenemünde #2."

38. Thiel report, 20.3.1942, and WvB minutes of 23.4.1942 meeting in NASM, FE692f.

39. WD minutes of 3.3.1942 meeting, in NASM, FE357; WD order, 6.6.1942, in BA/MA, RH8/v.1959.

40. Speer, *Inside*, 367; MvB to WvB, 9.2.1958, in BAK, N1085/84.

41. Speer, *Inside*, 367; Steinhoff? report, 31.7.1942, NASM, PGM, P. Archive Report 96/24; WvB to *Missiles and Rockets*, 21.4.1959 (porcupine quote), in WvBP-H, file 201-6.

42. WvB to Stegmaier, 29.7.1942, in BA/MA, RH8/v.1954; Neufeld, *The Rocket*, 105–7.

43. WvB, "Behind the Scenes," ms. 1950, WvBP-H, file 702-20; Thiel minutes of 21.8.1942 meeting in NASM, FE358.

44. WD minutes of 13.6.1942 meeting, and WD to Heeresanstalt Peenemünde (HAP), 29.9.1942, in NASM, FE342.

45. WvB to parents, 29.9.1956, in BAK, N1085/84.

CHAPTER 7

1. Klemperer, *I Will Bear Witness*, 2:118.

2. The following launch description is largely drawn from WD, *V-2*, 3–14, with material on the countdown in Michels, *Peenemünde*, 40. Von Braun always mentioned the launch's importance in his various memoirs but never left a detailed description.

3. WD, *V-2*, 6–7; Michels, *Peenemünde*, 40; Dannenberg, "Present at the Creation," 62.

4. Ibid., 8–13.

5. Ibid., 13–14; WvB, "Behind the Scenes," WvBP-H, file 702-20, p. 25.

6. Speer-Chronik, 4.–6.10.1942, in BABL, R3/1736, S.87; WD to Hartmann/Arm. Min., 6.10.1942, in FE342; WvB, "Programm S," 10.10.1942, in NASM file "Peenemünde #2."

7. Stegmaier, "Sonderbefehl," 10.10.1942, in NASM file "Peenemünde #2."

8. WvB, Protokoll of 26.9.1942 meeting, BA/MA, RH8/v.1258; v. Axthelm cover memo, 18.9.1942, and Göring Flak program, 1.9.1942, in NASM, FE738/4; WvB, "Die Entwicklung einer gesteuerten Flakrakete," 2.11.1942, NASM, PGM, P. Archive Report 58/3.

9. WD to Stegmaier (for WvB), 9.10.1942, in NASM FE728f, and WvB to WD, 16.10.1942, in DM, Peenemünde records.

10. Führer-Protokoll, 13.–14.10.1942, in Boelcke, *Deutschlands Rüstung*, 194; Führer-Protokoll, 22.11.1942, in Hillgruber, ed., *Kriegstagebuch*, 2:1312.

11. WvB, "Behind the Scenes," ms. 1950, WvBP-H, file 702-20; WvB, "Die befestigte Abschussstelle für A 4," 27.11.1942, in DM, Peenemünde records; Reisig OHI, 55–56.

12. "Versuchsschiessen A4," c. 7.1943, in DM, Peenemünde records, pictured in Michels, *Peenemünde*, 43; Reisig, *Raketenforschung*, 475–78; Schubert chronicle, 11.12.1942, in BA/MA, RH8/v.1209.

13. WD, "Aktenvermerk," 24.12.1942, in NASM, FE355; WD, *V-2*, 73–74, describes a similar meeting with WvB present, but gives a different (very likely incorrect) date. Dornberger's memoirs are a valuable source but are egocentric, unreliable, and, when it comes to the SS and concentration camp issues, dishonest.

14. WD, *V-2*, 75; Degenkolb to WvB, 29.1.1943, in NASM, FE732; WvB, "Behind the Scenes," ms. 1950, WvBP-H, file 702-20 ("which made"); WvB to Degenkolb, 17.2.1954 ("often"), WvBP-H, file 412-7.

15. Raithel OHI, 22.4.1994, 11–12; Allen, *Business of Genocide*, 210–11.

16. Schubert chronicle, 11.12.1942, in BA/MA, RH8/v.1209; Berger to Himmler, 16.12.1942, in NARA, T-175/R117/2642360 (quote).

17. Stegmaier to Berger, 16.1.1943, Berger to Himmler, 1.2.1943, and Himmler to Berger, 8.2.1943, in T-175/R124/2599320-322; WD, *V-2*, chap. 18. Note that Dornberger's date for Himmler's first visit is also off by five months.

18. Himmler's file on the Zanssen affair is in NACP, T-175/R124/25999300-319, -323; see also Neufeld, *The Rocket*, 180–83. Von Braun later believed that this affair was due to a conspiracy by SS-General Hans Kammler—see, e.g., his "Reminiscences," 142. This presumption is wrong.

19. Kershaw, *Hitler 1936–1945*, 551; Fest, *Speer*, 210–11; Hölsken, *Die V-Waffen*, 93–114; Degenkolb, "Fertigungsprogramm A4," 2.4.1943, and WvB "Rundschreiben," 30.4.1943, in NASM, FE732; WD memo, 24.4.1943, in BA/MA, RH8/v.1959; Freund and Perz, *Das KZ*, 62.

20. Wagner, "Zwangsarbeit," 17; Stegmaier "Sonderbefehl," 10.10.1942, in NASM file "Peenemünde #2"; Rudolph Aktennotiz, 9.2.1943, BA/MA, RH8/v.1210.

21. Schubert chronicle, 8.–9.4., Rudolph Aktennotiz, 16.4.1943, in BA/MA, RH8/v.1210. See Allen, *Business of Genocide*, for an entrée into the literature on SS concentration camp labor.

22. Schubert chronicle, 2.6., 17.6., and 11.7.1943, and Storch Aktenvermerk of 2.6.1943 meeting, all ibid.; WD memo, 24.4.1943, in BA/MA, RH8/v.1959; Wagner, "Zwangsarbeit," 18–19. For further elaboration on the army side, see Neufeld, *The Rocket*, 184–89.

23. One searches WvB's published 1950s memoirs "Why I Chose America," "Reminiscences," and "Space Man" in vain for any such mention; references even to the later horrors of Dora are generally vague and unspecific. Dornberger, on the other hand, explicitly lies in denying the use of foreign labor in Peenemünde (see WD, *V-2*, 192) and completely omits any reference to the later use of concentration camp labor in the program.

For commentary on the myth of a clean Peenemünde, see Wagner, "Zwangsarbeit in Peenemünde," 15–16; for a shorter version, see Wagner's article in Erichsen and Hoppe, *Peenemünde*, 43–52.

24. K. F. Baudrexl in Hess and Seidel, *Vernichtung*, 17 ("murderers . . ."); Huzel, *From Peenemünde*, 112–13; Gellately, *Backing Hitler*, esp. chaps. 3 and 9 and "Conclusions."

25. Clarke, *Astounding Days*, 184.

26. WvB, "Space Man," 20.7.1958, 24 (quote). For Speer's denials, see Schmidt, *Albert Speer*, and above all Sereny, *Albert Speer*. For public knowledge, see Johnson, *Nazi Terror*, chaps. 10–12, and Gellately, *Backing Hitler*, chap. 6.

27. WD, *V-2*, chap. 19 and photo insert; Heimburg OHI, 9.11.1989; WvB SS file card, NACP and BABL, BDC records on SS officers; Schubert chronicle, 12.6.1943, and Stegmaier program for Himmler visit, 28.6.1943, BA/MA, RH8/v.1210. Dornberger's chapter makes it appear that he was an apolitical engineer who even gently questioned Himmler about atrocities, but his own notebooks show him publicly declaring himself a Nazi enthusiast. See WD draft talk, 12.5.1943, in DM, WD notebook #1. The lowest German general's rank at the time was Generalmajor, equivalent to a British brigadier or an American one-star general.

28. WvB-Brill engagement announcement, 1.1.1943, copy from O. Halmburger/Loopfilm, original owned by Harald Tresp; WvB SS 1943 marriage file in NACP, BDC microfilm, RuSHA roll A5161, frames 1364–1406, original in BABL (WvB letters, 25.3. and 5.4.1943, frames 1378 and 1386).

29. Warsitz form dated 24.4.1943, NACP, BDC microfilm, RuSHA roll A5161, frames 1398–1400. Warsitz gives his party number as 379,289, a pre-1933 number. The Einwohnermeldekartei in the Landesarchiv Berlin has a card for Brill, which gives her father's title as "Dr. Reg. Rat [Regierungs-Rat]," a fairly high civil service title; she moved to Dresden 1.5.1936, presumably for university, and returned to her parents' house on 20.1.1940. On 10.4.1943 they moved to an address in Berlin-Wilmersdorf. WvB gave a different address for her five days earlier, presumably temporary lodging after the raid. No further moves are noted, undoubtedly due to the chaos at the end of the war in Berlin. Berlin researcher Dr. Frank Stucke's attempts in the late 1990s to trace Brill got nowhere; she may well have been killed or became a refugee, or married and changed her name. Klaus Riedel's widow made a passing reference to the failed engagement in a 1987 interview in Günzel, *Die fliegenden Flüssigkeitsraketen*, 104.

30. WvB-parents correspondence, fall 1946, in BAK, N1085/83; interview with Christina vB, Berlin, 20.9.2002; Hürter et al., *Biographisches Handbuch*, 263–64; SvB, "Memoiren," courtesy Christina vB, 36, 39–40; MvB Sr. to Frau Margis, 8.9.1939, "Kurze Bericht," c. 1.1943, and SS-Ahnentafel, c. 1943, in MvB Papers in possession of C.-F. vB, Munich; D. Kersten Schlidt filmed interview by Mausbach/Loopfilm, 1.5.2004, courtesy ZDF. I still wonder about the latter's explanation, as his mother had already approved the engagement. One alternative possibility is Jewish ancestry on Brill's side that violated the strict SS criteria. Rigg, *Hitler's Jewish Soldiers*, describes many cases of the unwanted discovery of previously unknown Jewish ancestors.

31. G. Friede filmed interview by Loopfilm, c. 2003, courtesy ZDF; Frederick Cook draft article, c. 11.1948, in NACP, RG319, IRR/PNF WvB, Box 657A.

32. Fernande to WvB, 30.3.1963 (stamped received 9.4.1963), and handwritten German translation by WvB, in WvBP-H, file 422-2. Translated passages are from the German version. Unlike Brill, her name has never been published; thus the last name is withheld.

33. Ibid.

34. WvB to Degenkolb, 6.3., WvB to WD, 7.5., and WvB to Steinhoff et al., 26.6.1943, in NASM, FE732; Thiel to WvB, 16.3.1943, in NASM, FE692f; WvB Protokolle of 7.5. and 14.5.1943 meetings in NASM, FE738/1.

35. WD Aktennotiz of 26.5. event, 29.5.1943, in BA/MA, RH8/v.1954 (=FE1092); Waeger/Arm. Min. "DE" order, 2.6.1943, in NASM file "Peenemünde #2."

36. WD, *V-2*, 100–101; Himmler notes on Hitler visit, 10.7.1943, in BABL, NS19/1474.

37. Ibid., 101; Speer, *Inside*, 368; Tessmann OHI, 23.1.1990.

38. WD, *V-2*, 102–6. For evidence of Dornberger's earlier statements, see Neufeld, *The Rocket*, chaps. 4–6.

39. Ruland, *WvB*, 141; see also Ward, *WvB Anekdotisch*, 85–86.

40. Ruland, *WvB*, 141–2 (diploma pictured on 141), Speer minutes of Hitler meeting, 8.7.1943, in Boelcke, *Deutschlands Rüstung*, 280.

41. Kehrl, *Krisenmanager*, 336; Speer, *Inside*, 368 ("extremely cordial . . .").

42. Ward, *WvB Anekdotisch*, 28. In his WvB SS 1943 marriage application, 5.4.1943, in NACP, BDC microfilm, RuSHA roll A5161, frame 1382, he gives his confession as "evangelisch" (Protestant).

43. For details and sources, see Neufeld, *The Rocket*, 192–95.

44. WD, *V-2*, 147–54; O&S, *Rocket Team*, 114; Stüwe, *Peenemünde-West*, 244–45, 657. I have found no document that confirms the 17.8.1943 meeting so vividly depicted in Dornberger's memoirs. It may be a dramatization based in part on other meetings, but the problems were real.

45. O&S, *Rocket Team*, 114; Ruland, *WvB*, 159; Klee and Merk, *Birth of the Missile*, 66; MvB Jr. IRR file, INSCOM FOIA; MvB Jr. "Basic Personnel Record," 11.1945, NACP, RG165, E.179, Box 703, file "Boston." The initial attempt to get him had been overruled, and he had been sent to fighter school, indicating that such service may have been imminent.

46. WvB quoted in O&S, *Rocket Team*, 114–15.

47. For a careful examination of what happened, see Middlebrook, *Peenemünde Raid*.

48. Werner Magirus quoted ibid., 152. See also WD, *V-2*, 158–60, which has him and von Braun leaving while the bombs are still falling, which is unlikely.

49. Bornträger to WvB, 25.6.1959, in WvBP-H, file 414-6; Kersten quoted in Ruland, *WvB*, 167 (he attributes it to Hannelore Bannasch, but this is a mistake, as Kersten Schlidt gives virtually a word-for-word identical story in her filmed interview by Mausbach/Loopfilm, 1.5.2004, courtesy ZDF); O&S, *Rocket Team*, 116–17, copies Ruland's mistake.

50. WD, *V-2*, 166–68.

51. Huzel, *From Peenemünde*, 58.

52. Werner Jagenow interview, 15.7.2000; WvB to Schneer, 2.1.1959, in WvBP-H, file 208-2.

53. Speer minutes of Hitler meetings, 19.–22.8.1943, in Boelcke, *Deutschlands Rüstung*, 291; Magirus to WvB, Rees, and Maus, ?.8.1943, and WvB? Protokoll, 25.8.1943, in NASM, FE732.

54. WvB? Protokoll, 25.8.1943, in NASM, FE732; WvB pilot log, 1943–44, in WvBP-H, file 700-17; Speer office chronicle, 26.8.1943, in BABL, R3/1738, S.10.

55. WvB pilot log, 1943–44, in WvBP-H, file 700-17; Bornemann, *Geheimprojekt Mittelbau*, 21–30; Wagner, *Produktion*, 184–86. The repeated statements of S&O, *WvB*, that he first visited the Mittelwerk on 25.1.1944 is a commentary on the competence of their research.

56. "Bericht" on Komm. f. Fernschiessen meeting, 9.9.1943, in NARA, T-971/R11/11-

22; WvB pilot log, 1943–44, in WvBP-H, file 700-17; Speer minutes of Hitler meetings, 19–22.8.1943, in Boelcke, *Deutschlands Rüstung,* 291.

57. Freund, *Arbeitslager Zement,* 52–62; WvB pilot log, 1943–44, in WvBP-H, file 700-17; WvB, "Vorschläge zur künftigen Sicherung der Weiterentwicklung gegen feindliche Luftangriffe," 2.10.1943, in NASM, FE692f.

58. See Neufeld, *The Rocket,* 203–4, 287–88, for details.

59. WD, *V-2,* 108–9; WvB to parents, 30.10.1946, in BAK, N1085/83. On Kammler's biography, see Allen, *Business of Genocide,* esp. 53–56, 140–64.

60. WvB pilot log, 1943–44, in WvBP-H, file 700-17; Wagner, *Produktion,* 216–17.

61. Michel, *Dora,* 70; Wagner, *Produktion,* 184–91; Sellier, *History,* 58–86. For another powerful memoir by a French survivor see Béon, *Planet Dora;* Sellier is also a survivor.

62. WvB deposition, 7.2.1969, New Orleans, NWHSA, Zweigarchiv Schloss Kalkum, Ger. Rep. 299/160, S. 69–80; excerpt from 1976 interview in WGBH transcript of *Frontline* program, "The Nazi Connection," broadcast 24.2.1987, courtesy Robert Smith. See also WvB's answers to Georg Rickhey's defense lawyers in the Nordhausen war crimes trial at Dachau for an early classified reference to the "primitive" conditions at the outset of the Mittelwerk: WvB, "Sworn Statement," Fort Bliss, 14.10.1947, NARA, M-1079/R4/168-175 (German, R12/337-48).

63. Ruland, *WvB,* 236; WvB to *Paris Match,* 26.4.1966, quoted in S&O, *WvB* (Amer. ed.), 53 (for a much fuller quotation of the letter in German translation, see the German ed., 113–17). My interpretation here is influenced by Weyer, *WvB,* 60–62.

64. Ward, *WvB Anekdotisch,* 31.

65. According to SS-Colonel Gerhardt Maurer, who was involved in labor allocation to the camps (and was thus himself a major war criminal), Kammler deliberately violated his promise to build the aboveground camp at Dora quickly. See NARA, M-1079/R9/447-50.

66. S&O, *WvB* (German ed.), 103–5 and (Amer. ed.) 44–45. The other eight sites were Peenemünde, Friedrichshafen, Rax-Werke, Heidelager, Schlier, Zement, Mitte, and Rebstock (underground production of A-4 operational vehicles)—and this list does not even include any subcontractors other than Zeppelin.

67. Kunze Protokoll, 1.11.1943, and WvB to Degenkolb, 12.11.1943, with his draft of 10.11. and written and typed calculations in NASM, FE732. On "Mitte" near Lehesten, see Gropp, *Aussenkommando Laura.* According to locals, WvB visited at least twice: see 36–37. On the Nuremberg standard for crimes against humanity, I am grateful to Eli Rosenbaum of OSI for his 23.7.1985 paper "Rudolph: The Speer Analogy."

68. "Lagebericht A 4," 5.12.1944, in BA/MA, RH8/v.1954; WvB pilot log, 1943–44, in WvBP-H, file 700-17.

69. "Lagebericht A 4," 5.12.1944, in BA/MA, RH8/v.1954.

70. WvB "Rundschreiben," 4.2.1944, in NASM, FE692f; Wegener, *Peenemünde Wind Tunnels,* 65–67, 85 ("tug-of-war," 65).

71. Franklin, *An American,* 78–79, 311.

72. Kettler and Förschner, "Sonder-Direktionsanweisung D," 8.1.1944, in BABL, NS 4 Anhang/3; WvB deposition, 7.2.1969, New Orleans, NWHSA, Zweigarchiv Schloss Kalkum, Ger. Rep. 299/160, S. 76; E. Verheyn interrogation, in NARA, M-1079/R4/788, 790, and Sawatzki interrogation, 14.4.1945, same, R4/761-62; Seidenstücker accusation in U.N. War Crimes Commission file 1192/Fr/G/523, kindly supplied by Eli Rosenbaum.

73. Rossmann Protokoll of Kammler visit, 11.2.1944, in NASM, FE692c; Walter II and K?, "Bericht zur Dienstreise vom 12.2. bis 19.2.44 nach MW," NASM, PGM, P. Archive Report 72/31.

CHAPTER 8

1. Lindbergh, *Autobiography of Values*, 348–49.

2. WvB pilot log, 1943–44, in WvBP-H, file 700-17; Ruland, *WvB*, 187; WD, *V-2*, 185. There is no independent evidence as to this meeting, other than the dubious recollection of Helmut Hoelzer that WvB told the tale in the Peenemünde Officers' Club: Hoelzer, OHI, 10.11.1989. But he told it often enough and consistently enough, and there is no obvious reason why he would make up such a tall tale. As to timing, he usually remembered it as February. He told Ruland that the call came in after his return from a very difficult, weather-plagued flight from Heidelager, which appears to coincide with the flight log trip of 30.–31.1.1944, but it ended in the morning at Prenzlau, instead of Peenemünde at night. Moreover, Himmler was not in Hochwald on 1 February, so von Braun must have mixed up the two flights. Himmler was there 7–11 and 18–22 February: Himmler Kalendarnotizen, 1944, in BABL, NS19/1444. So the most likely date is the twenty-second in the morning, before Himmler's train left for the south.

3. WvB undated note to Bart Slattery, re: 16.6.1964 letter of David Irving, and Slattery to Irving, 20.7.1964, in WvBP-H, file 437-12; WvB, "Behind the Scenes," in same, file 702-20, pp. 30–31; WvB, "Space Man," 20.7.1958, 24; Ruland, *WvB*, 193.

4. Rossmann's Protokoll of Kammler's visit to Peenemünde, 11.2.1944, in NASM, FE692c.

5. Speer, *Inside*, 323–35; Schmidt, *Albert Speer*, 87–99; Fest, *Speer*, 268–78.

6. Ruland, *WvB*, 202; WvB, "Behind the Scenes," WvBP-H, file 702-20, p. 31 ("payoff"); WvB, "Why I Chose America," 112. Regarding timing, there is a gap in flights from 19.3. to 5.4.1944 in WvB's pilot log, 1943–44, in WvBP-H, file 700-17, and there are minutes for a meeting at Dornberger's headquarters in Schwedt on 21.3.1944, in NASM, FE692c, which show Gröttrup and "Braun" (WvB?) as present. Perhaps this was the long, exhausting trip. Gröttrup wrote a note about the arrest on 10.8.1955, after he had returned from the USSR, dating it at 21.3.1944, which might be interpreted as that night (copy of note from G. Papers courtesy O. Przybilski).

7. Ruland, *WvB*, 202; MvB, *Weg*, 168–69.

8. Jodl diary, 8.3.1944, NARA, T-77/R1429/144-45, typed version T-77/R1430/923; Luise Jodl to WvB, 16.2.1938 [*sic:* 1958], in WvBP-H, file 405-1; Bergaust, *WvB*, 78–79; Ruland, *WvB*, 193–95. Ruland's assertion that the party was on 5.3.1944 is contradicted by WvB's flight log; perhaps it was Saturday the fourth.

9. For a nonconspiratorial interpretation, see Allen, *Business of Genocide*, 264–65, 343n77.

10. WD, *V-2*, 200–201; Kershaw, *Hitler 1936–1945*, 623.

11. WD, *V-2*, 201–3.

12. WvB note to Wiesman, 24.2.1959, in WvBP-H, file 208-2; Ward, *WvB Anekdotisch*, 98; Ruland, *WvB*, 203, 205, 207.

13. WD, *V-2*, 203–5; O&S, *Rocket Team*, 46–47; Ruland, *WvB*, 209.

14. Ruland, *WvB*, 203, 207–8; WvB, "Why I Chose America," 112 ("political remarks").

15. Ruland, *WvB*, 207–8; WvB, "Space Man," 20.7.1958, 24 ("red trouser stripes"); WD, *V-2*, 206.

16. Speer, *Inside*, 371–72; Speer minutes of Hitler meetings, 13.5.1944, in Boelcke, *Deutschlands Rüstung*, 362.

17. WvB in *Proceedings of "The Next Ten Thousand Years": A Scientific Symposium* (New York, 22.11.1957), 59–60, copy in NASER, RG 255, WvB's Speeches, Box 5.

18. WvB responses to Reid questionnaire, attached to Slattery to Reid, 17.5.1968, in WvBP-H, file 228-38; Wegener, *Peenemünde Wind Tunnels,* 48–49.

19. WvB, "Organisation der Abschlussentwicklung A4 und seiner Bodeneinrichtungen," 25.4.1944, in DM, Pers. 00019 (with thanks to J. Weyer); Sawatzki Aktenvermerk, 16.4.1944, in NASM, FE694a.

20. Wagner, *Produktion,* 95–96, 224–26; Bornemann, *Geheimprojekt,* 81; Speer (Saur) minutes of Hitler meeting, 5.3.1944, in Boelcke, *Deutschlands Rüstung,* 341; König to Steinhoff, 1.4.1944, and König to WvB, 11.4.1944, in NASM, FE738/1; Allen, *Business of Genocide,* 232–39; Irving, *Mare's Nest,* 220–22.

21. Sawatzki Aktenvermerk, 16.4.1944, in WvB circular to all sections, 10.7.1944, in NASM, FE694a; Neufeld, *The Rocket,* 224–25.

22. "Niederschrift über die Besprechung am 6.5.1944 . . . ," NASM FE331; Boerner testimony, 10.11.1947, in NARA, M-1079/R10/786-87 ("push back").

23. Rickhey and Kettler, "Sonder-Direktions-Anweisung," 22.6.1944, in BABL, NS4 Anhang/3; Wagner, *Produktion,* chap. 6 (on "mobile selection").

24. Georges Jouanin account attached to letter to MJN, 9.9.1997, translated by G. de Syon.

25. Jouanin to Neufeld, 17.12.1997. See Neufeld, "Wernher von Braun, the SS . . . ," 69–72, for further discussion of the problematic evidence, and another case that is more likely his brother Magnus. In this article I described incidents as being possible cases of mistaken identity, but the Jouanin case still seems intriguingly believable as Wernher von Braun.

26. Charles Sadron, "Á la Usine de Dora," 198–99; "Sadron (Charles, Louis)," *Who's Who in France,* 1969–70 ed., excerpt supplied by André Sellier; Sellier, *History,* 105–6, 129–30, 134. The visit to Sadron is confirmed by Sellier, who worked with Sadron. Sellier to MJN, 27.10.1999.

27. WvB to Sawatzki, 15.8.1944, DM, GD 638.8.2 (= NASM, FE694a); for context see also Röhner to WvB, 8.8.1944, ibid. On Dr. Hellmut Simon (not to be confused with SS-Oberscharführer Wilhelm Simon, responsible for the Arbeitseinsatzbüro of Mittelbau-Dora), see Wagner, *Produktion,* 197n69.

28. Neufeld, "Wernher von Braun, the SS . . . ," and Stuhlinger response in Neufeld and Stuhlinger, "Wernher von Braun and Concentration Camp Labor: An Exchange"; Röhner to WvB, 8.8., and WvB to Sawatzki, 15.8.1944, DM, GD 638.8.2; Wagner, *Produktion,* 641; Eli Rosenbaum, "Rudolph: The Speer Analogy," 23.7.1985, courtesy of the author. No flight is shown in von Braun's log for 18.–31.7.1944, and indeed none to Nordhausen after 29.6., but it is just at this point that his flying declined drastically, no doubt because Allied heavy bomber attacks on refineries in June and July caused a crippling fuel crisis.

29. WvB to Heinrich Walther, 1.10.1955, copy from Walther's memoir in WvBP-H, file 429-1; Seidel, *Nachbarn auf dem Ettersberg.*

30. WvB "Qualification Sheet . . . ," 10.6.1945, NACP, RG319, IRR PNF WvB, Box 657A.

31. Hölsken, *Die V-Waffen,* 106–7, 129–36; 190–91; Speer minutes of Hitler meetings, 19.–22.6.1944, in Boelcke, *Deutschlands Rüstung,* 385; Irving, *Mare's Nest,* 229–60; Gestapo Sonderkommission minutes of interrogation of Hildegard Margis, 21.9.1944, courtesy Christina vB.

32. WvB minutes, 4.4.1944, and Reissinger minutes of 1.6.1944 meeting, in BA/MA, RH8/v.1278; Kiefer Aktenvermerk to WvB and others, 8.7.1944, in NASM, FE388; WD, *V-2*, 217–21.

33. Steinhoff to T10, 23.6.1944, in BA/MA, RH8/v.1278; WvB to Arthur C. Clarke, 30.8.1951, in WvBP-H, file 400-2; WD, *V-2*, 228–30.

34. WD, *V-2*, 220–24; WvB, "Space Man," 20.7.1958, 25 ("was standing . . ."), and "Behind the Scenes" (ms., 1950), ibid., file 702-20, 32 (insert) ("got up . . ."); Raithel OHI, 22.4.1993.

35. WD to Fromm, 31.5.1944, in BA/MA, RH8/v.3730; "Die Aufgaben der Elektro-mechanischen Werke G.m.b.H. (EMW)," 28.6.44, in FE692f; WD, *V-2*, 209; "Abschrift, Durchführungsbestimmungen," c. 1.8.1944, in DM, Peenemünde archives (FE1224/1).

36. Storch to WvB, 1.2., and WvB marg. comment, 10.2.1944, in DM, GD 620.0.10 (FE1727); Huzel, *From Peenemünde*, 106, 123–26 (quote, 123); EW GmbH "Organisa-tionsplan," 1.8.1944, in NASM, FE424; Rees OHI, 8.11.1989; "Werdegang, Arbeiten der Vorkriegszeit und Leistungen im Kriege des Professors Dr. von Braun," c. late 1943, in NASM, FE341.

37. WvB pilot log, 1943–44, in WvBP-H, file 700-17; S&O, *WvB* (Amer. ed.), 56; Huzel, *From Peenemünde*, 102–5, 110–15; Dannenberg OHI, 7.1.1989; Kunze "Fahrbe-fehl," 20.10.1944, in NASM, FE732; Nimwegen to Sawatzki, 9.1.1945, in NASM, FE694a; Riedel death announcement, 5.8.1944, in BA/MA, RH8/v.1941. One persistent rumor has it that the Gestapo sawed through Riedel's axle to kill him, but this story lacks credi-bility.

38. See Neufeld, *The Rocket*, 239, 244–46, for details and sources.

39. WD, *V-2*, 236–37.

40. Huzel, *From Peenemünde*, 118–19; Kersten Schlidt to Stuhlinger, 1987, quoted in S&O, *WvB* (Amer. ed.), 55; Hölsken, *Die V-Waffen*, 108–9. Another oft-repeated story, which first surfaces in the 1950s, was that von Braun remarked that "we hit the wrong planet." He actually first used that phrase in question form as a section title in his 1950 manuscript memoir. After publication six years later, it took on a life of its own. See WvB, "Behind the Scenes," WvBP-H, file 702-20, 32, "Reminiscences," 144, and "Space Man," 20.7.1958, 25 (where the ghostwriter puts the words in his mouth).

41. Bergaust, *WvB*, 95; Heimburg OHI, 9.11.1989; Herken, *Brotherhood*, 139–40; Weyer, *WvB*, 71.

42. MvB, *Weg*, 305–6; SvB, *Flüchtige Gäste*, 40–59, 118–20; Hürter et al., *Biograph-isches Handbuch*, 263–64; WvB to Schneer, 2.1.1959, in WvBP-H, file 208-2; Carola vB interview, 18.12.2000, Berlin; SvB, "Memoiren," 40, 46–49, courtesy Christina vB; MvB Jr. testimony for Dachau Nordhausen trial, Fort Bliss, Tex., 14.10.1947, NARA, M-1079/R4/184; Huzel, *From Peenemünde*, 116–17.

43. Captured Personnel and Materiel Branch report, 26.–27.3.1945, in NACP, RG 165, G-2 Library "P" File 1940–45, Box 435, Captured Personnel Material Reports AL61-100 German 1944–45; DeVorkin, *Science*, chap. 3, for Regener; Zippelius answers to MI 14/4 questionnaire, 11.10.1945, in UKNA, WO 208/3155.

44. WD, *V-2*, 210 (quote); WvB marginalia on WD, Aktenvermerk, 20.11.1944, in DM, Peenemünde records, and Contag Wasserfall monthly report, 5.11.1944, in NASM, FE738/1; WvB to Brée/RLM, 30.9., and reply, 10.10.1944, in NASM, FE333.

45. Himmler notes on Hitler meetings, 26.–27.9.1944, in BABL, NS 19/1474; Speer to Himmler, 11.11.1944, in BABL, R3/1583; W. Riedel to Rickhey, 11.12.1944, in NASM, FE694a.

46. Dungan, *V-2*, 158–59; WD quoted in O&S, *Rocket Team*, 49; W. Riedel to Rickhey,

11.12.1944, in NASM, FE694a; photos in S&O, *WvB: An Illustrated Memoir*, 27, and Hölsken, *V-Missiles*, 10. According to notes kindly supplied by T. D. Dungan, the Division z.V. war diary in BA/MA, RH26/1022/3, mentions the Varlar award ceremony for WvB.

47. Roth to WvB, 13.6.1944, in NASM, FE738/1; WvB to Rossmann, 11.8., Roth to Storch, 1.9., and Roth to Kurzweg/WVA, 6.9.1944, in DM, P. files (FE1604 and FE1081).

48. Hermann Aktenvermerke, 15.9. and 12.10., Hellebrand minutes of 4.10. meeting, and Kurzweg Aktenvermerk, 24.10.1944, in DTM, Lehnert Nachlass, A4b file; A-4b documents, fall 1944, incl. WvB minutes of 24.10.1944 meeting, in DM, GD 636.0.1; Dahm OHI, 25.1.1990; launch report, 29.12.1944, in DM, Peenemünde archive (FE1604); WD, *V-2*, 250–51.

49. See Neufeld, *The Rocket*, 252–55, for details and references.

50. Huzel Aktennotiz, 26.12.1944, in NASM, FE731; WvB to Kunze, 20.11.1944, in NASM, FE694; Freund, *Arbeitslager Zement*, 80–114; Huzel, *From Peenemünde*, 124–26; Gottschalk order, 12.12.1944, and Huzel to Geschäftsleitung EW, 23.1.1945, in NASM, FE734.

51. Zeyss interview translation courtesy of the BBC; WvB to Schneer, 2.1.1959, in WvBP-H, file 208-2; Lang, "A Romantic Urge," 78.

52. Ruland, *WvB*, 239; DeVorkin, *Science*, 36; Paetzold to Weiss, 19.1.1945, in NASM, FE679; Huzel, *From Peenemünde*, 132–33.

53. WvB, "Space Man," 27.7.1958, 11; Ruland, *WvB*, 241–43. The version of von Braun's story in Ruland's biography is short and does not mention spaceflight. Rees confirms that such discussions took place but does not describe the meeting: Rees OHI by MJN, 1989.

54. WD, *V-2*, 260–63; WD telegrams to WvB, 25.1.1945 (received 26.1.), in DM, GD 620.0.1; Kammler orders and circulars, 6.2.1945 in BABL, R26III/52; Bornemann, *Geheimprojekt Mittelbau*, 135–37.

55. Buch quoted in Bornemann, *Geheimprojekt Mittelbau*, 137–38.

56. Huzel, *From Peenemünde*, 133–36; WvB minutes of 31.1.1945 meeting, in NASM, file "Peenemünde #2"; "Wichtige Punkte aus Sch. Prof. v. B an Aufsichtsrat v. 11.2.45," in NASM, FE731.

57. Ward, *WvB Anekdotisch*, 36 (quote); Ruland, *WvB*, 245; WvB, "Why I Chose America," 112.

58. WvB and MvB Jr. to parents, 31.7. and 13.8.1946, in BAK, N1085/83; Kamenicky to WvB, 27.3.1945, in NASM, FE333; Ward, *WvB Anekdotisch*, 33; WvB, "Space Man," 27.7.1958, 11; WvB to C. Zanssen, 23.2.1955, in WvBP-H, file 412-7.

59. WvB, "Space Man," 27.7.1958, 11; WvB, "Affidavit," 18.6.1947, NACP, RG 330, Accession 70A4398; WvB, handwritten "Kommentar," undated, c. 5.1957, WvBP-H, file 208-12 (see WvB to Mainz, 29.5.1957, in file 208-7).

60. Huzel, *From Peenemünde*, 139–40.

61. WvB, minutes of 2.3.1945 meeting in NASM, FE738/1; WvB, Antrag, 6.3.1945, in BA/MA, RH8/v.852; Henze and Hebestreit, *Raketen aus Bleicherode*, 112–13.

62. Ibid.; Huzel, *From Peenemünde*, 145; Reichsnährstand inventory, 10.3.1945, in NASM, FE333; Henze and Hebestreit, *Raketen aus Bleicherode*, 80–81.

63. Wagner, *Produktion*, 267–78, 354–55; Major Eugene Smith, report on interrogations of Rudolph and others at Fort Bliss, 10.6.1947, in NARA, M1079/R1/344-59, Rudolph interrogation, 2.6.1947, R1/418–19, and WvB and MvB Jr. questionnaires, 10.14.1947, on R4/168–75, 184–88; WvB, Antrag, 6.3.1945, in BA/MA, RH8/v.852; Entwicklungsgemeinschaft docs., 16.–27.3.1945, in NASM, FE333.

64. U.S. Army file card on WvB, 4.–6.1945, in NACP, RG319, IRR PNF WvB, Box

657A, gives accident as "app. 11/3/45. . . . Entered Knappschaft Hospital Bleicherode 12/3/45"; WvB says 12.3.1945 in his interr. of 8.3.1947 in FIAT "Brief Interrogation Report" on WvB, 8.7.1947, in UKNA, FO1031/128; WvB and MvB Jr. to parents, 31.7.1946, in BAK, N1085/83; WvB, "Space Man," 27.7.1958, 11; Ruland, *WvB*, 251–52; A. Gerlach (senior nurse, Knappschaftskrankenhaus) telephone interview by MJN, 1.12., and Gerlach to MJN, 2.12.2004; Wegener/WVA trip report, 3.4.1945 (meeting with WvB in hospital, 27.3.), DTM, Lehnert Nachlass.

65. WD, *V-2*, 266–67.

66. WvB questionnaire, 14.10.1947, NARA, M1079/R4/174 (quote); Ruland, *WvB*, 253.

67. Ruland, *WvB*, 255–56; WvB questionnaire, 14.10.1947, NARA, M1079/R4/174; A. Gerlach telephone interview by MJN, 1.12., and Gerlach to MJN, 2.12.2004; WvB deposition, 7.2.1969, New Orleans, NWHSA, Zweigarchiv Schloss Kalkum, Ger. Rep. 299/160, S. 69-80; U.S. Army file card on WvB, 4.–6.1945, in NACP, RG319, IRR PNF WvB, Box 657A.

68. Ruland, *WvB*, 256–57; WvB, "Space Man," 27.7.1958, 12.

69. Ruland, *WvB*, 257–58 (quotes); WvB, "Space Man," 27.7.1958, 12–13.

70. Lang, "A Romantic Urge," 78; WD, *V-2*, 271.

71. Jak. van den Driesch to WvB, 6.1.1969, in WvBP-H, file 423-4.

CHAPTER 9

1. Diary entry, 6.2.1937, quoted in Clary, *Rocket Man*, 169.

2. Kershaw, *Hitler 1936–1945*, 832; Huzel, *From Peenemünde*, 187; WvB/MvB Jr. to parents, 31.7.1946, in BAK, N1085/83 (signed by both, but clearly written by WvB); McGovern, *Crossbow*, 142 (WD quote). WvB would later continue to remember their surrender as coming after the German one: Lang, "A Romantic Urge," 79; WvB, "Space Man," 27.7.1958, 13; Bergaust, *WvB*, 96.

3. O&S, *Rocket Team*, 1–7; Jerry Cahill, "Wis. GI Held U.S. Space Future Fate," *Milwaukee Sentinel*, 12.2.1958, copy in NASM, WvB bio. file; McGovern, *Crossbow*, 143–45.

4. O&S, *Rocket Team*, 7–10; Huzel, *From Peenemünde*, 187–90; Lang, "A Romantic Urge," 79 (von Braun quotes).

5. Quoted in Bergaust, *WvB*, 96.

6. Bergaust, *WvB*, 96–97 (GI quote); WvB quoted in "V-2 Inventor Says He Could Have Won the War If He Had Been Given Two More Years," *Beachhead News*, 11.5.1945, copy in NASM, WvB bio. file.

7. Huzel, *From Peenemünde*, 190–92; O&S, *Rocket Team*, 11. (The latter puts WvB in an assembly point in Peiting, but Huzel doesn't remember him there.) The best general discussions of U.S. policy are found in Gimbel's works and in Judt and Ciesla, *Technology Transfer*. Still useful are Lasby, *Project Paperclip*, and McGovern, *Crossbow*.

8. Captured Personnel Material reports B-519, 6.12.1943, and B-761, 31.10.44, in NACP, RG 165, G-2 Library "P" File, Box 430; "German Scientists and Research Workers" sheet, c. 4.1945, in NACP, RG319, IRR/PNF WvB, Box 657A; Uhl, *Stalins V-2*, 32–40; Wagner, *Produktion*, 267–88; Sellier, *History*, 265–394.

9. Von Braun family correspondence, 1945–46, in BAK, N1085/83. On the impact of the expulsion on German memory of the Third Reich, see Moeller, *War Stories*, 1–87. For post-1945 memory, see also Herf, *Divided Memory*, and Frei, *Adenauer's Germany*.

10. Jessel, "Special Screening Report," 12.6.1945, Appendix A to Osborne to G-2/ USFET, 29.10.1945, NACP, RG260, OMGUS/FIAT, Box 8, file 471.94; Huzel, *From Peenemünde*, 193; Eisfeld, *Mondsüchtig*, 161–63.

11. Jessel report, 12.6.1945, NACP, RG260, OMGUS/FIAT, Box 8, file 471.94; Rudolph "Qualification Sheet for German Scientific Personnel," ?.6.1945, in NACP, RG319, IRR/PNF A.L.H. Rudolph, Box 636.

12. Jessel report, 12.6.1945, NACP, RG260, OMGUS/FIAT, Box 8, file 471.94; WvB "Qualification Sheet," 10.6.1945, in NACP, RG319, IRR/PNF WvB, Box 657A; Chertok, *Rockets*, 306–7.

13. Interrogation by Gollin and Stokes, 15.5.1945, and WvB, "Survey," in U.S. Army Ordnance, *Story of Peenemünde* (also known as *Peenemünde-East*), 241–54; quotes from corrected version of "Survey" in Zwicky, *Report*, 66–72 (quotes, 66).

14. WvB, "Survey," in Zwicky, *Report*, 66–72.

15. WvB interrogations in *Story of Peenemünde*, 212–19, 229–32, 235–46, 255–56; Trichel to Quinn, 23.5.1945, in NASM, Porter Papers, Box 4; McGovern, *Crossbow*, 151–55.

16. Bromley report to Chief, E.E.I.S., 7.6.1945, in NACP, RG156, E.1039A, Box 87; McGovern, *Crossbow*, 155–60.

17. Staver to Quinn, 26.5. and 16.6.1945, Staver to Ritchie, 23.5.1946, and Peifer notes on interview with Staver, 4.6.1962, in NACP, RG156, E.1039A, Box 87; Staver to Quinn, 29.5.45, in NASM, Porter Papers, Box 4; McGovern, *Crossbow*, 163–70. See Lasby, *Project Paperclip*, and Gimbel, *Science*, and "Project Paperclip," on the pre–Cold War origins of U.S. policy.

18. Staver to Quinn, 26.5. and 16.6.1945, Staver to Ritchie, 23.5.1946, and Peifer notes on interview with Staver, 4.6.1962, in NACP, RG156, E.1039A, Box 87; Staver to Quinn, 29.5. and 8.6.45, in NASM, Porter Papers, Box 4.

19. Huzel, *From Peenemünde*, 191–94; Gordon Young, "V2 Inventor Reveals His Secrets," *Daily Express*, 18.6.1945, copy in NASM, Willy Ley Collection, Box 5, file 165; "Antwerp Got More V-Hits Than London," *NYT*, 18.6.1945.

20. Boyle order, 17.6.1945, and file card, NACP, RG319, IRR/PNF WvB, Box 657A; Porter OHI by DeVorkin, 16.4.1984, NASM (Porter quote); WvB, handwritten "Kommentar," c. 5.1957, WvBP-H, file 208-12 (quote).

21. Gimbel, "U.S. Policy and German Scientists"; Lasby, *Project Paperclip*, 43–46; Uhl, *Stalins V-2*, 61–62.

22. McGovern, *Crossbow*, 195–96; Ruland, *WvB*, 281 (quotes); Ruth Schumacher to WvB, 15.11.1945, in WvBP-H, file 703-19.

23. Porter to Quinn, 7.7. and 9.7.1945, in NACP, RG156, E.1039A, Box 93, "Seizure of Personnel and Equipment"; Porter OHI by DeVorkin, 16.4.1984, NASM (quote).

24. "Progress Report on . . . the Hermes II Missile," 2.1947, in NACP, RG156, E.1129, Box K-781, courtesy L. Peterkin; WvB interrogation by Hull, Hausz, and Porter, 7.6.1945, in U.S. Army Ordnance, *Story of Peenemünde*, 237. See also discussion of an A-9 with ramjet in latter, 102–12.

25. Staver, "Miscellaneous Notes," 6.6.1962, in NACP, RG 156, E.1039A, Box 87.

26. Chertok, *Rockets*, 303–4; Uhl, *Stalins V-2*, 81–82; Lasby, *Project Paperclip*, 140–41; O&S, *Rocket Team*, 290–91; Peifer notes on Steinhoff interview, 17.6.1962, in NACP, RG156, E.1039A, Box 76, Steinhoff file; Staver to Quinn, 16.5., and to Chief, R&D Branch, 17.6.1945, in Box 87; Gröttrup interrogation, 28.5.1945, in NACP, RG165, G-2 Library "P" File, Box 685, CIOS Report XXXI-71, 4.

27. McGovern, *Crossbow*, 194–97; Hunt, *Secret Agenda*, 24–25; Toftoy speech,

2.6.1959, in USSRC, Toftoy Papers; Daily Journal, Army Branch, FIAT, 30.7.–31.7.45, in NACP, RG260, OMGUS/FIAT, Box 15; mimeographed list, 2.8.1945, in WvBP-H, file 702-22.

28. Staver to Ordnance R&D, 17.6.1945, in NACP, RG156, E.1039A, Box 87; O&S, *Rocket Team*, 294–300; McGovern, *Crossbow*, 200–204; Backfire documents, 1945, in NACP, RG260, OMGUS/FIAT, Box 8, Wilson "Dustbin" list, 19.7.1945, in Box 1, file 254.78, and Cameron, Backfire Report No. 2, 30.7.1945, in Box 13, file 471.2.

29. Boyle/FIAT to TI Branch, USFET, 18.7.1945, in NACP, RG260, OMGUS/FIAT, Box 2, file 254-86, and Robertson to Osborne, 23.8.1945, in Box 13, file 471.2; Crow to Wilson, 14.8. and Wilson to Boyle, 17.8.1945, in NACP, RG319, IRR/PNF WvB, Box 657A; WvB to Huzel, 28.8.1945, in USSRC, Huzel Papers; WvB/MvB Jr. to parents, 28.8.1945, in BAK, N1085/83.

30. Klein, *Vom Geschoss*, 223.

31. Lang, "A Romantic Urge," 79–80 (quote, 80); O&S, *Rocket Team*, 291; McGovern, *Crossbow*, 201–2; Gimbel, "Deutsche Wissenschaftler." The latter books assert that Dornberger was also in Wimbledon, but documentary evidence is lacking.

32. Rees time line of trip, n.d., in WvBP-H, file 702-8; M. Sipser telephone interview, 28.8.2001; Sassard travel orders for WvB, et al., 12.9., in NACP, RG319, IRR/PNF WvB, Box 657A; O&S, *Rocket Team*, 310–11 (quote, 310).

33. Rees time line of trip, n.d., in WvBP-H, file 702-8; M. Sipser telephone interview, 28.8.2001; WvB contracts, 14.9. and 15.9.1945, in NACP, RG319, IRR/PNF WvB, Box 657A.

34. Rees time line of trip, n.d., in WvBP-H, file 702-8; travel orders, Baur et al., 15.9.1945, in NACP, RG319, IRR/PNF WvB, Box 657A; WvB/MvB Jr. to parents, 31.7.1946, in BAK, N1085/83 (quote); O&S, *Rocket Team*, 311–12; Adjutant General order, 26.7.1945, in NACP, RG319, G-2 E.47B, G-2 Decimal File, 1941–1948, Box 989, file 400.112.

35. Basic Personnel Record, 20.7.1945, NACP, IRR/PNF WvB, Box 657A; Basic Personnel Record, 26.9.1945, in NACP, RG330, Acc. No. 70A4398; O&S, *Rocket Team*, 312; WvB/MvB Jr. to parents, 31.7.1946, in BAK, N1085/83 (quote); hepatitis A info.: http://www.cdc.gov/ncidod/diseases/hepatitis/a/fact.htm.

36. Travel orders, 2.10.1945, in NACP, RG 330, Acc. No. 70A4398; McGovern, *Crossbow*, 206–7, 242; WvB, "Why I Chose America," 112 (quote). The earliest was Dr. Herbert Wagner, designer of the Henschel company's tactical missiles, already imported by the navy in May.

37. WvB, "Why I Chose America," 112 (quote).

38. Koppes, *JPL*, 1–29; O&S, *Rocket Team*, 345–46.

39. Hamill speech in "Old Timers Reunion," 18.–19.10.1961, WvBP-H, file 112-11.

40. Ibid.

41. Ibid.

42. WvB, "Why I Chose America," 112 (quote); WvB/MvB Jr. to parents, 31.7.1946, in BAK, N1085/83; Rees time line of trip, n.d., in WvBP-H, file 702-8, and WvB speech, "How Big Is Space," 3.7.1959, in file 106-7.

43. MvB Jr. to parents, 31.7.1946, in BAK, N1085/83; Lange, itineraries of first four groups, n.d., in WvBP-H, file 702-22; O&S, *Rocket Team*, 314–17.

44. Basic Personnel Records, 29.11.1945–15.2.1946, in NACP, RG165, E.179, Box 703, file "Boston."

45. WvB, "Lorin-Rohr," beg. 10.12.1945, in WvBP-H, file 702-14; correspondence with Riedel and Hermann, 1.–2.1946, in same, file 701-8; Wegener, *Peenemünde Wind Tunnels*, chap. 10; Hunt, *Secret Agenda*, 23; Hamill to Toftoy, 25.12.1945, "A Christmas Tale," in USSRC, Toftoy Papers.

46. Lang, "A Romantic Urge," 81 (WvB quote); DeVorkin, *Science,* 115–16, 121 ("intolerable," 115); Rosen, *Viking Rocket Story,* 42–43.

47. Boehm et al., memo to Lord/Aberdeen, 22.1.1946, and "Memorandum für Aussprachepunkte mit Hamill," 10.2.1946, in WvBP-H, file 701-19; "black hand" letter, before 15.2.1946, in file 701-12; WvB to Frau Steinhoff et al., 20.5.1946, and other correspondence and drafts, spring 1946, in file 703-18.

48. Toftoy speech, 2.6.1959, in USSRC, Toftoy Papers; WvB to Bussmann, 30.5.1946, in WvBP-H, file 701-21, and Fleischer "Quitting," 11.12., and "Programm" for 13–22.12.1945, in file 702-12.

49. O&S, *Rocket Team,* 347 (WvB quote); Hamill to WvB, 7.2.1946, in WvBP-H, file 701-19.

50. DeVorkin, *Science,* 121; and "Memorandum für Aussprachepunkte mit Hamill," 10.2.1946, in WvBP-H, file 701-19, and "black hand" letter, before 15.2.1946, in WvBP-H, file 701-12.

51. Lang, "A Romantic Urge," 81 (WvB quote); Hauessermann OHI.

52. Toftoy speech, 13.6.1946, in NACP, RG156, E.1039A, Box 35 (quote); J. Neufeld, *Development,* chaps. 1–3; Dennis, " 'Our First Line,' " 430–40.

53. Rosen OHI by Neufeld; S&O, *WvB* (Amer. ed.), 78; Technical Report 10, 19.4.1946, in NACP, RG319, IRR/PNF WvB, Box 657A; interrogation of 1.7.1946, in JPL History Collection, files 5-308 and 5-313.

54. Bain to Hamill, 24.6. and Hamill reply, 8.7.1946, with "Questions and Answers on A-9, A-10 and A-11," in NACP, RG156, E.1039A, Box 79, file "Ch. II."; O&S, *Rocket Team,* 350.

55. Singles to Toftoy, 12.4.1946, in WvBP-H, file 701-7, and "Briefentwurf an Los Alamos Laboratory, Dr. J. R. Oppenheimer," in file 701-11. See also Hamill to Toftoy, 16.2.1946, in file 701-8, "Brief Description and Main Data of Long-Range Rocket 'Comet'," c. 4.1946, in file 701-10, and "Beschreibung der Fernrakete 'Comet'," and WvB, handwritten "Comet A," n.d., in file 701-11.

56. Singles to Toftoy, 12.4.1946, in WvBP-H, file 701-7; "Questions and Answers on A-9, A-10 and A-11," in NACP, RG 156, E.1039A, Box 79, file "Ch.II"; Eisfeld, *Mondsüchtig,* 186–90; Erichsen, "Präfiguration," in Erichsen and Hoppe, *Peenemünde,* 23–34.

57. DeVorkin, *Science,* 135–47; DeVorkin, "War Heads."

58. WvB/MvB Jr. to parents, 31.7. and 28.8.1946, in BAK, N1085/83.

CHAPTER 10

1. WvB, "Mars Project" English ms., 159–60, in WvBP-H, file 205-1. The USSRC has recently published this long-lost novel under the title *Project Mars.*

2. Frederick Cook ("uniform"), draft news story, late 1948, in NACP, RG319, IRR/PNF WvB, Box 657A; Ted Entlich interview, 29.10.2000; WvB, "Why I Chose America," 112 (El Paso quote); Patterson, *Grand Expectations,* 61–62; Hamill, "Itinerary of Personnel," 30.4.1946, in WvBP-H, file 701-18, and WvB to Babs Riedel in file 703-17 (California quote); Lang, "A Romantic Urge," 190; WvB to G.W. Crabbe/JCS, 16.3.1955, in NACP, RG330, Acc. 70A4398.

3. WvB note on report, 2.1.1947, in WvBP-H, file 701-10.

4. "Chronologische Folge der Personnel-forderung aus Deutschland," after 7.1947, in WvBP-H, file 703-20; WvB/MvB Jr. to parents, 27.9. (quote) and 13.10.1946, in BAK, N1085/83; Patterson, *Grand Expectations,* 121, 145–46.

5. SvB to WvB/MvB Jr., 6.2.1946, WvB/MvB Jr. to parents, 27.7.1946, in BAK, N1085/83; Spohn to WvB, 29.1. and Funk to WvB, 24.6.1946, in WvBP-H, file 703-17; MvB Sr., *Weg,* 309–39 ("Sensation," 338); Sibert to G-2 Captured Personnel and Material Branch, 27.5.1946, in NACP RG319, IRR/PNF WvB, Box 657A.

6. MvB Sr., *Weg,* 350–55; WvB/MvB Jr. to parents, and MvB Jr. to same, 31.7.1946, in BAK, N1085/83.

7. WvB/MvB Jr. to parents, 31.7., 11.8., 13.8., 21.8.1946 (quotes), in BAK, N1085/83.

8. MvB Sr. to WvB, 29.7. and WvB/MvB Jr. to parents, 2.9. and 22.9.1946, in BAK, N1085/83.

9. MvB Sr. to WvB, 29.7., WvB to parents, 3.9 and 22.9., MvB Jr./WvB to parents, 15.9., MvB Jr. to parents, 25.10.1946, in BAK, N1085/83.

10. WvB to parents, 3.9. and 4.11.1946, in BAK, N1085/83.

11. FBI report, 28.2.1949, FBI FOIA MvB Jr.; Vanech to Hoover/FBI, 17.2.1947, in NACP, RG330, JOIA Gen. Corr., 1946–52, Box 7; FBI report, 25.9.1948, in NACP, RG65, E.A1-136AB, Box 151, FBI file WvB 105-10747; MvB Jr. card file entry, c. 1948–49, in INSCOM FOIA MvB Jr.

12. WvB to parents, 3.9. (quote) and 4.11.1946, in BAK, N1085/83.

13. Ibid.; Maria vB?, "Betr. Alexander v. Quistorp," c. 1952, in WvBP-H, file 610-9; WvB, "Space Man," 3.10.1958, p. 14 ("father").

14. WvB/MvB Jr. to parents, 31.7., 11.8, 2.9. (music quotes), WvB to parents, 15.9.1946, in BAK, N1085/83.

15. MvB Jr. to parents, 31.7., 15.9.1946, in BAK, N1085/83.

16. WvB to parents, 22.10. and 30.10.1946, ibid.

17. John L. Sherrill, "Wernher von Braun," *Guideposts* (Oct. 1960), 1-5 (quote, 4–5). See also WvB, "Why I Chose America," 114–15; Lang, "A Romantic Urge," 84–85; Noble, *Religion of Technology,* 124. It was a fundamentalist Church of the Nazerene, but that did not make him a fundamentalist.

18. WvB/MvB Jr. to parents, 2.9. and 9.9.1946, in BAK, N1085/83.

19. WvB to parents, 30.10.1946 (Kammler), in BAK, N1085/83.

20. Toftoy speech, 2.6.1959, in USSRC, Toftoy Papers; WvB/MvB Jr. to parents, 21.8., 27.9., MvB Jr. to parents, 25.10.1946, in BAK, N1085/83 (quotes).

21. WvB to parents, 30.10., 25.11., 8.12.1946, 15.1.1947, in BAK, N1085/83.

22. Ibid.; SvB, "Memoiren," courtesy Christina vB.

23. WvB to parents, 8.12.1946, in BAK, N1085/83; El Paso clippings, 12.1946, in NACP, RG319, IRR/PNF WvB, Box 657A, in KSC, Debus Collection, and in Fort Bliss DOE; "V-2 Rocket Result of Moon Dream," *WP,* 4.12.1946; "Nazi Scientists Aid Army on Research," *NYT,* 4.12.1946; "We Want with the West," *Time,* 9.12.1946, p. 67.

24. WvB to parents, 8.12.1946, in BAK, N1085/83; Ley to Schaefer, 8.12.1946, in NASM, Ley Collection, Box 5, file 165; Generales to WvB, 6.12.1946, in WvBP-H, file 400-1. WvB got permission to send G. a letter and did so on 10.9.1946, also in file 400-1, but G.'s letter does not read like a reply.

25. WvB to parents, 10.2.1947, in BAK, N1085/83; Toftoy to Director of Intelligence, 11.2.1947, in NACP, RG319, IRR/PNF WvB, Box 657A; Adjutant General, WvB travel orders, 12.2.1947, in NACP, RG330, Acc. 70A4398 ; WvB telegrams to MvB Sr., 14.2. and 27?.2.1947, in MvB Papers in possession of C.-F. vB, Nr. 12, and MvB Sr. speech for wedding reception, 1.3.1947, in Nr. 67; Ruland, *WvB,* 320.

26. Konstantin v. Bayern, "Prof. v. Braun," and same to MvB Sr., 28.1.1955, in BAK, N1085/49; "Landshuter Flitterwoche," *Der Stern,* 19.7.1958, copy in NASM, Ley Collec-

tion, Box 30, folder 5; WvB, "Space Man," 3.10.1958, p. 14 (quote: "two . . ."); FIAT "Brief Interrogation Report" on WvB, 8.7.1947, in UKNA, FO1031/128.

27. MvB Sr., *Weg*, 360; Emmy vB to Anna Plewe, 10.4.1947, in BAK, N1085/73 (quotes on trip); WvB to "Peter" (Liesl Felsch), 11.8.1947, in WvBP-H, file 703-17.

28. Sherrill, "Wernher von Braun," *Guideposts* (Oct. 1960), 5; WvB to "Peter" (Liesl Felsch), and WvB to Robert G. Kiel Jr. ("nervous tension"), both 29.4.1947, in WvBP-H, file 703-17.

29. Lasby, *Project Paperclip*, 188–207; Hunt, *Secret Agenda*, 44–48; Bower, *Paperclip Conspiracy*, 264–67; Osborne to G-2/USFET, 29.10.1945, NACP, RG260, OMGUS/FIAT, Box 8, file 471.94; Joesten, "This Brain for Hire."

30. Hunt, *Secret Agenda*, 60–64; Smith to Air Provost Marshal, 10.6.1947, in NARA, M-1079/R1/344-59 (quote, 352).

31. 7708th War Crimes Group cable, 31.7., and reply, 7.8.1947, in NARA, M-1079/R1/432-33; WvB statement, M-1079/R4/168-75 (English), M-1079/R12/337-48 (German and questionnaire); Bornemann, *Geheimprojekt Mittelbau*, 153.

32. Lasby, *Project Paperclip*, 207–14, 224–29; Patterson, *Grand Expectations*, 128–29; Fort Bliss security reports, 28.2. and 1.7.1947, in NACP, RG156, E.1039A, Box 35, and Sestito to CSGID, 2.10.1947, in Box 93, and White report, 26.11.1947, in Box 101; Cone report on meetings, 4.–6.11.1947, in NACP, RG319, G-2 Decimal File 1941–48, Box 990; WvB/MvB Jr. to parents, 21.8., 27.9., WvB to parents, 14.11.1946, in BAK, N1085/83.

33. Toftoy to G-2, 13.11.1946, in NACP, RG330, JIOA General Corr., 1946–52, Box 2; OMGUS Sec. Rep. WvB, 21.1.1947, WvB application and Bio. and Prof. Data forms ("I want . . ."), 10.2.1947, WvB "Affidavit," 18.6.1947, in RG330, Acc. 70A4398; Revised Sec. Rep., 18.9.1947, in NACP, RG319, IRR/PNF WvB, Box 657A. Assertions by Bower, *Paperclip Conspiracy*, and Hunt, *Secret Agenda*, that there was a conspiracy to doctor files in violation of the law have been demolished by Gimbel in "German Scientists." The WvB case shows this even more clearly than most. Revised reports were openly labeled as such and still did not solve the problem of clearing his file.

34. Navy Intell. Rep., 23.9.1947, in NACP, RG330, Acc. 70A4398; FIAT, "Brief Interrogation Report" on WvB, 8.7.1947, in UKNA, FO1031/128; SvB, "Memoiren," courtesy Christina vB, 57; RJB to Chief, Exploitation Section, after 13.10.1947, NACP, RG319, G-2 Decimal File, 1941–1948, Box 1005, file 230.741 ("Oberusel").

35. Singles, "Security Report" on WvB, 14.2.1947, Sayler, "Certificate," 24.2.1947, WvB "Meldebogen," 8.2.1948, in NACP, RG330, Acc. 70A4398; Revised Sec. Rep., 26.2.1948, in NACP, RG319, IRR/PNF WvB, Box 657A; Fallwell, Routing Slip, 10.5.1949 in RG319, G-2 E.4713, G-2 Decimal File, 1941–48, Box 993, 400.112 ("problem cases"); 1948–49 docs. there and in RG330, Acc. 70A4398.

36. Toftoy draft for Hughes to G-2, 6.5.1948, in NACP, RG319, G-2 E.4713, G-2 Decimal File, 1941–48, Box 993, 400.112; FBI interview with Seale/GE, 22.5.1960, in NACP, RG 319, IRR/PNF WvB, Box 657A ("hypercritical"); Winterstein ("on the verge") quoted in S&O, *WvB*, 84; O&S, *Rocket Team*, 351; Reisig OHI; WvB to Hamill, 12.1.1948, in WvBP-H, file 703-11.

37. WvB et al., "Rocket Launching from Ships," 3.1948, in NASA/HD, HRC2561; GE Guided Missiles Dept., "A Brief History," 1954, in NACP, RG156, E.1039A, Box 90; DeVorkin, *Science*, 170, 187; Bumper launch list, http://history.msfc.nasa.gov/mm/lk_bump.html.

38. Lutjens to G-2, 20.6.1947, transcript in NACP, RG156, E.1039A, Box 35; "Special

Report: Missile 0," in RG156, E.1129, Box K-782, courtesy L. Peterkin; Hamill speech in "Old Timers Reunion," 18.–19.10.1961, WvBP-H, file 112-11; O&S, *Rocket Team*, 355.

39. RDB docs. on Hermes II, 1947–48, in NACP, RG156, E.1039A, Box 10, file GM8, and Box 84, Facilities, and Box 35; Guided Missile Research and Development: Fort Bliss and Redstone Arsenal, c. 1952–53, in Box 82; WvB et al., "A Large Multipurpose Booster Rocket," 4.1949, WvBP-H, current location unknown.

40. WvB to Schneer, 2.1.1959, in WvBP-H, file 208-2 ("reluctant"); Rotary Club speech, 16.1.1947, in same, file 101-3; S&O, *WvB* (Amer. ed.), 82–83.

41. WvB ARS applic., 3.2.1950, in WvBP-H, file 610-1; Oberth to Sänger, 28.4.1948, in HORM, Oberth Papers; Sänger to WvB, 7.5.1950, in WvBP-LC, Box 43, Corr. GfW 1950-52; Carter/BIS to WvB, 27.8.1949, reply, 29.9.1949. and Cleaver to WvB, 2.11.1949, in WvBP-H, file 400-2.

42. Lang, "A Romantic Urge," 83; WvB, "Mars Project" ms., WvBP-H, file 205-1 (English), file 204-7 (German), preface; WvB, *The Mars Project*, 2–3.

43. WvB, *Das Marsprojekt (The Mars Project)*, xv (preface to the 1962 edition), 7. In the "Mars Project" English ms., WvBP-H, file 205-1, the technical appendix is pp. 440–567 (the novel text runs to p. 439k, thus actually 450 pp.). In the German original, WvBP-H, file 204-7, part of the appendix is lost. There are also a number of drafts, loose calculations, and drawings for "Mars Project" in Box 206. See Lang, "A Romantic Urge," 82, on cramped quarters. Iris was born on 9 Dec. 1948.

44. WvB, *The Mars Project*, 3–4, 40–41, 61–62, 65–66; "Mars Project" English ms., WvBP-H, file 205-1, , pp. v–vi ,19–23.

45. WvB, *The Mars Project*, 2–4, 9–36; "Mars Project" English ms., WvBP-H, file 205-1, pp. 19–23, 29, 218–35.

46. WvB, *The Mars Project*, 1 (quotes); "Mars Project" English ms., WvBP-H, file 205-1, pp. iii–iv, 1–2.

47. WvB, "Mars Project" English ms., WvBP-H, file 205-1, pp. 157–62.

48. Ibid., 1–2; German ms., WvBP-H, file 204-7, pp. 1–3.

49. WvB, "Mars Project" English ms., WvBP-H, file 205-1, pp. iv–v; "Die Quistorps in Stalins Lagern," http://www.quistorp.de/quistorp_buch.htm.

50. WvB, "Mars Project" English ms., WvBP-H, file 205-1, pp. 159–60.

51. Ibid., passim.

52. WD to WvB, 8.8. and 21.11.1949, in WvBP-H, file 430-5; J.P. Layton to WvB, 19.11.1949, and WvB to Paul Reynolds, 7.2.1950, in file 612-1.

53. "Guided Missile Facility Budget Proposals for FY 1951," 29.9.1949, and Helmick to Crichlow, 19.1.1950, in NACP, RG156, E.1039A, Box 4, GM41; Hamby, *Man*, 524–25; S&O, *WvB*, 97; "Army Will Move Bliss Scientists," *El Paso Herald-Post*, 4.11.1949; "E.P. to Lose Rocket Center," *El Paso Times*, 5.11.1949.

54. Immigration Card, WvB, in NACP, RG319, IRR/PNF WvB, Box 657A; JIOA, "Standard Operating Procedure," 12.1.1950, in NACP, RG319, G-2 E.47B, G-2 Decimal File, 1941–48, Box 993, 400.112; S&O, *WvB* (Amer. ed.), 85–86.

CHAPTER 11

1. Quoted in Westrum, *Sidewinder*, 62.

2. WvB to Gatland, 10.3.1950, in WvBP-H, file 400-2; WvB to Reynolds, 7.2., Bradbury/Doubleday to Swan/Reynolds, 24.3., Hart/Macmillan to Swan, 9.5.19, and WvB to Swan, 7.8. and 2.10.1950, in same, file 400-7; Bergaust, *WvB*, 155–56; WvB to Koelle,

4.11.1950, in WVBP-LC, Box 43, German Corr. 1949–54 (quote). Koelle is the form he adopted in the United States after his 1955 arrival; it was originally spelled Kölle.

3. WvB travel orders, 29.3.1950, in WvBP-H, file 704-6; WvB to Koelle, 13.6.1950, in WvBP-LC, Box 43, German Corr. 1949–54.

4. WvB to parents, 18.4., 5.5., 20.6.1950, in BAK, N1085/84; MvB Jr. "Petition for Naturalization," 4.10.1954, NASER; WvB to Lang, 29.12.1950, in WvBP-LC, Box 44, Publications . . . 1949–53; WvB to Zaehringer, 25.2.1951, in WvBP-H, file 610-5 (quote).

5. Bergaust, *Rocket City U.S.A.*, 77–80; S&O, *WvB*, 97–99; Ward, *Dr. Space*, 74.

6. Bergaust, *WvB*, 184–86, and *Rocket City U.S.A.*, 40–42.

7. Joiner and Jolliff, *Redstone Arsenal Complex*, 1–12; Subcomm. on Guided Missiles to Ord. Tech. Comm., 18.6.1951, in NACP, RG156, E.320, Box I-144, courtesy L. Peterkin; "Transcript . . . Special Interdepartmental Guided Missiles Board 23 January 1950," in NACP, RG156, E.1039A, Box 83; Hermes chronology in same, Box 71.

8. Patterson, *Grand Expectations*, 177–78, 210–15; Halberstam, *Fifties*, 67–75; WvB to parents, 11. and 29.7.1950, in BAK, N1085/84.

9. Hamby, *Man*, 553.

10. Hermes chronology in NACP, RG156, E.1039A, Box 71, and Haas to Simon, 20.9.1950, in Box 20.

11. Redstone report 1, 1.1.–30.9.1951, in NACP, RG156, E.1039A, Box 30; WvB draft talk to Air War College, 28.5.1953, in WvBP-H, file 101-17; phone interview with Doug Hege, 1.10.2003; Kraemer, *Rocketdyne*, 31–43.

12. WvB draft talk to Air War College, 28.5.1953, in WvBP-H, file 101-17; WvB to Hamill, 29.3.1951, in NASER, RG255, MSFC/ULMF, #89-064, Box 6, Booster/Warhead 1951–61; Hamill/WvB/Moore, "Summary of Presentation: Hermes (XSSM-G-14)," 25.1.1951, in NACP, RG156, E.1039A, Box 13, file GM207, Redstone "Progress Report No. 1," 1.1.–30.9.1951, in Box 30, and "Presentation for Mr. K.T. Keller," 18.10.1951, in Box 77.

13. Redstone report 5, 1.7.–30.9.1952, in NACP, RG156, E.1039A, Box 30, and Satterfield/Akens, "Historical Monograph: Government-Contractor Relationships at ABMA," 1.7.1959, in Box 53; Bullard, "A History," 61–65, 74–78; J. Neufeld, *Development*, 86–92; Dunar and Waring, *Power*, 19–23, 39–51.

14. "Report of Agency Check," 13.10.1953 in NACP, RG319, Box 657A, IRR/PNF WvB; Redstone report 6, 1.10.–31.12.1952, in NACP, RG156, E.1039A, Box 30, Redstone budget document, 29.9.1954, in Box 20, and Ordnance memoranda, 15. and 20.10.1958, in Box 90, "Army Support to NASA"; WvB to MvB Sr., 2.2.1953, in BAK, N1085/84 ("regime").

15. "Mars Project" corr., 1950, in WvBP-H, file 400-7; Crouch, *Rocketeers*, 129.

16. Ley to WvB, 8.2.1950, in same, file 406-8; Ley and Bonestell, *Conquest*; Kilgore, *Astrofuturism*, 73–74; Ananoff et al., to WvB, 1.10.1950, in WvBP-LC, Box 43, Corr. GfW 1950–52.

17. WvB-Koelle-Bechtle-Neher-Loeser corr., 1950–51, in WvBP-LC, Box 43, German Corr. 1949–54.

18. Ibid.

19. Shepherd/BIS to WvB, 1.2., and reply, 3.3.1951 (quote) in WvBP-H, file 400-2, and WvB to Hodo-Weaver Companies, 24.3., and Richardson, 9.7.1951, in file 600-9; WvB to Hase, 27.12.1951, in WvBP-LC, Box 43, German Corr. 1949–54. The house was at 907 (now 1406) McClung St.

20. WvB-Cleaver corr., spring 1951, in WvBP-H, file 400-2; Koelle to WvB, 28.10., WvB reply, 4.11.1950, and WvB to Bechtle, 9.3.1951, in WvBP-LC, Box 43, German Corr. 1949–54; Wilhite, "The British Interplanetary Society."

21. WvB to Cleaver 21.5. and 20.6.1951, in WvBP-H, file 400-2; Kilgore, *Astrofuturism*, 66–68, 84–88. The block quotation comes from a loose page to which page 1 has been lost, but a clear reference in Cleaver's 1.7. letter dates it to 20.6.1951.

22. WvB, "Importance of . . . ," 9.1951, WvBP-H, file 101-7; WvB-Bechtle-Loeser corr., spring-summer 1951, in WvBP-LC, Box 43, German Corr. 1949–54; WvB, *Marsprojekt*.

23. WvB-Chillson/ARS, and WvB-Cleaver corr., spring 1951, in WvBP-H, file 400-2; Durant-WvB corr., 8.1951, in same, file 400-7; Neufeld-Durant conversations, c. 1999; WvB to Bechtle, 23.3.1951, in WvBP-LC, Box 43, German Corr. 1949–54.

24. *NYT*, 7.9.1951, p. 30; "Space, Here We Come," *Time*, 17.9.1951; *Huntsville Times*, 9.9.1951, p. 1; "Giant Doughnut Is Proposed as Space Station," *Popular Science* (Oct. 1951), 120–21.

25. Ordway and Liebermann, *Blueprint*, 128–29, 135–36; San Antonio conference program and invitation in WvBP-H, file 134-3.

26. WvB handwritten draft for 11.2.1953 speech in WvBP-H, file 101-15, and in WvBP-LC, Box 49, "Speeches and Writings Undated"; WvB to Lovelace Foundation, 25.10.1951, in WvBP-H, file 134-3.

27. Whipple memoir in Ordway and Liebermann, *Blueprint*, 129.

28. WvB to Ryan, 23.11., and Bonestell to WvB, 30.11., in WVBP-LC, Box 42, Collier's correspondence, 1951–52. How the memoir, "Behind the Scenes . . . ," WvBP-H, file 702-20, came to be written is revealed in the WvB-Gatland correspondence, mid-1950, in file 400-2. The *JBIS* eventually published a revised version in 1956 as "Reminiscences of German Rocketry."

29. WvB to Generales, 1.12., Ryan to WvB, 4.12., Manning to WvB letter contract, 11.12.1951, in WvBP-LC, Box 42, Collier's Corr., 1951–52; WvB to Haber, 18.9.1951, in same, Box 44, Publications . . . 1949–1953.

30. WvB to Ryan, 2.2., and Ley to WvB, 9.2.1952, in WvBP-LC, Box 42, Collier's Corr., 1951–52; WvB to Ryan, 26.12.1951, CRC/OU, Box 159, folder 9; WvB draft ms. "Man's Last Frontier," in NACP, RG 156, E.1039A, Box 72, Project von Braun.

31. Bonestell to WvB, 20.12., and reply 26.12.1951, and WvB to Ryan, 2.2., in WvBP-LC, Box 42, Collier's Corr., 1951–52. For an analysis of his booster, see Mark Wade, "Von Braun," www.astronautix.com/lvfam/vonbraun.htm.

32. WvB to Ryan, 26.2., and reply, 5.3.1952, in CRC/OU, Box 159, folder 9; WvB to Bechtle, 6.3.1952, in WvBP-LC, Box 43, German Corr. 1949–54, and WvB-Moseley-Ryan-Haley corr., 2.–3.1952 in Box 42, Collier's Corr., 1951–52.

33. WvB-Moseley-Ryan-Haley corr., 2.–3.1952, plus news release, media appearance lists, and WvB handwritten notes, in WvBP-LC, Box 42, Collier's Corr., 1951–52. The magazine's cover date was 22.3., but it always came out eight days early.

34. Ibid.; "Von Braun Lecture Takes 5,000 on Interplanetary Rocket Trip," *Washington Star*, 20.3.1952, clipping in WvBP-LC, Box 55, Scrapbook #7; WvB to Schindler/NOL, 26.3.1952, in WvBP-H, file 101-9 (quote); McCurdy, *Space*, 29–39.

35. *Collier's*, 22.3.1952, 22–36, 38–39, 65–67, 70–72, 74; Launius, *Space Stations*, 25–50.

36. Ibid., 23–26, 74; *Collier's* news release, 13.3., WvB "Lantern-Slide Cue Sheet," 11.3.1952, "Bill Slater Interview (TV)" notes, and draft script for interview, in WvBP-LC, Box 42, Collier's Corr., 1951–52; WvB notes, c. 3.1952, in same, Box 49, Speeches and Writings: Across the Moon.

37. WvB-parents corr., spring 1952, in BAK, N1085/84; WvB to Bechtle, 7.6.1952, in WvBP-LC, Box 43, German Corr. 1949–54; Moseley to WvB, 20.3., and reply 26.3.1952, in Box 42, Collier's corr., 1951–52; 1952–53 fan mail in Box 14; May to WvB, 15.3.1952, in WvBP-H, file 207-1; WvB to Cleaver, in same, file 400-2.

38. WvB to Duke/USN, 30.4.1952, in WvBP-H, file 134-1.

39. WvB to parents, 2.6.1952, in BAK, N1085/84 (quotes); Ryan to WvB, 2.4. and 3.4.1952, CRC/OU, Box 159, folder 9.

40. Grosse to WvB, 24.4., Truax to WvB, 2.4., 1.5., 5.6., WvB to Truax, 2.6., and WvB to Grosse, 21.6.1952, in WvBP-LC, Box 42, A.V. Grosse Action 1951–1957; Grosse interview in Ermenc, *Atomic Bomb Scientists*, 305–6 (Truman quote); Hamby, *Man*, 564, 600–5; Patterson, *Grand Expectations*, 232–42.

41. WvB-Grosse-Truax-Bossart corr., 4.–7.1952, in WvBP-LC, Box 42, A.V. Grosse Action 1951–1957.

42. WvB to Grosse, 21.6.1952, ibid.

43. Grosse-WvB telegrams 6.–7.1952, and WvB to Zucrow, 11.7.1952, in WvBP-LC, Box 42, A.V. Grosse Action 1951–1957; Patterson, *Grand Expectations*, 250–56.

44. WvB to Bechtle, 10.2.1952, in WvBP-LC, Box 43, German Corr. 1949–54.

45. WvB-Bechtle, WvB-Gartmann, and WvB-White corr., 4.–7.1952, ibid.; WvB–U. of Illinois Press corr., 1951–52, in WvBP-H, file 400-7.

46. WvB to Koelle, in WvBP-LC, Box 43, German Corr., GfW, 1950–52; WvB to parents, 2.6.1952, 10.10.1953, in BAK, N1085/84; WvB to parents, 21.6.1952, in MvB Papers in possession of C.-F. vB; Oberth to Sänger, 28.4.1948, Oberth to Weyl, 15.1.1952, in HORM, Oberth Papers.

47. WvB to Ley, 28.1., 6.2.1952, in NASM, Ley Collection, Box 30, folder 4; WvB-Oberth corr., 1952–55, in HORM, Oberth Papers; Toftoy to Oberth, 30.9., and WvB to Oberth, 18.11.1952, in WvBP-LC, Box 43, German Corr., GfW, 1952–53; Oberth IRR file, INSCOM FOIA Oberth; Nottrodt to Chief of Ord., 18.11.1952, in NACP, RG319, IRR/PNF WvB, Box 657A.

48. WvB to Gartmann, 17.2.1952, in WvBP-LC, Box 43, German Corr. 1952–53, and WvB to Koelle, 14.7.1952, in same box, Corr. GfW 1950–52; WvB to parents, 21.6.1952, in MvB Papers in possession of C.-F. vB (quote re: WD); WvB to McHugh/Ordnance, 13.8.1952, in NACP, RG156, E.1039A, Box 72, Project von Braun. Durant's CIA status has been publicly revealed in one document: Logsdon, ed., *Exploring*, 1:201–5.

49. WvB speech in WvBP-H, file 101-10.

50. WvB-Bechtle corr., 1951–52, in WvBP-LC, Box 43, German Corr. 1949–54; EvB to WvB, 31.7.1952, in BAK, N1085/73 (quotes).

51. WvB to Ley, 4.6.1952, and Ley to WvB, 7.8.1953, in WvBP-H, file 401-1; WvB-Ley-Hayden corr., 6.1952, in file 401-2; WvB to *Collier's*, 5.9.1952, in file 207-2; Ryan to WvB, 11.7., WvB to Ryan, 2.8.1952, in CRC/OU, Box 159, folder 9; WvB to parents, c. 18.9.1952, in BAK, N1085/84.

52. WvB to Ryan, 14.7.1952, in CRC/OU, Box 159, folder 9; WvB Moon manuscripts and clearances, 8.–9.1952, NACP, RG156, E.1039A, Box 72, Project von Braun; WvB to parents, 12.7.1952, in BAK, N1085/84.

53. WvB to parents, c. 18.9.1952, in BAK, N1085/84; WvB to Grosse, 25.9.1952, in WvBP-LC, Box 1, 1952 A to Z; "Space Superiority" speech and related corr., 9.1952, in WvBP-H, file 101-12; printed speech also in NASM, WvB bio. file.

54. "Space Superiority" speech in NASM, WvB bio. file; WvB, "Race of Armament" ms., in WvBP-H, file 225-14, and WvB to Ryan, 15.5.1952, in file 207-1; Ryan, ed., *Across*, 55–56. Rainer Eisfeld in *Mondsüchtig*, 186–89, first pointed out von Braun's advocacy of preemptive strikes.

55. "Space Superiority" speech in NASM, WvB bio. file; WvB, "Space Superiority"; clearance paperwork for pub., 9.–11.1952, in NACP, RG156, E.1039A, Box 72, Project von Braun; WvB speech, 26.10.1956, in WvBP-H, file 101-30.

56. WvB to Grosse, 25.9.1952, in WvBP-LC, Box 1, 1952 A to Z, and WvB-Grosse corr., 9.–11.1952, and WD to WvB, 20.10.1952, in Box 42, A. V. Grosse Action 1951–1957.

57. Grosse report, 25.8.1953, in NASA/HD, HRC 945, excerpt in Logsdon, ed., *Exploring,* 1:266–69; Neufeld, *Development,* 93–103.

58. WvB-Moseley corr., schedules and notes, in WvBP-H, file 207-2.

59. WvB-Ley-Hayden corr. in file 401-2, and Hayden 13.10.1952 program, in WvBP-H, file 101-13; *Collier's* press releases and media schedules in NACP, RG156, E.1039A, Box 72, Project von Braun.

60. *Collier's,* 18.10.1952, 51–58, 60, and 25.10.1952, 38–40, 42, 44–48.

61. Quoted in S&O, *WvB* (Amer. ed.), 115, presumably from Stuhlinger's memory.

62. Rosen OHI, 24.7.1998, NASM.

63. *NYT,* 14.10.1952, 33; "Journey into Space," *Time,* 8.12.1952, 62–64, 67–70, 73.

64. WvB, "Why I Chose America"; cover of same in WvBP-LC, Box 52, Clippings, 1934, 1952–58, and corr. with *American Magazine* in Box 44, Publications, 1949–53; WvB to WD, 29.4.1953, in WvBP-H, file 430-5; Ryan interview with WvB, 14.–15.7.1969, in CRC/OU, Box 163, folder 3 ("human skin").

65. Holmes to WvB, 23.3.1972, in WvBP-H, file 602-9; *Time,* 8.12.1952, 73; WvB to Leonard, 9.10.1953, in WvBP-LC, Box 1, 1953 A to H; Crouch, *Rocketeers,* 127–37.

66. WvB "ARS-Luncheon" handwritten talk, 6.5.1953, in WvBP-LC, Box 46, Speeches and Writings, 1951–1955; Edler to WvB, 23.11.1953, re: LA ARS speech, in same, Box 12, Invitations, 1952–April 1954; Kraemer OHI by Neufeld and Winter, 21.11. and 12.12.2000, NASM.

67. "Man's Survival in Space" series, *Collier's,* 28.2.1953, 40–48, 7.3.1953, 56–63, and 14.3.1953, 38–44.

68. WvB Mars sketches, 27.9.1952, in WvBP-LC, Box 46, Speeches and Writings, 1951–1955; Manning to WvB, letter contract 1.10.1952, in WvBP-H, file 207-4; WvB-Ley-Ryan-Haber corr., 1952–53, in same, file 207-8; WvB to Ryan, 3.1. and WvB to Ley, 18.1.1953, in CRC/OU, Box 159, folder 9; WvB-Ley-Ryan corr., 4.–9.1953, in WvBP-LC, Box 49, Speeches and Writings: Across the Moon; Ryan, ed., *Conquest.*

69. WvB to Ryan, 18.4.53, in WvBP-LC, Box 42, Collier's Corr. 1953; WvB "Baby Space Station" materials in CRC/OU, Box 153, folder 1, and Box 159, folder 9; Manning to WvB, letter contract, 1.5.1953, in WvBP-H, file 207-4; WvB, "Baby Space Station," *Collier's,* 27.6.1953, 33–35, 38, 40.

70. WvB to Oberth, 31.12.1952, in HORM, Oberth Papers (quote); WvB to parents, 10.10.1953, in BAK, N1085/84.

71. WvB to lab chiefs, 17.6.1953, in WvBP-LC, Box 43, Guided Missile Development; Patterson, *Grand Expectations,* 261; Braun, "Redstone's First Flight"; Eifler-Toftoy phone call, 13.5.1953, in WvBP-H, file 800-5, and Toftoy-Simon and Toftoy-Eifler phone calls, 11.–12.2.1954, in file 800-6; Eifler to Vincent, 2.3., and Toftoy to ORDTU, 16.7.1953, in NASER, RG255, MSFC/ULMF, 1973–2102, Series 5: Juno, Box 13, Ramjets.

72. WvB to parents, 13.6.1953 and 5.5.1955, in BAK, N1085/84; MvB Jr. to parents, 11.5. and 19.12.1955 (quote) in MvB Papers in possession of C.-F. vB; Hürter et al., *Biographisches Handbuch,* 1:264; SvB, "Memoiren," courtesy Christina vB, 58–60.

73. Harris, "The Year"; Dannenberg OHI by Launius, 25.7.2000, NASA/HD; Huzel, *From Peenemünde,* 16–17, 228–30.

74. Braun, "Redstone's First Flight"; Redstone report 9, 1.7.–9.30.1953, in NACP, RG156, E.1039A, Box 30.

75. Bechtle to WvB, 27.6.1953, in WvBP-LC, Box 43, German Corr. 1949–54; Neher, *Menschen;* WvB–U. of Illinois Press corr., in same, Box 1, 1953 I to R; WvB-Bonestell-

Collier's corr., contract, and WvB outline, 7.–8.1953, in same, Box 42, Collier's Corr. 1953; WvB to Ryan, 3.1.1953, in CRC/OU, Box 159, folder 9; WvB-Ley corr., 8.–9.1953, in WvBP-H, file 401-1.

76. WvB-Ley corr., 8.–9.1953, in WvBP-H, file 401-1; Bonestell to Ryan, 30.9.1953, in WvBP-LC, Box 50, Conquest of the Moon.

77. WvB to Bonestell, 9.10., in WvBP-LC, Box 42, Collier's Corr. 1953; and Bonestell to WvB, 13.10.1953, in Box 50, Conquest of the Moon.

78. WvB-Bonestell-Ley-*Collier's* corr., 10.–12.1953, in WvBP-LC, Box 50, Conquest of the Moon, Bonestell to WvB corr., 11.1953, in Box 42, Collier's corr. 1953, WvB to Neher, 4.6.1954, in Box 43, German corr. 1952–54 ("edited to death"); WvB to Bonestell, 17.11.1953 and 13.1.1954, in WvBP-H, file 600-5; *Collier's*, 30.4.1954, 21–29.

79. Day, "Von Braun Paradigm"; McCurdy, *Space*, 29–41, 47–51; Launius, *Space Stations*, chap. 2.

80. WvB to Brown, 4.6.1954, WvBP-H, file 207-13; WvB to parents, c.18.9.1952 ("businesslike"), 13.6.1953 (on aristocracy), and 20.12.1953 ("Cabin cruiser"), in BAK, N1085/84; Ward, *Dr. Space*, 79. Piszkiewicz, *WvB*, 66, first made the point about WvB's choice of the Episcopal Church.

81. Bullard, "History," 162, 164; WvB to Haley, 2.11.1954, in WvBP-H, file 610-4.

CHAPTER 12

1. Quoted in S&O, *WvB* (Amer. ed.), 122, apparently from Stuhlinger's memory.

2. WvB to parents, 3.6.1954, in BAK, N1085/84 ("more . . ."); Patterson, *Grand Expectations*, 264, 267–70 (quotes, 269), 294–96, 389–90; "Von Braun Deplores Ban on Oppenheimer," *NYT*, 15.3.1958.

3. S&O, *WvB* (Amer. ed.), 123, and O&S, *Rocket Team*, 375, give two different versions of Hoover's opening statement but with the same import.

4. McDougall, *Heavens*, 99–111.

5. Needell, *Science*, 325–26.

6. J. Neufeld, *Development*, 98–108.

7. McDougall, *Heavens*, 115–18; Day in Launius et al., *Reconsidering Sputnik*, 161–65; Hall, "The Eisenhower Administration," 61–63.

8. Needell, *Science*, 325–31.

9. S&O, *WvB* (Amer. ed.), 122–23; O&S, *Rocket Team*, 350–51; WvB to Toftoy, 15.1.1954, in WvBP-LC, Box 43, Guided Missile Development . . . 1952–65. The possibility of a "Super-Viking" upper stage is mentioned in Durant's notes to the 25.6.1954 meeting, Durant Papers, Orbiter file, courtesy Fred Durant, so it is not as if von Braun had entirely ignored such an idea.

10. WvB draft presentation for Sec. of Army, ?.8.1955, in WvBP-LC, Box 61, "Speeches and Writings, 1953–56"; Cleaver to Singer, 26.5.1954, in NASM, Singer Papers.

11. Cleaver to Singer, 26.5.1954, in NASM, Singer Papers; Durant notes of 25.6.1954 meeting, Durant Papers; the first extensive written description of the cluster is in WvB, "A Minimum Satellite Vehicle," 15.9.1954, copies in various places including WvBP-H, file 800-2.

12. WvB, "A Minimum Satellite Vehicle," 15.9.1954, WvBP-H, file 800-2.

13. S&O, *WvB*, 123; Durant notes of 6.9.1954 meeting in Durant Papers, Orbiter file; WvB, "The Story," 8–9 (quotes); WvB desk calendar entry, 17.6.1954, in WvBP-H, file 306-2. Several accounts, stemming from a 1956 Hoover speech, begin with Durant phon-

ing Hoover on 23.6., confirming von Braun's attendance two days later. However, the desk calendar makes it clear that it was not the first call.

14. Bergaust, *WvB*, 235–36; agenda and Durant notes of 25.6.1954 meeting, Durant Papers, Orbiter file.

15. Bergaust, *WvB*, 325–26; Clarke, *Astounding Days*, 181–82; WvB-Clarke corr., 1951–53, in WvBP-H, files 400-2 and 400-3.

16. WvB to Marché Goddard, 29.4.1954, in WvBP-H, file 207-13; Smith, "They're Following," 54–57 (Kimball quote, 55); Watts, *Magic Kingdom*, 268–71, 308–9, 365–66.

17. WvB corr. with Goddard, Bonestell, and Ned Brown/MCA, 4.–6.1954, and WvB to Brown, 17.1.1955, in WvBP-H, file 207-13. On Pal, see esp. Bonestell to Ley, 16.9.1953, in WvBP-H, file 600-5, and WvB to Brown, 17.1.1955, in file 207-13.

18. WvB corr. with Goddard, Brown, and Ley, 5–6.1954, in WvBP-H, file 207-13.

19. WvB to Ley, 1.7.1954, in NASM, Ley Collection, Box 10; WvB-Bonestell-Ley corr., 11.53-5.54, in WvBP-H, files 401-1 and 600-5, and WvBP-LC, Box 50, Conquest of the Moon; WvB to Bosché, 28.7.1954, in WvBP-H, file 207-13; WvB to Ley, 3.4. and 11.6.1955, in WvBP-LC, Box 45; WvB to J. Engel/Der Spiegel, 18.10.1957, NASER, RG255, 77-0021, For. Corr. of WvB, Box 2465, 1961 E.

20. WvB to Ley, 1.7.1954, in NASM, Ley Collection, Box 10; transcripts of story meetings, 17.–19.7.1954, in WDA, von Braun Notes, and TWA press release, 7.7.1955, and *Disneyland News* clipping, 10.3.56, in same, Flight to the Moon (Tomorrowland, DL); WvB to parents, 26.7.1954, in BAK, N1085/84; WvB-Stuart/MCA corr., 7.–12.1954, in WvBP-H, file 207-13. Both the press release and *Disneyland News* claim the consultation of WvB and Ley in the ride, but no evidence for WvB doing so survives in the WDA or the WvB Papers. That Ley had a role is shown in his memo to Adelquist, 22.10.1954, WDA, Prod. 5576 Moon Picture, Correspondence.

21. Shows, *Walt*, 29–30; Smith, "They're Following" 57 ("accent"); Piszkiewicz, *WvB*, 85; Ward, *Dr. Space*, 105. In 1970 he told the FBI, in response to a spurious claim by a Czech spy to have been his mistress, that he had been a "pretty good boy" in his marriage, which is less than a flat denial: NACP, RG65, E.A1-136AB, Box 152, file 105-10747.

22. Shows, *Walt*, 30; WvB to parents, 26.7.1954, in BAK, N1085/84; Kimball to WvB, 9.10.1954, in WvBP-H, file 207-13; Bosché quoted in Ward, *Dr. Space*, 91.

23. Shows, *Walt*, 31; Piszkiewicz, *WvB*, 85–86; WvB FBI file in NACP, RG65, E.A1-136AB, Boxes 151-152, file 105-10747; army surveillance in RG319, IRR/PNF WvB, Box 657A.

24. Quoted in Smith, "They're Following," 61, based on a Kimball interview by Smith available at WDA. The 1956 Mars show correspondence is missing from the WvB Papers but can be found in WDA, Misc.-Correspondence and Memos-5563.

25. WvB to parents, 26.7.1954, in BAK, N1085/84; WvB to Kimball, 28.8., partial Moon ms., and Bosché to WvB, 15.9 and 9.12., and reply 14.12.1954, in WvBP-H, file 207-13; typed Moon ms. in file 207-14; sketches, 8.1954, in WvBP-LC, Box 51, Voyage to the Moon; Disney program "Man and the Moon," first broadcast 28.12.1955, on DVD *Tomorrowland: Disney in Space and Beyond.* They also put a reactor on the space station.

26. WvB-Kimball-Bosché-Ley corr., 9–10.1954, in WvBP-H, file 207-13, receipt for airfare check in file 207-14; Watts, *Magic Kingdom*, 310; "Man in Space" on DVD *Tomorrowland.*

27. Kimball to WvB, 22.2., and WvB to Bosché, 27.2.1955, in file 207-14; "Man in Space" on DVD *Tomorrowland*; Smith, "They're Following," 57.

28. Quoted in *Nashville Banner*, 15.4.1955, copy in NACP, RG156, E.1039A, Box 72,

Project von Braun; WvB to parents, 5.5.1955, in BAK, N1085/84; security clearance paperwork, 1954–55, in NACP, RG319, IRR PNF WvB, Box 657A; WvB testimony, 14.12.1957, in U.S. Congress, *Hearings Before the Preparedness Investigating Subcommittee*, 582. Magnus vB Jr. had already become a citizen with a smaller group in 11.1954, as he had crossed the Juárez bridge sooner.

29. WvB to Martz, 30.8.1954, in WvBP-H, file 409-9; WvB desk calendar entry, 3.8.1954, in WvBP-H, file 306-2, and WvB, "A Minimum Satellite Vehicle," 15.9.1954, in file 800-2. For further detail on the satellite project, see my "Orbiter" article in Launius, *Reconsidering*, 231–57.

30. WvB, "A Minimum Satellite Vehicle," 15.9.1954, in WvBP-H, file 800-2; Durant notes to 6.9.1954 meeting in Durant Papers, Orbiter file; WvB to A. Thiel et al., 9.11.1954, in USSRC, Ordway Coll., Project SLUG/ORBITER.

31. WvB, "A Minimum Satellite Vehicle," 15.9.1954, in WvBP-H, file 800-2.

32. Ibid.," 15.9.1954, in WvBP-H, file 800-2; Durant to WvB, 4.9., and reply 10.9.1954, in same, file 401-8; Bissell to Dulles, end 9.1954, and related documents in NACP Library, RG263, CREST database of released CIA documents, courtesy Dwayne Day; Orbiter proposal, 1.1955, in NACP, RG156, E.1039A, Box 91, ORBITER (File #1); conversations with Fred Durant, c. 1999.

33. Durant notes of 6.10. and 6.12.1954 meetings, attendance list to latter, and timeline in Durant Papers, Orbiter file; Hoover memo to Rear Admiral Furth and Major General Simon, 14.12.1954, in AMCOM/HO, Satellite Info. 1953–56, copy courtesy Matt Bille; Orbiter proposal, 1.1955, in NACP, RG156, E.1039A, Box 91, ORBITER (File #1); S&O, *WvB* (Amer. ed.), 124, quote Durant on the hotel meeting but wrongly place it on 25.6.1954.

34. WvB to Flickinger, 23.12.1954, in AMCOM/HO, Satellite Info. 1953–56.

35. Chatfield to ORDTU, 30.7.1954, and McCormack/USAF to DCAS, Logistics, 4.1.1955, in NASER, RG255, MSFC/ULMF, Series 5: Juno, Box 13, New Projects; Simon to Chief of Ordnance, 8.2.1955, in NACP, RG156, E.1039A, Box 96, Misc. Docs. (Redstone); James Coolbaugh memoir on origins of USAF sat. program, courtesy D. Day; Yates/AFMTC to Power, 22.11.1954, in USAF History Support Office, Schriever Papers, roll 35254/F1258, and Schriever to Power, 30.3.1955, roll 35257/F407-08, courtesy J. Neufeld; J. Neufeld, *Development*, 144.

36. Hoover to Fortune on 17.3. meeting, 28.3.1955, and schedule, guest list, and related documents on 23.–24.5.1955 trip, in Durant Papers, courtesy Fred Durant; photos of trip in NACP, RG156, E.1039A, Box 91, Orbiter (File #1).

37. McDougall, *Heavens*, 119–21; Hall in Logsdon, ed., *Exploring*, 1:221–22 and Day in 2:238–42; Neufeld, "Orbiter," in Launius, *Reconsidering*, 239–40.

38. For a detailed analysis of the Committee, see Neufeld, "Orbiter," in Launius, *Reconsidering*, 240–47.

39. Stewart to Pickering, "Review," 19.4., and Stewart Comm. "Report," 4.8.1955, JPL Archives, roll 10-3/F547-61 and 775 (the army proposal is Appendix C, frames 765–94), and Froehlich, "Feasibility Study," 15.7.1955, doc. 3-593; WvB memo, 9.6.1955, on April meetings at JPL in AMCOM/HO, Satellite Info. 1953–56; minutes of 16.7.1955 meeting at JPL in NACP, RG156, E.1039A, Box 91, Orbiter (File #1); Rosen OHI by MJN, 24.7.1998, 6–7.

40. Stewart Comm. "Report," 4.8.1955, JPL Archives, roll 10-3/F820-21; WvB, "1000 Mile Missile Presentation," 8.7, in WvBP-H, file 800-9, and Bosché to WvB, 27.6.1955, and script in file 207-14; minutes of 8.7.1955 meeting in NACP, RG156, E.1039A, Box 34; Redstone Arsenal history, 1.7.–31.12.1955, in same, Box 44; WvB statement, 5.8.1955,

and drafts in same, Box 72, Project von Braun; WvB-Ley corr., 7.-8.1955, in WvBP-LC, Box 45; WvB to parents, late 7.1955, in BAK, N1085/84. The book is Ley, WvB, and Bonestell, *Exploration of Mars.*

41. Copies of DDEL docs., 7.1955, on satellite announcement in NASA/HD, HRC 12401 and 12402; CIA/OSI Scientific Intelligence Digest excerpt, 9.5.1955, in NACP, RG156, E.1039A, Box 91, Orbiter (File #1), and WvB statement, 5.8.1955, and drafts in Box 72, Project von Braun; Nickerson and WvB talks, 3.8.1955, in AMCOM/HO, Satellite Info. 1953–56. Needell, *Science,* 340–42, provides excellent commentary on the preparation for the satellite announcement, but the specific timing remains a mystery.

42. S&O, *WvB* (Amer. ed.), 127; minutes of 16.7.1955 meeting at JPL in NACP, RG156, E.1039A, Box 91, Orbiter (File #1), and Edson to Hirshhorn, 22.7.1955, in same box, Search for Natural Satellites of Earth; Sampson to Rechtin, 25.7.1955, in JPL Archives, roll 33-2. For von Braun's later summary of his emotional reaction, see WvB to Mainz, 1.11.1957, in WvBP-H, file 208-7.

43. Stewart Comm. "Report," 4.8.1955, JPL Archives, roll 10-3/F682-821; Neufeld, "Orbiter," in Launius, *Reconsidering,* 240–47.

44. Kaplan to Waterman, 6.5.1955, in Logsdon, *Exploring,* 1:302–3 ("German V-2 . . ."); McMath to Stewart, 1.8.1955, in JPL Archives, roll 10-3/F684; Green and Lomask, *Vanguard,* 48; WvB to Singer, 9.9.1955, in USSRC, Ordway Collection, Project Slug/Orbiter.

45. Nickerson cable to Toftoy, 4.8., JPL to WvB, Nickerson et al., 9. and 12.8., Simon to Quarles, 15.8., and GMDD/OML "Comments on Project Slug," 17.8.1955, in AMCOM/HO, Satellite Info. 1953–56.

46. R&D Policy Council minutes, 16.8.1955 meeting, in NACP, RG319, E.39, Records Relating to the R&D Policy Council, Box 2; Rosen OHI by MJN, 24.7.1998, 16; Green and Lomask, *Vanguard,* 51–53.

47. Rosen OHI by MJN, 24.7.1998, 16; WvB to Mainz, 1.11.1957, in WvBP-H, file 208-7; Stewart to Chair, R&D Policy Council, 24.8.1955, in JPL Archives, roll 10-3/F86-87; R&D Policy Council minutes, 24.8.1955 meeting, in NACP, RG319, E.39, Records Relating to the R&D Policy Council, Box 2.

48. Singer to WvB, 24.8., and reply 9.9.1955, in USSRC, Ordway Collection, Project Slug/Orbiter; Singer to WvB, 21.9.1955, in WvBP-LC, Box 2, 1955 R to Z. Again, see the analysis in Neufeld, "Orbiter," in Launius, *Reconsidering,* 240–47.

49. WvB insertion in WvB and Robinson, "How We Did It," ms. for *This Week,* 2.1958, in WvBP-LC, Box 46, Speeches and Writings, Jan.–Apr. 1958 (pub. version: "The Story . . .") and Nickerson draft letter for WvB to Brucker, 3.1.1961, in Box 11, 1965 H-N; Morris to ORDTB, 2.9.1955, in NACP, RG156, E.1039A, Box 91, Orbiter (File #1); JPL to WvB, Nickerson et al., 9. and 12.8., and WvB, "Missions and Equipment of RS 27," 8.9.1955, in AMCOM/HO, Satellite Info. 1953–56.

50. Grimwood and Stroud, *History,* 5–13; Armacost, *Politics,* 49–73.

51. WvB to parents, 24.11.1955, in BAK, N1085/84; Armacost, *Politics,* 127.

52. WvB to WD, 4.11.1953 and 7.1.1955, in WvBP-H, file 430-5.

53. Medaris, *Countdown,* 13, 68–75; WvB to parents, 5.3.1956, in BAK, N1085/84; ABMA staff meeting, 9.3.1956, in MP/FIT, DJ; Glennan quote ("spit and polish") in Hunley, *Birth of NASA,* 9.

54. Transcript of 5.1.1956 meeting with WvB, Medaris, in NASER, RG255, MSFC/ULME, Series 4, Box 41, file I-H-1, and WvB, "Justification for Super Grades," 1.2.1956, in Box 40, I-D-1; WvB to parents, 5.3. and 18.6.1956 ("Big-Time"), in BAK, N1085/84.

55. WvB to parents, 18.6.1956, and other letters, 1954–57, in BAK, N1085/84; Ward, *Dr. Space*, 80.

56. Grimwood and Stroud, *History*, 14–16; Tompkins, *Organizational Communication Imperatives*, 62–63.

57. Stubno, "Von Braun Rocket Team," 447–48; Bucher to WvB, 28.2.1972, in UHCL, Bilstein, "Stages," 3–17. Board minutes for mid-1956 to mid-1960 can be found in NASER, RG255, MSFC/ULMF, Series 4, Box 42, II-B-14.

58. WvB, "Teamwork"; Dunar and Waring, *Power*, 39–51; Ward, *Dr. Space*, 152–53.

59. Medaris report, 9.–12.1.1956 trip to L.A. with WvB et al., in MP/FIT, "Trip Reports," Nickerson memo, 28.1.1956 meeting with navy, in same, "Invitations, Conferences . . . ," minutes of 1.2. Medaris-WvB meeting in Memoranda (Internal) 1955 & 1956, and 2.2.1956 meeting in DJ of that date; Grimwood and Stroud, *History*, 55–56.

60. Grimwood and Stroud, *History*, 28, 30; Tousley memo, 15.2.1956, in MP/FIT, Memoranda (Internal) 1955 & 1956; Medaris to Zierdt, 16.2.1956, in AMCOM/HO, Jupiter C (Redstone #27); Hibbs, "Development of the High-Speed Stages . . . ," 13.4.1956, JPL Archives, doc. 3-594; Nickerson talk to Stewart Comm., 23.4.1956, in AMCOM/HO, Satellite Info. 1953–56.

61. WvB to Stanton, 17.2. (quotes) and 7.4.1956, in WvBP-H, file 401-16; Stewart to Furnas, 23.2.1956, in JPL Archives, roll 10-3/F160-63; Schulze memo, 27.3.1956, in NASER, RG255, MSFC/ULMF, Series 2, Box 2, Redstone-Propellants UDMH Fuels; Hibbs, "Development . . . ," 13.4.1956, JPL Archives, doc. 3-594; Green and Lomask, *Vanguard*, 67–95.

62. Stewart Comm. docs., 3.–5.1956, in JPL Archives, roll 10-3; Nickerson and Medaris docs., 4.1956, in AMCOM/HO, Satellite Info. 1953–56; minutes of NSC meeting, 3.5.1956, in DDEL, Ann Whitman File, NSC Series, Box 7, courtesy D. Day.

63. WvB, "The Story," 36 ("danced"); Medaris, *Countdown*, 119–20; Small to Harris, 27.10.1973, citing Medaris 14.12.1957 Preparedness Hearings testimony, in MP/FIT, "Dagger A"; Orman report, 26.9.1956, in AMCOM/HO, Jupiter C (Redstone #27); Mrazek to WvB, 10.9.1956, in NASER, RG255, MSFC/ULMF, Series 2, Box 1, Redstone—Missions of Missiles, and ABMA "Satellite Capability" report, 4.1957, in MSFC/ULMF, Acc. 89-064, Box 6, Misc. Jupiter Program Reports 1957–58.

64. WvB to parents, 29.9.1956, in BAK, N1085/84; Medaris, *Countdown*, 121–22.

65. Memo, 15.8., and Medaris to Gavin and Cummings, 21.8.1956, in MP/FIT, Acceleration of the Jupiter, Project "Blast" 1956; minutes of Dev. Board, 4.9.1956, in NASER, RG255, MSFC/ULMF, Series 4, Box 42; Heppenheimer, *Countdown*, 114–16.

66. Armacost, *Politics*, 104–17.

67. Ambrose, *Eisenhower*, 2:354–73.

68. Armacost, *Politics*, 117–24; Medaris to Gavin et al., 20.11., in "Dagger A," ABMA Staff Meeting minutes, 23. and 30.11., in Minutes 1956, and Cummings to Medaris, 8.12.1956, in Confidential Corr., 1956–58, all MP/FIT; "Dagger Report," 11.1956, in NACP, RG156, E.1039A, Box 29; Stuhlinger to Medaris, 8.3.1957 (transcript of interview), in NASER, RG255, MSFC/ULMF, Series 4, Box 39, I-B-19, and WvB remarks, Board meeting minutes, 10.12.1956, in Box 42; Harris to WvB, 1.12.1956 in WvBP-LC, Box 2, 1956 H to R, and WvB to Roth, 10.4.1957, in Box 3, 1957 O to S.

69. Medaris, *Countdown*, 127–33; Armacost, *Politics*, 124–28; transcript, 3.1.1956, in MP/FIT, Nickerson Case 1957; Bergaust, *WvB*, 247–51 (quotes, 248); "Expert Attacks Missile Secrecy," *NYT*, 27.6.1957.

70. WvB memo, 12.12.1956, in NASER, RG255, MSFC/ULMF, Series 3, Box 2, IV.C.3, and Zierdt memo, 25.1.1957, in Series 5, Box 13, MRBM and Redstone II; Redstone rep.,

1.10.1956–30.6.1957, in NACP, RG156, E.1039A, Box 29; Medaris, *Countdown*, 137 (Rees quote).

71. Medaris, *Countdown*, 137–38; Heppenheimer, *Countdown*, 116–18; Grimwood and Stroud, *History*, 157; Thor chronology at http://www.geocities.com/thor_irbm/ chronology.htm.

72. Medaris, *Countdown*, 137–38; Grimwood and Stroud, *History*, 157; Heppenheimer, *Countdown*, 118–19.

73. Grimwood and Stroud, *History*, 156; Heller to Lucas, 9.4.1962, in WvBP-H, file 612-3; WvB to Schmidt, 14.9.1969, in NASER, RG 255, MSFC/ULMF, Acc. 01-0002, Box 24; Lucas presentation to "Rocketry in the 1950s" seminar, 28.10.1971, in JPL Archives, doc. 5-608.

74. Ibid. The second Jupiter-C was RS-34, the third RS-40.

75. WvB to parents, 21.4. (quotes), 20.6., and 1(?).7.1957, in BAK, N1085/84; army documents and clipping regarding the trip in NACP, RG319, IRR/PNF WvB, Box 657A.

76. WvB to Durant, 23.4.1957, in WvBP-H, file 401-19; Stewart to Furnas, 8.4., Smith to Stewart, 22.4., and Stewart to Holaday, 12.6.1957, in JPL Archives, roll 10-3/F274-76 and 302, and Van Allen telegram to Pickering, and Odishaw to Pickering, 18.4.1957, in roll 10-7; Stuhlinger to Van Allen, 23.11.1956, and reply, 13.2.1957, in U. Iowa Library Spec. Coll., Van Allen Papers, courtesy D. Day; ABMA "Satellite Capability" report, 4.1957, in NASER, RG255, MSFC/ULMF, Acc. 89-064, Box 6, "Misc. Jupiter Program Reports 1957–1958"; ABMA docs., 6.–7.1957, in AMCOM/HO, Satellite Info. 1953–56; Medaris DJ, 26.6., in MP/FIT, and Medaris memo to WvB, 27.6.1957, in same, Memoranda (Internal) 1957.

77. OCO, "Earth Satellite Situation," 5.1957, in NACP, RG319, E.185(UD), IGY Records, 1955–60, Box 2; OCB meeting minutes, 13. and 17.6.1957, NASA/HD, HRC 012403; WvB to Ehricke, 6.9.1957, in WvBP-LC, Box 42, A.V. Grosse Action 1951–57.

CHAPTER 13

1. In WvBP-H, file 401-1.

2. WvB, "The Story," 36 ("As told to Donald R. Robinson").

3. Ibid. ("If . . ."); Medaris, *Countdown*, 155; Harris, *Selling Uncle Sam*, 81. According to Harris, the British journalist called him at home with the news, seeking WvB's number. Harris phoned an aide to Medaris, who allegedly conveyed the news to the general and WvB. As the three memoirs conflict, it is impossible to construct a coherent story of how word reached the party, but WvB's memoir is so close to the event, that it carries the most credibility, even if it is ghostwritten based on an interview. All stories agree on the "sixty" and "ninety days" statements, however.

4. Medaris, *Countdown*, 157; Dickson, *Sputnik*, 23–25, 124–25; WvB to parents, 9.11.1957, in BAK, N1085/84.

5. McDougall, *Heavens*, 141–48.

6. Maria vB to vB parents, hand-dated 14.10.1957 (likely receipt date), in BAK, N1085/77; ABMA Staff Meeting minutes and Medaris DJ, 7.10.1957, in MP/FIT; Dickson, *Sputnik*, 108–33.

7. Dickson, *Sputnik*, 123–24 (quoting Yates, "top . . ."); Medaris DJ, 14.10.1957, in MP/FIT; Medaris cable to WvB, 16.10., meeting minutes, 18.10., Medaris memo, 23.10., WvB Notes, c. 23.10.1957, in AMCOM/HO, Satellite Info. 1957; Stewart to Holaday, 28.10.1957, in JPL roll 10-3/F352-54.

8. Zierdt memo on 24.10.1957 meeting in NASER, RG255, MSFC/ULMF, Series 5, Box 13, "Project 6/13"; Medaris DJ, 24.10.1957, in MP/FIT; Pickering OHI by Steve Henke/U. Iowa ("silence"); Green and Lomask, *Vanguard*, 196–99.

9. Medaris, "Jupiter Story," 12.1959, in AMCOM/HO, file 870-5e; Armacost, *Politics*, 166–72; Grimwood and Stroud, *A History*, 37–47, 157.

10. Harford in Launius et al., *Reconsidering*, 86–87; George R. Price in *Life*, 18.11.1957, 125–26.

11. Dickson, *Sputnik*, 145–47; Medaris DJ, 8.11.1957, in MP/FIT; Medaris, *Countdown*, 165–70; WvB, "The Story," 36.

12. WvB desk calendar notes, 14.10.1957, in WvBP-H, file 306-6; Medaris, *Countdown*, 174; Brucker to McElroy, 20.11., and Daley cable to Medaris, 26.12.1957, in AMCOM/HO, Satellite Info. 1957; Jean memo, 25.11.1957, in NASER, RG255, MSFC/ULMF, Series 5, Box 13, Project 6/13; Pickering cable to Medaris, 18.11.1957, in JPL roll 21-17.

13. *Life*, 18.11.1957, 133–39; *NYT Magazine*, 20.10.1957, 14, 86–88.

14. AP interview in *WP* and *NYT*, 10.11.1957; Medaris DJ, 9.11.1957, in MP/FIT; *Life*, 18.11.1957, 136; "Symington Victory Seen," *NYT*, 24.11.1957; "Butler Holds von Braun Responsible for Missiles," *WP*, 9.12.1957; "Von Braun Denies Top Missiles Role," *NYT*, 10.11.1957; Dickson, *Sputnik*, 201 ("publicity seeking").

15. AP interview in *WP* and *NYT*, 10.11.1957; *Life*, 18.11.1957, 136 (quote).

16. AP interview in *WP* and *NYT*, 10.11.1957; WvB, "The Meaning of Space Superiority," 1.1958?, in WvBP-H, file 200-21. The article was written for *This Week* (Chesnutt to WvB, 5.3.1958, in WvBP-H, file 200-30) and eventually appeared in much modified form as "How Satellites Will Change Your Life," 8.6.1958, 8–9, 36–37. Orbital bombs are included.

17. Siddiqi, *Challenge*, 153–54; Stuhlinger memo, 29.10.1957, in NASA/HD, HRC 1974. Von Braun became friendly with Sedov and other Soviet delegates at later IAF meetings, but he and Korolev never met.

18. McDougall, *Heavens*, 151–55; Medaris, *Countdown*, 177–78.

19. Bosché to WvB, 17.5.1956, and Bosché to Durant, 15.11.1957, in WDA, Misc.-Correspondence and Memos-5563; Smith, "They're Following," 60–63; Kimball interview by Smith, c. 1977, WDA; Green and Lomask, *Vanguard*, 207–12; Dickson, *Sputnik*, 155–59.

20. "Bigger Rocket an Urgent Need, Von Braun and Medaris Warn," *NYT*, 15.12.1957; "All-Out Push to Dominate Space Urged," *WP*, 15.12.1957; U.S. Congress, *Inquiry*, 597, 602–32; Clark to Medaris, unclassified summary of memo, 4.11.1957, in MP/FIT, Memoranda, Internal 1957–59.

21. U.S. Congress, *Inquiry*, 602–32; WvB to MvB Sr., 2.2.1958 and 1.2.1959, in BAK, N1085/84; Pickering OHI by MJN, 13.1.1999.

22. ABMA/DOD, "A National Integrated . . . ," DDEL, Office of the Staff Secretary, Subject Series, Defense Subseries, Box 8, copy courtesy D. Day; McDougall, *Heavens*, 197.

23. McDougall, *Heavens*, 166.

24. WvB, "Firing of Explorer I," 18.3.1958, NASER, RG255, WvB's Speeches, Box 5, and ABMA Board meetings, 11.1957–1.1958, in same, RG255, MSFC/ULMF, Series 4, Box 42, II-B-14, and WvB meeting with Rocketdyne, 20.3.1958, in Series 5, Box 15, New Engines; Grimwood and Stroud, "History," 155, 157–58; Bullard, "History," 149–50; WvB to Stanton, 4.3.1958, in WvBP-H, file 401-16; "Redstone Modernization Program" documents, 8.1957, in DDEL, Office of the Staff Secretary, Subject Series, Defense Sub-

series, Box 6, copies courtesy GWU/SPI; Medaris, "Jupiter Story," 12.1959, in AMCOM/HO, file 870-5e, III-10.

25. WvB desk calendar 1958, WvBP-H, file 303-3; Green and Lomask, *Vanguard*, 213–14.

26. WvB handwritten insertion ("It was . . .") in WvB and Robinson, "How We Did It," ms. for WvB, "The Story," in WvBP-LC, Box 46, Speeches and Writings, Jan.–Apr. 1958; WvB to MvB Sr., 2.2.1958, in BAK, N1085/84; Ops. Coord. Board memo, 29.1.1958, in NASA/HD, HRC 12403, 194–97.

27. Medaris, *Countdown*, 203–9; WvB desk calendar 1958, WvBP-H, file 303-3.

28. Hinrichs, "Friday, 31 January 1958," in MP/FIT, Booklets, Letters, Explorer I Anniversary Items; army teletype, 31.1.1958, copy attached to WvB to Schuppener, 23.8.1969, in WvBP-LC, Box 58, 1969 Congratulatory Letters.

29. Ibid.

30. Ibid.; WvB, "The Story," 37.

31. Ibid.; Stuhlinger, "The Story of Explorer I," NASM speech 31.1.1978, in NASA/HD, HRC 2241.

32. Army teletype, 31.1.1958, copy attached to WvB to Schuppener, 23.8.1969, in WvBP-LC, Box 58, 1969 Congratulatory Letters.

33. Hinrichs, "Friday, 31 January 1958," in MP/FIT, Booklets, Letters, Explorer I Anniversary Items; Ward, *Dr. Space*, 100; Dickson, *Sputnik*, 174.

34. Ibid.; WvB to MvB Sr., 2.2.1958, in BAK, N1085/84.

35. Pickering OHI by MJN, 13.1.1999; Dickson, *Sputnik*, 175–76; WvB to MvB Sr., 2.2.1958, in BAK, N1085/84.

36. WvB to MvB Sr., 2.2.1958, in BAK, N1085/84; S&O, *WvB*, 139.

37. WvB desk calendar 1958, WvBP-H, file 303-3; *Time*, 17.2.1958, cover, 21–25; *Der Spiegel*, 12.2.1958, cover, 36–42, and 28.12.1955, cover, 25–34; MvB Sr. to WvB, 5.5.1958, in BAK, N1085/84.

38. Ibid.; WvB, "Reminiscences" and "Space Man"; corr. about latter in WvBP-H, file 200-30.

39. Chesnutt to WvB, 5.3.1958, in WvBP-H, file 200-30, and *This Week* corr. in files 200-25, 200-31, and 200-35.

40. "First Men" corr. in WvBP-H, file 200-31; WvB, *First Men* (book version); WvB–*This Week* corr. on Mars story, 10.–11.1959, in WvBP-H, file 200-35, and ms. and memos, 3.1960, in file 201-18.

41. WvB corr. with Harry Walker agency, 1958–59, in WvBP-H, file 600-1; Medaris DJ, 4.9.1958 (quote), in MP/FIT, and Medaris to WvB, 8.2.1958, in same, Memoranda (Internal) 1958; von Braun speeches in WvBP-H, 100 series boxes, with less complete sets in NASER and NASA/HD.

42. WvB to Tischendorf, 14.4.1958, in WvBP-H, file 208-5, and Mainz to WvB, 12.6.1958, in file 208-7; Medaris to Clifton, 6.6.1958, in MP/FIT, Official Corr. A-D 1958. WvB's "I Aim at the Stars" files are in WvBP-H, Boxes 208 to 210. Material on the Pentagon's involvement is in Georgetown University's Lauinger Library, Special Collections, DOD Film Collection, Boxes 22 and 23.

43. Rhombus-Film to WvB, 15.6., and check, 24.6.1957, in WvBP-H, file 208-5; 1516 Big Cove Road house paperwork in same, files 600-10 to 601-3; WvB to parents, 12.5. and 13.6.1958, in BAK, N1085/84; Ward, *Dr. Space*, 102.

44. Maria vB to Emmy vB, 24.2.1958, in BAK, N1085/73; Ward, *Dr. Space*, file 103-04, 149; WvB to Grogan, 4.6.1958, in WvBP-H, file 103-1 (quote).

45. Ward, *Dr. Space*, 107; Ordway-WvB corr., spring 1956, in WvBP-H, files 401-11

and 815-9; Sherrod notes, 20.8.1970, in NASA/HD, HRC 13287. The basis for my observation lies primarily in the inspection of hundreds of files in the WvB Papers in both places.

46. Medaris-Holaday phone call, Medaris DJ, 5.2.1958, in MP/FIT, and Storke to Chief of Staff, 14.3.1958, in same, Official Corr. R–Z 1958; WvB speech, 27.3.1958, in WvBP-LC, Box 46, Speeches and Writings, Jan.–Apr. 1958; Harford in Launius et al., *Reconsidering,* 88–92.

47. News release, 4.1959, "The Argus Experiment," in NACP, RG338, E.69B-0587, Box 3, Historian's Background Material, Redstone Missile #44, 1958–61; Medaris-Pickering-ARPA mtg., 17.4.1958, in AMCOM/HO, Satellite Info. 1958–60; Medaris to Daley, 25.4.1958, in MP/FIT, Official Corr. A–D 1958 (quote).

48. Medaris-York phone call, Medaris DJ, 7.3.1958, in MP/FIT; WvB to Stanton, 4.3.1958, in WvBP-H, file 401-16; Johnson/ARPA to Medaris, 3.7.1958, and news release, 4.1959, "The Argus Experiment," in NACP, RG338, E.69B-0587, Box 3, Historian's Background Material, Redstone Missile #44, 1958–61; WvB to parents, 12.5.1958, in BAK, N1085/84.

49. "Dick" to Medaris, 1.3.1958, in MP/FIT, Confidential Corr., 1956–58; Johnson to Medaris, "ARPA Order #1-58," and attached Johnson to Brucker, both 27.3.1958, in AMCOM/HO, Satellite Info. 1958–60.

50. Stuhlinger memo to WvB on "Moon-Rocket," 24.10.1957, copy in USSRC, Ordway Collection, Project Vanguard Documents, ABMA-1957; Small and Bank, "Red Socks Project" memo, 19.11.1957, in JPL roll 211-2, Deal & Red Socks 10/57–2/58; Johnson to Medaris, "ARPA Order #1-58," 27.3.1958, and Medaris-Pickering-ARPA mtg., 17.4.1958, in AMCOM/HO, Satellite Info. 1958–60; Craig Waff, draft chap. 1, DSN History, courtesy of author.

51. Adam chronology, 2.9.1958, in NASA/HD, HRC 12057; Springer, "Project Adam"; Swenson et al., *This New Ocean,* 77–82, 91–93, 99–100.

52. ABMA, "Development Proposal for Project Adam," 17.4.1958, copy in NASA/HD, HRC 12057; Durant to "Phil" (Strong/CIA?), 24.3.1958, in NASM, Durant bio. file.

53. U.S. Congress, *Astronautics and Space Exploration,* 74, 117; Medaris-WvB conversation, Medaris DJ, 10.2.1958, in MP/FIT.

54. Grimwood and Stroud, "History," 158–60; ABMA-RCA docs., 10.1956, in NACP, RG156, E.1039A, Box 91; Brucker to Holaday, 26.10.1957, Gavin cable to Medaris, 4.11.1957, in AMCOM/HO, Satellite Info. 1957; ABMA–Signal Corps–RCA meeting, 18.2., Medaris-Pickering-ARPA meeting, minutes, 17.4., and Schuppener to Zierdt, 2.5.1958, transmitting Johnson to Medaris, in AMCOM/HO, Satellite Info. 1958–60; Day, "The Clouds Above," 306 ("Let's . . .").

55. Satterfield and Akens, "Government-Contractor Relationships at ABMA," 1.7.59, in NACP, RG156, E.1039A, Box 53; WvB memo on Pershing, 28.1.1958, NASER, RG255, MSFC/ULMF, Series 4, Box 42, II-B-14. In March 1958 General Medaris was promoted to head a new Army Ordnance Missile Command (AOMC), including ABMA, Redstone Arsenal, and all Arsenal rocket projects reorganized into an Army Rocket and Guided Missile Agency (ARGMA), plus White Sands and indirect command over JPL. Medaris appointed his former deputy Brigadier General Jack Barclay to head ABMA but remained in effective command. Holger Toftoy was briefly deputy commanding general for AOMC but disliked Medaris intensely and escaped to command the Aberdeen Proving Ground in Maryland.

56. ABMA Staff Meeting, 27.3.1959, in MP/FIT, Minutes–1959 (quote); Dev. Ops. Board meetings, 20.1., 19.2., and 24.3.1958, NASER, RG255, MSFC/ULMF, Series 4,

Box 42, II-B-14, and Rees to WvB, 5.4.1958, in Box 40, I-F ABMA, and Millane memo, "Management of Jupiter IOC Program," 6.6.1958, in Series 3, Box 2, Organization and Procedures.

57. Minutes of meeting with ARPA and Medaris memo, both 27.6.1958, in MP/FIT, Memoranda (Internal) 1958; Medaris to Barclay, 18.4., and Medaris to Johnson, 20.5.1958, in AMCOM/HO, Satellite Info. 1958–60; ABMA-JPL Juno IV conference, 19.–21.8.1958, and Froehlich trip report, 11.9.1958, JPL roll 33-1A; Burke Juno IV report, 27.10.1958, JPL roll 211-4; JPL minutes of 31.10.1958 meeting with ABMA, JPL roll 211-3 (WvB quote).

58. Bilstein, *Stages*, 26–31; Belew memo on WvB visit to Rocketdyne on 20.3.1958, in NASER, RG255, MSFC/ULMF, Series 5, Box 15, X-L-2, and "Fact Sheet for Juno V Meeting at ARPA," 23.9.1958 in Series 4, Box 35, 9.a.1; WvB-Canright phone call, 4.8.1958, and WvB-York phone call, 18.9.1958, in WvB DJ, copies in UHCL, Bilstein "Stages," file 2-13, and ARPA order 14-59, 15.8.1958, in file 3-12; Zierdt to Barclay, 26.9.1958, in AMCOM/HO, Satellite Info. 1958–60. Von Braun preferred four Rocketdyne E-1 engines of twice the thrust, but the E-1 had been dying on the vine for lack of support in the air force and ARPA.

59. WvB speech, 9.7.1959, in NASER, RG255, WvB's Speeches, Box 6 (quote); Dev. Ops. Board meeting, 27.3.1959, NASER, RG255, MSFC/ULMF, Series 4, Box 42, II-B-14, WvB to parents, 22.5., 13.6, 12.7., 28.7.1958, in BAK, N1085/84.

CHAPTER 14

1. York, *Making Weapons*, 175.

2. WvB to parents, 13.6, 28.7., and 15.8.1958, in BAK, N1085/84; WvB to Dr. Frenkel, 30.9., and attached clipping, 25.8.1958, in WvBP-LC, Box 19, Aug.–Sept. 1958; Medaris DJ, 18. and 29.9.1958 (quote from latter), MP/FIT. For further detail see my article, "The End of the Army Space Program."

3. McDougall, *Heavens*, 195–200.

4. Silverstein to Glennan, 25.9.1958, attached to "Considerations Preparatory to . . . ," 20.8.1959, in NASER, RG255, MSFC/ULMF, Series 13, Box 15, NASA-Army Transfer Plan; Bonney to Glennan, 30.9.1958, in NASA/HD, HRC 12051.

5. Glennan memoir in Hunley, *Birth of NASA*, 10.

6. WvB to parents, 16.11.1958, BAK, N1085/84; Medaris DJ, 10. and 16.10., and 4.11.1958, MP/FIT; Ordnance memoranda, 15. and 20.10.1958, NACP, RG156, E.1039A, Box 90, Army Support to NASA.

7. Medaris, *Countdown*, 246; WvB statement, 15.10.1958, in NASER, RG255, MSFC/ULMF, Series 13, Box 15, NASA-Army Transfer Plan; "New Agency 'Requests' Scientists," *Baltimore Sun*, 15.10., and "Protest Led by Von Braun," 16.10.1958; "Missile Unit Shift Awaits Ike's Decision," *WP*, 16.10.1958; "Army Scientists Balk at Change," *NYT*, 16.10.1958; "Von Braun Hits Plan to Shift Missile Team," *Washington Star*, 16.10.1958; Hunley, *Birth of NASA*, 11.

8. NASA-Army agreements, 3.12 1958, in Logsdon, *Exploring*, 2:287–90; Koppes, *JPL*, 94–99; Medaris, *Countdown*, 247.

9. Purser to Gilruth, 13.10.1958, in UHCL, JSC Center Series, Paul Purser Logs to Gilruth, Box 1. For early discussions of women as astronauts, see Weitekamp, *Right Stuff, Wrong Sex*. Von Braun was as sexist as most other engineers then. In 1961–62 public speeches—see, e.g., 9. and 10.10.1961, in NASA/HD, HRC 2674—he often told a

crude joke he attributed to Bob Gilruth: in future spacecraft they would set aside "110 pounds. for recreational equipment." As a result of the controversy over women astronauts, he would learn to drop that line: Slattery to WvB, 9.9.1964, in WvBP-H, file 202-48.

10. Murray and Cox, *Apollo,* 29; Kraft, *Flight,* 83 (quote).

11. Kraft, *Flight,* 103–4.

12. Swenson et al., *This New Ocean,* 123, 151, 171–73, 178–87; Glenn, *John Glenn,* 282–83; Kuettner memo on 20.3.1959 meeting at Langley, in NASER, RG255, MSFC/ULMF, Series 1, Box 2, Project Adam-Mercury.

13. WvB to Pickering, 30.6.1959, in JPL roll 10-6, Pickering 1959 Corr.

14. Swenson et al., *This New Ocean,* 151; North memo, 4.12.1958, in NASWR, RG255, E.70, Box 2; Purser to Gilruth, 5.12.1958, 23.6. and 14.7.1959, in UHCL, JSC Center Series, Paul Purser Logs to Gilruth, Box 1.

15. ABMA staff meetings, 8.1. and 27.3.1959, in MP/FIT, Minutes-1959, and Medaris to Brucker, 26.1.1959, in Official Corr. A-D 1959; Nash, *The Other Missiles;* "Can Use $50 Million More: Rocket Expert," *New York News,* 21.1.1959; "Space Plans Seen Hurt by Economy," *WP,* 31.1.1959; WvB to Barclay and Medaris, 16.1.1959, in MP/FIT, Personal and Confidential Correspondence 1959.

16. WvB to Barclay and Medaris, 16.1.1959, in MP/FIT, Personal and Confidential Correspondence 1959.

17. Ibid.

18. Medaris DJ, 29.5.1959, MP/FIT.

19. Heppenheimer, *Countdown,* 151–53; Furniss, "The Early Pioneers," 428–30. The first launch attempt, on 17.8.1958, failed during launch and got no designation.

20. Medaris DJ, 2.–5.12.1958, in MP/FIT; Pioneer III press conference, 6.12.1958, in JPL roll 33-2; Furniss, "The Early Pioneers," 430; "Meet the Press" transcript, 7.12.1958 in WvBP-H, file 104-4.

21. Medaris-Pickering phone calls, Medaris DJ, 31.12.1958, in MP/FIT; Debus memo on Jupiter AM-14, 13.2.1959, in NASER, RG255, MSFC/ULMF, Series 5, Box 3, IX-1; Heppenheimer, *Countdown,* 153–55 (*Time* quote, 155).

22. ABMA, "Pioneer in Space," 1959, in NACP, RG156, E.1039A, Box 77; Furniss, "The Early Pioneers," 430; WvB to parents, 4.3.1959, in BAK, N1085/84.

23. Bergaust, *Rocket City, U.S.A.,* 142–43; Bilstein, *Stages,* 36–39; "Brief Resume of Missile Programs," c. 6.1959, in NASER, RG255, MSFC/ULMF, Series 4, Box 41, II-B-1, and Medaris to Johnson/ARPA, 23.6.1959, in Box 35, 9.a.1; Johnson to Medaris, 9.7.1959, ARPA Order 14-60, copy in UHCL, Bilstein "Stages" collection, 3–12.

24. Armacost, *Politics,* 234–37; York, *Making Weapons,* 166–74. For further detail on the second crisis, see my article, "The End of the Army Space Program."

25. Zierdt cable to Chief of Ordnance, 31.8.1959, in AMCOM/HO, Satellite Info. 1958–60; Medaris DJ, 31.8.1959, MP/FIT.

26. Kaiser, "Notes for General Barclay and Col Paul," 1.9. (quote), in AMCOM/HO, Satellite Info. 1958–60; "Considerations Preparatory to . . . ," 20.8.1959, in NASER, RG255, MSFC/ULMF, Series 13, Box 15, NASA-Army Transfer Plan; Medaris to Brucker, 3.9.1959 (quote from Glennan), MP/FIT, Personal and Confidential Correspondence 1959.

27. Harford, *Korolev,* 142; Medaris DJ, 14.9.1959, MP/FIT.

28. Medaris DJ, 14.9.1959, MP/FIT; Sloop, *Liquid Hydrogen,* 227–29; "Can Use $50 Million More: Rocket Expert," *New York News,* 21.1.1959. For York's attitude, see the epigraph to this chapter.

29. WvB OHI by Emme and Ray, 27.8.1970, in NASA/HD, HRC 2630; Medaris "<u>EYES ONLY</u>" memo to Hinrichs or Schomburg, 21.9.1959, MP/FIT, Personal and Confidential Correspondence 1959.

30. Medaris, "<u>EYES ONLY</u>" memo to Hinrichs or Schomburg, 21.9.1959, MP/FIT, Personal and Confidential Correspondence 1959; Medaris press conference on retirement, 27.10.1959, in MP/FIT, Corr. Re: Retirement; Glennan memoir in Hunley, *Birth of NASA,* 23.

31. Glennan to Dryden et al., 7.10.1959, with draft proposal of 6.10.1959, and Glennan press statement, 21.10.1959, copies in NASA/HD, HRC 12051, and Glennan and Gates, Memorandum for the President, 21.10.1959, copy in HRC 12054; Medaris DJ, 14. and 21.10.1959, MP/FIT; Harford, *Korolev,* 143–44; "Battle on to Control New Rocket," *New York Herald-Tribune,* 2.10.1959; "Ike Calls His Top Aides in Space-Missile Crisis," *Washington Daily News,* 21.10.1959; "Eisenhower Acts to Strip the Army of Its Space Role," *NYT,* 22.10.1959.

32. WvB to parents, 4.10.1959, BAK, N1085/84; Horner OHI by Emme and Sloop, 13.3.1974, NASA/HD, HRC 1083.

33. WvB to Wiesman, 26.10.1959, in WvBP-H, file 209-7; "Von Braun Cites Work with Army," *NYT,* 22.10.1959.

34. Bilstein, *Stages,* 45–46; Sloop, *Liquid Hydrogen,* 230–39; A. Hyatt OHI 26.4.1974, in NASA/HD, HRC 1093 and E. Hall OHI, 7.6.1973, in HRC 917, both by Sloop?, and Hall minutes of Saturn meeting on 27.11.1959, in HRC 922.

35. Hyatt memo on phone conversation with Horner, 18.12.1959, in NASA/HD, HRC 2563; "Rocket Booster 'Saturn' Is Given High Priority," *WP,* 24.10.1959; "President Orders Speed-Up in Plans For Super-Rocket," *NYT,* 15.1.1960; "Von Braun Glum on Space Race," *NYT,* 3.2.1960; Bilstein, *Stages,* 50.

36. McGrory, "Von Braun's Fan Club," clipping from unidentified paper, 4.2.1960, in NASA/HD, file not found, photocopy in my possession.

37. Glennan to Persons, 17.12.1959, in Johns Hopkins U. Special Collections, Ms. 147: Dryden Papers, Box 3.12, 1958 Dec.; Hyatt to Horner, 11.1.1960, in UHCL, Bilstein "Stages" collection, Author Resource Files, Box 5, file 5-9; Glennan diary entry, 8.3.1960, in Hunley, *Birth of NASA,* 87; ABMA Board meeting, 18.3.1960, NASER, RG255, MSFC/ULMF, Series 4, Box 42, II-B-14.

38. See esp. "I Aim . . ." script corr. in WvBP-H, file 208-2; Mainz to WvB, 9.10.1958, in same, file 208-7 ("that no film . . ."); Defense Dept. vetting process in Georgetown U. Special Collections, DOD Film Collection, Box 22, files 22 and 23.

39. Froeschel, "The Wernher von Braun Story," 29.7.1958, in WvBP-H, file 208-11; Dratler, "I Aim at the Stars" script, 30.4.1959, in same, file 209-5; WvB to Irmgard Riedel, 28.10.1959, in same, file 405-1; "Das Baby," *Der Spiegel,* 21.10.1959.

40. WvB, comments on Froeschel draft, c. 8.1959, in WvBP-H, file 208-12, and WvB to Schneer, 2.1.1959, in same, file 208-2; partial draft script, 10.10.1959, in file 209-8.

41. Dratler, "I Aim at the Stars" script, 30.4.1959, in WvBP-H, file 209-5, partial draft script, 10.10.1959, in file 209-8, and WvB to Dornberger, 27.7.1959, in file 209-10; videotape of *I Aim at the Stars* (1960).

42. "V2 Man Von Braun Puts the Film Men Straight . . . ," *Daily Express,* 16.9.1959, clipping in WvBP-H, file 208-8, and WvB to Wiesman, 16.10.1959, in file 209-7; "Das Baby," *Der Spiegel,* 21.10.1959.

43. SvB-WvB corr., 8.1959, in WvBP-H, file 419-15a, Bourland/ABMA to Army Adjutant General, n.d. (1959), in file 604-11, and translation of *Izvestia* report, 10.9.1959, in

file 106-11; WvB speech text in "Raketen verlängern die dritte Dimension," *Frankfurter Allgemeine Zeitung,* 9.9.1959, copy in DM, Pers. 00020; English in WvBP-LC, Box 47, Speeches and Writings, Sept.–Oct. 1959.

44. WvB-parents corr, 8.1959–1.1960, in BAK, N1085/73 and 85; C.-F. vB interview by MJN, 29.3.2001; Ward, *Dr. Space,* 213; Bergaust, *WvB,* 350.

45. Mainz to WvB, 14.1., and WvB reply, 20.1.1960, in WvBP-H, file 208-7, and WvB-Schneer-Thompson-Baruch corr., 25.2.–24.3.1960 in file 208-2; WvB to father, 4.1, 14.1, 24.1., and 23.2.1960 (quote), in BAK, N1085/85.

46. WvB to father, 24.1. and 5.6.1960 (quote), in BAK, N1085/85; Ruland, *WvB,* 318.

47. WvB to father, 2.7.1960 (quote), in BAK, N1085/85; "Von Braun Story Told," *Washington Star,* 22.6.1960; Ward, *Dr. Space,* 80.

48. WvB to father, 2.7.1960, in BAK, N1085/85; corr. regarding premiere, 3.–8.1960, in WvBP-H, file 210-1.

49. "Film on Von Braun Has a Stormy Bow," *NYT,* 20.8.1960; "Krach um den Raketen-Braun," *Süddeutsche Zeitung,* 20.–21.8.1960, copy in DM, Pers. 00024; "Raketenstar im grellen Scheinwerfer," *Badisches Tageblatt,* 22.8.1960, copy in WvBP-H, file 416-5.

50. "The festival Opens with Rockets . . . ," *Evening Standard,* 22.8.1960, copy in WvBP-H, file 210-1; "Von Braun Film Banned," *WP,* 24.9., and "Suspects Soviets of Short-Cut," 29.9.1960; "Missile Film Picketed," *NYT,* 20.10., and "Britons Protest Film," 25.11.1960; "Londoners Protest Film on Von Braun," *Los Angeles Times,* 25.11.1960; Bergaust, *WvB,* 368–69.

51. Richard Coe, "Aim Is High in Space Film," *WP,* 29.9.1960; Bosley Crowther, "Screen: About von Braun," *NYT,* 20.10.1960; "Cinema" page, *Time,* 17.10.1960, WvB's copy in WvBP-H, file 210-5; WvB to Cleaver, 8.11.1960, WvBP-H, file 416-5; WvB to MvB Sr., 14.1.1961, in BAK, N1085/85.

52. WvB to MvB Sr., 11.9.1960, in BAK, N1085/85; Eisenhower to WvB, 8.9.1960, in WvBP-LC, Box 4, 1960 E to G; McDougall, *Heavens,* 229; York, *Arms,* 147 (Ike quote).

53. Horst von Kunkel, "Wernher von Braun: The Ex-Nazi Who Runs Our Space Program," *Confidential* 8 (Oct. 1960), no. 8, pp. 16–17, 42–43, copy in NASA/HD, HRC 2556. The "sometimes I hit London" joke even made it into an episode of the TV show *West Wing* in 2005.

CHAPTER 15

1. From interviews by Cornelius Ryan, 14.–16.7.1969, in OU/CRC, Box 163, folder 3.

2. Kraft, *Flight,* 118–20; Kranz, *Failure,* 29–30.

3. Ibid.; Murray and Cox, *Apollo,* 62–65.

4. Swenson et al., *This New Ocean,* 273–97, 300; Murray and Cox, *Apollo,* 65–67.

5. Maria vB to MvB Sr., 3.11.1960, in BAK, N1085/77, WvB to parents, 20.12.1953, in N1085/84, WvB to EvB, 26.11.59, in N1085/73, and WvB to MvB Sr., 14.1.1961, in N1085/85; WvB OHI by Sohier and Emme for JFK Library, 31.3.1964, in NASA/HD, HRC 2627. In 1953 the two discussed Kennedy's brother Joe, who had been killed in 1944 while flying an explosive-laden bomber to be radio-directed on a V-2 bunker site in France. It blew up over England.

6. Murray and Cox, *Apollo,* 55–56, 66–67.

7. See "Von Hopes to Fly in Space Ship to Moon," *NYT,* 24.8.1960, and his reaction to the story's inaccuracies in WvB DJ, 23.8.1960, in NASA/HD, HRC 13255.

8. WvB, *First Men to the Moon;* Brooks et al., *Chariots,* 4–6; Ordway et al., "Project Horizon." See also WvB presentation to JCS Joint Space Logistics Conference, 20.5.1959, in WvBP-H, file 801-21.

9. Rosen and Schwenk, "A Rocket"; Rosen OHI by MJN, 24.7.1998; Bilstein, *Stages,* 50–53.

10. WvB Memo for Record, 22.12.1959, and Hyatt to Horner, 11.1.1960, w/WvB marg. comments, in NASER, RG255, MSFC/ULMF, #89-064, Box 13; Hyatt to WvB, 18.1.1960, in NASA/HD, HRC 2563; Bilstein, *Stages,* 48–50, 157–59. The "A" and "B" versions of Saturn, with nonhydrogen upper stages, had been discarded in the Silverstein committee.

11. Hyatt to Horner, 11.1.1960, in NASER, RG255, MSFC/ULMF, #89-064, Box 13; Hyatt to WvB, 22.1.1960, in NASA/HD, HRC 2563; Kraemer, *Rocketdyne,* 144–47; Bilstein, *Stages,* 129–41. The Centaur, when mounted on a Saturn, would be called the S-V, but that never came to pass, although the Block I version of Saturn C-1 had the shape of the projected three-stage vehicle.

12. Murray and Cox, *Apollo,* 56–57; Brooks et al., *Chariots,* 14–15; Bilstein, *Stages,* 209–10.

13. Swenson et al., *This New Ocean,* 297–99, 310–18.

14. Siddiqi, *Challenge,* 251–54, 259–60; Swenson et al., *This New Ocean,* 323–25; Debus DJ, 6.2., and Kuettner to WvB and attached memo, 7.2.1961, in NASWR, RG255, E.70, Box 17; WvB DJ, 15. and 16.2.1961 (quote), in NASA/HD, HRC 13256 and Low interview by Sherrod, 28.6.1972, in 13257.

15. Swenson et al., *This New Ocean,* 325, 328–30; Glenn, *John Glenn,* 312–14; Harford, *Korolev,* 159–60; Siddiqi, *Challenge,* 265–82; Siddiqi e-mail to MJN, 3.11.2005. The extra mission was dubbed MR-BD for "Booster Development."

16. "Von Braun Hails Feat," *NYT,* 13.4.1961; Day and Siddiqi, "Moon"; Ward, *Dr. Space,* 120 (U-2 story); Leake (CIA) to Morris, 9.2.1961, in NASER, RG255, MSFC/ULMF, Series 11, Box 7, Security-CIA 1961; WvB DJ, 9.3.1961, in NASA/HD, HRC 13256, re: CIA briefing for NASA.

17. Logsdon, *Decision,* 83–108. For Webb's biography, see Lambright, *Powering Apollo.*

18. Logsdon, *Decision,* 108–12; JFK to LBJ, 20.4.1961, in Logsdon, ed., *Exploring,* 1:423–24, original in JFK Library, copy courtesy LBJ Library; Beschloss in Launius and McCurdy, eds., *Spaceflight,* 56.

19. Logsdon, *Decision,* 112–14; WvB DJ, 21.4.1961, copy in NASA/HD, HRC 13256.

20. WvB DJ, 21.4.1961, NASA/HD, HRC 13256.

21. Logsdon, *Decision,* 112–15; Shapley interview by MJN, 26.6.2003; WvB to Johnson, 29.4.1961, unredacted copy in NASA/HD, HRC 12503; redacted version in Logsdon, ed., *Exploring,* 1:429–33. Murray and Cox, *Apollo,* 81, say WvB made an opening presentation on 24.4.1961 but give no source.

22. WvB to Johnson, 29.4.1961, in NASA/HD, HRC 12503.

23. See Logsdon, *Decision,* 113.

24. On the cultural influence, see McCurdy, *Space.*

25. WvB DJ, 30.4.–4.5.1961 in NASA/HD, HRC 13256; WvB to H. David, 5.2.1965, with answers to questions, in WvBP-H, file 228-21 (block quotation); WvB to MvB Sr., 22.6.1961, in BAK, N1085/85.

26. WvB DJ, 11.5. and 19.5.1961, in NASA/HD, HRC 13256; Logsdon, *Decision,* 127.

27. JFK speech excerpt in Logsdon, *Decision,* 128; Ward, *Dr. Space,* 128; WvB itinerary, 25.–27.5.1961, in NASA/HD, HRC 13256; speech and program in WvBP-H, file 111-14; "Experts Outline U.S. Space Plans," *NYT,* 27.5.1961.

28. Murray and Cox, *Apollo,* 81–82; "Lunar Plan Gives U.S. Chance to Beat Reds," *WP,* 26.6.1961.

29. WvB to MvB Sr., 22.6.1961, in BAK, N1085/85; WvB notes for 29.5. Board meeting in NASA/HD, HRC 13256.

30. WvB DJ, 9. and 14.6.1961, in NASA/HD, HRC 13256; Brooks et al., *Chariots,* 44–45, 50–51; Murray and Cox, *Apollo,* 109–10.

31. WvB notes on "Heaton report," after 10.7.1961, in WvB green notebook, WvBP-H, file 307-2; Brooks et al., *Chariots,* 44–45; Murray and Cox, *Apollo,* 109, 118–19.

32. WvB green notebook entry, 22.5.1961, WvBP-H, file 307-2; WvB notes for 29.5. Board meeting, WvB-Storms phone call, 23.6., WvB-Ostrander phone call, 6.7., and WvB DJ, 15.9.1961, in NASA/HD, HRC 13256; Brooks et al., *Chariots,* 51; Bilstein, *Stages,* 209–11.

33. Taylor, "NASA Looks for 'Super' Boss for Apollo," *Missiles and Rockets* (17.7.1961), 56, copy in NASA/HD, HRC 7201; Brooks et al., *Chariots,* 19; Seamans OHI by Emme and Putnam, 8.5.1968, in NASA/HD, HRC 3622; Seamans, *Aiming,* 93.

34. Seamans, *Aiming,* 93.

35. WvB-Frank Phillips call in WvB DJ, 21.8.1961, NASA/HD, HRC 13256; WvB and Rees notes, undated (c. 8.1961) in WvBP-H, file 606-6. Von Braun was away from Huntsville on travel and vacation from 13.7 to 7.8.

36. Seamans OHI by Emme and Putnam, 8.5.1968, in NASA/HD, HRC 3622, including formerly closed sections.

37. Murray and Cox, *Apollo,* 51–52; Freitag interview by Sherrod, 17.3.1971, in NASA/HD, HRC 13286 ("that damned Nazi"); Finger interview by MJN, 7.2.2002; Seamans OHI by Collins, 19.1.1988, NASM ("our big . . .").

38. Johnson, *Secret,* chap. 5; Dunar and Waring, *Power,* 48.

39. WvB to Dixon, 25.9.1961, in WNRC, RG255, A73-732, Box 8, Speeches—Werner [*sic*] von Braun, copy in WvBP-H, file 600-4, together with original Webb memo to WvB, n.d.; WvB DJ, 5.12.1961, in NASA/HD, HRC 13256, mentioning memo signing.

40. Webb OHI by Needell and Collins, 4.11.1985, NASM (quote); Dembling interviews by MJN, 28.–29.7.2004.

41. Benson and Faherty, *Moonport,* 60–64; "460 Ton Moon Rocket Tops Hopes in Test," *Chicago Tribune,* 28.10.1961; WvB to MvB Sr., 10. and 17.9.1961, in BAK, N1085/85. The H-1 engine had not yet been rated to a high enough thrust to make a total thrust of 1.5 million.

42. Bilstein, *Stages,* 336–38; WvB DJ, 31.10. and 2.11.1961, in NASA/HD, HRC 13256; NASA News Release, 1.6.1961, in NASER, RG255, MSFC/ULMF, Series 4, Box 35, 9a. Saturn Overall Program, and Frick to Holmes, 23.2.1962, in #01-0002, Box 14.

43. Purser to Gilruth, 23.10.1961, in JSC, Center Series, Purser Logs to Gilruth, Box 1; WvB-Gilruth phone call, 24.11., and WvB DJ with attached documents, 13.–14.12.1961, in NASA/HD, HRC 13256; WvB green notebook entries, 31.10., 6.11., and 14.11.1961, in WvBP-H, file 307-2; Swenson et al., *This New Ocean,* 377–78; Kraft, *Flight,* 118.

44. Rosen to Holmes, 6.11. and 20.11.1961, in NASM, Rosen Papers; Rosen OHI by MJN, 24.7.1998; WvB-Rosen phone call, 7.12.1961, in NASA/HD, HRC 13256, and Gilruth interview by Logsdon, 26.8.1969, in HRC 13286 ("the hole . . ."); MSMC minutes, 21.12.1961, in NASER, RG 255, 73-2102, MSFC/ULMF, Series 7, Box 15. Rosen still advocated direct ascent for the lunar landing method but was increasingly isolated.

45. The most complete account of the LOR story from Houbolt's standpoint is Hansen, *Spaceflight Revolution,* chap. 8, which also appeared as a NASA History monograph. On

WvB, see interview by Sherrod, 19.11.1969, in NASA/HD, HRC 13254; Ryan, ed., *Conquest of the Moon*.

46. WvB interviews by Sherrod, 19.11.1969 and 25.8.1970, in NASA/HD, HRC 13254 (quote, wording as revised by WvB, in 25.8.1970); Murray and Cox, *Apollo*, 113–14 (Faget quote).

47. Hansen, *Spaceflight Revolution*, 236–60.

48. WvB-Gilruth call, 24.11.1961, in NASA/HD, HRC 13256, Sherrod interviews of WvB, 25.8.1970, in 13254, Disher, 24.9.1970, in HRC 13286, and Low, 16.1.1974, in HRC 13287; "Moon Flight from Orbit Now Being Studied," *WP*, 12.10.1961; WvB speeches, e.g., 26.4.1962, in WvBP-H, file 113-6.

49. Ward, *Dr. Space*, 147–48; Bergaust, *WvB*, 343–44; WvB to Dryden, 20.11.1961, w/itinerary, in WvBP-H, file 113-1, and WvB to Warsitz, 27.4.1962, in file 418-2. Hanna Reitsch arranged for them to meet Indian prime minister Nehru, but Nehru was away. WvB to Reitsch, 21.11.1961, in NASER, RG255, 77-0021, For. Corr. of WvB, Box 2465, 1961R, and WvB to Reitsch, 18.1.1962, in Box 2466, 1962R.

50. Shea trip report, 18.1.1962, in NASA/HD, HRC 2026, Shea OHI by Emme, 6.5.1970, in HRC 2011 (quotes), and WvB DJ, 31.1.1962, in HRC 13257; Murray and Cox, *Apollo*, 120–23, 133–35.

51. Shea trip report, 18.1.1962, in NASA/HD, HRC 2026 (quotes); Geissler memos, 12. and 26.2. with WvB marg. comments, and MSMC agenda with Houbolt/Mathews viewgraphs, 6.2.1962, in NASER, RG255, MSFC/ULMF, #01-0002, Box 14.

52. Murray and Cox, *Apollo*, 111–12, 127–28.

53. Ibid., 137–38 (Frick and Faget quotes, 138); Shea-WvB call, 2.4., and WvB DJ, 16.4.1962, in NASA/HD 13257; Mattson to Donlan, 20.4.1962, in UHCL, Apollo Program Chron. Files, 062-64 ("Apparently . . .").

54. WvB green notebook entries, 30.4. and 7.5.1962, in WvBP-H, file 307-3; Shea-WvB call, 7.5.1962, in NASA/HD 13257.

55. Markley report, 28.4.1962 (shows Holmes still pro-EOR), in UHCL, Apollo Program Chron. Files, 062-64, and Rector memo, 30.4.1962, in 062-65; Sherrod interviews of Shea, 6.5.1971 and 10.3.1973, in NASA/HD, HRC 13289; Low to Shea, 16.5., and Shea memo on 29.5.1962 MSMC meeting in HRC 2012; WvB desk calendar for 1962, in WvBP-H, file 303-10.

56. WvB DJ, 31.5.1962, in NASA/HD 13257, and WvB memo, 30.3.1962, in HRC 2026; WvB desk calendar for 1962, in WvBP-H, file 303-10.

57. Sherrod interview of Shea, 6.5.1971, in NASA/HD, HRC 13289; Sherrod memo on LOR decision chronology, 19.8.1970, in HRC 7201; WvB DJ, 4.–7.7.1962, in HRC 13257; Agenda, 7.6.1962, in HRC 2012; PSAC agenda, 5.–6.6.1962, in WvBP-LC, Box 8, 1962 N-P. Geissler wrote concluding remarks for him on the fourth that Geissler then presented on the seventh as his pro-EOR summary: Geissler talk, 7.6.1962, in HRC 2027.

58. WvB "Concluding Remarks . . . ," 7.6.1962, copy in NASA/HD, HRC 13263; WvB DJ, 9. and 11.7.1962, in HRC 13257; S&O, *WvB*, 177–78. Stuhlinger puts this before 7.6.1962, but that makes the shock of that day incomprehensible.

59. WvB "Concluding Remarks . . . ," 7.6.1962, copy in NASA/HD, HRC 13263.

60. Ibid.

61. Shea OHI by Emme, 6.5.1970, in NASA/HD, HRC 2011.

62. Dawson and Bowles, *Taming*, 46–47; "Saturn Shot Is '100 Pct. Success' . . . ," *WP*, 26.4.1962 ("95 tons"); "N.A.S.A. Admits Deficiencies in Centaur Project," *NYT*, 16.5.1962.

63. Dawson and Bowles, *Taming*, 1–40 (Glennan quote, 31); Karth subcommittee hear-

ing, 15. and 18.5., and report, 2.7.1962, copies in NASA/HD, HRC 10203; Dunar and Waring, *Power*, 44–45.

64. Hammer story in D. Davis to Emme, 6.2.1983, in NASA/HD, HRC 190; Debus weekly note, 12.2.1962, in KSC Archives, Debus Collection, folder 125.

65. Dunar and Waring, *Power*, 45; Healey/MH to WvB, 5.10.1962, in WvBP-LC, Box 8, 1962 F-H; Hueter memo, 24.7.1962, in NASER, RG255, #01-0002, MSFC/ULMF, Box 14; WvB-Karth phone call, 24.8., WvB-Shea call, 10.9., WvB-Cortright call, 11.12., WvB DJ, 4.9., 24.–27.9., 21.12.1962, in NASA/HD, HRC 13257, Naugle OHI by McCurdy, 17.8.1987, in HRC 6722, and Karth hearing, 15.5.1962, in HRC 10203.

66. WvB quote in "Topics of Discussion" WvB-Ostrander, 5.12.1960, in NASA/HD, HRC 13255; WvB in agenda, 25.2., to 1.3.1963 Board meeting in HRC 13258.

67. Benson and Faherty, *Moonport*, 87–143; Dunar and Waring, *Power*, 70; WvB comment on Debus weekly note, 30.8.1961, in UHCL, Bilstein "Stages" coll., 5–17; WvB-Dixon phone call, 11.12., Rees to WvB, 19.12., and WvB DJ, 22.12.1961 in NASA/HD, HRC 13256; WvB DJ, 6.3., and WvB-Debus-Siepert call, 13.3.1962 in HRC 13257; Seamans OHI by Emme and Putnam, 8.5.1968, in HRC 3622. Debus never joined the party and never advanced beyond the rank of "SS-*Bewerber*" (applicant) but denounced someone to the Gestapo in 1942 for anti-Nazi remarks: NACP, RG330, JIOA Case Files, Debus file; BABL, BDC files, Debus SS marriage file, R.u.S-Fragebogen, 27.1.1942; WNRC, RG319, G-2 Project Decimal file:1957, Box 18, Debus file; Bower, *Paperclip Conspiracy*, 113–14.

68. Herring, *Way Station*, 1–92; Koelle weekly note to WvB, 26.8.1963, in UHCL, Bilstein "Stages" collection, 5–17; Webb-WvB call, 11.12.1963, in NASA/HD, HRC 13258.

69. Dunar and Waring, *Power*, 59–66, 74–76, 79; Ward, *Dr. Space*, 138.

70. Murray and Cox, *Apollo*, 140–43; "Moon Spat," *Time*, 21.9.1962; WvB OHI by Sohier and Emme, 31.3.1964, in NASA/HD, HRC 2627, and Clifton interview by Sherrod, in HRC 13286; handwritten notes, "v Br Luncheon," 25.10.1962, in NASER, RG255, MSFC/ULMF, Series 7, Box 28, 1.b.Civil Defense; 1516 Big Cove Rd. records, WvBP-H, file 601-3.

71. Johnson, *Secret*, 130–31; Brooks et al., *Chariots*, 127–28; transcript of JFK-NASA meeting, 21.11.1962, p. 17 ("I'm . . ."), and analysis by D. Day at http://history.nasa.gov/JFK-Webbconv/; WvB draft release, 20.8.1963, in WvBP-H, file 130-1. In fact, Khrushchev would not secretly approve a human lunar landing program until Aug. 1964—he and the Soviet leadership had just not taken Apollo seriously: Siddiqi, *Challenge*, 395–408.

72. Holmes-WvB call, 16.1., and Shea-WvB call, 17.1.1963, in NASA/HD, HRC 13258; "Back-Up Info. for Dr. von Braun" and WvB notes for MSMC meeting, 29.1.1963, in NASER, RG255, MSFC/ULMF, #01-0002, Box 15, and WvB to Holmes, 11.3.1963, and Rees memo on Freitag call, 21.6.1963, both in Box 23.

73. WvB-Gilruth call, 22.6., WvB DJ, 19.2, 4.6., 9.7. and 12.7., McCall cable, 11.7., and Shea-WvB call ("Berlin"), 15.8.1963, in NASA/HD, HRC 13258; GEM interview by Sherrod, 20.3.1973, in HRC 13287; GEM OHI by Putnam, 27.6.1967, in HRC 17783; Benson and Faherty, *Moonport*, 173–77; Sato, "Local Engineering."

74. GEM interview by Sherrod, 19.11.1969, in NASA/HD, HRC 13287; Webb OHI by Needell and Collins, 4.11.1985, NASM.

75. Gray, *Angle*, 20 ("slightly"), 150–59; "Notes on Discussion with Joe Shea," 8.1963, in LC, GEM Papers, Box 79; WvB DJ, 12.6.1962 ("behavior"), in NASA/HD, HRC 13257, memo on Storms-WvB call, 7.6.1963, in HRC 13258 ("crawled"); GEM OHI by Putnam, 27.6.1967, in HRC 17783; GEM interview by Sherrod, 19.11.1969, in HRC 13287; Bilstein, *Stages*, 209–22.

76. WvB DJ, 26.6.1963, in NASA/HD, HRC 13258; MSMC minutes, 25.6.1963, in NASER, RG 255, MSFC/ULMF, #01-0002, Box 15, and WvB memo, 16.8.1962, in MSFC/ULMF, Series 13, Box 20; Dunar and Waring, *Power,* 66.

77. WvB DJ and call to Seamans, 27.6., Webb-WvB call, 2.8., and WvB DJ, 13.8.1963, in NASA/HD, HRC 13258.

78. Katz to McCall, 28.3.1962, and WvB to Webb, 16.1.1962, in NASA/HD, HRC 13257; on Huntsville and MSFC, see Dunar and Waring, *Power,* chap. 4, and on Birmingham, McWhorter, *Carry Me Home.*

79. "Alabama Desegregation May Start at Huntsville," *WP,* 25.3., and "Policies of Gov. Wallace Unpopular in Huntsville," 10.6.1963; "Statement to LIFE Magazine Saturday, June 1, 1963," in WvBP-H, file 130-1; Gorman(?) memo on phone call, 23.5.1963, in NASER, RG255, MSFC/ULMF, #01-0002, Box 23, and Webb to WvB, 24.6., and reply, 15.7.1963, in MSFC/ULMF, 89-064, Box 13, copies in NASA/HD, HRC 8983.

80. GEM, "Constraints on Organizational Changes," n.d. (c. 8.1963), in LC, GEM Papers, Box 85, OMSF Org. and Mgmt., and "Notes on Discussion with Joe Shea," c. 8.1963., in Box 79; GEM OHI by Collins, 15.2.1988, NASM; GEM interview by Sherrod, 20.3.1973, in NASA/HD, HRC 13287 ("they would lose").

81. Johnson, *Secret,* 132–35.

82. WvB-Gilruth call, 8.10.1963, in NASA/HD, HRC 13258; WvB to GEM, and attached note, Holmes to Gorman, 14.10.1963, in NASER, RG255, MSFC/ULMF, #01-0002, Box 23; GEM OHI by Putnam, 27.6.1967, in HRC 17783 ("Wernher gave . . ."); WvB OHI by Bilstein et al., 17.11.1971, in NASA/HD, HRC 2632.

83. Murray and Cox, *Apollo,* 153–54; Mueller to Shea, 27.9.1963, and "Notes for Dr. Mueller . . . ," n.d., in LC, GEM Papers, Box 91, Saturn Program; WvB-GEM calls, 27.9., 30.9., and 3.10., in NASA/HD, HRC, 13258.

84. WvB itinerary, 19.10.–2.11.1963, in NASA/HD, HRC, 13258; MSMC minutes, 29.10.1963, in NASER, RG255, MSFC/ULMF, 73-2102, Series 7, Box 15; GEM telex, 1.11.1963, in UHCL, Apollo Chron. Files, 064-12. David Onkst/American U. in an unpublished paper, "Engineering All-Up," points out that Shea had earlier broached the idea, but Holmes rejected it.

85. WvB OHI by Emme?, 28.8.1970, in NASA/HD, HRC 2631 ("I said . . ."); WvB DJ, 29.10.–4.11.1963, in NASA/HD, HRC 13258.

86. WvB OHI by Bilstein et al., 17.11.1971, in NASA/HD, HRC 2632 ("management"); Bilstein, *Stages,* 350–51; WvB DJ, 4.–8.11., and WvB-GEM call, 8.11., in NASA/HD, HRC 13258, and Board meeting minutes, 8.11.1963, in HRC 16203; Mrazek viewgraphs, "Sequence of Events . . ." re: all-up decision, 1967?, in WvBP-LC, Box 12, 1967 I-Z; Disher interview by Murray, 11.7.1988, copy courtesy D. Onkst.

87. Launius, "Kennedy's Space Policy," 20; WvB OHI by Sohier and Emme, 31.3.1964, in NASA/HD, HRC 2627; WvB to Crossley/*Popular Science,* 27.11.1963, in WvBP-H, file 202-20, and WvB remarks, 16.11.1963, in file 802-20.

88. WvB DJ, 12.11., 25.11., 29.–30.12., and itinerary, 20.–22.11.1963, in NASA/HD, HRC 13258; Ward, *Dr. Space,* 132.

CHAPTER 16

1. Quote attributed to WvB on various Web sites, including: http://www.brainyquote .com/quotes/authors/w/wernher_von_braun.html. I cannot verify it, but it sounds authentic.

2. WvB to MvB Sr., 2.2.1964 in BAK, N1085/86; Benson and Faherty, *Moonport*, 203–14.

3. Johnson, *Secret*, 135–41; Sato, "Local Engineering," 577–79.

4. WvB quoted in Johnson, *Secret*, 140.

5. Johnson, *Secret*, 140–41; WvB to Directors of IO and R&DO, 8.4.1965, copy in UHCL, Bilstein "Stages" collection, 4–8; Phillips interview by Ordway, 29.1.1988, in LC, Phillips Papers, Box 138, folder 10 ("became," emphasis mine).

6. Phillips interview by Ordway, 29.1.1988, in LC, Phillips Papers, Box 138, folder 10.

7. GEM memo, 8.6.1964, in LC, GEM Papers, Box 76, MSFC file; WvB, "Remarks During Edgewater Conference, December 10 and 11, 1964," in NASER, RG255, MSFC/ULMF, Series 11, Box 1 (underlining in original). For other WvB remarks, see Magliato minutes, 11.3.1965, of Systems Engineering meeting in NASER, RG255, MSFC/ULMF, Series 9, Box 1; WvB speech, 29.3.1966, in WvBP-LC, Box 61, Speeches and Writings, Jan.–May 1966. See also Bilstein, *Stages*, 289–90.

8. Bilstein, *Stages*, 81–83, 192–95, 244–46; WvB, "Remarks . . . ," in NASER, RG255, MSFC/ULMF, Series 11, Box 1.

9. Bilstein, *Stages*, 269–73, 283–91.

10. Dunar and Waring, *Power*, 67; Phillips interview by Ordway, 29.1.1988, in LC, Phillips Papers, Box 138, folder 10.

11. Shepherd interview, 12.4.1971, and Young interview, 12.1.1972, both by Sherrod, in NASA/HD, HRC 13290, WvB DJ, 23.10., in HRC 13259, and "Campaign Charge: 'Blackmail' in the Space Program," *U.S. News & World Report*, 9.11.1964, copy in HRC 2625; "NASA May Leave Its Alabama Base," *NYT*, 24.10.1964.

12. WvB speech, "Huntsville in the Space Age," 8.12.1964, in WvBP-LC, Box 48, Speeches and Writings 1964; Slattery to Scheer, with attachments, ?.4.1965, in NASER, RG255, MSFC/ULMF, Public Affairs, Box 17; "Von Braun Fights Alabama Racism," *NYT*, 14.6.1965; Dunar and Waring, *Power*, 121–24.

13. Phone calls, 26.5.–6.4.1965, in NASA/HD, HRC 13260; "Wallace Is Given a NASA Warning," *NYT*, 9.6.1965, S&O, *WvB*, 188 (Wallace quote).

14. Ward, *Dr. Space*, 173 (Shepherd quote); Dunar and Waring, *Power*, 124–25.

15. "Happy Birthday for von Braun," *NYT*, 24.3.1965, and "Moon Program Takes Giant Step on Giant Tractor," 26.5.1966; Bilstein, *Stages*, 328–40; "A Man on the Moon in '68?," *U.S. News & World Report*, 12.12.1966, copy in WvBP-H, file 228-26. The interview got him in trouble with Webb, who was worried that excessive optimism would undermine NASA's already deteriorating budget prospects: Webb to WvB, 17.12.1966, in WvBP-H, file 406-5.

16. Bilstein, *Stages*, 114–15, 185–86; Benson and Faherty, *Moonport*, 324–39, 369–75; WvB-Debus call, 14.10., and WvB-O'Connor call, 15.12.1965, in NASA/HD, HRC 13260; Shepherd to WvB, 17.2., and Debus/WvB swing arms memo, 19.–25.2.1966, in NASER, RG255, MSFC/ULMF, #89-064, Box 15.

17. WvB/Gilruth to Storms, 14.7.1964, in UHCL, Bilstein "Stages" collection, 4-4, and Board minutes, 25.9.1964, in 5-22; Bilstein, *Stages*, 211–24.

18. Bilstein, *Stages*, 224–27; Gray, *Angle*, 159, 196–202; O'Connor to WvB, ?.10.1965, in UHCL, Bilstein "Stages" collection, 4-1.

19. Rees, "Personal Impressions," 8.12.1965, in UHCL, Bilstein "Stages" collection, 4-7; Rudolph to Rees, 5.11.1965, in WvBP-H, file 123-3; WvB-Rees call, 15.10.1965, in NASA/HD, HRC 13260; Phillips to GEM, 18.12., and GEM to Atwood, 19.12.1965, in LC, GEM Papers, Box 84, NAA 12/18/63–12/30/65.

20. Gray, *Angle*, 159; Ward, *Dr. Space*, 154–55 (Storms-WvB anecdotes and quotes).

21. Bilstein, *Stages,* 228–32; WvB-Storms call, 31.5.1966, in NASA/HD, HRC 13261 ("tear-choked").

22. WvB DJ, 30.11.–1.12.1966, in NASA/HD, HRC 13261 (WvB quote); Rees memo, 8.11., and WvB memo, 9.11.1966, in NASER, RG255, MSFC/ULMF, #01-0002, Box 23.

23. Koelle weekly note, 26.8.1963, in UHCL, Bilstein "Stages" collection, 5–17.

24. On nuclear programs, see NASER, RG255, MSFC/ULMF, #89-064, Box 15, and #01-0002, Box 23; Finger to WvB, 27.12.1963, and WvB to Fellows, 20.4.1964, in WvBP-LC, Box 10, 1964 A-J; WvB speech, 20.11.1963, in WvBP-H, file 804-3, and Dryden to Ferguson, 11.6.1964, in file 116-21.

25. Dunar and Waring, *Power,* 100; WvB comment on Koelle weekly note, 9.9.1963, in UHCL, Bilstein "Stages" collection, 5–17; WvB to Weidner, 18.12.1965, and attached memo in NASER, RG255, MSFC/ULMF, #89-064, Box 11; Portree, *Humans,* 11–29.

26. GEM-WvB-Gilruth-Debus meeting, 27.3.1964, in NASA/HD, HRC 910, MSFC-MSC meeting, 18.10.1965, in HRC 13260, and "Dr. von Braun's DISCUSSION on AAP with Bureau of Budget, March 31, 1966," in HRC 2625; "Impact of AES Concept on Present Apollo Program," before 17.11.1964, in NASER, RG255, MSFC/ULMF, #01-0002, Box 16; Compton and Benson, *Living,* 2–21. The program's 1964–65 acronym was AES, which variously stood for Apollo Experiment Support or Apollo Extension Systems.

27. Compton and Benson, *Living,* 40–46, 115; WvB-Rees-Debus-Siepert teleconference, 20.6.1968, in NASA/HD, HRC 13264, and WvB-Mettler/STL call, 8.4.1966, in 13261 (quote).

28. Lambright, *Powering Apollo,* 139.

29. Dunar and Waring, *Power,* 136–41; Compton and Benson, *Living,* 5; WvB to Geissler, 15.1.1965, in NASER, RG255, MSFC/ULMF, #01-0002, Box 15.

30. WvB note on McCall to WvB, 16.4.1962, in NASA/HD, HRC 13257, WvB drawing, 29.11.1964, in 2626, and Shepherd memo on Seamans visit, 30.11.1965, HRC 13261; WvB to Koelle, 10.8.1962, in MSFC Archives, drawer 52, Space Station (von Braun) 1962–68; Compton and Benson, *Living,* 22–30.

31. Compton and Benson, *Living,* 36–39, 69–76; Rees to WvB, 23.10.1965, in NASER, RG255, MSFC/ULMF, #01-0002, Box 23; Low to Disher, 22.7.1966, in RPI, Low Papers, Box 71, folder 3.

32. WvB note to O'Connor, 27.5. ("hard sell"), and WvB-GEM call, 14.7.1966 ("plant a . . ."), in NASA/HD, HRC 13261; Compton and Benson, *Living,* 72–73; WvB memo, 6.10.1966, in NASER, RG255, MSFC/ULMF, #01-0002, Box 23.

33. Compton and Benson, *Living,* 32–33, 49–52; Mueller to Teague, 19.10.1966, and attached copies in NASER, RG255, MSFC/ULMF, Series 9, Box 1, and Shepherd to WvB, 16.11.1966, in #01-0002, Box 23; "Briefing by Mr. Frank Williams," 11.5.1966, in NASA/HD, HRC 13261.

34. Board meeting minutes, 16.8.1966, in NASA/HD, HRC 13261; Rees to WvB, 22.8., and WvB to Shoemaker, 6.10.1966, in NASER, RG255, MSFC/ULMF, #01-0002, Box 23; Gilruth and WvB to GEM, 24.8., WvB memo, 22.9., and WvB to Gilruth, 19.10.1966, in UHCL, Center Series, Sullivan Management Series, Box 9, Lake Logan 1966.

35. Portree, *Humans,* 24, 29–31; Compton and Benson, *Living,* 40–43, 52–56; WvB to Weidner, 18.12.1965, in NASER, RG255, MSFC/ULMF, #89-064, Box 11; WvB speech, 29.3.1966, in WvBP-LC, Box 61, Speeches & Writings Jan.–May 1966; Board meeting minutes, 5.10.1966, in NASA/HD, HRC 13261 ("commented").

36. Webb to WvB, 20.12.1963, copies in NASA/HD, HRC 2563, and in Johns Hopkins University, MSE Library Special Collections, Dryden Papers, ms. 147, Box 3.16. WvB's

Mader file, and with it no doubt the original of this letter, has disappeared from the WvB Papers in Huntsville. The fact that the file once existed is revealed in the list of personal and "Sensitive" files attached to Ruth von Saurma's note to WvB, 22.8.1973, in WvBP-H, file 607-15. Most of those on the "Sensitive" list are missing too, primarily those relating to Mittelbau-Dora.

37. Mader, *Geheimnis;* WvB to Lehmann, 11.12.1962, in WvBP-H, file 417-10, and WvB to Weiss-Vogtmann, 14.1.1963, in file 418-2. The series was in *Forum* but not available to me; see also Mader, "Die Karriere des Wernher von Braun," *DDR in Wort und Bild,* 7.1963, 32–33, copy in NASM, WvB bio. file. WvB corresponded with Mader in 1961, as did his father. Both vBs were suspicious: Mader to WvB, 8.7., reply, 21.7., WvB to MvB Sr., 29.10., and reply, 7.11.1961, in BAK, N1085/85.

38. Mader, "Der skandlöse Doktorhut," *Der Sonntag* (East Berlin), no. 21 (c. 5.1963), and leaflet "Raketenboy Nummer 1" showing the cover, both in American Institute of Physics, Neils Bohr Library, Goudsmit Papers, Box 15, folder III./153. In Aug. 1963 Ruth von Saurma produced a translation of the leaflet and of excerpts of Mader's book, along with chapter summaries, a copy of which ended up in FBI file 105-130306, FBI FOIA WvB.

39. Webb to WvB, 20.12.1963, in NASA/HD, HRC 2563.

40. "Thought Police," *WP,* 6.8.1964; Huzel, *Peenemünde;* McGovern, *Crossbow;* Klee and Merk, *Birth* (German: *Damals in Peenemünde*); Irving, *Mare's Nest.*

41. Editors' note with copy of Robert Brustein, "Out of This World," *New York Review of Books* 1, no. 12 (6.2.1964), 3–4, in NASER, RG255, MSFC/ULMF, Public Affairs, box 16 (stamped received 29.1.1964); WvB to Clarke, 1.2.1965, in WvBP-H, file 410-4; Clarke, *Astounding Days,* 183 ("Stanley . . ."). Fred Kaplan, "Truth Stranger Than 'Strange-love,'" *NYT,* 10.10.2004, p. AR21, provides a convincing argument for Kahn. See also Frayling, *Mad, Bad,* 102–7, but his one-sided emphasis on WvB is unconvincing.

42. Lehrer, *That Was the Year That Was* (CD, Reprise Records); Lehrer phone interview by MJN, 28.1.2002; "For Tom Lehrer, the Parody's Not Over," *WP,* 16.7.2000. Lehrer kindly pointed out to me that the comedy duo Nichols and May did a sketch, "The Von Brauns at Home," on their record *Mike Nichols and Elaine May Examine Doctors* (1962). It is on the original LP but not on the later CD version.

43. Slattery to Scott Reuman, 26.1.1966, in WvBP-H, file 227-8; Fallaci, *When,* 219–23; Clarke, *Astounding Days,* 183.

44. Von Saurma note, 6.8.1965, and *Alphaville* materials and clippings in WvBP-H, file 224-5; plot summary quoted from "N.Y. Film Festival Opens with Fantasy," *Los Angeles Times,* 9.9.1965.

45. *New York Herald-Tribune,* Paris, 10.9.1965, clipping in WvBP-H, file 224-5, in which the quoted passage is marked in red pencil.

46. See the excellent analysis in Heimann and Ciesla, *"Die gefrorenen Blitze"* (quote, 161).

47. Ibid., 164–80. A veiled reference to the French broadcast issue appears in SvB to WvB, 18.3.1969, in WvBP-H, file 403-10. It is clear from context that this is not the first mention of it. Von Braun's file on the issue, entitled "Notes on East German film 'Die gefrorenen Blitze' 1969," probably by SvB, is in v. Saurma's list to WvB, 22.8.1973, in WvBP-H, file 607-15, but is missing. As noted above for Mader, this is part of a pattern of "Sensitive" files that have vanished from the WvB Papers in Huntsville, including SvB's 1965 notes on *Alphaville* and von Braun's file on *Paris Match* exchange (see below) and on the Essen war crimes case (discussed in the next chapter).

48. S&O, *WvB,* 51, including quotes; v. Saurma memo to WvB through Slattery, 2.5.1966, in WvBP-H, file 227-8. It seems from Stuhlinger and Ordway's text that they

had access to the missing file. When I asked Fred Ordway to get me a copy of the letter, he was as polite as always, but I never heard from him again.

49. WvB to Hertel, 14.11.1962, in WvBP-H, file 422-1, Slattery to Frutkin, 6.4.1965, in file 227-7 (Diesel Medal), v.Saurma memo, 25.8.1966, in file 125-4, Bölsche Prize program and clipping in file 125-4a, and Langley medal file, 3.-6.1967, in file 605-6; WvB to General Polk, in NASER, RG255, WvB's For. Corr., Box 2466, 1963P; Mader, "Der skandalöse Doktorhut," *Der Sonntag,* no. 21 (c. 5.1963), copy in American Institute of Physics, Neils Bohr Library, Goudsmit Papers, Box 15, folder III./153; "Dr. von Braun Will Receive Smithsonian Langley Medal," *NYT,* 6.6.1967.

50. Exchange on Meyer/RIAS, 9.1964, in NASER, RG255, WvB's For. Corr., Box 2467, 1964M; WvB to Hubmann (*Quick*), 2.9.1964, in WvBP-H, file 224-16 ("Because").

51. WvB to MvB Sr., 6.12.1964, in BAK, N1085/86, and MvB Sr. to Maria vB, 8.9.1966, in N1085/77 (quote); MvB, *Weg,* 445–67.

52. Christina vB interview by MJN, 23.3.2001; Carola vB interview by MJN, 18.12.2000; "Bonn Names von Braun's Brother," *NYT,* 24.8.1962, and "Bonn Aide Leaves U.N.," 18.7.1968.

53. Christina vB interview by MJN, 23.3.2001, MvB, *Weg,* 445–67; MvB Jr. to Sr., 5.7.1968, in BAK, N1085/76; "Pilot Chrysler Unit Irons Out Kinks in Cars," *NYT,* 27.8.1969, names MvB Jr. as "Chrysler's director of product warranty and service."

54. WvB to Irmgard Riedel, 8.8.1966, in WvBP-H, Pers. Corr. 1961–73 (file no. not found); Bergaust, *WvB,* 362–66; Ward, *Dr. Space,* 101.

55. Seamans, *Aiming,* 101–2; Ward, *Dr. Space,* 102–3, 144–45 (flying stories); WvB to Warsitz, 2.12.1968, in WvBP-H, file 421-5.

56. Ward, *Dr. Space,* 102–3, 109; S&O, *WvB,* 258, 278; WvB-Lowrey call, 4.4.1966, in NASA/HD, HRC 2625 ("getting drunk"), and WvB-Karth call, 19.5.1966, in HRC 13261. On paid speeches, see his Harry Walker agency files, WvBP-H, files 403-6 and -15.

57. Crossley, "Our Most Important Announcement in 91 Years," *Popular Science* 182, no. 1 (Jan. 1963), 55; article and book material in WvBP-H, files 203-1, 203-5, 211-1, 211-11, and other files.

CHAPTER 17

1. Mailer, *Of a Fire,* 65.

2. WvB to Jones, 8.8.1964, in WvBP-LC, Box 10, 1964 K-R (see also corr. in Box 11, 1965 H-N); WvB DJ, 28.3.1966 ("YES"), in NASA/HD, HRC 13261, and Vogel to Webb, 3.12.1966 ("in close . . ."), in 13254.

3. WvB itinerary, 26.12.1966–13.1.1967, in NASA/HD, HRC 13261; Stuhlinger trip report, c. 1.1967, copy in NASM, WvB bio. file; WvB to MvB Sr., 22.1.1967, in BAK, N1085/86 (quote); WvB, "Space Men in Antarctica" (ms. for *Popular Science*), 2.1967, in WvBP-H, file 214-9.

4. WvB itineraries, 23.-28.1.1967, in NASA/HD, HRC 13262, and Atwood interview by Sherrod, 24.6.1969, in 13285; Executives meeting schedule and WvB-Freitag notes, 27.-28.1.1967, in WvBP-H, file 805-12; Gray, *Angle,* 230; Murray and Cox, *Apollo,* 201–2; Shapley OHI by Collins, 13.7.1994, NASM.

5. Murray and Cox, *Apollo,* 215–20, 230–31; Lambright, *Powering,* 147–76.

6. WvB DJs and calls, 1.–3.2., WvB-Phillips call, 2.3., WvB DJ "Attachment," 27.2., staff luncheons, 10. and 17.4.1967, in NASA/HD, HRC 13262; WvB to B. Holmes, 9.2.1967, in WvBP-LC, Box 44, Misc. Office Notes 1963–68; S&O, *WvB,* 276 ("strange . . ."); GEM?,

handwritten "Webb Discussion with W.V.B.-H.G.," c. 5.1967, in LC, GEM Papers, Box 85, OMSF, Organization and Management. Early U.S. human spacecraft used five psi pure oxygen in space and were pumped above atmospheric pressure on the ground to keep nitrogen out before launch.

7. WvB DJ, 22.9., WvB-Elms call, 23.9.1965, in NASA/HD, HRC 13260, Board meeting minutes, 16.8., 20.10. luncheon, WvB-Debus call, 4.11.1966, in HRC13261, and "Voyager discussion with Mr. Webb . . . ," 18.1.1967, in HRC 13262; WvB memo on Saturn V/Voyager, 7.12.1965, in NASER, RG255, MSFC/ULMF, #01-0002, Box 23; WvB memos, 6.12.1966 and 8.3.1967, in WvBP-H, file 813-16. JPL was to do the lander and Langley the heat-shield capsule for entry.

8. Docs. on OSSA Senior Council Meeting, 3.1967, in WvBP-H, file 804-1; Shepherd memo, 28.6., WvB-Cortright call, 22.8.1967, in NASA/HD, HRC 13262; Patterson, *Grand Expectations*, 629–30, 663; Lambright, *Powering*, 184–85.

9. Maus to WvB, 16.6.1967, in NASER, RG255, MSFC/ULMF, #01-0002, Box 11, and Williams to WvB, 8.2.1968, in Box 24; Portree, *Humans*, 31–32, 35; Compton and Benson, *Living*, 86–87.

10. NASA press release, 3.2.1967, in WvBP-H, file 420-1; Murray and Cox, *Apollo*, 214–15; Bilstein, *Stages*, 326; *Space Daily* excerpt, 28.10.1966, in NASA/HD, HRC 13261 and Shepherd memos, 13.6.1967, in HRC 13262 ("necessity"); WvB memo, 28.6.1967, in NASER, RG255, MSFC/ULMF, #01-0002, Box 24.

11. Murray and Cox, *Apollo*, 240–42; Petrone interview by Sherrod, 25.9.1970, in NASA/HD, HRC 13288.

12. Murray and Cox, *Apollo*, 242–43; Bilstein, *Stages*, 353–55.

13. Bilstein, *Stages*, 355–59; Murray and Cox, *Apollo*, 244–50.

14. WvB quoted in Bilstein, *Stages*, 357; Rudolph weekly note, 13.11.1967, in UHCL, Bilstein "Stages" collection, 5–19.

15. Stuhlinger weekly note, 13.11.1967, in UHCL, Bilstein "Stages" collection, 5–19; WvB memo, 23.10.1967, and WvB to GEM, 17.9.1968 ("shattering") in NASER, RG255, MSFC/ULMF, #01-0002, Box 24; Dunar and Waring, *Power*, 142–44 ("grave").

16. Brooks et al., *Chariots*, 241–44; Compton and Benson, *Living*, 91–104; Madewell summary, 17.10., GEM to WvB, 1.12., with attachments, Board minutes, 8.12., Shepherd to WvB, 12. and 15.12.1967, and "Notes on Mr. Webb's Visit, 12/12/67," in NASA/HD, HRC 13262, and WvB-Mathews call, 19.2.1968, in HRC 13264; Stuhlinger, "Astronomy Missions Planning Board," 12.3., and "Trip Report," 16.–17.3.1968, in WvBP-H, file 807-7.

17. GEM interview by Sherrod, 19.11.1969, in NASA/HD, HRC 13287, and Board minutes, 5.4., and Slattery to WvB, 4.11.1968, in HRC 13264; Gilruth to Mathews, 29.3.1968, NASWR, RG255, E.15, Box 75; Compton and Benson, *Living*, 170; Dunar and Waring, *Power*, 187–88.

18. WvB, "The detective story . . . ," 8.1968, in WvBP-H, file 216-7 (*Popular Science*, 11.1968, reprinted in Logsdon, *Exploring*, 4:144–47); Bilstein, *Stages*, 360–61; Murray and Cox, *Apollo*, 308–13.

19. Showers to WvB, 8.4.1966, in MSFC Archives, Director's Files, drawer 52, POGO Working Group; Brown and Rudolph weekly notes, 8.4.1968, in UHCL, Bilstein "Stages" collections, 5–20; WvB, "The detective story . . . ," 8.1968, in WvBP-H, file 216-7; Bilstein, *Stages*, 361–63.

20. WvB-GEM call, 11.4.1968, in NASA/HD, HRC 2625, WvB note, 23.4., and Phillips cable, 26.4., in 13264; Phillips to O'Connor, 17.6.1968, in UHCL, Bilstein "Stages" collections, 5–16; Bilstein, *Stages*, 364.

21. Low, "Special Notes for August 9, 1968, and Subsequent," 19.8.1968, in RPI, Low Papers, Box 93, folder 4; Murray and Cox, *Apollo*, 315–18.

22. Ibid.; meeting minutes, 9.8.1968, in RPI, Low Papers, Box 93, folder 5.

23. Siddiqi, *Challenge*, 653–57, 662–65. The appendix to the 9.8.1968 minutes cited above gives APO (Apollo Program Office = Phillips?) the task of gathering an "Intelligence Estimate."

24. "Has the U.S. Settled for No. 2 in Space?," *U.S. News & World Report*, 14.10.1968, 74–75; "Von Braun Warns of Space Cuts," *WP*, 1.5.1968; O'Connor to WvB, 19.2.1968, with attached report on facilities, in MSFC Archives, Director's Files, drawer 51, Committees & Panels.

25. WvB to MvB Sr., 10.8.1968, in BAK, N1085/86, and MvB Jr. to Sr., 2.2.1969, in N1085/76; Compton and Benson, *Living*, 99–104; WvB phone calls, 25.–26.7.1968, in NASA/HD, HRC 13264.

26. Lambright, *Powering*, 197–200; Brooks et al., *Chariots*, 267–72.

27. Lambright, *Powering*, 200–204.

28. WvB remarks in staff luncheon, 29.4.1968, in NASA/HD, HRC 13264.

29. Belew memo, 7.2.1967, in NASA/HD, HRC 13262, and Shepherd memo, 22.4.1968, in HRC 13264; Shepherd to WvB, 7.8.1968, in WvBP-H, file 807-12; Finger to GEM 9.8., and WvB to GEM, 17.9.1968, in NASER, RG255, MSFC/ULMF, #01-0002, Box 24.

30. Board meeting minutes, 12.11., WvB-GEM call, 12.12.1968, in NASA/HD, HRC 13262; WvB to Gilruth, 17.1.1969, with announcement, UHCL, Apollo Chron. Files, 070-62, and WvB to GEM, 21.1.1969, 070-63; Johnson, *Secret*, 150–52; Dunar and Waring, *Power*, 144–48.

31. Murray and Cox, *Apollo*, 321–24; Brooks et al., *Chariots*, 272–76; Siddiqi, *Challenge*, chap. 15.

32. WvB DJ, 22.12.1968–5.1.1969, in NASA/HD, HRC 13265.

33. WvB to MvB Sr., 19.1.1969, in BAK, N1085/86.

34. Kaul Antrag, 4.12.1967, and Hueckel to WvB, 6.11.1968, in NWHSA, Zweigarchiv Schloss Kalkum, Ger. Rep. 299/160; Heimann and Ciesla, "*Die gefrorenen Blitze*," 179.

35. Dembling phone interview by MJN, 29.7.2004; WvB to Hueckel, 22.11.1968, in NWHSA, Zweigarchiv Schloss Kalkum, Ger. Rep. 299/160.

36. Dembling phone interview by MJN, 29.7.2004; Konopka phone interview by MJN, 5.10.2004; "Betty" to Paine, 3.1., re: Dembling call, and Dembling to Paine, 7.2.1969, in LC, Paine Papers, Box 32; "Von Braun Evidence in Nazi Trial Sought," *NYT*, 4.1.1969; Guilian to Hueckel, 6. and 21.1., and Kaul to Hueckel, 31.1.1969, in NWHSA, Zweigarchiv Schloss Kalkum, Ger. Rep. 299/160.

37. WvB deposition, 7.2.1969, in NWHSA, Zweigarchiv Schloss Kalkum, Ger. Rep. 299/160, S. 69-80, and West German newspaper clippings, 8.–10.2.1969, in Ger. Rep. 299/104; "War Crimes Trial Hears Dr. Von Braun," *Chicago Tribune*, 8.2.1969 ("nothing"); WvB to WD, 8.12.1969, in WvBP-H, file 423-4 (quote). No Feb. 1969 testimony stories were found in the *NYT* or *WP* or several other newspapers on Proquest.

38. Brooks et al., *Chariots*, chap. 12; Portree, *Humans*, 40–43; WvB to Burda, 25.7.1969, in WvBP-H, file 403-8; "Von Braun Looks to Mars Landing," *NYT*, 8.6.1969.

39. WvB-Rees-Debus-Siepert call, 20.6.1968 ("he didn't think"), in NASA/HD, HRC 13264, Phillips to WvB, 15.1., WvB-Newby call, 25.4., Soherer telegram, 27.5., Murphy to WvB, 2.6.1969, in HRC 13265, and WvB OHI by Bilstein et al., 17.11.1971, in HRC 2632; Rees LRV memo for von Braun, 16.6.1969, in NASER, RG255, MSFC/ULMF, #01-0002, Box 24; Dunar and Waring, *Power*, 100–102.

40. Compton and Benson, *Living*, 104–11; Belew to WvB, 1.5.1969, in NASER, RG255, MSFC/ULMF, #01-0002, Box 11; Belew to WvB, 22.5., and phone calls, 23.–29.5.1969, in NASA/HD, HRC 13265; WvB to GEM, 23.5., and Gilruth to GEM, 26.5.1969, in UHCL, Skylab, Box 500, file 4.

41. WvB to Olga Ley, 9.7.1969, in WvBP-H, file 406-8; WvB to MvB Sr., 8.6.1969, in BAK, N1085/86.

42. WvB agendas, misc. materials for Cape, 7.1969, in WvBP-H, file 809-15; WvB itinerary, 13.–18.7.1969, in NASA/HD, HRC 13265.

43. Mailer, *Of a Fire*, 71–73.

44. Ibid., 73–74; speech in WvBP-H, file 809-15.

45. C. Ryan, "Behind the Lines," ms. 1969, in OU/CRC, Box 163, folder 5; SvB to WvB, 4.7.1969, in WvBP-H, file 403-10, and speech and notes in 809-15; C.-F. vB interview by MJN, 29.3.2001.

46. Interviews by Cornelius Ryan, 14.–16.7.1969, in OU/CRC, Box 163, folder 3.

47. Hansen, *Spaceflight Revolution*, 268; WvB quoted in Ward, *Dr. Space*, 164.

CHAPTER 18

1. *Lady Windemere's Fan.*

2. Newby to WvB, 2.7., and celebration schedule for 24.7.1969 ("spontaneous"), in WvBP-H, file 809-16; "Soviets Join in Cheers at Astronauts' Return," *WP*, 25.7.1969, and "Festivities in Huntsville Have a German Flavor," *NYT*, 25.7.1969 (WvB quotes).

3. "Dr. von Braun's outline of proposed Mars presentation to STG," 23.7.1969, in NASA/HD, HRC 13265; " 'Mars Next' Remark by Agnew Stirs Row," *WP*, 17.7.1969; Portree, *Humans to Mars*, 40–43; Heppenheimer, *Space Shuttle Decision*, 125–50.

4. Fielder memo, 23.5.1969, in UHCL, JSC Center Series, Sullivan Management Series, Box 9, Lake Logan 1969; Heppenheimer, *Space Shuttle Decision*, 139–40; WvB OHI by Logsdon, 25.8.1970, in NASA/HD, HRC 13295 (WvB quote).

5. Portree, *Humans*, 42–44; "Von Braun Looks to Mars Landing," *NYT*, 8.6.1969.

6. WvB OHI by Logsdon, 25.8.1970, in NASA/HD, HRC 13295 (WvB quotes); Paine OHI by Logsdon, 3.9.1970, in NASA/HD, HRC 4185; WvB draft outline for *Reader's Digest*, typed after 27.5.1969, in WvBP-H, file 216-29; S&O, *WvB* (Amer. ed.), 212.

7. WvB OHI by Logsdon, 25.8.1970, in NASA/HD, HRC 13295, Shapley OHI by Logsdon, 12.8.1970, in HRC 1993; WvB presentation, 4.8., in HRC 4662, and copy of hearing, 5.8.1970, in HRC 2657.

8. WvB debriefing notes, 30.7.1969, in WvBP-H, file 225-7, and White House invitations in the presidential memorabilia binder; WvB itineraries, 29.7.–1.8., and 4.–8.8.1969, in NASA/HD, HRC 13265; " 'Historic' Party," in *WP*, 15.8.1969 ("thrilling"); Mark, *Space Station*, 37 ("A major . . ."); Portree, *Humans*, 43, 46–47.

9. Portree, *Humans*, 47–48; Heppenheimer, *Space Shuttle Decision*, 159–74; Hoff in Launius and McCurdy, *Spaceflight*, 98–100, 103–4; STG report, 9.1969, in Logsdon, *Exploring*, 1:522–43.

10. Heppenheimer, *Space Shuttle Decision*, 116–36; S&O, *WvB* (Amer. ed.), 241; MSFC Board meeting minutes, 11.7. and 8.8., WvB-Rees-Auter call, 18.8., and WvB DJ, 2.9.1969, in NASA/HD, HRC 13265; Weidner to WvB, 25.8.1969, in NASER, RG255, #01-0002, MSFC/ULMF, Box 24.

11. Hodge to "Bob" (Freitag?), 10.10.1969, in RPI, Low Papers, Box 79, folder 3; WvB-Rees call, 14.10.1969, in NASA/HD, HRC 13265; Heppenheimer, *Space Shuttle Decision*,

206–23; WvB, shuttle ms. for *Popular Science*, 3.5.1970, in WvBP-H, file 222-2. WvB advocated the two-stage reusable as early as the Sept. 1965 issue: "Coming . . . Ferries to Space," copy in 212–29.

12. WvB ms. and docs. on zero-G flight, 30.8.1968, in WvBP-H, file 216-10, and article "What It's Like to be Weightless," *Popular Science* (12.1968); WvB to Shepherd, 27.8.1968, in NASA/HD, HRC 13264; Ward, *Dr. Space*, 161; "Von Braun and Colleagues Designing Space Shuttle," *WP*, 25.7. 1969 ("grandfather").

13. Copy of Senate hearing, 5.8.1970, in NASA/HD, HRC 2657; "Von Braun Launches '76 Idea: Celebrate by Orbiting President," 20.9., *WP*, and "In Orbit," 22.9.1969 (editorial).

14. Shapley interview by Sherrod, 28.1.1970, in NASA/HD, HRC 13289.

15. Paine interview by Sherrod, 14.8.1970 ("I had . . ."), in NASA/HD, HRC 13288.

16. Ward, *Dr. Space*, 196–97; Shapley OHI by Collins, 30.8.1994, NASM. Webb was particularly worried about *The New York Times* because of its Jewish ownership, according to Shapley.

17. Paine interview by Sherrod, 10.9.1970, in NASA/HD, HRC 13288, and WvB-GEM call, 31.10.1969, in HRC 13265; Paine to Nixon, 19.9.1969, in LC, Paine Papers, Box 23; Low, "Personal Notes No. 1," 1.1.1970, in RPI, Low Papers, Box 70, folder 5.

18. Frank to Farley, 17.9.1969, in NASA/HD, HRC 4934, on D.A.A. history, and Shapley OHI by Mauer, 26.10.1986, in HRC 1991 ("monumentally"); Heppenheimer, *Space Shuttle Decision*, 108–10; Low, "Personal Notes No. 1," 1.1.1970, in RPI, Low Papers, Box 70, folder 5 ("some . . .").

19. WvB-Paine call, 1.12., and WvB DJ, 8.12.1969, in NASA/HD, HRC 13265; WvB desk calendar 1969–70, WvBP-H, file 304-7; Heppenheimer, *Space Shuttle Decision*, 174–76; S&O, *WvB* (Amer. ed.), 291; WvB speech to MSFC, 2.2.1970, in WvBP-LC, Box 61, Speeches & Writings 1970.

20. Paine interview by Sherrod, 14.8.1970, in NASA/HD, HRC 13288; S&O, *WvB* (Amer. ed.), 291, 295.

21. WvB desk calendar, 1969–70, WvBP-H, file 304-7; S&O, *WvB* (Amer. ed.), 292–93; Low, "Personal Notes No. 4," 13.1.1970, in Box 70, folder 5 (quote); Paine to Fleming/White House, 27.1.1970, in LC, Paine Papers, Box 24, Jan. 1970.

22. Low notes, 26.1., in RPI, Low Papers, Box 62, folder 5, and "Personal Notes No. 7," 31.1.1970, in Box 70, folder 5; Paine to Fleming, 27.1.1970, in LC, Paine Papers, Box 24, Jan. 1970, and press release 27.1.1970, in Box 54; press conf., 27.1., and press releases 27.–28.1.1970, in NASA/HD, HRC 2625; WvB speech outline and draft, 2.2.1970, in WvBP-LC, Box 61, Speeches and Writings 1970 (quotes); Ward, *Dr. Space*, 178–80.

23. Heppenheimer, *Space Shuttle Decision*, 175–77; Low, "Personal Notes No. 5," 17.1.1970, in RPI, Low Papers, Box 70, folder 5; Paine OHI by Logsdon, 3.9.1970, in NASA/HD, HRC 4185, and "NASA Shifts Von Braun to Post in Washington," *Washington Evening Star*, 28.1.1970, copy in HRC 2476; Shapley interview by MJN, 26.6.2003.

24. WvB itinerary, 7.–16.2.1970, in WvBP-H, file 810-22, and WvB Day schedule in file 611-6; Slattery memo, 27.2.1970., in NASER, RG255, MSFC/ULMF, #01-0002, Box 25; WvB DJ, 27.2.1970, in UHCL, Bilstein "Stages" Collection, 5–13. The house was at 816 Vicar Lane.

25. S&O, *WvB* (Amer. ed.), 303.

26. Memos on central planning, 2.–4.1970, in WNRC, RG255, 73A-772, Box 1, and 74-637, Box 2; ABC *Issues and Answers* transcript, 15.3.1970, in UHCL, JSC Shuttle Program Files, Box 005-65; WvB press conf., 31.3.1970, in NASA/HD, HRC 2640 (quotes).

27. WvB to MvB Sr., 5.4.1970, in BAK, N1085/86; "Washington Has a New Charmer," *Washington Star*, 22.3.1970; Apollo Shot Watched by Brandt," *WP*, 12.4.1970; "Post for von Braun's Brother," *NYT*, 14.4.1970; Hürter et al., *Biographisches Handbuch*, 265.

28. WvB to MvB Sr., 5.4. and 17.5.1970, in BAK, N1085/86.

29. Low, "Personal Notes No. 16" ("During . . ."), "18," and "19" ("This . . ."), 28.3., 12.4., and 25.4.1970, in RPI, Low Papers, Box 70, folder 5.

30. Newell to Low, 9.2., and reply, 13.2., Farley memo, 10.3.1970, in WNRC, RG255, 73A772, Box 1, Charter/Organization; Low, "Personal Notes No. 14," 7.3.1970, in RPI, Low Papers, Box 70, folder 5.

31. WvB presentation to Wallops, 13.6.1970, in NASA/HD, HRC 2628; "Ten Principal Action Items" from Wallops, 6.1970, LC, Paine Papers, Box 55, June 1970; Low notes, 14.6.1970, in RPI, Low Papers, Box 62, folder 4.

32. Launius, "A Waning of Technocratic Faith."

33. Paine to Nixon, 9.7., and Paine to Chapin/White House, 30.7.1970, in WNRC, RG255, 74-637, Box 2, Long Range Plans 1970; Heppenheimer, *Space Shuttle Decision*, 186–89; Low, "Personal Notes No. 28," 8.8.1970, in RPI, Low Papers, Box 70, folder 5.

34. Ward, *Dr. Space*, 192–93 (Kertes quote, 193).

35. Briefing papers and schedules, 11.6., and undated re: 4.8.1970 meeting, in WNRC, RG255, 73A772, Box 2; Farley memo, 5.8., and Sedlazek memo, 31.8.1970, in RPI, Low Papers, Box 87, folder 1; Paine to Findlay and to Townes, 1.9.1970, in LC, Paine Papers, Box 25. The decision was actually to cancel Apollo 15 (which had the last short-duration LM with no rover) plus 19, but the last missions were of course renumbered 15 to 17.

36. WvB OHI by Logsdon, 25.8., in NASA/HD, HRC 13295 (block quotes), and WvB interview by Sherrod, 25.8.1970., in HRC 13254 ("These"). In the latter case I have used his original words, not as he rewrote them in 1973 for Sherrod.

37. WvB itinerary, 7.–25.9., and WvB to Holden, 6.10.1970, in WvBP-H, file 814-12; Bergaust, *WvB*, 1–14; Ward, *Dr. Space*, 192–93 (Kertes quote, 193); Phillips interview by Ordway, 29.1.1988, in LC, Phillips Papers, Box 138, folder 10 (quote); Shapley interview by MJN, 26.6.2003.

38. Ward, *Dr. Space*, 194–96; Low interview by Sherrod, 5.7.1972, in NASA/HD, HRC 13287, and Scheer interview by Sherrod, 19.1.1971, in HRC 13289; Low, "Personal Notes No. 42," 21.2.1971, in RPI, Low Papers, Box 70, folder 3 ("quite . . ."); Kennick, "Biographical Note," in finding aid to the Low Papers. In June Low nominated him for the National Medal of Science, in a draft letter that WvB considered "very nice & flattering," although this was probably initiated by the new administrator, James Fletcher: WvB marg. comment on Seaton to WvB, 18.6.1971, in WNRC, RG255, 73A772, Box 1, von Braun's Chron File 1971; Low draft letter, c. 6.1971, in RPI, Low Papers, Box 52, folder 5.

39. Scheer interview by Sherrod, 19.1.1971, in NASA/HD, HRC 13289; Shapley OHI by Collins, 27.9.1994, NASM; Shapley interview by MJN, 26.6.2003.

40. WvB DJ by Kertes, 11.5. ("show biz"), in WvBP-H, file 308-1, and same, 28.10. and 4.11.1970, in file 308-3, and letters on Cavett show, in file 405-8; FBI cable, 16.9.1969, FBI FOIA WvB; protest leaflet for WvB talk, 30.10.1972, in NASA/HD, HRC 2477; Scheer interview by Sherrod, 19.1.1971, in HRC 13289; Ruland, *WvB*, 233–39; O'Donnell, "The Devil's Architect," *NYT Magazine*, 16.10.1969; Groesser to WvB, 31.1.1970, with clipping in WvBP-H, file 427-7(?). Speer sent his memoirs to WvB, who gratefully acknowledged Speer's role in rescuing him from his Gestapo arrest. Speer to WvB, ?.9.1969, in WvBP-H, file 433-9, and WvB reply, 14.10.1969, in file 424-1 and in BAK, N1340/7.

41. Pearson, "Prime Moon Credit Is Von Braun's," *WP*, 17.7.1969; WvB to General

Julius Klein, 2.8.1969, copy provided by Eli Rosenbaum, OSI. A 1960 attempt to down-grade the classification of WvB's army file was rejected on the ground that it contained damaging information. See NACP, RG319, E.A1-134B, Box 657A, IRR/PNF WvB.

42. Heppenheimer, *Space Shuttle Decision*, 270–72; WvB notes, 12.5.1971, in WvBP-H, file 811-12, copy in NASA/HD, HRC 2626.

43. Heppenheimer, *Space Shuttle Decision*, 336–60; S&O, *WvB* (Amer. ed.), 236, 298 (WvB quote), 307.

44. Memos on Fletcher meeting with AAD, 23.4.1971, in WNRC, RG255, 73A-772, Box 2; Farley memo, 28.5.1971, in WvBP-H, file 811-12; S&O, *WvB* (Amer. ed.), 236–37.

45. Heppenheimer, *Space Shuttle Decision*, 362–72; Low, "Personal Notes No. 38," 3.1.1971, in RPI, Low Papers, Box 70, folder 3, and "Personal Notes No. 52" and "53," 15. and 22.8.1971, in folder 2; WvB to Fletcher, 27.9.1971, in WvBP-H, file 812-16.

46. Heppenheimer, *Space Shuttle Decision*, 423–25; Low, "Personal Notes No. 48," 6.6.1971, in RPI, Low Papers, Box 70, folder 3; Fletcher to Schultz/OMB, 30.12.1971, in NASA/HD, HRC 13589.

47. Newell staff meeting, 28.9.1971, in NASA/HD, HRC 16790; Dethloff and Schorn, *Voyager's Grand Tour.*

48. Maria vB quoted in S&O, *WvB* (Amer. ed.), 303–4; WvB Tokyo remarks, 25.3., attached to Hachiya to WvB, 27.4.1971, in WvBP-H, file 143-3; Ward, *Dr. Space,* 197 (Goodrum quote), 199.

49. "Von Braun Warns Against Nation's Antiscience Mood," *Birmingham News,* 16.4.1971, and other clippings in NASA/HD, HRC 2476, and WvB speech, 27.5.1971, HRC 2651; WvB, "Hostility to Technology Is Irrational," *NAM Reports,* 23.8.1971, attached to Uhl/Fairchild to WvB, 30.8.1971, in WvBP-H, file 150-9, and WvB to Singer, 21.3.1972, in file 812-17.

50. WvB to Hubbard, 6.11.1970 (quote), and further corr. and memos, 1971, in WvBP-H, file 811-11; WvB to Seaton, 11.8.1971, in WNRC, RG255, 73A-772, Box 1, von Braun's Chron. File 1971; Michaud, *Reaching,* 41–45.

51. "Von Braun Hopes to Fly in Space Shuttle," *Houston Post,* 4.4.1972.

52. Low, "Personal Notes No. 57," 31.10.1971, in RPI, Low Papers, Box 70, folder 2.

53. Launius, "A Waning," 52-56; Heppenheimer, *Space Shuttle Decision,* 291–330, 362–415; Farley memo, 28.5.1971, in WvBP-H, file 811-12; Farley to WvB, 7.6.1971, in WNRC, RG255, 74-637, Box 2; WvB to Myers, 15.6.1971, in NASA/HD, HRC 8223.

54. Heppenheimer, *Space Shuttle Decision,* 408–18; Logsdon et al., *Exploring,* 3:10, 189–98.

55. Heppenheimer, *Space Shuttle Decision,* 416–23; WvB to Truax, 6.1.1972, in NASA/HD, HRC 2622, and Anderson memo, 17.3.1972, in HRC 2477.

56. Ward, *Dr. Space,* 199–200; WvB to Kawakami, 23.4.1971, in NASA/HD, HRC 2526; WvB to Coudenhove-Kalergi, 29.4.1971, in WvBP-H, file 427-6, WvB to Broglio, 27.5., and Zadotti, 22.9.1971, in file 422-4, and WvB to Uhl, 19.10.1971, in file 150-9 (quote).

57. Ward, *Dr. Space,* 200–201; WvB notes, 30.3.1972, in NASA/HD, HRC 2557.

58. Uhl phone interview, 10.7.2003; Low, "Personal Notes No. 71," 3.6.1972, in RPI, Low Papers, Box 69, folder 4.

59. Newell to Fletcher and Low, 10.5.1972, in RPI, Low Papers, Box 69, folder 4; WvB DJ by Kertes, 6.6.1972, in WvBP-H, file 308-9 (quotes).

60. Press release, 26.5.1972, in NASA/HD, HRC 2477; "Von Braun's Departure Marks the End of an Era," *NYT,* 27.5.1972; "Wernher von Braun and the Space Program" (editorial), *WP,* 3.6.1972; WvB DJ by Kertes, 24., 26., and 31.5.1972, in WvBP-H, file 308-9; Donnelly to WvB, 25.5.1972, in WvBP-H, file 817-22.

61. WvB DJ by Kertes, 8.6.1972, in WvBP-H, file 308-9; S&O, WvB (Amer. ed.), 307 (quotes).

CHAPTER 19

1. Quoted in "Man from NASA," *NYT,* 23.2.1975.

2. Ward, *Dr. Space,* 205; G. Wendt phone interview, 25.7.2006; Uhl phone interview, by MJN, 10.7.2003.

3. Uhl phone interview by MJN, 10.7.2003; "Big Fairchild Center in Md. Is Dedicated," *WP,* 18.10.1966; A-10 page, www.aerospaceweb.org/aircraft/attack/a10/; Bergaust, *WvB,* 463–65; "Fairchild Riding A-10 Wave," *NYT,* 23.2.1975.

4. WvB DJ by Kertes, 20.4., 24.4.1972, in WvBP-H, file 308-9, and WvB draft letter to "Carsbie" (Adams), c. 5.1974, 411–15 ("dynamic"); S&O, *WvB* (Amer. ed.), 238, 265, 309; WvB letter in Celestron ad, *Sky & Telescope* 46 (Oct. 1973), back cover, thanks to David DeVorkin.

5. Fletcher "Eyes Only" memo on Uhl call, and attached clipping, 14.4.1972, in RPI, Low Papers, Box 57, folder 5; WvB speech, 9.4.1971, in WvBP-H, file 150-2, and WvB DJ by Kertes, 18.5., 24.5.1972, in file 308-9; WvB speech, 11.10.1971, in NASA/HD, HRC 2639; WvB, "Prospective Space Developments," *Aeronautics & Astronautics* (Apr. 1972), 26–35.

6. "Von Braun's Departure—Why?" *Huntsville Times,* 28.5.1972, copy in WvBP-H, file 606-21.

7. Ward, *Dr. Space,* 204; "A Man with Thrust," *Today* (Florida), 4.6.1972, copy in WvBP-H, file 437-9; Bergaust, *WvB,* 498–99; S&O, *WvB* (Amer. ed.), 310.

8. WvB desk calendar, 6.–7.1972, in WvBP-H, file 305-4; Uhl phone interview, 10.7.2003; S&O, *WvB* (Amer. ed.), 309; "Fairchild Riding A-10 Wave," *NYT,* 23.2.1975.

9. Uhl phone interview by MJN, 10.7.2003; WvB notebook, 21.7.1972–26.1.1973, in WvBP-H, file 307-4; Hoban to Fletcher and Low, c. 18.12.1972, and Low "Personal Notes No. 85," 21.1.1973, in RPI, Low Papers, Box 68, folder 2; "Fairchild Riding A-10 Wave," *NYT,* 23.2.1975.

10. Low memo, 25.10.1972, in NASA/HD, HRC 13575; "Fairchild Riding A-10 Wave," *NYT,* 23.2.1975; WvB, "What the New Domestic Communications Satellites Will Do for You," *Popular Science* 202 (June 1973), 68–71, 144; WvB draft letter to "George," after 10.6.1974, in WvBP-H, file 411-14 (quote).

11. WvB desk calendar, 1.1973, WvBP-H, file 305-6; C.-F. vB interview, 29.3.2001; Uhl phone interview, 10.7.2003; Turner phone interview, 22.7.2003.

12. S&O, *WvB* (Amer. ed.), 314–17; WvB to Paine, 5.3.1974, in WvBP-H, file 411-12.

13. WvB draft letter to "Carsbie" (Adams), c. 5.1974, in WvBP-H, file 411-15, and to "Prof. Faust," c. 3.1975, in file 412-1 (block quote); WvB to Hewitt, 17.6.1976, in NSS, WvB file.

14. WvB to Hamill, 8.4.1974, in WvBP-H, file 817-17.

15. WvB desk calendar 1973, WvBP-H, file 305-6, and 1974, file 305-5, and 1974 travel itineraries in file 816-6; Turner phone interview, 22.7.2003; WvB draft letter to "Bill," c. 7.1974, in WvBP-H, file 411-14.

16. Hürter et al., *Biographisches Handbuch,* 265; "Magnus von Braun, 94, Dies; Ex-German Cabinet Minister," *WP,* 30.8.1972; MvB Sr. to WvB, 6.3.1972, in WvBP-H, file 405-3; Ward, *Dr. Space,* 205.

17. WvB to Hamill, 8.4.1974, in WvBP-H, file 817-17 (quotes); Bergaust, *WvB,* 470–71.

18. WvB DJ by Kertes, spring 1972, in WvBP-H, file 308-9; WvB draft letters to Wag-

ner and Janczarek, 8.1974., WvBP-H, file 411-4, and WvB draft letter to Wagner, after 30.3.1975, in file 412-1.

19. WvB to Hamill, 8.4.1974, in WvBP-H, file 817-17 (quotes), WvB to "Hermann" (Oberth), 17.1.1974, in file 430-9, and WvB desk calendar 6.–8.1973, file 305-6; S&O, *WvB,* 325.

20. WvB to "Hermann" (Oberth), 17.1.1974, in WvBP-H, file 430-9, WvB draft letter to "Carsbie" (Adams), c. 5.1974, in file 411-15, and WvB desk calendar 1973, file 305-6, and 1974, file 305-5.

21. WvB speech, 23.8.1974, in WvBP-H, file 150-19, WvB Iran itineraries, 6. and 10.1974, in file 816-6, WvB draft memo to Robinson, after 20.8., and draft letter to "Bill," c. 7.1974 (quote), in file 411-14.

22. Bergaust, *WvB,* 482–85; Ward, *Dr. Space,* 208; WvB desk calendar, 9.1974, in WvBP-H, file 305-5, WvB wire-ring notebook, 4.2.–4.10.1974, in file 307-5, Bergaust, "Final Schedule," 9.9.1974, in file 816-6, WvB draft letter to "Bruce" (Medaris?), c. 10.1974 ("ultimate"), and draft "Welcome and Opening Remarks," note dated 10.10.1974, both in file 412-2.

23. Uhl quoted in Ward, *Dr. Space,* 208; WvB quoted in S&O, *WvB,* 312; WvB outline for "Alaska Symposium," 2.10.1974, in WvBP-H, file 150-21, WvB draft letter to Governor Egan and Senator Hammond, c. 10.1974, and WvB draft letters to Fernandez-Moran, c. 11.1974, in file 412-2, and c. 1.1975, in file 411-16, and WvB draft letter to Cunningham, c. 4.1975, in file 412-1 ("dismayed").

24. WvB quoted in S&O, *WvB* (Amer. ed.), 318; Michaud, *Reaching,* 22–25.

25. Low "Personal Notes No. 98," 21.7.1973, in RPI, Low Papers, Box 68, folder 2; Uhl phone interview, 10.7.2003.

26. Uhl phone interview, 10.7.2003; Turner phone interview, 22.7.2003; WvB desk calendar entry, 4.3.1974, in WvBP-H, file 305-5; 1974 incorporation documents and meeting minutes, "Board of Directors" binder, and Turner, "A Plan for a National Space Association," mid-1974, all in NSS records; WvB to "Ted," c. 12.1974, in WvBP-H, file 412-2.

27. Meeting minutes and Hewitt reports, 11.1974–5.1975, in NSS records, "Board of Directors" binder.

28. Michaud, *Reaching,* 57–102, 207–13; WvB to Hubbard, c. late 1974, in WvBP-H, file 412-1, WvB handwritten "General Principles of NSI," c. 1975, in file 150-16, and Kertes WvB DJ, 16.3.1972, in file 308-8; S&O, *WvB* (Amer. ed.), 250–51.

29. WvB desk calendar, 5.–7.1975, in WvBP-H, file 305-7.

30. WvB desk calendar, 7.–9.1975, in WvBP-H, file 305-7; WvB draft letter to "John" (Young?), c. 11.1975, in file 412-1 (quotes); Ward, *Dr. Space,* 213.

31. WvB desk calendar, 10.–12.1975, in WvBP-H, file 305-7; S&O, *WvB* (Amer. ed.), 325–26; Bergaust, *WvB,* 544–45; Ward, *Dr. Space,* 216.

32. WvB, "Responsible Scientific . . . ," to be presented 29.10.1976, in NASA/HD, HRC 2643, and 1971–72 letters on religion in 2622 and 2623; ms. of "Responsible . . ." in WvBP-H, file 226-15, and speech, 23.11.1971, in file 143-16; WvB, "Von Braun's 'Search for God,' " *San Francisco Chronicle,* 28.2.1975. For WvB's design statements, see for example www.eadshome.com/VonBraun.htm.

33. WvB to Hewitt, 17.6. and 10.8.1976, in NSS, WvB file; S&O, *WvB* (Amer. ed.), 319–20; Michaud, *Reaching,* 49–54, 153. It later became the National Space Society.

34. S&O, *WvB* (Amer. ed.), 326–27.

35. Ibid., 327–28; excerpt from interview in WGBH transcript of *Frontline* program "The Nazi Connection," broadcast 24.2.1987; transcript of 5.4.1976 interview in NSS, Cinemaster file. See Chapter 7 for a fuller treatment of these excerpts.

36. White House correspondence, 1975–77, Gerald R. Ford Library, White House Central Files—Name Files, Box 3293, Wernher von Braun, also White House Central Files, MA2-32, Medals and Awards, Box 13, MA2-32 12/11/1976–20/1/1977, and David Gergen Files, Box 29, Wernher von Braun, including handwritten Gergen note, 21.7.1976 (quoted), on Muhlberg memo; Nicholson to Medal of Science committee, 3.2.1977, courtesy National Academies of Science Archives. The latter had nothing on the earlier nominations.

37. Higgins to Smith, 24.3.1977, courtesy Jimmy Carter Library, White House Central File, Subject File—Executive, Box MA-8, folder MA33, 1/20/77–12/31/78; Uhl phone interview by MJN, 10.7.2003 (quote); S&O, *WvB* (Amer. ed.), 328–29.

38. WvB draft letter to Speer, WvBP-H, file 412-1 (as mailed, 12.11.1975, in BAK, N1340/7).

39. WvB death certificate in WvBP-H, file 607-9; Ward, *Dr. Space*, 219–20.

EPILOGUE

1. Copy in NASA/HD, HRC 2475.

2. Statement and obits., ibid.

3. British obits., ibid; survey of the *Frankfurter Allegemeine,* the *Frankfurter Rundschau, Die Welt* (Hamburg), the *Süddeutsche Zeitung* (Munich), *Neues Deutschland* (official Communist Party daily, East Berlin), and the *Berliner Zeitung* (East), 17.–25.6.1977. Research is needed into former DDR archives to shed light on the campaign against WvB.

4. S&O, *WvB* (Amer. ed.), 329–31; memorial service program, 22.6.1977, and Collins and Stuhlinger eulogies in NASA/HD, HRC 2475; Fletcher's in NSS, Eulogies to Wernher von Braun.

5. "Wernher von Braun," *Washington Star,* 20.6., and "Wernher von Braun," *WP,* 23.6., and letters to *Star,* 26.6.1977, in NASA/HD, HRC 2475; Durant to *Star,* 23.6., and to *WP,* 25.6.1977, in NASM, WvB bio. file. Thanks to Tom Crouch.

6. Michel, *Dora* (originally published in French, 1975).

7. Rosenbaum interview by MJN, 26.7.2006; O&S, *Rocket Team;* Rudolph-OSI agreement, 28.11.1983, courtesy Rosenbaum/OSI; "German-Born NASA Expert Quits U.S. to Avoid War Crimes Suit," *NYT,* 18.10.1984; "Road to Departure of Ex-Nazi Engineer," *WP,* 4.11.1984. Rudolph's defenders subsequently claimed that the German government cleared him, when in fact the investigating prosecutor concluded only that under the narrow "base motive murder" statute, the one German crime for which the statute of limitations had not expired, he could not build a case against Rudolph. After a 1990 Canadian immigration trial, Rudolph was declared a minor war criminal and barred from further entry to that country; "Duhn report" of Landgericht Hamburg, 17.2.1987, and Canada deportation order, 11.1.1991, courtesy OSI. Ward's *Dr. Space,* 157–58, naively repeats the falsehoods of Rudolph's defenders regarding those two cases.

8. Rosenbaum interview by MJN, 26.7.2006; Hunt, "U.S. Coverup" and *Secret Agenda;* Bower, *Paperclip Conspiracy,* and his PBS *Frontline* program, "The Nazi Connection," broadcast 24.2.1987; Simpson, *Blowback.*

9. See especially S&O, *WvB,* and Ward, *Dr. Space,* as attempts to defend him.

10. WvB response to Reid questionnaire, attached to Slattery to Reid, 17.5.1968, in WvBP-H, file 228-38; see Chapter 8. On Goethe's Faust, see Hughes, *Human-Built World,* 18–20; Berman in Goethe, *Faust,* 718–26.

11. See Harford, *Korolev;* Uhl, *Stalins V-2;* and Siddiqi, *Challenge.*

SIGNIFICANT ABBREVIATIONS USED IN THE NOTES

AA/PA	Auswärtiges Amt, Politisches Archiv, Berlin
AMCOM/HO	Army Aviation and Missile Command History Office, Huntsville, Ala.
ARS	American Rocket Society
BABL	Bundesarchiv Berlin-Lichterfelde
BAK	Bundesarchiv Koblenz
BA/MA	Bundesarchiv/Militärarchiv, Freiburg
BDC	Berlin Document Center
BIS	British Interplanetary Society
CRC/OU	Cornelius Ryan Collection, Ohio University, Athens
CTR	Chemisch-Technisches Reichsanstalt
DDEL	Dwight D. Eisenhower Library, Abilene, Kans.
DJ	Daily Journal
DM	Deutsches Museum, Munich
EvB	Emmy von Braun
ETH	Eidgenössische Technische Hochschule, Zurich
EW	Entwicklungswerk or Elektromechanische Werke
FBI	Federal Bureau of Investigation
FE	Fort Eustis, Va.
FOIA	Freedom of Information Act
GD	German Document
GEM	George E. Mueller
GfW	Gesellschaft für Weltraumforschung
GStA	Geheimes Staatsarchiv, Berlin
GWU/SPI	George Washington University, Space Policy Institute, Washington, D.C.
HAP	Heeresanstalt Peenemünde
HAP 11	Heimat-Artillerie-Park 11
HORM	Hermann Oberth-Raumfahrtmuseum, Feucht
HRC	Historical Reference Collection, NASA History Office
HVP	Heeresversuchsstelle (or -versuchsanstalt) Peenemünde
IRR/PNF	Investigative Records Repository, Personal Name Files
IWM	Imperial War Museum, London
JPL	Jet Propulsion Laboratory, Pasadena, Calif.
JSC	Johnson Space Center, Houston (former Manned Spacecraft Center)
KSC	Kennedy Space Center, Fla.
LC	Library of Congress, Washington, D.C.
MJN	Michael J. Neufeld
MP/FIT	Medaris Papers, Florida Institute of Technology, Melbourne
Ms.	manuscript
MSC	Manned Spacecraft Center, Houston (now Johnson Space Center)
MSFC	Marshall Space Flight Center, Huntsville, Ala.
MSFC/ULMF	Marshall Space Flight Center, Upper-Level Management Files

MSMC	Manned Spaceflight Management Council
MvB	Magnus von Braun Sr.
MvB Jr.	Magnus von Braun Jr.
NACP	National Archives, College Park, Md.
NARA	National Archives and Records Administration
NASA	National Aeronautics and Space Administration
NASA/HD	NASA History Division
NASER	National Archives Southeast Region, Morrow, Ga.
NASM	National Air and Space Museum, Smithsonian Institution
NASWR	National Archives Southwest Region, Fort Worth, Tex.
NSDAP	Nationalsozialistische Deutsche Arbeiterpartei
NSS	National Space Society (formerly National Space Institute)
NWHSA	Nordrhein-Westfalisches Hauptstaatsarchiv, Düsseldorf
NYT	*New York Times*
O&S	Ordway and Sharpe
OKH	Oberkommando des Heeres
OKW	Oberkommando der Wehrmacht
OHI	oral history interview
OMGUS	Occupation Military Government of the United States
PGM	Peenemünde Guided Missiles microfilm
OSI	Office of Special Investigations, U.S. Justice Department
RG	record group
RLM	Reichsluftfahrtministerium
RPI	Renssalaer Polytechnic Institute, Troy, N.Y.
RSIC	Redstone Scientific Information Center, Huntsville, Ala.
S&O	Stuhlinger and Ordway
SA	Sturmabteilung
SS	Schutzstaffel
STG	Space Task Group
SvB	Sigismund von Braun
UHCL	University of Houston, Clear Lake, Tex.
UKNA	United Kingdom National Archives, Kew
USSRC	U.S. Space and Rocket Center, Huntsville, Ala.
vB	von Braun
VW	Versuchsserienwerk, Peenemünde
WD	Walter Dornberger
WDA	Walt Disney Archives, Burbank, Calif.
WNRC	Washington National Records Center, Suitland, Md.
WP	*Washington Post*
WvB	Wernher von Braun
WvBP-H	Wernher von Braun Papers, U.S. Space and Rocket Center, Huntsville, Ala.
WvBP-LC	Wernher von Braun Papers, Library of Congress

BIBLIOGRAPHY AND ARCHIVAL SOURCES

The discussion below covers the von Braun family papers in depth but otherwise lists only significant collections elsewhere used in my research.

Wernher von Braun Papers

Because of war destruction and the pillaging of his parents' former estate in Silesia in 1945–46, Wernher von Braun's papers, and those of his father and his brother Sigismund, contain little before 1945. Von Braun did salvage a small amount of treasured personal artifacts and miscellaneous Peenemünde documents from before 1945, but these fill scarcely more than 2 standard Hollinger archival boxes out of about 225 containing his papers, which are split between the Library of Congress Manuscript Division in Washington, D.C., and the U.S. Space and Rocket Center in Huntsville, Alabama.

The division of the papers is unfortunate and came about because, after von Braun had already begun giving records to the Library of Congress in the 1960s, he was convinced to give the rest of his papers—ultimately about 70 percent—to the new space museum in Huntsville. Like most museums, the Space and Rocket Center had no idea how to be an archive, with the result that the papers were improperly housed, somewhat jumbled, and only later reboxed. The files were, however, usefully renumbered as a result of the latter project. The Huntsville papers now comprise about 164 Hollinger boxes, plus some unboxed material, covering the years from 1927 to 1977. The Library of Congress has 61 boxes, almost entirely from 1950 to 1970, although there are copies of his early scrapbooks from the 1930s and 1940s. (The originals must still be in family hands.) The papers in both places are clogged with von Braun's huge foreign and fan correspondence, mostly from 1955 on, and his massive speeches and writings files from the 1950s and 1960s, but there is a lot of excellent material buried in all that dross. The few substantive surviving records of von Braun's group in Fort Bliss, 1945–50, are also part of the von Braun papers in Huntsville. Several boxes of his foreign correspondence and speech files from the 1960s ended up in the NASA Marshall Space Flight Center (MSFC) records in the National Archives Southeast Region (NASER) in Georgia. From what is missing from all of these locations, it appears that some family correspondence and the original von Braun scrapbooks remain in family hands. Several "sensitive" files relating to Mittelbau-Dora have also gone missing and may be held by someone in Huntsville.

As for von Braun's official papers regarding management, technical issues, and projects at Redstone Arsenal and MSFC, these papers have unfortunately been dispersed and are hard to trace. Some are in his papers, some are in NASER, some are in the MSFC history office, and most of those from nuclear missile work are still locked away in classified vaults at the Washington National Records Center (WNRC) or at the U.S. Army Aviation and Missile Command (AMCOM) in Huntsville. For the 1960s the Robert Sherrod collection at NASA History Division in Washington is absolutely invaluable, as Sherrod copied large segments of von Braun's Daily Journal and the attached correspondence and telephone transcripts, the originals of which vanished after the elimination of the first MSFC history office in 1975. They may turn up someday.

Other von Braun Family Papers

Most of the papers of Magnus von Braun Sr. are held at the Bundesarchiv Koblenz in Nachlass N1085, and they include a valuable collection of family correspondence from 1945 to 1972. There are only a couple of items from an earlier period, but there is a little more in the papers still held by Sigismund's only son, Dr. Christoph-Friedrich von Braun, in Munich. Magnus Sr.'s memoir *Weg durch vier Zeitepochen* (1st ed.: *Von Ostpreussen nach Texas*) gives some useful information but little on his wife and sons; it is essentially a political memoir. From his narrative of Soviet and Polish occupation in 1945–46, however, it is clear that there was once a large family archive that was destroyed in the pillaging of their Oberwiesenthal house.

Sigismund von Braun also has left a very small collection of papers at the German Foreign Office archive (Auswärtiges Amt, Politisches Archiv) in Berlin. He also published one memoir of his U.S. stay and world trip, 1933–35, and wrote another memoir that was kindly supplied to me by a daughter, Prof. Dr. Christina von Braun.

From the von Quistorp side of the family, there is very little in public archives, and the estate archives of Crenzow and Bauer were destroyed in 1945, as virtually all were. The library of the Landesarchiv Greifswald has a few rare publications about the family, and the archive itself has a couple of testaments.

Further Archival Sources Consulted

American Institute of Physics, Neils Bohr Library, College Park, Md.: Samuel Goudsmit Papers.

Archiv der Lietz-Schulen, Schloss Bieberstein: Von Braun file, photo files.

Bundesarchiv Koblenz: Magnus von Braun Papers (see above); Albert Speer Papers.

Bundesarchiv Berlin-Lichterfelde: Magnus von Braun Sr. Reich personnel records in R43I, Reich ministries, SS and Mittelbau-Dora camp records (NS 4 Anhang), former Berlin Document Center (BDC) party and SS records.

Bundesarchiv/Militärarchiv: Peenemünde records in RH8 (Heereswaffenamt).

Deutsches Museum, Munich: Peenemünde records; Walter Dornberger and Wernher von Braun files.

Eidgenössische Technische Hochschule, Zurich: Wernher von Braun student records.

Florida Institute of Technology Library, Special Collections, Melbourne: General John B. Medaris Papers.

Geheimes Staatsarchiv, Berlin: Prussian state records, Magnus von Braun personnel files.

Georgetown University, Lauinger Library, Special Collections, Washington, D.C.: Department of Defense Film Collection, "I Aim at the Stars" folders in boxes 22–23.

Gerald R. Ford Presidential Library, Ann Arbor, Mich.: Records relating to Wernher von Braun and the National Medals of Science and of Freedom.

Hermann Oberth-Raumfahrtmuseum: Oberth Papers.

Humboldt University Archive, Berlin: Wernher von Braun doctoral examination records; Karl Becker and Ernst Schumann records.

Imperial War Museum, London: Captured German records on V-weapons; Walter Riedel manuscript.

Jet Propulsion Laboratory Archives, Pasadena, Calif.: Stewart Committee records (roll 10-3); Pickering, Orbiter/RTV, Jupiter and Juno records.

Johns Hopkins University, Milton S. Eisenhower Library, Special Collections, Baltimore: Hugh Dryden Papers (Ms. 147).

Library of Congress, Manuscript Division: Wernher von Braun Papers (see above); George E. Mueller Papers; Thomas O. Paine Papers; Samuel Phillips Papers.

NASA History Division, Washington, D.C.: Historical Reference Collection of documents and copies, including the Sherrod collection.

NASA Kennedy Space Center Archives: Kurt Debus files, KSC files on Saturn/Apollo.

NASA Marshall Space Flight Center Archives, Huntsville, Ala.: MSFC Director's Office files on Saturn/Apollo.

National Air and Space Museum Archives, Smithsonian Institution, Washington, D.C., and Silver Hill, Md.: Peenemünde records on microfilm (FE and PGM); Willy Ley Collection, Richard Porter Papers; Fred Singer Papers; Fairchild Collection; oral history interview transcripts; biographical and reference files.

National Archives II, College Park, Md.: Army Ordnance records in RG156; Paperclip records in RG260, RG319, and RG330; FBI files of von Braun in RG65; captured German records on microfilm; Berlin Document Center microfilm of NSDAP and SS files; Mittelbau-Dora war crimes trial microfilm (M-1079).

National Archives Southeast Region, Atlanta, Ga.: NASA KSC and MSFC records in RG255, especially MSFC Upper-Level Management Files; WvB speech and foreign correspondence files; naturalization records.

National Archives Southwest Region, Fort Worth, Tex.: NASA MSC/JSC records in RG255, primarily Mercury and early 1960s.

National Space Society, Washington, D.C.: Files relating to Wernher von Braun and the founding of the National Space Institute.

Nordrhein-Westfalisches Haupstaatsarchiv, Zweigarchiv Schloss Kalkum: Essen Dora trial records.

Ohio University Library Special Collections, Athens, Oh.: Cornelius Ryan Collection.

Rensselaer Polytechnic Institute Library, Special Collections, Troy, N.Y.: George M. Low Papers.

United Kingdom National Archives (former Public Records Office), Kew: Foreign Office, War Office records.

University of Houston, Library, Special Collections, Clear Lake, Tex.: NASA MSC/JSC records, particularly Apollo and Skylab; Bilstein/*Stages to Saturn* collection.

U.S. Army Aviation and Missile Command, Historian's Office, Huntsville, Ala.: Jupiter, Redstone, Orbiter/RTV/Explorer files; official histories online.

U.S. Space and Rocket Center, Huntsville, Ala.: Wernher von Braun Papers (see above); Gen. Holger Toftoy Papers; Frederick Ordway collection.

Walt Disney Archives, Burbank, Calif.: Files relating to the Disney space shows and Rocket to the Moon ride.

Washington National Records Center, Suitland, Md.: NASA records (RG 255) on deposit.

BOOKS AND ARTICLES

Allen, Michael Thad. *The Business of Genocide: The SS, Slave Labor and Concentration Camps*. Chapel Hill: University of North Carolina Press, 2002.

Ambrose, Stephen E. *Eisenhower*. Vol. 2, *The President*. New York: Simon & Schuster, 1984.

Andreesen, Alfred, and Wernher von Braun. "Die gegenwärtige Situation der Landes-erziehungsheime," *Leben und Arbeit* 4 (1928–29), 134–40.

Armacost, Michael H. *The Politics of Weapons Innovation: The Thor-Jupiter Contro-versy*. New York: Columbia University Press, 1969.

Baranowski, Shelley. *The Sanctity of Rural Life: Nobility, Protestantism, and Nazism in Weimar Prussia*. New York: Oxford University Press, 1995.

Barth, Hans. *Hermann Oberth: Leben, Werk und Auswirkung auf die spätere Raum-fahrtentwicklung*. Feucht: Uni-Verlag, 1985.

Benson, Charles D., and William Barnaby Faherty. *Moonport: A History of Apollo Launch Facilities and Operations*. Washington, D.C.: NASA, 1978.

Béon, Yves. *Planet Dora*. Edited with an introduction by Michael J. Neufeld. Translated by Yves Béon and Richard L. Fague. Boulder, Colo.: Westview Press, 1997.

Bergaust, Erik. *Rocket City U.S.A.* New York: Macmillan, 1963.

———. *Wernher von Braun*. Washington, D.C.: National Space Institute, 1976.

Berlin und Umgebung: Kleine Ausgabe. Griebenreiseführer Band 25. Berlin: Grieben, 1931.

Bilstein, Roger E. *Stages to Saturn: A Technological History of the Apollo/Saturn Launch Vehicles*. Washington, D.C.: NASA, 1980.

Bode, Volkhard, and Gerhard Kaiser. *Raketenspuren: Peenemünde 1936–1994. Eine his-torische Reportage*. Berlin: Christoph Links, 1995.

Boelcke, Willi A., ed. *Deutschlands Rüstung im Zweiten Weltkrieg. Hitlers Konferenzen mit Albert Speer 1942–1945*. Frankfurt am Main: Athenaion, 1969.

Bornemann, Manfred. *Geheimprojekt Mittelbau: Vom zentralen Öllager des Deutschen Reiches zur grössten Raketenfabrik im Zweiten Weltkrieg*. 2nd ed. Munich: Bern-hard & Graefe, 1994.

Bornemann, Manfred, and Martin Broszat. "Das KL Dora-Mittelbau." In *Studien zur Geschichte der Konzentrationslager*. Schriftenreihe der Vierteljahreshefte für Zeit-geschichte, No. 21. Stuttgart: Deutsche Verlags-Anstalt, 1970.

Bower, Tom. *The Paperclip Conspiracy: The Battle for the Spoils and Secrets of Nazi Ger-many*. London: Michael Joseph, 1987.

Braun, Julius H. "Redstone's First Flight—Success or Failure?" In *History of Rocketry and Astronautics: Proceedings of the Thirtieth History Symposium of the Inter-national Academy of Astronautics*, edited by Hervé Moulin and Donald C. Elder, 81–91. AAS History Series, vol. 25. San Diego: Univelt, Inc., for the AAS, 2003.

Breitman, Richard. *The Architect of Genocide: Himmler and the Final Solution*. New York: Alfred A. Knopf, 1991.

Brooks, Courtney G., James M. Grimwood, and Loyd S. Swenson Jr. *Chariots for Apollo: A History of Manned Lunar Spacecraft*. Washington, D.C.: NASA, 1979.

Bullard, John W. *History of the Redstone Missile System*. Huntsville, Ala.: Army Missile Command, 1965. www.redstone.army.mil/history/pdf/welcome.html.

Bullmann, Franz, Wolfgang Rathert, and Dietmar Schenk, eds. *Paul Hindemith in Berlin*. Berlin: Hochschule der Kunst, 1997.

Cassidy, David. *Uncertainty: The Life and Science of Werner Heisenberg*. New York: W. H. Freeman, 1992.

Chertok, Boris. *Rockets and People*. Vol. 1. Washington, D.C.: NASA History Division, 2005.

Clarke, Arthur C. *Astounding Days: A Science Fictional Autobiography*. New York: Ban-tam, 1989.

Clary, David A. *Rocket Man: Robert H. Goddard and the Birth of the Space Age.* New York: Hyperion, 2003.

Compton, W. David, and Charles D. Benson. *Living and Working in Space: A History of Skylab.* Washington, D.C.: NASA, 1983.

Crouch, Tom D. *Aiming for the Stars.* Washington, D.C.: Smithsonian Institution Press, 1999.

———. *Rocketeers and Gentlemen Engineers: A History of the American Institute of Aeronautics and Astronautics . . . and What Came Before.* Reston, Va.: AIAA, 2006.

Dannenberg, Konrad. "Present at the Creation." *Aviation Week and Space Technology* 158 (24 March 2003), 62–63.

Dawson, Virginia P., and Mark D. Bowles. *Taming Liquid Hydrogen: The Centaur Upper Stage Rocket, 1958–2002.* Washington, D.C.: NASA, 2004.

Day, Dwayne A. "The Clouds Above, the Earth Below: The Secret Air Force Meteorological Programme." *Spaceflight* (2005), 302–11.

Dennis, Michael Aaron. " 'Our First Line of Defense': Two University Laboratories in the Postwar American State." *Isis* 85 (1994), 427–55.

Dethloff, Henry C., and Ronald A. Schorn. *Voyager's Grand Tour: To the Outer Planets and Beyond.* Washington, D.C.: Smithsonian Books, 2003.

DeVorkin, David H. *Race to the Stratosphere: Manned Scientific Ballooning in America.* New York and Berlin: Springer-Verlag, 1989.

———. *Science With a Vengeance: How the Military Created the U.S. Space Sciences after World War II.* New York and Berlin: Springer-Verlag, 1992.

———. "War Heads into Peace Heads: Holger N. Toftoy and the Public Image of the V-2 in the United States." *Journal of the British Interplanetary Society* 45 (1992), 439–44.

Dickson, Paul. *Sputnik: Shock of the Century.* New York: Walker, 2001.

Dornberger, Walter. "The German V-2." *Technology and Culture* 4 (Fall 1963), 393–408.

———. *L'arme secrète de Peenemünde (Les fusées V 2 et la conquête de l'espace).* Translated by Henri Daussy. Paris: Arthaud, 1954.

———. *Peenemünde: Die Geschichte der V-Waffen.* (Reprint of *V 2: Der Schuss ins Weltall,* 1952.) Frankfurt/Main and Berlin: Ullstein, 1989.

———. *V-2.* Translated by James Cleugh and Geoffrey Halliday. New York: Viking, 1954.

Dunar, Andrew, and Stephen Waring. *Power to Explore: A History of Marshall Space Flight Center, 1960–1990.* Washington, D.C.: NASA, 1999.

Dungan, T. D. *V-2: A Combat History of the First Ballistic Missile.* Yardley, Pa.: Westholme, 2005.

Eisfeld, Rainer. *Mondsüchtig: Wernher von Braun und die Geburt der Raumfahrt aus dem Geist der Barbarei.* Hamburg: Rowohlt, 1996.

Eisfeld, Rainer, and Wolfgang Jeschke. *Marsfieber: Aufbruch zum Roten Planeten. Phantasie und Wirklichkeit.* Munich: Droemer, 2003.

Erichsen, Johannes, and Bernhard M. Hoppe, eds. *Peenemünde: Mythos und Geschichte der Rakete, 1923–1989.* Berlin: Nicolai, 2004.

Ermenc, Joseph J. *Atomic Bomb Scientists: Memoirs, 1939–1945.* Westport, Conn.: Meckler, 1989.

Fallaci, Oriana. *When the Sun Dies.* Translated by Pamela Swinglehurst. New York: Atheneum, 1966.

Fest, Joachim. *Speer: Eine Biographie.* Berlin: Alexander Fest, 1999.

Fleischer, Wolfgang. *Die Heeresversuchsstelle Kummersdorf.* Wölfersheim-Berstadt: Podzun Pallas, 1995.

Frank, Bernhard. *Collège Français/Französisches Gymnasium Berlin, 1689–1989.* Berlin: Westkreuz, n.d. (1989).

Franklin, Thomas (pseud. for Hugh McInnish). *An American in Exile: The Story of Arthur Rudolph.* Huntsville, Ala.: Christopher Kaylor, 1987.

Frayling, Christopher. *Mad, Bad and Dangerous? The Scientist and the Cinema.* London: Reaktion, 2005.

Frei, Norbert. *Adenauer's Germany and the Nazi Past: The Politics of Amnesty and Integration.* Translated by Joel Golb. New York: Columbia University Press, 2002.

Freund, Florian. *Arbeitslager Zement: Das Konzentrationslager Ebensee und die Raketenrüstung.* Vienna: Verlag für Gesellschaftskritik, 1989.

Freund, Florian, and Bertrand Perz. *Das Kz in der Serbenhalle: Zur Kriegsindustrie in Wiener Neustadt.* Vienna: Verlag für Gesellschaftskritik, 1987.

Furniss, Tim. "The Early Pioneers." *Spaceflight* (Nov. 1972), 428–32.

Gartmann, Heinz. *The Men Behind the Space Rockets.* Translated by Eustace Wareing and Michael Glenny. New York: David McKay, 1956.

Gellately, Robert. *Backing Hitler: Consent and Coercion in Nazi Germany.* Oxford/New York: Oxford University Press, 2001.

Generales, Constantine D. J. "Recollections of Early Biomedical Moon-Mice Investigations." In *First Steps Toward Space,* edited by Frederick C. Durant III and George S. James, 75–80. San Diego: Univelt, Inc., for the AAS, 1985.

———. "Selected Events Leading to Development of Space Medicine." *New York State Journal of Medicine* 63 (1 May 1963), 1303–12.

Gievers, Johannes G. "Erinnerungen an Kreiselgeräte." *Jahrbuch der Deutschen Gesellschaft für Luft- und Raumfahrt E.V. (DGLR)* (1971), 263–91.

Gimbel, John. "German Scientists, United States Denazification Policy, and the 'Paperclip Conspiracy.' " *International History Review* 12 (August 1990), 441–85.

———. "Project Paperclip: German Scientists, American Policy and the Cold War." *Diplomatic History* 14 (1990), 343–65.

———. *Science, Technology and Reparations: Exploitation and Plunder in Postwar Germany.* Stanford, Calif.: Stanford University Press, 1990.

———. "U.S. Policy and German Scientists: The Early Cold War." *Political Science Quarterly* 101 (1986), 433–51.

Glenn, John, with Nick Taylor. *John Glenn: A Memoir.* New York: Bantam, 1999.

Goddard, Robert H. *The Papers of Robert H. Goddard.* Edited by Esther C. Goddard and G. Edward Pendray. New York: McGraw-Hill, 1970.

Goethe, Johann Wolfgang von. *Faust: A Tragedy.* Translated by Walter Arndt. Norton Critical Edition, 2nd ed. New York: W. W. Norton, 2001.

———. *Faust: Part One.* Translated by Bayard Taylor. New York: Colliers, 1962.

Gray, Mike. *Angle of Attack: Harrison Storms and the Race to the Moon.* New York: W. W. Norton, 1992.

Grigoleit, Eduard. "Die Ahnen des Weltraum- und Raketenforschers Wernher Freiherr von Braun." *Familie und Volk* 10 (1961), 261–71.

Green, Constance McLaughlin, and Milton Lomask. *Vanguard: A History.* Washington, D.C.: NASA, 1970.

Grimwood, James M., and Frances Stroud. *History of the Jupiter Missile System.* Huntsville, Ala.: U.S. Army Ordnance Missile Command, 1962.

Gropp, Dorit. *Aussenkommando Laura und Vorwerk Mitte Lehesten: Testbetrieb für V2-Triebwerke.* Bad Münstereifel: Westkreuz, 1999.

Gröttrup, Irmgard. *Rocket Wife.* London: André Deutsch, 1959.

Günzel, Karl Werner. *Die fliegenden Flüssigkeitsraketen: Raketenpioneer Klaus Riedel.* Höxter/Westfalen: privately printed, 1988.

Halberstam, David. *The Fifties.* New York: Fawcett, 1993.

Hall, R. Cargill. "The Eisenhower Administration and the Cold War: Framing American Astronautics to Serve National Security." *Prologue* 27 (Spring 1995), 58–72.

Hamby, Alonzo L. *Man of the People: A Life of Harry S. Truman.* New York/Oxford: Oxford University Press, 1995.

Hansen, James R. *Spaceflight Revolution: NASA Langley Research Center from Sputnik to Apollo.* Washington, D.C.: NASA, 1995.

Harford, James J. *Korolev: How One Man Masterminded the Soviet Drive to Beat America to the Moon.* New York: John Wiley, 1997.

Harris, Gary. "The Year the Rockets Came." *Air & Space Smithsonian* 14 (Apr.–May 1999), 56–63.

Harris, Gordon L. *Selling Uncle Sam.* Hicksville, N.Y.: Exposition, 1976.

Harrison, Mark. "The Soviet Market for Inventions: The Case of Jet Propulsion, 1932–1944." PERSA Working Paper No. 9, University of Warwick Department of Economics. Revised 21 July 2004. www2.warwick.ac.uk/fac/soc/economics/staff/faculty/Harrison/archive/persa/0091fulltext.pdf

Heimann, Thomas, and Burghard Ciesla. "*Die gefrorenen Blitze:* Wahrheit und Dichtung: FilmGeschichte einer 'Wunderwaffe.' " In *Apropos: Film 2002. Das Jahrbuch der DEFA-Stiftung,* 158–80. Berlin: DEFA-Stiftung/Bertz Verlag, 2002.

Henze, Bernd, and Gunther Hebestreit. *Raketen aus Bleicherode: Raketenbau und Entwicklung in Bleicherode am Südharz, 1943–1948.* Bleicherode: Stadtinformation Bleicherode, 1998.

Heppenheimer, T. A. *Countdown: A History of Spaceflight.* New York: John Wiley, 1997.

———. *The Space Shuttle Decision: NASA's Search for a Reusable Space Vehicle.* Washington, D.C.: NASA, 1999.

Herf, Jeffrey. *Divided Memory: The Nazi Past in the Two Germanys.* Cambridge, Mass.: Harvard University Press, 1997.

Herring, Mack R. *Way Station to Space: A History of the John C. Stennis Space Center.* Washington, D.C.: NASA, 1997.

Hess, Torsten, and Thomas A Seidel. *Vernichtung durch Fortschritt am Beispiel der Raketenproduktion im Konzentrationslager Mittelbau.* Bad Münstereifel: Westkreuz, 1995.

Herken, Gregg. *Brotherhood of the Bomb: The Tangled Lives and Loyalties of Robert Oppenheimer, Ernest Lawrence, and Edward Teller.* New York: Henry Holt, 2002.

Hillgruber, Andreas, ed. *Kriegstagebuch des Oberkommando der Wehrmacht (Wehrmachtführungsstab).* Vol. 2. Frankfurt: Bernard & Graefe, 1963.

Hinsley, F. H., et al. *British Intelligence in the Second World War: Its Influence on Strategy and Operations.* 3 vols. in 4. London: Her Majesty's Stationery Office, 1979–88.

Hoffmann, Dieter. "Das Physikalische Institut der Berliner Universität." *Physikalische Blätter* 55 (1999), 55–57.

———. "Die Physik an der Berliner Universität in der ersten Hälfte unseres Jahrhunderts." In *Berliner Wissenschaftshistorische Kolloquien VIII,* 5–29. Berlin: Akademie der Wissenschaften der DDR, 1984.

Hölsken, Heinz Dieter. *Die V-Waffen: Entstehung—Propaganda—Kriegseinsatz.* Stuttgart: Deutsche Verlags-Anstalt, 1984.

———. *V-Missiles of the Third Reich: The V-1 and V-2.* Sturbridge, Mass.: Monogram Aviation Publications, 1994. (Illustrated, revised edition of *Die V-Waffen.*)

Horeis, Heinz, ed. *Rolf Engel—Raketenbauer der ersten Stunde.* Munich: Lehrstuhl für Raumfahrttechnik, Technische Universität München, 1992.

Hughes, Thomas Parke. *Human-Built World: How to Think About Technology and Culture.* Chicago: University of Chicago Press, 2004.

———. *Rescuing Prometheus.* New York: Pantheon, 1998.

Hunley, J. D., ed. *The Birth of NASA: The Diary of T. Keith Glennan.* Washington, D.C.: NASA, 1993.

Hunt, Linda. *Secret Agenda: The United States Government, Nazi Scientists and Project Paperclip, 1945 to 1990.* New York: St. Martin's, 1991.

———. "U.S. Coverup of Nazi Scientists." *Bulletin of the Atomic Scientists* (Apr. 1985), 16–24.

Hürter, Johannes, Martin Kroger, Rolf Messerschmidt, and Christiane Scheidemann. *Biographisches Handbuch des deutschen Auswärtigen Dienstes, 1871–1945.* Band I. A–F. Paderborn: Ferdinand Schöningh, 2000.

Huzel, Dieter K. *Peenemünde to Canaveral.* Engelwood Cliffs, N.J.: Prentice-Hall, 1962.

Irving, David. *The Mare's Nest.* Boston: Little, Brown, 1965.

Joesten, Joachim. "This Brain for Hire." *Nation* 164, no. 2 (11 Jan. 1947), 36–38.

Johnson, Eric A. *Nazi Terror: The Gestapo, Jews and Ordinary Germans.* New York: Basic Books, 2000.

Johnson, Stephen B. *The Secret of Apollo: Systems Management in American and European Space Programs.* Baltimore, Md.: Johns Hopkins University Press, 2002.

Joiner, Helen Brents, and Elizabeth C. Jolliff. *The Redstone Arsenal Complex in Its Second Decade, 1950–1960.* Redstone Arsenal, Ala.: Historical Division, Army Missile Command, 1969.

Judt, Matthias, and Burghard Ciesla, eds. *Technology Transfer Out of Germany After 1945.* Amsterdam: Harwood, 1996.

Kehrl, Hans. *Krisenmanager im Dritten Reich: 6 Jahre Frieden, 6 Jahre Krieg: Erinnerungen.* Düsseldorf: Droste, 1973.

Kershaw, Ian. *Hitler 1889–1936: Hubris.* New York: W. W. Norton, 1999.

———. *Hitler 1936–1945: Nemesis.* New York: W. W. Norton, 2000.

———. *Popular Opinion and Political Dissent in the Third Reich: Bavaria, 1933–1945.* New York: Oxford University Press, 1983.

Kilgore, De Witt Douglas. *Astrofuturism: Science, Race and Visions of Utopia in Space.* Philadelphia: University of Pennsylvania Press, 2003.

Klee, Ernst, and Otto Merk. *The Birth of the Missile: The Secrets of Peenemünde.* Translated by T. Schoeters. New York: E. P. Dutton, 1965.

Klein, Heinrich. *Vom Geschoss zum Feuerpfeil: Der grosse Umbruch der Waffentechnik in Deutschland, 1900–1970.* Neckargemünd: Kurt Vowinckel, 1977.

Klemperer, Victor. *I Will Bear Witness.* 2 vols. New York: Random House, 1998–99.

Koerrenz, Ralf. *Hermann Lietz.* Frankfurt: Peter Lang, 1989.

———. *Landeserziehungsheime in der Weimarer Republik.* Frankfurt: Peter Lang, 1992.

Koppes, Clayton R. *JPL and the American Space Program: A History of the Jet Propulsion Laboratory.* New Haven and London: Yale University Press, 1982.

Kraemer, Robert. *Rocketdyne: Powering Humans into Space.* Reston, Va.: AIAA, 2005.

Kraft, Chris. *Flight: My Life in Mission Control.* New York: Dutton, 2001.

Kraft, Ruth. *Insel ohne Leuchtfeuer.* Berlin: Vision, 1994.

Kranz, Gene. *Failure Is Not an Option: Mission Control from Mercury to Apollo 13 and Beyond*. New York: Simon & Schuster, 2000.

Kutzer, Elisabeth. "Wernher von Braun." *Leben und Arbeit* (1977), 6–8.

Lambright, W. Henry. *Powering Apollo: James E. Webb of NASA*. Baltimore, Md.: Johns Hopkins University Press, 1995.

Lang, Daniel. "A Romantic Urge." In Daniel Lang, *From Hiroshima to the Moon: Chronicles of Life in the Atomic Age*, 175–93. New York: Simon & Schuster, 1959. Originally published in *The New Yorker* (21 Apr. 1951), 69–70, 72, 74, 76–84.

Large, David Clay. *Berlin*. New York: Basic Books, 2000.

Lasby, Clarence G. *Project Paperclip: German Scientists and the Cold War*. New York: Atheneum, 1971.

Launius, Roger D. "A Waning of Technocratic Faith: NASA and the Politics of the Space Shuttle Decision." *JBIS* 49 (1996), 49–58.

———. "Kennedy's Space Policy Reconsidered: A Post–Cold War Perspective." *Air Power History* 50, no. 4 (Winter 2003), 16–29.

———. *Space Stations: Base Camps to the Stars*. Washington, D.C.: Smithsonian Books, 2003.

Launius, Roger D., and Howard E. McCurdy, eds. *Spaceflight and the Myth of Presidential Leadership*. Urbana: University of Illinois Press, 1997.

Launius, Roger D., John M. Logsdon, and Robert W. Smith, eds. *Reconsidering Sputnik: Forty Years Since the Soviet Satellite*. Amsterdam: Harwood, 2000.

Lehman, Milton. *Robert H. Goddard: Pioneer of Space Research*. New York: Da Capo, 1988. (Reprint of *This High Man*, 1963.)

Ley, Willy. "Count von Braun." *Journal of the British Interplanetary Society* 6 (June 1947), 154–56.

———. "How It All Began." *Space World* 2 (June 1961), 23–25, 48–51.

———. *Rockets*. New York: Viking, 1944 (2nd ed., 1947).

———. *Rockets, Missiles and Space Travel*. New York: Viking, 1951 (expanded version of *Rockets*).

Ley, Willy, and Chesley Bonestell. *Conquest of Space*. New York: Viking, 1949.

Ley, Willy, Wernher von Braun, and Chesley Bonestell. *The Exploration of Mars*. New York: Viking, 1956.

Lindbergh, Charles A. *Autobiography of Values*. New York: Harcourt Brace Jovanovich, 1992.

Logsdon, John M. *The Decision to Go to the Moon: Project Apollo and the National Interest*. Chicago: University of Chicago Press, 1970.

———, ed. *Exploring the Unknown: Selected Documents in the History of the U.S. Civil Space Program*. 6 vols. Washington, D.C.: NASA History Office, 1995–2004.

Lomax, Judy. *Hanna Reitsch: Flying for the Fatherland*. London: John Murray, 1989.

Mader, Julius. *Geheimnis von Huntsville*. Berlin (-East): Deutscher Militär-Verlag, 1963 (3rd ed., 1967).

Mailer, Norman. *Of a Fire on the Moon*. New York: Grove Press, 1969.

Mark, Hans. *The Space Station: A Personal Journey*. Durham, N.C.: Duke University Press, 1987.

McDougall, Walter A. *The Heavens and the Earth: A Political History of the Space Age*. New York: Basic Books, 1985.

McGovern, James. *Crossbow and Overcast*. New York: William Morrow, 1964.

McWhorter, Diane. *Carry Me Home: Birmingham, Alabama. The Climatic Battle of the Civil Rights Revolution*. New York: Simon & Schuster, 2001.

Medaris, John B. *Countdown for Decision*. New York: G. P. Putnam's Sons, 1960.

Michaud, Michael A. G. *Reaching for the High Frontier: The American Pro-Space Movement, 1972–1984*. New York: Praeger, 1986.

Michel, Jean, with Louis Nucera. *Dora*. Translated by Jennifer Kidd. New York: Holt, Rinehart and Winston, 1979.

Michels, Jürgen. *Peenemünde und seine Erben in Ost und West*. Bonn: Bernhard & Graefe, 1997.

Middlebrook, Martin. *The Peenemünde Raid: The Night of 17–18 August 1943*. London: Penguin, 1988.

Moeller, Robert G. *War Stories: The Search for a Usable Past in the Federal Republic of Germany*. Berkeley: University of California Press, 2001.

Mosse, George L. *The Crisis of German Ideology*. New York: Grosset & Dunlap, 1964.

Murray, Charles, and Catherine Bly Cox. *Apollo: The Race to the Moon*. New York: Simon & Schuster, 1989.

Nash, Philip. *The Other Missiles of October: Eisenhower, Kennedy and the Jupiters, 1957–1963*. Chapel Hill: University of North Carolina Press, 1997.

Nebel, Rudolf. *Die Narren von Tegel. Ein Pioneer der Raumfahrt erzählt*. Düsseldorf: Droste, 1972.

———. *Raketenflug*. Berlin: Raketenflugplatz, 1932.

Needell, Allan A. *Science, Cold War and the American State: Lloyd V. Berkner and the Balance of Professional Ideals*. Amsterdam: Harwood, 2000.

Neufeld, Jacob. *The Development of Ballistic Missiles in the United States Air Force, 1945–1960*. Washington, D.C.: Office of Air Force History, 1990.

Neufeld, Michael J. "The End of the Army Space Program: Interservice Rivalry and the Transfer of the Von Braun Group to NASA, 1958–1959." *Journal of Military History* 69 (July 2005), 737–58.

———. "The Excluded: Hermann Oberth and Rudolf Nebel in the Third Reich." *Quest* 5, no. 4 (1996), 22–27.

———. "The Guided Missile and the Third Reich: Peenemünde and the Forging of a Technological Revolution." In *Science, Technology and National Socialism*, edited by Monika Renneberg and Mark Walker, 51–71, 352–56. Cambridge: Cambridge University Press, 1993.

———. *The Rocket and the Reich: Peenemünde and the Coming of the Ballistic Missile Era*. New York: Free Press, 1995 (paperback, Harvard University Press, 1996; German translation, *Die Rakete und Das Reich*, Brandenburgisches Verlagshaus, 1997, 2nd ed., Henschel Verlag, 1998).

———. "The Reichswehr, the Rocket and the Versailles Treaty: A Popular Myth Reexamined." *Journal of the British Interplanetary Society* 53 (2000), 163–72.

———. "Rocket Aircraft and the 'Turbojet Revolution': The Luftwaffe's Quest for High-Speed Flight, 1935–39." In *Innovation and the Development of Flight*, edited by Roger D. Launius, 207–34. College Station: Texas A&M University Press, 1999.

———. "Rolf Engel vs. the German Army: A Nazi Career in Rocketry and Repression." *History and Technology* 13 (1996), 53–72.

———. "Weimar Culture and Futuristic Technology: The Rocketry and Spaceflight Fad in Germany, 1923–1933." *Technology and Culture* 31 (October 1990), 725–52.

———. "Wernher von Braun, the SS, and Concentration Camp Labor: Questions of Moral, Political and Criminal Responsibility." *German Studies Review* 25 (2002), 57–78.

Neufeld, Michael J., and Ernst Stuhlinger. "Wernher von Braun and Concentration Camp Labor: An Exchange." *German Studies Review* 26 (2003), 121–26.

Noble, David. *The Religion of Technology: The Divinity of Man and the Spirit of Invention.* New York: Knopf, 1997.

Noordung, Hermann (pseudonym for Hermann Potoçnik). *Das Problem der Befahrung des Weltraums: Der Raketen-Motor.* Berlin: Richard Carl Schmidt, 1929.

———. *The Problem of Space Travel: The Rocket Motor.* Translation edited by Ernst Stuhlinger and J. D. Hunley. Washington, D.C.: NASA History Office, 1995.

Oberth, Hermann. *Die Rakete zu den Planetenräumen.* 1923. Reprint. Nuremberg: Uni-Verlag, 1960.

———. *Wege zur Raumschiffahrt.* 1929. Reprint. Bucharest: Kriterion, 1974.

Ordway, Frederick I., III, Mitchell R. Sharpe, and Ronald C. Wakeford. "Project Horizon: An Early Study of a Lunar Outpost." *Acta Astronautica* 17 (1988), 1105–21.

Ordway, Frederick I., III, and Mitchell R. Sharpe. *The Rocket Team.* New York: Thomas Y. Crowell, 1979.

Ordway, Frederick I., III, and Randy Liebermann. *Blueprint for Space: Science Fiction to Science Fact.* Washington, D.C.: Smithsonian Institution Press, 1992.

Patterson, James T. *Grand Expectations: The United States, 1945–1974.* Oxford History of the United States, vol. 10. New York: Oxford University Press, 1996.

Petzold, Joachim. *Franz von Papen.* Munich: Buchverlag Union, 1995.

Piszkiewicz, Dennis. *Wernher von Braun: The Man Who Sold the Moon.* Westport, Conn.: Praeger, 1998.

Portree, David S. F. *Humans to Mars: Fifty Years of Mission Planning, 1950–2000.* Monographs in Aerospace History #21. Washington, D.C.: NASA, 2001.

Powers, Thomas. *Heisenberg's War.* New York: Knopf, 1993.

Rakhmanin, V. F., and L. E. Sternin, eds. *Odnazhdy i navzegda . . . : dokumenty i liudi o sozdatele raketnykh dvigatelei i kosmicheskikh system akademike Valentine Petroviche Glushko.* Moscow: Mashinostroenie, 1998.

Reisig, Gerhard H. R. *Raketenforschung in Deutschland: Wie die Menschen das Weltall erobern.* Berlin: Wissenschaft und Technik, 1999.

Rielau, Hans. *Geschichte der Nebeltruppe.* Cologne: ABC- und Selbstschutzschule, 1965.

Rietz, Frank-E. *Die Magdeburger Pilotenrakete.* Halle: Mitteldeutscher Verlag, 1998.

Rigg, Bryan Mark. *Hitler's Jewish Soldiers: The Untold Story of Nazi Racial Laws and Men of Jewish Descent in the German Military.* Lawrence: University Press of Kansas, 2002.

Rohrwild, Karlheinz. *Die Geschichte der UFA-Rakete.* Feucht: Hermann Oberth-Raumfahrtmuseum, 1994.

Rose, Paul Lawrence. *Heisenberg and the Nazi Atomic Bomb Project: A Study in German Culture.* Berkeley: University of California Press, 1998.

Rosen, Milton W. *The Viking Rocket Story.* New York: Harper, 1955.

Rosen, Milton W., and F. C. Schwenk. "A Rocket for Manned Lunar Exploration." In *Xth International Astronautical Congress, London 1959: Proceedings,* 311–26. Vienna: Springer, 1960.

Ruland, Bernd. *Wernher von Braun: Mein Leben für die Raumfahrt.* Offenburg: Burda, 1969.

Ryan, Cornelius, ed. *Across the Space Frontier.* New York: Viking, 1952.

———. *Conquest of the Moon.* New York: Viking, 1953.

Sato, Yasushi. "Local Engineering and Systems Engineering: Cultural Conflict at NASA's

Marshall Space Flight Center, 1960–1966." *Technology and Culture* 46 (July 2005), 561–83.

Schmidt, Matthias. *Albert Speer: The End of a Myth*. Translated by Joachim Neugroschel. London: Harrap, 1985.

Schnepel, Wiard. "Die Quistorps," *Pommern* 25, no. 2 (1977), 14–19.

60 Jahre Hermann Lietz-Schule Spiekeroog, 1928–1988. Spiekeroog: Hermann Lietz-Schule, 1988.

Seamans, Robert C., Jr. *Aiming at Targets: The Autobiography of Robert C. Seamans, Jr.* Washington, D.C.: NASA, 1996.

Seidel, Thomas A., ed. *Nachbarn auf dem Ettersberg: Menschenverachtung und Erziehung zur Ehrfurcht*. Neudietendorf/Weimar: Evangelische Akademie Thüringen/Kuratorium Schloss Ettersburg e.V., 1995.

Sellier, André. *A History of the Dora Camp*. Translated by Stephen Wright and Susan Taponier. Chicago: Ivan Dee, 2003.

Sereny, Gitta. *Albert Speer: His Battle with Truth*. New York: Knopf, 1995.

Shows, Charles. *Walt: Backstage Adventures with Walt Disney*. La Jolla, Calif.: Communication Creativity, 1980.

Siddiqi, Asif A. *Challenge to Apollo: The Soviet Union and the Space Race, 1945–1974*. Washington, D.C.: NASA, 2000.

Sime, Ruth Lewin. *Lise Meitner: A Life in Physics*. Berkeley: University of California Press, 1996.

Simpson, Christopher. *Blowback: America's Recruitment of Nazis and Its Effects on the Cold War*. New York: Weidenfeld & Nicolson, 1988.

Sloop, John L. *Liquid Hydrogen as a Propulsion Fuel, 1945–1959*. Washington, D.C.: NASA, 1978.

Smith, David R. "They're Following Our Script: Walt Disney's Trip to Tomorrowland," *Future* (May 1978), 54–63.

Speer, Albert. *Infiltration*. Translated by Joachim Neugroschel. New York: Macmillan, 1981.

———. *Inside the Third Reich*. Translated by Richard and Clara Winston. New York: Avon, 1970.

Springer, Anthony M. "Project Adam: The Army's Man in Space Program." *Quest* (Summer–Fall 1994), 46–47.

Steinberg, Michael Stephen. *Sabers and Brown Shirts*. Chicago: University of Chicago Press, 1977.

Steinhoff, Johannes, Peter Pechel, and Dennis Showalter, eds. *Voices from the Third Reich*. Washington, D.C.: Regnery Gateway, 1989.

Stubno, William J., Jr. "The Von Braun Rocket Team Viewed as a Product of German Romanticism." *Journal of the British Interplanetary Society* 35 (1982), 445–49.

Stuhlinger, Ernst, and Frederick I. Ordway III. *Wernher von Braun: Crusader for Space*. 2 vols.: *A Biographical Memoir* and *A Pictorial Memoir*. Malabar, Fla.: Krieger, 1994.

———. *Wernher von Braun: Aufbruch in den Weltraum*. Esslingen: Bechtle, 1992.

Stüwe, Botho. *Peenemünde-West: Die Erprobungsstelle der Luftwaffe für geheime Fernlenkwaffen und deren Entwicklungsgeschichte*. Esslingen: Bechtle, 1995.

Sulloway, Frank J. *Born to Rebel: Birth Order, Family Dynamics and Creative Lives*. New York: Pantheon, 1996.

Swenson, Loyd S., Jr., James M. Grimwood, and Charles C. Alexander. *This New Ocean: A History of Project Mercury*. Washington, D.C.: NASA, 1966.

Szilard, Leo. "Reminiscences." In *The Intellectual Migration*, edited by Donald Fleming and Bernard Bailyn, 94–151. Cambridge, Mass.: Belknap Press of Harvard University Press, 1969.

Tompkins, Phillip K. *Organizational Communication Imperatives: Lessons of the Space Program.* Los Angeles: Roxbury, 1993.

Trischler, Helmuth. *Luft- und Raumfahrtforschung in Deutschland, 1900–1970: Politische Geschichte einer Wissenschaft.* Frankfurt: Campus, 1992.

Turner, Henry Ashby, Jr. *Hitler's 30 Days to Power.* Reading, Mass.: Addison-Wesley, 1996.

Uhl, Matthias. *Stalins V-2. Der Technologietransfer der deutschen Fernlenkwaffentechnik in die UdSSR und der Aufbau der sowjetischen Raketenindustrie 1945 bis 1959.* Bonn: Bernhard & Graefe, 2001.

U.S. Army Ordnance. *The Story of Peenemünde, or What Might Have Been.* (Also known as *Peenemünde East, through the Eyes of 500 Detained at Garmisch.*) Mimeographed. 1945.

U.S. Congress. House of Representatives. Select Committee on Astronautics and Space Exploration. *Astronautics and Space Exploration: Hearings . . . April 15 . . . [to] May 12, 1958.* Washington, D.C.: U.S. Government Printing Office, 1958.

U.S. Congress. Senate. Committee on Armed Services. *Inquiry into Satellite and Missile Programs: Hearings Before the Preparedness Investigating Subcommittee.* Part I. Washington, D.C.: U.S. Government Printing Office, 1958.

Velder, Christian. *300 Jahre Französisches Gymnasium Berlin.* Berlin: Nicolai, 1989.

von Braun, Magnus Freiherr. *Die Freiherren von Braun.* N.p.: Privately published, n.d. (1958).

———. *Weg durch vier Zeitepochen.* Limburg an der Lahn: Starke, 1965. (1st and 2nd ed.: *Von Ostpreussen nach Texas.* Stollham: Helmut Rauschenbusch, 1955.)

von Braun, Sigismund. *Flüchtige Gäste: Auf Weltenbummel, 1933–1935.* Frankfurt am Main: Haag + Herchen, 1993.

von Braun, Wernher. "Briefe als Vorwort." *Leben und Arbeit* 5 (1929–30), 154.

———. *First Men to the Moon.* Designed and illustrated by Fred Freeman. New York: Holt, Rinehart and Winston, 1960.

———. "Das Geheimnis der Flüssigkeitsrakete." *Die Umschau* 36 (4 June 1932), 449–52.

———. "Konstruktive, theoretische und experimentelle Beiträge zu dem Problem der Flüssigkeitsrakete." Ph.D. diss., University of Berlin, 1934. Reprint. *Raketentechnik und Raumfahrtforschung,* Sonderheft 1 (n.d., c. 1960).

———. "Lunetta." *Leben und Arbeit* 6 (1930–31), 88–92.

———. *Das Marsprojekt.* Frankfurt a.m.: Umschau, 1952.

———. *The Mars Project.* Urbana: University of Illinois Press, 1953 (Illini Books ed., 1991).

———. *Project Mars: A Technical Tale.* Burlington, Ont.: Apogee Books Science Fiction, 2006.

———. "Reminiscences of German Rocketry." *Journal of the British Interplanetary Society* 15 (May–June 1956), 125–45.

———. "Space Man—the Story of My Life." *American Weekly* (20 July 1958), 7–9, 22–25; (27 July 1958), 10–13; (3 August 1958), 12, 14–16.

———. "Space Superiority." *Ordnance* (Mar.–Apr. 1953), 770–75.

———. "Die Sternwarte." *Leben und Arbeit* 4 (1928–29), 173.

———. "The Story Behind the Explorers." *This Week* (13 April 1958), 8–9, 36–38.

———. "Teamwork: Key to Success in Guided Missiles." *Missiles and Rockets* (Oct. 1956), 38–42.

————. "Why I Chose America." *American Magazine* 154 (July 1952), 15, 111–12, 114–15.

von Quistorp, Barthold. *Geschichte der Familie Quistorp: Mittlere Hauptlinie seit 1718.* Berlin: Ernst Siegfried Mittler, 1901.

Wagner, Jens-Christian. *Produktion des Todes: Das KZ Mittelbau-Dora.* Göttingen, Wallstein, 2001.

————. "Zwangsarbeit in Peenemünde (1939–1945): Praxis und Erinnerung." *Zeitgeschichte Regional: Mitteilungen aus Mecklenburg-Vorpommern* 4, no. 1 (July 2000), 15–21.

Walker, Mark. *German National Socialism and the Quest for Nuclear Power, 1939–1949.* Cambridge: Cambridge University Press, 1989.

————. *Nazi Science: Myth, Truth, and the German Atomic Bomb.* New York: Plenum, 1995.

Ward, Bob. *Dr. Space: The Life of Wernher von Braun.* Annapolis, Md.: Naval Institute Press, 2005.

————. *Wernher von Braun Anekdotisch.* Esslingen: Bechtle, 1972.

Watts, Steven. *The Magic Kingdom: Walt Disney and the American Way of Life.* Boston: Houghton Mifflin, 1997.

Wegener, Peter P. *The Peenemünde Wind Tunnels: A Memoir.* New Haven: Yale University Press, 1996.

Weitekamp, Margaret A. *Right Stuff, Wrong Sex: America's First Woman-in-Space Program.* Baltimore, Md.: Johns Hopkins University Press, 2004.

Westrum, Ron. *Sidewinder: Creative Missile Development at China Lake.* Annapolis, Md.: Naval Institute Press, 1999.

Weyer, Johannes. *Wernher von Braun.* Hamburg: Rowohlt, 1999.

Wilson, Paul J. *Himmler's Cavalry: The Equestrian SS, 1930–1945.* Atglen, Pa.: Schiffer Military Publishing, 2000.

Winter, Frank H. *Prelude to the Space Age: The Rocket Societies, 1924–1940.* Washington, D.C.: Smithsonian Institution Press, 1983.

Winter, Frank H., and Michael J. Neufeld. "Heylandt's Rocket Cars and the V-2: A Little-Known Chapter in Rocket History." In *History of Rocketry and Astronautics: Proceedings of the Twenty-Sixth History Symposium of the International Academy of Astronautics. Washington, D.C., U.S.A., 1992.* Edited by Phillipe Jung. San Diego: Univelt, Inc., for the American Astronautical Society, 1997.

York, Herbert F. *Making Weapons, Talking Peace.* New York: Basic Books, 1987.

Zwicky, Fritz. *Report on Certain Phases of War Research in Germany.* Vol. 1. Pasadena: Aerojet Engineering Corporation, 1945.

Across the Space Frontier *(Ryan)*, 266–7, 275

Adam, Project, 329–30, 336, 368

Adams, Carsbie, 373, 462

Advanced Research Projects Agency (ARPA), 328–9, 331, 334, 336, 338, 341–2, 379

Aerobee, 282, 297–8

Aerojet, 220, 284, 385, 395

Agena, 379–80

Aggregat rockets
  A-1, 62–3, 67–8, 70
  A-2, 67, 70–5, 79, 81, 103, 111
  A-3
    briefings for Hitler on, 111, 128
    development and testing of, 75–7, 81, 84–5, 102–7
    failures of, 103–7, 109–10, 119
  A-4, *see* Vergeltungswaffe, V-2
  A-4b, 188–9, 192, 204–5
  A-5, 105–11, 113, 124, 128–9
  A-8, 129–30
  A-9, 126–9, 138, 158, 204–5, 212, 220–1
  A-10, 126–8, 205, 220–1
  A-11, 220–1

Agnew, Spiro, 430, 434, 436–7, 444

Air Force, U.S. (USAF), 175, 195, 197, 232, 235, 238–9, 267, 272, 280–1, 300, 328–31, 340–5, 347, 361, 369–70, 379–81, 400, 417, 434, 439
  Apollo and, 369, 395
  Centaur and, 379–80
  ICBMs and, 308, 387–9, 393
  IRBMs and, 262, 281, 293, 295, 298, 303, 305–6, 309, 314, 338
  NASA and, 334, 341–4
  Peenemünde and, 183, 201–2, 393
  Pioneer and, 328, 340
  satellites and, 280, 291, 293–4, 296–8, 305, 319–20, 330, 342

space conference of, 256–7
  U.S. rocket program and, 210, 213, 217, 220, 222

Air Ministry, German, *see* Luftwaffe, German

Alaska, 460, 464–6, 469

Aldrin, Buzz, 431, 433, 436

all-up decision, 388–9, 400, 419, 423

Alphaville, 407

Altvater, Karl Otto, 105–8

American Rocket Society (ARS), 240, 252, 255, 259, 261–2, 264–5, 278, 466
  and creation of NASA, 317–18
  and criticisms of von Braun's space proposals, 269, 271–2

Andreesen, Alfred, 22–3, 26, 31–5, 37

Antarctica, 414–15, 421

antiaircraft missiles, 204
  guidance and control of, 138, 149
  Loki and, 282–4, 291–5
  Luftwaffe and, 129, 137–9, 144, 149, 176, 189, 191
  Peenemünde and, 129, 138, 144, 149, 153, 158, 192, 282
  propulsion of, 138, 153, 155
  Taifun and, 189, 191–2, 282
  U.S. Army rocket program and, 209, 224
  Wasserfall and, 138–9, 144, 149, 153, 155, 158, 169, 176, 187–8, 191–2, 209, 224

Antwerp
  U.S. Army rocket program and, 206–7
  V-2 and, 188, 196, 351

Apollo, Project, 6, 161, 353–85, 387–93, 395, 397–404, 412, 415–50, 452, 473–4
  delays in, 380, 383, 415–16, 418, 423
  Earth-orbit rendezvous (EOR) in, 356–7, 365–6, 370, 372–4, 377–8
  fire in, 415–18, 420–1, 440
  guidance and control in, 372, 376

Apollo, Project (*cont.*)
  Kennedy and, 354–6, 358, 360, 362–4,
    378, 381–4, 387, 389–91, 399, 401,
    404, 418, 423, 425, 438, 440
  large launch vehicle for, 371–3
  lunar landings in, 32, 356, 366–9, 371,
    374–8, 429–34, 436–40, 442, 445–6,
    449–50, 454, 459, 462, 466, 473, 477
  lunar-orbit rendezvous (LOR) in, 372–8,
    382, 389, 400, 403, 423–5, 427–30,
    433
  media on, 383, 416, 419, 427, 431–3, 449
  near-fatal accident in, 445, 447
  plans for successor programs to, 391–2,
    399–404, 415–17, 420–1, 425–6,
    430–2, 434–6, 439, 441–4, 448, 459
  propulsion in, 357, 365, 372, 375–8, 397,
    416
  public opinion on, 362–3, 383
  secrecy in, 424–5
  test launches in, 419–22
  von Braun's management style and,
    356–7, 363–9, 371–2, 375–8, 383–5,
    387, 389, 391–3, 397, 422–4, 433
  see also Saturn program
Apollo Applications Program (AAP),
    399–404, 415–16, 430–1, 462
  see also Skylab
  von Braun's management style and,
    420–1, 425–6
Apollo-Soyuz Test Project, 454, 467–9
Apollo Telescope Mount (ATM), 402–4,
    420–1, 425–6, 430
Applications Technology Satellite-F
    (ATS-F), 460–1, 464–6
Ardennes, 184, 188
Argus, 327–30, 332
Armstrong, Neil, 40, 431, 433, 436
Army, German, 39, 48–88, 98–102, 110,
    167–9, 173, 182, 197, 233
  antiaircraft missiles and, 138–9
  and attempted assassination of Hitler,
    180–1, 184
  and campaign against rocketry amateurs,
    65–6
  interservice experimental rocket
    establishment and, 78–82, 86, 88,
    90, 93, 95, 99–101, 138–9
  and military uses for rockets, 48–53

  Peenemünde and, 90–6, 99–101, 106,
    112–13, 125–7, 156, 158–9, 191–3,
    339
  and rocket briefings for Hitler, 112,
    127–8, 150
  rocket fighter program and, 78–9, 82,
    100–2, 112, 114
  rocket program of, x, 4, 53–88, 90, 92,
    116, 204
  secret rocket testing and, 51–3, 57, 67–9,
    71–2, 77–8, 80
  Soviet campaign and, 128, 139, 142
  V-2 and, 119, 127–30, 132, 134–5, 137,
    140–1, 149, 158, 176, 476
  and von Braun's meeting with Himmler,
    168–9
  von Braun's politics and, 96, 99, 121
Army, U.S., 5–6, 96, 196–202, 206–25,
    231–40, 263–5, 279–80, 288, 291–301,
    305–7, 317–23, 327–32, 361, 373–4,
    381–2, 393, 395, 418, 459
  final World War II offensive of, 196–8,
    202
  Hermes II and, 224, 234, 238–9
  IRBMs and, 299–300, 305–6
  The Mars Project and, 245, 263
  and movies on von Braun, 347, 351–2
  NASA and, 334–6, 339, 341–3, 345
  Project Adam and, 329, 336
  Redstone and, 251, 258, 269
  rocket program of, 3, 6, 206–24, 227,
    231–5, 237–40, 245, 248, 251
  satellites and, 291–9, 303–4, 313–14, 317,
    319–23, 327, 331, 341
  von Braun's fame and, 260, 324–5
  von Braun's surrender to, 191–2, 199–201
Army Air Forces, U.S., *see* Air Force, U.S
Army Ballistic Missile Agency (ABMA),
    300, 306–10, 328–31, 340–4
  Apollo and, 356–7
  IRBMs and, 303, 306–8
  Mercury and, 336, 338
  NASA and, 334–6, 341–4, 346, 357
  satellites and, 309–10, 313–14, 319–20,
    322, 328, 330
astronauts, 353, 392, 420–3, 429–38, 469
  Apollo and, 6, 355, 372–3, 375, 378, 415,
    418, 422–3, 425, 427, 429–34,
    436–7, 449–50, 474

Collier's and, 272, 276
deaths of, 415, 418, 420
Gemini and, 371, 380
Mercury and, 338, 355, 358–9, 363,
  374–5
space shuttle and, 435, 438
and successor programs to Apollo,
  402–3, 420, 430
astronomy, 244, 248, 252, 256–7, 349, 390–2
Apollo and, 388, 390
Collier's and, 259, 272, 276
from orbit, 401–3, 420–1, 425–6
von Braun's early writings on, 28–9
von Braun's fascination with, 21–2,
  24–9, 33, 35, 48
Atlas, 262, 268, 280–1, 293, 299, 331, 358,
  371, 378–81
Mercury and, 336, 355, 375, 381
satellites and, 280, 296
atomic bombs, 5, 125–7, 162, 214, 230, 245
use of, 185, 205, 211, 221, 226, 261
see also nuclear weapons
Atomic Energy Commission, 400, 435
Atwood, Lee, 398–9, 415–16
Auschwitz, 99, 145, 159, 195
Austria, 25, 97, 101, 158, 173, 198, 463
V-2 and, 142–4, 149
World War I and, 13–15
Axster, Herbert, 196, 200, 207, 211, 217,
  235, 237
Axster, Ilse, 235

"Baby Space Station" (von Braun), 272–3,
  275–6
Backfire, Operation, 211
Bannasch, Hannelore, 92, 197
Barbarossa, Operation, 127, 130, 180
Bauer, 11, 80, 91, 156, 193, 243
Bäumker, Adolf, 79–80
Beale, Betty, 444
Bechtle, Otto Wolfgang, 252–5, 261–3, 265
Becker, Karl E., 39, 42, 101, 109–12
German Army rocket program and,
  53–6, 58–60, 64–5, 72, 75, 80–2, 88
and impact of World War II on rocket
  program, 116–17, 119
and military uses for rockets, 49–53
Peenemünde and, 92–3, 95, 106, 109
suicide of, 120–1

Bell Aircraft, 267–8, 300, 379, 458
Bergaust, Erik, 185, 284–5, 304, 306, 352,
  465
Berger, Gottlob, 141–2
Berlin, 7, 10–12, 14–19, 21–3, 26–8, 30, 32,
  35–40, 45–7, 51, 60–1, 65, 67, 69, 72,
  75–6, 83–6, 88, 90–2, 94–5, 98, 102, 105,
  111, 117, 120, 142, 153–9, 169, 183, 190
air raids on, 153–4, 185
M. von Braun's civil service career and,
  11, 15
Nebel-Riedel rocket tests and, 41–2, 47
Oberth's rocket project and, 39–40
Peenemünde and, 95, 157–9
political turmoil in, 16–17, 23
secrecy issues and, 53, 92
V-2 and, 133, 140, 156
W. von Braun's arrest and, 171–2
W. von Braun's childhood in, 16–19, 21
W. von Braun's higher education and,
  36–8, 45–6
W. von Braun's leisure activities and,
  83–5
and W. von Braun's romance with Brill,
  146–7
W. von Braun's trips to, 195–6, 409
blacks, 9
civil rights and, 279, 385–6, 395–7
race riots and, 404, 417, 422
Bleicherode, 194–8, 208, 210
Boeing, 381–2, 393–4, 438, 459, 467
Apollo and, 371, 393
Bonestell, Chesley, 252, 261, 285–6, 295
Collier's and, 257–9, 276
Mars book planned by, 275–6
Borkum, rocket tests at, 71–5, 102
Borsig locomotive and heavy machinery
  factory, 37–8, 40, 42
Bosché, Bill, 288, 290
Bossart, Karel "Charlie," 262, 379–80
Boykow, Johannes Maria, 77, 103
Brill, Dorothee, 146–7
British Interplanetary Society (BIS), 240,
  246, 253, 255, 257, 271, 280
Bromley, William, 206
Brucker, Wilber, 301, 306
NASA and, 335, 342–3
satellites and, 311, 314, 320–3
Brüning, Heinrich, 56

Buch, Alfred, 191–2
Buchenwald, 144, 194
  slave laborers and, 157, 178–80
Bumper, Project, 238, 274

"Can We Get to Mars?" (von Braun), 276
Cape Canaveral, Fla., 285, 304–5, 332, 361,
    375, 414–16, 433–4, 467
  Apollo and, 365–6, 377, 381, 397,
      415–16, 418, 424, 431, 433
  Kennedy's visits to, 389–90
  Mercury and, 358, 363
  Redstone and, 274, 294, 319
  satellites and, 296, 304, 319–22
Caro, Nicodem, 19
Carter, Jimmy, 471, 473
Centaur, 345, 358, 378–80
Central Intelligence Agency (CIA), 264,
    266, 284, 292, 329, 336, 360, 424
Charyk, Joseph, 343
Cherry Stone, *see* Vergeltungswaffe, V-1
Chertok, Boris, 210
China, Communist, 245, 249, 279, 477
Christofilos, Nicholas, 327
Chrysler Corporation, 331, 341, 381–2,
    394, 411, 463
  Jupiter and, 300–1
  Redstone and, 250–1, 274
Clarke, Arthur C., 145, 456
  von Braun's Nazi past and, 406–7
  von Braun's relationship with, 284–5
  Wallops Island retreat and, 445–6
Cleaver, A. V. "Val," 253–5, 283
Collier's, 282, 325, 431, 435
  astronaut issue of, 272, 276
  Ley-Bonestell Mars book and, 275–6
  Mars issue of, 272, 275–6, 285, 372
  Moon trip issues of, 266, 268, 270–2, 289
  space flight issues of, 6, 256–62, 264–73,
      275–8, 285–6, 289–90, 294, 316,
      368, 450
Collins, Michael, 431, 433, 436, 474
Communists, Communism, 42, 54, 56, 61,
    115, 160, 170, 181, 254, 261, 325, 349,
    353, 473
  in China, 245, 249, 279, 477
  von Braun's Nazi past and, 404–6, 408
  von Braun's politics and, 236, 238, 243,
      271, 316, 370

concentration camps, concentration camp
    prisoners, 171, 189, 201–2, 211, 230,
    271, 324, 348, 472–3
  enslavement of, ix, 5, 142–5, 154,
      156–65, 167, 175–80, 186, 195, 235,
      353, 405–6, 409, 429, 449, 476
  final Allied offensive and, 198, 202
  living and working conditions of,
      159–63, 177–8, 195
  mistreatment of, 165, 204, 256, 409, 429
  von Braun's awareness of, 145, 157,
      160–3, 173, 176–9, 204, 235
  von Braun's management style and,
      162–3, 176–9, 186
  von Braun's Nazi past and, 404–6, 408–9,
      428–9
  war crimes trials and, 235–6
Congress, U.S., 224, 236, 243, 316–18, 335,
    346, 350, 370, 387, 396, 412, 424–5,
    441, 443, 454–5
  Apollo and, 362, 364, 378–80, 382–3,
      402–3, 416–17
  proposed Martian expedition and, 434,
      436–7
  von Braun's testimonies for, 317–18,
      329, 361, 379, 425, 449
Conquest of Space, The (Ley and
    Bonestell), 252, 261, 275, 285
Conquest of the Moon (Ryan), 272–3
Crenzow, 11–16, 80, 91, 170, 243
Crow, Sir Alwyn, 211–12
cruise missiles, 149, 176, 180
  see also Vergeltungswaffen (vengeance
      weapons), missiles, V-1
Cuba, 360, 382

Dahm, Werner, 189
Debus, Kurt, 223, 328, 386, 397
  Apollo and, 380–1, 383, 415, 418, 424,
      431
  IRBMs and, 307–8
  Mercury and, 358, 418–19
  Redstone and, 274, 301, 304, 319
  satellites and, 304, 321
Defense Department, U.S. (DOD), 120, 193,
    213–14, 237, 266, 268, 317, 319–23,
    340–3, 361, 444, 459, 475
  Hermes II and, 248–9
  IRBMs and, 295, 299, 306, 309

and movies on von Braun, 325, 347, 350
NASA and, 341–3
Redstone and, 250, 307
satellites and, 281, 294–6, 304, 313–15,
 320–3, 327–8, 330, 341
U.S. Army rocket program and, 214, 232
Degenkolb, Gerhard, 157, 162–3, 187
 V-2 and, 140–3, 148–9, 152, 162
Delbrück, Clemens, 11, 14
Dembling, Paul, 428–9
"Design, Theoretical and Experimental
 Contributions to the Problem of the
 Liquid-Fuel Rocket" (von Braun),
 68–9
Disney, Walt, 6, 279–80, 287
 von Braun space shows for, 285–90, 295,
 301, 317, 368
Dr. Strangelove, 406
Dora (Michel), 474–5
Dora, *see* Mittelwerk, Mittelbau
Dornberger, Walter "Seppl," 51–4, 85–9,
 101–7, 119–21, 127–42, 144, 166–8,
 237, 245, 263–5, 267, 271, 300, 324,
 347, 379, 407, 431
 A-3 and, 102–5
 A-5 and, 105–7, 109, 111
 Allied internment of, 201, 203, 207–8,
 212
 antiaircraft missiles and, 129, 138, 149
 final Allied offensive and, 196–8
 German Army rocket program and,
 53–4, 58, 62, 65, 67, 71–2, 74, 76,
 81–2, 85, 87–8
 and impact of World War II on rocket
 program, 116–17, 119, 123
 and military uses for rockets, 49, 51–2
 and move to Oberammergau, 196–7
 Peenemünde and, 85–6, 92, 94–6, 99,
 102, 106, 109, 146, 154–9, 163, 191,
 193
 politics of, 97, 429
 and rocket briefings for Hitler, 110–12,
 127–8, 150–1
 secret rocket testing and, 52–3
 surrender of, 199–201, 203
 V-2 and, 81, 115, 119, 123, 127–37,
 139–42, 149–51, 153, 156, 158, 166,
 171–2, 174–6, 181–2, 184, 186–8,
 196, 265

von Braun's arrest and, 170–3, 175
 war crimes and, 211, 235
Douglas Aircraft, 220, 357, 372, 382
 IRBMs and, 305–7
 Saturn and, 384, 394, 397
Downs, Hugh, 471
Dratler, Jay, 347–8
Dryden, Hugh, 334, 360–1, 402, 404
 Adam and, 329–30
 Apollo and, 360, 364, 366–9, 378, 382
Durant, Frederick C., III, 329
 satellites and, 284, 292–3, 309
 von Braun's IAF papers and, 255, 264
Dyna-Soar space glider, 329, 341

Ehricke, Krafft, 241, 310, 379–80
Eisenhower, Dwight, 200, 203, 262, 268,
 273, 279–81, 289, 316, 319, 322–3,
 331, 338–9, 461
 Apollo and, 355, 358
 Argus and, 327–8
 farewell address of, 352–3
 IRBMs and, 299, 305, 309
 NASA and, 334–6, 344–5
 satellites and, 281, 294, 296–7, 304, 310,
 312–14, 322
 Saturn and, 338, 346, 352
 von Braun and, 312–13, 315–16, 323,
 346, 352–3
Elektromechanische Werke GmbH, 182,
 189
Engel, Rolf, 43, 48, 57, 65–6
 German Army rocket program and,
 54–5, 65
 Oberth's rocket project and, 39–40
Ettersburg, 22–9, 33, 180
Exploration of Mars, The (Ley, von Braun,
 and Bonestell), 286, 295
Explorer, 330–3, 419
 launches of, 319–27, 340, 347
 von Braun's fame and, 323–7, 333, 353

Faget, Max, 438
 Antarctic expedition of, 414–15
 Apollo and, 372–5
Fairchild Industries, 412, 458–67
 satellites and, 459–61, 464–6
 von Braun's employment at, 455–6,
 458–66, 469

Faust (Goethe), 5, 23, 349, 476
Federal Bureau of Investigation (FBI), 227, 238, 288, 346
Fieber, Karl, 107–9, 125
fighter-bombers, 459, 461–2, 465
First Annual Symposium on Space Travel, 255–7
First Men to the Moon (von Braun), 324–5, 356
Fleischer, Karl Otto, 206, 235, 237
Fletcher, James, 456, 471, 474
  NSI and, 466–7
  space shuttle and, 450–1, 453–4, 461
Fort Bliss, 224, 227–9, 234–7, 239, 301, 309
  everyday life at, 218–19, 228–9
  living conditions at, 217–18, 229, 231, 234
  The Mars Project and, 241, 245, 254
  U.S. Army rocket program and, 214–22, 232, 234, 245
  and von Braun's move to Huntsville, 245, 247
France, 82, 109, 115–16, 123, 188, 198–9, 206, 240, 279, 305, 407–9, 432, 463, 474, 477
  and movies on von Braun, 407–8
  slave labor and, 144, 160–1, 176–9
  U.S. Army rocket program and, 212–13
  V-2 and, 147, 164
  von Braun's Nazi past and, 408–9
  von Braun's romances and, 147–8
Frau im Mond, Die, 30, 36, 38–9, 44, 240
Freeman, Fred, 257–9, 266, 325
Frick, Charlie, 375–6
Froeschel, George, 347
Fromm, Fritz, 149, 158, 184

Gagarin, Yuri, 359–60, 383
Ganswindt, Hermann, 24, 39
Gavin, James, 306, 329
gefrorenen Blitze, Die, 408, 428
Geheimnis von Huntsville (Mader), 405–8
Geissler, Ernst, 377, 401
Gemini, 371, 373, 380–1, 384, 397, 415, 419
General Electric (GE), 383, 426, 446
  Hermes II and, 224, 238, 249
  satellites and, 294, 320, 460
  U.S. Army rocket program and, 206, 208–9, 214, 217–18, 222, 224

Generales, Constantine, 45–7, 52, 57–8, 63, 211, 232, 257, 350
Gergen, David, 471
German Democratic Republic (East Germany), 301, 349
  von Braun's Nazi past and, 392, 404–5, 408, 428–9
Germany, Federal Republic of (West Germany), 252, 263–5, 274, 346–51, 390, 409–11, 431–2, 436, 444
  and movies on von Braun, 346–9, 351
  von Braun's death and, 473–4
  von Braun's fame in, 309, 323–4, 405, 409–10, 473
  von Braun's Nazi past and, 405, 428–9
  von Braun's parents in, 260, 264–5, 309, 324, 332, 373
  von Braun's trips to, 309, 342, 348–51, 373, 409, 431, 447, 468–9
Germany, Nazi, ix–xi, xv, 3–6, 43, 48, 61–6, 73–4, 142–5, 183, 187–91, 201–3, 226, 231, 448–9
  anti-Semitism in, 23, 61–2, 86, 97–9, 368
  and campaign against rocketry amateurs, 65–6
  economy of, 97–8
  forced laborers used by, 142–4
  and movies on von Braun, 347–8, 351
  North African campaign of, 137, 139
  Poland invaded by, 114–16
  Soviet advances on, 180–1, 189–90, 193
  Soviet campaign against, 127–8, 130, 137, 139, 142–3, 150, 162
  surrender of, 199, 202–3
  U.S. Army rocket program and, 206–7
  V-2 and, 3, 162, 351
  von Braun's adaptation to, 63–5
  von Braun's Faustian bargain and, 4–5, 477
  von Braun's memoirs and, ix, 257
  von Braun's politics and, 315, 324, 326, 368, 392, 396, 449, 468, 471–2
  World War II setbacks of, 139–40, 142, 152, 167–8, 170–1, 175, 180–1, 188–91, 196–8
  see also Nazis, Nazi Party
Germany, occupied, 218, 225–37, 240, 266
  U.S. Army rocket program and, 206–12
  von Braun's family in, 225–9, 231–3, 243

von Braun's politics and, 236–7
von Braun's trip to, 233–4, 236
Germany, Weimar Republic of, 22–5,
  39–40, 110
  economy of, 17, 42, 56, 60
  education in, 22–4, 34–5
  politics in, 7, 15–17, 23, 42, 54–7, 60–1
  rocket fad in, 30–2, 34, 39, 50–1, 113
Gestapo, 87, 142, 145, 148, 152, 202
  and campaign against rocketry amateurs,
    65–6, 71
  von Braun's arrest and, 97, 169–70,
    172–3, 198, 227–8, 237, 271,
    315–16, 324, 476
Gilruth, Robert R. "Bob," 337, 349, 371–5,
  386, 398, 434, 438, 448
  Antarctic expedition of, 414–15, 421
  Apollo and, 366, 368, 372–5, 383–4, 389,
    403, 415, 421, 423
  Mercury and, 359, 423
Glennan, T. Keith, 357, 360
  NASA and, 334–6, 339, 342–6, 368
  Saturn and, 342, 379
Goddard, Robert, 25, 45, 47, 50, 73, 199,
  242, 261, 334, 410, 477
Goebbels, Josef, 69, 98, 111, 142, 185,
  187–8, 461
Göring, Hermann, 64, 74, 80–1, 100, 133,
  138, 157, 169, 461
Gorman, Harry, 396
Grand Tour, 451, 457
Great Britain, 9, 15, 109, 115–6, 143, 180,
  204–7, 210–12, 223, 240, 305, 447, 477
  and Allied interrogation of German
    scientists, 202, 204–5, 207
  Germany occupied by, 206–7, 225
  and movies on von Braun, 351–2,
    407–8
  rocket program of, 211–12
  U.S. Army rocket program and, 206–7,
    210
  V-2 and, 139, 182, 184–6, 188, 196, 348,
    351–2, 407, 449, 471, 473
  von Braun's arrest and, 172–3
  von Braun's IAF paper and, 254–6
  World War II and, 116, 123, 127, 138–9,
    147
Greece, 46, 236
Grissom, Virgil I "Gus," 371, 397, 415, 418

Grosse, Aristid V., 261–2, 266–8, 271
  satellites and, 261, 268, 284, 292
Gröttrup, Helmut, 170–4, 204, 210, 232
Grünow, Heinrich "Heini," 58–9, 71–2, 88
Gürtner, Franz, 69–70

Haber, Heinz, 271–2
  Collier's and, 257, 259, 272
  and von Braun's shows for Disney,
    286–7, 289–90
Haeussermann, Walter, 250–1, 394, 427
Hamburg, 154, 211
Hamill, James, 3, 206, 223–4, 229, 236–8,
  251, 273, 463
  U.S. Army rocket program and, 214–16,
    218–21, 224, 227, 231, 238, 248
Hardtack, Operation, 307, 319, 328, 330,
  332
Hayden Planetarium, 255–7, 266, 268–70
Heinisch, Kurt, 65, 87
Heinkel Aircraft, 87, 143
  rocket fighter program and, 79, 82–3,
    100, 112–14
Heisenberg, Werner, 125–6, 468
Hermann, Rudolf, 105–7, 124–5, 217
  A-4b and, 188–9
  Peenemünde and, 85–6, 92, 99
  V-2 and, 106–7, 165
Hermes, Project, 206, 208, 217, 248–9, 274,
  308, 330
  guidance and control in, 239, 251
  propulsion in, 239, 249
  test launches in, 238–9
  U.S. Army rocket program and, 224, 234,
    238–9
Heylandt, 40, 51, 67, 75–6, 152
Himmler, Heinrich, 63, 69, 168–72, 315,
  461
  Peenemünde and, 142, 145–6, 149, 158,
    192–3, 339
  V-2 and, 141–2, 146, 149–50, 156, 158,
    168–71, 175, 184, 187
  von Braun's meeting with, 168–9, 171, 187
  von Braun's politics and, 120–2
Hindemith, Paul, 27
Hinrichs, J., 320, 322
Hiroshima, 185, 205, 211, 221
History of Rocketry and Space Travel
  (von Braun and Ordway), 413

Hitler, Adolf, 3–4, 39, 48–9, 54, 64–6, 74, 81, 84, 86–7, 107, 114–15, 119–20, 132–4, 167–9, 171, 173–6, 191, 196, 201, 203, 226, 230, 309, 315, 448, 461, 472, 474
  anti-Semitism of, 97–8, 115, 185–6
  attempted assassination of, 180–1, 184
  briefings on rockets for, 110–12, 127–8, 149–53, 414
  death of, 198–9
  German Army rocket program and, 58, 64–5
  and impact of World War II on rocket program, 119, 123, 130
  and movies on von Braun, 347, 349
  Peenemünde and, 3, 99, 158, 193
  rise to power of, 42, 49, 56–8, 60–1, 194
  SA purge and, 69–70
  Soviet campaign and, 128, 150
  V-1 and, 139, 180
  V-2 and, 127–30, 133, 137, 139–42, 146, 149–53, 156, 158, 168–9, 174–6, 180–1, 186–8, 270, 326
  von Braun's encounters with, 64, 97, 110–12, 127–8, 150–2, 414
  and von Braun's meeting with Himmler, 168–9
  von Braun's politics and, 97, 126, 134
  war successes of, 122–3
Hoelzer, Helmut, 93–4, 117–18, 124, 133
Holmes, Bonnie, 271, 326, 360, 443
Holmes, Brainerd, 382–5, 387
  Apollo and, 368–9, 371, 374, 376, 378, 382–4
Holocaust, 60, 145, 159, 449
H-1 booster, 331, 341
Hoover, George, 279, 283–4, 291–2, 294–5
Horizon, Project, 357
Horner, Richard, 343–5
Houbolt, John C., 372–4, 377, 433
Huntsville, Ala., x, 253, 258, 260–1, 271, 274, 277, 300–2, 317, 328, 350, 356, 458, 468
  civil rights in, 386, 395–6
  IRBMs and, 295, 299, 302, 306, 308
  Mercury and, 336–8, 358–9
  Pioneer and, 340–1
  Redstone and, 250, 264, 283
  relationship between NASA and, 333–9, 341–6, 368

  satellites and, 283, 291, 294–5, 297–8, 304, 312–13, 320–1, 323
  Saturn and, 331, 342
  U.S. Army rocket program and, 3, 6, 234, 245, 247–9, 341
  von Braun's fame and, 434, 442–3
  von Braun's management style and, 282–3, 293, 306, 315
  von Braun's move to, 245, 247–9
  see also Marshall Space Flight Center
Huzel, Dieter, 156, 182, 206, 211, 274
  Peenemünde and, 144–5, 192, 194
  surrender of, 200, 203
  V-2 and, 184–5
hydrogen bomb, 279–80
  Soviet acquisition of, 280, 313
  see also nuclear weapons

I Aim at the Stars, 346–53, 406–8
"Importance of the Satellite Vehicle as a Step towards Interplanetary Flight, The" (von Braun), 254–6
India, 373, 460, 463–6, 470–1
intercontinental ballistic missiles (ICBMs), 126–7, 134, 267, 308, 316, 318, 331, 336, 341–3, 387–9, 393, 407, 476–7
  Minuteman and, 388–9
  nuclear weapons and, 313, 327
  Saturn and, 341–2
  Soviet Union and, 310, 313
  see also Atlas; Titan
intermediate-range ballistic missiles (IRBMs), 293, 298–309, 317–19, 328–31
  deployment of, 305–7, 319, 338
  Pershing and, 319, 330, 338, 351
  Polaris and, 306, 317
  press leaks and, 304–7
  satellites and, 304, 318
  von Braun's management style and, 295, 299, 304–9, 314, 319, 326
  see also Jupiter; Thor
International Astronautical Federation (IAF), 252–6, 316, 351
  satellites and, 295–8
  von Braun's papers for, 254–6, 264–5
International Geophysical Year (IGY), 281–2, 293–6, 298, 303, 313, 320, 328

Iran, 462–3, 465
Italy, 46, 98, 338, 455

Jaeger, Mr., 143
James, Lee, 395, 427, 433
Japan, 130, 210, 455
Jessel, Walter, 203–4
Jet Propulsion Laboratory (JPL), 214, 220,
        238, 249, 331, 340, 436
    NASA and, 334–6
    satellites and, 294–6, 304, 310, 313, 315,
        320, 322–3, 328
Jodl, Alfred, 150, 170–1, 173
Johnson, Lyndon B., 334, 381, 386, 422,
        446, 461
    Apollo and, 355–6, 360–2, 390, 404,
        425–8
    satellites and, 316–18
    Saturn and, 346, 392
Johnson, Roy, 328, 331
Johnson Space Center, *see* Manned
        Spacecraft Center
Jouanin, Georges, 177–8
Judaism, Jews, 160, 194–5, 212, 235, 410,
        448–9
    concentration camps and, 144–5
    discrimination against, 18, 23, 86, 448
    persecution of, 61–2, 97–9, 115, 145,
        185–6, 197, 368
    von Braun's Nazi past and, 406, 449, 468
Junkers Aircraft, 47, 77–80, 82, 176
Juno, 315, 318, 328, 330–1, 340
Jupiter, 300–5, 313–20, 328–31, 335–8,
        341–2, 351, 382
    deployment of, 319, 338
    Mercury and, 336–8, 342
    satellites and, 303, 309–10, 313, 315–16,
        318–20, 328
    test launches of, 304–5, 307–9, 314, 316
    von Braun's management style and, 302–3
Jupiter-Saturn mission, 451
Jürgens, Curd, 348, 351
Justice Department, U.S., 227, 474–5

Kahn, Herman, 406
Kammler, Hans, 156–7, 175–7, 191–7, 211,
        230, 236, 347
    Mittelwerk and, 159, 162–3
    and move to Oberammergau, 196–7

Peenemünde and, 157, 159, 163, 189,
        191–4
    V-2 and, 162, 169, 175–6, 182–4, 186–7,
        196
Kaplan, Joseph, 256–7, 259, 294, 296
Kapp Putsch, 16–17
Kaul, Friedrich, 428–9
Kehrl, Hans, 152
Keller, K. T., 250–1
Kennedy, John F., 446–7, 461
    Apollo and, 354–6, 358, 360, 362–4, 378,
        381–4, 386–7, 389–91, 399, 401,
        404, 418, 423, 425, 438, 440
Kennedy Space Center (KSC)
    Apollo and, 381, 418, 424
    Saturn and, 392, 397
Kerr, Robert, 360, 364
Kertes, Julia, 443, 446–7, 455
Khrushchev, Nikita, 310, 340, 351, 359
    satellites and, 312, 314, 327
Killian, James, 281–2, 294, 299, 335
Kimball, Ward, 285, 287–90, 317
King, Martin Luther, Jr., 386, 422
Klein, Heinrich, 212
Klemperer, Victor, 135
Klep, Rolf, 257–9, 266
Koelle, Heinz Hermann, 295, 361, 399
    Apollo and, 356–7
    The Mars Project and, 246–7, 252, 264–5
Konopka, Arthur, 429
Korean War, 249, 273, 280, 476
Korolev, Sergei Pavlovich, 5, 73, 314, 316,
        359, 477
    Soviet lunar probes and, 340, 342, 344
Kraft, Christopher Columbus, Jr., 337, 354,
        423
Kreiselgeräte, 72, 77, 102–9, 118
Kubrick, Stanley, 406, 413
Kummersdorf, 56–60, 75–80, 82–6, 94,
        116–17, 190, 202, 241–2
    A-3 and, 102, 104
    German Army rocket program and,
        58–60, 63–4, 69–71, 75–8, 80, 84–6,
        90, 92
    rocket aircraft program and, 78–9, 82,
        102
    rocket briefings for Hitler at, 110–12
    secret rocket testing at, 51–2
    V-2 and, 124, 139

Kunze, Heinz, 187, 191, 193
Künzel, Walter, 83, 87
Kurzweg, Herman, 105, 124
Kütbach, Ernst, 94, 122
Kutzer, Elisabeth, 35–7

Lake Logan agreements, 403, 430
Lang, Daniel, 3–4, 32, 198, 200, 240
  U.S. Army rocket program and, 217, 219
Lang, Fritz, 30, 36, 38
Leeb, Emil, 120, 140, 192
Lehrer, Tom, 406–7, 474
Leonard, Jonathan, 271
"Let's Tackle the Space Ship" (von Braun),
  259
Lewandowski, Mrs., 95, 168
Ley, Willy, 30, 39, 43, 52, 70, 232, 240, 252,
  261, 264, 285–90, 295, 311, 431
  Collier's and, 257, 259, 266, 272
  Germany Army rocket program and,
    55, 59
  Hayden symposia and, 255, 266, 270
  Mars book planned by, 275–6
  and von Braun's election to VfR board,
    57–8
  von Braun's higher education and, 35, 45
  and von Braun's shows for Disney,
    286–90
Lietz schools, 22, 33–6, 57
  von Braun's education at, 28, 31, 33–4,
    36, 40–1
Lighthouse, Operations, 102, 109, 116, 118
Lindbergh, Charles A., 167, 410
Logsdon, John, 435–6, 447
Loki, 282–4, 291–5
London, 10–12, 73, 180, 207–8, 280, 305,
  463
  M. von Braun's employment in, 10–11
  and movies on W. von Braun, 352–3
  V-2 and, 184–5, 188, 196, 212, 348, 352,
    473–4
  W. von Braun's IAF paper and, 254–6
  W. von Braun's trips to, 211–12, 350,
    373, 468
Low, George, 403, 440–5, 448–54, 466
  Apollo and, 366, 368, 389, 423–4, 440,
    445, 448, 452, 454
  space shuttle and, 445, 449–51, 453–4,
    457, 461

  and von Braun's departure from NASA,
    456–7
  von Braun's NASA appointment and,
    442–4
Luftwaffe, German, 74, 77–82, 86–7, 107–9,
  123, 126, 128–9, 153, 187, 189–91,
  194, 202, 209, 252–3
  antiaircraft missiles and, 129, 137–9, 144,
    149, 176, 189, 191
  interservice experimental rocket
    establishment and, 78–82, 86, 90,
    93, 95, 99–101, 138–9
  Peenemünde and, 90–3, 95, 99–102, 113
  rocket fighter program and, 78–9, 82,
    100–2, 113–14
  V-1 and, 134, 139, 176, 180, 191
  V-2 and, 113, 133–4, 139
  von Braun's flying for, 84, 113, 253
Luna, 340, 342, 344
Lunar Module (LM), 376–7, 420, 423–4,
  429–30, 433
lunar roving vehicles, 400–1, 414, 430, 450
"Lunetta" (von Braun), 40–1, 173, 243

Mader, Julius, 405–9
Mailer, Norman, 414, 431–2
Mainz, Friedrich, 325–6, 346, 348–9
Manhattan Project, 221, 242, 259–61, 267,
  279
Man in Space project, *see* Mercury, Project
Man in Space Soonest (MISS), 329
Manned Spacecraft Center (MSC), 371,
  381, 387, 414, 438
  Apollo and, 374, 377–8, 403–4, 416–17,
    420–3, 430, 433–4, 445, 448
  conflicts between MSFC and, 403–4,
    420–1, 440
"Man on the Moon: The Exploration" (von
  Braun and Whipple), 269, 272
"Man on the Moon: The Journey" (von
  Braun), 269, 272
Man Very High, 329
Mark, Hans, 436–7, 455
Mars, 29, 41, 325, 414, 430, 436–7
  Collier's and, 272, 275–6, 285, 372
  proposed expedition to, 234, 255, 268,
    275, 277, 295, 372, 399–400, 434–9,
    451–3
  von Braun's ambitions and, 76, 125, 240–1

and von Braun's shows for Disney, 286–8, 317

Voyager and, 417, 443, 451

Marshall, George C., 236, 352

Marshall Space Flight Center (MSFC), 6, 346, 351–2, 359–61, 370–89, 391–404, 411, 415–21, 438–44, 446, 452–4, 458–9, 475

    Apollo and, 356, 363–9, 371–9, 381–4, 389, 391–2, 399, 401–4, 416, 418–21, 423–4, 426, 430, 450

    blacks and, 386, 395, 397

    Centaur and, 379–80

    conflicts between MSC and, 403–4, 420–1, 440

    layoffs at, 420, 426, 459, 462

    Mercury and, 359, 381, 423

    proposed Martian expedition and, 435–6

    Saturn and, 370–1, 381–2, 388–9, 392, 394–5, 397–9, 401

    space shuttle and, 438, 454

    von Braun's departure from, 441–4

    von Braun's management style and, 382, 384–9, 391–9, 402–4, 413, 416, 420–1, 425–7, 438, 448–9, 452

    von Braun's Nazi past and, 407–8, 428–9

"Mars Project," (novel) (von Braun), 223–4, 234, 240–7, 252–5, 261–5, 325, 400, 435

    Neher's rewriting of, 252–3, 261–3, 265, 275

Mars Project, The (technical booklet) (von Braun), 263, 266, 275, 282

Martin Aircraft, 220, 298, 330, 338, 341

Martz, E. P., 291–2

Max (A-2), 71–4

Maxfield, Jim, 464, 469

May, Karl, 214, 222

McCarthy, Joseph, 279

McElroy, Neil, 317, 331, 344

    satellites and, 311–12, 314, 342

McGrory, Mary, 346

"Meaning of Space Superiority, The" (von Braun), 316

Medaris, John Bruce, 300, 325–31

    congressional testimonies of, 317–18

    IRBMs and, 303–8, 326

    and movies on von Braun, 325, 347

NASA and, 334–6, 339, 342–4

    satellites and, 303–4, 310–15, 320–2, 331

Mercury, Project, 371, 374–5, 381, 418–19, 423

    capsule in, 336–8, 354, 359

    launches, 354–5, 358–9, 363, 371, 374

    NASA and, 334–7, 355, 358, 363

    Saturn and, 341–6, 357

    von Braun's management style and, 337–8, 358–9, 363

"Method of Reaching Extreme Altitudes, A" (Goddard), 25

Mexico, 239, 245

Michaelis, Georg, 14

Michel, Jean, 160, 474–5

Milch, Erhard, 133–4, 149, 175

Minimum Orbital Unmanned Satellite of Earth (MOUSE), 280, 283

"Minimum Satellite Vehicle Based on Components from Missile Developments of the Army Ordnance Corps, A" (von Braun), 291–2

Minuteman, 388–9

Mirak, 42, 54

missiles, ix-x, 3, 5–6, 50, 75, 93, 209, 315–19, 343

    and gap between U.S. and Soviets, 315–16

    NASA-Huntsville relationship and, 334, 336, 339

    nuclear weapons on, 126, 221–2, 249–50, 259, 267, 281, 302–3, 305, 307–8, 313, 319, 327–8, 330, 332, 351, 400, 476

    proposed national program for, 318–19

    see also rockets, rocketry, rocket engineering; *specific missiles and types of missiles*

Mittelwerk, Mittelbau, 167, 169, 174–9, 191, 194–5, 197, 201–2, 204, 211, 220, 227, 348, 395, 471, 473, 475–6

    slave labor at, 157, 159–63, 165, 176–9, 186, 195, 353, 409, 476

    U.S. Army rocket program and, 206, 208, 217

    V-2 and, 165, 174, 176–9, 181, 186, 201, 206

    von Braun's awareness of conditions at, 160–3

    von Braun's Nazi past and, 392, 404–5, 408–9, 428–9

    war crimes trials and, 235–6, 449

Moon, 3–4, 25, 28, 41, 147, 201, 205, 208,
        232, 240–2, 277, 318, 380
    Collier's and, 266, 268, 270–2, 289
    manned flight to, *see* Apollo, Project
    Pioneer and, 328, 330–1, 334, 340–1
    proposed bases on, 357, 399, 414, 435,
        437, 445, 447
    proposed exploration of, 268–70, 336
    Soviet lunar program and, 340, 342, 344,
        424–7
    von Braun's ambitions and, 21, 36–7, 39,
        45, 48, 76, 84, 93, 111, 125, 152, 190,
        198, 240–1, 284, 354, 356, 368, 439
    von Braun's early writing on, 32–3
    and von Braun's shows for Disney, 287,
        289, 295, 301
Moritz (A-2), 71–4
Moseley, Seth, 258, 260, 268
Mrazek, Willi, 379–80, 388
Mueller, George, 386–9, 392–4, 414–16
    Apollo and, 383–4, 387–9, 392–3, 400–4,
        415–16, 418–21, 423–5, 430–1, 433,
        435–6, 440–1
    MSFC-MSC conflicts and, 403–4, 421
    Saturn and, 388, 398
    space shuttle and, 435, 438
    von Braun's Antarctic trip and, 414, 421
    von Braun's management style and, 384,
        387–8, 393–4, 396–7
Myers, Dale, 440, 444, 450

Nagasaki, 221, 261
Napoleon I, Emperor of France, 8, 151
National Advisory Committee for
        Aeronautics (NACA), 308, 329, 334,
        339, 368
National Aeronautics and Space
        Administration (NASA), x–xii, 5–6,
        147, 277, 330, 333–46, 349, 351,
        360–6, 368–9, 371, 373–4, 388–9,
        391–4, 396–8, 400–2, 410–12, 415–18,
        420, 422–4, 434–62, 464–8, 471, 474–5
    Apollo and, 355–8, 360, 362–6, 368, 374,
        377–84, 389, 393, 397, 401, 412,
        416–18, 422–3, 427–31, 446–7, 449
    Centaur and, 379–80
    Mercury and, 334–7, 355, 358, 363
    NSI and, 466–7
    Paine's appointees at, 440–4, 446, 448, 459

    Paine's departure from, 446–8
    proposed creation of, 317–8
    proposed Martian expedition and, 434–6
    relationship between Huntsville and,
        333–9, 341–6, 368
    satellites and, 334, 460, 464–6
    Saturn and, 341–6, 357, 394, 398, 447
    space shuttle and, 438–9, 449–50, 452–4,
        457, 459, 461
    and successor programs to Apollo, 391,
        401–2, 404, 432, 434–6, 441–4, 448,
        459
    von Braun's headquarters administrative
        appointment at, 441–6, 448–9, 459
    von Braun's departure from, 437, 455–60
    von Braun's fame and, 392, 410
    von Braun's Nazi past and, 407, 428–9,
        448, 475
    Wallops Island retreat and, 445–6
National Space Institute (NSI), 466–71
Naugle, John, 380, 444
Naval Research Laboratory (NRL), 220,
        222, 268, 294–8, 303–4, 319, 327
Navy, U.S., 239, 261, 272, 329, 334, 347,
        361, 415
    IRBMs and, 299–300, 302, 305–6
    satellites and, 279–80, 291–8, 303, 342
    U.S. rocket program and, 220, 222, 255,
        261
Nazis, Nazi Party, 49, 54–7, 63–5, 70, 77–8,
        80, 86, 96–9, 120–3, 140–2, 144–5,
        147, 162–3, 169, 185–7, 203–4, 208,
        217, 230, 252
    German Army rocket program and,
        54–5, 61, 64–5, 77
    and movies on von Braun, 326, 347–8,
        352
    Peenemünde and, 92, 96, 99, 109, 192
    rise to power of, 57, 60–1, 65
    V-2 and, 141–2, 152, 162, 181, 186
    von Braun's arrest and, 171, 174
    von Braun's Faustian bargain and, 125–6,
        137, 162, 174
    von Braun's politics and, 90, 96–7, 99, 116,
        121–2, 134, 144, 167, 186–7, 198, 204,
        224, 232–3, 235–7, 271, 290, 333, 337,
        347, 353, 392, 396–7, 404–9, 428–9,
        432, 440, 448–9, 468, 473–6
    see also Germany, Nazi

Nebel, Rudolf, 38–44, 47–55, 57, 108, 431
  entrepreneurship of, 43–4, 48, 62
  German Army rocket program and,
    54–5, 66–7, 87–8
  and military uses for rockets, 49–53
  Oberth's rocket project and, 38–41, 43–4
  politics of, 54–5, 65–6
  rocket tests of, 41–2, 47
  secret rocket testing and, 51–3, 65–6
  von Braun criticized by, 263–4
Neher, Franz Ludwig, 252–3, 261–3, 265, 275
Nernst, Walter, 56, 61
Netherlands, 184, 188, 193, 196
Neucken, 8–10, 14, 127, 226
Newell, Homer, 440–4, 448, 454–6
  space shuttle and, 454–5
  and successor programs to Apollo, 402,
    441
  von Braun's NASA appointment and,
    442–4
Nickerson, John C., 298–9, 303–6
  satellites and, 296, 298, 303–5
Nixon, Richard, 355, 426, 434, 439–44,
    446–7, 453–5, 461, 471
  Apollo and, 428, 430, 436–7
  space shuttle and, 439, 451, 453–4
Nordhausen, *see* Mittelwerk, Mittelbau
North African campaign, 137, 139
North American Aviation (NAA), 262, 272,
    293, 297, 318–19, 331, 341, 382
  Apollo and, 357, 366, 371, 375–6, 384,
    416–17, 421–2
  IRBMs and, 302, 319
  Redstone and, 250, 274, 284
  Saturn and, 384, 394, 398–9
North American Rockwell, 440, 461
Norton, Jonathan, 246
Nova, 357–8, 364–5, 371–2, 377–8, 383
nuclear energy, 205, 439
  rockets powered by, 125, 241, 287, 289,
    362, 400, 435, 437, 451, 454
Nuclear Engine for Rocket Vehicle Applica-
    tion (NERVA), 400, 435, 439, 451, 454
nuclear reactors, 125–6, 289, 400
nuclear weapons, 230, 243, 279–81, 312–13,
    369, 382, 462, 470, 476–7
  Collier's and, 259–60
  high-altitude detonation of, 307, 319,
    327–8, 330, 332

missiles and, 126, 221–2, 249–50, 259,
    267, 281, 302–3, 305, 307–8, 313,
    319, 327–8, 330, 332, 351, 400, 476
  and movies on von Braun, 351–2
  satellites and, 281, 314, 316, 327–8
  Soviet acquisition of, 245, 280, 313
  von Braun's space station advocacy and,
    271, 280
  see also atomic bombs
Oberammergau, 196–7
Oberth, Hermann, 24–6, 29–30, 34–6,
    43–5, 59, 75, 222, 240, 242, 263–4, 267,
    273, 295, 347, 409, 431, 477
  German Army rocket program, 86–7
  liquid-fuel rocket project of, 38–41, 43–4,
    50, 73
  Peenemünde and, 126, 155
  space mirror described by, 24, 29, 34, 41,
    205
Oberwiesenthal, 44–5, 69–70, 104, 115, 193
"Observatory, The" (von Braun), 33
O'Connor, Edmund, 395, 398
Of a Fire on the Moon (Mailer), 431–2
Office of Naval Research (ONR), 279–80,
    282–4, 291–5, 298
Office of Special Investigations (OSI),
    474–5
1B engines, 62
O'Neil, Gerard K., 468
1W engines, 59–60, 62
"On the Theory of the Long-Range
    Rocket" (von Braun), 34
Operation Crossbow, 407–8
Oppenheimer, J. Robert, 6, 185, 221, 265,
    279
Orbital Workshop, 402–4, 416, 425–6
  wet vs. dry, 420–1, 430
Orbiter, Project, 282, 293–9, 303–5, 309–10,
    320, 324, 329
  politics and, 293–8, 303
  press on, 312–13, 315
  as RTV, 298–9, 303, 309
  secrecy of, 304–5
Ordway, Frederick I., III, 326, 413, 466, 469,
    471, 475
Orion, Project, 400
Ostrander, Don, 359, 361, 363, 371
Overcast, Project, 210, 213, 215, 217–19

Pahlavi, Shah Reza, 463, 465
Paine, Thomas O., 434–49, 462
   Apollo and, 424, 426–7, 430, 445–6
   NASA appointees of, 440–4, 446, 448,
      459
   NASA departure of, 446–8
   proposed Martian expedition and, 434–7,
      439
   space shuttle and, 437–8, 445, 449
   and successor programs to Apollo, 430,
      434–6, 441–4, 448, 459
   Wallops Island retreat and, 445–6
Paperclip, Project, 3, 219, 226, 230, 233,
      251, 257, 264, 295, 324, 405, 449, 475
   public controversy over, 235–6, 240
Paris, 97–8, 184, 252, 305, 408, 444, 463
   U.S. Army rocket program and, 206–7,
      210, 212–13
   von Braun's trips to, 123, 147–8, 213, 468
Paris Gun, 81–2
Pauls, Uvo, 101
Peenemünde, Peenemünders, x, 3, 85–96,
      98–102, 104–10, 112–20, 122–35,
      141–65, 168–9, 172, 181–3, 188–96,
      200–3, 219–20, 228–9, 236, 251, 259,
      273, 294, 300, 326, 345, 354, 356, 379,
      393–4, 405, 462
   Aerodynamics Institute at, 85–6, 92, 154,
      165
   A-3 and, 102, 105
   A-5 and, 107–9
   air raids on, 153–6, 158, 164, 183, 393
   antiaircraft missiles and, 129, 138, 144,
      149, 153, 158, 192, 282
   construction and expansion of, 90, 92,
      106, 109, 112, 119, 127, 132, 143
   deteriorating conditions at, 183, 190
   establishing experimental rocket facility
      at, 80–2, 84–5, 87–8, 90–3, 95,
      99–101
   evacuations of, 157–8, 189, 191–4, 198,
      200, 207–9, 211, 213
   impact of World War II on, 116–17,
      119–20, 123, 127
   and integration of university
      researchers, 117–18
   internment of personnel from, 201–3
   movies on, 407–8
   and movies on von Braun, 347–8

politics and, 92, 96, 99, 109, 122, 142, 149
Regener barrel and, 186, 190, 222
and reorganization of rocket program,
   157–60, 163–4
rocket aircraft program and, 101, 112–14
rocket production of, 107, 110, 119, 123,
   131–2, 142–4, 154, 156, 162, 176
secrecy of, 110, 117, 143–4
slave labor at, 142–5, 154, 156, 160, 179,
   429
spaceflight and, 101, 125, 157–8
U.S. Army rocket program and, 206–8,
   210, 212–14, 217, 219, 234
V-2 and, 106, 118, 123–4, 126–35, 137–9,
   141–3, 146, 149, 151–2, 157–8,
   164–5, 174, 176, 178, 181, 188, 192,
   311, 330
von Braun's management style and,
   88–90, 93–6, 99, 101, 107–9, 113,
   116, 128–32, 134, 156–7, 176, 178,
   183, 207, 290, 339, 367, 460
von Braun's romances and, 147–8
Pegasus, 397, 412, 459
Pershing missiles, 319, 330, 338, 351
Petrone, Rocco, 418, 424
Phillips, Samuel, 392–5, 398, 448
   Apollo and, 389, 392–3, 395, 415–16,
      424, 427, 430, 433
   von Braun's management style and,
      393–5
Pickering, William, 318, 338
   satellites and, 294, 313–15, 320–4
Pietsch, Alfons, 75–6
Pioneer, 328, 330–1, 334, 340–1
Planetary Society, 468, 470
Pohl, Dieter, 32–3
Poland, 8, 12–14, 16, 98, 148, 158, 167, 183
   M. von Braun's civil service tenure and,
      12–13
   Nazi invasion of, 114–16
   slave labor and, 143, 160
   Soviet offensive and, 190, 225
   V-2 and, 145, 164, 181, 198
Polaris, 306, 317
Popular Science, 255, 412–13, 453
Porter, Richard
   satellites and, 294, 296–7, 320
   U.S. Army rocket program and, 208–10
Power, Thomas, 293

Prussia, 7–12, 18, 55, 150, 168, 171
  German politics and, 16, 57
  W. von Braun's heritage and family
    background in, 8–12, 15–16, 63, 82,
    96, 458
"Pupils as Researchers" (von Braun), 36
Purser, Paul, 336

Quarles, Donald, 268, 293–4, 297–8, 335
Quistorp, Bernhard Friedrich, 11

Raithel, Wilhelm, 99, 124, 141
Raketenflugplatz, 4, 47–55, 57–9, 62–3, 71,
    106, 131, 139, 183, 231–2, 431
  early period of, 42–4, 47–8
  German Army rocket program and,
    54–5, 58–9, 65, 76, 87–8
  and military uses for rockets, 49–53
  Oberth's rocket project and, 44, 73
  Repulsor tests at, 47–9
  staffing Peenemünde and, 87–8
Rakete zu den Planetenräumen, Die,
    (Oberth), 24–6
ramjets, 209, 214, 219–21, 224, 247, 308
  security concerns and, 219–20
  von Braun's management style and, 217,
    249
  see also Hermes, Project
RAND, 280–2, 284, 293
Rax-Werke, 142–4, 149, 156, 158
RCA, 330, 360, 368, 465
Redstone Arsenal, 3, 247–8, 251, 258, 271,
    278, 293, 300, 306, 311, 346, 395, 418
  satellites and, 291, 298, 304
Redstone ballistic missile, 249–52, 264,
    318–19, 328–32, 366
  guidance and control of, 250–1, 274–5
  Loki and, 282–4
  Mercury and, 336–8, 354, 358–9, 363,
    371, 419, 423
  nuclear weapons and, 250, 307, 319, 328,
    332
  propulsion of, 250, 275, 283–4, 303, 308,
    330, 354, 358
  satellites and, 279–80, 282–3, 296–9,
    303–4, 310
  secrecy of, 258, 271
  test launches of, 273–5, 278, 289, 294,
    301, 303–4, 307, 310

von Braun's management style and, 247,
    250–2, 261, 269, 273, 278, 282–3, 300
reentry test vehicles (RTVs), 308–9, 330
  satellites and, 298–9, 303, 309
Rees, Eberhard, 95, 157, 183, 206, 211–12,
    264, 307, 396, 403, 442
  Apollo and, 367–8, 398, 416–17, 421, 433
  Saturn and, 342, 398–9
  U.S. Army rocket program and, 212, 216
  von Braun's management style and,
    301–2, 330–1, 367, 385, 398–9
Regener barrel, 186, 190, 222
Reisig, Gerhard, 102, 104–5, 121
Reitsch, Hanna, 48, 153
Repulsor, 47–9, 52–3
"Responsible Scientific Investigation and
    Application" (von Braun), 469–70
Rickhey, Georg, 176, 187, 235–6
Riedel, Babs, 63, 231, 411
Riedel, Klaus, 59, 63, 66–7, 99, 183, 189,
    223–4, 231, 411
  arrest of, 170–3
  German Army rocket program and,
    54–5, 66, 76, 105–6
  Peenemünde appointment of, 87–8
  politics of, 54, 76, 174
  rocket testing and, 39–43, 47, 52, 76
  V-2 and, 139, 171–2
Riedel, Walter "Papa," 51, 75–7, 79, 96,
    102–3, 149, 187
  German Army rocket program and,
    67–8, 71–2, 76–7, 85
  V-2 and, 81, 111, 124, 128, 131
Riedel, Walther, 187, 223
  U.S. Army rocket program and, 206–7,
    216–17, 238
rocket aircraft programs, 78–80, 82–5, 116,
    129, 153, 267–8
  Luftwaffe and, 100–2, 113–14
  Peenemünde and, 101, 112–14
Rocket and the Reich, The (Neufeld), x–xi
Rocketdyne, *see* North American Aviation
rockets, rocketry, rocket engineering, xv,
    3–6, 29–36, 47–93, 167–8, 201–24,
    233–4, 236–46, 279–84, 327–8, 333–4,
    337–8, 405, 409
  aerodynamics of, 62–3, 67, 85, 89, 104,
    109, 124, 126, 129, 133, 149, 165,
    181–2, 188–9, 217, 239, 302, 370

rockets, rocketry, rocket engineering (*cont.*)
  Apollo and, 356, 365, 369, 374, 384, 395,
    419
  briefings for Hitler on, 110–12, 127–8,
    149–53, 414
  British program for, 211–12
  Collier's and, 258–9, 269, 273
  as fad, 30–2, 34, 39, 50–1, 113
  German Army program for, x, 4, 53–88,
    90, 92, 116, 204
  German government campaign against
    amateurs in, 65–6, 71, 76
  German interservice experimental
    establishment for, 78–82, 86, 88,
    90–3, 95, 99–102, 113–14, 138–9
  guidance and control of, 72, 75–7, 84–5,
    89, 102–10, 113, 116–19, 123–5,
    132–3, 138, 149, 162, 164, 178, 189,
    194, 209, 220, 238–9, 250–1, 274–5,
    282, 294, 302, 304, 340, 376, 380,
    394, 422
  impact of World War II on, 116–17,
    119–20, 123, 127, 130
  military uses of, 34, 39, 48–55, 59, 66, 71,
    74–5, 81–2, 161
  Mittelwerk and, 157, 159–63
  and movies on von Braun, 347, 350
  Nebel-Riedel tests and, 41–2, 47
  nuclear-powered, 125, 241, 287, 289, 362,
    400, 435, 437, 451, 454
  Oberth and, 24–5, 30, 34, 38–41, 43–4,
    50, 59, 73, 86–7, 126, 155, 264
  politics of, 54, 65
  propulsion of, 38–41, 43–4, 48, 50, 52,
    59–60, 62–3, 67–9, 72–3, 89, 92,
    100–3, 105, 111–13, 117, 124–5,
    129–31, 133, 135, 138, 148–9,
    152–3, 155, 159, 164, 177, 181–3,
    186, 189, 209, 217, 220, 238–9,
    241–2, 249–50, 275, 282–4, 302–3,
    308, 330–1, 334, 345, 354, 357–8,
    361–2, 371, 380, 385, 388, 390, 392,
    398, 400, 419, 423, 454, 476–7
  satellites and, 279–81, 283, 291–4, 297–8,
    303–4, 313, 316, 327
  secrecy about, 51–3, 57, 63, 65–9, 71–2,
    76–8, 80, 86–7, 92, 106, 110, 246, 265
  Soviet program for, 73, 210, 220, 232,
    290, 315–16
  trajectories of, 129, 133, 136, 140, 186
  USAF program for, 232, 238, 262, 281
  U.S. Army program for, 3, 6, 206–24,
    227, 231–5, 237–40, 245, 248, 251
  U.S. Navy and, 220, 222, 255, 261
  Valier's experiments with, 30, 40, 50–1,
    152
  von Braun's adolescent experiments in,
    25–6, 30–1
  von Braun's advocacy for, 240, 254
  von Braun's ambitions and, 93, 101, 107,
    111, 180, 185–6, 190, 284
  von Braun's early articles on, 34, 36, 44
  von Braun's enthusiasm for, 79, 93, 97,
    122, 173, 204, 208, 212
  von Braun's fascination with, 4–5,
    18–19, 24–7, 29, 31, 33–4, 38, 41, 45,
    48, 57, 62
  von Braun's Faustian bargain and, 4–5,
    174
  von Braun's management style and, 33,
    79, 134, 138, 301–2, 319, 347,
    426–7, 452, 476–7
  von Braun's politics and, 121–2
  von Braun's science fiction and, 41, 223,
    241–6, 324
  and von Braun's shows for Disney,
    286–7, 289–90
  see also missiles; Peenemünde,
    Peenemünders; space, space travel;
    specific rockets and types of
    rockets
Rocket Team, The (Ordway and Sharpe),
  475
Rosen, Milton, 220
  Apollo and, 357, 371, 373
  satellites and, 294–8
  von Braun criticized by, 268–71
Rosenbaum, Eli M., 474–5
Roth, Ludwig, 126, 138, 188–9, 306
Royal Air Force (RAF), British, 123, 129,
  202, 212, 349
  Pennemünde raids of, 153–6, 158, 164,
    183
Rudolph, Arthur, 51, 67, 111, 211, 216, 235,
  241, 330–1, 395, 427
  Apollo and, 374, 418–19
  German Army rocket program and,
    75–6

interservice experimental rocket
establishment and, 79–80
Mittelwerk and, 161, 163, 165
OSI case against, 475
Peenemünde and, 95, 99, 163
politics of, 99, 163, 203, 475
slave labor and, 143–4, 163, 195
V-2 and, 106–7, 123–4, 141, 143, 165
von Braun's management style and, 94,
301
Ruland, Bernd, 161, 168–70, 172, 192
Russian Empire, 13–15, 24
Russian Revolution, 15, 314, 363
Ryan, Cornelius, 266–7, 271–3, 294, 431
Collier's and, 256–7, 259, 266, 272, 275–6

SA (Stormtroopers), 56–7, 63–4, 122, 217
and campaign against rocketry amateurs,
66, 76
German Army rocket development and,
75–6
purge of, 69–70, 76, 97
Sadron, Charles, 178
Sagan, Carl, 468, 470
Sahl, Mort, 353, 406, 474
Sänger, Eugen, 101, 240
satellites, 6, 132, 239, 257–9, 271–3,
279–84, 303–5, 307, 309–34, 340–2,
356, 442, 453, 477
Collier's and, 259, 272–3
for communications, 341, 460–2, 464–6
Explorer and, 319–27, 330–3, 340, 347,
353, 419
Fairchild and, 459–61, 464–6
Grosse mission and, 261, 268, 284, 292
The Mars Project and, 223, 247
media on, 312–17, 323, 327
military interest in, 279–81
NASA and, 334, 460, 464–6
nuclear weapons and, 281, 314, 316,
327–8
politics and, 293–8, 303
for reconnaissance, 281–2, 294, 312, 330,
424
Redstone and, 279–80, 282–3, 296–9,
303–4, 310
Saturn and, 341, 346
science and, 281–2, 292–8, 304, 309–10,
313, 316, 318, 320, 327–8, 334, 403

secrecy of, 280–1, 294, 296, 304–5
Slug and, 291–3
Soviet Union and, 174, 268, 277, 280–2,
284, 292, 295–8, 304, 309–18,
324–5, 327, 329–30, 333, 353, 359,
379, 418–19, 466, 476–7
Stewart Committee on, 294–8, 303–4
tracking of, 291–2, 295–6, 320, 322
Vanguard and, 296–7, 303–4, 307, 309,
312–17, 319–20, 327
von Braun's fame and, 323–7, 333
von Braun's management style and,
283–4, 290–9, 303–4, 310, 312–13,
315, 318–20
see also Orbiter, Explorer
Saturn program, Saturn, 6, 242, 331, 338,
352, 360–1, 369–72, 392–5, 397–402,
411, 415–25, 435, 438–9, 475, 477
Apollo and, 357, 361, 363–6, 370–2,
374–8, 380–5, 388–90, 395, 397–9,
404, 415–16, 418–25, 427, 430–1,
438
crisis and delays in, 397–9
end of, 392, 441, 443, 447, 451
guidance and control of, 376, 394, 422
interservice rivalries and, 341–4
NASA and, 341–6, 357, 394, 398, 447
Pogo vibration in, 421–2
production plant for, 364–6
propulsion of, 345, 357–8, 385, 392, 398,
419, 423
satellites and, 341, 346
Skylab and, 446–7
and successor programs to Apollo,
400–2, 404, 420, 430
testing of, 381–2, 384, 388–9, 392, 394,
397–9, 401
von Braun's management style and, 341,
379, 381, 394–5, 398–9, 449
Saur, Karl Otto, 133, 152, 162, 175–6
Sawatzki, Albin, 162–3, 165, 174, 178–9,
197, 236
Scheer, Julian, 448–9
Schlidt, Dorothea Kersten "Dorette," 147,
155, 184, 241
Schmidt, Paul, 78
Schneer, Charles, 348, 350
Schneider, Erich, 62, 66, 72, 74, 77, 86, 95
Schneider, General, 95–6

Schriever, Bernard "Bennie," 281, 293, 300, 361, 393
  IRBMs and, 305, 307, 314
  NASA and, 341, 343
Schröder, Paul, 109
Schumann, Erich, 56, 58, 61–2, 68, 70, 85
Seamans, Robert C., 360–1, 404, 434, 440–1
  Apollo and, 360, 366–8, 373, 378, 382, 402, 416
Second Annual Symposium on Space Travel, 266, 268–70
"Secret of the Liquid-Fuel Rocket, The" (von Braun), 48
Sergeant missiles, 295, 298
Shapley, Willis, 361, 416, 436, 439, 441, 443, 449
Shea, Joseph, 374, 376, 378, 383–4, 387, 389, 416, 423
Shepard, Alan, 359, 363, 375, 418–19
Shepherd, James T., 396–7, 399, 426
Sher, Neal, 475
Shows, Charles, 287–8
Siemens, 42, 44, 87
  A-5 and, 105–9
  V-2 and, 119, 175, 182
Silverstein, Abraham "Abe," 334–5, 345, 357, 359, 361, 366–8, 380
Singer, S. Fred, 280–4, 298
Skylab, 360, 362, 402, 426, 431, 438, 446–7, 454, 462
Slattery, Bart, 406–7, 410
Slug, Project, 291–3
Smith, Eugene, 235
Smithsonian Institution, 25, 309, 410
Society for Space Research (GfW), 252–5, 264
Soviet Union, 5, 8, 25, 50, 115, 170, 201–4, 224–6, 260–1, 264, 301, 329–30, 333–4, 349, 351, 359–64, 389, 397, 408, 451
  advances on Germany of, 180–1, 189–90, 193
  Apollo and, 356, 360, 362–4, 382–3, 446
  German Army rocket program and, 54, 65
  Germany occupied by, 206–8, 210, 225, 228, 230, 243
  ICBMs and, 310, 313
  IRBMs and, 299, 303, 305
  lunar program of, 340, 342, 344, 424–7
  Mercury and, 355, 359
  Nazi campaign against, 127–8, 130, 137, 139, 142–3, 150, 162
  nuclear weapons acquired by, 245, 280, 313
  Poland offensive of, 190, 225
  rocket program of, 73, 210, 220, 232, 290, 315–16
  satellites and, 174, 268, 277, 280–2, 284, 292, 295–8, 304, 309–18, 324–5, 327, 329–30, 333, 353, 359, 379, 418–19, 466, 476–7
  Saturn and, 331, 342, 346
  slave labor and, 143–4, 160
  threat of, 193, 201, 203–4, 220, 222, 253–4, 261, 298
  U.S. Army rocket program and, 207–9, 237
  U.S. space rendezvous with, 454, 467–9
  von Braun's Nazi past and, 392, 404–5, 428
  von Braun's space station advocacy and, 267, 271
  and von Braun's trips to Germany, 233, 309
  Vostok and, 359–60
Soyuz, 454, 467–9
space, space travel, x, 19, 201, 203–5, 252–62, 312, 324–6, 332–7, 347–9, 355, 381, 397, 410, 413–14, 431, 456, 475–7
  and Allied interrogation of German scientists, 204–5
  Collier's and, 6, 256–62, 264–73, 275–8, 285–6, 289–90, 294, 316, 368, 450
  congressional hearings and, 317, 329
  and criticisms of von Braun's proposals, 268–72, 298
  freedom of, 281–2
  Hayden symposia on, 255–7, 266, 268–70
  Johnson's roundtable and, 361–2
  medical implications of, 45–7
  military control over exploration of, 253–4
  monkeys in, 272, 330, 341
  movies on, 30, 36, 38–9, 406, 413

and movies on von Braun, 347–8
NASA and, 334–6, 341–3, 345
nuclear weapons and, 221–2
Oberth and, 24–5, 39–40
Peenemünde and, 101, 125, 157–8
proposed national program for, 318–19
satellites and, 291, 294–6
USAF conference on, 256–7
V-2 and, 123, 181, 184, 190
von Braun's advocacy for, 6, 240–1, 247,
    252–4, 256–62, 265, 268–71, 276–8,
    283, 285–6, 290, 316–17, 326, 333,
    343, 353, 362, 368–9, 435, 438,
    442–3, 449, 452–3, 466–71, 476–7
von Braun's ambitions and, 21, 76, 93,
    101, 111, 180, 189–91, 255, 270,
    282, 284, 333, 438–9, 453, 458, 460,
    473, 475–6
von Braun's arrest and, 172–3
von Braun's early writings on, 28, 36
von Braun's enthusiasm for, 111–12,
    122, 125, 134, 168, 174, 204, 240–1,
    255, 400, 447, 473, 477
von Braun's fascination with, 4–6, 21,
    24–5, 29, 31–3, 36, 38, 41, 44, 48,
    55, 59
von Braun's Nazi past and, 392, 475
von Braun's science fiction and, 41,
    241–2, 325
see also rockets, rocketry, rocket
    engineering
"Space Man" (von Braun), 190, 324
space mirrors, 24, 29, 34, 41, 205
space planes, 316, 329, 334, 341, 451, 453
space shuttle, 356, 416, 437–9, 449–55, 459,
    461, 466, 468
    finances of, 438–9, 445, 449–50, 453–4,
        457
    propulsion of, 435, 437, 439, 450, 454–5
    von Braun's advocacy for, 438, 449–50
    von Braun's space flight ambitions and,
        438–9, 453
space station, 41, 316, 356, 435, 437–9, 445,
    452–3
    Collier's and, 257–9, 268–9, 286
    Grosse mission and, 261, 268
    The Mars Project and, 243–4
    and successor programs to Apollo,
        399–400, 402, 430

von Braun's advocacy for, 240, 266–9,
    271, 277, 280
and von Braun's shows for Disney, 286,
    289
"Space Superiority as a Means for
    Achieving World Peace" (von Braun),
    266–7
Space Task Group (presidential committee),
    434, 436–7
Space Task Group (STG) (NASA center),
    336–7, 358–9, 366
    see also Manned Spacecraft Center
Space Technologies Laboratories (STL),
    343, 386–7
"Space Travel" (von Braun), 265
Spain, 100, 462–3, 465
Speer, Albert, 145, 158–9, 173, 182, 191
    illness of, 169, 175
    memoirs of, 448–9, 472
    Peenemünde and, 120, 156–7, 339, 405
    and rocket briefings for Hitler, 149–52
    slave labor and, 143, 179, 449
    V-2 and, 115, 132–3, 139–42, 149–53,
        156, 158, 184, 187–8
Spiekeroog, 69–71, 91, 193
    von Braun's education at, 28–36, 39–40
Sputnik, 174, 277, 311–14, 318, 325, 327,
    329–30, 333, 353, 359, 379, 418–19,
    466, 476–7
SS (Protection Squad), 56–7, 63–5, 69, 129,
    141–6, 174–7, 179–80, 182, 191–8,
    211, 217, 228, 347, 428
    final Allied offensive and, 196–8, 202
    Peenemünde and, 122, 145–6, 191–2, 339
    slave labor and, 143–5, 157, 160–3
    V-2 and, 137, 141–2, 146, 156, 158,
        165–6, 169–70, 175–7, 179, 184,
        186–7, 196
    von Braun's arrest and, 171–2, 175
    von Braun's horseback riding and, 63–4
    von Braun's marriage application and,
        146–7
    and von Braun's meeting with Himmler,
        168–9
    von Braun's membership in, 121–2, 134,
        146, 152, 168, 172, 186, 191, 193,
        235–7, 271, 324, 381, 392, 404–6,
        409, 449, 473, 475
    von Braun's politics and, 120–2, 186

Stalin, Joseph, 8, 38, 98, 180, 190, 210, 226, 249, 253–4, 477
State Department, U.S., 218, 428–9
Staver, Robert, 206–10
Stegmaier, Gerhard, 142–3, 146
   V-2 and, 130, 133, 135, 138, 142
Steinhoff, Ernst, 109, 113, 117, 146, 170, 197, 207, 210–11, 294
   and rocket briefings for Hitler, 127, 149–50
   U.S. Army rocket program and, 216–17, 232, 238
   V-2 and, 124, 135, 149–50, 184
Stewart, Homer Joe, 294, 296–8, 304, 309
Stewart Committee, 294–8, 303–4
Storch, Paul, 175, 182–3, 189, 191
Storms, Harrison "Stormy," 398–9
   Apollo and, 366, 375–6, 384–5, 415–16
Stuhlinger, Ernst, ix–x, 179, 248, 275, 414, 416, 420, 427, 450–1, 457, 466, 471, 474
   Apollo and, 356–7, 377
   Mittelwerk and, 162–3
   satellites and, 279, 282–3, 292, 309–10, 316, 321–2
   and von Braun's shows for Disney, 288, 317
Sun, 28–9, 222
"Survey of Development of Liquid Rockets in Germany and Their Future Prospects" (von Braun), 204–5, 240
Szilard, Leo, 49

Taifun, 189, 191–2, 282
Teak, 332
Tessmann, Bernhard, 86, 196, 206
   surrender of, 200, 203
Test Stand XII, 189
Thiel, Walter, 85, 92, 124–5
   A-3 and, 102, 104–5
   death of, 154, 183
   V-2 and, 124, 128–9, 131, 136, 139
This Week, 324–5
Thompson, J. Lee, 348–51
Thor, 303, 305–8, 314, 317, 328, 331, 338, 357
Titan, 341–2, 417, 451
   Gemini and, 371, 373, 381
Todt, Fritz, 87, 120, 127, 132

Toftoy, Holger, 233, 237, 245, 251, 273, 282, 291, 293, 300, 347
   Hermes II and, 248–9
   U.S. Army rocket program and, 206–7, 210, 214, 216, 219, 221–2, 224, 231
Truax, Robert, 261–2, 292
Truman, Harry, 224, 236, 245, 315, 360
   Grosse mission and, 261–2
   Korean War and, 249, 261
Tsiolkovsky, Konstantin, 24–5, 242, 244, 477
Turkey, 236, 338, 382
Turner, Harold, 214–15
Turner, Tom, 462, 467

Uhl, Edward, 412, 455–6, 458–62, 464–7, 471
United Nations, 257, 389, 410–11
"Use of Atomic Warheads in Projected Mis-siles" (von Braun), 221
U-2 aircraft, 281, 312, 360

Valier, Max, 25, 39–40, 76, 112, 240
   death of, 40, 51, 67
   rocket experiments of, 30, 40, 50–1, 152
Van Allen, James, 309–10, 313, 320, 323–4, 327–8, 451
Van Allen belts, 327, 340
Vanguard, 327–8, 334, 347
   satellites and, 296–7, 303–4, 307, 309, 312–17, 319–20, 327
Verein für Raumschiffahrt (VfR), 30, 35, 38–40, 42, 52, 57–9, 65–6, 77–8
Vergeltungswaffen (vengeance weapons), missiles
   V-1, 78, 131, 185, 196
      Luftwaffe and, 134, 139, 176, 180, 191
   V-2, xv, 3, 5, 111–13, 123–53, 168–90, 211–12, 238–40, 252, 263, 265, 270, 290, 296, 308, 407, 471–7
      aerodynamics of, 126, 129, 133, 181–2
      airburst problem of, 164, 176, 181–2
      deployment of, 139–40, 142, 147, 149, 164, 166, 179, 181–2, 184–5
      discussions on successor to, 129–30
      guidance and control of, 116, 118–19, 123–4, 132–3, 164, 178, 275
      Hermes II and, 239, 249
      Hitler's briefings on, 112, 414

impact of World War II on, 116, 123, 127

legacy of, 476–7

and movies on von Braun, 326, 351–2

operational use of, 184–8, 196, 201, 212, 348, 351, 449, 471, 473–4

Peenemünde evacuation and, 157–8, 192

politics and, 130, 133–4, 137, 141–2, 175

production of, 106–7, 127–33, 137, 139–43, 148–9, 152–3, 156, 164–6, 174, 176–7, 201

propulsion of, 124–5, 129–31, 133, 135, 148–9, 152, 164, 177, 181–2, 186

Redstone and, 250, 282

slave labor and, 156, 158, 165, 175– 80, 186, 353, 449

specifications of, 81, 123–6, 136–7, 140, 250

testing and development of, 92, 101, 105, 115–16, 118–19, 123–5, 128–33, 135–8, 140–1, 145–6, 149, 152, 164– 6, 176, 181–2, 198, 206, 219, 222, 311

trajectory of, 136, 140

U.S. Army rocket program and, 206, 209, 214–15, 217, 219–22, 224, 232, 238–9

von Braun's arrest and, 170–3, 175

von Braun's management style and, 124, 126, 128–32, 134, 137–42, 148–9, 153, 157–8, 164–5, 175–9, 181, 185– 8, 255, 330, 348, 352, 414, 476

and von Braun's meeting with Himmler, 168–9

von Braun's surrender and, 199–201

as war-winning weapon, 162, 170–1

winged version of, 125–9, 138, 158, 188–9, 192, 204–5, 212, 220–1

V-2 (Dornberger), 265

Versailles Treaty, 9, 50, 74, 97

Vertikant guidance system, 108–9, 125

Vietnam, Vietnam War, 279, 391, 404, 415, 417, 422, 434, 437, 446, 449

Viking, 220, 268, 282, 294, 297

von Brauchitsch, Walther, 110, 116, 127

von Braun, Christoph-Friedrich (nephew), 225, 432, 462

von Braun, Emmy Freifrau (mother), x, 4, 11–22, 35–6, 60, 73, 134, 147, 172, 185, 193, 195, 202, 211, 213, 222, 225–9, 249, 264–6, 274, 277, 287–8, 290, 299–300, 304, 335, 344

children raised by, 7, 13–22, 26–7, 32, 35, 91, 229

death of, 349–50, 463, 469

education of, 12, 18

heritage of, 11, 19

husband's civil service career and, 13–15

illnesses of, 232–3

and movie on W. von Braun, 348–9

Oberwiesenthal estate of, 44–5, 69, 115

in occupied Germany, 225–7, 229, 231, 233, 243

Peenemünde and, 80, 90–1, 95, 159

Pioneer and, 340–1

scientific inclinations of, 12, 19

U.S. immigration of, 234, 247

W. von Braun's early rocket experiments and, 26–7

W. von Braun's fame and, 232, 309

in West Germany, 260, 264–5, 309, 332

World War I and, 13–15

von Braun, Friedrich "Fritz" (uncle), 8, 10, 127

von Braun, Gotthard Freiherr, 8

von Braun, Hildegard Margis (sister-in-law), 147

von Braun, Iris Careen (daughter), 241, 245, 247, 260, 277, 289, 326, 332, 341, 351, 431

education of, 411, 442

father's illness and, 470–1

teaching career of, 463–4

von Braun, Magnus, Jr. (brother), 27–8, 168, 195, 202, 207, 225–9, 231–2, 234, 245, 247, 274, 411, 425, 463

arrest of, 170–2, 227

childhood of, 15–17, 27, 91

education of, 45, 69–70, 153

and family members in occupied Germany, 225–7, 229, 232

final Allied offensive and, 197–8

military service avoided by, 185–6

Mittelwerk and, 186, 195

von Braun, Magnus, Jr. (brother) (*cont.*)
  Oberwiesenthal estate and, 44–5, 69–70
  post-Peenemünde attack reorganization
    and, 157–8
  surrender of, 199–200
  U.S. Army rocket program and, 211, 216,
    227
von Braun, Magnus Freiherr, Sr. (father), x–
    xi, 4, 7–22, 26–8, 35–7, 55–8, 73, 80,
    91, 127, 134, 147, 185, 193, 195, 202,
    211, 213, 222, 225–34, 249, 264–6,
    274, 287–8, 290, 299–300, 335, 344,
    349–51, 392, 415, 431, 447, 463
  Apollo and, 364–5, 425, 427–8
  banking career of, 16–17, 37, 44, 69
  childhood of, 9–10
  civil service career of, 7, 10–16, 28, 53,
    55–7, 60, 170, 260
  education of, 10, 18
  finances of, 10, 12, 14, 16–17, 19, 37, 277
  heritage of, 7–11, 19, 28, 44
  memoirs of, 9–10, 17–18, 28, 60, 69, 237,
    410–11
  and movie on W. von Braun, 349–50
  Oberwiesenthal estate of, 44–5, 69, 115
  in occupied Germany, 225–9, 231, 233, 243
  Peenemünde and, 95, 159
  politics of, 10, 15–16, 19–20, 28, 55–7,
    60–1, 69–70, 97, 243
  satellites and, 132, 304, 320, 322–3
  U.S. immigration of, 234, 247
  W. von Braun's arrest and, 172, 227
  W. von Braun's early rocket experiments
    and, 26–7, 31
  W. von Braun's fame and, 232, 309, 410
  W. von Braun's higher education and,
    36–7, 43
  W. von Braun's NASA employment and,
    444–5
  in West Germany, 260, 264–5, 309, 324,
    332, 373
  World War I and, 7, 13–15
von Braun, Margrit Cecile (daughter), 260,
    277, 289, 326, 332, 341, 350–1, 431
  education of, 411, 442, 464
  father's illness and, 470–1
von Braun, Maria (wife), x, 3, 193, 243, 257,
    264, 269, 309, 332, 355, 388, 390, 399,
    410–11, 451, 455, 464

Apollo and, 368, 431–3, 436
  heritage of, 441–2
  husband's courtship and engagement to,
    228–33
  husband's Fairchild employment and,
    459–60
  husband's fame and, 323, 326, 410
  husband's illnesses and, 469–72
  husband's NASA headquarters
    appointment and, 441–4
  married life of, 234, 241, 245, 247–8, 260,
    266, 277, 289, 301, 312, 328, 350–1,
    411, 427, 459
  Mercury and, 337, 363
  and movies on husband, 347, 350
  U.S. immigration of, 234, 247
von Braun, Maximilian Freiherr
    (grandfather), 8, 10, 12
von Braun, Peter Constantine (son), 350,
    433–4, 442, 460
  education of, 411, 464
von Braun, Siegfried (uncle), 8, 127
von Braun, Sigismund (brother), 26–8, 147,
    181, 202, 209, 225, 274, 349, 408, 444
  ambassadorships of, 408, 410–11, 432, 463
  childhood of, 13–17, 91
  education of, 15–18, 21, 27, 44
  Oberwiesenthal estate and, 44–5, 69–70
  in occupied Germany, 231–3, 237
  politics of, 70, 97–8, 185–6
  U.S. trip of, 70, 190
  World War I and, 13–15
von Braun, Wernher
  alcohol consumed by, 83–4, 170, 412, 455
  Allied internment and interrogation of,
    201–8, 233–4, 237, 243
  ambitions of, 4–7, 18–19, 21, 25–7,
    29–30, 35–7, 39, 45, 48, 55, 76, 84,
    93, 101, 107, 111, 125, 152, 180,
    185–6, 189–91, 198, 209, 222,
    240–1, 255, 263, 270, 273, 282, 284,
    288, 324, 333, 343, 354, 356, 368,
    438–9, 453, 458, 460, 473, 475–6
  on anti-Semitism, 97–9
  arrest of, 97, 167, 169–76, 183, 185, 187,
    191, 196, 198, 210, 227–8, 237, 271,
    315–16, 324, 476
  arrogance of, 36, 109, 118, 147, 186, 263,
    333, 337, 368

awards and honors of, 151–2, 155, 187–8,
191, 193, 240, 271, 309, 315, 323,
349, 409–10, 436, 443–4, 470–2,
birth of, 7, 13, 35
building as obsession of, 18–19, 21–2
cars of, 60, 83, 195–6, 198, 326
charisma of, 6, 20, 36, 93–4, 117, 153,
287
childhood of, 4, 7, 13–21, 23, 25–6, 28,
30–1, 91, 185, 356, 368, 447, 473
courage of, 155
death of, 6, 457, 470, 472–4
depressions of, 216, 263, 312, 451, 453
doctoral dissertation of, 49, 55–6, 68–9
education of, xv, 4, 15–18, 21–49, 52,
55–8, 60–2, 64, 68–9, 99, 117, 162,
180, 409
fame of, 3, 6, 19, 35, 147–8, 178, 183, 201,
232, 255–6, 258–60, 263, 265–6,
271, 277, 280, 285, 288, 309,
312–13, 315, 318, 323–7, 333,
335–6, 340–1, 349, 353, 361, 368,
392, 404–5, 409–10, 412, 414, 434,
442–3, 455, 458, 462–3, 467–8, 473,
475–6
Faustian bargain of, 4–5, 60–1, 125–6,
137–8, 162, 174, 348, 473–4,
476–7
finances of, 18, 42–4, 48, 57–8, 60, 69,
183, 213, 226, 231, 247, 253, 257,
264, 266, 272, 275, 277, 285, 287,
299–300, 309, 324–6, 369, 411–13,
443, 458, 460
flying of, 44–5, 48, 63, 79, 84, 91, 102,
113, 115, 118, 123, 134, 148–50,
153, 156–8, 164, 168, 173, 183, 186,
208, 247, 253, 257, 295, 301, 337,
390, 411–12, 415, 438–9, 453, 461,
464–5, 469
genius of, 89, 105, 108, 117
heritage of, 6–8, 11, 19, 21, 34–5, 37, 48,
55, 63–4, 76, 82, 96, 127, 277, 298,
300, 337–38, 441–2, 458, 476
horseback riding of, 63–4
hunting of, 28, 91, 103, 301, 412, 447,
455, 459, 465
illnesses of, 6, 213, 216, 260, 416, 460,
464, 469–72
injuries of, 195–8, 200–1, 207

legacy of, ix, 5–6, 476–7
leisure time of, 83–5, 90–1, 97, 99, 115,
123, 125, 170, 218–19, 222–4,
228–9, 232–4, 238, 241, 269, 277,
284–5, 287–9, 295, 301, 328, 351,
373, 399, 411, 415, 427, 431, 433,
441–2, 447, 455, 457, 460, 464,
468–9
management and leadership skills of, 6,
20, 30, 33, 43–4, 62, 68, 75, 78–9, 82,
84, 86–90, 93–6, 99, 101, 107–9,
113, 116–18, 124, 126, 128–32, 134,
137–42, 148–9, 153, 156–8, 162–5,
167, 175–9, 181, 183, 185–8, 194–5,
207, 217–19, 237, 247, 249–52, 255,
261, 269, 273–4, 278, 282–4,
290–310, 312–15, 318–20, 326–8,
330–1, 335–9, 341, 343, 346–8, 352,
356–9, 363–9, 371–2, 375–89,
391–9, 402–4, 409, 413–14, 416–17,
420–7, 433, 438, 448–9, 452, 458,
460, 476–7
manner and personality of, 3, 19–21, 26,
28–9, 43, 46, 48, 53, 55, 67, 70, 83–4,
93–5, 108, 130, 132, 156, 177–8,
183, 186, 191, 200, 208, 225, 255,
287–9, 297–8, 311–12, 314, 321,
338, 344, 374–6, 384–5, 390, 393,
412, 431–2, 444, 452, 460, 462,
464–5
marksmanship of, 122
married life of, 234, 241, 245, 247–8, 260,
266, 277, 287, 289, 301, 312, 315,
328, 350–1, 411, 427, 459, 463
media appearances of, 258–60, 268, 285,
289–90, 301, 317, 326, 340, 392,
444, 449, 469, 471
military service of, 84, 113, 253
movies on, 90, 99, 190, 309, 325–6, 333,
342, 345–53, 405–8, 428, 458
music enjoyed by, 26–8, 36, 43, 228–9,
269, 287–8
naiveté of, 448–9, 458
nicknames of, 28, 43, 276
nonconformist streak of, 18, 20–2,
26–7
opportunism of, 55, 121, 237, 254, 337,
343, 350, 399–400, 406–7, 413, 425,
428, 475

von Braun, Wernher (*cont.*)
  physical appearance of, 3, 15–16, 23, 26,
    40, 43, 53, 63, 93–4, 147, 178, 188,
    191–2, 201, 208, 315, 317, 348, 351,
    440, 442, 444, 469
  politics of, 4–5, 34–5, 48, 55, 61, 63–5,
    69–70, 76, 86–7, 90, 96–9, 116,
    120–2, 126, 134, 144, 167–8, 173–4,
    185–7, 198, 204, 224, 232–3, 235–8,
    243, 254–5, 266, 271, 290, 315–16,
    324, 326, 333, 337, 339, 347–9, 353,
    355, 368, 370, 385–6, 392, 396–7,
    404–9, 428–9, 432, 440, 448–9,
    461–2, 468, 471–6
  pragmatism of, 447
  pronunciation of his name, xv
  religious beliefs of, 4, 6, 21, 46, 152,
    229–30, 234, 244, 277, 287, 324,
    444, 469–70, 472
  romances of, 90–1, 146–8, 209, 237
  sailing of, 32, 91, 94, 455
  scuba diving of, 285, 287–8, 301, 328
  secrecy concerns of, 49, 55–6, 63, 66,
    68–9, 76–8, 80, 86–7, 95, 190, 201,
    215–16, 304–5, 309
  self-confidence of, 36, 321, 361, 409
  sense of humor of, 93, 156, 164, 212, 301,
    325, 407, 452, 455, 471
  and shows for Disney, 285–90, 295, 301,
    317, 368
  smoking of, 83
  speaking skills of, 6, 43, 48, 52, 84, 128,
    149–50, 240, 250, 255, 259–60,
    266–7, 270–2, 277–8, 289–90,
    295–7, 303, 325–7, 337, 342, 349,
    369–70, 372–3, 375, 377–8, 396,
    404, 412, 432, 436, 439, 442–4,
    452–3, 455, 458, 460, 462–4, 468,
    470
  surrender of, 190–2, 199–201, 203,
    271
  swimming of, 32, 459
  U.S. citizenship of, 290, 405, 477
  U.S. immigration of, 190, 212–16, 224–6,
    236–8, 245, 288, 475–7
  utopianism of, 223, 244
  wife courted by, 228–33
  womanizing of, 94, 287

  writing skills of, 6, 28–9, 32–6, 40–1, 44,
    48, 68–9, 173, 190, 204–5, 221,
    223–4, 234, 240–7, 252–7, 259,
    261–7, 269, 271–3, 275–7, 282, 286,
    289, 291–2, 295, 316, 324–7, 337,
    347–8, 356, 400, 409, 412–13, 431,
    435, 453, 458, 460, 464, 469–70
von Fritsch, Werner Freiherr, 74, 81–2
von Goethe, Johann Wolfgang, 5, 23, 180,
    207, 349, 476
von Hindenburg, Paul, 14, 42, 56, 60, 69
von Horstig, Ernst Ritter, 80
  German Army rocket program and, 58,
    75, 82
  and military uses for rockets, 49, 51–3
von Opel, Fritz, 30–1
von Papen, Franz, 56–7, 60, 69
von Quistorp, Alexander (uncle/father-in-
    law), 12, 17, 91, 193, 228, 243, 301,
    350, 370
von Quistorp, Hans (uncle), 12, 91, 243
von Quistorp, Johann Gottfried, 11
von Quistorp, Marie (grandmother), 11–12
von Quistorp, Theda (aunt/mother-in-law),
    193, 228–9, 264, 301, 350
von Quistorp, Wernher (grandfather),
    11–12, 80
von Richthofen, Wolfram Freiherr, 77–81
  interservice experimental rocket
    establishment and, 79–81, 100
  Luftwaffe rocket program and, 77–8
von Saurma, Ruth, 326, 407
von Schleicher, Kurt, 56, 60, 69
von Stauffenberg, Claus Schenk, 180–1,
    184
Vostok, 359–60
Voyager, 417, 443, 451

WAC Corporal sounding rockets, 238
Wagner, Dr., 192
Wahmke, Kurt, 58, 70–1, 76, 85
Wallace, George, 386, 395–6
Wallops Island retreat, 445–6
Walter, Hellmuth, 100–1, 112, 114
war crimes, war crimes trials, x, 179, 211,
    348, 472
  Dora and, 235–6, 449
  von Braun's deposition and, 160, 165

War Department, U.S, *see* Defense
   Department, U.S.
Warsitz, Erich, 109, 123, 374
   rocket fighter program and, 82–4, 100,
      113
   von Braun's relationship with, 83–4
   and von Braun's romance with Brill,
      146–7
Wasserfall, 138–9, 144, 149, 153, 155, 158,
   169, 176, 187–8, 191–2, 209, 224
Webb, James E., 360–1, 366–70, 389, 412,
   414–17, 440–1
   Apollo and, 360, 363–4, 366–8, 370, 378,
      382–4, 404, 415–17, 424–7
   civil rights and, 385–6, 395–7
   and successor programs to Apollo,
      400–1, 421, 425–6
   von Braun's management style and,
      384–5, 426
   von Braun's Nazi past and, 404–5
Webb, Patricia, 460
Wegener, Peter, 93, 174
Whipple, Fred, 256–7
   Collier's 259, 269, 272, 276
   satellites and, 284, 291
White, Henry J., 241, 245, 263, 266
White Sands Proving Ground, 235, 245,
   249, 291
   U.S. Army rocket program and, 214, 217,
      219, 221–2, 238
"Why I Chose America" (von Braun),
   271
Wiemer, Otto, 86–7
Wiesman, Walt (Wiesemann), 219, 345
Wiesner, Jerome, 355, 382
Wilde, Oscar, 43, 434
William II, Emperor of Germany, 7, 10, 90
   World War I and, 14–15
Wilson, Charles, 305–7, 319, 323
   IRBMs and, 299, 305–6, 317
Winkler, Johannes, 30, 39, 47, 77–8

Witzenhausen, 211–13, 216
   evacuation of Peenemünders to, 208–9,
      211, 213
women
   forced laborers and, 144, 154
   Peenemünde and, 94–5
World War I, 7–8, 12–15, 38, 77, 100, 112,
   190, 204
   Paris Gun and, 81–2
World War II, 6, 13, 28, 59–60, 89, 94, 96,
   98–9, 109, 114–17, 138–40, 152–3,
   245, 248–9, 261, 282–3, 300, 329, 337,
   351, 365, 393, 409, 426, 476
   end of, 199, 202–3
   final Allied offensive in, 196–8, 202
   Great Britain and, 116, 123, 127, 138–9,
      147
   impact on rocket program of, 116–17,
      119–20, 123, 127, 130
   Nazi anti-Semitism and, 98, 145
   Nazi setbacks in, 139–40, 142, 152,
      167–8, 170–1, 175, 180–1, 188–91,
      196–8
   Nazi successes of, 122–3
   in Pacific, 206, 210
   slave labor and, 143–4
   start of, 115–17, 120
   von Braun's arrest and, 170–1, 174

York, Herbert, 333, 341–4, 352

Zanssen, Leo, 94–6, 130
   German Army rocket program and, 62,
      72, 74, 77–8, 86
   Peenemünde and, 95–6, 109, 142, 158–9,
      163
   V-2 and, 135–6, 138, 142, 182
Zeppelin airship company, 130, 132, 142–4,
   149, 156
Zinnowitz, 14, 90–1, 115, 156, 170
Zond, 424, 427

PERMISSIONS ACKNOWLEDGMENTS

Grateful acknowledgment is made to the following for permission to reprint previously published material:

Alfred Publishing Co. Inc., Carlin Music Publishing Canada, Inc., and Ray Henderson Music Co., Inc.: Excerpt from "Sonny Boy" by Al Jolson, Buddy Desylva, Lew Brown, and Ray Henderson, copyright © 1928 (Renewed) by Chappell & Co., Stephen Ballentine Music, and Ray Henderson Music Co., Inc. (ASCAP). All rights reserved. Reprinted by permission of Alfred Publishing Co. Inc., Carlin Music Publishing Canada, Inc., on behalf of Redwood Music Ltd., and Ray Henderson Music Co., Inc.

Doris Dornberger and Sanford J. Greenburger Associates, Inc.: Excerpts from *V-2* by Walter Dornberger, translated by James Cleugh and Geoffrey Halliday, copyright © 1954 by The Viking Press, Inc. Reprinted by permission of Doris Dornberger and Sanford J. Greenburger Associates, Inc., on behalf of the Estate of Walter Dornberger.

The Free Press and Weidenfeld & Nicolson: Excerpts from *Inside the Third Reich* by Albert Speer, translated by Richard and Clara Winston, copyright © 1969 by Verlag Ullstein GmbH, translation copyright © 1970 by Macmillan Publishing Company. All rights reserved. Reprinted by permission of The Free Press, a division of Simon & Schuster Adult Publishing Group and Weidenfeld & Nicolson, a division of The Orion Publishing Group Ltd.

The Hearst Corporation: Excerpts from "Space Man—the Story of My Life" by Wernher von Braun, copyright © 1958 by Hearst Communications, Inc., successor in interest to The Hearst Corporation (published in *The American Weekly*, July 20 and 27, and August 3, 1958). All rights reserved. Reprinted by permission of The Hearst Corporation.

Krieger Publishing Company: Excerpt from *Wernher von Braun: Crusader for Space* by Ernst Stuhlinger and Frederick Ordway (published by Krieger Publishing Company, Malabar, Florida, 1994). Reprinted by permission of Krieger Publishing Company and the authors.

Tom Lehrer: Excerpt from "Wernher von Braun" by Tom Lehrer, copyright © by Tom Lehrer. Reprinted by permission of Tom Lehrer.

Simon & Schuster: Excerpts from "A Romantic Urge," from *From Hiroshima to the Moon: Chronicles of Life in the Atomic Age* by Daniel Lang, copyright © 1959 by Daniel Lang. Copyright renewed 1987 by Margaret Lang, Helen Lang, Frances Labaree, and Cecily Lang. "A Romantic Urge" was originally published in *The New Yorker*. All rights reserved. Reprinted by permission of Simon & Schuster Adult Publishing Group.

The Wylie Agency: Excerpt from *Of a Fire on the Moon* by Norman Mailer, copyright © 1970 by Norman Mailer. Reprinted by permission of The Wylie Agency.

Michael J. Neufeld is chair of the Space History Division of the Smithsonian's National Air and Space Museum. Born and raised in Canada, he received his doctorate in history from The Johns Hopkins University in Baltimore. His second book, *The Rocket and the Reich: Peenemünde and the Coming of the Ballistic Missile Era*, won the AIAA History Manuscript Award and the SHOT Dexter Prize. He lives in Takoma Park, Maryland.

A NOTE ON THE TYPE

The text of this book was set in a typeface called Aldus, designed by the celebrated typographer Hermann Zapf in 1952–53. Based on the classical proportion of the popular Palatino type family, Aldus was originally adapted for Linotype composition as a slightly lighter version that would read better in smaller sizes.

Hermann Zapf was born in Nuremberg, Germany, in 1918. He has created many other well-known typefaces including Comenius, Hunt Roman, Marconi, Melior, Michelangelo, Optima, Saphir, Sistina, Zapf Book, and Zapf Chancery.

Composed by North Market Street Graphics,
Lancaster, Pennsylvania

Printed and bound by Berryville Graphics,
Berryville, Virginia

Designed by Peter A. Andersen